Advanced Synchronization Control and Bifurcation of Chaotic Fractional-Order Systems

Abdesselem Boulkroune
Jijel University, Algeria

Samir Ladaci
National Polytechnic School of Constantine, Algeria

A volume in the Advances in Computer and
Electrical Engineering (ACEE) Book Series

Published in the United States of America by
   IGI Global
   Engineering Science Reference (an imprint of IGI Global)
   701 E. Chocolate Avenue
   Hershey PA, USA 17033
   Tel: 717-533-8845
   Fax: 717-533-8661
   E-mail: cust@igi-global.com
   Web site: http://www.igi-global.com

Library of Congress Cataloging-in-Publication Data

Names: Boulkroune, Abdesselem, 1972- editor. | Ladaci, Samir, 1971- editor.
Title: Advanced synchronization control and bifurcation of chaotic
    fractional-order systems / Abdesselem Boulkroune and Samir Ladaci, editors.
Description: Hershey, PA : Engineering Science Reference, [2018] | Includes
    bibliographical references.
Identifiers: LCCN 2017043501| ISBN 9781522554189 (hardcover) | ISBN
    9781522554196 (ebook)
Subjects: LCSH: Adaptive control systems. | Chaotic synchronization. |
    Fractional calculus. | Bifurcation theory.
Classification: LCC TJ217 .A3858 2018 | DDC 629.8/36--dc23 LC record available at https://lccn.loc.gov/2017043501

This book is published in the IGI Global book series Advances in Computer and Electrical Engineering (ACEE) (ISSN: 2327-039X; eISSN: 2327-0403)

British Cataloguing in Publication Data
A Cataloguing in Publication record for this book is available from the British Library.

All work contributed to this book is new, previously-unpublished material. The views expressed in this book are those of the authors, but not necessarily of the publisher.

For electronic access to this publication, please contact: eresources@igi-global.com.

Advances in Computer and Electrical Engineering (ACEE) Book Series

Srikanta Patnaik
SOA University, India

ISSN:2327-039X
EISSN:2327-0403

Mission

The fields of computer engineering and electrical engineering encompass a broad range of interdisciplinary topics allowing for expansive research developments across multiple fields. Research in these areas continues to develop and become increasingly important as computer and electrical systems have become an integral part of everyday life.

The **Advances in Computer and Electrical Engineering (ACEE) Book Series** aims to publish research on diverse topics pertaining to computer engineering and electrical engineering. **ACEE** encourages scholarly discourse on the latest applications, tools, and methodologies being implemented in the field for the design and development of computer and electrical systems.

Coverage

- Electrical Power Conversion
- Power Electronics
- Computer science
- Optical Electronics
- Digital Electronics
- Applied Electromagnetics
- Computer Architecture
- Analog Electronics
- Programming
- Qualitative Methods

IGI Global is currently accepting manuscripts for publication within this series. To submit a proposal for a volume in this series, please contact our Acquisition Editors at Acquisitions@igi-global.com or visit: http://www.igi-global.com/publish/.

Titles in this Series

For a list of additional titles in this series, please visit: www.igi-global.com/book-series

Handbook of Research on Power and Energy System Optimization
Pawan Kumar (Thapar University, India) Surjit Singh (National Institute of Technology Kurukshetra, India) Ikbal Ali (Jamia Millia Islamia, India) and Taha Selim Ustun (Carnegie Mellon University, USA)
Engineering Science Reference • copyright 2018 • 500pp • H/C (ISBN: 9781522539353) • US $325.00 (our price)

Big Data Analytics for Satellite Image Processing and Remote Sensing
P. Swarnalatha (VIT University, India) and Prabu Sevugan (VIT University, India)
Engineering Science Reference • copyright 2018 • 253pp • H/C (ISBN: 9781522536437) • US $215.00 (our price)

Modeling and Simulations for Metamaterials Emerging Research and Opportunities
Ammar Armghan (Aljouf University, Saudi Arabia) Xinguang Hu (HuangShan University, China) and Muhammad Younus Javed (HITEC University, Pakistan)
Engineering Science Reference • copyright 2018 • 171pp • H/C (ISBN: 9781522541806) • US $155.00 (our price)

Electromagnetic Compatibility for Space Systems Design
Christos D. Nikolopoulos (National Technical University of Athens, Greece)
Engineering Science Reference • copyright 2018 • 346pp • H/C (ISBN: 9781522554158) • US $225.00 (our price)

Soft-Computing-Based Nonlinear Control Systems Design
Uday Pratap Singh (Madhav Institute of Technology and Science, India) Akhilesh Tiwari (Madhav Institute of Technology and Science, India) and Rajeev Kumar Singh (Madhav Institute of Technology and Science, India)
Engineering Science Reference • copyright 2018 • 388pp • H/C (ISBN: 9781522535317) • US $245.00 (our price)

EHT Transmission Performance Evaluation Emerging Research and Opportunities
K. Srinivas (Transmission Corporation of Andhra Pradesh Limited, India) and R.V.S. Satyanarayana (Sri Venkateswara University College of Engineering, India)
Engineering Science Reference • copyright 2018 • 160pp • H/C (ISBN: 9781522549413) • US $145.00 (our price)

Fuzzy Logic Dynamics and Machine Prediction for Failure Analysis
Tawanda Mushiri (University of Johannesburg, South Africa) and Charles Mbowhwa (University of Johannesburg, South Africa)
Engineering Science Reference • copyright 2018 • 301pp • H/C (ISBN: 9781522532446) • US $225.00 (our price)

701 East Chocolate Avenue, Hershey, PA 17033, USA
Tel: 717-533-8845 x100 • Fax: 717-533-8661
E-Mail: cust@igi-global.com • www.igi-global.com

Editorial Advisory Board

Table of Contents

Detailed Table of Contents

Chapter 1

    Samir Ladaci, National Polytechnic School of Constantine, Algeria
    Karima Rabah, 20th August 1955 University of Skikda, Algeria
    Mohamed Lashab, University Larbi Ben M'Hidi of Oum El-Bouaghi, Algeria

This chapter investigates a new control design methodology for the synchronization of fractional-order Arneodo chaotic systems using a fractional-order sliding mode control configuration. This class of nonlinear fractional-order systems shows a chaotic behavior for a set of model parameters. The stability analysis of the proposed fractional-order sliding mode control law is performed by means of the Lyapunov stability theory. Simulation examples on fractional-order Arneodo chaotic systems synchronization are provided in presence of disturbances and noises. These results illustrate the effectiveness and robustness of this control design approach.

Chapter 2

    Shaobo He, Hunan University of Arts and Science, China
    Huihai Wang, Central South University, China
    Kehui Sun, Central South University, China

The fractional-order Lorenz hyperchaotic system is solved as a discrete map by applying Adomian decomposition method (ADM). Dynamics of this system versus parameters are analyzed by LCEs, bifurcation diagrams, and SE and C0 complexity. Results show that this system has rich dynamical behaviors. Chaos and hyperchaos can be generated by decreasing the fractional derivative order q in this system. It also shows that the system is more complex when q takes smaller values. Moreover, coupled synchronization of fractional-order chaotic system is investigated theoretically. The synchronization performances with synchronization controller parameters and derivative order varying are analyzed.

Synchronization and complexity of intermediate variables which generated by ADM are investigated. It shows that intermediate variables between the driving system and response system are synchronized and higher complexity values are found. It lays a technical foundation for secure communication applications of fractional-order chaotic systems.

Chapter 3

Farouk Zouari, Université de Tunis El Manar, Tunisia
Amina Boubellouta, University of Jijel, Algeria

This chapter focuses on the adaptive neural control of a class of uncertain multi-input multi-output (MIMO) nonlinear time-delay non-integer order systems with unmeasured states, unknown control direction, and unknown asymmetric saturation actuator. The design of the controller follows a number of steps. Firstly, based on the semi-group property of fractional order derivative, the system is transformed into a normalized fractional order system by means of a state transformation in order to facilitate the control design. Then, a simple linear state observer is constructed to estimate the unmeasured states of the transformed system. A neural network is incorporated to approximate the unknown nonlinear functions while a Nussbaum function is used to deal with the unknown control direction. In addition, the strictly positive real (SPR) condition, the Razumikhin lemma, the frequency distributed model, and the Lyapunov method are utilized to derive the parameter adaptive laws and to perform the stability proof.

Chapter 4

Khatir Khettab, University Mohamed Boudiaf of M'sila, Algeria
Yassine Bensafia, Bouira University, Algeria

This chapter presents a fractional adaptive interval type-2 fuzzy logic control strategy based on active fractional sliding mode controller (FAIT2FSMC) to synchronize tow chaotic fractional-order systems. The interval type-2 fuzzy logic systems (IT2FLS) are used to approximate the plant dynamics represented by unknown functions of the system, and the IT2F adaptation law adjusts the consequent parameters of the rules based on a Lyapunov synthesis approach. One of the main contributions in this work is the use of an IT2F and an adaptive fractional order $PI\lambda$ control law to eliminate the chattering action in the control signal. Based on fractional order Lyapunov stability criterion, stability analysis is performed for the proposed method for an acceptable synchronization error level. The performance of the proposed scheme is demonstrated through the synchronization of two different fractional order chaotic gyro systems. Simulations are implemented using a numerical method based on Grünwald-Letnikov approach to solve the fractional differential equations.

Chapter 5

Amina Boubellouta, University of Jijel, Algeria

In this chapter, one develops a fuzzy adaptive backstepping control-based projective synchronization scheme of a class of uncertain fractional-order nonlinear systems with unknown external disturbances. In each step, an uncertain nonlinear function is online modeled via a fuzzy logic system, and a virtual control term is determined based on the fractional Lyapunov stability. At the final step, a fuzzy adaptive control law ensuring the convergence of the projective synchronization error as well as the stability of the closed-loop control system is derived. Numerical simulations given at the end of this chapter confirm well the effectiveness of the proposed control method.

Over the past decades, chaos has stimulated the interest of researchers due to its existence in different fields of science and engineering. The chaotic systems are characterized by their sensitivity to the initial conditions. This property makes the system unpredictable long term. Similar to the integer-order differential systems, fractional-order differential systems can exhibit chaotic behaviors. This type of system contains one or more elements of fractional order. The fractional calculus is recognized in the early seventeenth century but it has been widely applied in many fields and with intense growth just over the past decades. To avoid troubles arising from unusual behaviors of a chaotic system, chaos control has gained increasing attention in recent years. An important objective of a chaos controller is to suppress the chaotic oscillations completely or reduce them to the regular oscillations. The goal of this chapter is to present the evolution of chaotic systems in open and closed loop in function of their parameters and designing a controller using bifurcation diagrams.

In this chapter, the projective synchronization problem of different multivariable fractional-order chaotic systems with both uncertain dynamics and external disturbances is studied. More specifically, a fuzzy adaptive controller is investigated for achieving a projective synchronization of uncertain fractional-order chaotic systems. The adaptive fuzzy-logic system is used to online estimate the uncertain nonlinear functions. The latter is augmented by a robust control term to efficiently compensate for the unavoidable fuzzy approximation errors, external disturbances as well as residual error due to the use of the so-called e-modification in the adaptive laws. A Lyapunov approach is employed to derive the parameter adaptation laws and to prove the boundedness of all signals of the closed-loop system. Numerical simulations are performed to verify the effectiveness of the proposed synchronization scheme.

Chapter 8

In this chapter, one investigates the chaos synchronization of a class of uncertain optical chaotic systems. More precisely, one also presents a systematic approach for designing a fractional-order (FO) sliding mode controller to achieve a rapid, robust, and perfect chaos synchronization. By this robust controller, it is rigorously proven that the associated synchronization error is Mittag-Leffler (or asymptotically) stable. In a numerical simulation framework, this synchronization scheme is tested on many chaotic optical systems taken from the open literature. The obtained results clearly show that the proposed chaos synchronization controller is not only strongly robust with respect to the unavoidable system's uncertainties (as unmodeled dynamics, and parameters' variation and uncertainty) and eventual dynamical external disturbances, but also can significantly reduce the chattering effect.

        Abdesselem Boulkroune, University of Jijel, Algeria
        Amina Boubellouta, University of Jijel, Algeria

This chapter addresses the fuzzy adaptive controller design for the generalized projective synchronization (GPS) of incommensurate fractional-order chaotic systems with actuator nonlinearities. The considered master-slave systems are with different fractional-orders, uncertain models, unknown bounded disturbances, and non-identical form. The suggested controller includes two keys terms, namely a fuzzy adaptive control and a fractional-order variable structure control. The fuzzy logic systems are exploited for approximating the system uncertainties. A Lyapunov approach is employed for determining the parameter adaptation laws and proving the stability of the closed-loop system. At last, simulation results are given to demonstrate the validity of the proposed synchronization approach.

        Bachir Bourouba, Setif-1 University, Algeria

In this chapter a new direct adaptive fuzzy optimal sliding mode control approach is proposed for the stabilization of fractional chaotic systems with different initial conditions of the state under the presence of uncertainties and external disturbances. Using Lyapunov analysis, the direct adaptive fuzzy optimal sliding mode control approach illustrates asymptotic convergence of error to zero as well as good robustness against external disturbances and uncertainties. The authors present a method for optimum tuning of sliding mode control system parameter using particle swarm optimization (PSO) algorithm. PSO is a robust stochastic optimization technique based on the movement and intelligence of swarm, applying the concept of social interaction to problem solving. Simulation examples for the control of nonlinear fractional-order systems are given to illustrate the effectiveness of the proposed fractional adaptive fuzzy control strategy.

        Ammar Soukkou, University of Jijel, Algeria
        Abdelkrim Boukabou, University of Jijel, Algeria

This chapter will establish the importance and significance of studying the fractional-order control of nonlinear dynamical systems and emphasize the link between the factional calculus and famous PID control design. It will lay the foundation related to the research scope, problem formulation, objectives and contributions. As a case study, a fractional-order PD-based feedback (Fo-PDF) control scheme with optimal knowledge base is developed in this work for achieving stabilization and synchronization of a large class of fractional-order chaotic systems (FoCS). Based and derived on Lyapunov stabilization arguments of fractional-order systems, the stability analysis of the closed-loop control system is investigated. The design and multiobjective optimization of Fo-PDF control law is theoretically rigorous and presents a powerful and simple approach to provide a reasonable tradeoff between simplicity, numerical accuracy, and stability analysis in control and synchronization of FoCS. The feasibility and validity of this developed Fo-PDF scheme have been illustrated by numerical simulations using the fractional-order Mathieu-Van Der Pol hyperchaotic system.

Chapter 12

Nasr-eddine Hamri, University of Mila, Algeria

The first steps of the theory of fractional calculus and some applications traced back to the first half of the nineteenth century, the subject only really came to life over the last few decades. A particular feature is that fractional derivatives provide an excellent instrument for the description of memory and hereditary properties of various materials and processes. This is the main advantage of fractional models in comparison with classical integer-order models; another feature is that scientists have developed new models that involve fractional differential equations in mechanics, electrical engineering. Many scientists have become aware of the potential use of chaotic dynamics in engineering applications. With the development of the fractional-order algorithm, the dynamics of fractional order systems have received much attention. Chaos cannot occur in continuous integer order systems of total order less than three due to the Poincare-Bendixon theorem. It has been shown that many fractional-order dynamical systems behave chaotically with total order less than three.

Chapter 13

Novel Cryptography Technique via Chaos Synchronization of Fractional-Order Derivative
Alain Giresse Tene, University of Dschang, Cameroon
Timoleon Crépin Kofane, University of Yaounde I, Cameroon

Synchronization of fractional-order-derivative systems for cryptography purpose is still exploratory and despite an increase in cryptography research, several challenges remain in designing a powerful cryptosystem. This chapter addresses the problem of synchronization of fractional-order-derivative chaotic systems using random numbers generator for a novel technique to key distribution in cryptography. However, there is evidence that researchers have approached the problem using integer order derivative chaotic systems. Consequently, the aim of the chapter lies in coding and decoding a text via chaos synchronization of fractional-order derivative, the performance analysis and the key establishment scheme following an application on a text encryption using the chaotic Mathieu-Van Der Pol fractional system. In order to improve the level of the key security, the Fibonacci Q-matrix is used in the key generation process and the initial condition; the order of the derivative of the responder system secretly shared between the responder and the receiver are also involved. It followed from this study that compared to the existing cryptography techniques, this proposed method is found to be very efficient due to the fact that, it improves the key security.

The aim of the chapter is twofold. First, a literature review on synchronization methods of fractional-order discrete-time systems is exposed. Second, a secure digital data communication based on synchronization of fractional-order discrete-time chaotic systems is proposed. Two synchronization methods based on observers are proposed to synchronize two fractional-order discrete-time chaotic systems. The first method concerns the impulsive synchronization where sufficient conditions for the synchronization error of the states are given. The second method concerns the exact synchronization which is based on a step-by-step delayed observer. In the same way, conditions are provided in order to allow the reconstruction of the states and the unknown input which is the message in this case. The two synchronization methods are combined in order to design a novel robust secure digital data communication. The performance of the proposed communication system is illustrated in numerical simulations where digital image signal is considered.

In this chapter, an adaptive control approach-based neural approximation is developed for a category of uncertain fractional-order systems with actuator nonlinearities and output constraints. First, to overcome the difficulties arising from the actuator nonlinearities and nonaffine structures, the mean value theorem is introduced. Second, to deal with the uncertain nonlinear dynamics, the unknown control directions and the output constraints, neural networks, smooth Nussbaum-type functions, and asymmetric barrier Lyapunov functions are employed, respectively. Moreover, for satisfactorily designing the control updating laws and to carry out the stability analysis of the overall closed-loop system, the Backstepping technique is used. The main advantage about this research is that (1) the number of parameters to be adapted is much reduced, (2) the tracking errors converge to zero, and (3) the output constraints are not transgressed. At last, simulation results demonstrate the feasibility of the newly presented design techniques.

Foreword

There are no more difficult problems to deal with than those confronting us with our relationship to the technical world. Thus, for example, we can quote the questions raised by Albert Einstein's father concerning the synchronization of train station clocks. The control of dynamic systems is part of these complex problems. As for the boldness of the engineers and scientists who decided, as in the present book, to approach such systems using among other things non-integer differential equations and their different vectored versions, it is no less important than that of Einstein's son deciding to treat the problems encountered by his father by using non-Euclidean geometries. In fact the epistemological option, which is implicit herein, is of the same geometrical nature: namely the hyperbolicity of complexity.

The choice of a cognitive upheaval based on the use of convolutions, fuzzy systems, nonlinear functions and analytically integro-differentiation operator characterized by a non-integer order, is henceforth to respond to an operational need: to give a conceptual representation of a technical world elusive otherwise with the usual tools of techno sciences. Fortunately for the scientific-engineer, the complexity of the world to be mastered exhibits standing features (dynamics specific to heterogeneous media, long-memory systems, recursive systems, attractors, correlations of divergent series, bifurcations, singular and/or residual characteristics) whose algebraic and geometric content can be explored by the means of most advanced mathematical notions, especially the algebraic geometry. An emerging subtle ontology, which complex content can no more be compared to that on which common linear and causal thought is based, defies today the engineer as yesterday the natural laws of physics challenged Ptolemy or Kepler, Eratosthenes or al Khwarizmi, Fresnel or Poisson.

"Let no one who is not geometer enter under my roof". This aphorism has been prevailing during 24 centuries; from Plato to Maryam Mizrakhani. Albert Einstein, for example, has understood the metaphysical and scientific characters tied within this stepping forward into the Plato's academy: namely, the step which consists of considering alongside all solutions of a given problem, also all of its singular algebraic sisters. As Bachelard, Heidegger or Simondon anticipated, the mental representation of the technical world can no longer be part of the simple set-theoretic perspective of a universe that would be given a priori to our senses as an unmatched object and unique *per se*. This vision, which reduces geometry to a series of embedding and makes of the exteriority of any scientist with respect to the object of his experiment a mere consequence of the axiom of choice (set theory), must now be revisited and addressed in the frame of category theory. As proved by Gauss local geometry exists, and it will be observed that externality is already questioned in the frame of a Quantum Mechanics which "stays to be understood" (Feynman). The nature itself became cultural under the leverage of the techniques and object and subject are nowadays irreversibly tied. The innate is now tied to the artefact and the tools developed to make the Cartesian man "like a master and possessor of nature" reach their limits conceptual limits but also their operational bounds. The tool creates a link with the content of the production (GAFA) and the clock creates a link with the Hausdorff content and the metric of the geometry where it is used (in fact to a capacity in the sense of Choquet). This is exactly what the non-integer differential equations tell us!

As Lee Smolinproved clearly, the question of time is, once again, at the heart of complexity and the question of time, as for Einstein, can be reduced to the question of the "synchronization" (including of geometrical states) which is precisely the first technical purpose of this book, in particular through the problem of control of so-called chaotic systems; in fact, correlated systems in scales. This technical book illustrates the state of the art in this matter. It highlights a couple of truths that is far from being obvious:

- The control cannot be a deterministic control. In analytic terms it will be asserted that the Lebesgue integrals cannot be relevant for the representation of basically non-additive systems.
- Stochastic control is irrelevant when long-range correlations do not fit to Gaussian conditions even if, in a very indirect way, this method can be used but with anomalous analytic confusions in the case of hyperscaled systems for instance.

It is precisely because these couple of constraints must be overcame that the time emerges as an implicit or explicitly complex variable associated to the operators of non-integer order (if different from 1/2 and of Riemann constraint) which possess the property of trapping the phase. Beyond the question of stability and in the absence of eigenstates, time emerges as a scale factor in the approximation of an object of representation then seen as a categorical co-limit. The lemma of Yoneda, which, accordingly to Philippe Riot's analysis, can be associated with the notion of Cauchy integral on any type of singularities, suggests that this limit can be analytic and / or vectored as done in this book. Many chapters play with implicit use of this lemma when the treatments discretizes. But it is also at this step that current research leads to the understanding that "analycity" is most often obtained through the use of a duality (Synchronization by coupling. Symmetry broken then reconstructed Construction / Partition of set. System / Controller. System / Environment. Use of Galois symmetries, etc.). This duality is implemented into hyper-chaotic systems; this dualityalso gives its adaptability to the neural network, or to the adjustment of 2-fuzzy processing. It is obviously this duality on which the notion of error, so useful to the efficiency of engineering processes, is based. In the general case and precisely for reasons of duality, that research leads us to think that time must be a complex variable, whereas the paradigm that time must be a real variable, often leads to confusion between both components of the tempo; the parametrization of a function on the one hand and the "history", on the other hand, both conveyed through the same parameter. This is exactly what the use of non-linear test-functions and that of fuzzy controllers under convolution constraints hide. The question of the bifurcation is for its part associated with the hyperbolic geometries on which the fractional dynamics develop, as well as their quadratic, fractional and/or projective control. The author of these lines suggests that the efficiency of the methods reported in the book and whose CRONE control, at the beginning of the eighties, was the flag, comes up within the self-similarity of the countable set of integer numbers

NxN=N, (Aleph zero) whose coherence with $N^{\alpha} \times N^{1-\alpha} = N^{2\alpha} \times N^{2(1-\alpha)}$ (Aleph 1) and its link with fractional operators remains to be probed.

This book is an expression of remarkable engineering work. The author of these lines, however, wanted to point out that these researches are based on very fundamental mathematical pillars that explain the effectiveness of the methods described. This book comes to enrich the state of the art of this problematic, otherwise constantly evolving and attracting a growing interest. Several contributions introduce innovative solutions mainly dedicated to the control and synchronization of fractional nonlinear systems. Therefore this book must henceforth take its place in any technical or mathematical library ... It is in this perspective that we have to thank the team that offers to us this work.

Alain Le Méhauté
Materials Design Inc., France

Alain Le Méhauté *was born and lived in Algeria up to 1965. He was graduated in Chemical Engineering in Lyon in 1972 and obtained his Doctorate in Solid State Chemistry in University of Nantes in 1979. ALM had a dual industrial career at CGE (later named Alcatel Alstom) where he was one of the inventors of Lithium Ion batteries (1977) and Additive Layer Technologies techniques (1984). Then as General Director of an Engineering School (1996-2010) he developed new methods using fully digital tools for engineers' curriculum, including in Quantum Mechanics and materials design. His scientific research on dynamics processes in fractal geometry in link with non-integer differential operator has earned him the honorary doctorate degree of Kazan University (2008). He is also the inventor of the Smart Passive Damping Device Systems for mechanical applications. Nowadays, he works with Philippe Riot about the Riemann Hypothesis and Goldbach Conjectures by starting from the Category theory.*

Preface

ABOUT THE SUBJECT

Fractional calculus is a natural generalization of the classical integer-order integral and differential calculus to non-integer orders (including complex orders). With the growing of computers, fractional calculus has recently become an increasingly attractive area of research in the scientific and industrial communities. In the last three decades there has been a considerable development in the use of fractional operators in various fields, such as: control system design, modeling and identification, observation and chaos synchronization. Before the 20th century, the theory of fractional calculus developed mainly as a pure theoretical field of mathematics useful just for mathematicians and theoretical physicists. A significant amount of discussions aimed at this subject has been presented by Oldham and Spanier (1974) and Podlubny (1999). However, it has been recently demonstrated that many real-world physical dynamical systems can be modelled by fractional-order differential equations rather than using classical integer-order ones. Notably, materials characterized by long memory and hereditary effects (Bagley & Torvik, 1984) and dynamical process such as mass diffusion and heat conduction (Jenson & Jeffreys, 1974) in fractal porous media can be mode precisely characterized by fractional-order models rather than integer-order models. There are also many examples of so-called fractal systems including transmission lines, electrochemical processes, viscoelastic materials, and so on. On the other hand, the fractional control has recently received great attention both from an academic and industrial viewpoint, because of their increasing flexibility (with respect to inter-order control systems) which allows the achievement of more challenging control requirements.

Up to the last decades, most engineers and practitioners were rather skeptical and hesitant to accept that chaotic behavior might have a practical application. Therefore, most research in this area has exclusively focused on how to suppress or avoid chaos. Although, now a much more exciting motivation has emerged to draw on and harness the very particular and strange characteristics of chaotic behavior. And essentially, self-synchronization of chaotic systems is a fascinating concept, which has been received considerable attention among nonlinear scientists in recent times. Chaos synchronization and chaos control play a significant role in information processing, control engineering, living organisms, image processing and neural networks, to name few. Besides, the synchronization property of chaotic circuits has revealed potential applications to secure modern communication systems, where the plain-text (-image) is encrypted by the (hyper-)chaotic signal at the transmitter and the cipher-text (-image) is transmitted to the receiver across a public channel (which can be an unsafe channel).

ABOUT THE BOOK

This new IGI Global book entitled *Advanced Synchronization Control and Bifurcation of Chaotic Fractional-Order Systems* contains 15 chapters contributed by subject experts who are specialized in the different topics addressed in this book. These chapters, which have been selected via a rigorous review process, are in the broad areas of chaos theory, fuzzy systems, chaos synchronization, fractional-order systems, secure data communication, modeling and identification, control systems and numerical simulation. A particular importance was given, in the selection of these chapters, to those offering practical solutions and novel theoretical contributions for the current research problems in the major topics of this present book, viz. synchronization and control of fractional-order chaotic systems, and secure data communication based on the synchronization of the fractional-order chaotic systems.

Objectives of This Book

This book presents some latest developments, tends, research solutions and applications of synchronization, control and bifurcations of fractional-order chaotic systems. Many methodologies have been presented for adequately achieving control and chaos synchronization. The proposed methods have been designed in order to overcome the limitations of the previous ones and to improve more advanced solutions for control and synchronization problems of fractional-order chaotic systems, also in order to develop more effective security keys for data communication based on the synchronization of the fractional-order chaotic systems. Most of these methods include the usage of intelligent approaches (as fuzzy systems) and optimization techniques. Besides, one has comprehensively reviewed some necessary tools available in the literature that are eventually used in study of fractional-order chaotic systems.

Organization of This Book

This book contains 15 chapters. Each chapter is briefly introduced below.

Chapter 1 proposes a new control design methodology for the synchronization of fractional-order Arneodo chaotic systems using a fractional-order sliding mode control configuration. The stability analysis of the proposed control law is performed by means of the Lyapunov stability theory.

Chapter 2 focuses on study of dynamics and synchronization of the fractional-order hyperchaotic system. In order to employ these hyperchaotic systems in the information security field, numerical solution algorithm, complex dynamical characteristics and synchronization control of the fractional-order Lorenz hyperchaotic system are investigated by combining means of theory analysis and numerical simulation.

Chapter 3 focuses on the design of a novel adaptive neural control of a class of uncertain multi-input multi-output (MIMO) nonlinear time-delay non-integer order systems with unmeasured states, unknown control direction and unknown asymmetric saturation actuator. First, a simple linear state observer is constructed to estimate the unmeasured states of the transformed system. Then, a neural network is incorporated to approximate the unknown nonlinear functions while a Nussbaum function is used to deal with the unknown control direction. In addition, a Lyapunov method is used to derive the parameter adaptive laws and to perform the stability proof.

Chapter 4 presents an adaptive interval type-2 fuzzy sliding mode control strategy to robustly synchronize two uncertain chaotic fractional-order systems with chattering elimination. The interval type-2 fuzzy logic systems are used to sufficiently approximate the uncertain plant dynamics. Based on fractional-order Lyapunov stability criterion, the stability analysis is performed for the proposed method for an acceptable synchronization error level.

Chapter 5 focuses on the development of a fuzzy adaptive backstepping control-based projective synchronization scheme of a class of uncertain fractional-order nonlinear systems with unknown external disturbances. The uncertain nonlinear functions are online modeled by using the adaptive fuzzy logic systems, and the virtual control terms are determined based on the fractional Lyapunov stability. This proposed control methodology ensures the convergence of the projective synchronization error as well as the stability of the closed-loop control system. Numerical simulations given at the end of this chapter confirm well the effectiveness of the proposed control method.

Chapter 6 focuses on study of the evolution of chaotic systems in open and closed loop in function of their parameters and designing a controller using bifurcation diagrams. A fractional order proportional integral derivative (FOPID) controller is proposed to stabilize the chaotic system on one of its fixed points. Then, using the bifurcation diagrams, we are able to define the variation interval for the three controller parameters, k_P, k_I and k_D where the system stabilizes the desired fixed point. The optimal values are then obtained by mean of a quadratic criterion, including the fractional orders.

Chapter 7 deals with the chaos synchronization problem of multivariable fractional-order chaotic systems subject to uncertain dynamics and external disturbances. More specifically, a novel fuzzy adaptive controller is proposed for achieving a projective synchronization of uncertain fractional-order chaotic systems. The adaptive fuzzy-logic systems are employed to online estimate the uncertain nonlinear functions. The latter is augmented by a robust control term to efficiently compensate for the unavoidable fuzzy approximation errors, external disturbances as well as residual error due to the use of the so-called e-modification in the adaptive laws. A Lyapunov approach is used to derive the parameter adaptation laws and to prove the boundedness of all signals of the closed-loop system.

Chapter 8 proposes a novel chaos synchronization system for a class uncertain optical chaotic systems. More precisely, a fractional-order (FO) sliding mode controller is designed to achieve a rapid, robust and perfect chaos synchronization. It is rigorously proven that the associated synchronization error is Mittag-Leffler stable. In a numerical simulation frame-work, this synchronization scheme is tested on many chaotic optical systems taken from the open control literature.

Chapter 9 addresses the fuzzy adaptive controller design for the generalized projective synchronization (GPS) of incommensurate fractional-order chaotic systems with input nonlinearities. The considered master-slave systems are supposed with different fractional-orders, uncertain models, unknown bounded disturbances and non-identical form. A Lyapunov approach is carefully employed for determining the parameter adaptation laws and proving the stability of the closed-loop system.

Chapter 10 focuses on solving the stabilization problem for a class of fractional chaotic systems subject to uncertainties and external disturbances, proposing a new direct adaptive fuzzy optimal sliding mode control approach. The sliding mode control system parameters are determined via a particle swarm optimization (PSO) algorithm. The numerical simulation results obtained confirm well the efficiency of this proposed fractional adaptive fuzzy control technique.

Chapter 11 focuses on the development of a new fractional-order PD-based feedback control scheme with optimal knowledge base for achieving stabilization and synchronization of class of fractional-order chaotic systems. Based on the Lyapunov stabilization principle of fractional-order systems, the stability analysis of the closed-loop controlled system is rigorously investigated. The control design methodology based a multiobjective optimization presents a powerful and simple approach to provide a reasonable tradeoff between simplicity, numerical accuracy and stability analysis.

Chapter 12 reports a rigorous theoretical study on the dynamical behavior of both integer and fractional-order nonlinear systems. Experience of dynamical behavior is considered. Bifurcation of the parameter-dependent system which provides a summary of essential dynamics is also investigated. Period-3 windows, coexisting limit cycles and chaotic zones are found. The occurrence and the nature of chaotic attractors are effectively verified by evaluating the largest Lyapunov exponents.

Chapter 13 focuses on the problem of synchronization of fractional order-derivative chaotic systems using as random numbers generator for a novel technique to key distribution in cryptography. Unlike the traditional cryptography approaches which are based on integer-order derivative chaotic systems, the aim of this chapter lies on coding and decoding a text via chaos synchronization of fractional order derivative, the performance analysis and the key establishment scheme following by an application on a text encryption using the chaotic Mathieu-Van Der Pol fractional system.

Chapter 14 aims to expose a literature review on synchronization methods of fractional-order discrete-time systems and to propose also a secure digital data communication based on synchronization of fractional-order discrete-time chaotic systems. Two effective synchronization methodologies based on observers are presented to synchronize two fractional-order discrete-time chaotic systems. The first method concerns the impulsive synchronization where sufficient conditions for the synchronization error of the states are given. The second method concerns the exact synchronization which is based on a step-by-step delayed observer. The performance of the proposed communication system is illustrated in numerical simulations where digital image signal is considered.

Chapter 15 focuses on the investigation of the tracking control problem of uncertain multi-input multi-output (MIMO) pure-feedback incommensurate fractional-order systems with output constraints and actuator nonlinearities. The Backstepping technique is applied for adequately determining the control updating laws and carrying out the stability analysis of the overall closed-loop system. Two simulation studies are worked out to illustrate the effectiveness and potential of the proposed adaptive control scheme.

Book Features

- These chapters comprehensively deal with the modern research problems in the topics of chaos synchronization and control of fractional-order systems, and cryptography approaches based on fractional-order systems.
- These chapters present a good literature review with a long list of closely-related references.
- These chapters are well organized and written with a good exhibition of the research problem, methodology, numerical simulation examples, and schematic illustrations/block diagrams.
- The chapters in this book talk about the details of engineering applications and future research topics.

Audience

This book is mainly aimed at researchers from academia and industry, who are working in the research area-synchronization, bifurcation and control of chaotic systems along with their applications in engineering, chaos and control engineering. Overall, this book can be used also as a major reference by undergraduate students for the following courses: control systems, cryptography, fractional calculus, fractional-order control systems, intelligent control, and many others.

REFERENCES

Bagley, R. L., & Torvik, P. J. (1984). On the appearance of the fractional derivative in the behavior of real materials. *Journal of Applied Mechanics*, *51*(2), 294–298. doi:10.1115/1.3167615

Jenson, V. G., & Jeffreys, G. V. (1977). *Mathematical Methods in Chemical Engineering*. London: Academic Press.

Oldham, K. B., & Spanier, J. (1974). *The fractional calculus*. New York: Academic Press.

Podlubny, I. (1999). *Fractional differential equations*. San Diego, CA: Academic Press.

Acknowledgment

The editors wish that these chapters in this edited book will motivate more research in the field of chaos synchronization and control of fractional-order chaotic systems and their real-world applications (as such cryptography, information processing, etc.).

We sincerely hope that this well-structured book, which covers so many different topics, will be very valuable for lecturers, professors, students, and practitioners.

We would like to also thank the reviewers for their valuable and constructive comments and effort to improve the chapters.

A special thank you goes to IGI Global and especially to Ms. Jordan Tepper and the book development team.

Abdesselem Boulkroune
Jijel University, Algeria

Samir Ladaci
National Polytechnic School of Constantine, Algeria

Chapter 1

Robust Synchronization of Fractional–Order Arneodo Chaotic Systems Using a Fractional Sliding Mode Control Strategy

Samir Ladaci
National Polytechnic School of Constantine, Algeria

Karima Rabah
20th August 1955 University of Skikda, Algeria

Mohamed Lashab
University Larbi Ben M'Hidi of Oum El-Bouaghi, Algeria

ABSTRACT

This chapter investigates a new control design methodology for the synchronization of fractional-order Arneodo chaotic systems using a fractional-order sliding mode control configuration. This class of non-linear fractional-order systems shows a chaotic behavior for a set of model parameters. The stability analysis of the proposed fractional-order sliding mode control law is performed by means of the Lyapunov stability theory. Simulation examples on fractional-order Arneodo chaotic systems synchronization are provided in presence of disturbances and noises. These results illustrate the effectiveness and robustness of this control design approach.

INTRODUCTION

For many decades ago, a huge number of research works have been carried out on mathematical topics of fractional calculus, dealing with derivatives and integrations of non-integer order. The fractional calculation was first introduced by (Oldham & Spanier, 1974), who presented the fractional derivative and the fractional integral. Several works have been done on the fractional calculation in electromagnetism

DOI: 10.4018/978-1-5225-5418-9.ch001

(Engheta, 1997; Jesus et al., 2006; Onufriyenko & Lewykin, 2002), they are generally based on the fractional derivative. Many other researchers investigated on fractional operators (Alexiadis et al., 2004; Harsoyo, 2007; Diethelm & Ford, 2005). Compared to the classical theory, fractional differential equations can be treated in very precise manner to describe many systems in various disciplinary scientific fields, such as material with vescoelasticity properties, dielectric polarization, chemical and electrolyte polarization, the nonlinear oscillation due to vibration of earthquakes, mechanics and electromagnetic wave systems (Lashab et al., 2010; Machado et al., 2011).

Very interesting performances and properties have been obtained based on fractional-order systems, and consequently great applications of such systems have been performed in various domains such as automatic control (Ladaci et al., 2009; Ladaci & Bensafia, 2015; Bettayeb et al., 2017), robotics and embedded systems (Duarte & Machado, 2002, Blu & Unse, 2007), analog and digital signal processing (Mandelbrot & Van Ness, 1968; Bhandari & Marziliano, 2010; Lamb et al., 2016; Li et al., 2017), image processing and digital video broad cast (Oustaloup, 1991), maximum power tracking and renewable energy (Neçaibia et al., 2015).

During the last decade, significant research efforts have been devoted to fractional systems that display chaotic behavior like: Newton–Leipnik formulation (Sheu et al., 2008), Rössler model (Li & Chen, 2004), Duffing model (Arena et al., 1997), Chua system (Hartley et al., 1995), Jerk model (Ahmad & Sprott, 2003), Chen dynamic circuit (Lu & Chen, 2006), characterization (Lu, 2006) ... The synchronization or control of these systems is a difficult task because the main characteristic of chaotic systems is their high sensitivity to initial conditions (N'doye et al. 2017). However, it is gathering more and more research effort due to several potential applications especially in cryptography (HosseinNia et al., 2010; Kadir et al., 2011, Rabah et al., 2015).

For the particular case of fractional-order systems with chaotic dynamics, many methods have been introduced to realize chaos synchronization, such as PC control (Miller & Ross, 1993), fractional-order $PI^\lambda D^\mu$ control (Rabah et al., 2016; Rabah et al., 2017), nonlinear state observer method (Wu et al., 2009), fuzzy adaptive control (Khettab et al. 2017), adaptive back-stepping control (Shukla & Sharma, 2017), sliding mode control (Bourouba & Ladaci, 2017; Hamiche et al, 2013; Guo & Ma, 2016) etc.

In the present work, we are interested by the problem of fractional-order Arneodo chaotic system synchronization by means of sliding mode control (Chen et al. 2012; Yin et al., 2012). Sliding mode control is a very suitable method for handling such nonlinear systems because of its robustness against disturbances and plant parameter uncertainties and its order reduction property (Xu et al., 2015).

The main objective is to design an appropriate control law such that the sliding mode is reached in a finite time. The system trajectory moves toward the sliding surface and stays on it. The conventional SMC uses a control law with large control gains yielding undesired chattering while the control system is in the sliding mode (Huanget al., 2008). Based on the Lyapunov stability theorem, an efficient control algorithm is proposed which guarantees feedback control system stability via the sliding mode robust tracking design technique.

This chapter is structured as follows. Section 2 presents an introduction to fractional calculus with some numerical approximation methods. The problem of fractional-order chaotic system synchronization is given in Section 3. Section 4 presents the proposed sliding mode synchronization technique and the control law design. The stability analysis is performed in Section 5. In Section 6, applications of the proposed control scheme on Arneodo fractional-order systems are investigated. Finally, conclusion remarks with future works are pointed out in Section 7.

ELEMENTS OF FRACTIONAL ORDER SYSTEMS

Fractional calculus theory deals with derivatives and integrals of arbitrary order that is not only integer orders as in the classical theory. This theory appeared and grows up mainly since three centuries. A recent reference presented by Miller & Ross (1993) provides a good source of documentation on fractional systems and operators. However, topics about the application of fractional-order operator theory to dynamic system control are just a recent focus of interest (Oustaloup, 1991; Ladaci & Charef, 2006).

1. Definitions

There are many mathematical definitions of fractional integration and derivation. We shall here, present two currently used definitions.

1.1 Riemann–Liouville (R–L) Definition

It is one of the most popular definitions of the fractional-order integrals and derivative (Miller & Ross, 1993). The R–L integral of fractional-order $\lambda > 0$ is given as:

$$I_{RL}^{\lambda} g\left(t\right) = D_{RL}^{-\lambda} g\left(t\right)$$
$$= \frac{1}{\Gamma(\lambda)} \int_{t_0}^{t} \left(t - \zeta\right)^{\pm-1} g\left(\zeta\right) d\zeta \tag{1}$$

and the R–L derivative of fractional-order μ is

$$D_{RL}^{\mu} g\left(t\right) = \frac{1}{\Gamma(n-\mu)} \frac{d^n}{dt^n} \int_{0}^{t} \left(t - \zeta\right)^{n-\mu-1} g\left(\zeta\right) d\zeta \tag{2}$$

where the integer n verifies: $(n - 1) < \mu < n$. The fractional-order derivative (2) may also be expressed from equation (1) as

$$D_{RL}^{\mu} g\left(t\right) = \frac{d^n}{dt^n} \left[I_{RL}^{n-\mu} g\left(t\right) \right] \tag{3}$$

1.2 Grünwald–Leitnikov (G–L) Definition

The G–L fractional-order integral with order $\lambda > 0$ is

$$I_{GL}^{\lambda} g\left(t\right) = D_{RL}^{-\lambda} g\left(t\right)$$
$$= \lim_{h \to 0} h^{\lambda} \sum_{j=0}^{k} \left(-1\right)^{j} \binom{-\lambda}{j} g\left(kh - jh\right) \tag{4}$$

Here, h is the sampling period with the coefficients $\omega(-\lambda)j$ verifying

$$\omega_0^{(-\lambda)} = \begin{pmatrix} -\lambda \\ 0 \end{pmatrix} = 1$$

which belong to the following polynomial:

$$\left(1-z\right)^{-\lambda} = \sum_{j=0}^{\infty} (-1)^j \begin{pmatrix} -\lambda \\ j \end{pmatrix} z^j = \sum_{j=0}^{\infty} \omega_j^{(-\lambda)} z^j \tag{5}$$

The G–L definition for fractional-order derivative with order $\mu > 0$ is

$$\begin{aligned} \mathrm{D}_{\mathrm{GL}}^{\mu} \mathrm{g}\left(\mathrm{t}\right) &= \frac{d^{\mu}}{dt^{\mu}} \mathrm{g}\left(\mathrm{t}\right) \\ &= \lim_{h \to 0} h^{-\mu} \sum_{j=0}^{k} (-1)^j \begin{pmatrix} \mu \\ j \end{pmatrix} g\left(kh - jh\right) \end{aligned} \tag{6}$$

where the coefficients

$$\omega_j^{(\mu)} = \begin{pmatrix} \mu \\ j \end{pmatrix} = \frac{\Gamma\left(\mu+1\right)}{\Gamma\left(j+1\right)\Gamma\left(\mu-j+1\right)}$$

with $\omega 0\ (\mu) = (\mu\ 0\ ) = 1$, are those of the polynomial:

$$\left(1-z\right)^{-\mu} = \sum_{j=0}^{\infty} (-1)^j \begin{pmatrix} \mu \\ j \end{pmatrix} z^j = \sum_{j=0}^{\infty} \omega_j^{(\mu)} z^j \tag{7}$$

2. Implementation Techniques

It is usual that industrial processes controls are sampled, and so a numerical approximation of the fractional operator is necessary. There exist several approximation approach classes depending on temporal or frequency domain. In the literature, the currently used approaches in frequency domain are those of Charef (Ladaci, &Bensafia, 2015) and Oustaloup (1991). In temporal domain, there are many approaches for the numerical solution of the fractional differential equations. Diethelm has proposed an efficient method based on the predictor–corrector Adams algorithm (Diethelm, 2003). Different definitions cited above have numerical approximations also (Bouroubaet al. 2017).

3. Fractional-Order System Stability

Let us recall the stability definition in the sense of Mittag–Leffler functions (Liet al. 2009).

Definition 1

The Mittag–Leffler function is frequently used in the solutions of fractional-order systems. It is defined as

$$E_\alpha(z) = \sum_{j=0}^{\infty} \frac{z^k}{\Gamma(k\alpha + 1)} \tag{8}$$

where $\alpha > 0$. The Mittag–Leffler function with two parameters has the following form:

$$E_{\alpha,\beta}(z) = \sum_{j=0}^{\infty} \frac{z^k}{\Gamma(k\alpha + \beta)} \tag{9}$$

where $\alpha > 0$ and $\beta > 0$. For $\beta = 1$, we have $E\alpha(z) = E\alpha,1(z)$.

Definition 2

Consider the Riemann–Liouville fractional non-autonomous system

$$D_{RL}^{\mu} x(t) = f(x, t) \tag{10}$$

where $f(x, t)$ is Lipschitz with a Lipschitz constant $l > 0$ and $\alpha \in (0, 1)$.

The solution of (10) is said to be Mittag–Leffler stable if

$$\|x(t)\| \le \left[m\left(x(t_0) \right) E_\alpha \left(-\lambda (t - t_0) \alpha \right) \right]^b \tag{11}$$

where t_0 is the initial time, $\alpha \in (0, 1)$, $\lambda > 0$, $b > 0$, $m(0) = 0$, $m(x) \ge 0$ and $m(x)$ is locally Lipschitz on $x \in B \subset R^n$ with Lipschitz constant m_0.

An important stability result is given below (Liet al. 2009).

Lemma 1: *Let $x = 0$ be a point of equilibrium for the fractional-order system* (10). *Suppose there exist a Lyapunov function $V(t, x(t))$ such that*

$$\in_1 \|x\|^\eta \le V(t, x) \le \in_2 \|x\| \tag{12}$$

$$\dot{V}(t, x) \leq \in_3 \left\| x(t) \right\| \tag{13}$$

where ϵ_1, ϵ_2, ϵ_3 and η are positive constants. Then the equilibrium point of system (10) is Mittag–Leffler (asymptotically) stable.

Synchronization of Fractional-Order Chaotic Systems

The following class of n-dimensional non-autonomous fractional-order chaotic system is considered (Jiang & Ma, 2013):

$$\begin{cases} D^q x_1 = x_2 \\ \vdots \\ D^q x_{n-1} = x_n \\ D^q x_n = f(x, t) \end{cases} \tag{14}$$

where $\mathbf{x} = [x1, x2, ..., xn]^T = [x, x^{(q)}, x^{(2q)}, ..., x^{((n-1)q)}]^T \in \mathbf{R}^n$, $f(\mathbf{x}, t)$ is a nonlinear function of $\mathbf{x}$ and

$0 < q < 1$.

Taking (14) as the drive system, the response system with a control input *u(t)* becomes

$$\begin{cases} D^q y_1 = y_2 \\ \vdots \\ D^q y_{n-1} = y_n \\ D^q y_n = g(y, t) + u \end{cases} \tag{15}$$

Where $\mathbf{y} = [y1, y2, ..., yn]^T \in \mathbf{R}^n$, $g(\mathbf{y}, t)$ is the nonlinear function of $\mathbf{y}$. Defining the error vector $\mathbf{e(t)}$ = $\mathbf{y(t)} - \mathbf{x(t)}$, and from equations (14) and (15), the error equation is as follows:

$$\begin{cases} D^q e_1 = e_2 \\ \vdots \\ D^q e_{n-1} = e_n \\ D^q e_n = g(y, t) - f(x, t) + u \end{cases} \tag{16}$$

Thus, the problem of synchronizing two fractional-order nonlinear systems is equivalent to the problem of finding a control *u(t)* ensuring that the error $\mathbf{e}$ in (16) converges to zero. A sliding mode controller is designed to achieve this objective in the next section.

Design of the Sliding Mode Controller

The main reason for the growing popularity of sliding mode control (SMC) is its robustness against disturbances under certain conditions (Xu & Wang, 2013; Xu et al. 2015). In this contribution, we propose a fractional-order sliding surface as

$$s\left(t\right) = k_1 D^{q-1} e_n + k_2 \int_0^t \sum_{i=1}^n c_i e_i \left(\xi\right) d\xi \tag{17}$$

where k_1, k_2 are positive coefficients and c_i, $i = 1, 2, ..., n$ are sliding surface parameters to be determined. The equivalent sliding mode control is obtained by taking the derivative of eq. (17) as follows:

$$\dot{s}\left(t\right) = k_1 D^q e_n + k_2 \sum_{i=1}^n c_i e_i = 0$$
$$\Rightarrow D^q e_n = \frac{k_2}{k_1} \sum_{i=1}^n c_i e_i \tag{18}$$

Hence, using eqs (16) and (17) we obtain the equivalent sliding mode control

$$u_{eq}\left(t\right) = -g(y,t) + f(x,t) - k \sum_{i=1}^n c_i e_i \tag{19}$$

Where $k = k_2/k_1$ is a positive real number. Choosing the following switch control law

$$u_{sw}\left(t\right) = -k sign\left(s\right) \tag{20}$$

The sliding mode control can be obtained as

$$u\left(t\right) = u_{eq}\left(t\right) + u_{sw(t)}$$
$$= -g\left(y,t\right) + f\left(x,t\right) - k \sum_{i=1}^n c_i e_i \tag{21}$$

The objective is that the state trajectories of the system described by eq. (15) converge towards the sliding surface. Thus, by defining;

$$c_i^* = -\frac{k_2}{k_1} c_i \tag{22}$$

The sliding mode dynamics are given by the following equations:

$$\begin{cases} D^q e_1 = e_2 \\ \vdots \\ D^q e_{n-1} = e_n \\ D^q e_n = \sum_{i=1}^{n} c_i^* e_i \end{cases}$$ (23)

or in a matrix equation form as:

$$D^q e(t) = A e(t)$$ (24)

where

$$e = [e_1, e_2, \ldots, e_n]^T$$

and

$$A = \begin{bmatrix} 0 & 1 & \cdots & 0 \\ \vdots & \vdots & \ddots & \vdots \\ 0 & 0 & \cdots & 1 \\ c_1^* & c_2^* & \cdots & c_n^* \end{bmatrix}$$

The selection of the fractional-order sliding surface parameters c^*_i $(i = 1, 2, ..., n)$ obeys the stability theorem of Matignon (Matignon, 1996, Ladaci & Moulay, 2008) which imposes for the sliding surface of eq. (17) to be asymptotically stable that the stability condition $|arg(eig(A))| > q\pi/2$ is verified.

STABILITY ANALYSIS

The principal result of this work is expressed by the following theorem:

Theorem 1: *Synchronization of systems (14) and (15) is perfectly achieved by the sliding mode control law (21) with $k = k_2/k_1$.*

Proof. We shall prove that the systems given by equations (14) and (15) are completely synchronized which means that the error dynamical system (16) is asymptotically stable. Let us choose a positive definite Lyapunov candidate function such that

$$V = |S|$$ (25)

(It is obvious that the Lyapunov function $V(t, e(t))$ satisfies the conditions in Lemma 1 for $\eta = 1$ and some positive constants ϵ_1 and ε_2.)

We get by simple derivative,

$$\dot{V} = sign\left(S\right)\dot{S}$$

$$= sign(S)\left[k_1 D^\alpha e_n + k_2 \sum_{i=1}^{n} c_i e_i\right]$$

$$= sign(S)\left[k_1\left(g(y,t) - f(x,t) + u\right) + k_2 \sum_{i=1}^{n} c_i e_i\right]$$

$$= sign(S)\left[k_1\left(-k\sum_{i=1}^{n} c_i e_i - k\, sign(S)\right) + k_2 \sum_{i=1}^{n} c_i e_i\right]$$

We set

$$k = \frac{k_2}{k_1} \tag{26}$$

Then we have

$$\dot{V} = sign(S)\left[k_1\left(-\frac{k_2}{k_1}\sum_{i=1}^{n} c_i e_i - \frac{k_2}{k_1} sign(S)\right) + k_2 \sum_{i=1}^{n} c_i e_i\right]$$

$$= sign(S)\left[-k_2\sum_{i=1}^{n} c_i e_i - k_2 sign(S) + k_2 \sum_{i=1}^{n} c_i e_i\right]$$

$$= sign(S)\left(-k_2 sign(S)\right)$$

$$= -k_2 \tag{27}$$

Then, it is always possible to find the positive constant ε_3 such that

$$\dot{V} = -k_2 \leq -\varepsilon_3 \|\mathbf{e}\|$$

and following lemma 1, system (16) is mittag–leffler stable and the error asymptotically converges to zero, which completes the proof.

APPLICATION TO FRACTIONAL ORDER ARNEODO SYSTEMS

The fractional order Arneodo system, belonging to the class of nonlinear systems (14) is defined by the following mathematical model,

$$\begin{cases} x^{(q)} = y \\ y^{(q)} = z \\ z^{(q)} = a\,x - b\,y - r\,z - x^3 \end{cases} \tag{28}$$

For $a = 5.5$, $b = 3.5$, $r = 0.4$ and $q = 0.9$ the fractional order system presents a chaotic behavior as shown in Figure 1.

Figure 1. Fractional order Arneodo Attractors

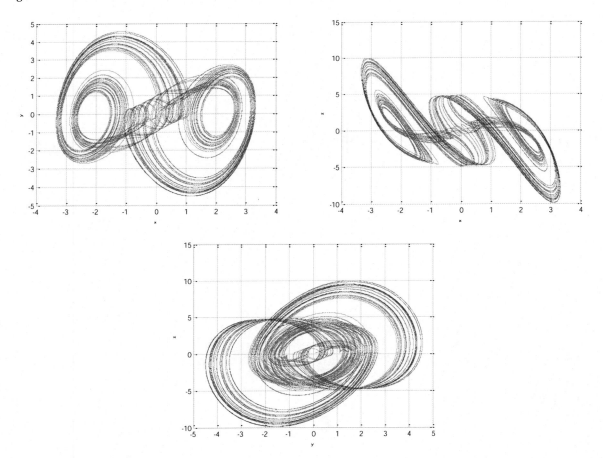

Now let us consider the problem of synchronizing two fractional order chaotic Arneodo systems. The state variables of the master and slave systems with initial conditions:

$$\left(0.2, 0.2, 0.2\right), \left(0.8, 0.4, 0.5\right)$$

are depicted respectively in Figures 2 and 3.

1. Synchronisation of Arneodo in Ideal Conditions (Without Disturbances)

We consider first that the system is free of disturbing signals. We take as sliding surface parameters the values $\left(c_1, c_2, c_3\right) = \left(6, 1, 5\right)$. After launching the sliding mode control action at $t = 10\,s$ with the gains values $\left(k_1, k_2\right) = \left(1, 0.08\right)$ with a sampling time of $h = 0.005$, the fractional order chaotic slave system is forced towards the sliding surface by the SMC controller. The simulation results are presented in Figures 4, 5, 6 and 7.

Figure 2. Chaotic behavior of the fractional order Arneodo master system

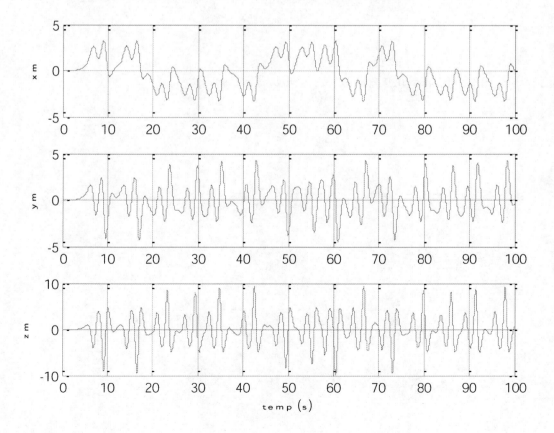

Figure 3. Chaotic behavior of the fractional order Arneodo slave system

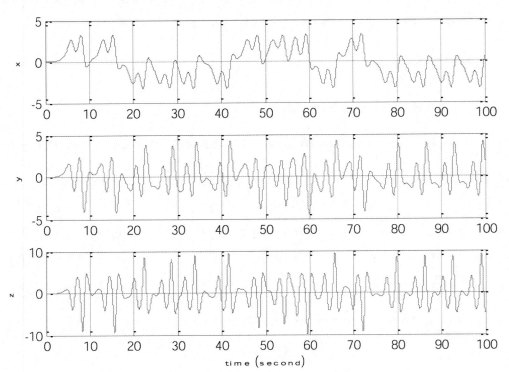

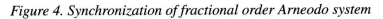

Figure 4. Synchronization of fractional order Arneodo system

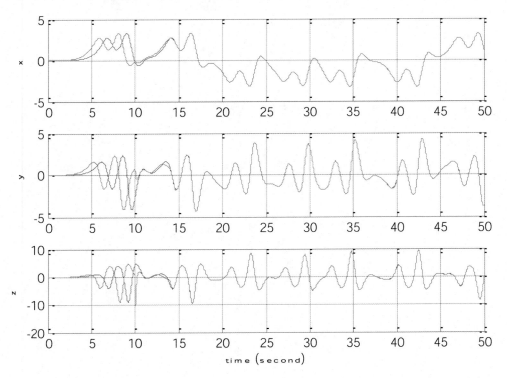

Figure 5. Synchronization errors of Arneodo fractional system

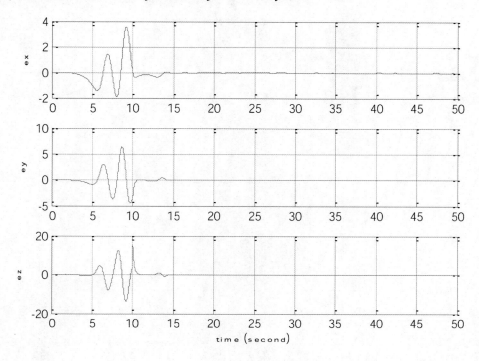

Figure 6. Control signal

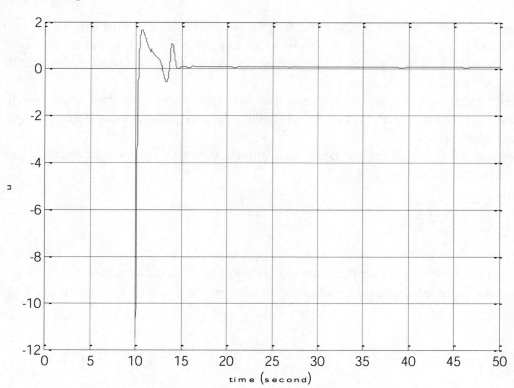

Figure 7. Sliding surface functions for the Arneodo fractional order system synchronization

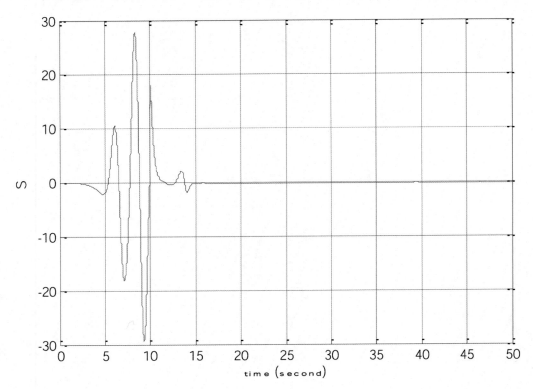

As shown in figure 4, there are three stages of the controlled system (Yang & Liu, 2013). In the first 20 s, Without controller, the system is chaotic as we can see in Figure 3. In the second phase (known as the reaching phase), after $t = 10$ s, the fractional-order chaotic system is forced towards the sliding manifold by the sliding mode controller.

When the trajectory touches the sliding surface, the system enters the third phase, which is called sliding mode operation. The results presented here show the good performance exhibited by the proposed synchronization schemes.

In order to point out the performance of the control system vs. the control parameter k, let us define the quadratic error criterion J as

$$J = \sqrt{\int_{t_c}^{t_f} \left(e_x^2 + e_y^2 + e_z^2 \right)}$$ (29)

where t_c is the time of control application and t_f is the simulation time duration.

The evolution of the quadratic error criterion J relatively to the controller parameters k_1 and k_2 is illustrated in Figure 8.

Figure 8. Quadratic error criterion J vs. the controller parameters k_1 and k_2

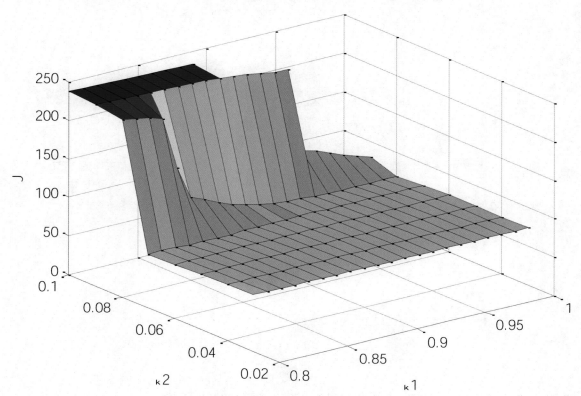

2. Synchronization of Arneodo Systems in Distributed Conditions

Now, we apply a random disturbance signal to the fractional order Arneodo system to investigate on the proposed SMC performance in bas operating conditions. The mathematical model is given by the equation,

$$\begin{cases} x^{(q)} = y \\ y^{(q)} = z \\ z^{(q)} = -ax - by - rz + x^3 + \xi \end{cases} \tag{30}$$

where $\xi(t) = B * rand$ is the random signal with $B = 0.01$.

The simulation results demonstrate the efficiency of the proposed SMC control method to achieve the synchronization of the two Arneodo systems with disturbance rejection (Plestan et al. 2010).

Figure 9. Synchronization of the fractional order disturbed Arneodo system

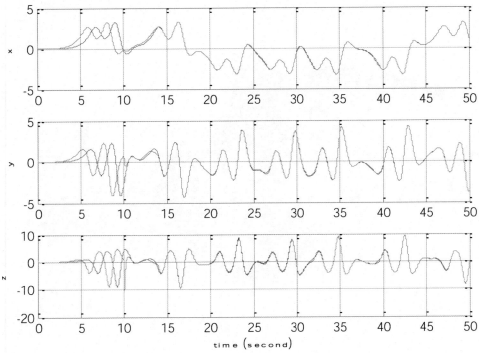

Figure 10. Synchronization errors of disturbed Arneodo fractional system

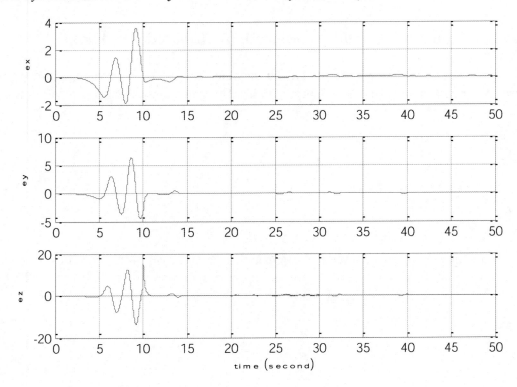

Figure 11. Control signal for disturbed fractional order Arneodo system

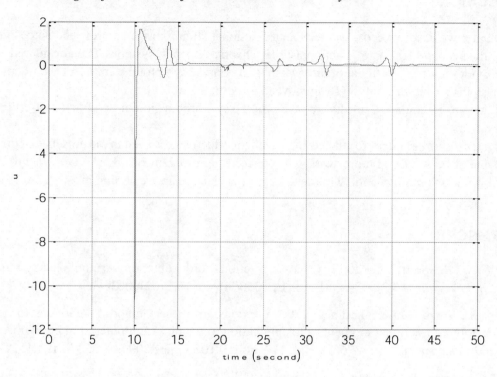

Figure 12. Sliding surface for the disturbed Arneodo fractional order system synchronization

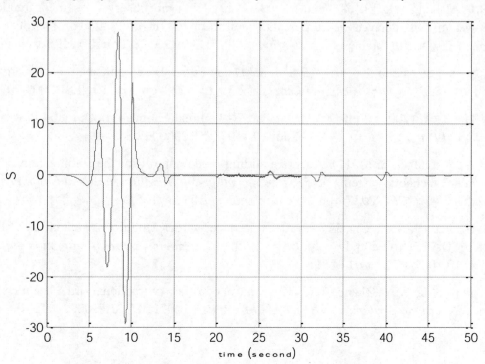

CONCLUSION

In this chapter we have studied a new efficient fractional sliding mode control scheme design in order to enable the synchronization of fractional-order chaotic Arneodo systems. The considered design approach provides a set of fractional order laws that guarantee asymptotic stability of the fractional-order chaotic systems in the sense of the Lyapunov stability theorem.

The illustrative simulation results are given for the synchronization of two fractional-order Arneodo chaotic systems.

The systems show good performance and excellent effectiveness even in the presence of disturbances affecting the slave system. Future work will concern the problem of control and synchronization of fractional-order uncertain chaotic with delays systems using adaptive sliding mode control laws.

REFERENCES

Ahmad, W. M., & Sprott, J. C. (2003). Chaos in fractional-order autonomous nonlinear systems. *Chaos, Solitons, and Fractals, 16*(2), 339–351. doi:10.1016/S0960-0779(02)00438-1

Alexiadis, A., Vanni, M., & Gardin, P. (2004). Extension of the method of moments for population balances involving fractional moments and application to a typical agglomeration problem. *Journal of Colloid and Interface Science, 276*(1), 106–112. doi:10.1016/j.jcis.2004.03.052 PMID:15219436

Arena, P., Caponetto, R., Fortuna, L., & Porto, D. (1997). Chaos in a fractional order duffing system. In *Proceedings of The International Conference of ECCTD* (pp. 1259-1262). Budapest: Academic Press.

Bettayeb, M., Al-Saggaf, U. M., & Djennoune, S. (2017). High gain observer design for fractional-order non-linear systems with delayed measurements: Application to synchronisation of fractional-order chaotic systems. *IET Control Theory & Applications, 11*(17), 3191–3178. doi:10.1049/iet-cta.2017.0396

Bhandari, A., & Marziliano, P. (2010). Fractional Delay Filters Based on Generalized Cardinal Exponential Splines. *IEEE Signal Processing Letters, 17*(3), 225–228. doi:10.1109/LSP.2009.2036386

Blu, T., & Unse, M. (2007). Self-Similarity: Part II- Optimal Estimation of Fractal Processes. *IEEE Trans. On Signal Proc, 55*(4), 1364–1378. doi:10.1109/TSP.2006.890845

Bourouba, B., & Ladaci, S. (2017). Adaptive sliding mode control for the stabilization of a class of fractional-order Lü chaotic systems. In *Proceedings of the 5th IEEE International Conference on Electrical Engineering – (ICEE'2017)* (pp.1-5). Boumerdes, Algeria: IEEE.

Bourouba, B., Ladaci, S., & Chaabi, A. (2017). Reduced-Order Model Approximation of Fractional-Order Systems Using Differential Evolution Algorithm. *Journal of Control, Automation and Electrical Systems*. doi: 10.1007/s40313-017-0356-5

Chen, D., Liu, Y., Ma, X., & Zhang, R. (2012). Control of a class of fractional-order chaotic systems via sliding mode. *Nonlinear Dynamics, 67*(1), 893–901. doi:10.100711071-011-0002-x PMID:22757537

Diethelm, K. (2003). Efficient Solution of Multi-Term Fractional Differential Equations Using P(EC) mE Methods. *Computing, 71*(4), 305–319. doi:10.100700607-003-0033-3

Diethelm, K., Ford, N. J., Freed, A. D., & Luchko, Y. (2005). Algorithms for the fractional calculus: A selection of numerical methods. *Computer Methods in Applied Mechanics and Engineering, 194*(6-8), 743–773. doi:10.1016/j.cma.2004.06.006

Duarte, F. B. M., & Machado, J. A. T. (2002). Chaotic Phenomena and Fractional-Order Dynamics in the Trajectory Control of Redundant Manipulators. *Nonlinear Dynamics, 29*(1–4), 315–342. doi:10.1023/A:1016559314798

Engheta, N. (1997). On the Role of Fractional Calculus in Electromagnetic Theory. *IEEE Transact. on Antennas Propagation, 39*(4), 35-46.

Guo, Y., & Ma, B. (2016). Stabilization of a class of uncertainnonlinear system via fractional sliding mode controller. In *Proceedings of 2016 Chinese Intelligent Systems Conference, Lecture Notes in Electrical Engineering.* Springer. 10.1007/978-981-10-2338-5_34

Hamiche, H., Guermah, S., Djennoune, S., Kemih, K., Ghanes, M., & Barbot, J.-P. (2013). Chaotic synchronisation and secure communication via sliding-mode and impulsive observers.*International Journal of Modelling. Identification and Control., 20*(4), 305–318. doi:10.1504/IJMIC.2013.057564

Harsoyo, A. (2007). Weyl's Fractional Operator Expression of Skin Effect of a Good Conductor. In *Proceedings of the International Conference on Electrical Engineering and Informatics.* InstitutTeknologi Bandung, Indonesia.

Hartley, T. T., Lorenzo, C. F., & Qammer, H. K. (1995). Chaos in fractional order Chua's System. *IEEE Transactions on Circuits and Systems. I, Fundamental Theory and Applications, 42*(8), 485–490. doi:10.1109/81.404062

HosseinNia, S. H. (2010). Control of chaos via fractional order state feedback controller. In New trends in nanotechnology and fractional calculus applications. Berlin: Springer-Verlag.

Huang, Y. J., Kuo, T. C., & Chang, S. H. (2008). Adaptive Sliding-Mode Control for NonlinearSystems with Uncertain Parameters. *IEEE Transactions on Systems, Man, and Cybernetics. Part B, Cybernetics, 38*(2), 534–539. doi:10.1109/TSMCB.2007.910740 PMID:18348934

Jesus, I. S., Machado, J. A. T., & Cunha, J. B. (2006).Application of genetic algorithms to the implementation of fractional electromagnetic potentials. *Proceedings of The Fifth International Conference on Engineering Computational Technology (ECT'06).* 10.4203/ccp.84.58

Jiang, W., & Ma, T. (2013). Synchronization of a class of fractional-order chaotic systems via adaptive sliding mode control. In *Proceedings of the Int. IEEE Conf. Vehicular Electronics and Safety (ICVES)* (pp. 229-233). Dongguan, China: IEEE. 10.1109/ICVES.2013.6619637

Kadir, A., Wang, X. Y., & Zhao, Y.-Z. (2011). Robust adaptive fuzzy neural tracking control for a class of unknown chaotic systems. *Pramana – Journal of Physics, 76*(6), 887–900.

Khettab, K., Ladaci, S., & Bensafia, Y. (2017). Fuzzy adaptive control of fractional order chaotic systems with unknown control gain sign using a fractional order Nussbaum gain. *IEEE/CAA Journal of Automatica Sinica, 4*(4). DOI: 10.1109/JAS.2016.7510169

Ladaci, S., & Bensafia, Y. (2015). Fractional order Self-Tuning Control. In *Proceedings of the IEEE 13th International Conference on Industrial Informatics (INDIN'15)* (pp. 544-549). Cambridge, UK: IEEE. 10.1109/INDIN.2015.7281792

Ladaci, S., & Charef, A. (2006). On Fractional Adaptive Control. *Nonlinear Dynamics, 43*(4), 365–378. doi:10.100711071-006-0159-x

Ladaci, S., Charef, A., & Loiseau, J. J. (2009). Robust fractional adaptive control based on the strictly positive realness condition. *International Journal of Applied Mathematics and Computer Science, 19*(1), 69–76. doi:10.2478/v10006-009-0006-6

Ladaci, S., & Moulay, E. (2008). Lp-stability analysis of a class of nonlinear fractional differential equations. *Journal of Automation and Systems Engineering, 2*(1), 40–46.

Lamb, D., Chamon, L. F. O., & Nascimento, V. H. (2016). Efficient filtering structure for Spline interpolation and decimation. *Electronics Letters, 52*(1), 39–41. doi:10.1049/el.2015.1957

Lashab, M., Ladaci, S., Abdelliche, F., Zebiri, C., & Benabdelaziz, F. (2010). Fractional spline wavelet for numerical analysis in electromagnetic. In *Proceedings of the International Multi-Conference on Systems Signals and Devices (SSD)*. Amman, Jordan: Academic Press. 10.1109/SSD.2010.5585573

Li, C., & Chen, G. (2004). Chaos and hyperchaos in the fractional-order Rössler equations. *Physica A, 341*(1–4), 55–61. doi:10.1016/j.physa.2004.04.113

Li, Y., Chen, Y. Q., & Podlubny, I. (2009). Mittag–Leffler stability of fractional order nonlinear dynamic systems. *Automatica, 45*(8), 1965–1969. doi:10.1016/j.automatica.2009.04.003

Li, Z., Santi, F., Pastina, D., & Lombardo, P. (2017). Passive Radar Array With Low-Power Satellite Illuminators Based on Fractional Fourier Transform. *IEEE Sensors Journal, 17*(24), 8378–8394. doi:10.1109/JSEN.2017.2765079

Lu, J. G. (2006). Chaotic dynamics of the fractional-order Lü system and its synchronization. *Physics Letters. [Part A], 354*(4), 305–311. doi:10.1016/j.physleta.2006.01.068

Lu, J. G., & Chen, G. (2006). A note on the fractional-order Chen system. *Chaos, Solitons, and Fractals, 27*(3), 685–688. doi:10.1016/j.chaos.2005.04.037

Machado, J. T., Kiryakova, V., & Mainardi, F. (2011). Recent history of fractional calculus. *Communications in Nonlinear Science and Numerical Simulation, 16*(3), 1140–1153. doi:10.1016/j.cnsns.2010.05.027

Mandelbrot, B., & Van Ness, J. W. (1968). Fractional Brownian motions, fractional noises and applications. *SIAM Review, 10*(4), 422–437. doi:10.1137/1010093

Matignon, D. (1996). Stability results for fractional differential equations with applications to control processing. *Proceedings of IMACS, IEEE-SMC, Computational Engineering in Systems and Application Multi-conference, 2*, 963–968.

Miller, K., & Ross, B. (1993). *An introduction to the fractional calculus and fractional differential equations*. New York: Wiley.

N'doye, I., Laleg-Kirati, T.-M., Darouach, M., & Voos, H. (2017). $\mathcal{H}\infty$ Adaptive observer for nonlinear fractional-order systems. *International Journal of Adaptive Control and Signal Processing*, *31*(3), 314–331. doi:10.1002/acs.2699

Neçaibia, A., Ladaci, S., Charef, A., & Loiseau, J. J. (2015). Fractional order extremum seeking approach for maximum power point tracking of photovoltaic panels. *Frontiers in Energy*, *9*(1), 43–53. doi:10.100711708-014-0343-5

Oldham, K. B., & Spanier, J. (1974). *The fractional Calculus, Theory and applications of Differentiation and integration to arbitrary order*. London: Academic Press Inc.

Onufriyenko, V. M., & Lewykin, V. M. (2002) Integro-Differential Potentials for the Analysis of a Fractal cover Properties. *Proceedings of the IX Conference on Mathematical Methods for electromagnetic Theory (MMET'02)*. 10.1109/MMET.2002.1106932

Oustaloup, A. (1991). *Commande Robuste d'ordre non Entier. In The CRONE control (La commande CRONE)*. Paris: Hermès.

Plestan, F., Shtessel, Y., Bregeault, V., & Poznyak, A. (2010). New methodologies for adaptive sliding mode control. *International Journal of Control*, *83*(9), 1907–1919. doi:10.1080/00207179.2010.501385

Rabah, K., Ladaci, S. & Lashab, M. (2016). Stabilization of a Genesio-Tesi Chaotic System Using a Fractional Order $PI^\lambda D^\mu$ Regulator. *International Journal of Sciences and Techniques of Automatic Control & Computer Engineering*, *10*(1), 2085–2090.

Rabah, K., Ladaci, S. & Lashab, M. (2017) Bifurcation-based Fractional Order $PI^\lambda D^\mu$ Controller Design Approach for Nonlinear Chaotic Systems. *Frontiers of Information Technology & Electronic Engineering*. DOI: 10.1613/FITEE.1601543

Rabah, K., Ladaci, S., & Lashab, M. (2015). Stabilization of Fractional Chen Chaotic System by Linear Feedback Control. In *Proceedings of the 3rd Int. IEEE Conf. on Control, Engineering & Information Technology (CEIT2015)*. Tlemcen, Algeria: IEEE. 10.1109/CEIT.2015.7232990

Sheu, L. J., Chen, H.-K., Chen, J.-H., Tam, L.-M., Chen, W.-C., Lin, K.-T., & Kang, Y. (2008). Chaos in the Newton-Leipnik System with Fractional Order. *Chaos, Solitons, and Fractals*, *36*(1), 98–103. doi:10.1016/j.chaos.2006.06.013

Shukla, M. K., & Sharma, B. B. (2017). Stabilization of a class of uncertain fractional order chaotic systems via adaptive backstepping control. In *Proceedings of the IEEE 2017 Indian Control Conference (ICC)*. IIT Guwahati. 10.1109/INDIANCC.2017.7846518

Wu, X. J., Lu, H. T., & Shen, S. L. (2009). Synchronization of a new fractional-order hyperchaotic system. *Physics Letters. [Part A]*, *373*(27–28), 2329–2337. doi:10.1016/j.physleta.2009.04.063

Xu, Y., & Wang, H. (2013). Synchronization of Fractional-Order Chaotic Systems with Gaussian Fluctuation by Sliding Mode Control. *Abstract and Applied Analysis*, *948782*, 1–7.

Xu, Y., Wang, H., Liu, D., & Huang, H. (2015). Sliding mode control of a class of fractional chaotic systems in the presence of parameter perturbations. *Journal of Vibration and Control, 21*(3), 435–448. doi:10.1177/1077546313486283

Yang, N., & Liu, C. (2013). A novel fractional-order hyperchaotic system stabilization via fractional sliding-mode control. *Nonlinear Dynamics, 74*(3), 721–732. doi:10.100711071-013-1000-y

Yin, C., Zhong, S., & Chen, W. (2012). Design of sliding mode controller for a class of fractional-order chaotic systems. *Communications in Nonlinear Science and Numerical Simulation, 17*(1), 356–366. doi:10.1016/j.cnsns.2011.04.024

Chapter 2
Dynamics and Synchronization of the Fractional–Order Hyperchaotic System

Shaobo He
Hunan University of Arts and Science, China

Huihai Wang
Central South University, China

Kehui Sun
Central South University, China

ABSTRACT

The fractional-order Lorenz hyperchaotic system is solved as a discrete map by applying Adomian decomposition method (ADM). Dynamics of this system versus parameters are analyzed by LCEs, bifurcation diagrams, and SE and C0 complexity. Results show that this system has rich dynamical behaviors. Chaos and hyperchaos can be generated by decreasing the fractional derivative order q in this system. It also shows that the system is more complex when q takes smaller values. Moreover, coupled synchronization of fractional-order chaotic system is investigated theoretically. The synchronization performances with synchronization controller parameters and derivative order varying are analyzed. Synchronization and complexity of intermediate variables which generated by ADM are investigated. It shows that intermediate variables between the driving system and response system are synchronized and higher complexity values are found. It lays a technical foundation for secure communication applications of fractional-order chaotic systems.

INTRODUCTION

In recent years, dynamical analyses of fractional-order chaotic systems have become a hot topic (Pham *et al.*, 2017; Matouk & Elsadany, 2016; Sun *et al.*, 2010). Fractional-order systems based secure communication and information encryption also aroused researchers' interests (Chen *et al.*, 2013; Wang *et al.*, 2013; Wang *et al.*, 2014). Currently, three numerical solution algorithms, namely, frequency domain

DOI: 10.4018/978-1-5225-5418-9.ch002

method (FDM) (Charef *et al.*, 1992), Adams-Bashforth-Moulton algorithm (ABM) (Sun *et al.*, 1984) and Adomian decomposition method (ADM) (Adomian, 1990), are mainly used to solve fractional-order chaotic systems. Meanwhile, Wang and Yu (2012) applied multistage homotopy-perturbation method and Arena *et al.* (2012) employed differential transform method to solve fractional-order chaotic systems. Obviously, the accuracy of different numerical algorithms is different, and the reliability of these algorithms should be investigated. For instance, Tavazoei *et al.* (2007) reported that FDM is not always reliable in detecting chaotic behaviors in nonlinear systems. Moreover, it is not difficult to find out that by applying different numerical algorithms, dynamical analysis results of fractional-order chaotic systems are different. Take fractional-order Chen system as an example, Tavazoei et al. (2007) showed that the minimum order to generate chaos by ABM is $q=0.83$ while solved by FDM, the system can generate chaos at $q=0.2$ and Cafagna and Grassi (2008) showed that chaos can be found even for $q=0.08$ when the system is analyzed by employing ADM. It is important to compare different solving algorithms and to figure out how to choose a proper algorithm in different application fields by analyzing their characteristics, including speed, computing precision, time and space complexity of different algorithms.

Lyapunov Characteristic Exponents (LCEs) are necessary and more convenient for detecting hyperchaos in fractional-order hyperchaotic system. Li *et al.* (2010) proposed a definition of LCEs for fractional differential systems based on a frequency-domain approximation, but the limitations of frequency-domain approximations are highlighted by Tavazoei *et al.* (2007). Time series based LCEs calculation methods like Wolf algorithm which is designed by Wolf *et al.* (1985), Jacobian method proposed by Ellner et al. (1991) and neural network algorithm presented by Maus and Sprott (2013) have difficulties when choosing the embedding dimension and the delay parameter inherent of the phase-space reconstruction. Recently, LCEs of fractional-order chaotic systems are calculated based on ADM by applying QR decomposition method (Caponetto and Fazzino, 2013). Currently, calculating LCEs of fractional-order chaotic systems versus their parameters and fractional order q has aroused people's interest.

Meanwhile, complexity measure is also an important way to analyze dynamics of a chaotic system. It can reflect the security of the system to some extent, if it is used in information security field. Currently, there are several methods to measure complexity of time series, including permutation entropy (PE) (Bandt and Pompe, 2002), statistical complexity measure (SCM) (Larrondo *et al.*, 2005), sample entropy (SampEn) (Richman and Moorman, 2000), fuzzy entropy (FuzzyEn) (Chen *et al.*, 2009), spectral entropy (SE) (Phillip *et al.*, 2009), and C_0 algorithm (Shen *et al.*, 2005). Among them, SE and C_0 algorithm are proper choices to estimate the complexity of a time series accurately and rapidly without any over-coarse graining preprocessing. Moreover, SE and C_0 algorithm are used to measure complexity of different kind of nonlinear time series. He *et al.* (2013) analyzed complexity integer-order chaotic system by applying SE algorithm. A quantitative analysis of brain optical images is carried out by Cao et al. (2007) by C0 algorithm and complexity of chaotic systems is calculated by Sun et al. (2013) with C_0 algorithm. Thus according to He *et al.* (2015; 2016), it is an interest topic to carry out complexity analysis of fractional-order chaotic systems.

Finally, synchronization of chaotic systems has aroused much interest of scholars, and it is found that fractional-order chaotic system can also be synchronized. A variety of approaches have been proposed for the synchronization of fractional-order chaotic systems. Chen et al. (2013) proposed a Takagi–Sugeno fuzzy model to a class of chaotic synchronization and anti-synchronization in fractional-order chaotic system. Zhang et al. (2016) discussed Lag-generalized synchronization of time-delay chaotic systems with stochastic perturbation. Meanwhile, Bhalekar and Daftardar-Gejji (2010) applied active control, Chen, et al. (2012) employed fuzzy sliding mode controller, Tavazoei and Haeri (2008) used active sliding mode control method, Gammoudi and Feki (2013) introduced robust observe and Gao and Yu (2005) coupled control to synchronize different fractional-order chaotic system. However, numerical solutions of the above reports are obtained by employing ABM and FDM, and there are no articles dealing with synchronization of fractional-order chaotic systems based on ADM. Meanwhile, among these methods, the coupled synchronization with simplest controller can be implemented easily. Thus, it is still a novel topic to investigate coupled synchronization of fractional-order hyperchaotic systems.

Currently, numerical solution, dynamical analysis, synchronization and real applications of fractional chaotic systems have been widely investigated. However, as mentioned above, at the moment study of fractional-order chaotic systems is still at an early stage. In order to employ the fractional-order hyperchaotic systems in the information security field, numerical solution algorithm, complex dynamical characteristics and synchronization control of the fractional-order Lorenz hyperchaotic system are investigated by combining means of theory analysis and numerical simulation.

The rest of this chapter is organized as follows. In Section "Definitions, solution algorithms and system model", comparisons between different numerical solutions of the fractional-order chaotic system are carried out and ADM solution of fractional-order Lorenz hyperchaotic system is obtained. In Section "Definitions, solution algorithms and system model", LCEs calculation method and complexity measure algorithms are presented. Dynamics and complexity of the system are analyzed and some interesting results are illustrated. In Section "Synchronization of fractional-order hyperchaotic system", coupled synchronization of the fractional-order Lorenz hyperchaotic system is investigated and synchronization in the intermediate variable of ADM solution is analyzed. Finally, we summarize the results in the last Section.

DEFINITIONS, SOLUTION ALGORITHMS AND SYSTEM MODEL

Fractional-Order Calculus

Currently, there are two fractional-order calculus definitions mainly used in real applications and mathematics, and these two definitions are Riemann-Liouville (R-L) definition and Caputo definition (Carpinteri and Mainardi, 1997).

Definition 2.1 (Carpinteri and Mainardi, 1997): Fractional-order Riemann-Liouville (R-L) derivative is given by

$$^*D_{t_0}^q x(t) = \begin{cases} \dfrac{d}{dt}\left[\dfrac{1}{\Gamma(1-q)} \int_{t_0}^t \dfrac{x(\tau)}{(t-\tau)^q} d\tau \right], 1 < q < 1 \\ \dfrac{d}{dt} x(t), q = 1 \end{cases}. \tag{1}$$

Definition 2.2 (Carpinteri and Mainardi, 1997): Fractional-order R-L integration is defined by

$$J_{t_0}^q x(t) = \frac{1}{\Gamma(q)} \int_{t_0}^t (t - \tau)^{q-1} x(\tau) d\tau , \tag{2}$$

in which $0 < q \leq 1$.

According to the $^*D_{t_0}^q J_{t_0}^q = x(t)$. When $t \in [t_0, t_1]$, $q \geq 0$, $\gamma > -1$, $r \geq 0$, and for the given constant C, the following properties are satisfied.

$$J_{t_0}^q (t - t_0)^\gamma = \frac{\Gamma(\gamma + 1)}{\Gamma(\gamma + 1 + q)} (t - t_0)^{\gamma + q} \tag{3}$$

$$J_{t_0}^q C = \frac{C}{\Gamma(q + 1)} (t - t_0)^q \tag{4}$$

$$J_{t_0}^q J_{t_0}^\Gamma x(t) = J_{t_0}^{q+r} x(t). \tag{5}$$

Definition 2.3 (Carpinteri and Mainardi, 1997): Fractional-order Caputo derivative is denoted as

$$D_{t_0}^q x(t) = \begin{cases} \dfrac{1}{\Gamma(m - q)} \displaystyle\int_{t_0}^t (t - \tau)^{m-q-1} x^{(m)}(\tau) d\tau, & m - 1 < q < m \\ \dfrac{d^m}{dt^m} x(t), & q = m \end{cases}. \tag{6}$$

where, $m \in N$, $m - 1 < q \leq m$. When $t \in [t_0, t_1]$, $m \in N$, $m-1 < q \leq m$, we have

$$D_{t_0}^0 x(t) = J_{t_0}^0 x(t) = x(t), \tag{7}$$

$$J_{t_0}^q D_{t_0}^q x(t) = x(t) - \sum_{k=0}^{m-1} x^{(k)}(t_0^+) \frac{(t - t_0)^k}{k!}. \tag{8}$$

In this chapter, Caputo fractional derivative is used.

Solution Algorithms

In fact, it is more difficult to obtain the numerical solution of fractional-order equations than that of integer-order equations. Generally, integer-order equations can be solved by Euler method or Runge-Kutta method. However, for fractional-order equations, there are any different methods due to different fractional order definitions and design thoughts. Here, we introduce three numerical approaches which are widely used for approximate of fractional-order chaotic systems.

Frequency Domain Method

Bode graphics approximating method is used in the frequency method and the idea is to obtain frequency domain expansion of fractional integral operator via solving $1/s^q$ in frequency domain. This transfer function $1/s^q$ is carried out by applying piecewise linear approximation in frequency domain (Charef, *et al.* 1992). As an example, if $q=0.9$, the transfer function is denoted by

$$\frac{1}{s^{0.9}} \approx \frac{1.766s^2 + 36.27s + 4.914}{s^3 + 36.15s^2 + 7.789s + 0.01},$$

(9)

where the error can be controlled within 2~3 dB. By applying Laplace transformation to the fractional-order calculus, we have

$$L\left\{ {}^*D_{t_0}^q x(t) \right\} = s^q L\left\{ x(t) \right\} - \sum_{k=0}^{n-1} s^k \left[{}^*D_{t_0}^{q-1-k} x(t) \right]_{t=0},$$

(10)

in which ${}^*D_{t_0}^q$ is R-L fractional-order derivative. When the initial conditions of the system is zero, the Laplace transform of above equation becomes to

$$L\left\{ D_{t_0}^q x(t) \right\} = s^q L\left\{ x(t) \right\}.$$

(11)

In real application, frequency domain method for fractional-order chaotic systems is usually carried out by the Simulink module of Matlab softer or by analogous circuit.

Adams-Bashforth-Moulton Algorithm

Consider the following fractional-order chaotic system

$$\begin{cases} D_{t_0}^q \mathbf{x}(t) = f(\mathbf{x}, \mathbf{x}(t)), 0 \le t \le T \\ \mathbf{x}^{(k)}(0) = \mathbf{x}_0^{(k)}, k = 0,1,2,\dots\dots,\lceil q \rceil - 1 \end{cases},$$

(12)

where $x(t)=[x(t), y(t), z(t), u(t)]^{\mathrm{T}}$ is the given variables, $\lceil \cdot \rceil$ is the ceil function, $D_{t_0}^q$ is the Caputo fractional-order derivative. It equals to the Volterra integral equation

$$x(t) = \sum_{k=0}^{n-1} x_0^{(k)} \frac{t^k}{k!} + \frac{1}{\Gamma(q)} \int_0^t (t-\tau)^{q-1} f(\tau, x(t))d\tau.$$

(13)

Obviously, the two parts of the right side in the above equation totally determined by the initial value. A typical state is $0<q<1$, and the Volterra equation has weak singularity. Let $h=T/N$, $t_j=jh(j=0, 1, 2, ..., N)$, where T is the integral upper limit of this equation. Then the corrector formula of Equation(13) is given by (Sun, *et al.* 1984)

$$x_h(t_{n+1}) = \sum_{k=0}^{\lceil q \rceil - 1} x_0^{(k)} \frac{t_{n+1}^k}{k!} + \frac{h^q}{\Gamma(q+2)} f(t_{n+1}, x_h^p(t_{n+1})) + \frac{h^q}{\Gamma(q+2)} \sum_{j=0}^{n} a_{j,n+1} f(t_j, x_h(t_j)), \qquad (14)$$

where

$$a_{j,n+1} = \begin{cases} n^{q+1} - (n-q)(n+1)^q & j = 0 \\ (n-j-2)^{q+1} + (n-j)^{q+1} - 2(n-j+1)^{q+1} & 1 \le j \le n \end{cases}, \qquad (15)$$

Then we use one-step Adams-Bashforth rule to replace one-step Adams-Moulton rule. The predictor term $x_h^p(t_{n+1})$ is given by (Sun, *et al.* 1984)

$$x_h^p(t_{n+1}) = \sum_{k=0}^{n-1} x_0^{(k)} \frac{t_{n+1}^k}{k!} + \frac{1}{\Gamma(q)} \sum_{j=0}^{n} b_{j,n+1} f(t_j, x_h(t_j)), \qquad (16)$$

where

$$b_{j,n+1} = \frac{h^q}{q}((n-j+1)^q - (n-j)^q), 0 \le j \le n. \qquad (17)$$

The basic algorithm of fractional-order Adams-Bashforth-Moulton method is shown as formula (14) and (16), where $a_{j,n+1}$, $b_{j,n+1}$ are presented by formula (15) and (17) respectively.

Adomian Decomposition Method

Let $\mathbf{x}(t)= [x(t), y(t), z(t), u(t)]^T$. System (12) is separated into two parts,

$$\begin{cases} D_{t_0}^q \mathbf{x}(t) = L\mathbf{x} + N\mathbf{x} \\ \mathbf{x}^{(k)}(t_0^+) = \mathbf{b}_k, k = 0, ..., m-1 \end{cases}. \qquad (18)$$

Here, m=ceil(q), and $\mathbf{b}_k$ is a specified constant relating to the initial values. $L\mathbf{x}$ represents the linear part of system (12), and $N\mathbf{x}$ represents the nonlinear part. By applying the fractional integral operator $J_{t_0}^q$ to both sides of Equation (18), the following equation is obtained

$$\mathbf{x} = J_{t_0}^q L\mathbf{x} + J_{t_0}^q N\mathbf{x} + \sum_{k=0}^{m-1} \mathbf{b}_k \frac{(t-t_0)^k}{k!}. \tag{19}$$

According to Adomian (1990) and Cafagna and Grassi (2008), the nonlinear terms are decomposed to

$$\begin{cases} A^i(\mathbf{x}^0, \mathbf{x}^1, \cdots, \mathbf{x}^i) = \dfrac{1}{i!} [\dfrac{d^i}{d\lambda^i} N(\mathbf{v}^i(\lambda))]_{\lambda=0}, \\ \mathbf{v}^i(\lambda) = \sum_{k=0}^i (\lambda)^k \mathbf{x}^k \end{cases} \tag{20}$$

where $i=0,1,\ldots$; then the nonlinear terms are expressed as

$$Nx = \sum_{i=0}^{\infty} A^i(x^0, x^1, \cdots, x^i) \tag{21}$$

According to Cafagna and Grassi (2008), the solution of Equation (12) is derived by

$$\begin{cases} \mathbf{x}^0 = \sum_{k=0}^{m-1} \mathbf{b}_k \dfrac{(t-t_0)^k}{k!} \\ \mathbf{x}^1 = J_{t_0}^q L\mathbf{x}^0 + J_{t_0}^q \mathbf{A}^0(\mathbf{x}^0) \\ \mathbf{x}^2 = J_{t_0}^q L\mathbf{x}^1 + J_{t_0}^q \mathbf{A}^1(\mathbf{x}^0, \mathbf{x}^1) \\ \cdots \\ \mathbf{x}^i = J_{t_0}^q L\mathbf{x}^{i-1} + J_{t_0}^q \mathbf{A}^{i-1}(\mathbf{x}^0, \mathbf{x}^1, \cdots, \mathbf{x}^{i-1}) \\ \cdots \end{cases} \tag{22}$$

The analytical solution of the fractional-order system is presented by

$$\mathbf{x}(t) = \sum_{i=0}^{\infty} \mathbf{x}^i = F(\mathbf{x}(t_0)). \tag{23}$$

Obviously, it is impossible to calculate infinite items of $\mathbf{x}^i$, although it is the exact solution of system (18).

Comparison of Different Algorithms

Both of ABM and ADM are time domain algorithms for fractional-order equations. A further investigation of ABM, ADM and fourth order Runge-Kutta method is carried out by comparing their accuracy, speed, time complexity and space complexity. It provides a basis for the choice of numerical solution of fractional-order chaotic systems.

Firstly, we analyze the accuracy of the three numerical algorithms. When $q=1$, the fractional-order system is actual an integer-order system. It can also be solved by many other algorithms such as Runge-

Kutta algorithm, Euler algorithm, where Runge-Kutta algorithm has more satisfying result. Here, by employing ADM, ABM and fourth order Runge-Kutta method, the following initial question is solved.

$$\begin{cases} D_{t_0}^q y(t) = y \\ y(0) = 1 \end{cases}.$$

(24)

When $q=1$, the exact solution is $y=e^t$. The numerical solutions obtained from the three numerical solution algorithms are denoted as $y_n^{(R)} y_n^{(A)}$, and $y_n^{(r)}$, and they are calculated by

$$y^{(A)} = y_0 [1 + \frac{(t-t_0)^q}{\Gamma(q+1)} + \cdots + \frac{(t-t_0)^{8q}}{\Gamma(8q+1)}],$$

(25)

$$\begin{cases} K_1 = y_n^{(R)} \\ K_2 = y_n^{(R)} + \frac{h}{2} K_1 \\ K_3 = y_n^{(R)} + \frac{h}{2} K_2 \\ K_4 = y_n^{(R)} + h K_3 \\ y_{n+1}^{(R)} = y_n^{(R)} + \frac{h}{6} (K_1 + 2K_2 + 2K_3 + K_4) \end{cases},$$

(26)

$$\begin{cases} y_{n+1}^{(Y)} = y_0 + \frac{h^q}{\Gamma(q+2)} (y_{n+1}^p + \sum_{j=0}^{n} \alpha_{j,n+1} y_j^{(Y)}) \\ \alpha_{j,n+1} = \begin{cases} n^q - (n-2)(n+1)^q & j = 0 \\ (n-j+2)^{q+1} + (n-j)^{q+1} - 2(n-j+1)^{q+1} & 1 \le j \le n \end{cases} \\ y_{n+1}^p = y_0 + \frac{1}{\Gamma(q)} \sum_{j=0}^{n} b_{j,n+1} y_j^{(Y)} \\ b_{j,n+1} = \frac{h^q}{q} ((n-j+1)^q - (n-j)^q) \quad 0 \le j \le n \end{cases}.$$

(27)

Errors produced by different algorithms are given in Figure 1.

The error increases with time going on and follows the exponential curve as shown in Figure 1. According to Figure 1, ABM has the largest error at the level 10^{-2}. Compared with ABM, Runge-Kutta method is much better and its error is at the level of 10^{-5}. However, ADM has the best results. So, we can see that ADM is the best choice for solving this kind of initial problem. Furthermore, we can check the truncation error of the three algorithms. ABM is given by

Figure 1. Error of different numerical solutions (a) ADM;(b) Runge-Kutta algorithm;(c) ABM

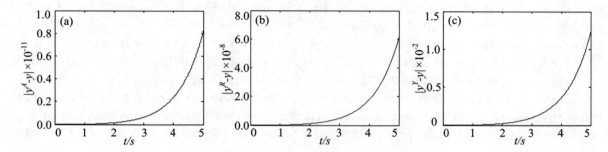

$$e = \max_{j=0,1,\cdots,N} | x(t_j) - x_h(t_j) | = o(h^p) . \tag{28}$$

where $p = \min(2, 1+q)$. When $q=1$, $e = o(h^2)$. The truncation error of the Runge-Kutta algorithm is defined as

$$e = \max_{j=0,1,\cdots,N} | x(t_j) - x_h(t_j) | = o(h^5) . \tag{29}$$

Obviously, it has higher accuracy. The convergence of ADM is similar with that of Taylor series, and it has very fast convergence speed. According to Abbaoui and Cherruault (1994), the error converges to

$$e \leq k \frac{M^P}{P!} , \tag{30}$$

where P represent the item number. For example, in Equation (30), $P=8$; $\| N^{(P)}(0) \| \leq k$, $\sum_{i=0}^{\infty} | u_i | \leq M$. In fact, we just need certain number items of ADM to obtain a solution with high accuracy. Table 1 shows the comparison results of the three algorithms

According to Table 1, time complexity and space complexity of ABM are $O(n^2)$, which is much worse than that of FDM and ADM. The reason is that ABM needs all history data in each iteration. Moreover,

Table 1. Comparison of the three numerical algorithms

	FDM	ABM	ADM
Domain	Frequency domain	Time domain	Time domain
Time complexity	$O(n)$	$O(n^2)$	$O(n)$
Space complexity	$O(n)$	$O(n^2)$	$O(n)$
Accuracy	$\leq$3dB	$O(h^p)$, $p=\min(2,1+q)$	$e \leq k \cdot M^P/P!$
Definition used	R-L definition	Caputo definition	Caputo definition
Application	Theoretical analysis and analog circuit	Theoretical analysis	Theoretical analysis and digital circuit

accuracy should be considered. ADM solution has exact solution when infinite items used, and it has high accuracy even with finite items as shown above. In addition, ADM has higher accuracy than ABM which is given as O(h^p), p=min(2,1+q). The error of FDM can be controlled within 3dB, but the result is not satisfying at the low and high frequency region. Furthermore, FDM can be used to design analog circuit of fractional-order chaotic system and ADM can be employed to design the digital circuit. Finally, we make a comparison of ADM and ABM on their time consumed and results are shown in Table 2. In Table 2, N represents the length of time series. These simulations are finished in a computer with Intel Dual CPU E2180 2.0 GHz. It shows that ABM needs much more time when the simulation time or length of time series increases. In this Chapter, ADM is used to solve the fractional-order hyperchaotic system.

Model of Fractional-Order Lorenz Hyperchaotic System

By introducing a nonlinear quadratic controller u to the second equation of Lorenz system, Gao *et al.* (2007) proposed a four dimensional dynamic system which is given by

$$\begin{cases} \dot{x} = 10(y - x) \\ \dot{y} = 28x - xz + y - u \\ \dot{z} = xy - 8z / 3 \\ \dot{u} = kyz \end{cases}, \qquad (31)$$

where k ($0<k\leq1$) is the system parameter. According to Gao *et al.* (2007), when $k\in(0, 0.152)$, the system is hyperchaotic, when $k\in[0.152, 0.21)\cup[0.34, 0.49)$, the system is chaotic, while the system undergoes periodic orbits for the rest region of k. By introducing fractional derivative to this system, He *et al.* (2015) analyzed dynamics of the fractional-order hyperchaotic Lorenz which is given by

$$\begin{cases} D_{t_0}^q x = 10(y - x) \\ D_{t_0}^q y = 28x - xz + y - u \\ D_{t_0}^q z = xy - 8z / 3 \\ D_{t_0}^q u = kxy \end{cases}. \qquad (32)$$

Obviously, it is a representative fractional order chaotic system and investigation of this system has typical meaning. Moreover, He *et al.* (2015) solved this fractional-order system by ADM, and a rapid iteration scheme of the fractional-order hyperchaotic Lorenz system is obtained which is denoted as

Table 2. Time consumed by ADM and ABM

	ADM	ABM
N=1000	0.9701s	2.0154s
N=2000	1.8403s	7.7051s
N=5000	4.5162s	51.3995s

$$
\begin{cases}
x_{n+1} = \sum_{j=0}^{6} \dfrac{c_1^j h^{jq}}{\Gamma(jq+1)} \\[2mm]
y_{n+1} = \sum_{j=0}^{6} \dfrac{c_2^j h^{jq}}{\Gamma(jq+1)} \\[2mm]
z_{n+1} = \sum_{j=0}^{6} \dfrac{c_3^j h^{jq}}{\Gamma(jq+1)} \\[2mm]
u_{n+1} = \sum_{j=0}^{6} \dfrac{c_4^j h^{jq}}{\Gamma(jq+1)}
\end{cases}
\tag{33}
$$

where the intermediate variables c_i^j ($i=1, 2, 3, 4$; $j=1, 2,..., 6$) are calculated by

$$
c_1^0 = x_n, c_2^0 = y_n, c_3^0 = z_n, c_4^0 = u_n,
\tag{34}
$$

$$
\begin{cases}
c_1^1 = 10(c_2^0 - c_1^0) \\[1mm]
c_2^1 = 28c_1^0 - c_1^0 c_3^0 + c_2^0 - c_4^0 \\[1mm]
c_3^1 = c_1^0 c_2^0 - 8c_3^0 / 3 \\[1mm]
c_4^1 = k c_2^0 c_3^0
\end{cases}
\tag{35}
$$

$$
\begin{cases}
c_1^2 = 10(c_2^1 - c_1^1) \\[1mm]
c_2^2 = 28c_1^1 - c_1^0 c_3^1 - c_1^1 c_3^0 + c_2^1 - c_4^1 \\[1mm]
c_3^2 = c_1^1 c_2^0 + c_1^0 c_2^1 - 8c_3^1 / 3 \\[1mm]
c_4^2 = k\left(c_2^1 c_3^0 + c_2^0 c_3^1\right)
\end{cases}
\tag{36}
$$

$$
\begin{cases}
c_1^3 = 10(c_2^2 - c_1^2) \\[1mm]
c_2^3 = 28c_1^2 - c_1^0 c_3^2 - c_1^1 c_3^1 \dfrac{\Gamma(2q+1)}{\Gamma^2(q+1)} - c_1^2 c_3^0 + c_2^2 - c_4^2 \\[2mm]
c_3^3 = c_1^0 c_2^2 + c_1^1 c_2^1 \dfrac{\Gamma(2q+1)}{\Gamma^2(q+1)} + c_1^2 c_2^0 - 8c_3^2 / 3 \\[2mm]
c_4^3 = k\left(c_2^0 c_3^2 + c_2^1 c_3^1 \dfrac{\Gamma(2q+1)}{\Gamma^2(q+1)} + c_2^2 c_3^0\right)
\end{cases}
\tag{37}
$$

$$
\begin{cases}
c_1^4 = 10(c_2^3 - c_1^3) \\[2mm]
c_2^4 = 28c_1^3 - c_1^0 c_3^3 - (c_1^2 c_3^1 + c_1^1 c_3^2)\dfrac{\Gamma(3q+1)}{\Gamma(q+1)\Gamma(2q+1)} - c_1^3 c_3^0 + c_2^3 - c_4^3 \\[3mm]
c_3^4 = c_1^0 c_2^3 + (c_1^2 c_2^1 + c_1^1 c_2^2)\dfrac{\Gamma(3q+1)}{\Gamma(q+1)\Gamma(2q+1)} + c_1^3 c_2^0 + 8c_3^3 / 3 \\[3mm]
c_4^4 = k\left(c_2^0 c_3^3 + (c_2^2 c_3^1 + c_2^1 c_3^2)\dfrac{\Gamma(3q+1)}{\Gamma(q+1)\Gamma(2q+1)} + c_2^3 c_3^0\right)
\end{cases}
\tag{38}
$$

$$
\begin{cases}
c_1^5 = 10(c_2^4 - c_1^4) \\[2mm]
c_2^5 = 28c_1^4 - c_1^0 c_3^4 - (c_1^3 c_3^1 + c_1^1 c_3^3)\dfrac{\Gamma(4q+1)}{\Gamma(q+1)\Gamma(3q+1)} - c_1^2 c_3^2 \dfrac{\Gamma(4q+1)}{\Gamma^2(2q+1)} \\[3mm]
\qquad - c_1^4 c_3^0 + c_2^4 - c_4^4 \\[2mm]
c_3^5 = c_1^0 c_2^4 + (c_1^3 c_2^1 + c_1^1 c_2^3)\dfrac{\Gamma(4q+1)}{\Gamma(q+1)\Gamma(3q+1)} + c_1^2 c_2^2 \dfrac{\Gamma(4q+1)}{\Gamma^2(2q+1)} \\[3mm]
\qquad + c_1^4 c_2^0 - 8c_3^4 / 3 \\[2mm]
c_4^5 = k(c_2^0 c_3^4 + (c_2^3 c_3^1 + c_2^1 c_3^3)\dfrac{\Gamma(4q+1)}{\Gamma(q+1)\Gamma(3q+1)} + c_2^2 c_3^2 \dfrac{\Gamma(4q+1)}{\Gamma^2(2q+1)} \\[3mm]
\qquad + c_2^4 c_3^0)
\end{cases}
\tag{39}
$$

$$
\begin{cases}
c_1^6 = 10(c_2^5 - c_1^5) \\[2mm]
c_2^6 = 28c_1^5 - c_1^0 c_3^5 - (c_1^1 c_3^4 + c_1^4 c_3^1)\dfrac{\Gamma(5q+1)}{\Gamma(q+1)\Gamma(4q+1)} - \\[3mm]
\qquad (c_1^2 c_3^3 + c_1^3 c_3^2)\dfrac{\Gamma(5q+1)}{\Gamma(2q+1)\Gamma(3q+1)} - c_1^5 c_3^0 + c_2^5 - c_4^5 \\[3mm]
c_3^6 = c_1^0 c_2^5 + (c_1^1 c_2^4 + c_1^4 c_2^1)\dfrac{\Gamma(5q+1)}{\Gamma(q+1)\Gamma(4q+1)} + \\[3mm]
\qquad (c_1^2 c_2^3 + c_1^3 c_2^2)\dfrac{\Gamma(5q+1)}{\Gamma(2q+1)\Gamma(3q+1)} + c_1^5 c_2^0 - 8c_3^5 / 3 \\[3mm]
c_4^6 = k(c_2^0 c_3^5 + (c_2^1 c_3^4 + c_2^4 c_3^1)\dfrac{\Gamma(5q+1)}{\Gamma(q+1)\Gamma(4q+1)} + \\[3mm]
\qquad (c_2^2 c_3^3 + c_2^3 c_3^2)\dfrac{\Gamma(5q+1)}{\Gamma(2q+1)\Gamma(3q+1)} + c_2^5 c_3^0)
\end{cases}
\tag{40}
$$

In Equation (33), $h=t_{n+1}-t_n$ and $\Gamma(\cdot)$ is the Gamma function. This rapid iteration scheme starts at c_i^0 ($i=1, 2, 3, 4$). To get c_i^j, it needs to calculate c_1^{j-1}, c_2^{j-1}, c_3^{j-1} and c_4^{j-1} in advance. Based on the discrete map (33), it is not difficult to get the time series by the way of computer programming. The Jacobian matrix of this map is easy to get through symbolic operation of mathematical software like Matlab and Mathematica. In this chapter, we set h=0.01. Dynamics and complexity under two parameter k and derivative order q are analyzed in the following section.

DYNAMICS AND COMPLEXITY ANALYSES

LCEs Calculation of Fractional-Order Chaotic System

For a given map $\mathbf{X}(m+1)=F(\mathbf{X}(m))$, QR decomposition method (Ellner, *et al.*, 1991) is an effective way to calculate the LCEs. The computational process is shown by

$$
\begin{aligned}
qr[J_m J_{m-1} \cdots J_1] &= qr[J_m J_{m-1} \cdots J_2 (J_1 Q_0)] \\
&= Q_m R_m \cdots R_2 R_1
\end{aligned}
\tag{41}
$$

where $qr[\cdot]$ represents QR decomposition function, and J is the Jacobian matrix of the given map. Q is an orthogonal matrix and R is upper triangular matrix. All LCEs are calculated by

$$
\lambda_\eta = \frac{1}{Mh} \sum_{i=1}^{M} \ln | R_i(\eta, \eta) |,
\tag{42}
$$

where η=1, 2, ..., d (dimension of the system), and M is the maximum iteration number. When q=1.0, the sum of LCEs of the fractional-order hyperchaotic Lorenz system is Δ=-10+1-8/3. Let Δ_M denote the sum of estimated Lyapunov exponents $(\lambda_1, \lambda_2, \lambda_3, \lambda_4)$ at each time step. Figure 2 shows the global error $|\Delta - \Delta_M|$. So we set M=20000 for accurate and stable outputs.

Complexity Measure Algorithms

Definition of Shannon entropy is used in the Spectral Entropy (SE) algorithm (Phillip, *et al.* 2009), so SE is an entropy method. C_0 (Shen, *et al.* 2005) is designed based on the ratio of irregular in the time series, and it works very well for complexity measure. Details of these two algorithms are shown in this section.

1.   Spectral Entropy (SE)

SE reflects the disorder in the Fourier transformation domain. A flatter spectrum has a larger value of SE, which shows a higher complexity of the time series. SE is described as follows. Given a time series $\{x(n), n$=0, 1, 2, ..., N-1$\}$ with a length of N, let $x(n) = x(n) - \overline{x}$, where $\overline{x}$ is the mean value of time series. Its corresponding Discrete Fourier Transformation (DFT) is defined by

$$
X(k) = \sum_{n=0}^{N-1} x(n) e^{-j2\pi nk/N} ,
\tag{43}
$$

Figure 2. Error vs. iterations for integer order hyperchaotic Lorenz system

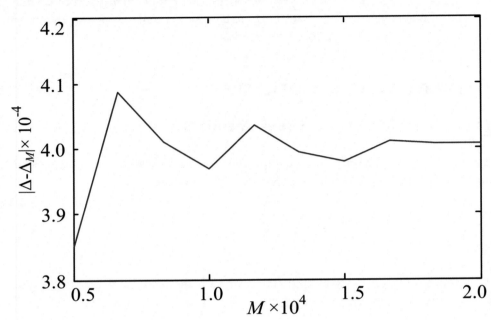

where $k=0, 1, ..., N-1$ and j is the imaginary unit. If the power of a discrete power spectrum with the k_{th} frequency is $|X(k)|^2$, then the "probability" of this frequency is defined as

$$P_k = \left|X(k)\right|^2 \Big/ \sum\nolimits_{k=0}^{N/2-1} \left|X(k)\right|^2. \tag{44}$$

When the DFT is employed, the summation runs from $k=0$ to $k=N/2-1$. Phillip, *et al.* (2009) designed the normalization entropy and it is denoted by

$$\text{SE} = -\sum\nolimits_{k=0}^{N/2-1} P_k \ln P_k \Big/ \ln(N/2), \tag{45}$$

where $\ln(N/2)$ is the entropy of completely random signal. In this paper, the length N for SE is 4×10^4 after removing the first 10^4 points of data.

2. C_0 complexity algorithm

C_0 complexity is also based on the DFT, and it reflects the ratio of irregular in the series. The corresponding DFT process the time series $\{x(n), n=0, 1, 2, ..., N-1\}$ is shown as formula (43). Define the mean square value of $X(k)$ as

$$G_N = (1/N)\sum_{k=0}^{N-1} |X(k)|^2. \tag{46}$$

Let

$$\tilde{X}(k) = \begin{cases} X(k) & if \mid X(k) \mid^2 > rG_N \\ 0 & if \mid X(k) \mid^2 \le rG_N \end{cases}, \tag{47}$$

where r ($r>0$) is the control parameter. The inverse Fourier Transformation of $X(k)$ is

$$\tilde{x}(n) = (1 / N)\sum_{k=0}^{N-1} \tilde{X}(k)e^{j2\pi nk/N}, \tag{48}$$

where $n=0, 1, ..., N$-1. Finally, the C_0 complexity is defined as

$$C_0(r, N) = \sum_{n=0}^{N-1} \mid x(n) - \tilde{x}(n) \mid^2 \Big/ \sum_{n=0}^{N-1} \mid x(n) \mid^2. \tag{49}$$

In this paper, we set $r=15$ and $N=4\times10^4$ to calculate the C_0 complexity.

LCEs and Bifurcation Analysis

There are a system parameter k and a derivative order q in the fractional-order hyperchaotic Lorenz system as given in Equation (31). Obviously, there are four Lyapunov characteristic exponents since the dimension of the system is four. But we just show the first three (λ_1, λ_2, λ_3) for better observation. Lyapunov characteristic exponents (LCEs) and the corresponding bifurcation diagrams are shown in Figures 3 and 5. Some typical phase diagrams generated by system (31) are presented in Figures 4 and 6.

1. Fix $k=0.21$ and set $q\in[0.60\ 1.00]$ varying with step size of $\Delta q=0.001$. The bifurcation diagram and LCEs results are shown in Figure 3 (a) and (b), respectively. It illustrates that the states of the system are different as q increases. The period windows can be observed at $q\in[0.635\ 0.662]$ U

Figure 3. Bifurcation and LCEs with different q (k=0.21) (a) Bifurcation diagram; (b) Lyapunov characteristic exponents

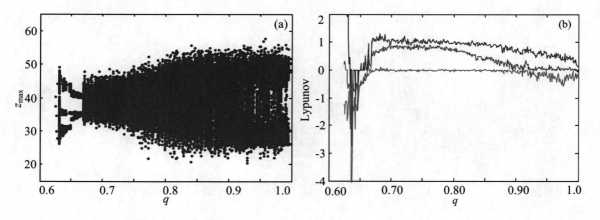

(0.999 1]. When $q\in(0.662\ 0.920]$, the system is hyperchaotic. When $q\in(0.920\ 0.999]$, this system is chaotic. It should be pointed out that the integer-order system is periodic while chaos or hyperchaoes can be found when order q changes to fractional order. Phase diagrams of the hyperchaotic system with different derivative order q varying are shown in Figure 4.

2.   Fix $q=0.96$ and vary k from 0 to 1 with the step of $\Delta k=0.0025$. The bifurcation diagram and LCES results are shown in Figure 5. It illustrates that the system is hyperchaotic at $k\in[0\ 0.1875]$. When $k\in(0.1875\ 0.2275]\cup(0.3400\ 0.4975]$, the system is in chaotic state, and it is periodic for $k\in(0.2275\ 0.3400]\cup(0.4975\ 1]$. Phase diagrams with different parameter k are shown in Figure 6 which illustrates that the system has different states as k takes different values.

Remark 1: We summarize dynamics of the system with k varying under different q. For the integer-order hyperchaotic Lorenz system ($q=1$), when $k\in(0, 0.152)$, the system is hyperchaotic, when $k\in[0.152, 0.210)\cup[0.34, 0.49]$, the system is chaotic, and the system is periodical for the rest values of bifurcation parameter k (Gao *et al.* 2007). For $q=0.96$, when $k\in[0, 0.1875]$, the system is hyperchaotic, when $k\in(0.1875, 0.2275]\cup(0.3400, 0.4975]$, the system is chaotic, while for rest interval, the system is periodical. It shows that when solved by ADM, the fractional-order hyperchaotic Lorenz system has wider range of k for hyperchaos.

According to the above analysis, the system has relative wider hyperchaotic interval with the variation of derivative order q. Moreover, rich dynamics has been found in this system since hyperchaotic state, chaotic state and periodic circles are observed.

Figure 4. Phase diagrams of fractional-order hyperchaotic Lorenz system (k=0.21) (a) q=1.00; (b) q=0.92; (c) q=0.90; (d) q=0.82; (e) q=0.72; (f) q=0.65

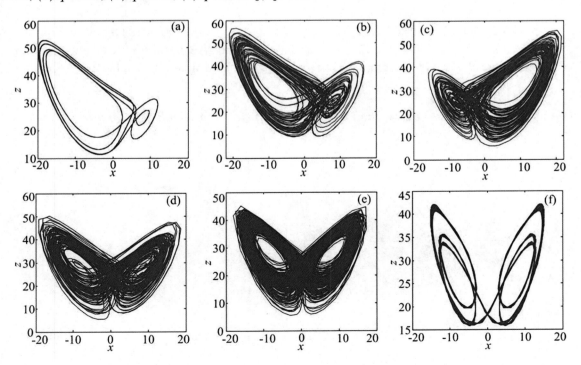

Figure 5. Bifurcation and LCEs with different k (q=0.96) (a) Bifurcation diagram; (b) Lyapunov characteristic exponents

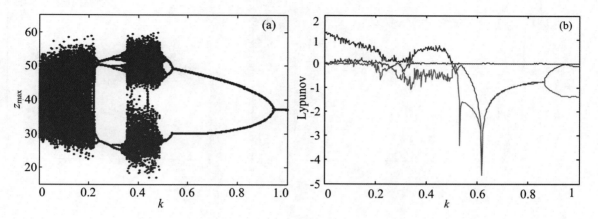

Figure 6. Phase diagrams of fractional-order hyperchaotic Lorenz system (q=0.96) (a) k=0.05; (b) k=0.20; (c) k=0.30; (d) k=0.40; (e) k=0.50; (f) k=0.80

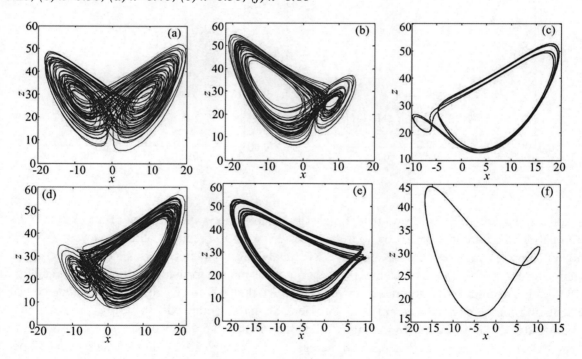

Complexity Analysis

Complexity of x series in the fractional-order Lorenz hyperchaotic system is calculated. SE and C_0 analysis results for increasing q ($k=0.21$) or increasing k ($q=0.96$) are illustrated in Figures 7 and 8, respectively. As it is the same with maximum LECs, SE and C_0 complexity also cannot be used to distinguish chaos and hyperchaos. But when the system has high complexity, it means that the system is chaotic or hyper-

Figure 7. Complexity for increasing q (k=0.21) (a) SE complexity; (b) C_0 complexity

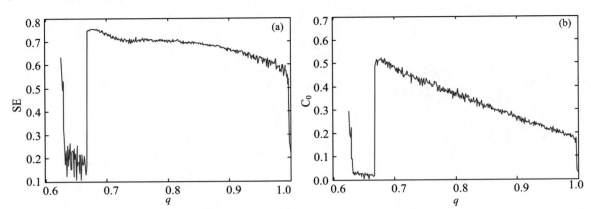

Figure 8. Complexity for increasing k (q=0.96) (a) SE complexity; (b) C_0 complexity

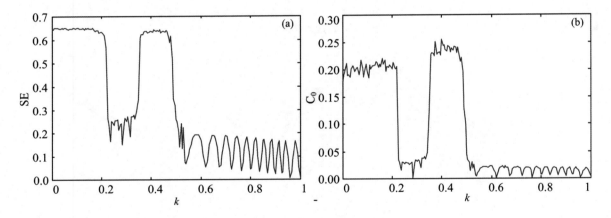

chaotic. Meanwhile, it also shows that complexity results agree well with that of maximum LCEs and bifurcation diagram. It is better to choose smaller values of q in real applications since the system has higher complexity in these cases. Compared with analyzing complexity versus only a single parameter, analyzing complexity in the parameter plane can show us more information. Moreover, SE and C_0 algorithm estimate complexity of time series very fast, so both of SE and C_0 algorithm are good choices for calculating complexity in the parameter plane. Here, SE and C_0 complexity in the q-k parameter plane are calculated and results are shown in Figure 9. It is shown that complexity of the fractional-order chaotic system decreases when fractional order q increases. High complexity region takes up about 40 percent of total parameter plane. It presents a practical basis for parameter choice in the real applications.

Remark 2: Complexity analysis results agree with the dynamical analysis results, which means that complexity measure is an effective method for characteristic analysis of fractional order chaotic systems.

Remark 3: According to analysis results, fractional-order chaotic system has higher complexity than its integer-order counterpart. It indicates the potential application value of fractional chaotic systems.

Figure 9. Complexity in the parameter plane q-k (a) SE complexity; (b) C_0 complexity

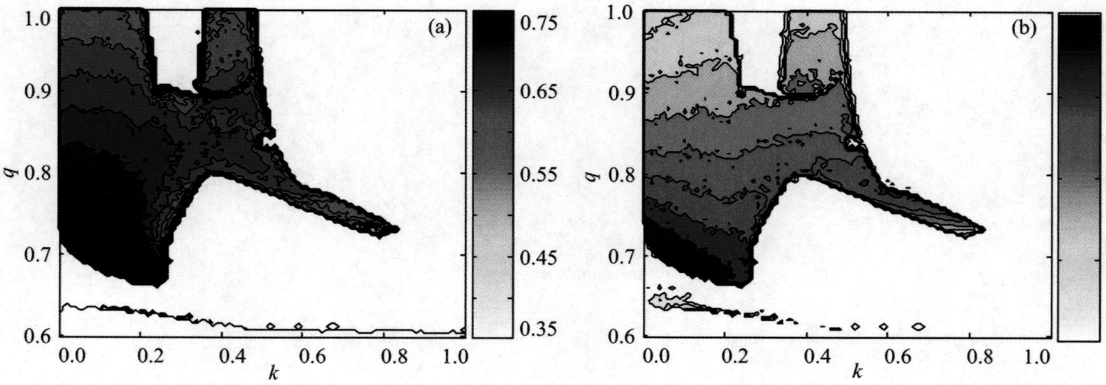

SYNCHRONIZATION OF FRACTIONAL-ORDER HYPERCHAOTIC SYSTEM

Fractional-Order Coupled Synchronization

Consider the following the system

$$D_{t_0}^q \mathbf{x}(t) = f(\mathbf{x}(t)) + C\mathbf{x}(t),$$ (50)

then its coupled system is defined as

$$D_{t_0}^q \mathbf{y}(t) = f(\mathbf{y}(t)) + C\mathbf{y}(t) + \rho(\mathbf{x}(t) - \mathbf{y}(t)).$$ (51)

where ρ is the coupled strength. When the errors satisfy

$$\lim_{t \to \infty} \left\| y(t) - x(t) \right\| = 0,$$ (52)

then the two systems can be synchronized.

Synchronization of fractional-order Lorenz hyperchaotic systems is considered. Let us rewrite the system as

$$\begin{cases} D_{t_0}^q x_1 = 10(x_2 - x_1) \\ D_{t_0}^q x_2 = 28x_1 - x_1 x_3 + x_2 - x_4 \\ D_{t_0}^q x_3 = x_1 x_2 - 8x_3 / 3 \\ D_{t_0}^q x_4 = kx_2 x_3 \end{cases}.$$ (53)

According to Equation(51) the coupled system is denoted as

$$\begin{cases} D_{t_0}^q y_1 = 10(y_2 - y_1) + \rho(x_1 - y_1) \\ D_{t_0}^q y_2 = 28y_1 - y_1y_3 + y_2 - y_4 + \rho(x_2 - y_2) \\ D_{t_0}^q y_3 = y_1y_2 - 8y_3 / 3 + \rho(x_3 - y_3) \\ D_{t_0}^q y_4 = ky_2y_3 + \rho(x_4 - y_4) \end{cases} \tag{54}$$

Define

$$\mathbf{C} = \begin{bmatrix} -10 & 10 & 0 & 0 \\ 28 & 1 & 0 & -1 \\ 0 & 0 & -8/3 & 0 \\ 0 & 0 & 0 & 0 \end{bmatrix}, f(x(t)) = \begin{bmatrix} 0 \\ -x_1x_3 \\ x_1x_2 \\ kx_2x_3 \end{bmatrix}, \tag{55}$$

and denote

$$\begin{cases} \mathbf{e} = \mathbf{y} - \mathbf{x} = [e_1, e_2, e_3, e_4]^T \\ e_i = y_i - x_i, i = 1, 2, 3, 4 \end{cases}, \tag{56}$$

then the error system of the two hyperchaotic systems can be given by

$$D_{t_0}^q \mathbf{e}(t) = D_{t_0}^q \mathbf{y}(t) - D_{t_0}^q \mathbf{x}(t) = (\mathbf{C} - \acute{\mathbf{A}})\mathbf{e}(t) + f(\mathbf{y}(t)) - f(\mathbf{x}(t)), \tag{57}$$

in which

$$f(\mathbf{x}(t)) - f(\mathbf{y}(t)) = \begin{bmatrix} 0 \\ x_1x_3 - y_1y_3 \\ -x_1x_2 + y_1y_2 \\ -kx_2x_3 + ky_2y_3 \end{bmatrix} = \mathbf{Be}, \tag{58}$$

and

$$\mathbf{B} = \begin{bmatrix} 0 & 0 & 0 & 0 \\ -y_3 & 0 & -x_1 & 0 \\ x_2 & y_1 & 0 & 0 \\ 0 & ky_3 & kx_2 & 0 \end{bmatrix}. \tag{59}$$

Obviously, when $t \to \infty$, if $e_i \to 0$ (i=1, 2, 3, 4), system (53) and system (54) are synchronized.

Lemma 1 (He, *et al.*, 2016): For $q \in (0,1]$, $D_{t_0}^q \left| x(t) \right| = \text{sgn}(x(t)) D_{t_0}^q x(t)$.

Theory 1: If the coupled strength $\rho > \lambda_{\max}\left(\tilde{\mathbf{C}}\right) + \psi \lambda_{\max}\left(\tilde{\mathbf{B}}\right)$, system (50) and system (51) can be synchronized, where $\tilde{\mathbf{C}} = 0.5\left(\mathbf{C} + \mathbf{C}^T\right)$, $\psi = \max\{\left|x_i\right|, i = 1, 2, 3, 4\}$, $\tilde{\mathbf{B}} = 0.5(\mathbf{B}_1 + \mathbf{B}_1^{\ T})$, $\boldsymbol{B}_1 = \{[0, 0, 0, 0], [1, 0, 1, 0], [1, 1, 0, 0], [0, 1, 1, 0]\}$ and $\lambda_{\max}\left(\cdot\right)$ is the maximum eigenvalue.

Proof: Define the Lyapunov function as

$$V = \|\mathbf{e}\|, \tag{60}$$

According to Lemma 1, differentiation of the Lyapunov function is calculated by

$$D_{t_0}^q V(t) = D_{t_0}^q \sum_{i=1}^{4} \left|e_i\right| = \text{sgn}(\mathbf{e}^T) D_{t_0}^q \mathbf{e}. \tag{61}$$

Since the parameter of $k \in [0, 1]$, the following relationship can be obtained

$$\text{sgn}(\mathbf{e}^T)\mathbf{B}\mathbf{e} \leq \psi \, \text{sgn}(\mathbf{e}^T)\tilde{\mathbf{B}}\mathbf{e} \leq \psi \lambda_{\max}\left(\tilde{\mathbf{B}}\right)\text{sgn}(\mathbf{e}^T)\mathbf{e}. \tag{62}$$

Thus

$$
\begin{aligned}
D_{t_0}^q V(t) &= \text{sgn}(\mathbf{e}^T)\left(\mathbf{C} + \mathbf{B} - \boldsymbol{\rho}\right)\mathbf{e} \\
&\leq \text{sgn}(\mathbf{e}^T)\frac{\mathbf{C} + \mathbf{C}^T}{2}\mathbf{e} + \psi\,\text{sgn}(\mathbf{e}^T)\frac{\mathbf{B} + \mathbf{B}^T}{2}\mathbf{e} - \rho\,\text{sgn}(\mathbf{e}^T)\mathbf{e} \\
&\leq \text{sgn}(\mathbf{e}^T)\lambda_{\max}\left(\tilde{\mathbf{C}}\right)\mathbf{e} + \text{sgn}(\mathbf{e}^T)\psi\lambda_{\max}\left(\tilde{\mathbf{B}}\right)\mathbf{e} - \text{sgn}(\mathbf{e}^T)\rho\mathbf{e} \\
&= \text{sgn}(\mathbf{e}^T)\left(\lambda_{\max}\left(\tilde{\mathbf{C}}\right)I + \psi\lambda_{\max}\left(\tilde{\mathbf{B}}\right)I - \boldsymbol{\rho}\right)\mathbf{e} \\
&= \text{sgn}(\mathbf{e}^T)\mathbf{P}\mathbf{e}
\end{aligned}
\tag{63}
$$

where

$$
\begin{cases}
\boldsymbol{\rho} = diag(\rho, \rho, \rho, \rho) \\
\mathbf{P} = \left(\lambda_{\max}\left(\tilde{\mathbf{C}}\right) + \psi\lambda_{\max}\left(\tilde{\mathbf{B}}\right) - \rho\right)\mathbf{I}
\end{cases}
\tag{64}
$$

So, when $\rho > \lambda_{\max}\left(\tilde{\mathbf{C}}\right) + \psi\lambda_{\max}\left(\tilde{\mathbf{B}}\right)$, $D_{t_0}^q V(t) < 0$. It means that the fractional-order derivative of the error system is negative and the global synchronization of the two coupled system can be obtained.

Remark 4: Theorem 1 is a sufficient condition for the coupling synchronization of the fractional-order Lorenz hyperchaotic system. It means that if the condition is satisfied, the two systems are synchronized. However, the two systems can also be synchronized with much smaller coupling strength which will be verified by numerical simulation in the following section.

Remark 5: Until now, the minimum coupling strength of coupled synchronization has not been found yet. However, compared with other controllers, coupled controller is much easier to be implemented in real applications

Remark 6: Coupled strength ρ is the main design parameter of the proposed synchronization scheme. In the real applications, we should choose a proper r ρ for a short synchronization set-up time. Meanwhile, although derivative order q is not the parameter of the proposed synchronization scheme, it affects the synchronization set-up time. Numerical simulation in the following section will give proper values of these two parameters.

Simulation of the Coupled Synchronization

Numerical solution of the master is presented above. By employing ADM, numerical solution of the coupled system is given by

$$\begin{cases} y_{1,n+1} = \sum_{j=0}^{6} \xi_1^j \, h^{jq} \Big/ \Gamma(jq+1) \\ y_{2,n+1} = \sum_{j=0}^{6} \xi_2^j \, h^{jq} \Big/ \Gamma(jq+1) \\ y_{3,n+1} = \sum_{j=0}^{6} \xi_3^j \, h^{jq} \Big/ \Gamma(jq+1) \\ y_{4,n+1} = \sum_{j=0}^{6} \xi_4^j \, h^{jq} \Big/ \Gamma(jq+1) \end{cases} \tag{65}$$

where ξ_i^j (i=1, 2, 3, 4; j=1, 2,..., 6) are calculated by

$$\xi_1^0 = y_{1,n}, \xi_2^0 = y_{2,n}, \xi_3^0 = y_{3,n}, \xi_4^0 = y_{4,n}, \tag{66}$$

$$\begin{cases} \xi_1^1 = 10(\xi_2^0 - \xi_1^0) + \rho(c_1^0 - \xi_1^0) \\ \xi_2^1 = 28\xi_1^0 - \xi_1^0\xi_3^0 + \xi_2^0 - \xi_4^0 + \rho(c_2^0 - \xi_2^0) \\ \xi_3^1 = \xi_1^0\xi_2^0 - 8\xi_3^0 / 3 + \rho(c_3^0 - \xi_3^0) \\ \xi_4^1 = k\xi_2^0\xi_3^0 + \rho(c_4^0 - \xi_4^0) \end{cases}, \tag{67}$$

$$\begin{cases} \xi_1^2 = 10(\xi_2^1 - \xi_1^1) + \rho(c_1^1 - \xi_1^1) \\ \xi_2^2 = 28\xi_1^1 - \xi_1^0\xi_3^1 - \xi_1^1\xi_3^0 + \xi_2^1 - \xi_4^1 + \rho(c_2^1 - \xi_2^1) \\ \xi_3^2 = \xi_1^1\xi_2^0 + \xi_1^0\xi_2^1 - 8\xi_3^1 / 3 + \rho(c_3^1 - \xi_2^1) \\ \xi_4^2 = k\left(\xi_2^1\xi_3^0 + \xi_2^0\xi_3^1\right) + \rho(c_4^1 - \xi_2^1) \end{cases}, \tag{68}$$

$$
\begin{cases}
\xi_1^3 = 10(\xi_2^2 - \xi_1^2) + \rho(c_1^2 - \xi_1^2) \\[2mm]
\xi_2^3 = 28\xi_1^2 - \xi_1^0\xi_3^2 - \xi_1^1\xi_3^1\dfrac{\Gamma(2q+1)}{\Gamma^2(q+1)} - \xi_1^2\xi_3^0 + \xi_2^2 \\[2mm]
\qquad -\xi_4^2 + \rho(c_2^2 - \xi_2^2) \\[2mm]
\xi_3^3 = \xi_1^0\xi_2^2 + \xi_1^1\xi_2^1\dfrac{\Gamma(2q+1)}{\Gamma^2(q+1)} + \xi_1^2\xi_2^0 - 8\xi_3^2 \,/\, 3 + \rho(c_3^2 - \xi_3^2) \\[2mm]
\xi_4^3 = k\left(\xi_2^0\xi_3^2 + \xi_2^1\xi_3^1\dfrac{\Gamma(2q+1)}{\Gamma^2(q+1)} + \xi_2^2\xi_3^0\right) + \rho(c_4^2 - \xi_4^2)
\end{cases}
\tag{69}
$$

$$
\begin{cases}
\xi_1^4 = 10(\xi_2^3 - \xi_1^3) + \rho(c_1^3 - \xi_1^3) \\[2mm]
\xi_2^4 = 28\xi_1^3 - \xi_1^0\xi_3^3 - (\xi_1^2\xi_3^1 + \xi_1^1\xi_3^2)\dfrac{\Gamma(3q+1)}{\Gamma(q+1)\Gamma(2q+1)} - \xi_1^3\xi_3^0 + \\[2mm]
\qquad \xi_2^3 - \xi_4^3 + \rho(c_2^3 - \xi_2^3) \\[2mm]
\xi_3^4 = \xi_1^0\xi_2^3 + (\xi_1^2\xi_2^1 + \xi_1^1\xi_2^2)\dfrac{\Gamma(3q+1)}{\Gamma(q+1)\Gamma(2q+1)} + \xi_1^3\xi_2^0 + 8\xi_3^3 \,/\, 3 + \rho(c_3^3 - \xi_3^3) \\[2mm]
\xi_4^4 = k\left(\xi_2^0\xi_3^3 + (\xi_2^2\xi_3^1 + \xi_2^1\xi_3^2)\dfrac{\Gamma(3q+1)}{\Gamma(q+1)\Gamma(2q+1)} + \xi_2^3\xi_3^0\right) + \rho(c_4^3 - \xi_4^3)
\end{cases}
\tag{70}
$$

$$
\begin{cases}
\xi_1^5 = 10(\xi_2^4 - \xi_1^4) + \rho(c_1^4 - \xi_1^4) \\[2mm]
\xi_2^5 = 28\xi_1^4 - \xi_1^0\xi_3^4 - (\xi_1^3\xi_3^1 + \xi_1^1\xi_3^3)\dfrac{\Gamma(4q+1)}{\Gamma(q+1)\Gamma(3q+1)} \\[2mm]
\qquad -\xi_1^2\xi_3^2\dfrac{\Gamma(4q+1)}{\Gamma^2(2q+1)} - \xi_1^4\xi_3^0 + \xi_2^4 - \xi_4^4 + \rho(c_2^4 - \xi_2^4) \\[2mm]
\xi_3^5 = \xi_1^0\xi_2^4 + (\xi_1^3\xi_2^1 + \xi_1^1\xi_2^3)\dfrac{\Gamma(4q+1)}{\Gamma(q+1)\Gamma(3q+1)} - 8\xi_3^4 \,/\, 3 , \\[2mm]
\qquad +\xi_1^2\xi_2^2\dfrac{\Gamma(4q+1)}{\Gamma^2(2q+1)} + \xi_1^4\xi_2^0 + \rho(c_3^4 - \xi_3^4) \\[2mm]
\xi_4^5 = k(\xi_2^0\xi_3^4 + (\xi_2^3\xi_3^1 + \xi_2^1\xi_3^3)\dfrac{\Gamma(4q+1)}{\Gamma(q+1)\Gamma(3q+1)} \\[2mm]
\qquad +\xi_2^2\xi_3^2\dfrac{\Gamma(4q+1)}{\Gamma^2(2q+1)} + \xi_2^4\xi_3^0) + \rho(c_4^4 - \xi_4^4)
\end{cases}
\tag{71}
$$

$$
\left\{
\begin{aligned}
\xi_1^6 &= 10(\xi_2^5 - \xi_1^5) + \rho(c_1^5 - \xi_1^5) \\[4pt]
\xi_2^6 &= 28\xi_1^5 - \xi_1^0\xi_3^5 - (\xi_1^1\xi_3^4 + \xi_1^4\xi_3^1)\frac{\Gamma(5q+1)}{\Gamma(q+1)\Gamma(4q+1)} - \xi_1^5\xi_3^0 + \xi_2^5 \\[4pt]
&\quad -(\xi_1^2\xi_3^3 + \xi_1^3\xi_3^2)\frac{\Gamma(5q+1)}{\Gamma(2q+1)\Gamma(3q+1)} - \xi_4^5 + \rho(c_2^5 - \xi_2^5) \\[4pt]
\xi_3^6 &= \xi_1^0\xi_2^5 + (\xi_1^1\xi_2^4 + \xi_1^4\xi_2^1)\frac{\Gamma(5q+1)}{\Gamma(q+1)\Gamma(4q+1)} - 8\xi_3^5 \big/ 3 + \\[4pt]
&\quad (\xi_1^2\xi_2^3 + \xi_1^3\xi_2^2)\frac{\Gamma(5q+1)}{\Gamma(2q+1)\Gamma(3q+1)} + \xi_1^5\xi_2^0 + \rho(c_3^5 - \xi_3^5) \\[4pt]
\xi_4^6 &= k(\xi_2^0\xi_3^5 + (\xi_2^1\xi_3^4 + \xi_2^4\xi_3^1)\frac{\Gamma(5q+1)}{\Gamma(q+1)\Gamma(4q+1)} + \xi_2^5\xi_3^0) + \\[4pt]
&\quad (\xi_2^2\xi_3^3 + \xi_2^3\xi_3^2)\frac{\Gamma(5q+1)}{\Gamma(2q+1)\Gamma(3q+1)} + \rho(c_4^5 - \xi_4^5)
\end{aligned}
\right.
\tag{72}
$$

Remark 7: In the solution of response system, $c_i^j \left(i = 1, \cdots, 4; j = 0, 1, \cdots, 5\right)$ is used. It means that, compared with coupled synchronization between integer-order chaotic systems, coupled synchronization between fractional-order chaotic systems need more information for driving the response system.

Remark 8: ADM based numerical solution of fractional-order systems can be implemented in the digital circuit, which means that the synchronized system can be realized in the digital circuit by employing the DSP or FPGA technology.

Let parameter k=0.2, fractional derivative order q=0.96, and set the time step size h=0.01, the initial conditions of drive system are $x_1(0)$=1, $x_2(0)$=2, $x_3(0)$=3 and $x_4(0)$=4, and the initial conditions of drive system are $y_1(0)$=5, $y_2(0)$=6, $y_3(0)$=7 and $y_4(0)$=8. If we define the errors are $e_i = y_i - x_i$, the results are shown in Figure 10. According to Figure 10, system (53) and system (54) are synchronized at $t \approx 1.2s$.

Furthermore, synchronization set-up time under different derivative order q and coupled strength ρ is worth investigating as well. In Figure 11 (a), when order q equals to 0.7, 0.8, 0.9 and 1.0, the synchronization set-up time decreases with the increase of q. In Figure 11 (b), when the coupled strength ρ takes values of 2, 4, 6 and 8, synchronization set-up time decreases with the increase of ρ, which means that we should choose relatively larger ρ in real applications. According to Theory 1, $\lambda_{\max}\left(\tilde{\mathbf{C}}\right)$=24.284, ψ =81.555, $\lambda_{\max}\left(\tilde{\mathbf{B}}\right)$=1.618, the theoretical value of coupled strength ρ should be 156.24. However, in our simulation, values of coupled strength ρ are smaller than 156.24, thus *Remark 4* is verified.

When solved by ADM, some intermediate variables ξ_i^j and c_i^j (i=1, 2, 3, 4, j=0, 1, 2, ..., 6) are used. Define the synchronization error between those intermediate variables as

$$
E_k = \sum_{i=1}^{4} \left| \xi_i^\eta - c_i^\eta \right|, \eta = 0, 1, \cdots, 6 .
\tag{73}
$$

Figure 10. Coupled synchronization error of fractional-order hyperchaotic Lorenz system (a) e_1 ;(b) e_2 ;(c) e_3 ;(d) e_4

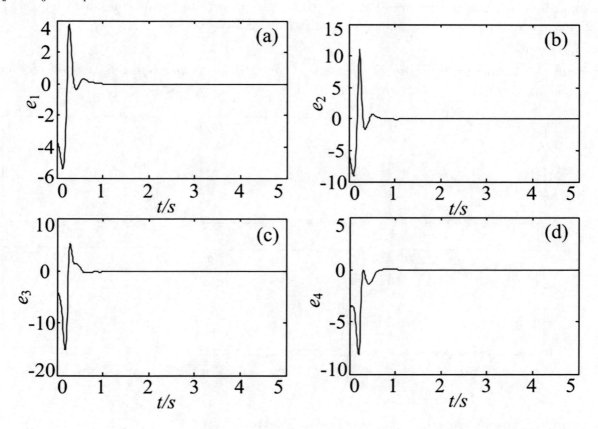

Figure 11. Coupled synchronization error of fractional-order hyperchaotic Lorenz system with different parameters varying (a) fractional derivative order q varying;(b) coupled strength ρ varying

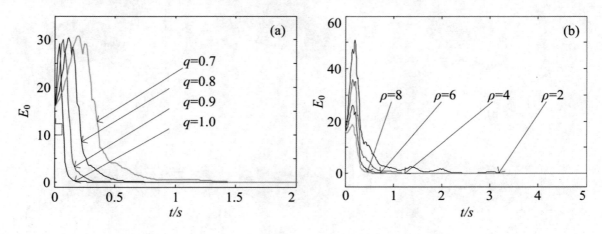

Obviously, when $\eta=0$, E_0 is the sum of synchronization error between state variables. The synchronization errors of intermediate variables are shown in Figure 12. It indicates that synchronization exists within these intermediate variables. Actually, chaotic attractors can be found as illustrated in Figure 13. In the next section, complexity of intermediate variables is analyzed.

Figure 12. Synchronization error of intermediate variables in fractional-order Lorenz hyperchaotic system (a) E_0 ;(b) E_1 ;(c) E_2 ;(d) E_3 ;(e) E_4 ;(f) E_5

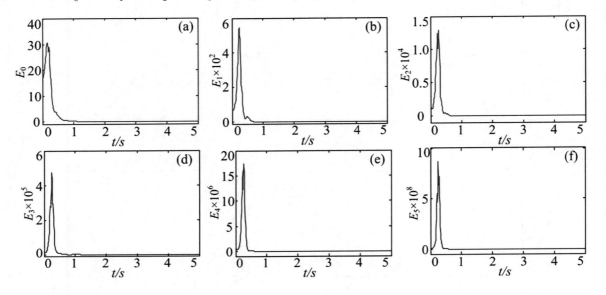

Figure 13. Phase diagrams of the intermediate variables (a) $\xi_1^0(x_1) - \xi_3^0(x_2) - \xi_2^0(x_3)$; (b) $\xi_1^1 - \xi_3^1 - \xi_2^1$; (c) $\xi_1^2 - \xi_3^2 - \xi_2^2$; (d) $\xi_1^3 - \xi_3^3 - \xi_2^3$; (e) $\xi_1^4 - \xi_3^4 - \xi_2^4$; (f) $\xi_1^5 - \xi_3^5 - \xi_2^5$

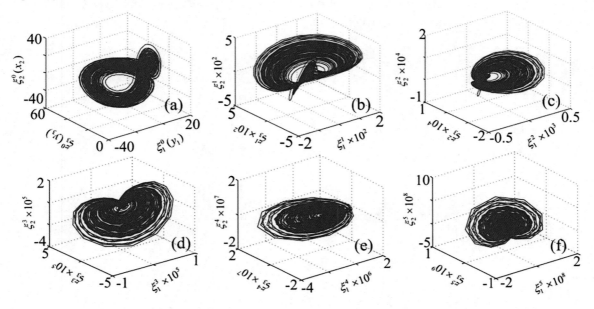

Remark 9: It is significant and interesting to find that synchronization exists between intermediate variables of two coupled systems.

Complexity Analysis of the Synchronization

C_0 and SE algorithms are applied to measure complexity of intermediate variables where those time series are c_i^j ($i=1, 2, 3, 4; j=0, 1, 2, \cdots, 6$) and the length of each time series is $N=5\times10^4$. As shown in Figure 14, C_0 and SE complexity increase with the increase of index j. It means that the intermediate variable time series have higher complexity than that of state variable time series. It shows that these intermediate variables time series can also be used in the secure communication application field.

CONCLUSION

Numerical solution, dynamics, complexity, and coupled synchronization of fractional-order hyperchaotic Lorenz system are investigated. Compared with ABM and FDM, ADM solution of fractional-order chaotic systems has higher accuracy, faster calculation speed and consumes less memory, and it can be used to realize fractional-order chaotic system in digital circuit. It is shown that the fractional-order hyperchaotic Lorenz system contains rich dynamical behaviors. Meanwhile, it is interesting that the system with integer-order is periodic, but chaos and hyperchaos can be found when changing the integer-order system into a fractional-order system. Furthermore, SE and C_0 complexity analysis of fractional-order Lorenz hyperchaotic system is carried out, and complexities agree with LCEs. Complexity of the fractional-order hyperchaotic system decreases when q increases. It also indicates that complexity analysis is a more convenient method to choose parameters of fractional-order chaotic system in the real applications. Moreover, by employing ADM, coupled synchronization of fractional-order Lorenz hyperchaotic systems is investigated. It is shown that the proposed synchronization controller is effective, theoretically and practically. When the synchronized systems are solved by ADM, intermediate variables in the drive

Figure 14. Complexity calculation results of intermediate variables (a) C_0 complexity result; (b) SE complexity result

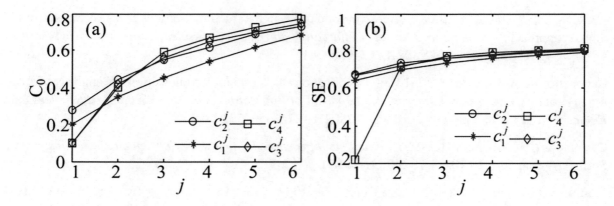

system are used in the solution of the response system. Synchronization between intermediate variables is also observed. It lays a technical foundation for secure communication application of fractional-order Lorenz hyperchaotic system. As for the further future topics, we think they can be carried out from two aspects. Firstly, FPGA implementation of fractional-order synchronization should be carried out since it is shown that the numerical solution is fast. Secondly, secret communication of synchronized fractional-order chaotic systems based on FPGA technology will be investigated.

ACKNOWLEDGMENT

This research was supported by the National Natural Science Foundation of China [grant number 11747150, 61161006 and 61073187], the Doctoral Research in Hunan University of Arts and Science [grant number E07016048], and the Fundamental Research Funds for the Central Universities of Central South University [grant number 72150050641].

REFERENCES

Abbaoui, K., & Cherruault, Y. (1994). Convergence of Adomian's method applied to differential equations. *Mathematical and Computer Modelling*, *28*(5), 103–109.

Adomian, G. (1990). A Review of the decomposition method and some recent results for nonlinear equations. *Mathematical and Computer Modelling*, *13*(7), 17–43. doi:10.1016/0895-7177(90)90125-7

Arena, F., Gatti, G., & Martra, G. (2012). Adaptation of differential transform method for the numeric-analytic solution of fractional-order Rössler chaotic and hyperchaotic systems. *Abstract & Applied Analysis,* (4), 305-309.

Bandt, C., & Pompe, B. (2002). Permutation entropy: A natural complexity measure for time series. *Physical Review Letters*, *88*(17), 174102. doi:10.1103/PhysRevLett.88.174102 PMID:12005759

Bhalekar, S., & Daftardar-Gejji, V. (2010). Synchronization of different fractional order chaotic systems using active control. *Communications in Nonlinear Science and Numerical Simulation*, *15*(11), 3536–3546. doi:10.1016/j.cnsns.2009.12.016

Cafagna, D., & Grassi, G. (2008). Bifurcation and chaos in the fractional-order Chen system via a time-domain approach. *International Journal of Bifurcation and Chaos in Applied Sciences and Engineering*, *18*(7), 1845–1863. doi:10.1142/S0218127408021415

Caponetto, R., & Fazzino, S. (2013). An application of Adomian decomposition for analysis of fractional-order chaotic systems. *International Journal of Bifurcation and Chaos in Applied Sciences and Engineering*, *23*(03), 1350050. doi:10.1142/S0218127413500508

Carpinteri, A., & Mainardi, F. (1997). *Fractal and Fractional Calculus in Continuum Mechanics*. Wien: Springer-Verlag. doi:10.1007/978-3-7091-2664-6

Charef, A., Sun, H. H., Tsao, Y. Y., & Onaral, B. (1992). Fractal system as represented by singularity function. *IEEE Transactions on Automatic Control*, *37*(9), 1465–1470. doi:10.1109/9.159595

Chen, D., Wu, C., Iu, H. H. C., & Ma, X. (2013). Circuit simulation for synchronization of a fractional-order and integer-order chaotic system. *Nonlinear Dynamics*, *73*(3), 1671–1686. doi:10.100711071-013-0894-8

Chen, D., Zhang, R., & Sprott, J. C. (2012). Synchronization between integer-order chaotic systems and a class of fractional-order chaotic systems via sliding mode control. *Chaos (Woodbury, N.Y.)*, *70*(2), 1549–1561. PMID:22757537

Chen, D., Zhao, W., Sprott, J. C., & Ma, X. (2013). Application of Takagi–Sugeno fuzzy model to a class of chaotic synchronization and anti-synchronization. *Nonlinear Dynamics*, *73*(3), 1495–1505. doi:10.100711071-013-0880-1

Chen, W. T., Zhuang, J., Yu, W. X., & Wang, Z. (2009). Measuring complexity using FuzzyEn, ApEn, and SampEn. *Medical Engineering & Physics*, *31*(1), 61–68. doi:10.1016/j.medengphy.2008.04.005 PMID:18538625

Ellner, S., Gallant, A. R., McCaffrey, D., & Nychka, D. (1991). Convergence rates and data requirements for Jacobian-based estimates of Lyapunov exponents from data. *Physics Letters. [Part A]*, *153*(6), 357–363. doi:10.1016/0375-9601(91)90958-B

Gammoudi, I. E., & Feki, M. (2013). Synchronization of integer order and fractional order Chua's systems using robust observer. *Communications in Nonlinear Science and Numerical Simulation*, *18*(3), 625–638. doi:10.1016/j.cnsns.2012.08.005

Gao, T. G., Chen, G. R., Chen, Z. Q., & Cang, S. (2007). The generation and circuit implementation of a new hyper-chaos based upon Lorenz system. *Physics Letters. [Part A]*, *361*(1), 78–86. doi:10.1016/j.physleta.2006.09.042

Gao, X., & Yu, J. (2005). Synchronization of two coupled fractional-order chaotic oscillators. *Chaos, Solitons, and Fractals*, *26*(1), 141–145. doi:10.1016/j.chaos.2004.12.030

He, S. B., Sun, K. H., & Wang, H. H. (2015). Complexity analysis and DSP implementation of the fractional-order Lorenz hyperchaotic system. *Entropy (Basel, Switzerland)*, *17*(12), 8299–8311. doi:10.3390/e17127882

He, S. B., Sun, K. H., & Wang, H. H. (2016). Solution and dynamics analysis of a fractional-order hyperchaotic system. *Mathematical Methods in the Applied Sciences*, *39*(11), 2965–2973. doi:10.1002/mma.3743

He, S. B., Sun, K. H., & Wang, H. H. (2016). Synchronisation of fractional-order time delayed chaotic systems with ring connection. *The European Physical Journal. Special Topics*, *225*(1), 97–106. doi:10.1140/epjst/e2016-02610-3

He, S. B., Sun, K. H., & Zhu, C. X. (2013). Complexity analyses of multi-wing chaotic systems. *Chinese Physics B*, *22*(5), 050506. doi:10.1088/1674-1056/22/5/050506

Larrondo, H. A., González, C. M., Martin, M. T., Plastino, A., & Rosso, O. A. (2005). Intensive statistical complexity measure of pseudorandom number generators. *Physica A*, *356*(1), 133–138. doi:10.1016/j.physa.2005.05.025

Li, C., Gong, Z., Qian, D., & Chen, Y. Q. (2010). On the bound of the Lyapunov exponents for the fractional differential systems. *Chaos (Woodbury, N.Y.)*, *20*(1), 013127. doi:10.1063/1.3314277 PMID:20370282

Matouk, A. E., & Elsadany, A. A. (2017). Dynamical analysis, stabilization and discretization of a chaotic fractional-order GLV model. *Nonlinear Dynamics*, *85*(3), 1597–1612. doi:10.100711071-016-2781-6

Maus, A., & Sprott, J. C. (2013). Evaluating Lyapunov exponent spectra with neural networks. *Chaos, Solitons, and Fractals*, *51*(51), 13–21. doi:10.1016/j.chaos.2013.03.001

Pham, V. T., Kingni, S. T., Volos, C., Jafari, S., & Kapitaniak, T. (2017). A simple three-dimensional fractional-order chaotic system without equilibrium: Dynamics, circuitry implementation, chaos control and synchronization. *International Journal of Electronics and Communications*, *78*(1), 220–227. doi:10.1016/j.aeue.2017.04.012

Phillip, P. A., Chiu, F. L., & Nick, S. J. (2009). Rapidly detecting disorder in rhythmic biological signals: A spectral entropy measure to identify cardiac arrhythmias. *Physical Review. E*, *79*(1), 011915. doi:10.1103/PhysRevE.79.011915 PMID:19257077

Richman, J. S., & Moorman, J. R. (2000). Physiological time-series analysis using approximate entropy and sample entropy. *American Journal of Physiology. Heart and Circulatory Physiology*, *278*(6), 2039–2049. doi:10.1152/ajpheart.2000.278.6.H2039 PMID:10843903

Shen, E. H., Cai, Z. J., & Gu, F. J. (2005). Mathematical foundation of a new complexity measure. *Applied Mathematics and Mechanics*, *26*(9), 1188–1196. doi:10.1007/BF02507729

Sun, H. H., Abdelwahab, A. A., & Onaral, B. (1984). Linear approximation of transfer function with a pole of fractional power. *IEEE Transactions on Automatic Control*, *29*(5), 441–444. doi:10.1109/TAC.1984.1103551

Sun, K. H., He, S. B., & Zhu, C. X. (2013). Analysis of chaotic complexity characteristics based on C_0 Algorithm. *Tien Tzu Hsueh Pao*, *41*(9), 1765–1771.

Sun, K. H., Wang, X., & Sprott, J. C. (2010). Bifurcations and chaos in fractional-order simplified Lorenz system. *International Journal of Bifurcation and Chaos in Applied Sciences and Engineering*, *20*(4), 1209–1219. doi:10.1142/S0218127410026411

Tavazoei, M. S., & Haeri, M. (2007). Unreliability of frequency-domain approximation in recognizing chaos in fractional-order systems. *Signal Processing IET*, *1*(4), 171–181. doi:10.1049/iet-spr:20070053

Tavazoei, M. S., & Haeri, M. (2008). Synchronization of chaotic fractional-order systems via active sliding mode controller. *Physica A*, *387*(1), 57–70. doi:10.1016/j.physa.2007.08.039

Wang, S., & Yu, Y. G. (2012). Application of multistage homotopy-perturbation method for the solutions of the chaotic fractional order systems. *International Journal of Nonlinear Science*, *13*(1), 3–14.

Wang, S., Yu, Y. G., Wang, H., & Rahmani, A. (2014). Function projective lag synchronization of fractional-order chaotic systems. *Chinese Physics B*, *23*(4), 040502. doi:10.1088/1674-1056/23/4/040502

Wang, Z., Huang, X., Li, Y. X., & Song, X.-N. (2013). A new image encryption algorithm based on the fractional-order hyperchaotic Lorenz system. *Chinese Physics B*, *22*(1), 010504. doi:10.1088/1674-1056/22/1/010504

Wolf, A., Swift, J. B., Swinney, H. L., & Vastano, J. A. (1985). Determining Lyapunov exponents from a time series. *Physica D. Nonlinear Phenomena*, *16*(3), 285–317. doi:10.1016/0167-2789(85)90011-9

Zhang, S., Yu, Y., Wen, G., & Rahmani, A. (2016). Lag-generalized synchronization of time-delay chaotic systems with stochastic perturbation. *Modern Physics Letters B*, *30*(1), 1550263. doi:10.1142/S0217984915502632

KEY TERMS AND DEFINITIONS

Complexity: Measured by spectral entropy and C_0 complexity algorithms (or other entropy algorithms and complexity algorithms), and it can reflect the degree of disorder of the time series.

Coupled-Synchronization: Two fractional-order chaotic systems which are controlled by coupled controllers and synchronization between corresponding state variables can be then found.

Dynamics: Behaviors of the fractional-order chaotic systems which can be analyzed by Lyapunov exponents and bifurcation diagrams.

Fractional Calculus: The derivative order q is not an integer number. There are many different kinds of definitions for fractional-order calculus including Riemann-Liouville (R-L) definition and Caputo definition.

Hyperchaotic System: Compared with chaotic system, a hyperchaotic system has two or more positive Lyapunov exponents.

Intermediate Variables: When the fractional-order chaotic system is solved by ADM algorithm, to simplify the numerical solution, some coefficients are introduced.

Secure Communication: The original information is encrypted by certain method, and ciphertext is send to the receiver through communication channel. Thus, other people cannot understand what the information has been sent. It should be pointed out that chaos-based secure communication is a hot topic at the present.

Chapter 3
Adaptive Neural Control for Unknown Nonlinear Time–Delay Fractional–Order Systems With Input Saturation

Farouk Zouari
Université de Tunis El Manar, Tunisia

Amina Boubellouta
University of Jijel, Algeria

ABSTRACT

This chapter focuses on the adaptive neural control of a class of uncertain multi-input multi-output (MIMO) nonlinear time-delay non-integer order systems with unmeasured states, unknown control direction, and unknown asymmetric saturation actuator. The design of the controller follows a number of steps. Firstly, based on the semi-group property of fractional order derivative, the system is transformed into a normalized fractional order system by means of a state transformation in order to facilitate the control design. Then, a simple linear state observer is constructed to estimate the unmeasured states of the transformed system. A neural network is incorporated to approximate the unknown nonlinear functions while a Nussbaum function is used to deal with the unknown control direction. In addition, the strictly positive real (SPR) condition, the Razumikhin lemma, the frequency distributed model, and the Lyapunov method are utilized to derive the parameter adaptive laws and to perform the stability proof.

INTRODUCTION

In the control literature, strict-feedback, pure-feedback and stochastic nonlinear systems are frequently encountered (Yu et al., 2016; Shi, 2015; Cui et al., 2015; Yu & Du, 2011; Chen et al., 2010). In addition, there exist several real systems described by non-integer order differential equations such as (Boulkroune et al., 2016a): regular variation in thermodynamics, viscoelastic systems, dielectric polarization, electrical circuits, biological and financial systems, electromagnetic waves, heat conduction in a semi-infinite slab,

DOI: 10.4018/978-1-5225-5418-9.ch003

robotics, biophysics, and so on. It is worth noting that integer order systems are a special case of non-integer order systems (Boulkroune et al., 2016a; Miao & Li, 2015; Shi, 2015a; Bouzeriba et al.,2016a; Boulkroune et al., 2012a; Boulkroune et al., 2012b; Boulkroune et al., 2014a; Boulkroune & M'Saad, 2011; Boulkroune et al., 2014b; Sui et al., 2015; Iqbal et al., 2015; Wang et al., 2015a; Wang et al., 2015b; Liu et al., 2015a; Du & Chen, 2009; Mizumoto et al., 2015; Shahnazi, 2016; Wei et al., 2015; Lan & Zhou, 2013; N'Doye & Laleg-Kirati, 2015; Li & Wang, 2014; Vargas-De-León, 2015; Chen & Chen, 2015; Stamova & Stamov, 2014; Stamova & Stamov, 2013). Additionally, it has been proved that the fractional calculus is an excellent mathematical tool for accurate descriptions of memory and hereditary properties of several materials and processes (Boulkroune et al., 2016a). Compared with integer order systems, there is very little research dealing with multi-input multi-output (MIMO) fractional-order systems (Yu et al., 2016; Stamova & Stamov, 2013; Lan et al., 2012; Zhang et al., 2015; Ladaci et al., 2009; Farges et al., 2010; Lazarević & Spasić, 2009; Lim et al., 2013; Domek & Dworak, 2016; Luo & Liu, 2014; Liu & Jiang, 2013a; Li et al., 2015a; Li et al., 2015b; Li et al.,2015c; McGarry et al., 2007; Rădac et al., 2014; Yacoub et al., 2014; Yan et al., 2016; Liu et al., 2016a; Gao & Liu, 2016; Liu & Tong, 2013b; Liu & Tong, 2014; Liu & Tong, 2015b; Bouzeriba et al., 2016b; Chen et al., 2016; Wang et al., 2017; Ibeas, & de la Sen, 2007; Tabatabaei & Arefi, 2016; Arefi et al., 2014a; Arefi et al., 2014b; Petras, 2011; Boulkroune et al., 2010; Ioannou & Sun, 1996; Boulkroune et al., 2016b; Yue & Li, 2012; Liu et al., 2016b). This fact can be explained by the specificity of MIMO systems and the difficulties with the extension of the approaches employed for integer order systems to fractional ones (Boulkroune et al., 2012a; Shahnazi, 2016; Domek & Dworak, 2016; Li et al., 2015b; Yan et al., 2016; Liu & Tong, 2014; Tabatabaei & Arefi, 2016).

This work is thus devoted to the control of MIMO fractional systems with some specific features of including some elements that are frequently encountered in control systems so that the contribution of the chapter is of interest in real applications of control. These features are:

Nonlinearity

Real world systems are usually nonlinear (Yu et al., 2016; Shi, 2015; Cui et al., 2015; Yu & Du, 2011; Chen et al., 2010; Miao & Li, 2015; Shi, 2015a; Bouzeriba et al., 2016a; Boulkroune et al., 2012a; Boulkroune et al., 2012b; Boulkroune et al., 2014a; Boulkroune & M'Saad, 2011; Boulkroune et al., 2014b; Sui et al., 2015; Iqbal et al., 2015; Wang et al., 2015a; Wang et al., 2015b; Liu et al., 2015a; Du & Chen, 2009; Mizumoto et al., 2015; Shahnazi, 2016; Wang et al., 2015a; Wang et al., 2015b; Lan & Zhou, 2013; N'Doye & Laleg-Kirati, 2015; Li & Wang, 2014; Vargas-De-León, 2015; Chen & Chen, 2015; Stamova & Stamov, 2014; Stamova & Stamov, 2013; Liu et al., 2016b). This fact implies that they are best described by nonlinear models rather than by linear ones (Boulkroune et al., 2016a; Bouzeriba et al.,2016a; Wei et al., 2015; Lan & Zhou, 2013; N'Doye & Laleg-Kirati, 2015; Li & Wang, 2014; Vargas-De-León, 2015; Chen & Chen, 2015; Stamova & Stamov, 2014; Stamova & Stamov, 2013; Lan et al., 2012; Zhang et al., 2015; Ladaci et al., 2009; Farges et al., 2010; Lazarević & Spasić, 2009; Lim et al., 2013; Domek & Dworak, 2016; Luo & Liu, 2014.; Liu & Jiang, 2013a; Li et al., 2015a; Li et al., 2015b; Li et al., 2015c; McGarry et al., 2007; Rădac et al., 2014; Yacoub et al., 2014;Yan et al., 2016; Liu et al., 2016a; Gao & Liu, 2016; Liu & Tong, 2013b; Liu & Tong, 2014; Yue & Li, 2012). Therefore, a general setting for the control problem is to consider a set of nonlinear equations describing the system (Li et al., 2015b; Li et al., 2015c; McGarry et al., 2007; Rădac et al., 2014; Yacoub et al., 2014 ;Yan et al., 2016; Liu et al., 2016a; Gao & Liu, 2016; Liu & Tong, 2013b; Liu & Tong, 2014; Liu &

Tong, 2015b; Bouzeriba et al., 2016b; Chen et al., 2016; Wang et al., 2017; Ibeas, & de la Sen, 2007; Tabatabaei & Arefi, 2016; Arefi et al.,2014a; Arefi et al.,2014b; Petras, 2011; Boulkroune et al., 2010; Ioannou & Sun, 1996; Boulkroune et al., 2016b; Yue & Li, 2012). This includes a nonlinear dynamical behavior along with a potential nonaffinity in the control input (Du & Chen, 2009). During the past decades, considerable attention has been paid to the adaptive control of classes of nonlinear fractional-order systems (see Boulkroune et al., 2016a; Bouzeriba et al., 2016a; Wei et al., 2015; Lan & Zhou, 2013; N'Doye & Laleg-Kirati, 2015; Li & Wang, 2014; Vargas-De-León, 2015; Chen & Chen, 2015; Stamova & Stamov, 2014; Stamova & Stamov, 2013; Lan et al., 2012; Ladaci et al., 2009; Farges et al., 2010; Lazarević & Spasić, 2009; Lim et al., 2013; Domek & Dworak, 2016; Luo & Liu, 2014.; Liu & Jiang, 2013a ; Bouzeriba et al.,2016b; Chen et al., 2016; Wang et al., 2017) and the references therein). In the recent research works (Boulkroune et al., 2016a; Bouzeriba et al.,2016a) nonlinear fractional-order systems with affine structures have been also investigated.

Nonaffinity

However, there exist several nonlinear nonaffine systems in practice, such as chemical reactors, biochemical processes, some aircraft and pendulum dynamical models, and so on (Yu et al., 2016; Boulkroune et al., 2012a; Boulkroune et al., 2014a; Liu et al., 2015a; Du & Chen, 2009; Wei et al., 2015; N'Doye & Laleg-Kirati, 2015; Li & Wang, 2014; Rădac et al., 2014; Liu & Tong, 2014; Tabatabaei & Arefi, 2016; Arefi et al., 2014b). Due to the great efforts devoted by researchers, remarkable adaptive control approaches have been developed for nonaffine systems (Liu et al., 2015a; Rădac et al., 2014; Liu & Tong, 2014; Tabatabaei & Arefi, 2016). It is worth noting that affine systems are a special case of nonaffine systems (Yu et al., 2016; Boulkroune et al., 2012a; Boulkroune et al., 2014a). In (Boulkroune et al., 2012a; Liu et al., 2015a; Du & Chen, 2009), it has been shown that the non-affine problem can be traditionally addressed by five approaches, namely: (i) approach based on Taylor series expansion, (ii) approach based on implicit function theorem, (iii) approach based on the mean value theorem, (iv) approach based on differentiating the original system equation, (v) approach based on a local inversion of the Takagi-Sugeno (TS) fuzzy affine model. Moreover, the knowledge of the sign of the control gain is required in (Du & Chen, 2009;Wei et al.,2015) to facilitate the design of the adaptive controls for nonlinear nonaffine systems.

Unknown Control Direction

As stated in (Shi, 2015a; Shi, 2015b; Boulkroune et al., 2012a; Boulkroune et al., 2012b; Li et al., 2015a; Arefi et al., 2014b; Boulkroune et al., 2016b), there are many systems with unknown control direction such as electrical systems, biochemical and biophysical processes, robotics, to name but a few. Various robust adaptive fuzzy sliding mode controllers have been presented for a class of nonlinear fractional order systems with unknown control direction (Boulkroune et al., 2016a; Bouzeriba et al., 2016a; Luo & Liu, 2014; Bouzeriba et al., 2016b). In Shi (2015a), Boulkroune et al. (2012a ; 2012b), Liu et al. (2016a), Gao & Liu (2016), Liu & Tong (2013b; 2014; 2015b), Boulkroune et al. (2010), Ioannou & Sun (1996), Boulkroune et al. (2016b), and Yue & Li (2012). Five methods have been used to cope with the unknown control direction problem: (i) a method based on a Nussbaum-type function, (ii) a method based on directly estimating unknown parameters, (iii) a method based on a monitoring function, (iv) a method based on a hysteresis-type function, (v) a method based on a hysteresis-dead zone type function and a Nussbaum function. Compared with the existing controls in Shi (2015a; 2015b), Boulkroune et al. (2012a; 2012b), Li et al. (2015a), Boulkroune et al. (2016b), the adaptive fuzzy control laws presented in Liu et al. (2016a), Gao & Liu (2016), Liu & Tong (2013b) have solved the tracking problem for non-linear uncertain Discrete-Time systems with unknown control direction and input nonlinearities (such as dead-zone, backlash-like hysteresis and backlash), by using the reinforcement learning algorithm.

Uncertainty

In most practical situations, the systems under control are unknown or partially unknown (Yu & Du, 2011; Miao & Li, 2015; Boulkroune et al., 2014a; Boulkroune & M'Saad, 2011; Wang et al., 2015a; Liu et al., 2015a; Shahnazi, 2016; Lan et al., 2012; Li et al., 2015c; Tabatabaei & Arefi, 2016; Arefi et al., 2014a; Ioannou & Sun, 1996). These facts require specific control tools to deal with the controller design process, being one of the most extended ones the adaptive control paradigm. The conventional controllers have been constructed thanks to the mathematical models of identified plants from the Input-Output data (McGarry et al., 2007; Rădac et al., 2014; Yacoub et al., 2014; Yan et al., 2016; Liu et al., 2016a). For coping with conventional controller problems, data-driven control techniques have been used in many researches (Rădac et al., 2014). As presented in McGarry et al. (2007), Rădac et al. (2014), Yacoub et al. (2014), and Yan et al. (2016), iterative feedback tuning, correlation-based tuning, frequency-domain tuning, iterative regression tuning, simultaneous perturbation stochastic approximation, data-driven predictive control, model-free adaptive control, model-free control, unfalsified control, adaptive online iterative feedback tuning, data-driven reinforcement learning control, and model-free or data-driven iterative learning control represent the main iterative data-driven controller tuning techniques. Besides, virtual reference feedback tuning is a "one-shot" direct data-based controller design method which converts the model-reference control problem into an identification problem (McGarry et al., 2007). Usually, virtual reference feedback tuning does not ensure the stability of closed loop control systems because it calculates the controller parameters by utilizing Input-Output data of the open-loop stable processes. In contrast to model-based control techniques, data-driven control techniques construct the controllers directly with the help of on-line or off-line Input-Output data of the controlled processes without mathematical models of the controlled systems and whose stability, convergence, and robustness can be ensured by mathematical analysis under some assumptions (Yacoub et al., 2014). On the other side, in wide industrial applications, adaptive sliding mode controllers, adaptive backstepping controls, robust adaptive controls and impulsive adaptive controls have been also applied theoretically and experimentally for nonlinear systems with linearly parameterized uncertainty (Li & Wang, 2014; Vargas-De-León, 2015; Chen & Chen, 2015; Stamova & Stamov, 2014; Stamova & Stamov, 2013; Lan et al., 2012; Ladaci et al., 2009; Farges et al., 2010). Furthermore, thanks to the universal approximation theorem (Boulkroune et al., 2016a; Bouzeriba et al., 2016a; Wei et al., 2015; Luo & Liu, 2014; Bouzeriba et al., 2016b; Chen et al., 2016; Wang et al., 2017), various neural network based-adaptive and fuzzy adaptive controllers have been developed for a class of nonlinear uncertain systems. Several intelligent control techniques like neural network-based control techniques and fuzzy control techniques are data-driven control techniques (McGarry et al., 2007; Rădac et al., 2014; Yacoub et al., 2014; Yan et al., 2016). By using a Lyapunov method, the adaptive control design and the stability analysis of integer nonlinear uncertain systems can be effectively carried out (Yu et al., 2016; Shi, 2015; Cui et al., 2015; Yu & Du, 2011; Chen et al., 2010; Boulkroune et al., 2016a; Miao & Li, 2015; Shi, 2015a; Bouzeriba et al.,2016a; Boulkroune et al., 2012a; Boulkroune et al., 2012b; Boulkroune et al., 2014a; Boulkroune

& M'Saad, 2011; Boulkroune et al., 2014b; Sui et al., 2015; Iqbal et al., 2015; Wang et al., 2015a;Wang et al., 2015b; Liu et al., 2015a; Du & Chen, 2009; Mizumoto et al., 2015; Shahnazi, 2016; Wei et al., 2015; Vargas-De-León, 2015; Liu et al., 2016b). Moreover, in the recent papers (Wei et al.,2015; Lan & Zhou, 2013; et al., 2015; Li & Wang, 2014), the frequency distributed model and the indirect Lyapunov method are used to design the adaptive controller and to analyze the stability of nonlinear uncertain fractional order systems. Compared to Boulkroune et al. (2016a), Bouzeriba et al. (2016a), Vargas-De-León, (2015), Chen & Chen (2015), Stamova & Stamov (2014), Luo & Liu, (2014), Bouzeriba et al. (2016b), Chen et al. (2016), and Wang et al. (2017), the main advantage of the works (Wei et al., 2015; Lan & Zhou, 2013; N'Doye & Laleg-Kirati, 2015; Li & Wang, 2014) is that the fractional derivatives of the Lyapunov functions have not been calculated and novel Lyapunov functions have been designed with the help of the frequency distributed model in order to tackle the limitation of conversational square type Lyapunov functions. Nevertheless, the works (Wei et al., 2015; Lan & Zhou, 2013; N'Doye & Laleg-Kirati, 2015; Li & Wang, 2014) have not studied the effect of actuator nonlinearities in the control design and stability analysis.

Saturation in the Control Input

In many industrial systems, the input (actuator) saturation can exist (Yu et al., 2016; Sui et al., 2015; Iqbal et al., 2015; Wang et al., 2015a; Wang et al., 2015b; Shahnazi, 2016; Li et al., 2015c). It usually gravely limits the system performance and sometimes even makes the closed-loop system unstable (Yu et al., 2016; Sui et al., 2015; Iqbal et al., 2015; Wang et al., 2015a; Wang et al., 2015b; Shahnazi, 2016). Therefore, the analysis and control of non-linear systems with input saturation are important fields in the practical control system design and have been receiving great attention in recent years (Sui et al., 2015; Iqbal et al., 2015; Wang et al., 2015a; Wang et al., 2015b). The output of the physical actuator has maximum and minimum amplitude limits (Yu et al., 2016; Shi, 2015a; Cui et al., 2015; Yu & Du, 2011; Chen et al., 2010; Boulkroune et al., 2016a; Miao & Li, 2015; Shi, 2015b; Bouzeriba et al., 2016a; Boulkroune et al., 2012a; Boulkroune et al., 2012b; Boulkroune et al., 2014a; Boulkroune & M'Saad, 2011; Boulkroune et al., 2014b; Sui et al., 2015). Moreover, in the control literature, few results are available for systems with saturation nonlinearities (Yu et al., 2016; Shi, 2015a; Cui et al., 2015; Yu & Du, 2011; Chen et al., 2010; Boulkroune et al., 2016a; Miao & Li, 2015; Shi, 2015b; Bouzeriba et al., 2016a; Boulkroune et al., 2012a; Boulkroune et al., 2012b; Boulkroune et al., 2014a; Boulkroune & M'Saad, 2011; Boulkroune et al., 2014b; Sui et al., 2015; Shahnazi, 2016; Lim et al., 2013). In Yu et al. (2016), the problem of adaptive tracking control has been investigated for a class of uncertain pure-feedback nonlinear time-delay systems in the presence of unknown asymmetric saturation actuators by means of a Gaussian error function-based continuous differentiable model. In Lim et al. (2013), a method has been provided for the asymptotic stabilization of fractional-order systems with input saturation. The major limitation of the adaptive controllers introduced in Yu et al. (2016), Wang et al. (2015b), and Lim et al. (2013) is that all of the state variables of the systems must be measurable.

Unavailability of State Measurements

In most practical situations, the state variables of the system may be unavailable for measurement (Shi, 2015a; Shi, 2015b; Du & Chen, 2009; Mizumoto et al., 2015). In these cases, output feedback control (or observer-based control) laws should be utilized to get the desired performance (Boulkroune et al.,

2012b; Boulkroune et al., 2014a; Boulkroune et al., 2014b). In general, there are three methods of output feedback control design (Du & Chen, 2009): (i) a method based on the separation principle paradigm, (ii) a method based on the non-separation principle, (iii) a method based on the Strictly Positive Real (SPR) condition. Under the separation principle, the observer and the controller may be constructed separately, in such a way that the combined observer-controller output feedback guarantee the main characteristics of the controller with the full state available (Shi, 2015a; Shi, 2015b; Du & Chen, 2009). However, under the non-separation principle, the observer does not depend on the uncertainties of the system and the design of observer gain is coupled with the control system design (Shi, 2015b; Du & Chen, 2009). The SPR condition of the observation error dynamics is required so that one may employ Meyer-Kalman-Yakubovich (MKY) Lemma to design the adaptation laws and for the stability analysis (Shi, 2015b; Boulkroune et al., 2014a; Boulkroune & M'Saad, 2011; Boulkroune et al., 2014b). In general, the SPR condition is a very restrictive condition and may not be satisfied by many systems. The filtering of the observation error dynamics (which are not SPR) by a stable filter has been performed in Shi, (2015a; 2015b), Boulkroune et al. (2014a), Boulkroune & M'Saad (2011), Boulkroune et al. (2014b), and Shahnazi, (2016) to meet the SPR condition of a transfer function associated with the Lyapunov stability analysis. In Lan & Zhou (2013), Li & Wang (2014), and Lan et al. (2012), the problem of output feedback control of a class of fractional-order systems has been investigated. It should be pointed out that the time-delay case has not been investigated in Shi (2015a; Shi, 2015b), Boulkroune et al. (2012b), Boulkroune et al. (2014a; 2014b), Du & Chen (2009), Mizumoto et al. (2015), Lan & Zhou (2013), Li & Wang (2014), and Lan et al. (2012).

Delays

Furthermore, in many practical control systems, delays are generally encountered (Yu et al., 2016; Cui et al., 2015; Yu & Du, 2011; Chen et al., 2010; Vargas-De-León, 2015; Chen & Chen, 2015; Stamova & Stamov, 2014; Stamova & Stamov, 2013; Liu & Jiang, 2013a; Li et al., 2015b; Chen et al., 2016; Wang et al., 2017; Yue & Li, 2012). In fact, the existence of delays causes poor performance and even instability of the system under control (Cui et al., 2015; Yu & Du, 2011; Chen et al., 2010). The Lyapunov-Krasovskii method and the Lyapounv-Razumikhin method are usually employed to perform the stability analysis and controller design for time-delay systems (Yu et al., 2016; Cui et al., 2015; Yu & Du, 2011; Chen et al., 2010; Vargas-De-León, 2015). Compared with the Krasovskii technique, the Lyapunov- Razumikhin technique is applied to many time-delay systems such that the control design and the stability analysis can be relatively simple (Yu et al., 2016; Cui et al., 2015; Yu & Du, 2011; Chen et al., 2010) and without the usual assumption that the derivative of the delay terms must be less than unity. Moreover, the Lyapunov-Krasovskii functionals which are always composed by quadratic and integral functions, have been extended for analyzing the nonlinear fractional order systems in (Yu et al., 2016; Cui et al.,2015; Liu & Jiang, 2013a; Yue & Li, 2012). However, the Lyapunov-Razumikhin functionals are selected as quadratic functions in order to design the control for fractional-order systems with constant delays, time-varying delays and distributed time-varying delays (Yu et al., 2016; Yu & Du, 2011; Chen et al., 2010; Vargas-De-León, 2015; Chen & Chen, 2015; Stamova & Stamov, 2014; Stamova & Stamov, 2013; Yue & Li, 2012). In Vargas-De-León (2015), Chen & Chen (2015), Stamova & Stamov (2014), and Stamova & Stamov (2013), stability theorems for fractional-order systems have been developed by using Riemann-Liouville derivatives, Caputo derivatives, a Lyapunov function and the Razumikhin technique. Based on a combination of the fractional Barbalat's lemma, the Lyapunov theorem and the Razumikhin functional approach, some stability conditions have been obtained for fractional-order neural networks with time delay (Wang et al., 2017). So far, to the best of the authors' knowledge, the problem of the adaptive control of a class of uncertain MIMO nonlinear time-delay non-integer order systems with unmeasured states, unknown control direction and unknown input saturation has not been studied before in the literature.

Inspired by the previous discussion, a novel robust output-feedback adaptive neural control approach is proposed in this paper for a class of uncertain MIMO nonlinear time delay non-integer order systems with unmeasured states, unknown control direction and unknown asymmetric saturation actuator. Note that the first time in the literature that this kind of systems is under consideration. Based on the semi-group property of fractional order derivative, the original system is transformed into a normalised fractional order one by a novel state transformation with the purpose of facilitating the control design. During this process, the mean value theorem and a Gaussian error function-based continuous differentiable model are used to describe the unknown asymmetric saturation actuator and to get an affine model in which the control input linearly appears, respectively. Then, a simple linear state observer and a neural network are employed to estimate the unmeasured states of the transformed system and to approximate the unknown nonlinear functions, respectively. A Nussbaum function is utilized in order to cope with the unknown control direction. In addition, the SPR condition, the Razumikhin Lemma, the frequency distributed model, the Lyapunov method and the Barbalat's lemma are adopted for deriving the parameter adaptive laws. The main contribution of this manuscript lies in the following:

1. Compared with the existing works (Yu et al., 2016; Shi, 2015a; Chen et al., 2010; Boulkroune et al., 2016a; Miao & Li, 2015; Shi, 2015b; Bouzeriba et al., 2016a; Boulkroune et al., 2012a; Boulkroune et al., 2012b; Boulkroune et al., 2014a; Boulkroune & M'Saad, 2011; Boulkroune et al., 2014b; Iqbal et al., 2015; Wang et al., 2015a; Wang et al., 2015b; Liu et al., 2015a; Du & Chen, 2009; Mizumoto et al., 2015; Shahnazi, 2016; Wei et al.,2015; Lan & Zhou, 2013; N'Doye & Laleg-Kirati, 2015; Li & Wang, 2014; Vargas-De-León, 2015; Chen & Chen, 2015; Stamova & Stamov, 2014; Stamova & Stamov, 2013; Lan et al., 2012; Zhang et al., 2015; Ladaci et al., 2009; Farges et al., 2010; Yue & Li, 2012), the considered class of systems is relatively large.

2. Unlike Boulkroune et al. (2016a), Miao & Li (2015), Bouzeriba et al. (2016a), Wei et al. (2015), Lan & Zhou (2013), N'Doye & Laleg-Kirati (2015), Li & Wang (2014), Lan et al. (2012), Zhang et al. (2015), Ladaci et al. (2009), Farges et al. (2010), the proposed design approach does not require a priori knowledge of the signs of control gains nor any information of the bound of input saturation.

3. In contrast to the adaptive control schemes (Yu et al., 2016; Shi, 2015a; Cui et al., 2015; Yu & Du, 2011; Chen et al., 2010; Boulkroune et al., 2016a; Miao & Li, 2015; Shi, 2015b; Bouzeriba et al., 2016a; Boulkroune et al., 2012a; Boulkroune et al., 2012b; Boulkroune et al., 2014a; Boulkroune & M'Saad, 2011; Boulkroune et al., 2014b; Sui et al., 2015; Iqbal et al., 2015; Wang et al., 2015a; Wang et al., 2015b; Liu et al., 2015a; Du & Chen, 2009; Mizumoto et al., 2015; Shahnazi, 2016; Lan & Zhou, 2013; N'Doye & Laleg-Kirati, 2015; Li & Wang, 2014; Lan et al., 2012; Zhang et al., 2015; Ladaci et al., 2009; Farges et al., 2010; Yue & Li, 2012), the number of adjustable parameters is reduced.

4. This proposed work can handle systems with both constant and distributed time-varying delays.

5. Unlike the closely related works (Yu et al., 2016; Yu & Du, 2011; Yue & Li, 2012), the tracking errors converge asymptotically to zero.

The remaining part of the chapter is outlined as follows. The problem statement is presented in Section 2. The neural adaptive output-feedback control is designed in Section 3. Some simulation examples are given to show the feasibility, validity and effectiveness of the proposed controller in Section 4. Finally, conclusions are provided in section 5.

Notations

D^q denotes the $q-$order Caputo differential operator. $\| \ \|$ indicates the Euclidean norm. $\mathrm{diag}\left(*\right)$ denotes a block diagonal matrix. $0_{n \times m}$ is the zero matrix of size $n \times m$. I_n represents the identity matrix of size n. $\lambda_{\min}\left(.\right)$ denotes the minimum eigenvalue of corresponding matrices. t denotes the time index. s is the Laplace variable. $\tanh\left(.\right)$ denotes the hyperbolic tangent function. The superscript T denotes the matrix transpose operation. $sat\left(.\right)$ is the saturation function. $\mathrm{sgn}\left(.\right)$ represents the sign function. L_∞ is the space of bounded functions. L_2 is the space of square-summable functions.

PROBLEM STATEMENT

Consider a class of MIMO uncertain nonlinear time-delay non-integer order systems as follows

$$
\begin{cases}
D^{q_i} x_i\left(t\right) = A_{0,i} x_i\left(t\right) + b_{0,i}\Bigg[f_{1,i}\left(x\left(t\right), x\left(t - \tau_{1,i}\left(t\right)\right)\right) + d_i\left(t\right) + f_{3,i}\left(x\left(t\right), \nu_i\left(t\right)\right) \\
\qquad + \int_{t-\tau_{2,i}(t)}^{t} f_{2,i}\left(x\left(\tau\right)\right) d\tau \Bigg] + \sum_{k=0}^{n_i-2} b_{1,k,i}\Bigg[f_{4,k,i}\left(x\left(t\right), x\left(t - \tau_{3,k,i}\left(t\right)\right)\right) \\
\qquad + \varpi_{k,i}\left(t\right) + \int_{t-\tau_{4,k,i}(t)}^{t} f_{5,k,i}\left(x\left(\tau\right)\right) d\tau \Bigg], \ \forall t \geq 0 \\
x_i\left(t\right) = \varphi_i\left(t\right), \ \forall t \leq 0 \\
\nu_i\left(t\right) = \mathrm{sat}\left(u_i\left(t\right)\right) \\
y_i\left(t\right) = c_{0,i}^{\ T} x_i\left(t\right) \quad , i = 1,\ldots,\mathrm{p}
\end{cases}
\tag{1}
$$

where $0 < q_i \leq m_i$, $i=1,\ldots,\mathrm{p}$ are known constants with m_i, $i=1,\ldots,\mathrm{p}$ being known strictly positive integers.

$$
A_{0,i} = \begin{bmatrix} 0_{\left(n_i-1\right)\times 1} & I_{n_i-1} \\ & 0_{1\times n_i} \end{bmatrix} \in \mathbb{R}^{n_i \times n_i} , \ b_{0,i} = \begin{bmatrix} 0_{1\times\left(n_i-1\right)} & 1 \end{bmatrix}^T \in \mathbb{R}^{n_i} ,
$$

$$
b_{1,k,i} = \begin{bmatrix} 0_{1\times k} & 1 & 0_{1\times\left(n_i-k-1\right)} \end{bmatrix}^T \in \mathbb{R}^{n_i} , \ c_{0,i} = \begin{bmatrix} 1 & 0_{1\times\left(n_i-1\right)} \end{bmatrix}^T \in \mathbb{R}^{n_i} ,
$$

$$x_i\left(t\right) = \left[x_{i,1}\left(t\right), \quad x_{i,2}\left(t\right), \quad \dots, \quad x_{i,n_i}\left(t\right)\right]^T \in \mathbb{R}^{n_i},$$

$k = 0, \dots, n_i - 2$, $i = 1, \dots, \mathrm{p}$ and $n_1 + n_2 + \cdots + n_p = n$.

$$x\left(t\right) = \left[x_1^T\left(t\right), \quad x_2^T\left(t\right), \quad \dots, \quad x_p^T\left(t\right)\right]^T \in \mathbb{R}^n,$$

$$u\left(t\right) = \left[u_1\left(t\right), \quad u_2\left(t\right), \quad \dots, \quad u_p\left(t\right)\right]^T \in \mathbb{R}^p$$

and

$$y\left(t\right) = \left[y_1\left(t\right), \quad y_2\left(t\right), \quad \dots, \quad y_p\left(t\right)\right]^T \in \mathbb{R}^p$$

are the state variable, the control input and the output of the system, respectively.

$$\nu\left(t\right) = \left[\nu_1\left(t\right), \quad \nu_2\left(t\right), \quad \dots, \quad \nu_p\left(t\right)\right]^T \in \mathbb{R}^p$$

is the output of the asymmetric saturation actuator.

$$f_{1,i}\left(x\left(t\right), x\left(t - \tau_{1,i}\left(t\right)\right)\right) \in \mathbb{R}, \quad f_{2,i}\left(x\left(t\right)\right) \in \mathbb{R}, \quad f_{3,i}\left(x\left(t\right), \nu_i\left(t\right)\right) \in \mathbb{R}$$

$$f_{4,\mathrm{k},i}\left(x\left(t\right), x\left(t - \tau_{3,\mathrm{k},i}\left(t\right)\right)\right) \in \mathbb{R}$$

and $f_{5,\mathrm{k},i}\left(x\left(t\right)\right) \in \mathbb{R}$, $k = 0, \dots, n_i - 2$, $i = 1, \dots, \mathrm{p}$ are unknown smooth functions.

The initial condition functions $\varphi_i\left(t\right) \in \mathbb{R}^{n_i}$, $i = 1, \dots, \mathrm{p}$, are unknown, smooth and bounded $\forall t \leq 0$.

$\varpi_{\mathrm{k},i}\left(t\right) \in \mathbb{R}$ and $d_i\left(t\right) \in \mathbb{R}$, $k = 0, \dots, n_i - 2$, $i = 1, \dots, \mathrm{p}$ are the external disturbances.

For $j = 1, 2$, $k = 0, \dots, n_i - 2$, $i = 1, \dots, \mathrm{p}$, $\tau_{j,i}\left(t\right)$, $\tau_{3,\mathrm{k},i}\left(t\right)$ and $\tau_{4,\mathrm{k},i}\left(t\right)$, represent unknown time-varying delays satisfying $0 \leq \tau_{j,i}\left(t\right) \leq \tau^*$, $0 \leq \tau_{3,\mathrm{k},i}\left(t\right) \leq \tau^*$, $0 \leq \tau_{4,\mathrm{k},i}\left(t\right) \leq \tau^*$ with τ^* being an unknown strictly positive constant.

$\mathrm{sat}\left(u_i\left(t\right)\right)$, $i = 1, \dots, p$, are defined as (Yu et al., 2016; Sui et al.,2015; Iqbal et al., 2015; Wang et al., 2015a; Wang et al., 2015b; Shahnazi, 2016; Lim et al., 2013; Ibeas, & DelaSen, 2007)

$$\nu_i\left(t\right) = \text{sat}\left(u_i\left(t\right)\right) = \begin{cases} u_{min}, & if\ u_i\left(t\right) < u_{min} < 0 \\ u_i\left(t\right), & if\ u_{min} \le u_i\left(t\right) \le u_{max} \\ u_{max}, & if\ u_i\left(t\right) > u_{max} > 0 \end{cases}, \ i = 1,\ldots,p \tag{2}$$

where u_{min} and u_{max} are unknown constants.

Remark 1

It is worth pointing out that the considered system (1) can be used to describe a relatively large class of uncertain nonlinear systems, such as: communication networks, chemical processes, underwater vehicles, Duffing chaotic system, aircraft wing rock, induction servo-motor drive, fractional-order Lü system, fractional-order Lorenz system, fractional-order unified chaotic system, fractional-order Chen system, and so on (Yu et al., 2016; Shi, 2015; Cui et al., 2015; Yu & Du, 2011; Chen et al., 2010; Boulkroune et al., 2016a; Miao & Li, 2015; Shi, 2015a; Bouzeriba et al.,2016a; Boulkroune et al., 2012a; Boulkroune et al., 2012b; Boulkroune et al., 2014a; Boulkroune & M'Saad, 2011; Boulkroune et al., 2014b; Sui et al.,2015; Iqbal et al., 2015; Wang et al., 2015a; Wang et al., 2015b; Liu et al., 2015a; Du & Chen, 2009; Mizumoto et al., 2015; Shahnazi, 2016; Wang et al., 2015; Wei et al., 2015; Lan & Zhou, 2013; N'Doye & Laleg-Kirati, 2015; Li & Wang, 2014; Vargas-De-León, 2015; Chen & Chen, 2015; Stamova & Stamov, 2014; Stamova & Stamov, 2013; Yue & Li, 2012; Liu et al., 2016b).

Remark 2

The most frequently used definitions for non-integer derivatives are: Riemann–Liouville, Grünwald–Letnikov, and Caputo definitions (Boulkroune et al., 2016a; Bouzeriba et al., 2016a; Wei et al., 2015; Lan & Zhou, 2013; N'Doye & Laleg-Kirati, 2015; Li & Wang, 2014; Vargas-De-León, 2015; Chen & Chen, 2015; Stamova & Stamov, 2014; Stamova & Stamov, 2013; Lan et al., 2012; Ladaci et al., 2009; Farges et al., 2010; Lazarević & Spasić, 2009; Lim et al., 2013; Domek & Dworak, 2016; Luo & Liu, 2014). As the Caputo fractional operator is more consistent than another ones, then this operator will be employed in the rest of this chapter.

Remark 3

From (2), it is clear that the saturation actuator $\nu_i\left(t\right)$ has sharp corners when $\nu_i\left(t\right) = u_{min}$ and $\nu_i\left(t\right) = u_{max}$. Therefore, several techniques cannot be directly applied for designing adaptive controllers (Sui et al., 2015; Iqbal et al., 2015). To overcome such a problem, the system (2) is usually modeled by smooth functions (Yu et al., 2016; Sui et al., 2015; Iqbal et al., 2015; Wang et al., 2015a; Wang et al., 2015b; Shahnazi, 2016; Lim et al., 2013; Li et al., 2015b; Li et al., 2015c).

Throughout this chapter, the following assumptions are made for the system (1).

Assumption 1: Only the system output $y\left(t\right)$ is measured.

Assumption 2: For $j_1 = 1, \ldots, 3$, $j_2 = 4, \ldots, 6$, $k = 0, \ldots, n_i - 2$, $i = 1, \ldots, \text{p}$, there exist unknown class $-k_\infty$ functions $\alpha_{j_1,i}(\ )$ and $\alpha_{j_2,k,i}(\ )$, such that

$$
\begin{cases}
\displaystyle\sum_{i=1}^{p}\left|f_{1,i}\left(x(t), x(t-\tau_{1,i}(t))\right)\right| \leq \sum_{i=1}^{p}\alpha_{1,i}\left(\left\|x(t-\tau_{1,i}(t))\right\|\right) + \sum_{i=1}^{p}\alpha_{2,i}\left(\left\|x(t)\right\|\right) \\[2ex]
\displaystyle\sum_{i=1}^{p}\left|f_{2,i}\left(x(t)\right)\right| \leq \sum_{i=1}^{p}\alpha_{3,i}\left(\left\|x(t)\right\|\right) \\[2ex]
\displaystyle\sum_{i=1}^{p}\sum_{k=0}^{n_i-2}\left|f_{4,k,i}\left(x(t), x(t-\tau_{3,k,i}(t))\right)\right| \leq \sum_{i=1}^{p}\sum_{k=0}^{n_i-2}\alpha_{4,k,i}\left(\left\|x(t-\tau_{3,k,i}(t))\right\|\right) + \sum_{i=1}^{p}\sum_{k=0}^{n_i-2}\alpha_{5,k,i}\left(\left\|x(t)\right\|\right) \\[2ex]
\displaystyle\sum_{i=1}^{p}\sum_{k=0}^{n_i-2}\left|f_{5,k,i}\left(x(t)\right)\right| \leq \sum_{i=1}^{p}\sum_{k=0}^{n_i-2}\alpha_{6,k,i}\left(\left\|x(t)\right\|\right)
\end{cases} \tag{3}
$$

Assumption 3: The sign of the matrix

$$
g_1\left(x(t), \nu(t)\right) = \text{diag}\left(\frac{\partial f_{3,1}\left(x(t), \nu_1(t)\right)}{\partial \nu_1(t)}, \ldots, \frac{\partial f_{3,\text{p}}\left(x(t), \nu_p(t)\right)}{\partial \nu_p(t)}\right)
$$

is unknown. However, the matrix $g_1\left(x(t), \nu(t)\right)$ must be strictly positive-definite or strictly negative-definite such that there exist two unknown positive constants $g_{\min}$ and $g_{\max}$, satisfying:

$$
0 < g_{\min} < \left|\frac{\partial f_{3,i}\left(x(t), \nu_i(t)\right)}{\partial \nu_i(t)}\right| < g_{\max} \quad, i = 1, \ldots, \text{p} \tag{4}
$$

Assumption 4: There exists an unknown constant d^* such that $\left|d_i(t)\right| < \mathrm{d}^*$ and $\left|\varpi_{k,i}(t)\right| < d^*$, $k = 0, \ldots, n_i - 2$, $i = 1, \ldots, \text{p}$.

Remark 4

Several practical systems satisfy Assumptions 1 and 4 (Shi, 2015a; Shi, 2015b; Boulkroune et al., 2012b; Boulkroune et al., 2014a; Boulkroune et al., 2014b; Shahnazi, 2016; Lan & Zhou, 2013; Li & Wang, 2014; Lan et al., 2012; Li et al., 2015a; Arefi et al., 2014b). Assumption 2 is not restrictive and is crucial for applying the Razumikhin Lemma in the controller design (Yu et al., 2016; Cui et al., 2015; Yu & Du, 2011; Chen et al., 2010). Assumption 3 is frequently required for global controllability of systems, e.g. see Yu et al. (2016), Shi (2015a), Cui et al. (2015), Yu & Du, (2011), Chen et al. (2010), Boulkroune et al. (2016a), Miao & Li (2015), Shi (2015b), Bouzeriba et al. (2016a), Boulkroune et al. (2012a), Boulkroune et al. (2012b), Boulkroune et al. (2014a), Boulkroune & M'Saad (2011), Boulkroune et al. (2014b), Sui et al. (2015), Iqbal et al. (2015), Wang et al. (2015a), Wang et al. (2015b), Liu et al. (2015a), Du & Chen (2009), Mizumoto et al. (2015), Shahnazi (2016), Wei et al. (2015), and Arefi et al. (2014b). Unlike Zhang et al. (2015), Li et al. (2015b), Boulkroune et al. (2016b), the assumption on the derivative of the time-varying delays (being less than one) is relaxed in this chapter.

The main objective of this chapter is to design an adaptive control for the system (1) such that the system output $y(t)$ tracks a specified desired trajectory $y_d(t) = \left[y_{d1}(t), \quad y_{d2}(t), \quad \dots, \quad y_{dp}(t) \right] \in \mathbb{R}^p$, while all the closed-loop signals remain bounded.

CONTROLLER DESIGN

Under Assumptions 1-4, in order to design the controller for the system (1), one will use:

- A Gaussian error function-based continuous differentiable model to describe the unknown asymmetric saturation actuator,
- The mean value theorem to get an affine model in which the control input appears in a linear fashion,
- A set of new state variables for transforming the system (1) into a normalized fractional order system in order to facilitate the control design,
- An adaptive observer of the new defined state variables to estimate the unmeasured states of the transformed system,
- A neural network to approximate the unknown continuous functions,
- A Nussbaum gain function to deal with the unknown control direction,
- The SPR condition, the Razumikhin Lemma, the frequency distributed model, the Lyapunov method and the Barbalat's lemma to construct the adaptation laws.

Approximation of Saturation Functions

According to Yu et al. (2016), Shahnazi, (2016), the saturation functions can be approximated as follows

$$\text{sat}\left(u_i(t)\right) = \beta_{0,i}\left(u_i(t)\right) + \gamma_i(t), \ i = 1,\dots,p \tag{5}$$

where

$$\beta_{0,i}\left(u_i(t)\right) = u_{M_i} erf\left(\frac{\sqrt{\pi}}{2u_{M_i}} u_i(t)\right),$$

$$u_{M_i} = \frac{\left(u_{\max} + u_{\min}\right)}{2} + \frac{\left(u_{\max} - u_{\min}\right)}{2} \text{sgn}\left(u_i(t)\right),$$

$$erf\left(\frac{\sqrt{\pi}}{2u_{M_i}} u_i(t)\right) = \frac{2}{\sqrt{\pi}} \int_0^{\frac{\sqrt{\pi}}{2u_{M_i}}u_i(t)} \exp\left(-\tau^2\right) d\tau$$

and $\gamma_i(t) = \mathrm{sat}\left(u_i(t)\right) - \beta_{0,i}\left(u_i(t)\right)$, $i = 1, \ldots, p$ are bounded functions.

System Transformation

By applying the mean value theorem (Yu et al., 2016; Wang et al., 2015a; Liu et al., 2015a), one can obtain

$$
\begin{cases}
\displaystyle\int_{t-\tau_{2,i}(t)}^{t} f_{2,i}\left(x(\tau)\right) d\tau = \tau_{2,i}(t) f_{2,i}\left(x\left(t - \tau_{5,i}(t)\right)\right) \\[2mm]
\displaystyle\int_{t-\tau_{4,k,i}(t)}^{t} f_{5,k,i}\left(x(\tau)\right) d\tau = \tau_{4,k,i}(t) f_{5,k,i}\left(x\left(t - \tau_{6,k,i}\right)\right), k = 0, \ldots, n_i - 2 \\[2mm]
f_{3,i}\left(x(t), \nu_i(t)\right) = f_{3,i}\left(x(t), 0\right) + g_{1,i}\left(x(t), \nu_{\Lambda_{1,i}}(t)\right)\nu_i(t) \\[2mm]
\nu_i(t) = \beta_{1,i}\left(u_{\Lambda_{2,i}}(t)\right)u_i(t) + \gamma_i(t), \quad i = 1, \ldots, \mathrm{p}
\end{cases}
\tag{6}
$$

with

$$
g_{1,i}\left(x(t), \nu_{\Lambda_{1,i}}(t)\right) = \left.\frac{\partial f_{3,i}\left(x(t), \nu_i(t)\right)}{\partial \nu_i(t)}\right|_{\nu_i(t) = \nu_{\Lambda_{1,i}}(t)},
$$

$$
0 \le \tau_{5,i}(t) \le \tau_{2,i}(t) \le \tau^*, \ \nu_{\Lambda_{1,i}}(t) = \Lambda_{1,i}\nu_i(t), \ 0 < \Lambda_{1,i} < 1,
$$

$$
\beta_{1,i}\left(u_{\Lambda_{2,i}}(t)\right) = \left.\frac{\partial \beta_{0,i}\left(u_i(t)\right)}{\partial u_i(t)}\right|_{u_i(t) = u_{\Lambda_{2,i}}(t)}, \ 0 < \beta_{1,i}\left(u_{\Lambda_{2,i}}(t)\right) \le 1,
$$

$$
u_{\Lambda_{2,i}}(t) = \Lambda_{2,i}u_i(t), \ 0 \le \tau_{6,k,i} \le \tau_{4,k,i} \le \tau^*
$$

and $0 < \Lambda_{2,i} < 1$, $k = 0, \ldots, n_i - 2$, $i = 1, \ldots, \mathrm{p}$.

Now, by introducing the new state variables

$$
\begin{cases}
z_{i,j}(t) = \left[x_{i,j}(t), \quad D^{\delta_i}x_{i,j}(t), \quad \ldots \quad D^{m_i\delta_i}x_{i,j}(t)\right]^T \in \mathbb{R}^{m_i+1}, \ j = 1, \ldots, n_i \\[2mm]
z_i(t) = \left[z_{i,1}^{\ T}(t), \quad z_{i,2}^{\ T}(t), \quad \ldots, \quad z_{i,n_i}^{\ T}(t)\right]^T \in \mathbb{R}^{r_i}, \ i = 1, \ldots, p \\[2mm]
z(t) = \left[z_1^{\ T}(t), \quad z_2^{\ T}(t), \quad \ldots, \quad z_p^{\ T}(t)\right]^T \in \mathbb{R}^r
\end{cases}
\tag{7}
$$

Consequently, the system (1) can be transformed into the following normalized fractional order system

$$\begin{cases} D^{\delta_i} z_i(t) = A_{1,i} z_i(t) + b_{2,i} \Big[f_{1,i}\big(x(t), x(t-\tau_{1,i}(t))\big) + d_i(t) + f_{3,i}\big(x(t), 0\big) \\ \qquad\qquad + \tau_{2,i}(t) f_{2,i}\big(x(t-\tau_{5,i}(t))\big) + g_{1,i}\big(x(t), \nu_{\Lambda_{1,i}}(t)\big) \nu_i(t) \Big] \\ \qquad\qquad + \sum_{k=0}^{n_i-2} b_{3,k,i} \Big[f_{4,k,i}\big(x(t), x(t-\tau_{3,k,i}(t))\big) + \varpi_{k,i}(t) \\ \qquad\qquad + \tau_{4,k,i}(t) f_{5,k,i}\big(x(t-\tau_{6,k,i}(t))\big) \Big] \Big], \ \forall t \geq 0 \\[2mm] x_i(t) = \varphi_i(t), \ \forall t \leq 0 \\ \nu_i(t) = \mathrm{sat}\big(u_i(t)\big) \\ y_i(t) = c_{1,i}^{\ T} z_i(t) \quad , \ i = 1,\dots,\mathrm{p} \end{cases} \tag{8}$$

with

$$0 < \delta_i = \frac{q_i}{m_i + 1} < 1, \ r_i = (m_i + 1) n_i, \ A_{1,i} = \begin{bmatrix} 0_{(r_i-1)\times 1} & I_{r_i-1} \\ & 0_{1\times r_i} \end{bmatrix} \in \mathbb{R}^{r_i \times r_i},$$

$$b_{2,i} = \begin{bmatrix} 0_{(r_i-1)\times 1} \\ 1 \end{bmatrix} \in \mathbb{R}^{r_i}, \ c_{1,i} = \begin{bmatrix} 1 & 0_{1\times(r_i-1)} \end{bmatrix}^T \in \mathbb{R}^{r_i},$$

$$b_{3,k,i} = \begin{bmatrix} 0_{1\times(m_i+(m_i+1)k)} & 1 & 0_{1\times(r_i-(m_i+1)(k+1))} \end{bmatrix}^T \in \mathbb{R}^{r_i},$$

$$k = 0,\dots,n_i - 2, \ i = 1,\dots,\mathrm{p} \text{ and } r_1 + r_2 + \cdots + r_p = r.$$

Remark 5

It is clear that the control objective of system (1) can be achieved by controlling system (8). In fact, controlling the normalized system instead of the original one is easier because most of the adaptive control design and stability analysis methods are available for the $0 < \delta_i < 1, \ i = 1,\dots,\mathrm{p}$ cases (Bouzeriba et al., 2016a; Wei et al.,2015; Lan & Zhou, 2013; N'Doye & Laleg-Kirati, 2015; Li & Wang, 2014; Vargas-De-León, 2015; Chen & Chen, 2015; Stamova & Stamov, 2014; Stamova & Stamov, 2013; Lan et al., 2012; Ladaci et al., 2009; Farges et al., 2010; Lazarević & Spasić, 2009; Lim et al., 2013; Luo & Liu, 2014; Liu & Jiang, 2013a).

Let us now define

$$\begin{cases} \vartheta_{di}(t) = z_i(t) - x_{di}(t) \\ \vartheta_i(t) = y_i(t) - y_{di}(t) \\ x_{di}(t) = \left[y_{di}(t), \quad D^{\delta_i} y_{di}(t), \quad \ldots, \quad D^{(r_i-1)\delta_i} y_{di}(t) \right]^T \in \mathbb{R}^{r_i}, \ i = 1, \ldots, p \end{cases} \tag{9}$$

where the functions

$$y_{di}(t), \quad D^{\delta_i} y_{di}(t), \quad \ldots, \quad D^{(r_i-1)\delta_i} y_{di}(t), \quad D^{r_i\delta_i} y_{di}(t),$$

$i = 1, \ldots, p$, are known, continuous and bounded.

On the other hand, we have

$$\vartheta_d(t) = \left[\vartheta_{d1}^T(t), \quad \vartheta_{d2}^T(t), \quad \ldots, \quad \vartheta_{dp}^T(t) \right]^T \in \mathbb{R}^r,$$

$$\vartheta(t) = \left[\vartheta_1(t), \quad \vartheta_2(t), \quad \ldots, \quad \vartheta_p(t) \right]^T \in \mathbb{R}^p,$$

$$x_d(t) = \left[x_{d1}^T(t), \quad x_{d2}^T(t), \quad \ldots, \quad x_{dp}^T(t) \right]^T \in \mathbb{R}^r$$

and

$$x_D(t) = \left[D^{r_1\delta_1} y_{d1}(t), \quad D^{r_2\delta_2} y_{d2}(t), \quad \ldots, \quad D^{r_p\delta_p} y_{dp}(t) \right]^T \in \mathbb{R}^p.$$

Adaptive Observer for the New Defined State Variables

For the system (8), the state observer is designed as (Shi, 2015a; Du & Chen, 2009; Shahnazi, 2016; Lan et al., 2012):

$$\begin{cases} D^{\delta_i} \hat{\vartheta}_{di}(t) = \left[A_{1,i} + b_{2,i} k_{ci} \right] \hat{\vartheta}_{di}(t) - k_{oi} \tilde{y}_i(t) \\ \hat{y}_i(t) = c_{1,i}^T \hat{z}_i(t), \\ \tilde{y}_i(t) = y_i(t) - \hat{y}_i(t), \\ \hat{z}_i(t) = x_{di}(t) + \hat{\vartheta}_{di}(t), \ i = 1, \ldots, p \end{cases} \tag{10}$$

where the gain matrices $k_{ci} \in \mathbb{R}^{1 \times r_i}$ and $k_{oi} \in \mathbb{R}^{r_i}$, are chosen such that the matrices $\left[A_{1,i} + b_{2,i} k_{ci} \right] \in \mathbb{R}^{r_i \times r_i}$ and $\left[A_{1,i} + k_{oi} c_{1,i}^T \right] \in \mathbb{R}^{r_i \times r_i}$, $i = 1, \ldots, p$ are strictly Hurwitz.

$$\hat{z}_i\left(t\right) = \left[\hat{z}_{i,1}{}^T\left(t\right), \quad \hat{z}_{i,2}{}^T\left(t\right), \quad \ldots, \quad \hat{z}_{i,n_i}{}^T\left(t\right)\right]^T \in \mathbb{R}^{r_i}$$

is the estimate of $z_i\left(t\right)$ with

$$\hat{z}_{i,j}\left(t\right) = \left[\hat{x}_{i,j}\left(t\right), \quad D^{\delta_i}\hat{x}_{i,j}\left(t\right), \quad \ldots \quad D^{m_i \delta_i}\hat{x}_{i,j}\left(t\right)\right]^T \in \mathbb{R}^{m_i+1},$$

$j = 1, \ldots, n_i$, $i = 1, \ldots, p$.

Also, one has

$$\hat{z}\left(t\right) = \left[\hat{z}_1{}^T\left(t\right), \quad \ldots, \quad \hat{z}_p{}^T\left(t\right)\right]^T \in \mathbb{R}^r,$$

$$\tilde{y}\left(t\right) = \left[\tilde{y}_1\left(t\right), \quad \ldots, \quad \tilde{y}_p\left(t\right)\right]^T \in \mathbb{R}^p$$

and

$$\hat{\vartheta}_d\left(t\right) = \left[\hat{\vartheta}_{d1}{}^T\left(t\right), \quad \hat{\vartheta}_{d2}{}^T\left(t\right), \quad \ldots, \quad \hat{\vartheta}_{dp}{}^T\left(t\right)\right]^T \in \mathbb{R}^r.$$

Remark 6

Unlike in (Lan & Zhou, 2013; Li & Wang, 2014), the proposed observer has a simple linear form.

Neural Network for Approximating Uncertain Functions

Based on Razumikhin Lemma (Yu et al., 2016 ; Cui et al., 2015 ; Yu & Du, 2011 ; Chen et al., 2010 ; N'Doye & Laleg-Kirati, 2015 ; Vargas-De-León, 2015; Chen & Chen, 2015; Stamova & Stamov, 2014; Stamova & Stamov, 2013 ; Wang et al., 2017). and using the new state variables (7), it is proven that there exists a constant $\Gamma > 1$ such that

$$\begin{cases} \left\|x\left(t - \tau_{j,i}\left(t\right)\right)\right\| \leq \Gamma \left\|x\left(t\right)\right\| \leq \Gamma \left\|z\left(t\right)\right\|, \ j = 1,2 \\ \left\|x\left(t - \tau_{3,k,i}\left(t\right)\right)\right\| \leq \Gamma \left\|x\left(t\right)\right\| \leq \Gamma \left\|z\left(t\right)\right\|, \\ \left\|x\left(t - \tau_{4,k,i}\left(t\right)\right)\right\| \leq \Gamma \left\|x\left(t\right)\right\| \leq \Gamma \left\|z\left(t\right)\right\|, \\ \left\|x\left(t - \tau_{6,k,i}\left(t\right)\right)\right\| \leq \Gamma \left\|x\left(t\right)\right\| \leq \Gamma \left\|z\left(t\right)\right\|, k = 0, \ldots, n_i - 2 \\ \left\|x\left(t - \tau_{5,i}\left(t\right)\right)\right\| \leq \Gamma \left\|x\left(t\right)\right\| \leq \Gamma \left\|z\left(t\right)\right\|, \ i = 1, \ldots, p \end{cases} \qquad (11)$$

with $\left\| z\left(t\right) \right\| = \sqrt{ \left\| x\left(t\right) \right\|^{2} + \sum_{i=1}^{p} \sum_{j=1}^{n_i} \sum_{k=1}^{m_i} \left| D^{k\delta_i} x_{i,j}\left(t\right) \right|^{2} }$.

Remark 7

The Razumikhin condition (11) has been demonstrated in (Yu et al., 2016; Cui et al., 2015; Yu & Du, 2011; Chen et al., 2010; N'Doye & Laleg-Kirati, 2015; Vargas-De-León, 2015; Chen & Chen, 2015; Stamova & Stamov, 2014; Stamova & Stamov, 2013; Wang et al., 2017) and will be used in the procedure of controller design later.

Moreover, one has

$$
\begin{cases}
\alpha_{1,i}\left(\left\| x\left(t - \tau_{1,i}\left(t\right)\right) \right\| \right) \leq \alpha_{1,i}\left(\Gamma \left\| x\left(t\right) \right\| \right) \leq \alpha_{1,i}\left(\Gamma \left\| z\left(t\right) \right\| \right) \\
\alpha_{4,k,i}\left(\left\| x\left(t - \tau_{3,k,i}\left(t\right)\right) \right\| \right) \leq \alpha_{4,k,i}\left(\Gamma \left\| x\left(t\right) \right\| \right) \leq \alpha_{4,k,i}\left(\Gamma \left\| z\left(t\right) \right\| \right), \\
\alpha_{6,k,i}\left(\left\| x\left(t - \tau_{6,k,i}\left(t\right)\right) \right\| \right) \leq \alpha_{6,k,i}\left(\Gamma \left\| x\left(t\right) \right\| \right) \leq \alpha_{6,k,i}\left(\Gamma \left\| z\left(t\right) \right\| \right), k = 0,\ldots,n_i - 2 \\
\alpha_{3,i}\left(\left\| x\left(t - \tau_{5,i}\left(t\right)\right) \right\| \right) \leq \alpha_{3,i}\left(\Gamma \left\| x\left(t\right) \right\| \right) \leq \alpha_{3,i}\left(\Gamma \left\| z\left(t\right) \right\| \right), \ i = 1,\ldots,p
\end{cases} \tag{12}
$$

Based on the universal approximation theorem (Yu & Du, 2011; Boulkroune et al., 2016a ; Miao & Li, 2015 ; Shi, 2015b ; McGarry et al., 2007 ; Rădac et al., 2014 ; Yacoub et al., 2014 ; Yan et al., 2016 ; Wang et al., 2017; Ibeas, & de la Sen, 2007 ; Tabatabaei & Arefi, 2016 ; Arefi et al.,2014a ; Chen et al., 2016), The unknown function

$$
\begin{aligned}
F\left(z\left(t\right), \hat{z}\left(t\right) \right) = &\sum_{i=1}^{p} \alpha_{1,i}\left(\Gamma \left\| z\left(t\right) \right\| \right) + \sum_{i=1}^{p} \left| f_{3,i}\left(x\left(t\right), 0\right) \right| + \tau^{*} \sum_{i=1}^{p} \alpha_{3,i}\left(\Gamma \left\| z\left(t\right) \right\| \right) \\
&+ \sum_{i=1}^{p} \alpha_{2,i}\left(\left\| z\left(t\right) \right\| \right) + \sum_{i=1}^{p} \left| k_{ci} \hat{z}_i\left(t\right) \right| + \sum_{i=1}^{p} \left| D^{r_i\delta_i} y_{di}\left(t\right) \right| + \left\| x_D\left(t\right) \right\| \\
&+ \sum_{i=1}^{p} \sum_{k=0}^{n_i-2} \alpha_{4,k,i}\left(\Gamma \left\| z\left(t\right) \right\| \right) + \sum_{i=1}^{p} \sum_{k=0}^{n_i-2} \alpha_{5,k,i}\left(\left\| z\left(t\right) \right\| \right) + n\, \mathrm{d}^{*} + \left\| x_d\left(t\right) \right\| \\
&+ \tau^{*} \sum_{i=1}^{p} \sum_{k=0}^{n_i-2} \alpha_{6,k,i}\left(\Gamma \left\| z\left(t\right) \right\| \right) + \left[\left| u_{\min} \right| + u_{\max} \right] p g_{\max}
\end{aligned}
$$

can be approximated on the compact set

$$
\Omega = \left\{ \begin{matrix} z\left(t\right) \in \mathbb{R}^{r}, \\ \hat{z}\left(t\right) \in \mathbb{R}^{r} \end{matrix} \middle| \ \left\| z\left(t\right) \right\| + \left\| \hat{z}\left(t\right) \right\| \leq M \right\},
$$

by a three-layer neural network as follows

$$F\left(z\left(t\right),\hat{z}\left(t\right)\right) = w^{*T}\xi\left(\hat{z}\left(t\right)\right) + \varepsilon \tag{13}$$

where M is an unknown strictly positive constant. $\varepsilon \in \mathbb{R}$, is unknown and bounded over the compact set Ω, i.e., $\left|\varepsilon\right| \leq \varepsilon^{*}$, with ε^{*} being an unknown strictly positive constant. $\hat{z}\left(t\right) \in \mathbb{R}^{r}$ is the input of the neural network. $\xi\left(\hat{z}\left(t\right)\right) \in \mathbb{R}^{\ell}$, is the neural activation function with $\ell \geq 1$ being the number of neural network nodes.

The optimal neural network parameter, $w^{*} \in \mathbb{R}^{\ell}$, is defined as follows (Shi, 2015a; Yu & Du, 2011; Chen et al., 2010; Boulkroune et al., 2016a; Miao & Li, 2015; Shi, 2015b ; Bouzeriba et al.,2016a; Boulkroune et al., 2012a; Boulkroune et al., 2012b; Boulkroune et al., 2014a; Boulkroune et al., 2014b; Sui et al., 2015; Wang et al., 2015a; Yacoub et al., 2014; Yan et al., 2016; Bouzeriba et al.,2016b; Wang et al., 2017; Tabatabaei & Arefi, 2016; Arefi et al., 2014a).

$$w^{*} = \arg \min_{w^{*} \in \mathbb{R}^{\ell}} \left(\sup_{(z,\hat{z}) \in \Omega} \left| F\left(z\left(t\right),\hat{z}\left(t\right)\right) - w^{T}\xi\left(\hat{z}\left(t\right)\right) \right| \right), \tag{14}$$

Typically, $\left\| w^{*} \right\|$, is unknown, constant and bounded. Moreover, $\left\| \xi\left(\hat{z}\left(t\right)\right) \right\|$ is known, and bounded (Yu et al., 2016; McGarry et al.,2007; Rădac et al., 2014; Yacoub et al., 2014; Yan et al., 2016)

Remark 8

Similar to (Yu et al., 2016; Cui et al., 2015; Yu & Du, 2011; Miao & Li, 2015; Wang et al., 2015a; Du & Chen, 2009; Tabatabaei & Arefi, 2016; Arefi et al., 2014a; Arefi et al., 2014b), the neural network $w^{*T}\xi\left(\hat{z}\left(t\right)\right)$ employed in this chapter for approximating the unknown functions contains a single hidden layer with ℓ neurons and a single output layer with one neuron. The hidden-layer activation function can be a logistic sigmoid function, a hyperbolic tangent function or a radial basis function. Besides, the output-layer activation function is a linear function. To reduce the complexity and burden of computation, the weight matrix between the input layer and the hidden layer is randomly initialized and fixed. Only, the weight vector between the hidden layer and the output layer w^{*} is unknown and must be estimated in controller design. It is worth noting that radial basis function (RBF) neural networks are widely employed in practical control systems thanks to its simple architectures and satisfactory approximation properties (Yu et al., 2016 Cui et al., 2015; Yu & Du, 2011; Wang et al., 2015a; Du & Chen, 2009; Tabatabaei & Arefi, 2016; Arefi et al., 2014a; Arefi et al., 2014b).

Adaptive Control Law

To meet the control objective, the following adaptive control law is proposed

$$\begin{cases} u(t) = N\big(\varsigma(t)\big)\hat{\theta}(t)\dfrac{\rho^2\big(\hat{z}(t)\big)}{\sigma(t) + \rho\big(\hat{z}(t)\big)\big\|\tilde{y}(t)\big\|}\tilde{y}(t) \\[3mm] \dot{\hat{\theta}}(t) = \chi\dfrac{\rho^2\big(\hat{z}(t)\big)\big\|\tilde{y}(t)\big\|^2}{\sigma(t) + \rho\big(\hat{z}(t)\big)\big\|\tilde{y}(t)\big\|} - \chi\sigma(t)\hat{\theta}(t) \\[3mm] \dot{\varsigma}(t) = \hat{\theta}(t)\dfrac{\rho^2\big(\hat{z}(t)\big)\big\|\tilde{y}(t)\big\|^2}{\sigma(t) + \rho\big(\hat{z}(t)\big)\big\|\tilde{y}(t)\big\|} \\[3mm] \rho\big(\hat{z}(t)\big) = \big\|\hat{z}(t)\big\| + \big\|\tilde{y}(t)\big\| + \big\|\xi\big(\hat{z}(t)\big)\big\| + 1 \end{cases} \tag{15}$$

where $N\big(\varsigma(t)\big) = \cos\left(\dfrac{\pi}{2}\varsigma(t)\right)\exp\big(\varsigma^2(t)\big)$ is a Nussbaum function (Shi, 2015a; Boulkroune et al., 2012a; Boulkroune et al., 2012b). χ is a known strictly positive constant. $\sigma(t)$ is a known strictly positive function such that $\int_0^t \sigma(\tau)d\tau$ is bounded, $\forall t \geq 0$. $\hat{\theta}(t)$ is the estimate of the unknown strictly positive constant θ^*, which is defined by (30).

Remark 9

Similar to Yu et al. (2016), Shi (2015a), Cui et al. (2015), Yu & Du (2011), Wang et al. (2015a), Du & Chen (2009), Zhang et al. (2015), it is always reasonable to choose $\hat{\theta}(0) \geq 0$ because for any given initial condition $\hat{\theta}(0) \geq 0$, $\hat{\theta}(t) \geq 0$ holds $\forall t \geq 0$.

To recapitulate, Figure 1 shows the overall scheme of the proposed neural adaptive control. Similar to controllers in Yu et al. (2016), Shi (2015a), Cui et al. (2015), Yu & Du (2011), Chen et al. (2010), Boulkroune et al. (2016a), Miao & Li (2015), Shi (2015b), Bouzeriba et al. (2016a), Boulkroune et al. (2012a), Boulkroune et al. (2012b), Boulkroune et al. (2014a), Boulkroune & M'Saad (2011), Boulkroune et al. (2014b), Sui et al. (2015), Iqbal et al. (2015), Wei et al. (2015), Lan & Zhou (2013), Li et al. (2015a), Bouzeriba et al. (2016b), Arefi et al. (2014a), Arefi et al. (2014b), Boulkroune et al. (2010), and Yue & Li (2012), the proposed adaptive neural controller in this chapter is running online without any offline-learning process.

Remark 10

Unlike in McGarry et al. (2007), Rădac et al. (2014), Yacoub et al. (2014), Yan et al. (2016), the requirements of an off-line learning phase and a validation phase (by using the training data and the validation data, respectively) are not required at all in this chapter. In fact, the learning of the neural networks used in this chapter is made online.

Remark 11

As mentioned in Lan & Zhou (2013), Li & Wang (2014), and Lan et al. (2012), the fractional order controller and observer are a generalization of the traditional integer controller and observer.

Stability Analysis

The main results of the proposed controller are summarized in the following theorem.

Theorem 1

For given reference signals, let us consider the system (1) with the newly defined states (7) and the transformed system (8), satisfying Assumptions 1–4. Then, for any bounded initial condition, the state observer (10) and the control law (15) ensure that:

- All signals of the closed-loop system remain bounded, i.e., $\hat{\theta}(t)$, $\zeta(t)$, $u(t)$, $\hat{z}(t)$, $\rho(\hat{z}(t))$ and $\tilde{y}(t) \in L_{\infty}$,
- The tracking errors converge asymptotically to zero, i.e., $\vartheta_i(t) \to 0$ as $t \to +\infty$, for $i = 1, \dots, p$.

Proof

Two steps compose the proof of Theorem 1. In Step 1, a suitable change of coordinates is used to satisfy a SPR condition of the transfer function of the observation error dynamics. In step 2, a novel class of Lyapunov functions is designed by the aid of the frequency-distributed model to analyze the stability of the system under the proposed controller.

Figure 1. Proposed neural adaptive control scheme

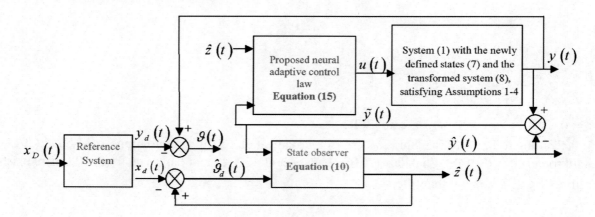

Step 1

Let the observation error be defined as $\tilde{z}(t) = z(t) - \hat{z}(t)$. Then, by using (8) and (10), the dynamics of the observation error can be expressed as

$$
\begin{cases}
D^{\delta_i}\tilde{z}_i(t) = \left[A_{1,i} + k_{oi}c_{1,i}{}^T\right]\tilde{z}_i(t) + b_{2,i}\left[f_{1,i}\left(x(t), x\left(t - \tau_{1,i}(t)\right)\right) - k_{ci}\hat{\vartheta}_{di}(t) + f_{3,i}\left(x(t), 0\right)\right. \\
\qquad\quad + \tau_{2,i}(t)f_{2,i}\left(x\left(t - \tau_{5,i}(t)\right)\right) + g_{1,i}\left(x(t), \nu_{\Lambda_{1,i}}(t)\right)\nu_i(t) - D^{r_i\delta_i}y_{di}(t) + d_i(t)\right] \\
\qquad\quad + \displaystyle\sum_{k=0}^{n_i-2} b_{3,k,i}\left[f_{4,k,i}\left(x(t), x\left(t - \tau_{3,k,i}(t)\right)\right) + \tau_{4,k,i}(t)f_{5,k,i}\left(x\left(t - \tau_{6,k,i}(t)\right)\right) + \varpi_{k,i}(t)\right] \\
\tilde{y}_i(t) = c_{1,i}{}^T\tilde{z}_i(t), \quad i = 1, \dots, p
\end{cases}
\tag{16}
$$

In the frequency domain, the dynamics (16) can be rewritten by using the mixed notation (i.e. time-frequency) (Shi, 2015a; Shi, 2015b; Boulkroune et al., 2014a; Boulkroune & M'Saad, 2011; Boulkroune et al., 2014b).

$$
\begin{aligned}
\tilde{y}_i(t) = H_{0,i}(s)\Big[&f_{1,i}\left(x(t), x\left(t - \tau_{1,i}(t)\right)\right) + \tau_{2,i}(t)f_{2,i}\left(x\left(t - \tau_{5,i}(t)\right)\right) \\
&- k_{ci}\hat{\vartheta}_{di}(t) + f_{3,i}\left(x(t), 0\right) + g_{1,i}\left(x(t), \nu_{\Lambda_{1,i}}(t)\right)\nu_i(t) - D^{r_i\delta_i}y_{di}(t) + d_i(t)\Big] \\
&+ \sum_{k=0}^{n_i-2} H_{1,k,i}(s)\Big[f_{4,k,i}\left(x(t), x\left(t - \tau_{3,k,i}(t)\right)\right) + \varpi_{k,i}(t) \\
&+ \tau_{4,k,i}(t)f_{5,k,i}\left(x\left(t - \tau_{6,k,i}(t)\right)\right)\Big], \quad i = 1, \dots, p
\end{aligned}
\tag{17}
$$

where the stable transfer functions

$$
H_{0,i}(s) = c_{1,i}{}^T\left[s^{\delta_i}I_{r_i} - \left[A_{1,i} + k_{oi}c_{1,i}{}^T\right]\right]^{-1}b_{2,i}
$$

and

$$
H_{1,k,i}(s) = c_{1,i}{}^T\left[s^{\delta_i}I_{r_i} - \left[A_{1,i} + k_{oi}c_{1,i}{}^T\right]\right]^{-1}b_{3,k,i},
$$

$k = 0, \dots, n_i - 2$, $i = 1, \dots, p$ are not SPR.

According to Shi (2015a), Shi (2015b), Boulkroune et al. (2014a), Boulkroune & M'Saad (2011), Boulkroune et al. (2014b), Shahnazi (2016), Ladaci et al. (2009), and Farges et al. (2010), there exists matrices $b_{ci} \in \mathbb{R}^{r_i}$, and stable filters

$$
\left(\Upsilon_{0,i}(s), \ \Upsilon_{1,k,i}(s), \ k = 0, \dots, n_i - 2, \ i = 1, \dots, p\right)
$$

such that

$$\begin{cases} H_{1,k,i}\left(s\right) = H_{fi}\left(s\right)\Upsilon_{1,k,i}\left(s\right),\ k = 0,\ldots,n_i - 2 \\ H_{0,i}\left(s\right) = H_{fi}\left(s\right)\Upsilon_{0,i}\left(s\right),\ i = 1,\ldots,p \\ H_{fi}\left(s\right) = c_{1,i}^{\ T}\left[s^{\delta_i}I_{r_i} - \left[A_{1,i} + k_{oi}c_i^{\ T}\right]\right]^{-1}b_{ci} \end{cases} \tag{18}$$

where $H_{fi}\left(s\right)$, $i = 1,\ldots,p$ are SPR.

By defining the auxiliary errors as

$$\begin{aligned} e_{a,i}\left(t\right) = {}&\Upsilon_{0,i}\left(s\right)\Big[f_{1,i}\left(x\left(t\right),x\left(t - \tau_{1,i}\left(t\right)\right)\right) + \tau_{2,i}\left(t\right)f_{2,i}\left(x\left(t - \tau_{5,i}\left(t\right)\right)\right) \\ &- k_{ci}\hat{\vartheta}_{di}\left(t\right)\ + f_{3,i}\left(x\left(t\right),0\right) + g_{1,i}\left(x\left(t\right),\nu_{\Lambda_{1,i}}\left(t\right)\right)\nu_i\left(t\right) + d_i\left(t\right) - \mathrm{D}^{r,\delta_i}\,y_{di}\left(t\right)\Big] \\ &- \Big[f_{1,i}\left(x\left(t\right),x\left(t - \tau_{1,i}\left(t\right)\right)\right) + \tau_{2,i}\left(t\right)f_{2,i}\left(x\left(t - \tau_{5,i}\left(t\right)\right)\right) - k_{ci}\hat{z}_i\left(t\right) \\ &+ f_{3,i}\left(x\left(t\right),0\right) + g_{1,i}\left(x\left(t\right),\nu_{\Lambda_{1,i}}\left(t\right)\right)\nu_i\left(t\right)\Big] + g_{1,i}\left(x\left(t\right),\nu_{\Lambda_{1,i}}\left(t\right)\right)\gamma_i\left(t\right) \\ &+ \sum_{k=0}^{n_i-2}\Upsilon_{1,k,i}\left(s\right)\Big[f_{4,k,i}\left(x\left(t\right),x\left(t - \tau_{3,k,i}\left(t\right)\right)\right) + \tau_{4,k,i}\left(t\right)f_{5,k,i}\left(x\left(t - \tau_{6,k,i}\left(t\right)\right)\right) + \varpi_{k,i}\left(t\right)\Big] \\ &- \sum_{k=0}^{n_i-2}\Big[f_{4,k,i}\left(x\left(t\right),x\left(t - \tau_{3,k,i}\left(t\right)\right)\right) + \tau_{4,k,i}\left(t\right)f_{5,k,i}\left(x\left(t - \tau_{6,k,i}\left(t\right)\right)\right)\Big],\ \ i = 1,\ldots,p \end{aligned} \tag{19}$$

One can write

$$\begin{aligned} \tilde{y}_i\left(t\right) = {}&H_{fi}\left(s\right)\Big[f_{1,i}\left(x\left(t\right),x\left(t - \tau_{1,i}\left(t\right)\right)\right) + \tau_{2,i}\left(t\right)f_{2,i}\left(x\left(t - \tau_{5,i}\left(t\right)\right)\right) \\ &+ f_{3,i}\left(x\left(t\right),0\right) + g_{2,i}\left(x\left(t\right),\nu_{\Lambda_{1,i}}\left(t\right),u_{\Lambda_{2,i}}\left(t\right)\right)u_i\left(t\right) + e_{a,i}\left(t\right) \\ &+ \sum_{k=0}^{n_i-2}\tau_{4,k,i}\left(t\right)f_{5,k,i}\left(x\left(t - \tau_{6,k,i}\left(t\right)\right)\right) - k_{ci}\hat{z}_i\left(t\right) \\ &+ \sum_{k=0}^{n_i-2}f_{4,k,i}\left(x\left(t\right),x\left(t - \tau_{3,k,i}\left(t\right)\right)\right)\Big],\ \ i = 1,\ldots,p \end{aligned} \tag{20}$$

with

$$g_{2,i}\left(x(t),\nu_{\Lambda_{1,i}}(t),u_{\Lambda_{2,i}}(t)\right) = \beta_{1,i}\left(u_{\Lambda_{2,i}}(t)\right)g_{1,i}\left(x(t),\nu_{\Lambda_{1,i}}(t)\right)$$

and

$$0 < \left|g_{2,i}\left(x_i(t),\nu_{\Lambda_{1,i}}(t),u_{\Lambda_{2,i}}(t)\right)\right| \le g_{\max}, \quad i = 1,\dots,p.$$

Based on (13) and the previous works (Shi, 2015a; Shi, 2015b; Boulkroune et al., 2014a; Boulkroune & M'Saad, 2011; Boulkroune et al., 2014b; Shahnazi, 2016), one can obtain

$$\begin{cases} \displaystyle\sum_{i=1}^{p}\left|f_{1,i}\left(x(t),x\left(t-\tau_{1,i}(t)\right)\right)\right| + \sum_{i=1}^{p}\left|f_{3,i}\left(x(t),0\right)\right| \\[2mm] \displaystyle +\sum_{i=1}^{p}\left|\tau_{2,i}(t)f_{2,i}\left(x\left(t-\tau_{5,i}(t)\right)\right)\right| \\[2mm] \displaystyle +\sum_{i=1}^{p}\left|k_{ci}\hat{z}_i(t)\right| + \sum_{i=1}^{p}\sum_{k=0}^{n_i-2}\left|\tau_{4,k,i}(t)f_{5,k,i}\left(x\left(t-\tau_{6,k,i}(t)\right)\right)\right| \\[2mm] \displaystyle +\sum_{i=1}^{p}\sum_{k=0}^{n_i-2}\left|f_{4,k,i}\left(x(t),x\left(t-\tau_{3,k,i}(t)\right)\right)\right| \le F\left(z(t),\hat{z}(t)\right) \\[3mm] \displaystyle \sum_{i=1}^{p}\left|e_{a,i}(t)\right| \le \Delta_1 F\left(z(t),\hat{z}(t)\right) + \Delta_2 \end{cases} \tag{21}$$

where Δ_1 and Δ_2 are unknown strictly positive constants.

By using (8), the state space realization of (20) is given by

$$\begin{cases} D^{\delta_i}\tilde{z}_i(t) = \left[A_{1,i} + k_{oi}c_{1,i}{}^T\right]\tilde{z}_i(t) + b_{ci}\Big[f_{1,i}\left(x(t),x\left(t-\tau_{1,i}(t)\right)\right) \\[2mm] \qquad\qquad + \tau_{2,i}(t)f_{2,i}\left(x\left(t-\tau_{5,i}(t)\right)\right) + \sum_{k=0}^{n_i-2}f_{4,k,i}\left(x(t),x\left(t-\tau_{3,k,i}(t)\right)\right) \\[2mm] \qquad\qquad + \sum_{k=0}^{n_i-2}\tau_{4,k,i}(t)f_{5,k,i}\left(x\left(t-\tau_{6,k,i}(t)\right)\right) - k_{ci}\hat{z}_i(t) + e_{a,i}(t) \\[2mm] \qquad\qquad + f_{3,i}\left(x(t),0\right) + g_{2,i}\left(x(t),\nu_{\Lambda_{1,i}}(t),u_{\Lambda_{2,i}}(t)\right)u_i(t)\Big] \\[3mm] \tilde{y}_i(t) = c_{1,i}{}^T\tilde{z}_i(t), \quad i = 1,\dots,p \end{cases} \tag{22}$$

From (10) and (22), one can get

$$\begin{cases} D^{\delta_i} \mathrm{X}_i\left(t\right) = A_{di} \mathrm{X}_i\left(t\right) + b_{di}\Bigg[f_{1,i}\Big(x\left(t\right), x\left(t - \tau_{1,i}\left(t\right)\right)\Big) + \tau_{2,i}\left(t\right) f_{2,i}\Big(x\left(t - \tau_{5,i}\left(t\right)\right)\Big) \\ \qquad\qquad + \sum_{k=0}^{n_i - 2} f_{4,\mathrm{k},i}\Big(x\left(t\right), x\left(t - \tau_{3,\mathrm{k},i}\left(t\right)\right)\Big) - k_{ci}\hat{z}_i\left(t\right) + f_{3,i}\Big(x\left(t\right), 0\Big) \\ \qquad\qquad + \sum_{k=0}^{n_i - 2} \tau_{4,\mathrm{k},i}\left(t\right) f_{5,\mathrm{k},i}\Big(x\left(t - \tau_{6,\mathrm{k},i}\left(t\right)\right)\Big) + e_{a,i}\left(t\right) \\ \qquad\qquad + g_{2,i}\Big(x\left(t\right), \nu_{\Lambda_{1,i}}\left(t\right), u_{\Lambda_{2,i}}\left(t\right)\Big) u_i\left(t\right) \Bigg] \\ \tilde{y}_i\left(t\right) = c_{di}{}^T \mathrm{X}_i\left(t\right), \quad i = 1, \ldots, p \end{cases} \qquad (23)$$

with

$$A_{di} = \begin{bmatrix} \left[A_{1,i} + b_{2,i}k_{ci}\right] & -k_{oi}c_{1,i}{}^T \\ 0_{r_i \times r_i} & \left[A_{1,i} + k_{oi}c_{1,i}{}^T\right] \end{bmatrix} \in \mathbb{R}^{2r_i \times 2r_i},$$

$$\mathrm{X}_i\left(t\right) = \begin{bmatrix} \hat{\vartheta}_{di}\left(t\right) \\ \tilde{z}_i\left(t\right) \end{bmatrix} \in \mathbb{R}^{2r_i},$$

$$b_{di} = \begin{bmatrix} 0_{1 \times r_i} & b_{ci}{}^T \end{bmatrix}^T \in \mathbb{R}^{2r_i}$$

and

$$c_{di} = \begin{bmatrix} 0_{1 \times r_i} & c_{1,i}{}^T \end{bmatrix}^T \in \mathbb{R}^{2r_i}, \quad i = 1, \ldots, p.$$

Since

$$H_f\left(s\right) = \mathrm{diag}\Big(H_{f1}\left(s\right), \quad \ldots, \quad H_{fp}\left(s\right)\Big)$$

is a proper SPR transfer function and the matrix

$$A_d = \mathrm{diag}\Big(A_{d1}, \quad \ldots, \quad A_{dp}\Big) \in \mathbb{R}^{2r \times 2r}$$

is stable, there exist constant symmetric positive definite matrices

$$P = \mathrm{diag}\Big(P_1, \quad P_2, \quad \ldots, \quad P_p\Big) \in \mathbb{R}^{2r \times 2r}$$

and $Q = Q^T > 0$, such that:

$$
\begin{cases}
A_d^T P + P A_d = -Q \\
\qquad P B_d = C_d
\end{cases}
\tag{24}
$$

with

$$
B_d = \mathrm{diag}\left(b_{d1}, \quad b_{d2}, \quad \ldots, \quad b_{dp} \right) \in \mathbb{R}^{2r \times p}
$$

and $C_d = \mathrm{diag}\left(c_{d1}, \quad c_{d2}, \quad \ldots, \quad c_{dp} \right) \in \mathbb{R}^{2r \times p}$.

$P_i = P_i^T > 0$, $i = 1, \ldots, \mathrm{p}$ are constant symmetric positive-definite matrices.

Step 2

Based on the frequency-distributed model (Wei et al., 2015; Lan & Zhou, 2013; N'Doye & Laleg-Kirati, 2015; Li & Wang, 2014), the dynamic system (23) can be expressed as

$$
\begin{cases}
\dfrac{\partial Z_i\left(\omega, t\right)}{\partial t} = -\omega Z_i\left(\omega, t\right) + A_{di} X_i\left(t\right) + b_{di}\Big[f_{1,i}\left(x\left(t\right), x\left(t - \tau_{1,i}\left(t\right)\right)\right) - k_{ci}\hat{z}_i\left(t\right) \\
\qquad + \tau_{2,i}\left(t\right) f_{2,i}\left(x\left(t - \tau_{5,i}\left(t\right)\right)\right) + \displaystyle\sum_{k=0}^{n_i - 2} f_{4,k,i}\left(x\left(t\right), x\left(t - \tau_{3,k,i}\left(t\right)\right)\right) \\
\qquad + \displaystyle\sum_{k=0}^{n_i - 2} \tau_{4,k,i}\left(t\right) f_{5,k,i}\left(x\left(t - \tau_{6,k,i}\left(t\right)\right)\right) + f_{3,i}\left(x\left(t\right), 0\right) + e_{a,i}\left(t\right) \\
\qquad + g_{2,i}\left(x\left(t\right), \nu_{\Lambda_{1,i}}\left(t\right), u_{\Lambda_{2,i}}\left(t\right)\right) u_i\left(t\right) \Big], \\[1em]
X_i\left(t\right) = \displaystyle\int_0^{+\infty} \mu_i\left(\omega\right) Z_i\left(\omega, t\right) d\omega, \\
\tilde{y}_i\left(t\right) = c_{di}^T X_i\left(t\right), \quad i = 1, \ldots, p
\end{cases}
\tag{25}
$$

with $\mu_i\left(\omega\right) = \dfrac{\sin\left(\delta_i \pi\right)}{\pi} \omega^{-\delta_i}$ and $Z_i\left(\omega, t\right) \in \mathbb{R}^{2r_i}$, $i = 1, \ldots, p$.

Remark 12

It follows from Wei et al. (2015), Lan & Zhou (2013), N'Doye & Laleg-Kirati (2015), and Li & Wang (2014), that a fractional order system can be transformed into its equivalent frequency distributed model. Moreover, the traditional Lyapunov method can be used to analyze the stability of the frequency-distributed model.

Now, let us consider the following Lyapunov function candidate

$$V(t) = \sum_{i=1}^{p} V_i(t) + \frac{1}{2\chi} \tilde{\theta}^2(t) \tag{26}$$

with

$$V_i(t) = \frac{1}{2} \int_0^{+\infty} \mu_i(\omega) Z_i^T(\omega, t) P_i Z_i(\omega, t) d\omega,$$

$i = 1, \ldots, p$ and $\tilde{\theta}(t) = \theta^* - \hat{\theta}(t)$.

From (23) -(25), it is easy to show that

$$\begin{cases} -\sum_{i=1}^{p} \int_0^{+\infty} \omega \mu_i(\omega) Z_i^T(\omega, t) P_i Z_i(\omega, t) d\omega \leq 0 \\ \tilde{y}(t) = B_d^T P \mathrm{X}(t) \end{cases} \tag{27}$$

with $\mathrm{X}(t) = \begin{bmatrix} \mathrm{X}_1^T(t), & \mathrm{X}_2^T(t), & \ldots, & \mathrm{X}_p^T(t) \end{bmatrix}^T \in \mathbb{R}^{2r}$.

By using (21), (24) and (27), the time derivative of $V(t)$ along the solutions of (25) can be expressed as follows

$$\dot{V}(t) \leq -\frac{\lambda_{\min}(Q)}{2} \|\mathrm{X}(t)\|^2 + \|\tilde{y}(t)\| \left(1 + \Delta_1 + \Delta_2\right) \left(1 + F(z(t), \hat{z}(t))\right)$$
$$+ \tilde{y}^T(t) G_2\left(x(t), \nu_{\Lambda_1}(t), u_{\Lambda_2}(t)\right) u(t) + \frac{\tilde{\theta}(t) \dot{\hat{\theta}}(t)}{\chi} \tag{28}$$

with

$$G_2\left(x(t), \nu_{\Lambda_1}(t), u_{\Lambda_2}(t)\right) =$$
$$\mathrm{diag}\left(g_{2,1}\left(x(t), \nu_{\Lambda_{1,1}}(t), u_{\Lambda_{2,1}}(t)\right), \quad \ldots, \quad g_{2,p}\left(x(t), \nu_{\Lambda_{1,p}}(t), u_{\Lambda_{2,p}}(t)\right)\right) \in \mathbb{R}^{p \times p}.$$

On the other hand, based on the neural network parameterization (13), the following inequality holds

$$\dot{V}(t) \leq -\frac{\lambda_{\min}(Q)}{2} \|\mathrm{X}(t)\|^2 + \|\tilde{y}(t)\| \left(1 + \Delta_1 + \Delta_2\right) \left(1 + \|w^*\| \|\xi(\hat{z}(t))\| + \varepsilon^*\right)$$
$$+ \tilde{y}^T(t) G_2\left(x(t), \nu_{\Lambda_1}(t), u_{\Lambda_2}(t)\right) u(t) + \frac{\tilde{\theta}(t) \dot{\hat{\theta}}(t)}{\chi} \tag{29}$$

Let us denote

$$\theta^* = \left(1 + \Delta_1 + \Delta_2\right)\left(1 + \left\|w^*\right\| + \varepsilon^*\right) \tag{30}$$

Then, by utilizing (15) and (30), (29) can be rewritten as

$$
\begin{aligned}
\dot{V}(t) \leq & -\frac{\lambda_{\min}(Q)}{2}\left\|\mathrm{X}(t)\right\|^2 + \theta^*\left\|\tilde{y}(t)\right\|\rho\left(\hat{z}(t)\right) + \frac{\tilde{\theta}(t)\dot{\hat{\theta}}(t)}{\chi} \\
& + N\left(\zeta(t)\right)\hat{\theta}(t)\frac{\rho^2\left(\hat{z}(t)\right)}{\sigma(t) + \rho\left(\hat{z}(t)\right)\left\|\tilde{y}(t)\right\|}\tilde{y}^T(t)G_2\left(x(t), \nu_{\Lambda_1}(t), u_{\Lambda_2}(t)\right)\tilde{y}(t)
\end{aligned} \tag{31}
$$

From Boulkroune et al. (2016a), Shi (2015b), Miao & Li (2015), Zhang et al. (2015), and Bouzeriba et al. (2016b), one can deduce that

$$
\begin{cases}
\tilde{y}^T(t)G_2\left(x(t), \nu_{\Lambda_1}(t), u_{\Lambda_2}(t)\right)\tilde{y}(t) = \Phi(t)\left\|\tilde{y}(t)\right\|^2 \\
\theta^*\left\|\tilde{y}(t)\right\|\rho\left(\hat{z}(t)\right) - \theta^*\dfrac{\rho^2\left(\hat{z}(t)\right)\left\|\tilde{y}(t)\right\|^2}{\sigma(t) + \rho\left(\hat{z}(t)\right)\left\|\tilde{y}(t)\right\|} \leq \theta^*\sigma(t) \\
\sigma(t)\hat{\theta}(t)\tilde{\theta}(t) \leq -\dfrac{1}{2}\sigma(t)\tilde{\theta}^2(t) + \dfrac{1}{2}\sigma(t)\theta^{*2}
\end{cases} \tag{32}
$$

where $\Phi(t) \in \mathbb{R}$ is an unknown bounded function satisfying $\Phi(t) \neq 0$, $\forall t \geq 0$.

From (31) and (32), it is easy to obtain that

$$\dot{V}(t) \leq -\frac{\lambda_{\min}(Q)}{2}\left\|\mathrm{X}(t)\right\|^2 + \theta^*\sigma(t) + \frac{1}{2}\sigma(t)\theta^{*2} + \left(1 + N\left(\zeta(t)\right)\Phi(t)\right)\dot{\zeta}(t) \tag{33}$$

After integrating (33) over $\left[0, \quad t\right]$, one has

$$
\begin{aligned}
V(t) + \frac{\lambda_{\min}(Q)}{2}\int_0^t\left\|\mathrm{X}(\tau)\right\|^2 d\tau \leq & \int_0^t\left(1 + N\left(\zeta(\tau)\right)\Phi(\tau)\right)\dot{\zeta}(\tau)d\tau \\
& + V(0) + \left[\theta^* + \frac{1}{2}\theta^{*2}\right]\int_0^t\sigma(\tau)d\tau
\end{aligned} \tag{34}
$$

According to (15), (34), and Shi (2015a), Shi (2015b), Boulkroune et al. (2014a), Boulkroune & M'Saad (2011), Boulkroune et al. (2014b), Shahnazi (2016), $V(t)$, $\dfrac{\lambda_{\min}(Q)}{2}\displaystyle\int_0^t\left\|\mathrm{X}(\tau)\right\|^2 d\tau$, $\left[\theta^* + \dfrac{1}{2}\theta^{*2}\right]\displaystyle\int_0^t\sigma(\tau)d\tau$ and $\displaystyle\int_0^t\left(1 + N\left(\zeta(\tau)\right)\Phi(\tau)\right)\dot{\zeta}(\tau)d\tau$ are bounded $\forall t \in \left[0, +\infty\right[$.

Therefore, it is clear that $X(t) \in L_2$.

From (23), since the functions

$$f_{1,i}\left(x(t), x\left(t - \tau_{1,i}(t)\right)\right), \ f_{2,i}\left(x\left(t - \tau_{5,i}(t)\right)\right),$$

$$f_{3,i}\left(x(t), \nu_i(t)\right), \ f_{4,k,i}\left(x(t), x\left(t - \tau_{3,k,i}(t)\right)\right)$$

and $f_{5,k,i}\left(x\left(t - \tau_{6,k,i}(t)\right)\right)$, $k = 0, \ldots, n_i - 2$, are continuous, and the variables

$$\left(X_i(t), \ \hat{z}_i(t), \ g_{2,i}\left(x(t), \nu_{\Lambda_{1,i}}(t), u_{\Lambda_{2,i}}(t)\right) u_i(t), \ e_{a,i}(t)\right)$$

are bounded, then one has $D^{\delta_i} X_i(t) \in L_\infty$, for $i = 1, \ldots, p$.

Finally, since $X(t) \in L_2 \cap L_\infty$ and $D^{\delta_i} X_i(t) \in L_\infty$ for $i = 1, \ldots, p$, one can deduce that $\lim\limits_{t \to +\infty} \|X(t)\| = 0$. Furthermore, by using Barbalat's lemma (Shi, 2015a; Boulkroune et al., 2012a; Zhang et al., 2015; Wang et al., 2017), it follows that the tracking errors converge asymptotically to zero, i.e., $\lim\limits_{t \to +\infty} \|\vartheta(t)\| = 0$ because $\|\vartheta(t)\| \leq \|X(t)\|$.

The proof is completed here.

Remark 13

As presented in Boulkroune et al. (2016a), Bouzeriba et al. (2016a), Wei et al. (2015), Vargas-De-León (2015); Lan et al. (2012), Ladaci et al. (2009), Farges et al. (2010); Lazarević & Spasić (2009), Lim et al. (2013), Domek & Dworak (2016), Liu & Jiang (2013a), Wang et al. (2017), and Liu et al. (2016b), the traditional stability tools for integer order systems cannot be directly applicable to non-integer ones. For example in Boulkroune et al. (2016a) and Bouzeriba et al. (2016a), the stability of fractional-order chaotic systems has been studied by using the semigroup property of fractional order derivative, the Lipschiz condition and the Lyapunov approach. In Wei et al. (2015), Lan & Zhou (2013), N'Doye & Laleg-Kirati (2015), and Li & Wang 2014), some stability analysis for fractional-order nonlinear systems have been performed by utilizing a combination of continuous frequency distributed equivalent model and indirect Lyapunov approach. In Vargas-De-León (2015), sufficient stability conditions for fractional-order epidemic systems have been obtained by Volterra-type Lyapunov functions. In Chen & Chen (2015), and Liu & Jiang (2013a), stability analysis problem of fractional-order systems with delays have been solved by Lyapunov approaches, Razumikhin-type stability theorems and Lyapunov-Krasovskii approaches. In (Liu et al., 2016b), simple criteria of Mittag-Leffler stability have been proposed for fractional nonlinear systems.

COMPARISON TO AVAILABLE METHODS

Compared to some available control schemes in Yu et al. (2016), Boulkroune et al., (2016a), Bouzeriba et al., (2016a), Wei et al. (2015), Lan & Zhou (2013), Lan et al. (2012), Zhang et al. 2015); Ladaci et al. (2009), Farges et al. (2010), Domek & Dworak (2016), Yue & Li (2012), the most important advantages of our work are that:

- It solves the input saturation and the unmeasured state problem of nonlinear systems,
- It does not require a priori knowledge of the signs of control gains nor any information of the bound of input saturation,
- It can handle systems with constant, time-varying and distributed time-varying delays,
- The considered class of systems is relatively large,
- The tracking errors asymptotically converge to zero,
- The proposed control is continuous and has a simple structure, i.e., the number of tuning parameters is reduced.

SIMULATION EXAMPLES

In this section, two simulation examples are conducted to illustrate the effectiveness of the proposed controller.

Example 1: An Academic Mimo Uncertain Nonlinear System

Consider the non-integer order system (1), under Assumptions 1–4 with

- The integers $p = 2$, $m_1 = m_2 = 2$, $n_1 = n_2 = 2$, $n = n_1 + n_2 = 4$,
- The constants $q_1 = 1.99$, $q_2 = 1.98$,
- The matrices $A_{0,1} = A_{0,2} = \begin{bmatrix} 0 & 1 \\ 0 & 0 \end{bmatrix}$,
- The vectors $b_{0,1} = b_{0,2} = \begin{bmatrix} 0 & 1 \end{bmatrix}^T$, $c_{0,1} = c_{0,2} = \begin{bmatrix} 1 & 0 \end{bmatrix}^T$, $b_{1,0,1} = b_{1,0,2} = \begin{bmatrix} 1 & 0 \end{bmatrix}^T$,
- The state variables $x_1(t) = \begin{bmatrix} x_{1,1}(t), & x_{1,2}(t) \end{bmatrix}^T$, $x_2(t) = \begin{bmatrix} x_{2,1}(t), & x_{2,2}(t) \end{bmatrix}^T$, $x(t) = \begin{bmatrix} x_1^T(t), & x_2^T(t) \end{bmatrix}^T$,
- The output of the system $y(t) = \begin{bmatrix} y_1(t), & y_2(t) \end{bmatrix}^T$,
- The control input $u(t) = \begin{bmatrix} u_1(t), & u_2(t) \end{bmatrix}^T$,
- The parameters of the asymmetric saturation actuator (2) $u_{min} = -15$, $u_{max} = 20$,
- The output of the asymmetric saturation actuator $v(t) = \begin{bmatrix} v_1(t), & v_2(t) \end{bmatrix}^T$,
- The functions

$$f_{1,1}\left(x(t), x\left(t - \tau_{1,1}(t)\right)\right) = \frac{\sin\left(\left\|x(t) + x\left(t - \tau_{1,1}(t)\right)\right\|\right)}{2 + \left\|x(t) + x\left(t - \tau_{1,1}(t)\right)\right\|},$$

$$f_{2,1}\left(x(t)\right) = \sin\left(\left\|x(t)\right\|^2\right), \; f_{3,1}\left(x(t), \nu_1(t)\right) = \tanh\left(\left\|x(t)\right\| + \nu_1(t)\right),$$

$$f_{4,0,1}\left(x(t), x\left(t - \tau_{3,0,1}(t)\right)\right) = \sin\left(2\left\|x(t)\right\| + \left\|x\left(t - \tau_{3,0,1}(t)\right)\right\|\right),$$

$$f_{5,0,1}\left(x(t)\right) = 0, \; f_{1,2}\left(x(t), x\left(t - \tau_{1,2}(t)\right)\right) = \sin\left(\left\|x(t) - x\left(t - \tau_{1,2}(t)\right)\right\|^2\right),$$

$$f_{2,2}\left(x(t)\right) = \sin\left(\left\|x(t)\right\|^3\right), \; f_{3,2}\left(x(t), \nu_2(t)\right) = \tanh\left(-4\left\|x(t)\right\|^2 + \nu_2(t)\right),$$

$$f_{4,0,2}\left(x(t), x\left(t - \tau_{3,0,2}(t)\right)\right) = \frac{\sin\left(\left\|x(t)\right\|\left\|x\left(t - \tau_{3,0,2}(t)\right)\right\|\right)}{1 + \left\|x(t)\right\|\left\|x\left(t - \tau_{3,0,2}(t)\right)\right\|}, \; f_{5,0,2}\left(x(t)\right) = 0$$

- The time-varying delays $\tau_{1,1}(t) = 1.1 + \sin(t), \tau_{2,1}(t) = 2.1 + \sin(t), \; \tau_{3,0,1}(t) = 4 + 2\cos(t),$ $\tau_{4,0,1}(t) = 0, \quad \tau_{1,2}(t) = 1.5 + \cos(t), \quad \tau_{2,2}(t) = 3.2 + \sin(t), \quad \tau_{3,0,2}(t) = 3 + \cos(t),$ $\tau_{4,0,2}(t) = 0,$

- The external disturbances $\varpi_{0,1}(t) = \varpi_{0,2}(t) = \cos(t), \; d_1(t) = d_2(t) = \sin(t),$

- The initial condition functions $\varphi_1(t) = \begin{bmatrix} 1, & -\cos(2t) \end{bmatrix}^T, \; \varphi_2(t) = \begin{bmatrix} 10\sin(t), & -5 \end{bmatrix}^T,$

The objective is to force the output $y(t)$ to track the desired trajectory $y_d(t) = \begin{bmatrix} 10, & 5\sin\left(\frac{2}{\pi}t\right) \end{bmatrix}^T.$

From section 3, the design of the proposed controller is carried out based on the following five steps:

Step 1: Transform our academic MIMO system into the system (8) with

- The integers $r_1 = r_2 = 6, r = r_1 + r_2 = 12,$

- The constants $\delta_1 = \dfrac{q_1}{m_1 + 1}, \; \delta_2 = \dfrac{q_2}{m_2 + 1},$

- The matrices $A_{1,1} = A_{1,2} = \begin{bmatrix} 0_{5\times 1} & I_5 \\ 0_{1\times 6} \end{bmatrix},$

- The vectors $b_{2,1} = b_{2,2} = \begin{bmatrix} 0_{1\times 5} & 1 \end{bmatrix}^T, \; b_{3,0,1} = b_{3,0,2} = \begin{bmatrix} 0_{1\times 2} & 1 & 0_{1\times 3} \end{bmatrix}^T, \; c_{1,1} = c_{1,2} = \begin{bmatrix} 1 & 0_{1\times 5} \end{bmatrix}^T,$

○ The state variables. $z_1\left(t\right) = \left[x_{1,1}\left(t\right),\ D^{\delta_1}x_{1,1}\left(t\right),\ D^{2\delta_1}x_{1,1}\left(t\right),\ x_{1,2}\left(t\right),\ D^{\delta_1}x_{1,2}\left(t\right),\ D^{2\delta_1}x_{1,2}\left(t\right)\right]^T,$

$z_2\left(t\right) = \left[x_{2,1}\left(t\right),\ D^{\delta_2}x_{2,1}\left(t\right),\ D^{2\delta_2}x_{2,1}\left(t\right),\ x_{2,2}\left(t\right),\ D^{\delta_2}x_{2,2}\left(t\right),\ D^{2\delta_2}x_{2,2}\left(t\right)\right]^T,$

$z\left(t\right) = \left[z_1^{\,T}\left(t\right),\ z_2^{\,T}\left(t\right)\right]^T.$

Step 2: Select the design parameters used in the observer (10) and the control law (15) as follows

$$\chi = 100,\ \sigma\left(t\right) = \frac{1}{\left(1+t\right)^2},$$

$$k_{c1} = k_{c2} = \begin{bmatrix} -1 & -6 & -15 & -20 & -15 & -6 \end{bmatrix}$$

and

$$k_{o1} = k_{o2} = \begin{bmatrix} -6 & -15 & -20 & -15 & -6 & -1 \end{bmatrix}^T.$$

Step 3: Construct the State Observer $\hat{z}\left(t\right)$ By Using (10).

Step 4: For approximating the unknown nonlinear functions, choose a radial basis function (RBF) neural network $w^{*T}\xi\left(\hat{z}\left(t\right)\right)$ containing 20 nodes with centers evenly distributed in the interval

$$\hat{z}\left(t\right) \in \left[-30,30\right] \times \left[-30,30\right] \times \left[-30,30\right] \times \left[-30,30\right]$$
$$\times \left[-30,30\right] \times \left[-30,30\right] \times \left[-30,30\right] \times \left[-30,30\right]$$
$$\times \left[-30,30\right] \times \left[-30,30\right] \times \left[-30,30\right] \times \left[-30,30\right]$$

and widths being equal to 60.

Step 5: Determine the control law according to (15).

Remark 14

The approximation properties of radial basis function (RBF) neural networks have been presented in the works Yu et al. (2016), Cui et al. (2015), Yu & Du (2011), Wang et al. (2015a), Du & Chen (2009), McGarry et al. (2007), Rădac et al. (2014), Yacoub et al. (2014), Yan et al. (2016), Tabatabaei & Arefi (2016), Arefi et al. (2014a), and Arefi et al. (2014b)

The Simulation results obtained by applying the proposed controller, are depicted in Figures 2-8 with the initial conditions $\hat{\theta}(0) = 0$, $\zeta(0) = 1.2$,

$$\hat{z}_1(0) = \begin{bmatrix} 1, & 0, & 0, & -0.9, & 0, & 0 \end{bmatrix}^T$$

and

$$\hat{z}_2(0) = \begin{bmatrix} 0, & 0, & 0, & -4.9, & 0, & 0 \end{bmatrix}^T.$$

From Figures 2-3, it can be seen that the system output $y(t)$ satisfactorily follows the desired reference signal $y_d(t)$. Figures 4-5 illustrate the control input $u(t)$ and the output of the asymmetric saturation actuator $\nu(t)$. Figures 6-7 clearly show that the designed observer for the unmeasured states is valid. Figure 8 demonstrates that the Euclidean norm of the tracking error vector $\|\vartheta(t)\|$ goes very rapidly to zero. From these figures, it is easy to observe that the signals $\left(u(t),\ \nu(t),\ \hat{x}_{1,2}(t),\ \hat{x}_{2,2}(t)\right)$ are bounded and a good tracking control performance is achieved. In addition, the robustness of the proposed adaptive control scheme with respect to asymmetric saturation actuator, uncertain dynamics and disturbances is visibly confirmed by these simulation results.

Figure 2. System output $y_1(t)$ and reference signal $y_{d1}(t)$

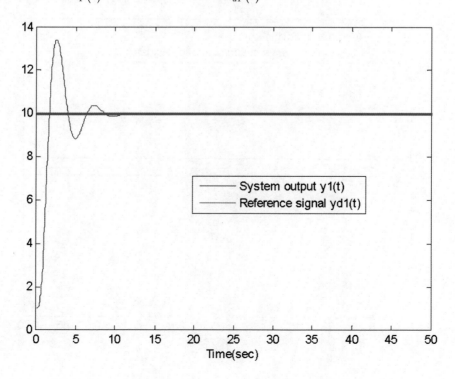

Figure 3. System output $y_2(t)$ and reference signal $y_{d2}(t)$

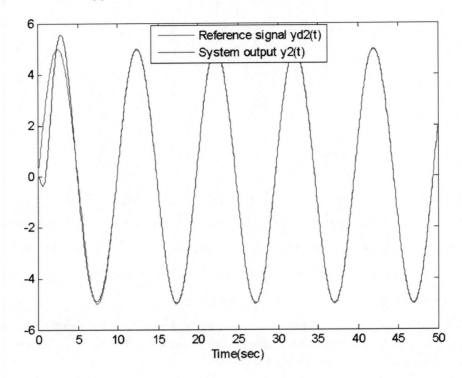

Figure 4. Control input $u_1(t)$ and output of the asymmetric saturation actuator $v_1(t)$

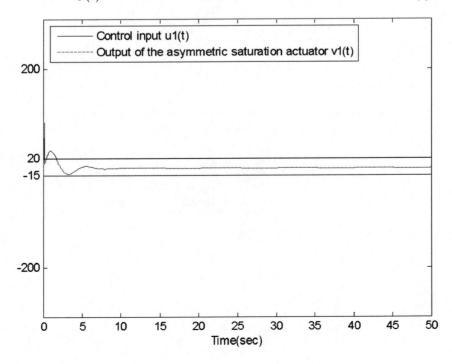

Figure 5. Control input signals $u_2(t)$ and output of the asymmetric saturation actuator $v_2(t)$

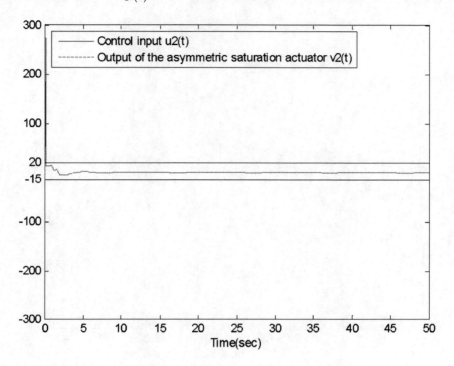

Figure 6. Observer state $\hat{x}_{1,2}(t)$

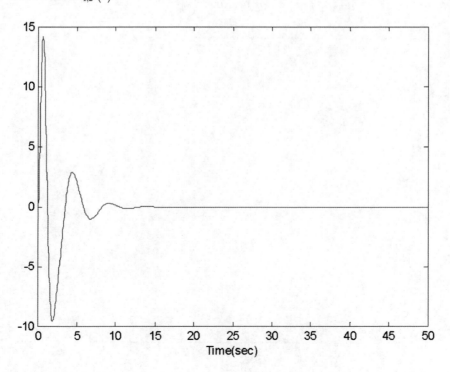

Figure 7. Observer state $\hat{x}_{2,2}(t)$

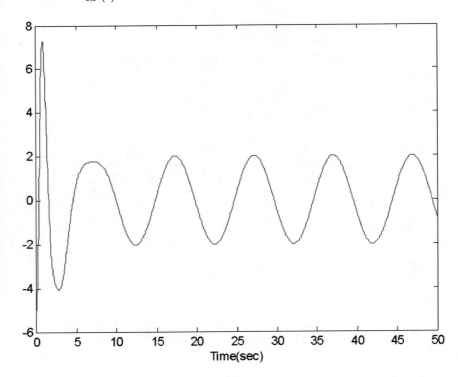

Figure 8. Euclidian norm of the tracking error vector $\|\vartheta(t)\|$

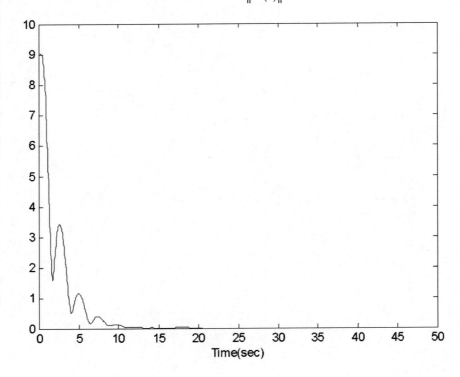

Example 2

A two-stage chemical reactor with delayed recycle streams and external disturbances (Yu et al., 2016; Yue & Li, 2012), under Assumptions 1–4, can be described by system (1) with

- The integers $\mathrm{p} = 1$, $m_1 = 1$, $n_1 = 2$, $n = n_1 = 2$,
- The constant $q_1 = 1$,
- The matrix $A_{0,1} = \begin{bmatrix} 0 & 1 \\ 0 & 0 \end{bmatrix}$,
- The vectors $b_{0,1} = \begin{bmatrix} 0 & 1 \end{bmatrix}^T$, $c_{0,1} = \begin{bmatrix} 1 & 0 \end{bmatrix}^T$, $b_{1,0,1} = \begin{bmatrix} 1 & 0 \end{bmatrix}^T$,
- The state variables $x(t) = x_1(t) = \begin{bmatrix} x_{1,1}(t), & x_{1,2}(t) \end{bmatrix}^T$,
- The output of the system $y(t) \in \mathbb{R}$,
- The control input $u(t) \in \mathbb{R}$,
- The parameters of the asymmetric saturation actuator (2) $u_{\min} = -3$, $u_{\max} = 5$,
- The output of the asymmetric saturation actuator $\nu(t) \in \mathbb{R}$,
- The functions $f_{3,1}\big(x(t), \nu(t)\big) = \nu(t) - 0.8 x_{1,2}(t)$, $f_{2,1}\big(x(t)\big) = x_{1,1}(t) x_{1,2}(t)$,

$$f_{1,1}\big(x(t), x(t - \tau_{1,1}(t))\big) = x_{1,1}\big(t - \tau_{1,1}(t)\big) + x_{1,1}\big(t - \tau_{1,1}(t)\big) x_{1,2}^{2}\big(t - \tau_{1,1}(t)\big)\cos(t),$$

$$f_{4,0,1}\big(x(t), x(t - \tau_{3,0,1}(t))\big) = -0.8 x_{1,1}(t) + 2 x_{1,1}(t) x_{1,1}\big(t - \tau_{3,0,1}(t)\big)\exp(-t),$$

$$f_{5,0,1}\big(x(t)\big) = x_{1,1}(t) x_{1,2}(t)$$

- The time-varying delays $\tau_{1,1}(t) = 1.2 + 1.1\sin(t)$, $\tau_{2,1}(t) = 1.5 + 1.2\sin(t)$, $\tau_{3,0,1}(t) = 1.2 + \sin(t)$, $\tau_{4,0,1}(t) = 1.5 + 1.2\sin(t)$,
- The external disturbances $\varpi_{0,1}(t) = \varpi_{1,1}(t) = \varpi_{1,2}(t) = 2\sin(t)$, $d_1(t) = 5\cos(t)$,
- The initial condition function $\varphi_1(t) = \begin{bmatrix} 2.5, & -3 \end{bmatrix}^T$

The objective is to steer the system output $y(t)$ to follow the reference trajectory $y_d(t) = 3\cos\left(\dfrac{2}{\pi}t\right)$.

By using the design process in Section 3, the considered two-stage chemical reactor with delayed recycle streams and external disturbances can be transformed into the system (8), with

- The integers, $r = r_1 = 4$,
- The constant $\delta_1 = \dfrac{q_1}{m_1 + 1}$,

- The matrices $A_{1,1} = \begin{bmatrix} 0_{3 \times 1} & I_3 \\ 0_{1 \times 4} \end{bmatrix}$,

- The vectors $b_{2,1} = \begin{bmatrix} 0_{1 \times 3} & 1 \end{bmatrix}^T$, $c_{1,1} = \begin{bmatrix} 1 & 0_{1 \times 3} \end{bmatrix}^T$, $b_{3,0,1} = \begin{bmatrix} 0 & 1 & 0_{1 \times 2} \end{bmatrix}^T$,

- The state variables $z(t) = z_1(t) = \begin{bmatrix} x_{1,1}(t), & D^{\delta_1} x_{1,1}(t) & x_{1,2}(t) & D^{\delta_1} x_{1,2}(t) \end{bmatrix}^T$,

The design parameters employed in the observer (10) and the control law (15), are specified as follows $\chi = 100$, $\sigma(t) = \dfrac{1}{(1+t)^2}$, $k_{c1} = \begin{bmatrix} -1 & -4 & -6 & -4 \end{bmatrix}$ and $k_{o1} = \begin{bmatrix} -4 & -6 & -4 & -1 \end{bmatrix}^T$.

For dealing with the unknown functions, a radial basis function (RBF) neural network $w^{*T} \xi(\hat{z}(t))$ containing 30 nodes with centers evenly distributed in the interval

$$\hat{z}(t) \in \begin{bmatrix} -30, 30 \end{bmatrix} \times \begin{bmatrix} -30, 30 \end{bmatrix} \times \begin{bmatrix} -30, 30 \end{bmatrix} \times \begin{bmatrix} -30, 30 \end{bmatrix}$$

and widths being equal to 70 is used.

Figures 9-12 show the simulation results of our proposed controller with the initial conditions $\hat{\theta}(0) = 0$, $\zeta(0) = 1.1$ and $\hat{z}(0) = \begin{bmatrix} 2.5, & 0, & -2.8, & 0 \end{bmatrix}^T$. From Figure 9, it can be clearly seen that

Figure 9. System output $y(t)$ and reference signal $y_d(t)$

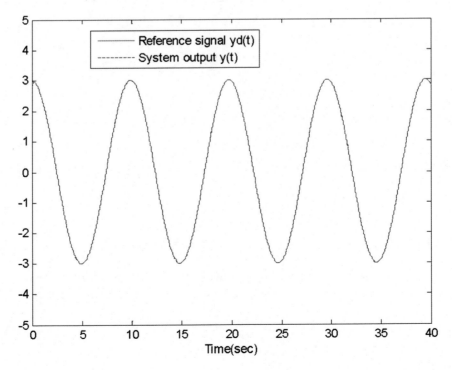

Figure 10. Control input $u(t)$ and output of the asymmetric saturation actuator $\nu(t)$

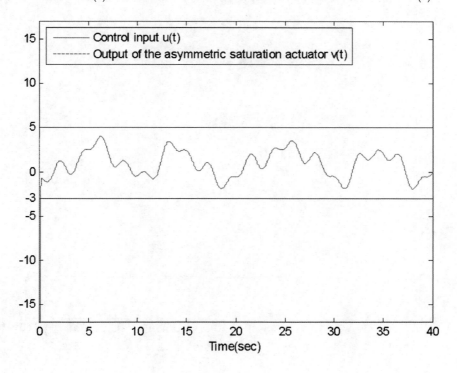

Figure 11. Observer state $\hat{x}_{1,2}(t)$

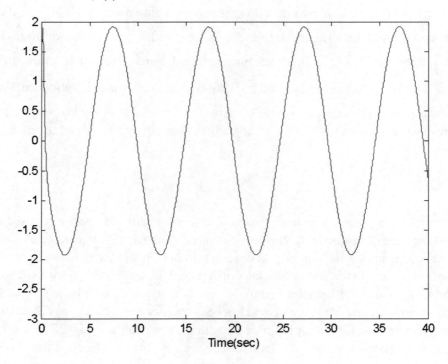

Figure 12. Tracking error $\vartheta\left(t\right)$

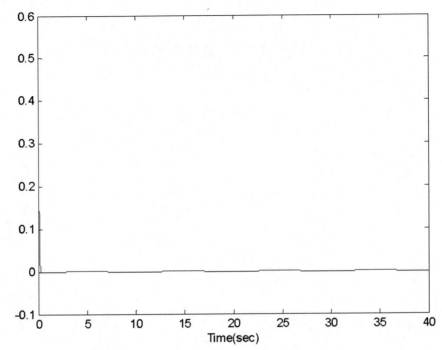

the system output $y\left(t\right)$ effectively tracks the desired reference signal $y_d\left(t\right)$ very fast. The control input $u\left(t\right)$ and the output of the asymmetric saturation actuator $\nu\left(t\right)$ are presented in Figure 10. From Figure 11, it is easy to deduce that the observer state $\hat{x}_{1,2}\left(t\right)$ is bounded. Figure 12 demonstrates that the tracking error $\vartheta\left(t\right)$ converges to zero in finite time. From Figures 9-12, it is clear that the signals $\left(u\left(t\right),\ \nu\left(t\right),\ \hat{x}_{2,2}\left(t\right)\right)$ are bounded and a good tracking control performance is obtained. From the above analysis of simulation results, one can visibly confirm the robustness of the proposed adaptive control scheme with respect to asymmetric saturation actuator, uncertain dynamics and disturbances.

CONCLUSION

In this research, an adaptive neural output-feedback control scheme has been proposed for a class of uncertain MIMO nonlinear time-delay non-integer order systems with unmeasured states, unknown control direction and unknown asymmetric saturation actuator. In this scheme, the mean value theorem and a Gaussian error function-based continuous differentiable model have been used to describe the unknown asymmetric saturation actuator and to get an affine model in which the control input appears in a linear fashion, respectively. First, the system has been transformed into a normalized fractional order system by using a state transformation in order to facilitate the control design. Then, in the controller design, a neural network has been used to approximate the unknown nonlinear functions. A simple linear state observer has been designed to estimate the unmeasured states of the transformed system and a Nussbaum-type function has been incorporated for dealing with the unknown control direction. Indeed, the SPR condition, the Razumikhin Lemma, the frequency distributed model, the Lyapunov method and the Barbalat's lemma have been employed to construct the adaptation laws. The proposed scheme has the following advantages: (1) the number of the adjustable parameters is reduced, (2) the tracking errors converge asymptotically to zero and (3) all signals of the closed-loop system remain bounded. The effectiveness of the proposed scheme has been illustrated by simulation examples. In our future research works, one will focus on the design of an observer-based adaptive fuzzy control for nonlinear fractional-order systems with faults and input nonlinearities (dead-zone, saturation, hysteresis…) based on the results of this chapter.

ACKNOWLEDGMENT

The authors would like to thank Prof. Abdesselem Boulkroune for his valuable comments that have helped to improve this chapter.

REFERENCES

Arefi, M. M., Jahed-Motlagh, M. R., & Karimi, H. R. (2014a). Adaptive Neural Stabilizing Controller for a Class of Mismatched Uncertain Nonlinear Systems by State and Output Feedback. *IEEE Transactions on Cybernetics*, *45*(8), 1587–1596. doi:10.1109/TCYB.2014.2356414 PMID:25265641

Arefi, M. M., Ramezani, Z., & Jahed-Motlagh, M. R. (2014b). Observer-based adaptive robust control of nonlinear nonaffine systems with unknown gain sign. *Nonlinear Dynamics*, *78*(3), 2185–2194. doi:10.100711071-014-1573-0

Boulkroune, A., Bounar, N., M'Saad, M., & Farza, M. (2014b). Indirect adaptive fuzzy control scheme based on observer for nonlinear systems: A novel SPR-filter approach. *Neurocomputing*, *135*, 378–387. doi:10.1016/j.neucom.2013.12.011

Boulkroune, A., Bouzeriba, A., & Bouden, T. (2016a). Fuzzy generalized projective synchronization of incommensurate fractional-order chaotic systems. *Neurocomputing*, *173*(3), 606–614. doi:10.1016/j.neucom.2015.08.003

Boulkroune, A., & M'Saad, M. (2011). A practical projective synchronization approach for uncertain chaotic systems with dead-zone input. *Communications in Nonlinear Science and Numerical Simulation*, *16*(11), 4487–4500. doi:10.1016/j.cnsns.2011.02.016

Boulkroune, A., & M'Saad, M. (2012b). On the design of observer-based fuzzy adaptive controller for nonlinear systems with unknown control gain sign. *Neurocomputing*, *201*, 71–85.

Boulkroune, A., M'Saad, M., & Chekireb, H. (2010). Design of a fuzzy adaptive controller for MIMO nonlinear time-delay systems with unknown actuator nonlinearities and unknown control direction. *Information Sciences*, *180*(24), 5041–5059. doi:10.1016/j.ins.2010.08.034

Boulkroune, A., M'Saad, M., & Farza, M. (2012a). Adaptive fuzzy tracking control for a class of MIMO nonaffine uncertain systems. *Neurocomputing*, *93*, 48–55. doi:10.1016/j.neucom.2012.04.006

Boulkroune, A., M'saad, M., & Farza, M. (2016b). Adaptive fuzzy system-based variable-structure controller for multivariable nonaffine nonlinear uncertain systems subject to actuator nonlinearities. *Neural Computing & Applications*. doi:10.100700521-016-2241-8

Boulkroune, A., Tadjine, M., M'Saad, M., & Farza, M. (2014a). Design of a unified adaptive fuzzy observer for uncertain nonlinear systems. *Information Sciences*, *265*, 139–153. doi:10.1016/j.ins.2013.12.026

Bouzeriba, A., Boulkroune, A., & Bouden, T. (2016a). Fuzzy adaptive synchronization of uncertain fractional-order chaotic systems. *International Journal of Machine Learning and Cybernetics*, *7*(5), 893–908. doi:10.100713042-015-0425-7

Bouzeriba, A., Boulkroune, A., & Bouden, T. (2016b). Projective synchronization of two different fractional-order chaotic systems via adaptive fuzzy control. *Neural Computing & Applications*, *27*(5), 1349–1360. doi:10.100700521-015-1938-4

Chen, B., & Chen, J. (2015). Razumikhin-type stability theorems for functional fractional-order differential systems and applications. *Applied Mathematics and Computation*, *254*, 63–69. doi:10.1016/j.amc.2014.12.010

Chen, B., Liu, X., Liu, K., Shi, P., & Lin, C. (2010). Direct adaptive fuzzy control for nonlinear systems with time-varying delays. *Information Sciences*, *180*(5), 776–792. doi:10.1016/j.ins.2009.11.004

Chen, L., Liu, C., Wu, R., He, Y., & Chai, Y. (2016). Finite-time stability criteria for a class of fractional-order neural networks with delay. *Neural Computing & Applications*, *27*(3), 549–556. doi:10.100700521-015-1876-1

Cui, G., Wang, Z., Zhuang, G., Li, Z., & Chu, Y. (2015). Adaptive decentralized NN control of large-scale stochastic nonlinear time-delay systems with unknown dead-zone inputs. *Neurocomputing*, *158*, 194–203. doi:10.1016/j.neucom.2015.01.048

Domek, S., & Dworak, P. (2016). Theoretical Developments and Applications of Non-Integer Order Systems. *Lecture Notes in Electrical Engineering, 357.*

Du, H., & Chen, X. (2009). NN-based output feedback adaptive variable structure control for a class of non-affine nonlinear systems: A nonseparation principle design. *Neurocomputing*, *72*(7-9), 2009–2016. doi:10.1016/j.neucom.2008.12.015

Farges, C., Moze, M., & Sabatier, J. (2010). Pseudo-state feedback stabilization of commensurate fractional order systems. *Automatica*, *46*(10), 1730–1734. doi:10.1016/j.automatica.2010.06.038

Gao, Y., & Liu, Y. J. (2016). Adaptive fuzzy optimal control using direct heuristic dynamic programming for chaotic discrete-time system. *Journal of Vibration and Control*, *22*(2), 595–603. doi:10.1177/1077546314534286

Ibeas, A., & DelaSen, M. (2007). Robust Sliding Control of Robotic Manipulators Based on a Heuristic Modification of the Sliding Gain. *Journal of Intelligent & Robotic Systems*, *48*(4), 485–511. doi:10.100710846-006-9124-7

Ioannou, P. A., & Sun, J. (1996). *Robust adaptive control.* Englewood Cliffs, NJ: Prentice Hall.

Iqbal, M., Rehan, M., Hong, K. S., Khaliq, A., & Saeed-ur-Rehman. (2015). Sector-condition based results for adaptive control and synchronization of chaotic systems under input saturation. *Chaos, Solitons, and Fractals, 77,* 158–169. doi:10.1016/j.chaos.2015.05.021

Ladaci, S., Charef, A., & Loiseau, J. (2009). Robust Fractional Adaptive Control Based on the Strictly Positive Realness Condition. *International Journal of Applied Mathematics and Computer Science, 19*(1), 69–76. doi:10.2478/v10006-009-0006-6

Lan, Y.-H., Huang, H.-X., & Zhou, Y. (2012). Observer-based robust control of a ($1 \leq a < 2$) fractional-order uncertain systems: A linear matrix inequality approach. *IET Control Theory & Applications, 6*(2), 229–234. doi:10.1049/iet-cta.2010.0484

Lan, Y.-H., & Zhou, Y. (2013). Non-fragile observer-based robust control for a class of fractional-order nonlinear systems. *Systems & Control Letters, 62*(12), 1143–1150. doi:10.1016/j.sysconle.2013.09.007

Lazarević, M.-P., & Spasić, A.-M. (2009). Finite-time stability analysis of fractional order time-delay systems: Gronwall's approach. *Mathematical and Computer Modelling, 94*(3-4), 475–481. doi:10.1016/j.mcm.2008.09.011

Li, C., & Wang, J. (2014). Robust adaptive observer for fractional order nonlinear systems: an LMI approach. In *Control and Decision Conference (2014 CCDC), The 26th Chinese* (pp. 392-397). IEEE. 10.1109/CCDC.2014.6852179

Li, Y., Tong, S., & Li, T. (2015a). Observer-Based Adaptive Fuzzy Tracking Control of MIMO Stochastic Nonlinear Systems with Unknown Control Directions and Unknown Dead Zones. *IEEE Transactions on Fuzzy Systems, 23*(4), 1228–1241. doi:10.1109/TFUZZ.2014.2348017

Li, Y., Tong, S., & Li, T. (2015b). Hybrid Fuzzy Adaptive Output Feedback Control Design for MIMO Time-Varying Delays Uncertain Nonlinear Systems. *IEEE Transactions on Fuzzy Systems.* doi:10.1109/TFUZZ.2015.2486811

Li, Y., Tong, S., & Li, T. (2015c). Composite Adaptive Fuzzy Output Feedback Control Design for Uncertain Nonlinear Strict-Feedback Systems with Input Saturation. *IEEE Transactions on Cybernetics, 45*(10), 2299–2308. doi:10.1109/TCYB.2014.2370645 PMID:25438335

Lim, Y.-H., Oh, K.-K., & Ahn, H.-S. (2013). Stability and Stabilization of Fractional-Order Linear Systems Subject to Input Saturation. *IEEE Transactions on Automatic Control, 58*(4), 1062–1067. doi:10.1109/TAC.2012.2218064

Liu, K., & Jiang, W. (2013a). Uniform stability of fractional neutral systems: A Lyapunov-Krasovskii functional approach. *Advances in Difference Equations, 2013*(1), 379. doi:10.1186/1687-1847-2013-379

Liu, S., Jiang, W., Li, X., & Zhou, X. F. (2016b). Lyapunov stability analysis of fractional nonlinear systems. *Applied Mathematics Letters, 51,* 13–19. doi:10.1016/j.aml.2015.06.018

Liu, Y.-H., Huang, L., Xiao, D., & Guo, Y. (2015a). Global adaptive control for uncertain nonaffine nonlinear hysteretic systems. *ISA Transactions, 58,* 255–261. doi:10.1016/j.isatra.2015.06.010 PMID:26169122

Liu, Y. J., Gao, Y., Tong, S., & Li, Y. (2016a). Fuzzy Approximation-Based Adaptive Backstepping Optimal Control for a Class of Nonlinear Discrete-Time Systems With Dead-Zone. *IEEE Transactions on Fuzzy Systems*, *24*(1), 16–28. doi:10.1109/TFUZZ.2015.2418000

Liu, Y. J., & Tong, S. (2013b). Adaptive Fuzzy Control for a Class of Nonlinear Discrete-Time Systems with Backlash. *IEEE Transactions on Fuzzy Systems*, *22*(5), 1359–1365. doi:10.1109/TFUZZ.2013.2286837

Liu, Y. J., & Tong, S. (2014). Adaptive Fuzzy Identification and Control for a Class of Nonlinear Pure-Feedback MIMO Systems with Unknown Dead Zones. *IEEE Transactions on Fuzzy Systems*, *23*(5), 1387–1398. doi:10.1109/TFUZZ.2014.2360954

Liu, Y. J., & Tong, S. (2015b). Adaptive fuzzy control for a class of unknown nonlinear dynamical systems. *Fuzzy Sets and Systems*, *263*, 49–70. doi:10.1016/j.fss.2014.08.008

Luo, J., & Liu, H. (2014). Adaptive Fractional Fuzzy Sliding Mode Control for Multivariable Nonlinear Systems. *Discrete Dynamics in Nature and Society*.

McGarry, K., Sarfraz, M., & MacIntyre, J. (2007). Integrating gene expression data from microarrays using the self-organising map and the gene ontology. *Pattern Recognition in Bioinformatics*, 206-217.

Miao, B., & Li, T. (2015). A novel neural network-based adaptive control for a class of uncertain nonlinear systems in strict-feedback form. *Nonlinear Dynamics*, *79*(2), 1005–1013. doi:10.100711071-014-1717-2

Mizumoto, I., Fujii, S., & Ikejiri, M. (2015). Control of a magnetic levitation system via output feedback based two DOF control with an adaptive predictive feedforward input. In *Control Applications (CCA), 2015 IEEE Conference on* (pp. 71-76). IEEE. 10.1109/CCA.2015.7320612

N'Doye, I., & Laleg-Kirati, T. M. (2015). Fractional-order adaptive fault estimation for a class of nonlinear fractional-order systems. In American Control Conference (ACC), 2015 (pp. 3804-3809). IEEE. doi:10.1109/ACC.2015.7171923

Petras, I. (2011). *Fractional-Order Nonlinear Systems: Modeling, Analysis and Simulation*. Berlin: Springer-Verlag; doi:10.1007/978-3-642-18101-6.

Rădac, M. B., Precup, R. E., Petriu, E. M., & Preitl, S. (2014). Iterative Data-Driven Tuning of Controllers for Nonlinear Systems With Constraints. *IEEE Transactions on Industrial Electronics*, *61*(11), 6360–6368. doi:10.1109/TIE.2014.2300068

Shahnazi, R. (2016). Observer-based adaptive interval type-2 fuzzy control of uncertain MIMO nonlinear systems with unknown asymmetric saturation actuators. *Neurocomputing*, *171*, 1053–1065. doi:10.1016/j.neucom.2015.07.098

Shi, W. (2015a). Observer-based fuzzy adaptive control for multi-input multi-output nonlinear systems with a nonsymmetric control gain matrix and unknown control direction. *Fuzzy Sets and Systems*, *236*, 1–26. doi:10.1016/j.fss.2014.05.015

Shi, W. (2015b). Observer-based direct adaptive fuzzy control for single-input single-output non-linear systems with unknown gain sign. *IET Control Theory & Applications*, *9*(17), 2506–2513. doi:10.1049/iet-cta.2015.0076

Stamova, I., & Stamov, G. (2013). Lipschitz stability criteria for functional differential systems of fractional order. *Journal of Mathematical Physics*, *54*(4), 043502. doi:10.1063/1.4798234

Stamova, I., & Stamov, G. (2014). Stability analysis of impulsive functional systems of fractional order. *Communications in Nonlinear Science and Numerical Simulation*, *19*(3), 702–709. doi:10.1016/j.cnsns.2013.07.005

Sui, S., Tong, S., & Li, Y. (2015). Observer-based fuzzy adaptive prescribed performance tracking control for nonlinear stochastic systems with input saturation. *Neurocomputing*, *158*, 100–108. doi:10.1016/j.neucom.2015.01.063

Tabatabaei, S. M., & Arefi, M. M. (2016). Adaptive neural control for a class of uncertain non-affine nonlinear switched system. *Nonlinear Dynamics*, *83*(3), 1773–1781. doi:10.100711071-015-2446-x

Vargas-De-León, C. (2015). Volterra-type Lyapunov functions for fractional-order epidemic systems. *Communications in Nonlinear Science and Numerical Simulation*, *24*(1-3), 75–85. doi:10.1016/j.cnsns.2014.12.013

Wang, F., Yang, Y., Xu, X., & Li, L. (2017). Global asymptotic stability of impulsive fractional-order BAM neural networks with time delay. *Neural Computing & Applications*, *28*(2), 345–352. doi:10.100700521-015-2063-0

Wang, H., Liu, X., & Liu, K. (2015a). Adaptive neural data-based compensation control of non-linear systems with dynamic uncertainties and input saturation. *IET Control Theory & Applications*, *9*(7), 1058–1065. doi:10.1049/iet-cta.2014.0709

Wang, Q., Zhou, B., & Duan, G.-R. (2015b). Robust gain scheduled control of spacecraft rendezvous system subject to input saturation. *Aerospace Science and Technology*, *42*, 442–450. doi:10.1016/j.ast.2015.02.002

Wei, Y., Chen, Y., Liang, S., & Wang, Y. (2015). A novel algorithm on adaptive backstepping control of fractional order systems. *Neurocomputing*, *165*, 395–402. doi:10.1016/j.neucom.2015.03.029

Yacoub, R. R., Bambang, R. T., Harsoyo, A., & Sarwono, J. (2014). *DSP* Implementation of Combined FIR-Functional Link Neural Network for Active Noise Control. *International Journal of Artificial Intelligence*, *12*(1), 36–47.

Yan, P., Liu, D., Wang, D., & Ma, H. (2016). Data-driven controller design for general MIMO nonlinear systems via virtual reference feedback tuning and neural networks. *Neurocomputing*, *171*, 815–825. doi:10.1016/j.neucom.2015.07.017

Yu, Z., & Du, H. (2011). Adaptive neural control for uncertain stochastic nonlinear strict-feedback systems with time-varying delays: A Razumikhin functional method. *Neurocomputing*, *74*(12-14), 2072–2082. doi:10.1016/j.neucom.2010.12.030

Yu, Z., Li, S., & Yu, Z. (2016). Adaptive neural control for a class of Pure-Feedback Nonlinear Time-Delay Systems with Asymmetric Saturation Actuators. *Neurocomputing*, *173*(3), 1461–1470. doi:10.1016/j.neucom.2015.09.020

Yue, H., & Li, J. (2012). Output-feedback adaptive fuzzy control for a class of non-linear time-varying delay systems with unknown control directions. *IET Control Theory & Applications*, 6(9), 1266–1280. doi:10.1049/iet-cta.2011.0226

Zhang, Z., Xu, S., & Zhang, B. (2015). Exact tracking control of nonlinear systems with time delays and dead-zone input. *Automatica*, 52, 272–276. doi:10.1016/j.automatica.2014.11.013

KEY TERMS AND DEFINITIONS

Fractional-Order Systems: Described in time domain by a fractional-order differential equation or by systems of fractional-order differential equations.

Lyapunov's Second Method: Also called Lyapunov's direct method, a method of stability assessment that is based on the use of energy-like functions without resorting to explicit solution of the associated evolution equations.

Neural Control: A control system that incorporates artificial neural networks.

Neural Network: A parallel distributed information processing structure consisting of processing elements, called neurons, interconnected via unidirectional signal channels called connections.

Neural Output Feedback Control: A neural control based on feedback of a system output, or a neural control based on a state observer.

Nussbaum Function: A function incorporated in the control law to deal with the unknown control direction (i.e., with the unknown control gain sign).

State Observer: Algorithm constructed to estimate the unmeasured states of plant.

Chapter 4
An Adaptive Interval Type-2 Fuzzy Sliding Mode Control Scheme for Fractional Chaotic Systems Synchronization With Chattering Elimination:
Fractional Adaptive PI-Regulator Approach

Khatir Khettab
University Mohamed Boudiaf of M'sila, Algeria

Yassine Bensafia
Bouira University, Algeria

ABSTRACT

This chapter presents a fractional adaptive interval type-2 fuzzy logic control strategy based on active fractional sliding mode controller (FAIT2FSMC) to synchronize tow chaotic fractional-order systems. The interval type-2 fuzzy logic systems (IT2FLS) are used to approximate the plant dynamics represented by unknown functions of the system, and the IT2F adaptation law adjusts the consequent parameters of the rules based on a Lyapunov synthesis approach. One of the main contributions in this work is the use of an IT2F and an adaptive fractional order PIλ control law to eliminate the chattering action in the control signal. Based on fractional order Lyapunov stability criterion, stability analysis is performed for the proposed method for an acceptable synchronization error level. The performance of the proposed scheme is demonstrated through the synchronization of two different fractional order chaotic gyro systems. Simulations are implemented using a numerical method based on Grünwald-Letnikov approach to solve the fractional differential equations.

DOI: 10.4018/978-1-5225-5418-9.ch004

INTRODUCTION

Fractional order systems (Hilfer, 2001; Machado et al., 2011) have shown very attractive performances and properties, and there for many applications of such systems have been reported in different areas such as signal processing, image processing (Oustaloup, 1995), automatic control (Slotine, 1991), robotics (Duarte et al., 2002), and renewable energy. A great number of research works focused on fractional systems that display chaotic behavior like: Chua circuit (Hartley, 1995), Duffing system (Arena et al., 1997), Chen dynamic (Lu and Chen, 2006), characterization (Lu et al., 2006), Rössler system and Newton-Leipnik formulation (Sheu et al., 2008). Synchronization or control of these systems is a difficult task because a main characteristic of chaotic systems is their high sensitivity to initial conditions, but it is gathering more and more research effort due to several potential applications especially in cryptography (Hosseinnia et al., 2010).

Fractional adaptive control is a growing research topic gathering the interest of a great number of researchers and control engineers (Ladaci and Charef, 2012). The main argument of this community is the significant enhancement obtained with these new real-time controllers comparatively to integer order ones (Podlubny, 1999).

Since the pioneering works of Vinagre et al. (2002) and Ladaci and Charef (2002), an increasing number of works are published focusing on various fractional order adaptive schemes such as: fractional order model reference adaptive control (Chen et al., 2016; Ladaci & Charef, 2006); Wei, 2015), fractional order adaptive pole placement control (Ladaci & Bensafia, 2016), fractional high-gain adaptive control (Ladaci et al., 2008), fractional multi-model adaptive control(Ladaci and Khettab, 2012), robust fractional adaptive control (Ladaci, 2009), fractional extremum seeking control (Neçaibia et al., 2014), Fractional IMC-based adaptive control (Ladaci, 2014), fractional adaptive sliding mode control (Efe, 2008), fractional adaptive PID control (Ladaci & Charef, 2006; Neçaibia & Ladaci, 2014).

The study and design of fractional adaptive control laws for nonlinear systems is also an actual leading research direction (Azar & Vaidyanathan, 2015; Tian et al., 2014). Many control strategies have been proposed in literature to deal with the control and synchronization problems of various nonlinear and chaotic fractional order systems (Aguila et al., 2016; Rabah et al., 2016). Nonlinear fractional adaptive control is wide meaning concept with many different control approaches such as: fractional order adaptive backstepping output feedback control scheme (Wei et al, 2016), adaptive feedback control scheme based on the stability results of linear fractional order systems (Odibat, 2010), Adaptive Sliding Control (Lin et al., 2010; Yuan et al., 2014), Adaptive synchronization of fractional-order chaotic systems via a single driving variable (Zhang & Yang, 2011), H∞ robust adaptive control (Khettab et al., 2014), etc. Whereas, in order to deal with nonlinear systems presenting uncertainties or unknown model parameters, many authors have used fuzzy systems (Boulkroune et al., 2016). In this work, we use Type-2 Fuzzy logic systems (Azar et al., 2012; Lin, 2011).

Chaos theory concerns deterministic systems whose behavior can in principle be predicted. Chaotic systems are predictable for a while and then 'appear' to become random (Boeing et al., 2016). The amount of time that the behavior of a chaotic system can be effectively predicted depends on three things: How much uncertainty can be tolerated in the forecast, how accurately its current state can be measured and a time scale depending on the dynamics of the system, called the Lyapunov time. Some examples of Lyapunov times are: chaotic electrical circuits, about 1 millisecond; weather systems, a few days (unproven); the solar system, 50 million years. In chaotic systems, the uncertainty in a forecast increases exponentially with elapsed time. Hence, mathematically, doubling the forecast time more than squares the proportional uncertainty in the forecast. This means, in practice, a meaningful prediction cannot be made over an interval of more than two or three times the Lyapunov time. When meaningful predictions cannot be made, the system appears random (Sync, 2003).

For the particular case of fractional order chaotic systems, many approaches have been proposed to achieve chaos synchronization, such as PC control (Li & Deng, 2006), nonlinear state observer method (Wu et al., 2009), adaptive control (Khettab et al., 2017) and sliding mode control (Zeghlache et al., 2017).

Synchronization or control of these systems is a difficult task because a main characteristic of chaotic systems is their high sensitivity to initial conditions, but it is gathering more and more research effort due to several potential applications especially in cryptography. For the particular case of fractional order chaotic systems, many approaches have been proposed to achieve chaos synchronization, such as PC control, nonlinear state observer method, adaptive control and sliding mode control...

In this work we are interested by the problem of uncertain fractional order chaotic systems synchronization by mean of adaptive fuzzy sliding mode control. Sliding mode control is a very suitable method for handling such nonlinear systems because of low sensitivity to disturbances and plant parameter variations and its order reduction property, which relaxes the burden of the necessity of exact modeling.

In the proposed control configuration, an interval type-2 fuzzy logic approximation method is used to modelize the uncertain fractional order system. We consider interval type-2 fuzzy sets which are extension of type-1 fuzzy sets introduced in the first time by Zadeh (1975). Basic concepts of type-2 fuzzy sets and systems were advanced and well established in (Karnik & Mende,l 1998; Mendel & John, 2002). Mendel and Karnik (1998) introduced five different kinds of type reduction methods which are extended versions of type-1 defuzzification methods. Qilian and Mendel (2000) proposed an efficient and simplified method for computing the input and antecedent operations for interval type-2 fuzzy logic systems (IT2FLS) using the concept of upper and lower Membership functions. Karnik and Mendel developed the centroid of an interval type-2 fuzzy set (IT2FS), not only for an IT2FS and IT2FLCs but also for general type-2 FSs and introduced an algorithm for its computation. Mendel described important advances for both general and interval type-2 fuzzy sets and systems in 2007. Because of the calculation complexity especially in the type reduction, use of IT2FLC is still controversial. Seplveda et al. showed that using adequate hardware implementation, IT2FLS can be efficiently utilized in applications that require high speed processing. Thus, the type-2 FLS has been successfully applied to several fuzzy controller designs (Cazarez-Castro et al., 2012; Lin et al., 2009; Wang et al., 2002).

Based on the fractional order Lyapunov stability theorem, an efficient adaptive control algorithm by means of interval type-2 fuzzy logic models is proposed that guarantees the feedback control system stability and that is able to attenuate the effects of additive noises and estimation errors on the tracking performance to any prescribed error level via the sliding mode robust tracking design technique. However, the important problem of sliding mode techniques from the control perspective is the discontinuity of the control signal required to obtain robustness. This destructive phenomenon, so-called chattering may affect control accuracy or incur an unwanted wear of a mechanical component. Various solutions to reduce the chattering have been studied in the literature. Comparing with a similar previous work, an improved synchronization technique is proposed here for a robust sliding mode control of nonlinear systems with fractional order dynamics that is able to eliminate the chattering phenomena for uncertain systems with unknown parameters' variation. The main contribution of this work consists in combining an adaptive fractional PI^λ control law with the sliding mode controller in order to improve the control signal quality by eliminating the undesirable chattering. The Grünwald-Letnikov numerical approximation method is used for fractional order differential equation resolution with improved performance result.

Stability analysis is performed for the proposed control strategy using fractional order Lyapunov theory and numerical simulation results on the synchronization of two fractional order chaotic systems illustrate the effectiveness of the proposed fractional fuzzy adaptive synchronization strategy.

The main contribution of this work consists in combining an adaptive fractional PI^λ control law with the sliding mode controller in order to improve the control signal quality by eliminating the undesirable chattering. The Grünwald-Letnikov numerical approximation method is used for fractional order differential equation resolution with improved performance result.

This chapter is organized as follows: Section 2 presents basics of fractional Order Systems and calculus with some numerical approximation methods, a brief description of interval type-2 fuzzy systems is given in section 3. In Section 4 the proposed adaptive sliding mode interval type-2 fuzzy synchronization technique of uncertain fractional order systems is described. The stability analysis is performed in section 5. In section 6, application of the obtained control scheme on a two fractional chaotic gyro is investigated. Finally, concluding remarks with future works are presented in section 7.

BASICS OF FRACTIONAL ORDER SYSTEMS

Fractional Derivatives and Integrals

There exists many formulations for the fractional order derivative definition; the most popular are those of Grünwald-Letnikov (GL), Riemann-Liouville (RL) and Caputo (Li and Tong 2013) (Ladaci and Khettab 2012).

Riemann-Liouville (RL) fractional order integral is expressed as:

$$^{RL}_{a}D_t^{-\alpha}f(t) = \frac{1}{\Gamma(\alpha)} \int_a^t (t-\tau)^{\alpha-1}f(\tau) \tag{1}$$

The fractional order derivative is defined as:

$$^{RL}_{a}D_t^{\alpha}f(t) = \frac{1}{\Gamma(1-\alpha)} \frac{\mathrm{d}}{\mathrm{d}t}\left[\int_a^t \frac{f(\tau)}{(t-\tau)^{\alpha}}\mathrm{d}\tau\right] \tag{2}$$

where,

$$\Gamma(x) = \int_t^a y^{\alpha-1}e^{-y}dy \tag{3}$$

$\Gamma(.)$ is the Gamma function, a, t and α are real numbers, and alpha verifies $0 < \alpha < 1$. In we assume that $a = 0$ without loss of generality. Also we use $_aD_t^{\alpha} = D^{\alpha}$.

Numerical Approximation Method

The specialized literature proposes different ways and techniques for approaching non-integer order operators. They result in various algorithms for the numerical simulation of these systems. The most common approach used in the fractional order chaotic systems literature is a modified version of the Adams-Bashforth-Moulton method based on predictor-correctors (Diethelm et al 2002). However, we will use in this work a simpler approach consist on the fractional order operator discretization following the Grünwald-Letnikov definition (Pétras 2011).

The Grünwald-Letnikov fractional order derivative definition is expressed as (Diethelm et al., 2002; Pétras, 2011):

$$
{}^{GL}_{t_0}D^\alpha_t f(t) = \lim_{n \to 0} \frac{1}{h^n} \times \left(\sum_{j=0}^{\left[\frac{t-\alpha}{h}\right]} (-1)^j \binom{\alpha}{j} f(t-jh) \right)
\tag{4}
$$

where $\left[\frac{t-\alpha}{h}\right]$ indicates the integer part and $(-1)^j \binom{\alpha}{j}$ are binomial coefficients $c_j^{(\alpha)}$ $(j = 0, 1, ...)$.

The calculation of these coefficients is done by the formula of following recurrence:

$$
c_0^{(\alpha)} = 1, \quad c_j^{(\alpha)} = (1 - \frac{1+\alpha}{j})c_{j-1}^{(\alpha)}
$$

now, if we consider the fractional order differential equation: ${}^{GL}_{t_0}D^\mu_t y(t) = f(y(t), t)$ then, the numerical solution is expressed as:

$$
y(t_k) = f(y(t_k), t_k)h^\mu - \sum_{j=v}^{k} c_j^{(\mu)} y(t_{k-j})
\tag{5}
$$

This approximation of the fractional derivative within the meaning of Grünwald-Letnikov is on the one hand equivalent to the definition of Riemman-Liouville for a broad class of functions (Caponetto et al., 2010), on the other hand, it is well adapted to the definition of Caputo (Adams method) because it requires only the initial conditions and has a physical direction clearly.

BRIEF DESCRIPTION OF INTERVAL TYPE-2 FUZZY SYSTEMS

Simple Fuzzy Logic Systems

The uncertain fractional order chaotic system may be directly addressed by fuzzy logic systems by using the linguistic models (e.g., small, medium and large) (Khettab et al., 2015; Takagi & Sugeno, 1985).

The Takagi-Sugeno (T-S) configuration of the system (Takagi & Sugeno, 1985) includes a fuzzy rule base, represented by a number of fuzzy IFTHEN rules in the form:

$$R^{(l)} : \text{IF } x_1 \text{ is } F_1^l, \text{ and } ..., x_n \text{ is } F_n^l \text{ THEN}$$

$$y_l = \alpha_0^l + \alpha_1^l x_1 + ... + \alpha_n^l x_n = \theta_l^T [1 \ x^T]^T \tag{6}$$

where $(F_1^l, ..., F_i^l, ..., F_n^l)$ are input fuzzy sets and $\theta_l^T = [\alpha_0^l + \alpha_1^l + ... + \alpha_n^l]$ represents the adjustable factors of the consequence part. y_l is a crisp value, and a fuzzy inference engine to combine the fuzzy IF-THEN rules in the fuzzy rule base into a mapping from an input linguistic vector $\mathbf{x} = [x_1, x_2, ..., x_n]^T \in \Re^n$ to an output variable $y \in \Re$. The output of the fuzzy logic systems with central average defuzzifier, product inference and singleton fuzzifier can be expressed as

$$y(\mathbf{x}) = \frac{\sum_{l=1}^M v^l y_l}{\sum_{l=1}^M v^l} = \frac{\sum_{l=1}^M v^l \theta_l^T [1 \ x^T]^T}{\sum_{l=1}^M v^l} \tag{7}$$

where M is the number of rules, $v^l = \prod_{i=1}^n \mu_{F_i^l(x_i)}$ is the true value of the lth implication and $\mu_{F_i^l(x_i)}$ is the membership function value of the x_i (Lin et al., 2011). Equation (7) can be rewritten as

$$y(\mathbf{x}) = \theta_l^T \xi(\mathbf{x}) \tag{8}$$

where $\theta_l^T = [\theta_1^T, \theta_2^T, ..., \theta_M^T]$ is the parameter vector and $\xi^l(\mathbf{x}) = [\xi^1(x), \xi^2(x), ... , \xi^M(x)]$ a fuzzy basis function vector defined as:

$$\xi^l(\mathbf{x}) = \frac{v^l [1 \ x^T]}{\sum_{l=1}^M v^l}$$

The output (7) is pumped out by the mean of the common defuzzification strategy.

The above fuzzy logic system is able to provide a uniform approximation of any well-defined non-linear function over a compact set U_c to any degree of accuracy, as proved in the universal approximation theorem (Wang & Mendel, 1992; Khettab et al., 2017).

Interval Type-2 Fuzzy Logic

A brief overview of the basic concepts of Interval type-2 fuzzy systems is presented in the following (Karnik et al., 1999). If we consider a type-1 membership function, as in Figure 1, then a type-2 mem-

Figure 1. Example of a type-1 membership function

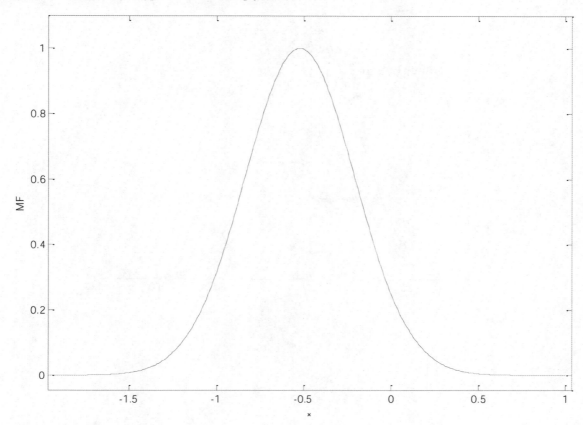

bership function can be produced. In this case, for a specific value x' the membership function (u'), takes on different values, which are not all weighted the same, so we can assign membership grades to all of those points.

A type-2 fuzzy set in a universal set X is denoted as $\tilde{A}$ and can be characterized in the following form:

$$\tilde{A} = \int_{x \in X} \mu_{\tilde{A}}(x, v) / x \ , \ \forall v \in J_x \subseteq [0, 1]$$

$$\mu_{\tilde{A}}(x) = \int_{v \in J_x} f_x(v) / v,$$

in which $0 \leq \mu_{\tilde{A}}(x) \leq 1$

The 2-D interval type-2 Gaussian membership function with uncertain mean $m \in [m_1, \ m_2]$ and a fixed deviation σ is shown in Figure 2.

Figure 2. Interval type-2 membership function

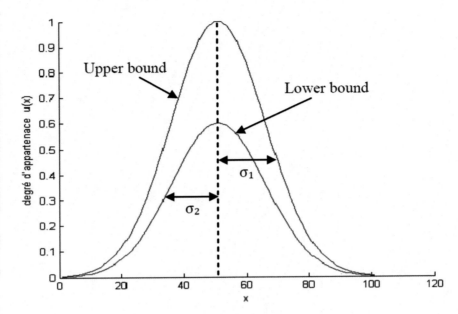

$$\mu_{\tilde{A}}\left(\mathrm{x}\right) = \exp\left[-\frac{1}{2}\left(\frac{\mathrm{x - m}}{\sigma}\right)^2\right]$$

A fuzzy logic system (FLS) described using at least one type-2 fuzzy set is called a type-2 FLS. Type-1 FLSs are unable to directly handle rule uncertainties, because they use type-1 fuzzy sets that are certain. On the other hand, type-2 FLSs, are useful in circumstances where it is difficult to determine an exact numeric membership function, and there are measurement uncertainties (Lin et al 2011).

A type-2 FLS is characterized by IF–THEN rules, where their antecedent or consequent sets are now of type-2. Type-2 FLSs, can be used when the circumstances are too uncertain to determine exact membership grades such as when the training data is affected by noise. Similarly, to the type-1 FLS, a type-2 FLS includes a fuzzifier, a rule base, fuzzy inference engine, and an output processor, as we can see in Figure 3 for a Mamdani-model.

An IT2FS is described by its Lower $\underline{\mu}_{\tilde{A}}\left(x\right)$ and Upper $\overline{\mu}_{\tilde{A}}\left(x\right)$ membership functions. For an IT2FS, the footprint of uncertainty (FOU) is described in terms of lower and upper MFs as:

$$FOU\left(\tilde{A}\right) = \bigcup_{x \in X}\left[\underline{\mu}_{\tilde{A}}\left(x\right), \ \overline{\mu}_{\tilde{A}}\left(x\right)\right]$$

The type-reducer generates a type-1 fuzzy set output, which is then converted in a numeric output through running the defuzzifier. This type-1 fuzzy set is also an interval set, for the case of our FLS we used center of sets type reduction, $y\left(X\right)$ which is expressed as (Castillo and Melin 2012):

Figure 3. Type-2 fuzzy logic system

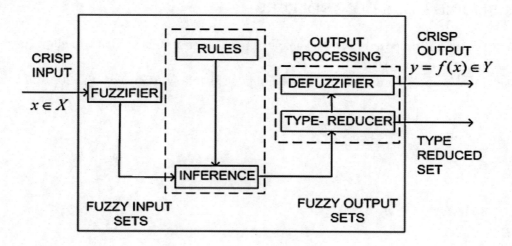

$$y\left(X\right) = \left[y_l, y_r\right]$$

where $y_l = \dfrac{\sum_{i=1}^{M} f_l^i y_l^i}{\sum_{i=1}^{M} f_l^i}$ and $y_r = \dfrac{\sum_{i=1}^{M} f_r^i y_r^i}{\sum_{i=1}^{M} f_r^i}$

The values of y_l and y_r define the output interval of the type-2 fuzzy system, which can be used to verify if training or testing data are contained in the output of the fuzzy system. This measure of covering the data is considered as one of the design criteria in finding an optimal interval type-2 fuzzy system. The other optimization criteria, is that the length of this output interval should be as small as possible.

From the type-reducer, we obtain an interval set $y\left(X\right)$, to defuzzify it we use the average of y_l and y_r, so the defuzzified output of an interval singleton type-2 FLS is (Castillo and Melin 2012):

$$y\left(X\right) = \left(\frac{1}{2}\right)\left(y_l + y_r\right)$$

where y_l .and y_r .are the left most and right most points of the Interval type-1 set:

$$y_l = \sum_{i=1}^{M} y_l^i \xi_l^i = \underline{\xi}_l^T \underline{\theta}_l \text{ and } y_r = \sum_{i=1}^{M} y_r^i \xi_r^i = \underline{\xi}_r^T \underline{\theta}_r$$

$$y\left(X\right) = \left(y_l + y_r\right)/2 = \underline{\xi}^T \underline{\theta}.$$

where $\underline{\xi}^T = \left(1/2\right)\left[\underline{\xi}_r^T \ \ \underline{\xi}_l^T\right]$ and $\underline{\theta} = \left[\underline{\theta}_r \ \ \underline{\theta}_l\right]$.

PROBLEMATIC: FRACTIONAL ADAPTIVE INTERVAL TYPE-2 FUZZY SLIDING MODE CONTROLLERS

Let us now present the proposed fractional adaptive fuzzy control strategy that will allow the control of nonlinear fractional order systems.

Consider the fractional order nonlinear system given as follows (Khettab et al 2017d; Lin and Kuo 2011),

$$
\begin{cases}
x_1^{(q_1)} = x_2 \\
\vdots \\
x_{n-1}^{(q_{n-1})} = x_n \\
\quad x_n^{(q_n)} = f(\mathbf{x}, t) + g(\mathbf{x}, t)u + d(t) \\
y = x_1
\end{cases}
\tag{9}
$$

This system is called commensurate if $q_1 = q_2 = ... = q_n = q$ and can be rewritten as,

$$
x^{(nq)} = f(\mathbf{x}, t) + g(\mathbf{x}, t)u + d(t)
$$
$$
y = x_1
\tag{10}
$$

where $\mathbf{x} = [x_1, x_2, ..., x_n]^T = [x, x^{(q)}, ..., x^{((n-1)q)}]^T$. $f(\mathbf{x}, t)$ and $g(\mathbf{x}, t)$ are unknown but bounded non-linear functions, $d(t)$ is the external bounded disturbance, assuming that the upper bound of the disturbance $d(t)$ is D, that is $|d(t)| \leq D$, and $u(t)$ is the control input.

The nonlinear system (10) is assumed to be controllable and the input gain $g(\mathbf{x}, t) \neq 0$ has to be non-zero. Consequently, without loss of generality, we assume that $g(\mathbf{x}, t) > 0$.

The control objective is to force the system output $\mathbf{y}$ to follow a given bounded reference signal $\mathbf{y}_d$, under the constraint that all signals involved must be bounded.

Let us now define the reference signal vector $\mathbf{y}_d$ and the tracking error vector $\mathbf{e}$ as follows:

$$
\mathbf{y}_d = \left[y_d, y_d^{(q)}, ..., y_d^{((n-1)q)} \right]^T \in \Re^n
\tag{11}
$$

$$
\mathbf{e} = \mathbf{y}_d - \mathbf{y} = \left[e, e^{(q)}, ..., e^{((n-1)q)} \right]^T \in \Re^n,
$$
$$
\mathbf{e}^{(iq)} = \mathbf{y}_d^{(iq)} - \mathbf{y}^{(iq)}
\tag{12}
$$

where $0 < q < 1$. Let $\mathbf{k} = [k_1, k_2, ..., k_n]^T \in \Re^n$ to be chosen in a way that $h(p) = \sum_{i=1}^{n} k_i p^{(i-1)q}$, $k_n = 1$ is Hurwitz polynomial.

The sliding surface is defined as:

$$s(\mathbf{x}, t) = -(\mathbf{k}e)$$
$$= -(k_1 e + k_2 e^{(q)} + \dots + k_{n-1} e^{((n-2)q)}$$
$$+ e^{((n-1)q)}) \tag{13}$$

when $e(0) = 0$, the tracking problem $x = y_d$ implies that the sliding surface $s(\mathbf{e}) = 0$, $\forall t \geq 0$. Correspondingly, the sliding mode control will be designed in two phases:

1. The reaching phase when $s(\mathbf{x}, t) \neq 0$, and
2. The sliding phase by $s(\mathbf{x}, t) = 0$, for initial error $e(0) = 0$.

With the following sliding condition:

$$s(x, t)\dot{s}(x, t) \leq -\eta \left| s(x, t) \right|, \quad \eta > 0 \tag{14}$$

which must be satisfied.

In absence of uncertainty and external disturbance, the corresponding equivalent control force $u_{eq}(t)$, can be obtained by $\dot{s}(\mathbf{x}, t) = 0$. This later classic derivative can be decomposed into a fractional type,

$$\dot{s}(\mathbf{x}, t) = D^{(1-q)}(D^q(s(\mathbf{x}, t))) = 0$$
$$\text{then} \quad D^q(s(\mathbf{x}, t)) = 0 \tag{15}$$

If the functions $f(\mathbf{x}, t)$ and $g(\mathbf{x}, t)$ are known and the system is free of external disturbance i.e., $d(t) = 0$. The control signal in the following equation drives the dynamic to reach to the sliding surface:

$$s^{(q)} = -\left(\sum_{i=1}^{n-1} k_i e^{(iq)} + e^{(nq)} \right)$$
$$= -\left(\sum_{i=1}^{n-1} k_i e^{(iq)} + y_d^{(nq)} - y^{(nq)} \right)$$
$$= -\left(\sum_{i=1}^{n-1} k_i e^{(iq)} - f(x, t) - g(\mathbf{x}, t)u_{eq} \right) - \mathbf{y}_d^{(nq)} \tag{16}$$
$$= -\sum_{i=1}^{n-1} k_i e^{(iq)} + f(\mathbf{x}, t) + g(\mathbf{x}, t)u_{eq} - \mathbf{y}_d^{(nq)}$$
$$= 0$$

Therefore, the equivalent control law is given by:

$$u_{eq} = \frac{1}{g(\mathbf{x},t)} \left(\sum_{i=1}^{n-1} k_i e^{(iq)} - f(\mathbf{x},t) + \mathbf{y}_d^{(nq)} \right) \tag{17}$$

Substituting (17) into (10), we have

$$e^{(nq)} + k_n e^{(n-1)q} + \ldots + k_1 e = 0 \tag{18}$$

which is the main objective of control $\lim_{t \to \infty} e(t) = 0$.

In the reaching phase we get $s(\mathbf{x},t) \neq 0$, and a switching-type control u_{sw} must be added in order satisfy the sufficient condition (14) which implies that the global control will be written as:

$$u_i = u_{eq} - u_{sw} \tag{19}$$

with

$$u_{sw} = \frac{1}{g(\mathbf{x},t)} \Big(\psi_p \, \text{sgn}(s) \Big) \tag{20}$$

where $\psi_p \geq \eta > 0$ and,

$$\text{sgn}(s) = \begin{cases} 1 & \text{for} \quad s > 0 \\ 0 & \text{for} \quad s = 0 \\ -1 & \text{for} \quad s < 0 \end{cases} \tag{21}$$

Therefore the global sliding mode control law is given by:

$$u^* = \frac{1}{g(\mathbf{x},t)} \left(\sum_{i=1}^{n-1} k_i e^{(iq)} - f(\mathbf{x},t) + y_d^{(nq)} - \psi_p \, \text{sgn}(s) \right) \tag{22}$$

We can show by taking a Lyapunov function candidate defined as

$$V = \frac{1}{2} s^2(\mathbf{e}) \tag{23}$$

And differentiating (23) with respect to time to the fractional order q, $V^{(q)}(t)$ along the system trajectory, we obtain

$$
\begin{aligned}
V^{(q)} = ss^{(q)} &= s\left(\sum_{i=1}^{n-1} k_i e^{(iq)} + e^{(nq)}\right) \\
&= -s\left(\sum_{i=1}^{n-1} k_i e^{(iq)} - y_d^{(nq)} + y^{(nq)}\right) \\
&= -s\left(\sum_{i=1}^{n-1} k_i e^{(iq)} + f(\mathbf{x},t) + g(\mathbf{x},t)u_{eq} - y_d^{(nq)}\right) \\
&\leq -\eta\left|s(\mathbf{x},t)\right|
\end{aligned}
\tag{24}
$$

Hence, the sliding mode control u^* guarantees the sliding condition of (14).

However, as mentioned in (Ho et al., 2009), the functions f and g are usually unknown in practice and it is difficult to apply the control law (22) for an unknown nonlinear plant. Moreover, the chattering problem appears when adding the switching control term u_{sw}.

To deal with these problems, we consider the adaptive sliding mode control scheme using a fuzzy logic system and the fractional order PI^λ control law to avoid chattering problem.

The input and output of the continuous time fractional order PI^λ controller, where $\lambda = q$, are in the form:

$$
u_{PI} = p\left(\mathbf{s}\big|\theta_p\right) = \theta_{p_1} z_1 + \theta_{p_2} z_2
\tag{25}
$$

where $z_1 = s$, $z_2 = s^{(q)}$, θ_{p_1} and θ_{p_2} are control gains to be designed. Equation (25) can be rewritten as:

$$
u_{PI} = p\left(\mathbf{s}\big|\theta_p\right) = \frac{p_r + p_l}{2} = \frac{1}{2}\left(\xi_{pr}^T \theta_{pr} + \xi_{pl}^T \theta_{pl}\right) = \xi_p^T(\mathbf{s})\theta_p
\tag{26}
$$

where $\xi^T(\mathbf{s}) = [s, s^{(q)}] \in \Re^2$ and $\theta_p = [\theta_{p1}, \theta_{p2}]^T \in \Re^2$ is an adjustable parameter vector.

The resulting control law, which includes a fuzzy system to approximate the unknown functions $f(\mathbf{x})$ and $g(\mathbf{x})$ and a fractional adaptive PI^q controller that attenuates the chattering and improve performance, is as follows:

$$
u_i = \frac{1}{g(\mathbf{x}|\theta_g)}\left(\sum_{i=1}^{n-1} k_i e^{(iq)} - f(\mathbf{x}|\theta_f) + y_d^{(nq)} - u_{PI}\right)
\tag{27}
$$

The switching control u_{sw} is replaced by the action of the fractional adaptive PI^q controller to avoid the problem of chattering when the state is within a limited layer $\left|s(x,t)\right| < \phi$; the control action is maintained in the saturated state when the value is outside the boundary layer.

Hence, we set $\left|p(s|\theta_p)\right| = D + \psi_p + \omega_{\max}$ when $s(\mathbf{x}, t)$ is outside of the boundary layer, i.e., $\left|s(x,t)\right| \geq \phi$, where ϕ is the thickness of the boundary layer.

Note that the control law (22) is realizable only while $f(\mathbf{x}, t)$ and $g(\mathbf{x}, t)$ are well known.

However, $f(\mathbf{x}, t)$ and $g(\mathbf{x}, t)$ are unknown and external disturbance $d(t) \neq 0$, the ideal control effort (22) cannot be implemented. We replace $f(\mathbf{x}, t)$, $g(\mathbf{x}, t)$ and u_{PI} by the fuzzy logic system $f(\mathbf{x}|\theta_f)$, $g(\mathbf{x}|\theta_g)$ and $p(\mathbf{s}|\theta_p)$ in a specified form as (9), i.e.,

$$f(x|\theta_f) = \frac{f_r + f_l}{2} = \frac{1}{2}\left(\xi_{fr}^T \theta_{fr} + \xi_{fl}^T \theta_{fl}\right) = \xi^T(\mathbf{x})\theta_f,$$

$$g(x|\theta_g) = \frac{g_r + g_l}{2} = \frac{1}{2}\left(\xi_{gr}^T \theta_{gr} + \xi_{gl}^T \theta_{gl}\right) = \xi^T(\mathbf{x})\theta_g, \tag{28}$$

$$p(s|\theta_p) = \frac{p_r + p_l}{2} = \frac{1}{2}\left(\xi_{pr}^T \theta_{pr} + \xi_{pl}^T \theta_{pl}\right) = \xi^T(\mathbf{s})\theta_p$$

where $\theta_f = [\theta_{fr} \ \theta_{fl}]$, $\theta_g = [\theta_{gr} \ \theta_{gl}]$ and $\theta_p = [\theta_{pr} \ \theta_{pl}]$

Here the fuzzy basis function $\xi_f(\mathbf{x}) = \xi_g(\mathbf{x}) = \frac{1}{2}[\xi_r(\mathbf{x}) \quad \xi_l(\mathbf{x})]$, $\xi_p(\mathbf{s}) = \frac{1}{2}[\xi_r(\mathbf{s}) \quad \xi_l(\mathbf{s})]$ depends on the type-2 fuzzy membership functions and is supposed to be fixed, while θ_f, θ_g and θ_p are adjusted by adaptive laws based on a Lyapunov stability criterion (Lin et al., 2011; Duarte-Mermoud et al., 2015). Therefore, the resulting control effort (27) can be obtained as:

$$u_i = \frac{1}{\frac{1}{2}\left(\xi_{gr}^T \theta_{gr} + \xi_{gl}^T \theta_{gl}\right)}\left(\sum_{i=1}^{n-1} k_i e^{(iq)} - \frac{1}{2}\left(\xi_{fr}^T \theta_{fr} + \xi_{fl}^T \theta_{fl}\right) + y_d^{(nq)} - \frac{1}{2}\left(\xi_{pr}^T \theta_{pr} + \xi_{pl}^T \theta_{pl}\right)\right) \tag{29}$$

The optimal parameter estimations θ_f^*, θ_g^* and θ_g^* are defined as

$$\theta_f^* = [\theta_{fr}^* \ \theta_{fl}^*] = \arg\min_{\theta_f \in \Omega_f}\left[\sup_{x \in \Omega_x}\left|f(x|\theta_f) - f(x,t)\right|\right]$$

$$\theta_g^* = [\theta_{gr}^* \ \theta_{gl}^*] = \arg\min_{\theta_g \in \Omega_g}\left[\sup_{x \in \Omega_x}\left|g(x|\theta_g) - g(x,t)\right|\right]$$

$$\theta_p^* = [\theta_{gr}^* \ \theta_{gl}^*] = \arg\min_{\theta_p \in \Omega_p}\left[\sup_{x \in \Omega_x}\left|p(s|\theta_p) - u_{sw}\right|\right]$$

where $\Omega_f, \Omega_g, \Omega_p$ and Ω_x are constraint sets of suitable bounds on $\theta_f, \theta_g, \theta_p$ and x respectively and they are defined as $\Omega_f = \left\{\theta_f \middle| \left|\theta_f\right| \leq M_f\right\}$, $\Omega_g = \left\{\theta_g \middle| \left|\theta_g\right| \leq M_g\right\}$, $\Omega_p = \left\{\theta_p \middle| \left|\theta_p\right| \leq M_p\right\}$ and

$\Omega_x = \left\{ x \middle| \; |x| \leq M_x \right\}$ where M_f, M_g, M_p and M_x are positive constants. Assuming that the fuzzy parameters θ_f, θ_g and θ_p never reach the boundaries.

Let us define the minimum approximation error,

$$
\begin{aligned}
\omega = & \left[f(x,t) - f(x|\theta_f^*) \right] \\
& + \left[g(x,t) - g(x|\theta_g^*) \right] u_i
\end{aligned}
\tag{30}
$$

and define the errors: $\tilde{\theta}_f = \theta_f - \theta_f^*$, $\tilde{\theta}_g = \theta_g - \theta_g^*$ and $\tilde{\theta}_p = \theta_p - \theta_p^*$. Then, the equation of the sliding surface (16) can be rewritten as

$$
\begin{aligned}
s^{(q)} = & \; \omega + \left[f(\mathbf{x}|\theta_f^*) - f(\mathbf{x}|\theta_f) \right] + \left[g(\mathbf{x}|\theta_g^*) - g(\mathbf{x}|\theta_g) \right] u_i \\
& - p(\mathbf{s}|\theta_p) + p(\mathbf{s}|\theta_p^*) - p(\mathbf{s}|\theta_p^*) + d(t) \\
= & \; \omega - \left[\tilde{\theta}_{pr}^T \quad \tilde{\theta}_{pl}^T \right] \xi(\mathbf{s}) - \left[\tilde{\theta}_{fr}^T \quad \tilde{\theta}_{fl}^T \right] \xi(\mathbf{x}) - \left[\tilde{\theta}_{gr}^T \quad \tilde{\theta}_{gl}^T \right] \xi(\mathbf{x}) u_i - p(\mathbf{s}|\theta_p^*) + d(t)
\end{aligned}
\tag{31}
$$

STABILITY ANALYSIS

The following theorem establishes the asymptotic stability of the proposed control system.

Theorem 1

Consider the fractional order SISO nonlinear system (10) with the control input (29), if the fuzzy-based adaptive laws are chosen as:

$$
\begin{aligned}
\left[\theta_{fr}^{(q)} \quad \theta_{fl}^{(q)} \right] &= \left[r_1 s \xi_{fr}(\mathbf{x}) \quad\quad r_2 s \xi_{fl}(\mathbf{x}) \right] \\
\left[\theta_{gr}^{(q)} \quad \theta_{gl}^{(q)} \right] &= \left[r_3 s \xi_{gr}(\mathbf{x}) u_i \quad r_4 s \xi_{gl}(\mathbf{x}) u_i \right] \\
\left[\theta_{pr}^{(q)} \quad \theta_{pl}^{(q)} \right] &= \left[r_5 s \xi_{pr}(\mathbf{s}) \quad\quad r_6 s \xi_{pl}(\mathbf{s}) \right]
\end{aligned}
\tag{32}
$$

where $\theta_f^{(q)} = [\theta_{fr}^{(q)} \; \theta_{fl}^{(q)}]$, $\theta_g^{(q)} = [\theta_{gr}^{(q)} \; \theta_{gl}^{(q)}]$ and $\theta_p^{(q)} = [\theta_{pr}^{(q)} \; \theta_{pl}^{(q)}]$ and

$$
\xi_f^T(\mathbf{x}) = \xi_g^T(\mathbf{x}) = \left(\frac{1}{2} \right) \left[\xi_r^T(\mathbf{x}) \quad \xi_l^T(\mathbf{x}) \right], \quad \xi_p^T(\mathbf{s}) = \left(\frac{1}{2} \right) \left[\xi_{pr}^T(\mathbf{s}) \quad \xi_{pl}^T(\mathbf{s}) \right]
$$

where r_1, r_2 and r_3 are positive constants, then, the overall adaptation scheme ensures the overall stability of the closed-loop system resulting in the sense that the tracking error converges to zero and all the variables of the closed-loop system are bounded.

Proof

Let us choose the Lyapunov function candidate as:

$$V = \frac{1}{2}s^2 + \frac{1}{2r_1}\tilde{\theta}_{fr}^T\tilde{\theta}_{fr} + \frac{1}{2r_2}\tilde{\theta}_{fl}^T\tilde{\theta}_{fl} + \frac{1}{2r_3}\tilde{\theta}_{gr}^T\tilde{\theta}_{gr} + \frac{1}{2r_4}\tilde{\theta}_{gl}^T\tilde{\theta}_{gl} + \frac{1}{2r_5}\tilde{\theta}_{pr}^T\tilde{\theta}_{pr} + \frac{1}{2r_6}\tilde{\theta}_{pl}^T\tilde{\theta}_{pl} \tag{33}$$

The derivative of (33) with respect to time using the Caputo derivative Lemma (Khettab et al., 2017) (Aguila-Camacho et al., 2014; Li and Sun, 2015), gives

$$V^{(q)} \leq ss^{(q)} + \frac{1}{r_1}\tilde{\theta}_{fr}^T\tilde{\theta}_{fr}^{(q)} + \frac{1}{r_2}\tilde{\theta}_{fl}^T\tilde{\theta}_{fl}^{(q)} + \frac{1}{r_3}\tilde{\theta}_{gr}^T\tilde{\theta}_{gr}^{(q)} + \frac{1}{r_4}\tilde{\theta}_{gl}^T\tilde{\theta}_{gl}^{(q)} + \frac{1}{r_5}\tilde{\theta}_{pr}^T\tilde{\theta}_{pr}^{(q)} + \frac{1}{r_6}\tilde{\theta}_{pl}^T\tilde{\theta}_{pl}^{(q)} \tag{34}$$

$$V^{(q)} \leq s\left(\omega - \begin{bmatrix} \tilde{\theta}_{pr}^T & \tilde{\theta}_{pl}^T \end{bmatrix}\xi(\mathbf{s}) - \begin{bmatrix} \tilde{\theta}_{fr}^T & \tilde{\theta}_{fl}^T \end{bmatrix}\xi(\mathbf{x}) - \begin{bmatrix} \tilde{\theta}_{gr}^T & \tilde{\theta}_{gl}^T \end{bmatrix}\xi(\mathbf{x})u_i - p(\mathbf{s}|\theta_p^*) + d(t)\right)$$
$$+ \frac{1}{r_1}\tilde{\theta}_{fr}^T\tilde{\theta}_{fr}^{(q)} + \frac{1}{r_2}\tilde{\theta}_{fl}^T\tilde{\theta}_{fl}^{(q)} + \frac{1}{r_3}\tilde{\theta}_{gr}^T\tilde{\theta}_{gr}^{(q)} + \frac{1}{r_4}\tilde{\theta}_{gl}^T\tilde{\theta}_{gl}^{(q)} + \frac{1}{r_5}\tilde{\theta}_{pr}^T\tilde{\theta}_{pr}^{(q)} + \frac{1}{r_6}\tilde{\theta}_{pl}^T\tilde{\theta}_{pl}^{(q)} \tag{35}$$

$$\begin{aligned} V^{(q)} \leq & \ s\omega - s\tilde{\theta}_{pr}^T\xi(\mathbf{s}) - s\tilde{\theta}_{pl}^T\xi(\mathbf{s}) - s\tilde{\theta}_{fr}^T\xi(\mathbf{x}) - s\tilde{\theta}_{fl}^T\xi(\mathbf{x}) \\ & - s\tilde{\theta}_{gr}^T\xi(\mathbf{x})u_i - s\tilde{\theta}_{gl}^T\xi(\mathbf{x})u_i - sp(\mathbf{s}|\theta_p^*) + sd(t) \\ & + \frac{1}{r_1}\tilde{\theta}_{fr}^T\tilde{\theta}_{fr}^{(q)} + \frac{1}{r_2}\tilde{\theta}_{fl}^T\tilde{\theta}_{fl}^{(q)} + \frac{1}{r_3}\tilde{\theta}_{gr}^T\tilde{\theta}_{gr}^{(q)} + \frac{1}{r_4}\tilde{\theta}_{gl}^T\tilde{\theta}_{gl}^{(q)} + \frac{1}{r_5}\tilde{\theta}_{pr}^T\tilde{\theta}_{pr}^{(q)} + \frac{1}{r_6}\tilde{\theta}_{pl}^T\tilde{\theta}_{pl}^{(q)} \\ \leq & \ \frac{1}{r_1}\tilde{\theta}_{fr}^T\left(\tilde{\theta}_{fr}^{(q)} - r_1 s\xi(\mathbf{x})\right) + \frac{1}{r_2}\tilde{\theta}_{fl}^T\left(\tilde{\theta}_{fl}^{(q)} - r_2 s\xi(\mathbf{x})\right) \\ & + \frac{1}{r_3}\tilde{\theta}_{gr}^T\left(\tilde{\theta}_{gr}^{(q)} - r_3 s\xi(\mathbf{x})u_i\right) + \frac{1}{r_4}\tilde{\theta}_{gl}^T\left(\tilde{\theta}_{gl}^{(q)} - r_4 s\xi(\mathbf{x})u_i\right) \\ & + \frac{1}{r_5}\tilde{\theta}_{pr}^T\left(\tilde{\theta}_{pr}^{(q)} - r_5 s\xi(\mathbf{s})\right) + \frac{1}{r_6}\tilde{\theta}_{pl}^T\left(\tilde{\theta}_{pl}^{(q)} - r_6 s\xi(\mathbf{s})\right) \\ & - s(D + \eta)\operatorname{sgn}(s) + sd(t) + s\omega \end{aligned} \tag{36}$$

By considering the fractional robust compensator (27) and the fractional fuzzy adaptations laws (32), we get after a simple manipulation

$$V^{(q)} \leq s\omega - s\psi_p\operatorname{sgn}(s) = s\omega - |s|\psi_p \leq 0 \tag{37}$$

Since ω it the minimum approximation error, (37) is the best result that we can obtain. Therefore, all signals in the system are bounded. Obviously, if $e(0)$ is bounded, then $e(t)$ is also bounded for all t.

Since the reference signal $\mathbf{y}_d$ is bounded, then the system states $\mathbf{x}$ is bounded as well. Form (37) and (Duarte-Mermoud et al., 2015; Gallegos et al., 2015), we can conclude that all errors are Lyapunov uniformly stable.

SIMULATION RESULTS

Let us apply the proposed controller to synchronize two different fractional order chaotic gyro systems (Lin et al., 2011).

We will apply in this section our adaptive hybrid fuzzy sliding mode controller to force the fractional order chaotic gyro response system to track the trajectory of the fractional order chaotic gyro drive system.

Consider two fractional order chaotic gyro systems (Lin et al., 2011):

Drive System:

$$\begin{cases} D^q y_1 = y_2 \\ D^q y_2 = -\dfrac{100}{4} y_1 + \dfrac{1}{12} y_1^3 - 0.5 y_2 - 0.05 y_2^3 + \sin\left(y_1\right) + 35.5 \sin\left(2t\right) y_1 - \dfrac{1}{6} x_1^3 + d\left(t\right) \end{cases} \tag{38}$$

Response System:

$$\begin{cases} D^q y_1 = x_2 \\ D^q y_2 = -\dfrac{100}{4} x_1 + \dfrac{1}{12} x_1^3 - 0.7 x_2 - 0.08 x_2^3 + \sin\left(x_1\right) + 33 \sin\left(2t\right) x_1 - \dfrac{1}{6} x_1^3 \\ \qquad\quad -0.1 \sin\left(x_1\right) + d\left(t\right) + u\left(t\right) \end{cases} \tag{39}$$

where $d(t) = 0.1\sin(t)$ is an external disturbance. In this study we consider the case $q = 0.98$. The main objective is to control the trajectories of the response system to track the reference trajectories obtained from the drive system.

The initial conditions of the drive and response systems are chosen as:

$$\left(y_1(0) \quad y_2(0)\right)^T = \left(0.25 \quad 0.25\right)^T \text{ and } \left(x_1(0) \quad x_2(0)\right)^T = \left(0.2 \quad 0.2\right)^T \text{ respectively.}$$

The membership functions of x_i, for $f\left(\mathbf{x}|\theta_f\right)$ and $g\left(\mathbf{x}|\theta_g\right)$ are selected as (Lin et al., 2011):

$$\mu_{F_i^l}(x_i) = \exp\left[-0.5\left(\frac{x_i - \bar{x}}{0.8}\right)^2\right] \tag{40}$$

where $i = 1 \sim 2$ and $l = 1,\dots,7$, and $\bar{x}$ is selected from the interval $\left[-1, 2\right]$.

Figure 4. Interval Type-2 Fuzzy sets Gaussian with uncertain standard deviation σ

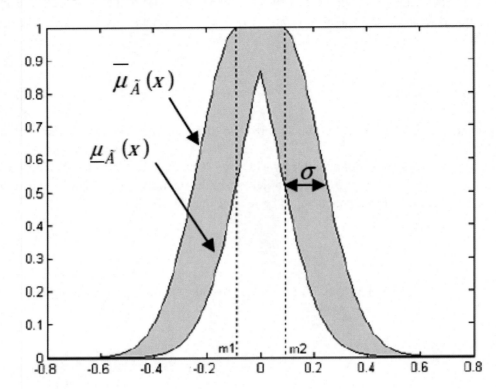

From (32) and (26) the control law (27) can be obtained as:

$$u_i = \frac{1}{\frac{1}{2}\left(\xi_{gr}^T \theta_{gr} + \xi_{gl}^T \theta_{gl}\right)}\left(\sum_{i=1}^{n-1} k_i e^{(iq)} - \frac{1}{2}\left(\xi_{fr}^T \theta_{fr} + \xi_{fl}^T \theta_{fl}\right) + y_d^{(nq)} - \frac{1}{2}\left(\xi_{pr}^T \theta_{pr} + \xi_{pl}^T \theta_{pl}\right)\right) \tag{41}$$

Specifying the simulation parameters as: $\mathbf{k} = \begin{bmatrix} 1 & 1 \end{bmatrix}$, $r_1 = r_2 = 150$, $r_3 = r_4 = 35$ and $r_5 = r_6 = 7$, the simulation time window $T = 35\,\sec$ and the sampling period $\Delta = 0.001\,\sec$; the simulations results are illustrated as follows.

Figure 5 shows the 3-D phase portrait of the drive and response systems before the application of the proposed control scheme. The synchronization performance is very bad at this initial stage.

Step 1: Fractional Sliding Mode Control

Figure 6 shows the synchronization trajectory after the integration of the proposed control law: we can notice a fast and perfect synchronization of the fractional chaotic systems (drive and response).

Figure 7 shows the trajectories of the states x_1, y_1 and x_2, y_2. The sliding surface is shown in Figure 8(a) and the control effort trajectory is given in Figure 8(b).

Figure 5. Phase portrait of master and slave systems (without control action)

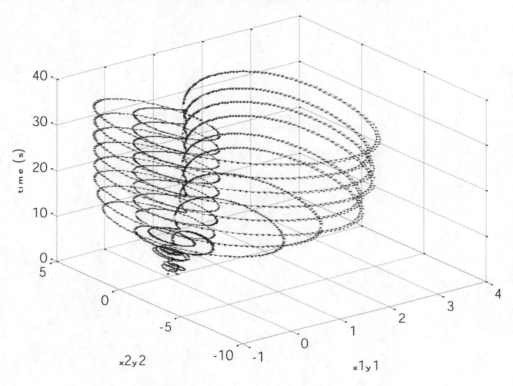

Figure 6. Synchronization performance of fractional chaotic gyro systems (with control action)

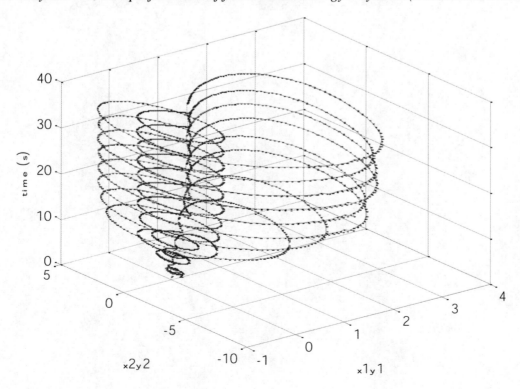

Figure 7. State trajectories for the IT2FSMC controller - (a): States x_1 and y_1, (b): States x_2 and y_2

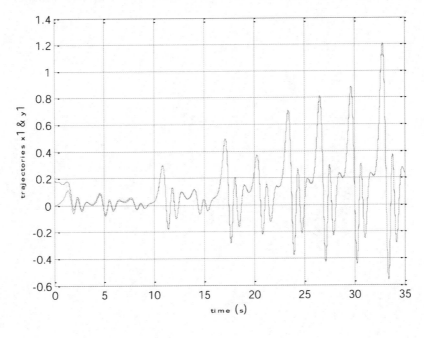

(a)

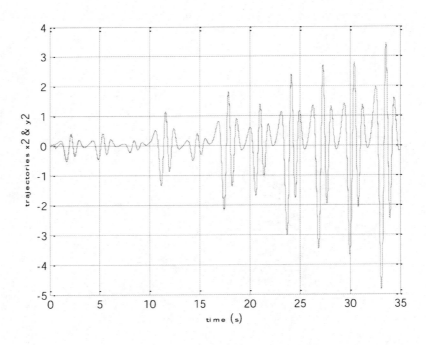

(b)

Figure 8. IT2FSMC controller - (a): Sliding surface $s(t)$, (b): Control signal $u(t)$

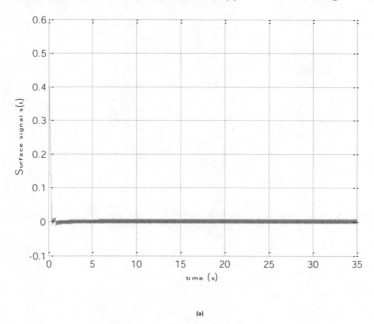

(a)

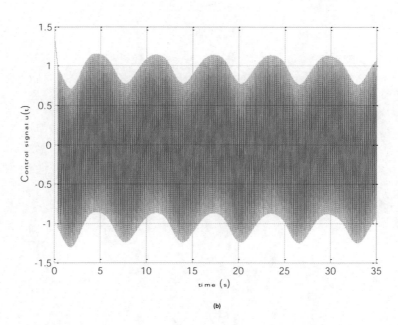

(b)

Figure 9 illustrates the fast convergence of response system output to that of the drive one. However, the chattering phenomena appears like a big inconvenient for this control strategy, as illustrated in the sliding surface and the control effort trajectories in Figure 8.

Figure 9. Errors signals - (a): Error $e_1(t)$, (b): Error $e_2(t)$

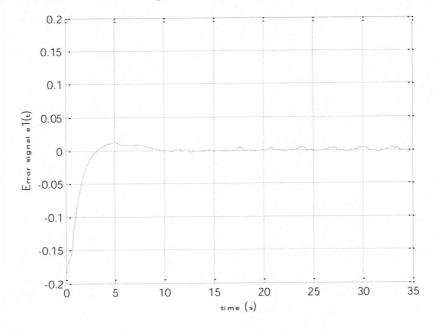

(a)

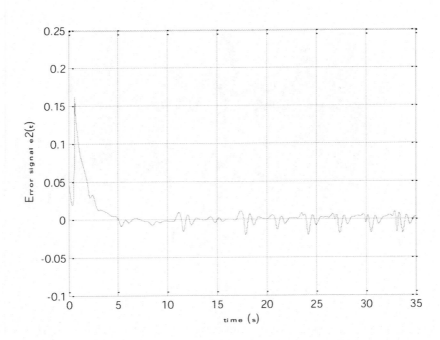

(b)

Step 2: Integration of FA-PI^λ-Regulator

Let us consider now the problem of eliminating the chattering that appeared in the above results, and introduce the complementary FA-PI^λ controller. The simulation results are given in Figure 10 for the synchronization performance of the gyro chaotic master and slave systems.

We see that the synchronization performance is enhanced even in presence of disturbance $d(t)$ and the chattering phenomena is eliminated in the sliding surface trajectory *s(t)* and the control signal $u(t)$ as illustrated from Figure 11.

CONCLUSION

In this chapter an improved fractional adaptive fuzzy sliding mode control strategy is proposed based on Interval type-2 fuzzy sets theory to deal with chaos synchronization of different uncertain fractional order gyro chaotic systems. A major contribution of this work is introducing an adaptive fractional PI^λ controller to eliminate the chattering phenomena in the fractional sliding mode controller. Thus, the

Figure 10. Synchronization performance for the IT2FSMC with the fractional order adaptive PI^λ controller

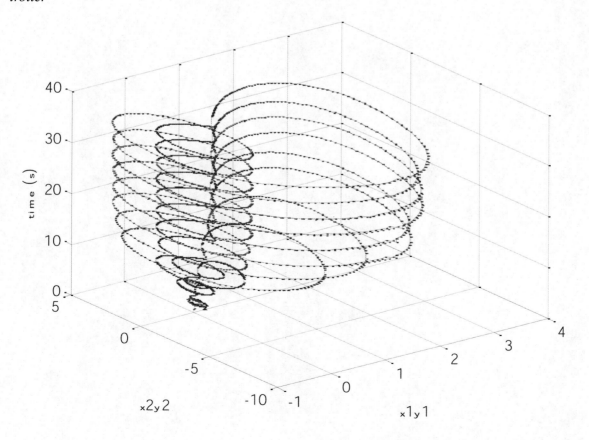

Figure 11. IT2FSMC with the fractional order adaptive PI^λ controller - (a): Sliding surface $s(t)$, (b): Control signal $u(t)$

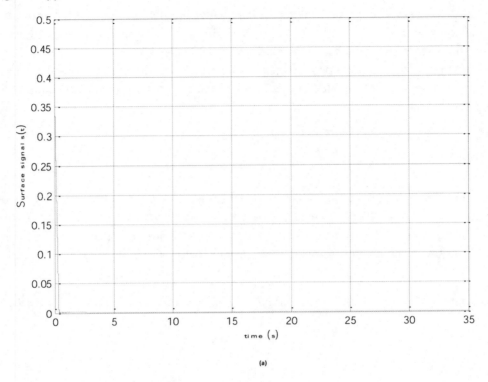

(a)

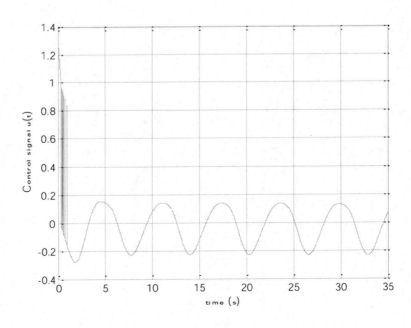

(b)

well-known disadvantage of sliding mode techniques from the control perspective, i.e. the discontinuity of the control signal necessary to achieve robustness, is no longer pertinent in this context.

The proposed indirect adaptive interval type-2 fuzzy PI^λ sliding mode controller uses interval type-2 fuzzy logic and adapts consequent parameters to approximate the unknown nonlinear system functions. The use of interval type-2 helps to minimize the added computational burden, and hence renders the overall system to be more practically applicable. To eliminate the chattering problem, a fractional PI^λ controller is designed where its parameters are also adjustable. Finally, since the backbone of the proposed approach is based on sliding mode control, Lyapunov analysis is applied to prove asymptotic stability of the proposed approach.

Based on the Lyapunov stability theorem, free parameters of the adaptive fuzzy controller can be tuned on line by the output feedback control law and adaptive laws to achieve fractional order chaotic systems synchronization.

Besides, the asymptotic stability of the overall control system is established and an illustrative simulation example, chaos synchronization of two fractional order gyro systems, is realized with the Grünwald-Letnikov numerical approximation approach to demonstrate the effectiveness of the proposed methodology.

Future research efforts will concern fractional order discrete adaptive control of uncertain or unknown fractional order systems. Another topic of interest is the design of new robust adaptive control laws for the class of fractional nonlinear systems based on various control configurations: discrete MRAS, the Strictly Positive realness property ...

ACKNOWLEDGMENT

The authors are grateful to Professor Samir Ladaci for his contribution and helpful comments on an early version of this Chapter.

REFERENCES

Aguila-Camacho, N., Duarte-Mermoud, M. A., & Delgado-Aguilera, E. (2016). Adaptive synchronization of fractional Lorenz systems using a re duce d number of control signals and parameters. *Chaos, Solitons, and Fractals*, *87*, 1–11. doi:10.1016/j.chaos.2016.02.038

Aguila-Camacho, N., Duarte-Mermoud, M. A., & Gallegos, J. A. (2014). Lyapunov functions for fractional order systems. *Communications in Nonlinear Science and Numerical Simulation*, *19*(9), 2951–2957. doi:10.1016/j.cnsns.2014.01.022

Arena, P., Caponetto, R., Fortuna, L., & Porto, D. (1997). Chaos in a fractional order Duffing system. *Proc. Int. Conf. of ECCTD*, 1259-1262.

Azar, A. T. (2012). Overview of Type-2 Fuzzy logic systems. *International Journal of Fuzzy System Applications*, *2*(4), 1–28. doi:10.4018/ijfsa.2012100101

Azar, A. T., & Vaidyanathan, S. (2015). *Chaos Modeling and Control Systems Design, Studies in Computational Intelligence* (Vol. 581). Springer-Verlag.

Boeing, G. (2016). *Visual Analysis of Nonlinear Dynamical Systems: Chaos, Fractals, Self-Similarity and the Limits of Prediction. Systems, 4(4).* doi:10.3390ystems4040037

Boulkroune, A., Bouzeriba, A., Bouden, T., & Azar, A. T. (2016). *Fuzzy Adaptive Synchronization of Uncertain Fractional-order Chaotic Systems. In Advances in Chaos Theory and Intelligent Control. Studies in Fuzziness and Soft Computing* (Vol. 337). Springer-Verlag.

Caponetto, R., Dongola, G., Fortina, L., & Petráš, I. (2010). *Fractional Order Systems: Modeling and control application.* World Scientific Publishing. doi:10.1142/7709

Castillo, O., & Melin, P. (2012). *Recent Advances in Interval Type-2 Fuzzy Systems.* Springer Briefs in Computational Intelligence; doi:10.1007/978-3-642-28956-9

Cazarez-Castro, N. R., Aguilar, L. T., & Castillo, O. (2012). Designing type-1 and type-2 fuzzy logic controllers via fuzzy Lyapunov synthesis for non-smooth mechanical systems. *Engineering Applications of Artificial Intelligence, 25*(5), 971–979. doi:10.1016/j.engappai.2012.03.003

Chen, Y., Wei, Y., Liang, S., & Wang, Y. (2016). Indirect model reference adaptive control for a class of fractional order systems. *Communications in Nonlinear Science and Numerical Simulation, 39,* 458–471. doi:10.1016/j.cnsns.2016.03.016

Diethelm, K., Ford, N. J., & Freed, A. D. (2002). A predictor-corrector approach for the numerical solution of fractional differential equations. *Nonlinear Dynamics, 29*(1/4), 3–22. doi:10.1023/A:1016592219341

Duarte, F. B. M., & Machado, J. A. T. (2002). Chaotic phenomena and fractional-order dynamics in the trajectory control of redundant manipulators. *Nonlinear Dynamics, 29*(1/4), 315–342. doi:10.1023/A:1016559314798

Duarte-Mermoud, M. A., Aguila-Camacho, N., Gallegos, J. A., & Castro-Linares, R. (2015). Using general quadratic Lyapunov functions to prove Lyapunov uniform stability for fractional order systems. *Communications in Nonlinear Science and Numerical Simulation, 22*(1-3), 650–659. doi:10.1016/j.cnsns.2014.10.008

Efe, M. O. (2008). Fractional Fuzzy Adaptive Sliding-Mode Control of a 2-DOF Direct-Drive Robot Arm. *IEEE Transactions on Systems, Man, and Cybernetics. Part B, Cybernetics, 38*(6), 1561–1570. doi:10.1109/TSMCB.2008.928227 PMID:19022726

Gallegos, J. A., Duarte-Mermoud, M. A., Aguila-Camacho, N., & Castro-Linares, R. (2015). On fractional extensions of Barbalat Lemma. *Systems & Control Letters, 84,* 7–12. doi:10.1016/j.sysconle.2015.07.004

Hartley, T. T., Lorenzo, C. F., & Qammer, H. K. (1995). Chaos in a fractional order Chuas system. *IEEE Transactions on Circuits and Systems I, 42*(8), 485–490. doi:10.1109/81.404062

Hilfer, R. (2001). *Applications of fractional calculus in physics.* World Scientific.

Ho, H. F., Wong, Y. K., & Rad, A. B. (2009). Adaptive fuzzy sliding mode control with chattering elimination for nonlinear SISO systems. *Simulation Modelling Practice and Theory, 17*(7), 1199–1210. doi:10.1016/j.simpat.2009.04.004

Hosseinnia, S. H., Ghaderi, R., Ranjbar, A., Abdous, F., & Momani, S. (2010). *Control of Chaos via Fractional-Order State Feedback Controller: New Trends in Nanotechnology and Fractional Calculus Applications.* Springer Verlag-Berlin. doi:10.1007/978-90-481-3293-5_46

Karnik, N. N., & Mendel, J. M. (1998). Type-2 fuzzy logic systems: type-reduction. *Proceedings of the IEEE International Conference on Systems, Man, and Cybernetics*, 2046-2051.

Karnik, N. N., Mendel, J. M., & Liang, Q. (1999). Type-2 fuzzy logic systems. *IEEE Transactions on Fuzzy Systems, 7*(6), 643–658. doi:10.1109/91.811231

Khettab, Ladaci, & Bensafia. (2017). Fuzzy adaptive control of fractional order chaotic systems with unknown control gain sign using a fractional order Nussbaum gain. IEEE/CAA Journal of Automatica Sinica, 4(3), 1-8.

Khettab, K., Bensafia, Y., & Ladaci, S. (2017). Robust Adaptive Interval Type-2 Fuzzy Synchronization for a Class of Fractional Order Chaotic Systems. In A. T. Azar & ... (Eds.), *Fractional Order Control and Synchronization of Chaotic Systems, Series: Studies in Computational Intelligence 688* (pp. 203–224). Springer-Verlag Germany. doi:10.1007/978-3-319-50249-6_7

Khettab, K., Bensafia, Y., & Ladaci, S. (2017d). Chattering Elimination in Fuzzy Sliding Mode Control of Fractional Chaotic Systems Using a Fractional Adaptive Proportional Integral Controller. *International Journal of Intelligent Engineering and Systems, 10*(5), 255–265. doi:10.22266/ijies2017.1031.28

Khettab, K., Bensafia, Y., & Ladaci, S. (2017). Robust Adaptive Fuzzy Control for a Class of Uncertain Nonlinear Fractional Systems. In Lecture Notes in Electrical Engineering: Vol. 411. Recent Advances in Electrical Engineering and Control Applications. Springer International Publishing.

Khettab, K., Bensafia, Y., & Ladaci, S. (2015). Fuzzy adaptive control enhancement for non-affine systems with unknown control gain sign. *Proc. 16th Int. IEEE Conf. on Sciences and Techniques of Automatic control and computer engineering, STA'2015*, 616-621. 10.1109/STA.2015.7505141

Khettab, K., Bensafia, Y., & Ladaci, S. (2014). Robust Adaptive Fuzzy control for a Class of Uncertain nonlinear Fractional Systems. *Proceedings of the Second International Conference on Electrical Engineering and Control Applications ICEECA'2014.*

Ladaci, S., & Bensafia, Y. (2016). Indirect fractional order pole assignment based adaptive control. *Engineering Science and Technology, an International Journal, 19*, 518-530.

Ladaci, S., & Charef, A. (2002). Commande adaptative à modèle de référence d'ordre fractionnaire d'un bras de robot. (in French) Communication Sciences & Technologie. *ENSET Oran, Algeria., 1*, 50–52.

Ladaci, S., & Charef, A. (2006). On Fractional Adaptive Control. *Nonlinear Dynamics, 43*(4), 365–378. doi:10.100711071-006-0159-x

Ladaci, S., & Charef, A. (2006). An Adaptive Fractional PIλDμ Controller. *Proceedings of the Sixth Int. Symposium on Tools and Methods of Competitive Engineering, TMCE 2006*, 1533-1540.

Ladaci, S., & Charef, A. (2012). Fractional order adaptive control systems: A survey. In Classification and Application of Fractals. Nova Science Publishers, Inc.

Ladaci, S., Charef, A., & Loiseau, J. J. (2009). Robust Fractional Adaptive Control Based on the Strictly Positive Realness Condition. *International Journal of Applied Mathematics and Computer Science*, *19*(1), 69–76. doi:10.2478/v10006-009-0006-6

Ladaci, S., & Khettab, K. (2012). Fractional Order Multiple Model Adaptive Control. *International Journal of Automation & Systems Engineering*, *6*(2), 110–122.

Ladaci, S., Loiseau, J. J., & Charef, A. (2008). Fractional Order Adaptive High-Gain Controllers for a Class of Linear Systems. *Communications in Nonlinear Science and Numerical Simulation*, *13*(4), 707–714. doi:10.1016/j.cnsns.2006.06.009

Ladaci, S., Loiseau, J. J., & Charef, A. (2010). Adaptive Internal Model Control with Fractional Order Parameter. *International Journal of Adaptive Control and Signal Processing*, *24*(11), 944–960. doi:10.1002/acs.1175

Li, C., & Deng, W. H. (2006). Chaos synchronization of fractional order differential systems. *International Journal of Modern Physics B*, *20*(07), 791–803. doi:10.1142/S0217979206033620

Li, C., & Tong, Y. (2013). Adaptive control and synchronization of a fractional-order chaotic system. *Pramana Journal of Physics*, *80*(4), 583–592. doi:10.100712043-012-0500-5

Li, L., & Sun, Y. (2015). Adaptive Fuzzy Control for Nonlinear Fractional-Order Uncertain Systems with Unknown Uncertainties and External Disturbance. *Entropy (Basel, Switzerland)*, *17*(12), 5580–5592. doi:10.3390/e17085580

Lin, T.-C., Chen, M.-C., Roopaei, M., & Sahraei, B. R. (2010). Adaptive type-2 fuzzy sliding mode control for chaos synchronization of uncertain chaotic systems. *Proceedings of the IEEE International Conference on Fuzzy Systems (FUZZ)*. 10.1109/FUZZY.2010.5584444

Lin, T.-C., & Kuo, C. H. (2011). synchronization of uncertain fractional order chaotic systems: Adaptive fuzzy approach. *ISA Transactions*, *50*(4), 548–556. doi:10.1016/j.isatra.2011.06.001 PMID:21741648

Lin, T. C., Kuo, C. H., & Balas, V. E. (2011). Uncertain Fractional Order Chaotic Systems Tracking Design via Adaptive Hybrid Fuzzy Sliding Mode Control. *Int. J. of Computers, Communications & Control*, *6*(3), 418-427.

Lin, T. C., Kuo, M. J., & Hsu, C. H. (2010). Robust Adaptive Tracking Control of Multivariable Nonlinear Systems Based on Interval Type-2 Fuzzy approach. *International Journal of Innovative Computing, Information, & Control*, *6*(1), 941–961.

Lin, T. C., Lee, T.-Y., & Balas, V. E. (2011). Synchronization of Uncertain Fractional Order Chaotic Systems via Adaptive Interval Type-2 Fuzzy Sliding Mode Control. *Proceedings of the IEEE International Conference on Fuzzy Systems*. 10.1109/FUZZY.2011.6007354

Lin, T. C., Liu, H. L., & Kuo, M. J. (2009). Direct adaptive interval type-2 fuzzy control of multivariable nonlinear systems. *Engineering Applications of Artificial Intelligence*, *22*(3), 420–430. doi:10.1016/j.engappai.2008.10.024

Lu, J. G. (2006). Chaotic dynamics of the fractional order LRu system and its synchronization. *Physics Letters. [Part A]*, *354*(4), 305–311. doi:10.1016/j.physleta.2006.01.068

Lu, J. G., & Chen, G. (2006). A note on the fractional-order Chen system. *Chaos, Solitons, and Fractals*, *27*(3), 685–688. doi:10.1016/j.chaos.2005.04.037

Machado, J. T., Kiryakova, V., & Mainardi, F. (2011). Recent history of fractional calculus. *Communications in Nonlinear Science and Numerical Simulation*, *16*(1), 1140–1153. doi:10.1016/j.cnsns.2010.05.027

Mendel, J. M., & John, R. I. B. (2002). Type-2 fuzzy sets made simple. *IEEE Transactions on Fuzzy Systems*, *10*(2), 117–127. doi:10.1109/91.995115

Neçaibia, A., & Ladaci, S. (2014). Self-tuning fractional order $PI\lambda D\mu$ controller based on extremum seeking approach. International Journal of Automation and Control. *Inderscience*, *8*(2), 99–121.

Neçaibia, A., Ladaci, S., Charef, A., & Loiseau, J. J. (2014). Fractional Order Extremum Seeking Control. *Proceedings of the 22nd Mediterranean Conference on Control and Automation*, 459-462.

Odibat, Z. M. (2010). Adaptive feedback control and synchronization of non-identical chaotic fractional order systems. *Nonlinear Dynamics*, *60*(4), 479–487. doi:10.100711071-009-9609-6

Oustaloup, A. (1995). *La dérivation non entière: théorie, synthèse et applications*. Hermès-Paris.

Pétras, I. (2011). *Fractional-Order Nonlinear Systems: Modeling, Analysis and Simulation, Series: Nonlinear Physical Science*. Springer-Verlag. doi:10.1007/978-3-642-18101-6

Podlubny, I. (1999). *Fractional differential equations*. San Diego, CA: Academic Press.

Qilian, L., & Mendel, J. M. (2000). Interval type-2 fuzzy logic systems: Theory and design. *IEEE Transactions on Fuzzy Systems*, *8*(5), 535–550. doi:10.1109/91.873577

Rabah, K., Ladaci, S., Lashab, M. (2016). Stabilization of a Genesio-Tesi Chaotic System Using a Fractional Order $PI\lambda D\mu$ Regulator. *International Journal of Sciences and Techniques of Automatic Control & Computer Engineering*, *10*(1), 2085–2090.

Sastry, S., & Bodson, M. (1989). *Adaptive Control: Stability, Convergence and Robustness*. New York: Prentice-Hall.

Sheu, L. J., Chen, H. K., Chen, J. H., Tam, L. M., Chen, W. C., Lin, K. T., & Kang, Y. (2008). Chaos in the Newton-Leipnik system with fractional order. *Chaos, Solitons, and Fractals*, *36*(1), 98–103. doi:10.1016/j.chaos.2006.06.013

Slotine, J. J. E. (1991). *Applied Nonlinear Control*. Prentice Hall.

Takagi, T., & Sugeno, M. (1985). Fuzzy Identification of Systems and Its Applications to Modeling and Control. *IEEE Transactions on Systems, Man, and Cybernetics*, *15*(1), 116–132. doi:10.1109/TSMC.1985.6313399

Tian, X., Fei, S., & Chai, L. (2014). Adaptive Control of a Class of Fractional-order Nonlinear Complex Systems with Dead-zone Nonlinear Inputs. *Proceedings of the 33rd Chinese Control Conference*. 10.1109/ChiCC.2014.6896919

Vinagre, B. M., Petras, I., Podlubny, I., & Chen, Y.-Q. (2002). Using Fractional Order Adjustment Rules and Fractional Order Reference Models in Model-Reference Adaptive Control. *Nonlinear Dynamics*, *29*(1/4), 269–279. doi:10.1023/A:1016504620249

Wang, C.-H., Liu, H.-L., & Lin, T.-C. (2002). Direct Adaptive Fuzzy-Neural Control with State Observer and Supervisory Controller for Unknown Nonlinear Dynamical Systems. *IEEE Transactions on Fuzzy Systems*, *10*(1), 39–49. doi:10.1109/91.983277

Wang, L. X., & Mendel, J. M. (1992). Fuzzy basis function, universal approximation, and orthogonal least square learning. *IEEE Transactions on Neural Networks*, *3*(5), 807–814. doi:10.1109/72.159070 PMID:18276480

Wei, Y., Sun, Z., Hu, Y., & Wang, Y. (2015). On fractional order composite model reference adaptive control. *International Journal of Systems Science*. doi:10.1080/00207721.2014.998749

Wei, Y., Tse, P. W., Yao, Z., & Wang, Y. (2016). Adaptive backstepping output feedback control for a class of nonlinear fractional order systems. *Nonlinear Dynamics*, *86*(2), 1047–1056. doi:10.100711071-016-2945-4

Wu, X. J., Lu, H. T., & Shen, S. L. (2009). Synchronization of a new fractional-order hyperchaotic system. *Physics Letters. [Part A]*, *373*(27-28), 2329–2337. doi:10.1016/j.physleta.2009.04.063

Yuan, J., Shi, B., & Yu, Z. (2014). Adaptive Sliding Control for a Class of Fractional Commensurate Order Chaotic Systems. *Mathematical Problems in Engineering*.

Zadeh, L. A. (1975). The concept of a linguistic variable and its application to approximate reasoning. *Information Sciences*, *8*(3), 199–249. doi:10.1016/0020-0255(75)90036-5

Zeghlache, S., Ghellab, M. Z., & Bouguerra, A. (2017). Adaptive Type-2 Fuzzy Sliding Mode Control Using Supervisory Type-2 Fuzzy Control for 6 DOF Octorotor Aircraft. *International Journal of Intelligent Engineering and Systems*, *10*(3), 47–57. doi:10.22266/ijies2017.0630.06

Zhang, R., & Yang, S. (2011). Adaptive synchronization of fractional-order chaotic systems via a single driving variable. *Nonlinear Dynamics*, *66*(4), 831–837. doi:10.100711071-011-9944-2

Chapter 5
Backstepping Control for Synchronizing Fractional-Order Chaotic Systems

Amina Boubellouta
University of Jijel, Algeria

ABSTRACT

In this chapter, one develops a fuzzy adaptive backstepping control-based projective synchronization scheme of a class of uncertain fractional-order nonlinear systems with unknown external disturbances. In each step, an uncertain nonlinear function is online modeled via a fuzzy logic system, and a virtual control term is determined based on the fractional Lyapunov stability. At the final step, a fuzzy adaptive control law ensuring the convergence of the projective synchronization error as well as the stability of the closed-loop control system is derived. Numerical simulations given at the end of this chapter confirm well the effectiveness of the proposed control method.

INTRODUCTION

In the last four decades, *fractional calculus* has attracted much attention from physicists and engineers owing to its attractive properties and potential applications, for reviews in this topic one can refer to Podlubny (1999), Shen & Lam (2014), Aguila-Camacho et al. (2014), Duarte-Mermoud et al. (2015), Liu et al. (2017a), Bao & Cao, (2015), Bao et al. (2015), Liu et al. (2017), Geng et al. (2016), Bouzeriba et al. (2015), Bouzeriba et al. (2016a), Boulkroune et al. (2015a), and Boubellouta & Boulkroune (2016). It has been proved that the fractional-order differential equation is an effective means for a precise modeling of the nonlinear and complex dynamics of many physical systems and some particular materials (Podlubny, 1999; Shen & Lam, 2014; Aguila-Camacho et al., 2014; Duarte-Mermoud et al., 2015; Liu et al., 2017a; Bao & Cao, 2015). The fractional-order differential equation is considered as a natural generalization of the classical integer-order differential equation. For more information about the fractional calculus, for instance one can refer to Liu et al. (2015a), Liu et al. (2015b), Wen et al. (2016), Yu et al. (2017). Numerous attractive fundamental results have been recently reported, in the literature, on the stability

DOI: 10.4018/978-1-5225-5418-9.ch005

analysis and control design problems of fractional-order systems. For instance, a novel fractional-order Lyapunov stability method has been proposed for a class of fractional-order nonlinear dynamic systems in Li et al. (2009). A robust nonlinear fractional-order state observer has been designed in Boroujeni & Momeni (2012) for a class of nonlinear fractional-order systems. In Yang & Chen (2015), a finite-time stabilization approach for impulsive switched systems with fractional-order dynamics has been proposed. In Liu et al. (2015a), Liu et al. (2015b), and Liu et al. (2015c), an adaptive control methodology has been used also to effectively stabilize a class of uncertain fractional-order systems. Some intelligent (fuzzy or neural networks) feedback control approaches for uncertain fractional-order chaotic systems have been proposed in Huang et al. (2014), Boulkroune et al. (2016a), and Bouzeriba et al. (2016b; 2016c). Considering this important number of works related to fractional-order (linear or nonlinear) systems, it is very clear that its stability analysis and their control design problems are becoming hot research areas.

One of the most generally used approaches for nonlinear control is the *backstepping control* concept (Kwan & Lewis, 2000; Pan & Yu, 2015; Pan & Yu, 2016). This control methodology has been considered as an efficient approach for integer-order nonlinear systems having a model with a triangular structure. Its key idea is that the control law is designed by using states as virtual control signals (in other words, as desired signals), and their derivatives are required. Theoretically, calculation of the virtual control signal derivatives is simple, but it can be quite complicated and tedious in applications when the number of the system states is greater than three. It is worth mentioning that the standard backstepping control approaches (Kwan & Lewis, 2000; Pan & Yu, 2015; Pan & Yu, 2016), which are only valid for integer-order nonlinear systems, cannot be straightforwardly extended for nonlinear fractional-order systems, because the fractional-order differentiation of a quadratic Lyapunov function is very complicated. Some researchers have tried to use the backstepping concept to control fractional-order systems (Efe, 2011; Baleanu et al., 2011; Ding et al., 2014). In Sheng et al. (2017), Wei et al. (2015), and Wei et al. (2016), adaptive backstepping control schemes have been proposed for uncertain nonlinear systems with fractional-order dynamics and triangular configuration. To analyze the stability, an integer-order standard Lyapunov approach has been used. In Liu et al. (2017c), Bigdeli & Ziazi (2017), Nikdel et al. (2016), and Shukla & Sharma (2017a, 2017b, 2018), some adaptive backstepping control schemes for triangular fractional-order nonlinear systems have been designed via a fractional-order Lyapunov stability method. However, these fractional-order backstepping controllers suffer from some limitations:

- Some schemes have not been rigorously derived in mathematics: the virtual control laws have been designed as non-derivable functions in Liu et al. (2017c), Shukla & Sharma (2017a), and Nikdel et al. (2016).
- System models in almost schemes are assumed to be known, see Sheng et al. (2017), Wei et al. (2015), Wei et al. (2016), Nikdel et al. (2016), and Shukla & Sharma (2017a, 2017b, 2018).
- Unmatched disturbances (in some cases, even matched disturbances) have not been considered in the system models (Liu et al., 2017c; Sheng et al., 2017; Wei et al., 2015, 2016; Bigdeli & Ziazi, 2017; Nikdel et al., 2016; Shukla & Sharma, 2017a, 2017b, 2018).

It is well-known that quadratic Lyapunov candidate functions are generally employed in the stability analysis of adaptive backstepping controllers of non-fractional-order nonlinear systems. However, the fractional-order derivatives of a quadratic Lyapunov function is very complicated. Consequently, how to design an adaptive backsteeping controller for fractional-order nonlinear systems via a fractional Lyapunov stability criterion is a challenging and open issue. Motivated by this issue and the above limitations of the existing adaptive backstepping control schemes of fractional-order systems (Liu et al., 2017c; Sheng et al., 2017; Wei et al., 2015, 2016; Bigdeli & Ziazi, 2017; Nikdel et al.,2016; Shukla & Sharma, 2017a, 2017b, 2018), a novel adaptive fuzzy backstepping control methodology is proposed, in this paper, to achieve a projective synchronization, for a class of unknown fractional-order chaotic systems with a lower triangular structure. In each step, an uncertain nonlinear function is online approximated via a fuzzy logic system, and a virtual control term is determined based on the fractional Lyapunov stability. At the final step, a fuzzy adaptive controller ensuring the convergence of the projective synchronization error as well as the stability of the closed-loop control system is derived. Compared to the previous works, the contributions of this chapter can be summarized as follows:

1. A novel fuzzy adaptive backstepping control law is proposed to deal with a projective synchronization issue of uncertain fractional-order chaotic systems
2. The stability associated to the closed-loop control system is rigorously analyzed via a fractional Lyapunov method.
3. The uncertain nonlinear functions are online approximated by using adaptive fuzzy systems. And novel fractional-order updating laws are constructed to adjust the unknown fuzzy parameters.
4. Unlike the previous works Liu et al. (2017c), Sheng et al. (2017), Wei et al. (2015; 2016), Bigdeli & Ziazi (2017), Shukla & Sharma (2017a; 2017b; 2018), Nikdel et al. (2016), both matched and unmatched disturbances have been considered in the system models.
5. Compared to Bigdeli & Ziazi (2017) and Shukla & Sharma (2017a; 2017b; 2018), the proposed controller is scalar. So, its practical implementation is simple and inexpensive.
6. Unlike the works in Sheng et al. (2017), Wei et al. (2015; 2016), Nikdel et al. (2016), Shukla & Sharma (2017a; 2017b; 2018), the master-slave models are assumed to be uncertain. And the controller designed does not depend on those models.
7. To robustly and conjointly compensate for the matched and unmatched disturbances, and unavoidable fuzzy approximation errors, a novel dynamical adaptive compensator is proposed.
8. Unlike Liu et al. (2017c), Bigdeli & Ziazi (2017), Shukla & Sharma (2017a), and Nikdel et al. (2016), the proposed controller is rigorously derived and the virtual control laws have been designed as derivable functions.

The rest of this chapter is organized as follows. A description of the fuzzy logic systems which will be used for online approximation of uncertainties and some concepts related to the fractional calculus are presented in Section 2. the detailed control law design and the stability analysis are given in Section 3. Simulation results are shown in Section 4. Finally, Section 5 concludes this chapter and gives possible future directions of this research.

FUZZY LOGIC SYSTEM AND FRACTIONAL CALCULUS

Description of the Fuzzy Logic System

The basic configuration of a fuzzy logic system consists of a fuzzifier, some fuzzy IF–THEN rules, a fuzzy inference engine and a defuzzifier, as shown in Figure 1. The fuzzy inference engine uses the fuzzy

Figure 1. Basic configuration of a fuzzy logic system

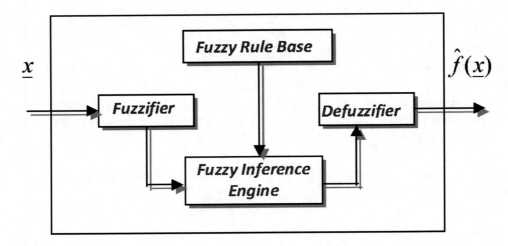

IF–THEN rules to perform a mapping from an input vector $\underline{x}^T = \left[x_1, x_2, \ldots, x_n \right] \in R^n$ to an output $\hat{f} \in R$. The *ith* fuzzy rule is written as

$$R^{(i)} : if \ x_1 \ is \ A_1^i \ and \ \ldots and \in x_n \ is \ A_n^i \ then \ \hat{f} \ is \ f^i, \tag{1}$$

where $A_1^i, A_2^i, \ldots,$ and A_n^i are fuzzy sets and f^i is the fuzzy singleton for the output in the *ith* rule.

By using the singleton fuzzifier, product inference, and center-average defuzzifier, the output of the fuzzy system can be expressed as follows:

$$\hat{f}\left(\underline{x} \right) = \frac{\sum_{i=1}^m f^i \left(\prod_{j=1}^n \mu_{A_j^i} \left(x_j \right) \right)}{\sum_{i=1}^m \left(\prod_{j=1}^n \mu_{A_j^i}(x_j) \right)} = \theta^T \psi \left(\underline{x} \right), \tag{2}$$

where $\mu_{A_j^i}(x_j)$ is the degree of membership of x_j is proposed to deal with a x_j to A_j^i, m is the number of fuzzy rules, $\theta^T = \left[f^1 f^2 \ldots f^m \right]$ is the adjustable parameter vector (composed of consequent parameters), and $\psi^T = \left[\psi^1 \psi^2 \ldots \psi^m \right]$ with

$$\psi^i \left(\underline{x} \right) = \frac{\left(\prod_{j=1}^n \mu_{A_j^i} \left(x_j \right) \right)}{\sum_{i=1}^m \left(\prod_{j=1}^n \mu_{A_j^i} \left(x_j \right) \right)} \tag{3}$$

Being the fuzzy basis function (FBF). Throughout the paper, it is assumed that the FBFs are selected so that there is always at least one active rule (Wang, 1994), i.e.

$$\sum_{i=1}^{m}(\prod_{j=1}^{n}\mu_{A_j^i}(x_j)) > 0. \tag{4}$$

Note that the fuzzy system (2) is widely applied in modeling and control of nonlinear systems, because it has been proven by Wang (1994) that this fuzzy logic system can estimate an arbitrary nonlinear smooth function $f(\underline{x})$ defined on a compact operating space to a given accuracy. Of particular importance, it is assumed that the FBFs, $\psi(\underline{x})$, are properly specified beforehand by designer. But, the consequent parameters, θ, are determined by some appropriate adaptation algorithms which will be designed later (Bounar et al., 2014, 2015; Boulkroune et al., 2008a, 2011, 2015b, 2016b, 2017; Li et al.,2016a; Liu & Tong, 2017d; Benzaoui et al., 2016; Rigatos et al., 2016).

Some Concepts Related to the Fractional Calculus

In fractional calculus, the classical definitions of the integral and derivative of a function are generalized from integer orders to real orders. In the literature, there are several definitions regarding the fractional-derivative of order $\alpha \geq 0$, but the Caputo definition is used in the most engineering applications, because the latter incorporates initial conditions for $f(.)$ and its integer order derivatives, in other words initial conditions are physically appealing in the traditional way.

Unlike the fractional-order (FO) derivative, the definition of the fractional-order integral is unique and it is given by:

$$I_t^\alpha f(t) = \frac{1}{\Gamma(\alpha)} \int_0^t \frac{f(\tau)}{(t-\tau)^{1-\alpha}} d\tau , \tag{5}$$

where

$$\Gamma(\alpha) = \int_0^{+\infty} \tau^{\alpha-1} e^{-\tau} d\tau \tag{6}$$

is the so-called Gamma function.

The *ath* fractional derivative is defined by:

$$D_t^\alpha f(t) = \frac{1}{\Gamma(n-\alpha)} \int_0^t \frac{f^{(n)}(\tau)}{(t-\tau)^{\alpha+1-n}} d\tau \tag{7}$$

where $n-1 \leq \alpha < n$. Note that the fractional derivative which will be used in the rest of this chapter.

Taking Laplace's transform on (7) gives

$$\int_0^\infty e^{-st} D_t^\alpha f(t) \, dt = s^\alpha F(s) - \sum_{k=0}^{n-1} s^{\alpha-k-1} f^{(k)}(0) \tag{8}$$

with $F(s)$ being the Laplace transform of $f(t)$.

In the rest of this chapter, one will consider only the case where $0 < \alpha \leq 1$. The following lemmas are important in the stability analysis and the control law design for fractional-order chaotic systems.

Lemma 1 (Li et al., 2009): Assume that the origin is the unique equilibrium point of the following non-autonomous fractional-order nonlinear system

$$D_t^\alpha x(t) = f(t, x(t)) \tag{9}$$

with $f : I \times \Omega \to \Re$ being Lipschitz and continuous. If there exists a Lyapunov function $V(t, x(t))$ and class$-K$ functions g_i (for $i = 1, 2, 3$) to satisfy

$$g_1(\|x(t)\|) \leq V(t, x(t) \leq g_2(\|x(t)\|) \tag{10}$$

$$D_t^\alpha V(t, x(t)) \leq -g_3(\|x(t)\|) \tag{11}$$

Then (9) is asymptotically stable, i.e. $\lim_{x \to \infty} x(t) = 0$.

Lemma 2 (Aguila-Camacho et al., 2014): If $x(t)$ is a continuous and derivable function, then the Caputo's derivative operator satisfies the following important relation:

$$\frac{1}{2} D_t^\alpha (x^T(t)x(t)) \leq x^T(t)D_t^\alpha x(t) \quad \text{(for } 0 < \alpha \leq 1) \tag{12}$$

Lemma 3 (Duarte-Mermoud, et al., 2015): (Lyapunov Stability and Uniform stability of fractional order systems). Let $x = 0$ be an equilibrium point for the non autonomous fractional-order system (9). Let us assume that there exists a continuous Lyapunov function $V(x(t), t)$ and a scalar *class-K* function $\gamma_1(.)$ such that, $\forall x \neq 0$:

$$\gamma_1(\|x\|) \leq V(x(t), t) \tag{13}$$

and

$$D_t^\beta V(x(t), t) \leq 0 \text{, with } \beta \in \left]0, 1\right] \tag{14}$$

then the origin of the system (9) is Lyapunov stable.

If, furthermore, there is a scalar *class-K* function $\gamma_2(.)$ satisfying

$$V(x(t), t) \leq \gamma_2(\|x\|) \tag{15}$$

then the origin of the system (9) is Lyapunov uniformly stable.

In the rest of this chapter, for convenience, the simple and short notation D^{α} (instead of D_t^{α}) will be used for indicating the Caputo fractional derivative.

ADAPTIVE FUZZY BACKSTEPPING CONTROLLER DESIGN

Consider the following class of uncertain FO chaotic *master systems:*

$$Master \begin{cases} D^{\alpha}x_1 = f_{m1}(\underline{x}_1) \\ D^{\alpha}x_2 = f_{m2}(\underline{x}_2) \\ \vdots \\ D^{\alpha}x_{n-1} = f_{mn-1}(\underline{x}_{n-1}) \\ D^{\alpha}x_n = f_{mn}(\underline{x}_n) \end{cases} \tag{16}$$

where $0 < \alpha \leq 1$ is the fractional-order, $\underline{x}_n = x = \left[x_1, x_2, \ldots, x_n\right]^T \in R^n$ is the pseudo-states' vector of the master system, $\underline{x}_i = \left[x_1, x_2, \ldots, x_i\right]^T \in R^i$, $f_{mi}(\underline{x}_i) \in R$, for $i = 1, 2, \ldots, n$, is an unknown smooth nonlinear functions.

Its *slave system* is given by

$$Slave \begin{cases} D^{\alpha}y_1 = f_{s1}(\underline{y}_1) + g_{s1}y_2 + d_{s1}(t) \\ D^{\alpha}y_2 = f_{s2}(\underline{y}_2) + g_{s2}y_3 + d_{s2}(t) \\ \vdots \\ D^{\alpha}y_{n-1} = f_{sn-1}(\underline{y}_{n-1}) + g_{sn-1}y_n + d_{sn-1}(t) \\ D^{\alpha}y_n = f_{sn}(\underline{y}_n) + g_{sn}u + d_{sn}(t) \end{cases} \tag{17}$$

where $0 < \alpha \leq 1$ is the fractional-order, $y(t) = \left[y_1, y_2, \ldots, y_n\right]^T \in R^n$ is the slave pseudo-states vector, $\underline{y}_j = \left[y_1, y_2, \ldots, y_i\right]^T \in R^i$, $f_{si}(\underline{x}_i) \in R$, for $i = 1, 2, \ldots, n$, are unknown smooth nonlinear functions. $g_{si} \neq 0$, for $i = 1, 2, \ldots, n$, are known real constants. u denotes the control input vector and d_{si} stands for the unknown external disturbances. One assumes that those disturbances are bounded as follows: $\left|d_{si}(t)\right| \leq \overline{d}_{si}$, for $i = 1, 2, \ldots, n$.

Remark 1: The master-slave model (16) and (17) considered in this chapter represents a relatively large class of uncertain FO chaotic systems. It is worth noting that several FO chaotic systems can be described by (16) and (17), such as: FO Lu system, FO Lorenz system, FO unified chaotic system, FO Chen system, and so on.

Remark 2: To the best of authors' knowledge, many fractional-order systems can chaotically behave for $0 < \alpha \leq 1$, and most of the previous works on the synchronization of the chaotic systems also mainly consider this case. Although the restriction on the system order, our work can deal with most of the fractional chaotic systems with theoretical rigorousness, and in the view of application oriented, one believes that the consideration of $0 < \alpha \leq 1$ can give a satisfactory result.

Remark 3: It should be noted that some recent backstepping control schemes have been also proposed for a class of fractional-order nonlinear systems in Sheng et al. (2017), Wei et al. (2015; 2016), Nikdel et al. (2016), Shukla & Sharma (2017a; 2017b; 2018). However, in these schemes, the system models are assumed to be known or almost known. In our present work, the system models can be fully unknown.

Remark 4: Unlike many previous works, Liu et al. (2017c), Sheng et al. (2017), Wei et al. (2015; 2016), Bigdeli & Ziazi (2017), Shukla & Sharma (2017a; 2017b; 2018), Nikdel et al. (2016), the matched and unmatched disturbances are considered in the slave models. Note that the control design problem for triangular chaotic systems with unmatched disturbances is very challenge.

Our main objective consists in designing a fuzzy adaptive backstepping control law u which achieves a projective synchronization between the master system (16) and the slave one (17), while assuring that all variables involved in the closed-loop system (including the synchronization errors) are Lyapuonv uniformly stable.

To quantify our objective, one can define the synchronization errors as follows:

$$
\begin{cases}
e_1 = y_1(t) - \lambda_1 x_1(t) \\
e_2 = y_2(t) - \lambda_2 x_2(t) \\
\vdots \\
e_{n-1} = y_{n-1}(t) - \lambda_{n-1} x_{n-1}(t) \\
e_n = y_n(t) - \lambda_n x_n(t)
\end{cases}
\tag{18}
$$

where λ_i is a scaling factor defining a proportional relation between the synchronized systems.

$$
\begin{cases}
D^\alpha e_1 = f_{s1}(\underline{y}_1) + g_{s1} e_2 - \lambda_1 f_{m1}(\underline{x}_1) + \lambda_1 g_{s1} x_2 + d_{s1} \\
D^\alpha e_2 = f_{s2}(\underline{y}_2) + g_{s2} e_3 - \lambda_2 f_{m2}(\underline{x}_2) + \lambda_2 g_{s2} x_3 + d_{s2} \\
\vdots \\
D^\alpha e_{n-1} = f_{sn-1}(\underline{y}_{n-1}) + g_{sn-1} e_n - \lambda_{n-1} f_{mn-1}(\underline{x}_{n-1}) + \lambda_{n-1} g_{sn-1} x_n + d_{sn-1} \\
D^\alpha e_n = f_{sn}(\underline{y}_n) + g_{sn} u - \lambda_n f_{mn}(\underline{x}_n) + d_{sn}
\end{cases}
\tag{19}
$$

or equivalently

$$\begin{cases} D^\alpha e_1 = h_1(\underline{y_1}, \underline{x_2}) + g_{s1}e_2 + d_{s1} \\ D^\alpha e_2 = h_2(\underline{y_2}, \underline{x_3}) + g_{s2}e_3 + d_{s2} \\ \vdots \\ D^\alpha e_{n-1} = h_{n-1}(\underline{y_{n-1}}, \underline{x_n}) + g_{sn-1}e_n + d_{sn-1} \\ D^\alpha e_n = h_{n-1}(\underline{y_n}, \underline{x_n}) + g_{sn}u + d_{sn} \end{cases} \tag{20}$$

where

$$h_i(\underline{y_i}, \underline{x_{i+1}}) = f_{si}(\underline{y_i}) - \lambda_i f_{mi}(\underline{x_i}) + \lambda_i g_{si}x_{i+1},$$

for $i = 1, ..., n-1$ and $h_n(\underline{y_n}, \underline{x_n}) = f_{sn}(\underline{y_n}) - \lambda_n f_{mn}(\underline{x_n})$.

The backstepping recursive design procedure will be used here to construct of the Lyapunov function candidate and to derive the control law. It can be detailed in the following steps.

Step 1: Let the unknown smooth function $h_1(\underline{y_1}, \underline{x_2})$ be approximated by the linearly parameterized fuzzy system (2), on the compact set $\Omega_{\underline{y_1}}$, as follows:

$$\hat{h_1}(\underline{y_1}, \underline{x_2}, \theta_1) = \theta_1^T \psi_1(\underline{y_1}) \tag{21}$$

where $\psi_1(\underline{y_1})$ is the fuzzy basis function (FBF) vector, which is fixed a priori by the designer, and θ_1 is the adjustable parameter vector of the fuzzy system (Hamel & Boulkroune, 2016; Liu & Tong, 2015d; Tong & Li, 2013; Liu & Tong, 2014; Li et al., 2015; Li & Tong, 2016b; Liu et al., 2016; Sui et al., 2016; Boulkroune et al., 2008b; Boulkroune & M'saad, 2012).

Let us define

$$\theta_1^* = \arg\min_{\theta_1}\left[\sup_{\underline{y_1} \in \Omega_{\underline{y_1}}} \left| h_1(\underline{y_1}, \underline{x_2}) - \theta_1^T \psi_1(\underline{y_1}) \right| \right] \tag{22}$$

as the optimal value of θ_1 which is mainly introduced for analysis purposes as its value is not needed when implementing the controller.

Define also

$$\tilde{\theta}_1 = \theta_1 - \theta_1^* \text{ and } \varepsilon_1(\underline{y_1}, \underline{x_2}) = h_1(\underline{y_1}, \underline{x_2}) - \theta_1^{*T}\psi_1(\underline{y_1}) \tag{23}$$

as the parametric estimation error and the fuzzy reconstruction error, respectively.

As in Hamel & Boulkroune (2016), Liu & Tong (2015d), Tong & Li (2013), Liu & Tong (2014), Li et al. (2015), Li & Tong (2016b), Liu et al. (2016), Sui et al. (2016), Boulkroune et al. (2008b), Boulkroune & M'saad (2012), one assumes that this fuzzy reconstruction error is bounded for all $\underline{x}_2 \in \Omega_{\underline{x}_2}, \underline{y}_1 \in \Omega_{\underline{y}_1}$, i.e.

$$\left| \varepsilon_1 \left(\underline{y}_1, \underline{x}_2 \right) \right| \leq \bar{\varepsilon}_1, \quad \forall \underline{x}_2 \in \Omega_{\underline{x}_2}, \underline{y}_1 \in \Omega_{\underline{y}_1} \tag{24}$$

where $\bar{\varepsilon}_1$ is an unknown constant.

From the above analysis, one has

$$h_1(\underline{y}_1, \underline{x}_2) - \theta_1^T \psi_1 \left(\underline{y}_1 \right) = h_1(\underline{y}_1, \underline{x}_2) - \theta_1^{*T} \psi_1 \left(\underline{y}_1 \right) + \theta_1^{*T} \psi_1 \left(\underline{y}_1 \right) - \theta_1^T \psi_1 \left(\underline{y}_1 \right)$$

$$= -\tilde{\theta}_1^T \psi_1 \left(\underline{y}_1 \right) + \varepsilon_1 \left(\underline{y}_1, \underline{x}_2 \right) \tag{25}$$

It follows from (25) and (20) that

$$D^\alpha e_1 = h_1(\underline{y}_1, \underline{x}_2) + g_{s1} e_2 + d_{s1}$$

$$= -\tilde{\theta}_1^T \psi_1 \left(\underline{y}_1 \right) + \theta_1^T \psi_1 \left(\underline{y}_1 \right) + g_{s1} e_2 + d_{s1} + \varepsilon_1 \left(\underline{y}_1, \underline{x}_2 \right) \tag{26}$$

Let design the first virtual control input α_1 as follows

$$\alpha_1 = g_{s1}^{-1} \left(-\theta_1^T \psi_1 \left(\underline{y}_1 \right) - k_1 \omega_1 \right) \tag{27}$$

where $\omega_1 = e_1$ and $k_1 > 0$ is a design parameter.

Its adaptation law can be designed also

$$D^\alpha \theta_1 = \gamma_1 \omega_1 \psi_1 \left(\underline{y}_1 \right) - \gamma_1 \sigma_1 \left| \omega_1 \right| \theta_1 \tag{28}$$

with σ_1 and γ_1 being strictly positive design parameters.

Remark 5: Note that the virtual control input (27) is essentially comprised of two terms, namely:

  ◦   A *fuzzy term*, $\theta_1^T \psi_1 \left(\underline{y}_1 \right)$, employed to model the uncertain functions $h_1(\underline{y}_1, \underline{x}_2)$,
  ◦   A *linear control term*, $k_1 \omega_1$, introduced for stability purposes.

Remark 6: The update law (28) contains two terms, namely:

  ◦   An *e-modification term*, $\gamma_1 \sigma_1 \left| \omega_1 \right| \theta_1$, guarantees the boundedness of the updated parameters, and
  ◦   A *gradient term*, $\gamma_1 \omega_1 \psi_1 \left(\underline{y}_1 \right)$, is used to cancel a term produced by fractional-differentiating the quadratic Lyapunov function.

Because the Caputo fractional-order derivative of a constant is zero, one can write (28) as follows:

$$D^\alpha \theta_1 = D^\alpha \tilde{\theta}_1 = \gamma_1 \omega_1 \psi_1 \left(\underline{y}_1 \right) - \gamma_1 \sigma_1 \left| \omega_1 \right| \theta_1 \tag{29}$$

Now, let's denote $\omega_2 = e_2 - \alpha_1$. From (26) and (27), one has

$$D^\alpha \omega_1 = -\tilde{\theta}_1^T \psi_1 \left(\underline{y}_1 \right) + \theta_1^T \psi_1 \left(\underline{y}_1 \right) + g_{s1} e_2 + d_{s1} + \varepsilon_1 \left(\underline{y}_1, \underline{x}_2 \right)$$

$$= -\tilde{\theta}_1^T \psi_1 \left(\underline{y}_1 \right) + \theta_1^T \psi_1 \left(\underline{y}_1 \right) + g_{s1} \left(e_2 - \alpha_1 \right) + g_{s1} \alpha_1 + d_{s1} + \varepsilon_1 \left(\underline{y}_1, \underline{x}_2 \right)$$

$$= -\tilde{\theta}_1^T \psi_1 \left(\underline{y}_1 \right) - k_1 \omega_1 + g_{s1} \omega_2 + d_{s1} + \varepsilon_1 \left(\underline{y}_1, \underline{x}_2 \right) \tag{30}$$

Multiplying both sides of (30) by ω_1 yields

$$\omega_1 D^\alpha \omega_1 = -\omega_1 \tilde{\theta}_1^T \psi_1 \left(\underline{y}_1 \right) - k_1 \omega_1^2 + g_{s1} \omega_1 \omega_2 + \omega_1 d_{s1} + \omega_1 \varepsilon_1 \left(\underline{y}_1, \underline{x}_2 \right) \tag{31}$$

Choose a Lyapunov function candidate as follows

$$V_1 = \frac{1}{2} \omega_1^2 + \frac{1}{2\gamma_1} \tilde{\theta}_1^T \tilde{\theta}_1 \tag{32}$$

By using Lemma 2, the Caputo fractional derivative of (32) becomes:

$$D^\alpha V_1 = \frac{1}{2} D^\alpha \omega_1^2 + \frac{1}{2\gamma_1} D^\alpha \tilde{\theta}_1^T \tilde{\theta}_1 \le \omega_1 D^\alpha \omega_1 + \frac{1}{\gamma_1} \tilde{\theta}_1^T D^\alpha \tilde{\theta}_1 \tag{33}$$

Substituting (28) and (31) into (33) yields

$$\begin{aligned} D^\alpha V_1(\mathrm{t}) &\le -k_1 \omega_1^2 - \sigma_1 \left| \omega_1 \right| \tilde{\theta}_1^T \theta_1 + g_{s1} \omega_1 \omega_2 + \omega_1 d_{s1} + \omega_1 \varepsilon_1 \left(\underline{y}_1, \underline{x}_2 \right) \\ &\le -k_1 \omega_1^2 - \frac{\sigma_1}{2} \left| \omega_1 \right| \left\| \tilde{\theta}_1 \right\|^2 + g_{s1} \omega_1 \omega_2 + H_1 \left| \omega_1 \right| \end{aligned} \tag{34}$$

with $H_1 = \left(\overline{d}_{s1} + \overline{\varepsilon}_1 + \frac{\sigma_1}{2} \left\| \theta_1^* \right\|^2 \right)$.

The next step consists in stabilizing the error ω_2.

Step 2: From the second equation of (20), one has

$$D^{\alpha}\omega_2 = D^{\alpha}e_2 - D^{\alpha}\alpha_1 = h_2(\underline{y}_2, \underline{x}_3) + g_{s2}e_3 + d_{s2} - D^{\alpha}\alpha_1 \tag{35}$$

Let the unknown smooth function $h_2(\underline{y}_2, \underline{x}_3)$ be approximated by the linearly parameterized fuzzy systems (3), on the compact set $\Omega_{\underline{y}_2}$, as follows:

$$\hat{h}_2\left(\underline{y}_2, \underline{x}_3, \theta_2\right) = \theta_2^T \psi_2\left(\underline{y}_2\right) \tag{36}$$

where $\psi_2\left(\underline{y}_2\right)$ is the fuzzy basis function (FBF) vector, which is fixed a priori by the designer, and θ_2 is the adjustable parameter vector of this fuzzy system.

Let us define

$$\theta_2^* = \arg\min_{\theta_2}\left[\sup_{\underline{y}_2 \in \Omega_{\underline{y}_2}}\left|h_2(\underline{y}_2, \underline{x}_3) - \theta_2^T \psi_2\left(\underline{y}_2\right)\right|\right] \tag{37}$$

as the optimal value of θ_2 which is mainly introduced for analysis purposes as its value is not needed when implementing the controller (Boulkroune et al., 2017; Hamel & Boulkroune, 2016; Liu & Tong, 2015d; Tong & Li, 2013; Liu & Tong, 2014; Li et al., 2015; Li & Tong, 2016b; Liu et al., 2016; Sui et al., 2016; Boulkroune et al., 2008b; Boulkroune & M'saad, 2012).

Define also

$$\tilde{\theta}_2 = \theta_2 - \theta_2^* \text{ and } \varepsilon_2\left(\underline{y}_2, \underline{x}_3\right) = h_2(\underline{y}_2, \underline{x}_3) - \theta_2^{*T} \psi_2\left(\underline{y}_2\right) \tag{38}$$

as the parametric estimation error and the fuzzy reconstruction error, respectively.

As in Hamel & Boulkroune (2016), Liu & Tong (2015d), Tong & Li (2013), Liu & Tong (2014), Li et al. (2015), Li & Tong (2016b), Liu et al. (2016), Sui et al. (2016), Boulkroune et al. (2008b), Boulkroune & M'saad (2012), one assumes that this fuzzy reconstruction error is bounded for all $\underline{x}_3 \in \Omega_{\underline{x}_3}, \underline{y}_2 \in \Omega_{\underline{y}_2}$, i.e.

$$\left|\varepsilon_2\left(\underline{y}_2, \underline{x}_3\right)\right| \leq \bar{\varepsilon}_2, \quad \forall \underline{x}_3 \in \Omega_{\underline{x}_3}, \underline{y}_2 \in \Omega_{\underline{y}_2} \tag{39}$$

where $\bar{\varepsilon}_2$ is an unknown constant.

From the above analysis, one has

$$h_2(\underline{y}_2, \underline{x}_3) - \theta_2^T \psi_2\left(\underline{y}_2\right) = h_2(\underline{y}_2, \underline{x}_3) - \theta_2^{*T} \psi_2\left(\underline{y}_2\right) + \theta_2^{*T} \psi_2\left(\underline{y}_2\right) - \theta_2^T \psi_2\left(\underline{y}_2\right)$$

$$= -\tilde{\theta}_2^T \psi_2\left(\underline{y}_2\right) + \varepsilon_2\left(\underline{y}_2, \underline{x}_3\right) \tag{40}$$

It follows from (35) and (40) that

$$D^\alpha \omega_2 = h_2\left(\underline{y}_2, \underline{x}_3\right) + g_{s2} e_3 + d_{s2} - D^\alpha \alpha_1$$

$$= -\tilde{\theta}_2^T \psi_2\left(\underline{y}_2\right) + \theta_2^T \psi_2\left(\underline{y}_2\right) - D^\alpha \alpha_1 + g_{s2} e_3 + d_{s2} + \varepsilon_2\left(\underline{y}_2, \underline{x}_3\right) \tag{41}$$

Let design the virtual control input α_2 as follows

$$\alpha_2 = g_{s2}^{-1}\left(-\theta_2^T \psi_2\left(\underline{y}_2\right) - k_2 \omega_2 - g_{s1} \omega_1 + D^\alpha \alpha_1\right) \tag{42}$$

where $k_2 > 0$ is a design parameter.

Its adaptation law can be designed as

$$D^\alpha \theta_2 = \gamma_2 \omega_2 \psi_2\left(\underline{y}_2\right) - \gamma_2 \sigma_2 \left|\omega_2\right| \theta_2 \tag{43}$$

with σ_2 and γ_2 being strictly positive design parameters.

Because the Caputo fractional-order derivative of a constant is zero, one can write (43) as follows:

$$D^\alpha \theta_2 = D^\alpha \tilde{\theta}_2 = \gamma_2 \omega_2 \psi_2\left(\underline{y}_2\right) - \gamma_2 \sigma_2 \left|\omega_2\right| \theta_2 \tag{44}$$

Now, les's denote $\omega_3 = e_3 - \alpha_2$. From (41) and (42), one has

$$D^\alpha \omega_2 = -\tilde{\theta}_2^T \psi_2\left(\underline{y}_2\right) + \theta_2^T \psi_2\left(\underline{y}_2\right) + g_{s2} e_2 + d_{s2} + \varepsilon_2\left(\underline{y}_2, \underline{x}_3\right) - D^\alpha \alpha_1$$

$$= -\tilde{\theta}_2^T \psi_2\left(\underline{y}_2\right) + \theta_2^T \psi_2\left(\underline{y}_2\right) + g_{s2}\left(e_3 - \alpha_2\right) + g_{s2} \alpha_2 + d_{s2} + \varepsilon_2\left(\underline{y}_2, \underline{x}_3\right) - D^\alpha \alpha_1$$

$$= -\tilde{\theta}_2^T \psi_2\left(\underline{y}_2\right) - k_2 \omega_2 - g_{s1} \omega_1 + g_{s2} \omega_3 + d_{s2} + \varepsilon_2\left(\underline{y}_2, \underline{x}_3\right) \tag{45}$$

Multiplying both sides of (45) by ω_2 yields

$$\omega_2 D^\alpha \omega_2 = -\omega_2 \tilde{\theta}_2^T \psi_2\left(\underline{y}_2\right) - k_2 \omega_2^2 - g_{s1} \omega_2 \omega_1 + g_{s2} \omega_2 \omega_3 + \omega_2 d_{s2} + \omega_2 \varepsilon_2\left(\underline{y}_2, \underline{x}_3\right) \tag{46}$$

Choose a Lyapunov function candidate as follows

$$V_2 = V_1 + \frac{1}{2}\omega_2^2 + \frac{1}{2\gamma_2}\tilde{\theta}_2^T \tilde{\theta}_2 \tag{47}$$

By using Lemma 5, the fractional derivative of (47) becomes:

$$D^\alpha V_2 = D^\alpha V_1 + \frac{1}{2} D^\alpha \omega_2^2 + \frac{1}{2\gamma_2} D^\alpha \tilde{\theta}_2^T \tilde{\theta}_2 \le D^\alpha V_1 + \omega_2 D^\alpha \omega_2 + \frac{1}{\gamma_2} \tilde{\theta}_2^T D^\alpha \tilde{\theta}_2 \tag{48}$$

Substituting (46) and (44) into (48) yields

$$D^\alpha V_2 \le D^\alpha V_1 - k_2 \omega_2^2 - \sigma_2 \left| \omega_2 \right| \tilde{\theta}_2^T \theta_2 - g_{s1} \omega_1 \omega_2 + g_{s2} \omega_2 \omega_3 + \omega_2 d_{s2} + \omega_2 \varepsilon_2 \left(\underline{y}_2, \underline{x}_3 \right)$$

$$\le -k_1 \omega_1^2 - k_2 \omega_2^2 - \frac{\sigma_1}{2} \left| \omega_1 \right| \left\| \tilde{\theta}_1 \right\|^2 - \frac{\sigma_2}{2} \left| \omega_2 \right| \left\| \tilde{\theta}_2 \right\|^2 + g_{s2} \omega_2 \omega_3 + H_1 \left| \omega_1 \right| + H_2 \left| \omega_2 \right| \tag{49}$$

with $H_2 = \left(\overline{d}_{s2} + \overline{\varepsilon}_2 + \frac{\sigma_2}{2} \left\| \theta_2^* \right\|^2 \right)$.

In the next step (step 3), one will stabilize the error ω_3.

Step *i*: From the *ith* equation of (20), one has

$$D^\alpha \omega_i = D^\alpha e_i - D^\alpha \alpha_{i-1} = h_i \left(\underline{y}_i, \underline{x}_{i+1} \right) + g_{si} e_{i+1} + d_{si} - D^\alpha \alpha_{i-1}, \text{ for } i = 3, ..., n-1 \tag{50}$$

Let the unknown smooth function $h_i \left(\underline{y}_i, \underline{x}_{i+1} \right)$ be approximated by the linearly parameterized fuzzy systems (9), on the compact set $\Omega_{\underline{y}_i}$, as follows:

$$\hat{h}_i \left(\underline{y}_i, \underline{x}_{i+1}, \theta_i \right) = \theta_i^T \psi_i \left(\underline{y}_i \right), \text{ with } i = 3, ..., n-1, \tag{51}$$

where $\psi_i \left(\underline{y}_i \right)$ is the fuzzy basis function (FBF) vector, which is fixed a priori by the designer, and θ_i is the adjustable parameter vector of the fuzzy system.

Let us define

$$\theta_i^* = \arg \min_{\theta_i} \left[\sup_{\underline{y}_i \in \Omega_{\underline{y}_i}} \left| h_i(\underline{y}_i, \underline{x}_{i+1}) - \theta_i^T \psi_i \left(\underline{y}_i \right) \right| \right] \tag{52}$$

as the optimal value of θ_i which is mainly introduced for analysis purposes as its value is not needed when implementing the controller.

Define also

$$\tilde{\theta}_i = \theta_i - \theta_i^* \text{ and } \varepsilon_i(\underline{y}_i, \underline{x}_{i+1}) = h_i(\underline{y}_i, \underline{x}_{i+1}) - \theta_i^{*T} \psi_i \left(\underline{y}_i \right) \tag{53}$$

as the parametric estimation error and the fuzzy reconstruction error, respectively.

As in Hamel & Boulkroune (2016), Liu & Tong (2015d), Tong & Li (2013), Liu & Tong (2014), Li et al. (2015), Li & Tong (2016b), Liu et al. (2016), Sui et al. (2016), Boulkroune et al. (2008b), and Boulkroune & M'saad (2012), one assumes that this fuzzy reconstruction error is bounded for all $\underline{x}_{i+1} \in \Omega_{\underline{x}_{i+1}}, \underline{y}_j \in \Omega_{\underline{y}_j}$, i.e.

$$\left| \varepsilon_i(\underline{y}_j, \underline{x}_{i+1}) \right| \le \bar{\varepsilon}_i, \quad \forall \underline{x}_{i+1} \in \Omega_{\underline{x}_{i+1}}, \underline{y}_j \in \Omega_{\underline{y}_j} \tag{54}$$

where $\bar{\varepsilon}_i$ is an unknown constant.

From the above analysis, one has

$$h_i(\underline{y}_j, \underline{x}_{i+1}) - \theta_i^T \psi_i\left(\underline{y}_j\right) = h_i(\underline{y}_j, \underline{x}_{i+1}) - \theta_i^{*T} \psi_i\left(\underline{y}_j\right) + \theta_i^{*T} \psi_i\left(\underline{y}_j\right) - \theta_i^T \psi_i\left(\underline{y}_j\right)$$

$$= -\tilde{\theta}_i^T \psi_i\left(\underline{y}_j\right) + \varepsilon_i(\underline{y}_j, \underline{x}_{i+1}) \tag{55}$$

It follows from (55) and (50) that

$$D^\alpha \omega_i = h_i(\underline{y}_j, \underline{x}_{i+1}) + g_{si} e_{i+1} + d_{si} - D^\alpha \alpha_{i-1}$$

$$= -\tilde{\theta}_i^T \psi_i\left(\underline{y}_j\right) + \theta_i^T \psi_i\left(\underline{y}_j\right) + g_{si} e_{i+1} + d_{si} + \varepsilon_i\left(\underline{y}_j, \underline{x}_{i+1}\right) - D^\alpha \alpha_{i-1} \tag{56}$$

Let's design the virtual control input α_i as follows

$$\alpha_i = g_{si}^{-1}\left(-\theta_i^T \psi_i\left(\underline{y}_j\right) - k_i \omega_i - g_{si} \omega_{i-1} + D^\alpha \alpha_{i-1}\right) \tag{57}$$

where $k_i > 0$ is a design parameter.

Its adaptation law can be designed as

$$D^\alpha \theta_i = \gamma_i \omega_i \psi_i\left(\underline{y}_j\right) - \gamma_i \sigma_i |\omega_i| \theta_i \tag{58}$$

with σ_i and γ_i being strictly positive design parameters.

Because the Caputo fractional-order derivative of a constant is zero, one can write (58) as follows:

$$D^\alpha \theta_i = D^\alpha \tilde{\theta}_i = \gamma_i \omega_i \psi_i\left(\underline{y}_j\right) - \gamma_i \sigma_i |\omega_i| \theta_i \tag{59}$$

Now, let's denote $\omega_{i+1} = e_{i+1} - \alpha_i$. From (56) and (55), one has

$$D^{\alpha}\omega_i = -\tilde{\theta}_i^T \psi_i\left(\underline{y}_i\right) + \theta_i^T \psi_i\left(\underline{y}_i\right) + g_{si}e_{i+1} + d_{si} + \varepsilon_i\left(\underline{y}_i, \underline{x}_{i+1}\right) - D^{\alpha}\alpha_{i-1}$$

$$= -\tilde{\theta}_i^T \psi_i\left(\underline{y}_i\right) + \theta_i^T \psi_i\left(\underline{y}_i\right) + g_{si}(e_{i+1} - \alpha_i) + g_{si}\alpha_i + d_{si} + \varepsilon_i\left(\underline{y}_i, \underline{x}_{i+1}\right) - D^{\alpha}\alpha_{i-1}$$

$$= -\tilde{\theta}_i^T \psi_i\left(\underline{y}_i\right) - k_i\omega_i - g_{si-1}\omega_{i-1} + g_{si}\omega_{i+1} + d_{si} + \varepsilon_i\left(\underline{y}_i, \underline{x}_{i+1}\right) \qquad (60)$$

Multiplying both sides of (60) by ω_i yields

$$\omega_i D^{\alpha}\omega_i = -\omega_i\tilde{\theta}_i^T \psi_i\left(\underline{y}_i\right) - k_i\omega_i^2 - g_{si-1}\omega_i\omega_{i-1} + g_{si}\omega_i\omega_{i+1} + \omega_i d_{si} + \omega_i\varepsilon_i\left(\underline{y}_i, \underline{x}_{i+1}\right) \qquad (61)$$

Choose a Lyapunov function candidate as follows

$$V_i = V_{i-1} + \frac{1}{2}\omega_i^2 + \frac{1}{2\gamma_i}\tilde{\theta}_i^T\tilde{\theta}_i \qquad (62)$$

By using Lemma 2, the fractional derivative of (62) becomes:

$$D^{\alpha}V_i = D^{\alpha}V_{i-1} + \frac{1}{2}D^{\alpha}\omega_i^2 + \frac{1}{2\gamma_i}D^{\alpha}\tilde{\theta}_i^T\tilde{\theta}_i \le D^{\alpha}V_{i-1} + \omega_i D^{\alpha}\omega_i + \frac{1}{\gamma_i}\tilde{\theta}_i^T D^{\alpha}\tilde{\theta}_i \qquad (63)$$

Substituting (61) and (59) into (63) yields

$$D^{\alpha}V_i \le D^{\alpha}V_{i-1} - k_i\omega_i^2 - \sigma_i\left|\omega_i\right|\tilde{\theta}_i^T\theta_i - g_{si-1}\omega_i\omega_{i-1} + g_{si}\omega_i\omega_{i+1} + \omega_i d_{si} + \omega_i\varepsilon_i\left(\underline{y}_i, \underline{x}_{i+1}\right)$$

$$\le -\sum_1^i k_j\omega_j^2 - \sum_1^i \frac{\sigma_j}{2}\left|\omega_j\right|\left\|\tilde{\theta}_i\right\|^2 + g_{si}\omega_i\omega_{i+1} + \sum_1^i H_j\left|\omega_j\right| \qquad (64)$$

with $H_j = \left(\overline{d}_{sj} + \overline{\varepsilon}_j + \frac{\sigma_j}{2}\left\|\theta_j^*\right\|^2\right)$.

Step n: From the last equation of (20), one has

$$D^{\alpha}\omega_n = D^{\alpha}e_n - D^{\alpha}\alpha_{n-1} = h_n(\underline{y}_n, \underline{x}_n) + g_{sn}u + d_{sn} - D^{\alpha}\alpha_{n-1} \qquad (65)$$

where $\omega_n = e_n - \alpha_{n-1}$

Let the unknown smooth function $h_n(\underline{y}_n, \underline{x}_n)$ be approximated by the linearly parameterized fuzzy system (2), on the compact set $\Omega_{\underline{y}_n}$, as follows:

$$\hat{h}_n\left(\underline{y}_n, \underline{x}_n, \theta_n\right) = \theta_n^T \psi_n\left(\underline{y}_n\right) \tag{66}$$

where $\psi_n\left(\underline{y}_n\right)$ is the fuzzy basis function (FBF) vector, which is fixed a priori by the designer, and θ_n is the adjustable parameter vector of the fuzzy system.

Let us define

$$\theta_n^* = \arg\min_{\theta_n}\left[\sup_{\underline{y}_n \in \Omega_{\underline{y}_n}} \left| h_n(\underline{y}_n, \underline{x}_n) - \theta_n^T \psi_n\left(\underline{y}_n\right) \right|\right] \tag{67}$$

as the optimal value of θ_n which is mainly introduced for analysis purposes as its value is not needed when implementing the controller.

Define also

$$\tilde{\theta}_n = \theta_n - \theta_n^* \text{ and } \varepsilon_n\left(\underline{y}_n, \underline{x}_n\right) = h_n(\underline{y}_n, \underline{x}_n) - \theta_n^{*T} \psi_n\left(\underline{y}_n\right) \tag{68}$$

as the parametric estimation error and the fuzzy reconstruction error, respectively.

As in Hamel & Boulkroune (2016), Liu & Tong (2015d), Tong & Li (2013), Liu & Tong (2014), Li et al. (2015), Li & Tong (2016b), Liu et al. (2016), Sui et al. (2016), Boulkroune et al. (2008b), and Boulkroune & M'saad (2012), one assumes that this fuzzy reconstruction error is bounded for all

$$\underline{x}_n \in \Omega_{\underline{x}_n}, \underline{y}_n \in \Omega_{\underline{y}_n}, \text{ i.e}$$

$$\left|\varepsilon_n\left(\underline{y}_n, \underline{x}_n\right)\right| \leq \bar{\varepsilon}_n, \quad \forall \underline{x}_n \in \Omega_{\underline{x}_n}, \underline{y}_n \in \Omega_{\underline{y}_n} \tag{69}$$

where $\bar{\varepsilon}_n$ is an unknown constant.

From the above analysis, one has

$$\hat{h}_n(\underline{y}_n, \underline{x}_n) - \theta_n^T \psi_n\left(\underline{y}_n\right) = h_n(\underline{y}_n, \underline{x}_n) - \theta_n^{*T} \psi_n\left(\underline{y}_n\right) + \theta_n^{*T} \psi_n\left(\underline{y}_n\right) - \theta_n^T \psi_n\left(\underline{y}_n\right)$$

$$= -\tilde{\theta}_n^T \psi_n\left(\underline{y}_n\right) + \varepsilon_n(\underline{y}_n, \underline{x}_n) \tag{70}$$

It follows from (70) and (65) that

$$D^\alpha \omega_n = h_n(\underline{y}_n, \underline{x}_n) + g_{sn} u + d_{sn} - D^\alpha \alpha_{n-1}$$

$$= -\tilde{\theta}_n^T \psi_n\left(\underline{y}_n\right) + \theta_n^T \psi_n\left(\underline{y}_n\right) + g_{sn} u + d_{sn} + \varepsilon_n(\underline{y}_n, \underline{x}_n) - D^\alpha \alpha_{n-1} \tag{71}$$

The practical control law can now be designed as follows:

$$u = g_{sn}^{-1} \left(-\theta_n^T \psi_n \left(\underline{y}_n \right) - k_n \omega_n - g_{sn-1} \omega_{n-1} + D^\alpha \alpha_{n-1} + v_r \right) \tag{72}$$

where $k_n > 0$ is a design parameter.

The corresponding adaptation law can be designed as

$$D^\alpha \theta_n = \gamma_n \omega_n \psi_n \left(\underline{y}_n \right) - \gamma_n \sigma_n \left| \omega_n \right| \theta_n \tag{73}$$

and

$$D^\alpha \hat{H} = \gamma_h W \tag{74}$$

$$D^\alpha v_r = -\gamma_r v_r + \gamma_r \left[-\omega_n + \frac{v_r \left(-\hat{H}^T W \right)}{v_r^2 + \delta^2} \right] \tag{75}$$

$$D^\alpha \delta = -\gamma_\delta \frac{\delta \hat{H}^T W}{v_r^2 + \delta^2}, \ \delta(0) > 0 \tag{76}$$

with $\hat{H}$ being the estimate of the unknown vector $H^T = \left[H_1, H_2, ..., H_n \right]$ and $W^T = \left[\left| \omega_1 \right|, \left| \omega_2 \right|, ..., \left| \omega_n \right| \right]$, where σ_n, γ_n, γ_r, γ_δ, and γ_h are strictly positive design parameters.

From (71) and (72), one has

$$D^\alpha \omega_n = -\tilde{\theta}_n^T \psi_n \left(\underline{y}_n \right) + \theta_n^T \psi_n \left(\underline{y}_n \right) + g_{sn} u + d_{sn} + \varepsilon_n \left(\underline{y}_n, \underline{x}_n \right) - D^\alpha \alpha_{n-1}$$

$$= -\tilde{\theta}_n^T \psi_n \left(\underline{y}_n \right) - k_n \omega_n - g_{sn-1} \omega_{n-1} + d_{sn} + \varepsilon_n \left(\underline{y}_n, \underline{x}_n \right) + v_r \tag{77}$$

Multiplying both sides of (77) by ω_n yields

$$\omega_n D^\alpha \omega_n = -\omega_n \tilde{\theta}_n^T \psi_n \left(\underline{y}_n \right) - k_n \omega_n^2 - g_{sn-1} \omega_n \omega_{n-1} + \omega_n d_{sn} + \omega_n \varepsilon_n \left(\underline{y}_n, \underline{x}_n \right) + \omega_n v_r \tag{78}$$

Choose a Lyapunov function candidate as follows

$$V_n = V_{n-1} + \frac{1}{2}\omega_n^2 + \frac{1}{2\gamma_n}\tilde{\theta}_n^T\tilde{\theta}_n + \frac{1}{2\gamma_\delta}\delta^2 + \frac{1}{2\gamma_v}v_r^2 + \frac{1}{2\gamma_h}\tilde{H}^T\tilde{H} \tag{79}$$

By using Lemma 2, the fractional derivative of (79) becomes:

$$D^\alpha V_n = D^\alpha V_{n-1} + \frac{1}{2}D^\alpha\omega_n^2 + \frac{1}{2\gamma_n}D^\alpha\tilde{\theta}_n^T\tilde{\theta}_n + \frac{1}{2\gamma_\delta}D^\alpha\delta^2 + \frac{1}{2\gamma_v}D^\alpha v_r^2 + \frac{1}{2\gamma_h}D^\alpha\tilde{H}^T\tilde{H}$$

$$\leq D^\alpha V_{n-1} + \omega_n D^\alpha\omega_n + \frac{1}{\gamma_n}\tilde{\theta}_n^T D^\alpha\tilde{\theta}_n + \frac{1}{\gamma_\delta}\delta D^\alpha\delta + \frac{1}{\gamma_v}v_r D^\alpha v_r + \frac{1}{\gamma_h}\tilde{H}^T D^\alpha\tilde{H} \tag{80}$$

Substituting (78) and (73) into (80) yields

$$D^\alpha V_n \leq D^\alpha V_{n-1} - k_n\omega_n^2 - \sigma_n\left|\omega_n\right|\tilde{\theta}_n^T\theta_n - g_{sn-1}\omega_n\omega_{n-1} + \omega_n d_{sn} + \omega_n\varepsilon_n\left(\underline{y}_n,\underline{x}\right) + \omega_n v_r + $$
$$\frac{1}{\gamma_\delta}\delta D^\alpha\delta + \frac{1}{\gamma_v}v_r D^\alpha v_r$$

$$\leq -\sum_1^n k_j\omega_j^2 - \sum_1^n\frac{\sigma_j}{2}\left|\omega_j\right|\left\|\tilde{\theta}_i\right\|^2 + \sum_1^n H_j\left|\omega_j\right| + \omega_n v_r + \frac{1}{\gamma_\delta}\delta D^\alpha\delta + \frac{1}{\gamma_v}v_r D^\alpha v_r + \frac{1}{\gamma_h}\tilde{H}^T D^\alpha\tilde{H}$$

$$\leq -\sum_1^n k_j\omega_j^2 - \sum_1^n\frac{\sigma_j}{2}\left|\omega_j\right|\left\|\tilde{\theta}_i\right\|^2 + H^T W + \omega_n v_r + \frac{1}{\gamma_\delta}\delta D^\alpha\delta + \frac{1}{\gamma_v}v_r D^\alpha v_r + \frac{1}{\gamma_h}\tilde{H}^T D^\alpha H \tag{81}$$

with $H_n = \left(\bar{d}_{sn} + \bar{\varepsilon}_n + \frac{\sigma_n}{2}\left\|\theta_n^*\right\|^2\right)$.

Using (74)-(76), one gets finally

$$D^\alpha V_n \leq -\sum_1^n k_j\omega_j^2 \tag{82}$$

The stability result of the closed-loop system is given as follows.

Theorem 1: For the master-salve system (16)-(17), if the control input is designed as (27), (42), (57) and (72), and the adaptation laws are selected as (28), (43), (58), and (73)-(76), then synchronization errors as well as parametric estimation errors are Lyapunov uniformly stable.

Proof of Theorem 1: From Step1 to Step n, and from (82), and according to Lemma 3, one can conclude that all errors are Lyapunov uniformly stable.

SIMULATION RESULTS

Two simulation examples are presented in this section to show the effectiveness of the theoretical results obtained.

Example 1

In this example, one will verify the effectiveness of the proposed scheme for the synchronization of two fractional-order Duffing's systems (Xu et al., 2013; Rostami & Haeri, 2015). The dynamical equations of those systems are given below.

The Master System:

$$\begin{cases} D^{\alpha}x_1(t) = x_2 \\ D^{\alpha}x_2(t) = x_1 - x_1^{3} - 0.15x_2 - 0.3\cos(t) \end{cases} \tag{83}$$

The Slave System:

$$\begin{cases} D^{\alpha}y_1(t) = y_2 + d_1(t) \\ D^{\alpha}y_2(t) = y_1 - y_1^{3} - 0.15y_2 + d_2(t) + u \end{cases} \tag{84}$$

The external disturbances are selected as follows: $d_1(t) = 1,$ and $d_2(t) = 0.1 - 0.4\cos(t)$.

The no-controlled slave system (83) chaotically behaves when the fractional order $\alpha = 0.97$. The simulation is performed using the following initial conditions: $(x_1(0), x_2(0)) = (-0.2, 0.1)$, $(y_1(0), y_2(0)) = (-2.9, 2)$.

Figure 2 shows the chaotic attractor of the system (83). From this figure, it is clear that the chaos exists in this fractional-order Duffing's system. The Lyapunov exponents of the master system (83) are depicted in Figure 3.

The design parameters used in this simulation are specified as follows:

$$\gamma_2 = 700, \sigma_2 = 0.001, \ \gamma_h = 3, \ \gamma_r = 75, \gamma_\delta = 10^{-6},$$

and $k_1 = 5, k_2 = 1$.

The used fuzzy logic system, $\theta_2^T \psi_2(\underline{y}_2)$, has the vector $\underline{y}_2 = [y_1, y_2]^T$ as an input. For each input variable of this fuzzy system, as in (Boulkroune et al., 2008b), one defines three (one triangular and two trapezoidal) membership functions uniformly distributed on the intervals [-4, 4].

To test our proposed adaptive backstepping control for the master-slave system (83) and (84), four cases are considered here:

Figure 2. Dynamical behavior of the uncontrolled fractional-order Duffing's system

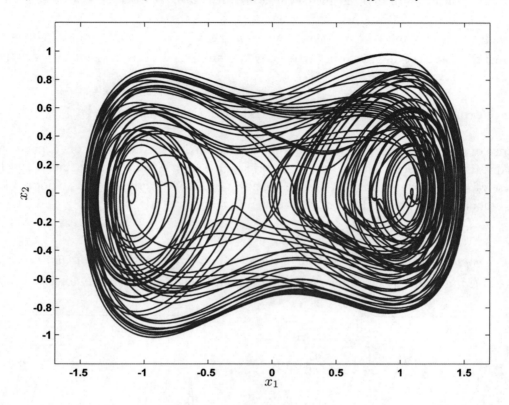

Figure 3. Lyapunov exponents of the uncontrolled fractional-order Duffing's system

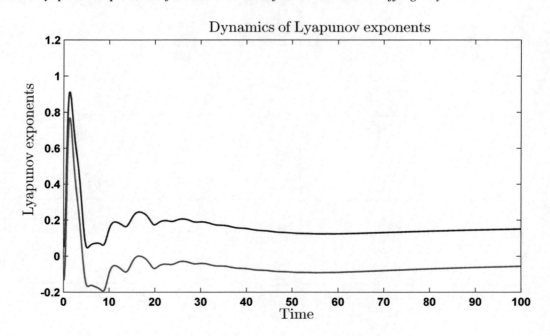

Case 1: Complete Synchronization Without External Disturbances $(\lambda_i = 1)$

The simulation results of this complete synchronization (i.e. for $\lambda_i = 1$) are presented in Figure 4. It can be seen that this backstepping controller efficiently synchronizes the slave system (84) with the master one (83).

Case 2: Complete Synchronization With External Disturbances $(\lambda_i = 1)$

In presence of the external disturbances, the simulation results for this controller are depicted in Figure 5. From this figure, it is clear that the state trajectories of the slave system (84) are quickly synchronized with those of the master system (83), despite unknown external disturbances. In addition, the control signal is smooth, admissible and free of chattering.

Figure 4. Complete synchronization without disturbances (example 1): (a) x_1 (solid line) and y_1 (dotted line). (b) x_2 (solid line) and y_2 (dotted line). (c) e_1 (solid line) and e_2 (dotted line). (d) u (solid line).

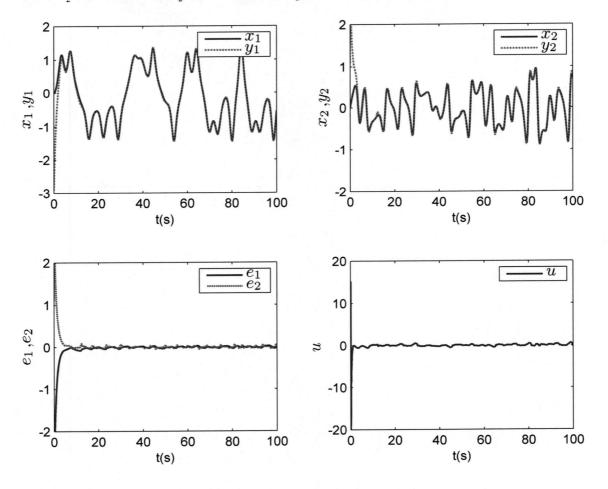

Figure 5. Complete synchronization with disturbances (example 1): (a) x_1 (solid line) and y_1 (dotted line). (b) x_2 (solid line) and y_2 (dotted line). (c) e_1 (solid line) and e_2 (dotted line). (d) u (solid line).

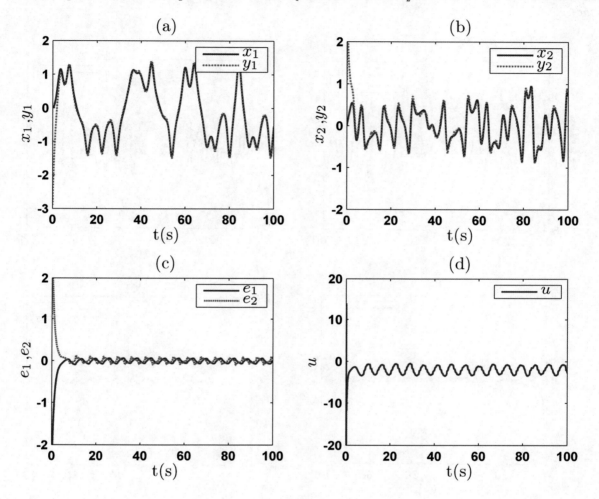

Case 3: Anti-Phase Synchronization Without External Disturbances $(\lambda_i = -1)$

Simulation results for this case are given in Figure 6. This figure shows that the proposed controller performs well.

Case 4: Anti-Phase Synchronization With External Disturbances $(\lambda_i = -1)$

The obtained simulation results for this case are given in Figure 7. It can be clearly seen that the slave trajectories are effectively anti-phase-synchronized with those of the master system, despite the presence of uncertainties and unknown external disturbances.

Figure 6. Anti-phase synchronization without disturbances (example 1): (a) x_1 (solid line) and y_1 (dotted line). (b) x_2 (solid line) and y_2 (dotted line). (c) e_1 (solid line) and e_2 (dotted line). (d) u (solid line).

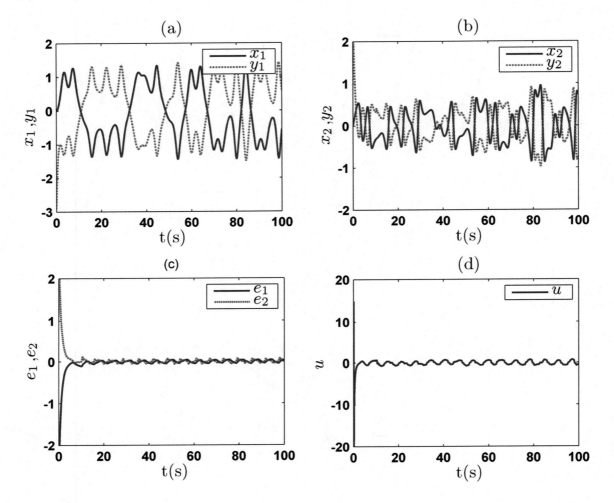

Example 2

Consider the synchronization of two different fractional-order chaotic systems: namely the fractional-order Arneodo's system (as master system), and the fractional-order hybrid optical system (as slave system).

The Master System (Lu, 2005; Roohi et al., 2015):

$$\begin{cases} D^\alpha x_1(t) = x_2 \\ D^\alpha x_2(t) = x_3 \\ D^\alpha x_3(t) = 5.5x_1 - 3.5x_2 - x_3 - x_3^3 \end{cases} \tag{85}$$

Figure 7. Anti-phase synchronization with disturbances (example 1): (a) x_1 *(solid line) and* y_1 *(dotted line). (b)* x_2 *(solid line) and* y_2 *(dotted line). (c)* e_1 *(solid line) and* e_2 *(dotted line). (d)* u *(solid line).*

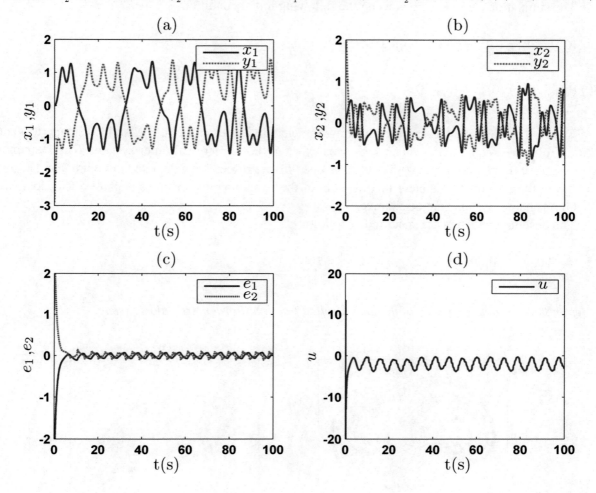

The Slave System (Mitschke & Flüggen, 1984; Abdelouahab & Hamri, 2014):

$$\begin{cases} D^\alpha y_1 = y_2 + d_1(t) \\ D^\alpha y_2 = y_3 + d_2(t) \\ D^\alpha y_3 = -\beta y_3 - y_2 + f(y_1) + d_3(t) + u \end{cases} \qquad (86)$$

where $\beta = 0.326$, and $f(y_1) = \mu y_1(1 - y_1)$, with $\mu = 0.761$. And without lost of generality, the external dynamic disturbances are chosen as:

$$d_1(t) = 1, d_2(t) = 0.1 + \cos(t), \ d_3(t) = 0.1 + 2\cos(3t) + \sin(5t).$$

The no-controlled slave system (86) and the master system (85) chaotically behave when the fractional order $\alpha = 0.99$ (Roohi et al., 2015, Abdelouahab & Hamri, 2014).

The simulations are performed using the following initial conditions

$$(x_1(0), x_2(0), x_3(0)) = (-3, -0.5, 0.1),$$

$$(y_1(0), y_2(0), y_3(0)) = (3, 1, -0.5).$$

Figure 8 and Figure 10 respectively show the chaotic attractors of both chaotic systems (85) and (86). From those figures, it is clear that chaos exists in those fractional-order systems. The Lyapunov exponents of the master system (85) and slave one (86) are respectively depicted in Figure 9 and Figure 11. From these figures, it is clear that the sum of the Lyapunov exponents is negative. This confirms that both chaotic systems are dissipative.

The design parameters are specified as follows:

$$\gamma_3 = 700, \sigma_3 = 0.001, \gamma_h = 2, \gamma_r = 73, \gamma_\delta = 10^{-6},$$

Figure 8. Dynamical behavior of the uncontrolled fractional-order Arneodo's system.

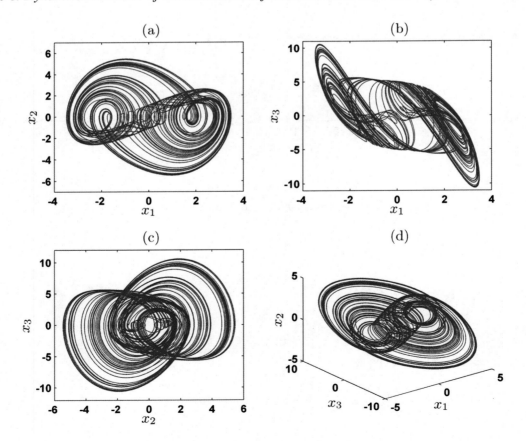

Figure 9. Lyapunov exponents. of the uncontrolled fractional-order Arneodo's system.

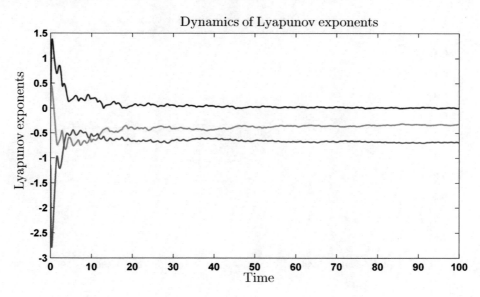

Figure 10. Dynamical behavior of the uncontrolled fractional-order hybrid optical system for $\mu = 0.761$ and $\beta = 0.326$.

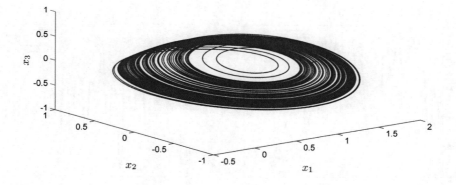

and $k_1 = 8, k_2 = 1, k_3 = 2$.

The used fuzzy logic system, $\theta_3^T \psi_3 \left(\underline{y}_3 \right)$, has the vector $\underline{y}_3 = \left[y_1, y_2, y_3 \right]^T$ as an input. For each input variable of this fuzzy system, as in (Boulkroune et al., 2008b), one defines three (one triangular and two trapezoidal) membership functions uniformly distributed on the intervals [-10, 10].

To test this backstepping controller for this master-slave system, four cases are considered here.

Case 1: Complete Synchronization Without External Disturbances $(\lambda_i = 1)$

The simulation results of this complete synchronization (i.e. for $\lambda_i = 1$) are presented in Figure 12. It can be seen that this backstepping controller efficiently synchronizes the slave system (86) with the master one (85).

Figure 11. Lyapunov exponents of the uncontrolled fractional-order hybrid optical system.

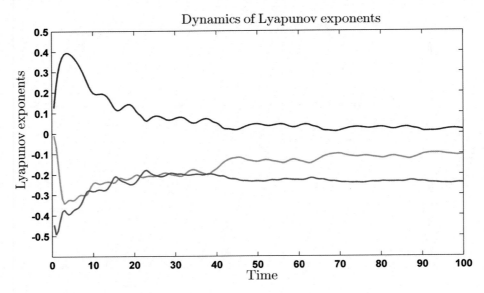

Figure 12. Complete synchronization without disturbances (example 2): (a) x_1 (solid line) and y_1 (dotted line). (b) x_2 (solid line) and y_2 (dotted line). (c) x_3 (solid line) and y_3 (dotted line). (d) u (solid line).

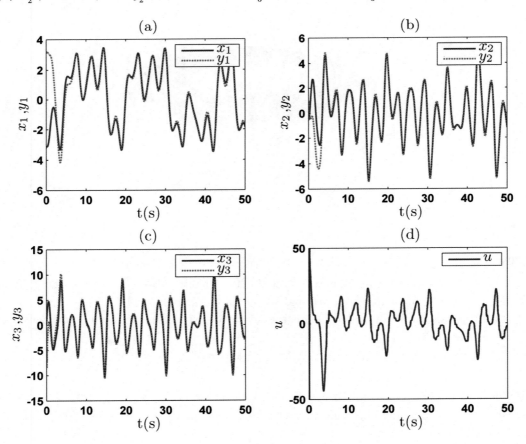

Case 2: Complete Synchronization With External Disturbances $(\lambda_i = 1)$

In presence of the external disturbances, the simulation results for this controller are depicted in Figure 13. From this figure, it is clear that the state trajectories of the slave system (86) are quickly synchronized with those of the master system (85) despite uncertainties and unknown external disturbances. In addition, the control signal is smooth, admissible and free of chattering.

Case 3: Anti-Phase Synchronization Without External Disturbances $(\lambda_i = -1)$

Simulation results are given in Figure 14. This figure shows that the proposed controller performs well.

Figure 13. Complete synchronization with disturbances (example 2): (a) x_1 (solid line) and y_1 (dotted line). (b) x_2 (solid line) and y_2 (dotted line). (c) x_3 (solid line) and y_3 (dotted line). (d) u (solid line).

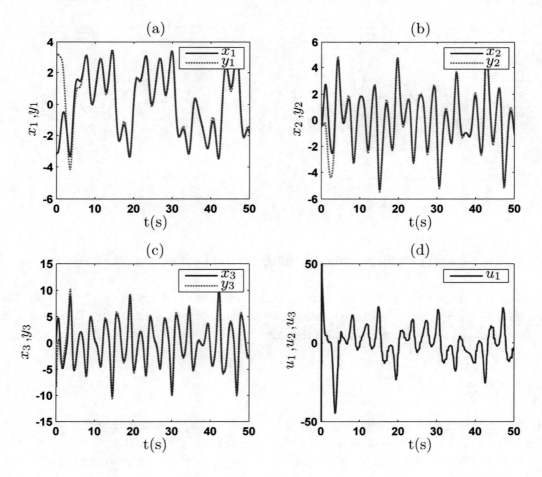

Figure 14. Anti-phase synchronization without disturbances (example 2): (a) x_1 *(solid line) and* y_1 *(dotted line). (b)* x_2 *(solid line) and* y_2 *(dotted line). (c)* x_3 *(solid line) and* y_3 *(dotted line). (d)* u *(solid line).*

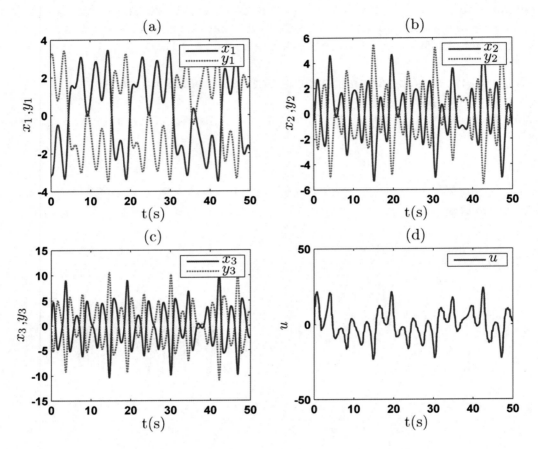

Case 4: Anti-Phase Synchronization With External Disturbances $(\lambda_i = -1)$

The obtained simulation results for this case are given in Figure 15. It can be clearly seen that the slave trajectories are effectively anti-phase-synchronized with those of the master system, despite the presence of uncertainties and unknown external disturbances.

CONCLUSION

In this chapter, an adaptive backstepping control has been investigated to achieve a projective synchronization of a class of uncertain chaotic systems. The backstepping concept has been used to systematically derive step by step our fundamental results. The fuzzy systems have been exploited to adaptively

Figure 15. Anti-phase synchronization with disturbances (example 2): (a) x_1 (solid line) and y_1 (dotted line). (b) x_2 (solid line) and y_2 (dotted line). (c) x_3 (solid line) and y_3 (dotted line). (d) u (solid line).

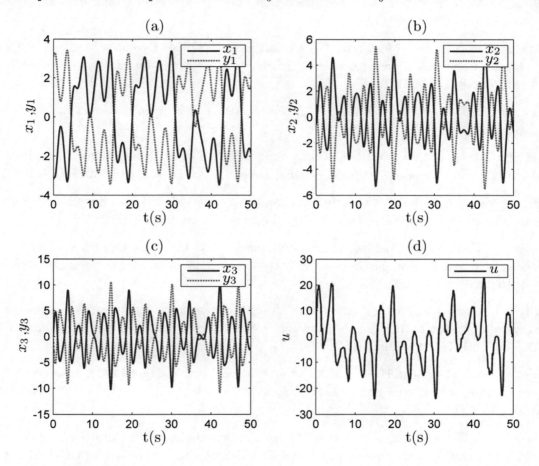

estimate the unknown nonlinear functions. The stability analysis associated to the closed-loop system has been rigorously performed by means of a fractional Lyapunov theory. The effectiveness of the proposed control methodology has been verified via two numerical simulation examples.

In future works, one can study the state and output feedback backstepping control design problems for fractional-order chaotic systems which are with dynamic disturbances, input nonlinearities (saturation, dead-zone or hysteresis), and immeasurable states.

ACKNOWLEDGMENT

The author would like to thank Prof. Abdesselem Boulkroune for his valuable comments which have helped to improve this chapter.

REFERENCES

Abdelouahab, M. S., & Hamri, N. (2014). Fractional-order hybrid optical system and its chaos control synchronization. *EJTP*, *11*(30), 49–62.

Aguila-Camacho, N., Duarte-Mermoud, M. A., & Gallegos, J. A. (2014). Lyapunov functions for fractional order systems. *Communications in Nonlinear Science and Numerical Simulation*, *19*(9), 2951–2957. doi:10.1016/j.cnsns.2014.01.022

Baleanu, D., Machado, J. A. T., & Luo, A. C. (Eds.). (2011). *Fractional dynamics and control*. New York: Springer.

Bao, H., Park, J. H., & Cao, J. (2015). Adaptive synchronization of fractional-order memristor-based neural networks with time delay. *Nonlinear Dynamics*, *82*(3), 1343–1354. doi:10.100711071-015-2242-7

Bao, H. B., & Cao, J. D. (2015). Projective synchronization of fractional-order memristor-based neural networks. *Neural Networks*, *63*, 1–9. doi:10.1016/j.neunet.2014.10.007 PMID:25463390

Benzaoui, M., Chekireb, H., Tadjine, M., & Boulkroune, A. (2016). Trajectory tracking with obstacle avoidance of redundant manipulator based on fuzzy inference systems. *Neurocomputing*, *196*, 23–30. doi:10.1016/j.neucom.2016.02.037

Bigdeli, N., & Ziazi, H. A. (2017). Finite-time fractional-order adaptive intelligent backstepping sliding mode control of uncertain fractional-order chaotic systems. *Journal of the Franklin Institute*, *354*(1), 160–183. doi:10.1016/j.jfranklin.2016.10.004

Boroujeni, E. A., & Momeni, H. R. (2012). Non-fragile nonlinear fractional order observer design for a class of nonlinear fractional order systems. *Signal Processing*, *92*(10), 2365–2370. doi:10.1016/j.sigpro.2012.02.009

Boubellouta, A., & Boulkroune, A. (2016). Chaos synchronization of two different PMSM using a fractional order sliding mode controller. In *Modelling, Identification and Control (ICMIC), 2016 8th International Conference on* (pp. 995-1001). IEEE. 10.1109/ICMIC.2016.7804259

Boulkroune, A., Bouzeriba, A., & Bouden, T. (2016a). Fuzzy generalized projective synchronization of incommensurate fractional-order chaotic systems. *Neurocomputing*, *173*, 606–614. doi:10.1016/j.neucom.2015.08.003

Boulkroune, A., Bouzeriba, A., & Hamel, S. (2015a). Projective synchronization scheme based on Fuzzy controller for uncertain multivariable chaotic systems. In *Chaos Modeling and Control Systems Design* (pp. 73–93). Springer International Publishing. doi:10.1007/978-3-319-13132-0_5

Boulkroune, A., Bouzeriba, A., Hamel, S., & Bouden, T. (2015b). Adaptive fuzzy control-based projective synchronization of uncertain nonaffine chaotic systems. *Complexity*, *21*(2), 180–192. doi:10.1002/cplx.21596

Boulkroune, A., Hamel, S., Zouari, F., Boukabou, A., & Ibeas, A. (2017). Output-Feedback Controller Based Projective Lag-Synchronization of Uncertain Chaotic Systems in the Presence of Input Nonlinearities. *Mathematical Problems in Engineering*.

Boulkroune, A., & M'saad, M. (2012). On the design of observer-based fuzzy adaptive controller for nonlinear systems with unknown control gain sign. *Fuzzy Sets and Systems*, *201*, 71–85. doi:10.1016/j.fss.2011.12.005

Boulkroune, A., M'saad, M., & Farza, M. (2016b). Adaptive fuzzy system-based variable-structure controller for multivariable nonaffine nonlinear uncertain systems subject to actuator nonlinearities. *Neural Computing & Applications*, 1–14.

Boulkroune, A., Tadjine, M., M'Saad, M., & Farza, M. (2008a). A unified approach for design of indirect adaptive output-feedback fuzzy controller. *International Journal of Intelligent Systems Technologies and Applications*, *5*(1-2), 83–103. doi:10.1504/IJISTA.2008.018168

Boulkroune, A., Tadjine, M., M'Saad, M., & Farza, M. (2008b). How to design a fuzzy adaptive controller based on observers for uncertain affine nonlinear systems. *Fuzzy Sets and Systems*, *159*(8), 926–948. doi:10.1016/j.fss.2007.08.015

Boulkroune, A., Tadjine, M., M'saad, M., & Farza, M. (2011). Adaptive fuzzy observer for uncertain nonlinear systems. *Control and Intelligent Systems*, *39*(3), 145–153. doi:10.2316/Journal.201.2011.3.201-1985

Bounar, N., Boulkroune, A., & Boudjema, F. (2014). Adaptive fuzzy control of doubly-fed induction machine. *Journal of Control Engineering and Applied Informatics*, *16*(2), 98–110.

Bounar, N., Boulkroune, A., Boudjema, F., & Farza, M. (2015). Adaptive fuzzy vector control for a doubly-fed induction motor. *Neurocomputing*, *151*, 756–769. doi:10.1016/j.neucom.2014.10.026

Bouzeriba, A., Boulkroune, A., & Bouden, T. (2015). Fuzzy adaptive synchronization of a class of fractional-order chaotic systems. In *Control, Engineering & Information Technology (CEIT), 2015 3rd International Conference on* (pp. 1-6). IEEE. 10.1109/CEIT.2015.7233073

Bouzeriba, A., Boulkroune, A., & Bouden, T. (2016a). Fuzzy adaptive synchronization of a class of fractional-order chaotic systems. In *Advances and Applications in Chaotic Systems* (pp. 363–378). Springer International Publishing. doi:10.1007/978-3-319-30279-9_15

Bouzeriba, A., Boulkroune, A., & Bouden, T. (2016b). Projective synchronization of two different fractional-order chaotic systems via adaptive fuzzy control. *Neural Computing & Applications*, *27*(5), 1349–1360. doi:10.100700521-015-1938-4

Bouzeriba, A., Boulkroune, A., & Bouden, T. (2016c). Fuzzy adaptive synchronization of uncertain fractional-order chaotic systems. *International Journal of Machine Learning and Cybernetics*, *7*(5), 893–908. doi:10.100713042-015-0425-7

Ding, D., Qi, D., Meng, Y., & Xu, L. (2014). Adaptive Mittag-Leffler stabilization of commensurate fractional-order nonlinear systems. *Decision and Control (CDC), 53rd Annual Conference on*, 6920-6926.

Duarte-Mermoud, M. A., Aguila-Camacho, N., Gallegos, J. A., & Castro-Linares, R. (2015). Using general quadratic Lyapunov functions to prove Lyapunov uniform stability for fractional order systems. *Communications in Nonlinear Science and Numerical Simulation*, *22*(1), 650–659. doi:10.1016/j.cnsns.2014.10.008

Efe, M. Ö. (2011). Fractional order systems in industrial automation—a survey. *IEEE Transactions on Industrial Informatics*, *7*(4), 582–591. doi:10.1109/TII.2011.2166775

Geng, L., Yu, Y., & Zhang, S. (2016). Function projective synchronization between integer-order and stochastic fractional-order nonlinear systems. *ISA Transactions*, *64*, 34–46. doi:10.1016/j.isatra.2016.04.018 PMID:27156677

Hamel, S., & Boulkroune, A. (2016). A generalized function projective synchronization scheme for uncertain chaotic systems subject to input nonlinearities. *International Journal of General Systems*, *45*(6), 689–710. doi:10.1080/03081079.2015.1118094

Huang, X., Wang, Z., Li, Y., & Lu, J. (2014). Design of fuzzy state feedback controller for robust stabilization of uncertain fractional-order chaotic systems. *Journal of the Franklin Institute*, *351*(12), 5480–5493. doi:10.1016/j.jfranklin.2014.09.023

Kwan, C., & Lewis, F. L. (2000). Robust backstepping control nonlinear systems using neural networks. *IEEE Transactions on Systems, Man, and Cybernetics. Part A, Systems and Humans*, *30*(6), 753–766. doi:10.1109/3468.895898

Li, H., Wang, J., Lam, H. K., Zhou, Q., & Du, H. (2016a). Adaptive sliding mode control for interval type-2 fuzzy systems. *IEEE Transactions on Systems, Man, and Cybernetics. Systems*, *46*(12), 1654–1663. doi:10.1109/TSMC.2016.2531676

Li, Y., Chen, Y., & Podlubny, I. (2009). Mittag–Leffler stability of fractional order nonlinear dynamic systems. *Automatica*, *45*(8), 1965–1969. doi:10.1016/j.automatica.2009.04.003

Li, Y., & Tong, S. (2016b). Adaptive fuzzy output-feedback stabilization control for a class of switched nonstrict-feedback nonlinear systems. *IEEE Transactions on Cybernetics*, *47*(4), 1007–1016. doi:10.1109/TCYB.2016.2536628 PMID:26992190

Li, Y., Tong, S., & Li, T. (2015). Composite adaptive fuzzy output feedback control design for uncertain nonlinear strict-feedback systems with input saturation. *IEEE Transactions on Cybernetics*, *45*(10), 2299–2308. doi:10.1109/TCYB.2014.2370645 PMID:25438335

Liu, H., Li, S., Cao, J., Li, G., Alsaedi, A., & Alsaadi, F. E. (2017b). Adaptive fuzzy prescribed performance controller design for a class of uncertain fractional-order nonlinear systems with external disturbances. *Neurocomputing*, *219*, 422–430. doi:10.1016/j.neucom.2016.09.050

Liu, H., Li, S., Wang, H., Huo, Y., & Luo, J. (2015c). Adaptive synchronization for a class of uncertain fractional-order neural networks. *Entropy (Basel, Switzerland)*, *17*(10), 7185–7200. doi:10.3390/e17107185

Liu, H., Li, S. G., Sun, Y. G., & Wang, H. X. (2015a). Adaptive fuzzy synchronization for uncertain fractional-order chaotic systems with unknown non-symmetrical control gain. *Acta Physica Sinica*, *64*(7), 070503.

Liu, H., Li, S.-G., Sun, Y.-G., & Wang, H.-X. (2015b). Prescribed performance synchronization for fractional-order chaotic systems. *Chinese Physics B*, *24*(9), 090505. doi:10.1088/1674-1056/24/9/090505

Liu, H., Li, S. G., Wang, H. X., & Li, G. J. (2017a). Adaptive fuzzy synchronization for a class of fractional-order neural networks. *Chinese Physics B*, *26*(3), 030504. doi:10.1088/1674-1056/26/3/030504

Liu, H., Pan, Y., Li, S., & Chen, Y. (2017c). Adaptive fuzzy backstepping control of fractional-order nonlinear systems. *IEEE Transactions on Systems, Man, and Cybernetics. Systems*, *47*(8), 2209–2217. doi:10.1109/TSMC.2016.2640950

Liu, Y. J., Gao, Y., Tong, S., & Li, Y. (2016). Fuzzy approximation-based adaptive backstepping optimal control for a class of nonlinear discrete-time systems with dead-zone. *IEEE Transactions on Fuzzy Systems*, *24*(1), 16–28. doi:10.1109/TFUZZ.2015.2418000

Liu, Y. J., & Tong, S. (2014). Adaptive fuzzy control for a class of nonlinear discrete-time systems with backlash. *IEEE Transactions on Fuzzy Systems*, *22*(5), 1359–1365. doi:10.1109/TFUZZ.2013.2286837

Liu, Y. J., & Tong, S. (2015d). Adaptive fuzzy control for a class of unknown nonlinear dynamical systems. *Fuzzy Sets and Systems*, *263*, 49–70. doi:10.1016/j.fss.2014.08.008

Liu, Y. J., & Tong, S. (2017). Barrier Lyapunov functions for Nussbaum gain adaptive control of full state constrained nonlinear systems. *Automatica*, *76*, 143–152. doi:10.1016/j.automatica.2016.10.011

Lu, J. G. (2005). Chaotic dynamics and synchronization of fractional-order Arneodo's systems. *Chaos, Solitons, and Fractals*, *26*(4), 1125–1133. doi:10.1016/j.chaos.2005.02.023

Mitschke, F., & Flüggen, N. (1984). Chaotic behavior of a hybrid optical bistable system without a time delay. *Applied Physics. B, Lasers and Optics*, *35*(2), 59–64. doi:10.1007/BF00697423

Nikdel, N., Badamchizadeh, M., Azimirad, V., & Nazari, M. A. (2016). Fractional-order adaptive backstepping control of robotic manipulators in the presence of model uncertainties and external disturbances. *IEEE Transactions on Industrial Electronics*, *63*(10), 6249–6256. doi:10.1109/TIE.2016.2577624

Pan, Y., & Yu, H. (2015). Dynamic surface control via singular perturbation analysis. *Automatica*, *57*, 29–33. doi:10.1016/j.automatica.2015.03.033

Pan, Y., & Yu, H. (2016). Composite learning from adaptive dynamic surface control. *IEEE Transactions on Automatic Control*, *61*(9), 2603–2609. doi:10.1109/TAC.2015.2495232

Podlubny, I. (1999). *Fractional differential equations*. San Diego, CA: Academic Press.

Rigatos, G., Zhu, G., Yousef, H., & Boulkroune, A. (2016). Flatness-based adaptive fuzzy control of electrostatically actuated MEMS using output feedback. *Fuzzy Sets and Systems*, *290*, 138–157. doi:10.1016/j.fss.2015.08.027

Roohi, M., Aghababa, M. P., & Haghighi, A. R. (2015). Switching adaptive controllers to control fractional-order complex systems with unknown structure and input nonlinearities. *Complexity*, *21*(2), 211–223. doi:10.1002/cplx.21598

Rostami, M., & Haeri, M. (2015). Undamped oscillations in fractional-order Duffing oscillator. *Signal Processing*, *107*, 361–367. doi:10.1016/j.sigpro.2014.03.042

Shen, J., & Lam, J. (2014). Non-existence of finite-time stable equilibria in fractional-order nonlinear systems. *Automatica, 50*(2), 547–551. doi:10.1016/j.automatica.2013.11.018

Sheng, D., Wei, Y., Cheng, S., & Shuai, J. (2017). Adaptive backstepping control for fractional order systems with input saturation. *Journal of the Franklin Institute, 354*(5), 2245–2268. doi:10.1016/j.jfranklin.2016.12.030 PMID:28683926

Shukla, M. K., & Sharma, B. B. (2017a). Backstepping based stabilization and synchronization of a class of fractional order chaotic systems. *Chaos, Solitons, and Fractals*.

Shukla, M. K., & Sharma, B. B. (2017b). Stabilization of a class of fractional order chaotic systems via backstepping approach. *Chaos, Solitons, and Fractals, 98*, 56–62. doi:10.1016/j.chaos.2017.03.011

Shukla, M. K., & Sharma, B. B. (2018). Control and Synchronization Of A Class Of Uncertain Fractional Order Chaotic Systems Via Adaptive Backstepping Control. *Asian Journal of Control*.

Sui, S., Li, Y., & Tong, S. (2016). Observer-based adaptive fuzzy control for switched stochastic nonlinear systems with partial tracking errors constrained. *IEEE Transactions on Systems, Man, and Cybernetics. Systems, 46*(12), 1605–1617. doi:10.1109/TSMC.2016.2523904

Tong, S., & Li, Y. (2013). Adaptive fuzzy output feedback control of MIMO nonlinear systems with unknown dead-zone inputs. *IEEE Transactions on Fuzzy Systems, 21*(1), 134–146. doi:10.1109/TFUZZ.2012.2204065

Wang, L. X. (1994). *Adaptive fuzzy systems and control: Design and stability analysis*. Englewood Cliffs, NJ: Prentice-Hall.

Wei, Y., Chen, Y., Liang, S., & Wang, Y. (2015). A novel algorithm on adaptive backstepping control of fractional order systems. *Neurocomputing, 165*, 395–402. doi:10.1016/j.neucom.2015.03.029

Wei, Y., Peter, W. T., Yao, Z., & Wang, Y. (2016). Adaptive backstepping output feedback control for a class of nonlinear fractional order systems. *Nonlinear Dynamics, 86*(2), 1047–1056. doi:10.100711071-016-2945-4

Wen, G., Zhao, Y., Duan, Z., Yu, W., & Chen, G. (2016). Containment of higher-order multi-leader multi-agent systems: A dynamic output approach. *IEEE Transactions on Automatic Control, 61*(4), 1135–1140. doi:10.1109/TAC.2015.2465071

Xu, Y., Li, Y., Liu, D., Jia, W., & Huang, H. (2013). Responses of Duffing oscillator with fractional damping and random phase. *Nonlinear Dynamics, 74*(3), 745–753. doi:10.100711071-013-1002-9

Yang, Y., & Chen, G. (2015). Finite-time stability of fractional order impulsive switched systems. *International Journal of Robust and Nonlinear Control, 25*(13), 2207–2222. doi:10.1002/rnc.3202

Yu, W., Li, Y., Wen, G., Yu, X., & Cao, J. (2017). Observer design for tracking consensus in second-order multi-agent systems: Fractional order less than two. *IEEE Transactions on Automatic Control, 62*(2), 894–900. doi:10.1109/TAC.2016.2560145

KEY TERMS AND DEFINITIONS

Adaptive Control: A control methodology in which one or more parameters are used to vary the feedback control signals in order to satisfy some required performance criteria.

Chaos: Erratic and unpredictable dynamic behavior of a deterministic system which never repeats itself. Necessary conditions for a system to display a chaotic behavior are that it be nonlinear and have at least three independent state variables.

Fractional-Order Control: A field of control theory that uses the fractional-order integrator and derivative as parts of the control system design toolkit.

Fractional-Order System: A dynamical system modelled by a fractional differential equation which contains derivatives of non-integer order.

Fuzzy Control System: A control system which is based on fuzzy logic system.

Nonlinear System: A system which can be modelled by a nonlinear differential equation.

Synchronization of Chaos: A phenomenon that may arise, when two or more chaotic systems are coupled.

Chapter 6
Behavior Studies of Nonlinear Fractional–Order Dynamical Systems Using Bifurcation Diagram

Karima Rabah
University of Skikda, Algeria

ABSTRACT

Over the past decades, chaos has stimulated the interest of researchers due to its existence in different fields of science and engineering. The chaotic systems are characterized by their sensitivity to the initial conditions. This property makes the system unpredictable long term. Similar to the integer-order differential systems, fractional-order differential systems can exhibit chaotic behaviors. This type of system contains one or more elements of fractional order. The fractional calculus is recognized in the early seventeenth century but it has been widely applied in many fields and with intense growth just over the past decades. To avoid troubles arising from unusual behaviors of a chaotic system, chaos control has gained increasing attention in recent years. An important objective of a chaos controller is to suppress the chaotic oscillations completely or reduce them to the regular oscillations. The goal of this chapter is to present the evolution of chaotic systems in open and closed loop in function of their parameters and designing a controller using bifurcation diagrams.

INTRODUCTION

Fractional systems, or more non-integer order systems, can be considered as a generalization of integer order systems (Oldham & Spanier, 2006; Sabatier et al., 2007; Kilbas et al., 2006; Das, 2008).

Emergence of effective methods to solve differentiation and integration of non-integer order equations makes fractional-order systems more and more attractive for the systems control community (Rabah et al., 2015). In order to improve the performance of linear feedback systems, Podlubny (1999) proposed a generalization of the classical PID controller to $PI^\lambda D^\mu$ form called the fractional PID, which has recently

DOI: 10.4018/978-1-5225-5418-9.ch006

become very popular due to its additional flexibility to meet design specifications. Since, fractional order PID (FOPID) controllers have found application in several power systems as cited in the following. In Pan & Das (2012), a fractional order PID controller is designed to take care of various contradictory objective functions for an automatic voltage regulator (AVR) system. Bouafoura & Braiek (2010), deals with the design of fractional order PID controller for integer and fractional plants. In Chen et al. (2014), a FOPID is designed for the hydraulic turbine regulating system (HTRS) with the consideration of conflicting performance objectives. As well, the comparative study between the optimum of PID and FOPID controllers improve the superiority of the fractional order controllers over the integer controllers. In Faieghiet al. (2011), the author makes a design of Fractional-Order PID for ship roll motion control using chaos embedded PSO algorithm. In Tang et al. (2012), optimum design of fractional order PID controller for AVR system using chaotic ant swarm. Based on the fractional high gain adaptive control approach, Ladaci et al. (2009) introduced new tuning parameters for the performance behavior improvement of the controlled plant.

In this chapter, we are interested in the analysis of fractional order nonlinear systems and controls in temporal domain fractional PID controllers based on bifurcation diagram to avoid troubles arising from unusual and undesired behaviors.

The bifurcation diagram is one of the most important tools for determining the behavior of the dynamical systems. It shows the values visited or approached asymptotically (fixed points, periodic orbits, or chaotic attractors) of a system as a function of a bifurcation parameter in the system. It rapidly evaluates all possible solutions of a system according to the variations of one of its parameters or its fractional order.

The aim of this work can be resumed in the following points:

1. Study of the fractional-order chaotic system evolution in function of fractional-order using also the bifurcation diagram.
2. Study of the newselected fractional-order nonlinear chaotic system behavior according to its own parameters using the bifurcation diagram.
3. Designing a controller with a bifurcation diagram, particularly a fractional order PID controller, adjusted using this tool.

Simulation examples are given for the different categories of fractional-order chaotic systems, analysis and control design to illustrate the effectiveness of this mathematical tool.

ELEMENTS OF FRACTIONAL CALCULUS THEORY

Fractional calculus is an old mathematical research topic, but it is retrieving popularity nowadays. Recent references Miller & Ross (1993) provide a good source of documentation on fractional systems and operators. However, the topics about application of fractional-order operator theory to dynamic systems control are just a recent focus of interest (Oustaloup, 1991, Ladaci & Charef, 2006, Rabah et al. 2017b).

Basic Definitions

The analysis of the fractional system can be done in the temporal or frequency domain. For that, researches developed several methods to answer this requirement.

1. In Frequency Domain

In this case, the two most used methods are those of Charef and Oustaloup.

Charef method is an approximation approach witch bring the system behavior in the frequency domain(Charefet al. 1992).This is done for a given q, creating a rapprochement with Bode of 20 times q dB / decade and which will therefore have a phase shift of about 90 degrees q times the frequency band required. The transfer function of the fractal order integrator is represented in the frequency domain by the following irrational function

$$H_I = \frac{1}{s^q} \tag{1}$$

Where $s = j\omega$ the complex and q is a positive fractional number such that $0 < q < 1$. In given frequency band of practical interest $\left[\omega_L, \omega_H\right]$. This fractional order operator can be modeled by a fractional power pole (FPP) whose transfer function is given as follows

$$\mathrm{H}(\mathrm{s}) = \frac{K_I}{\left(1 + \dfrac{s}{\omega_c}\right)^q} \tag{2}$$

If we suppose that for $\omega \in \left[\omega_L, \omega_H\right]$ we have $\omega >> \omega_c$ than we can write

$$H(s) = \frac{K_I}{\left(\dfrac{s}{\omega_c}\right)^q} = \frac{K_I \omega_c}{s^q} = \frac{1}{s^q} \tag{3}$$

With $K_I = \dfrac{1}{\omega_c^q}$ and ω_c is the FPP cutoff frequency which is obtained from the low frequency ω_L:

$$\omega_c = \sqrt{10^{\frac{\varepsilon}{10^q}} - 1} \tag{4}$$

Where ε is the maximum permissible error between the slope of the fractional power operator of (1), and the FPP of (2) in the given frequency band $\left[\omega_L, \omega_H\right]$.

The approximation method consists of approximating the slope of 20 dB/dec on the Bode plot of the FPP by a number of lines in the form of zigzag produced by alternating slope of 20q dB/dec and 0dB/dec corresponding to an alternating poles and zeros on the negative real axis of the s-plan such that

$$p_0 < z_0 < p_1 < z_1 < ... < z_{N-1} < p_N \tag{5}$$

Hence the following approximation

$$H(s) = \frac{K_I}{\left(1 + \dfrac{s}{\omega_c}\right)^q} = K_I \frac{\prod_{i=0}^{N-1}\left(1 + \dfrac{s}{z_i}\right)}{\prod_{i=0}^{N}\left(1 + \dfrac{s}{p_i}\right)} \tag{6}$$

Using the method of the singularity function, the poles and zeros of the approximation is in the form of a geometric progression. This graphical approximation method begins with the choice of an approximation error y in dB and approximation frequency band ω_{max}.

The frequency band ω_{max} can be chosen to be 100 times the high frequency of the frequency band of practical interest ω_H, the parameters a, b, p_0, z_0 and N can be easily determined as follows

$$a = 10^{\frac{y}{10(1-q)}} \text{ and } b = 10^{\frac{y}{10q}}$$

$$p_i = \left(ab\right)^i p_0 \text{ and } z_i = \left(ab\right)^i a p_0$$

$$\text{with } p_0 = \omega_c \sqrt{b}, z_0 = a p_0, N = \mathrm{int}\, eger\left[\frac{\log \dfrac{\omega_{max}}{p_0}}{\log\left(ab\right)}\right]$$

Hence, the fractional order integrator can be approximated by a rational function in a given frequency band of practical interest by

$$p_i = p_0 \left(ab\right)^i, \text{ for } i = 1, 2, ..., N$$

$$z_i = z_0 \left(ab\right)^i, \text{ for } i = 1, 2, ..., N$$

2. Temporal Domain

There are many mathematic definitions for fractional integration and derivation. We will here, present two current used one.

a. Riemann-Liouville (R-L) Definition

The R-L fractional order integral of order $\lambda > 0$ is defined as:

$$I_{RL}^{\lambda} f(t) = D^{-\lambda} f(t)$$

$$= \frac{1}{\Gamma(\lambda)} \int_0^t (t - \tau)^{\lambda - 1} f(\tau) d\tau \tag{7}$$

$$D_{RL}^{\mu} f(t) = \frac{1}{\Gamma(n - \mu)} \frac{d^n}{dt^n} \int_0^t (t - \tau)^{n - \mu - 1} f(\tau) d\tau \tag{8}$$

with $\Gamma(.)$ is the Euler's gamma function and the integer n is such that (n-1) < μ < n. This fractional order derivative of equation (8) can also be defined from equation (1) as:

$$D_{RL}^{\mu} f(t) = \frac{d^n}{dt^n} \left\{ I_{RL}^{(n-\mu)} f(t) \right\} \tag{9}$$

b. Grünwald-Leitnikov (G-L) Definition

For $\mu > 0$ the G-L fractional order derivative definition is:

$$D_{GL}^{\mu} f(t) = \frac{d^{\mu}}{dt^{\mu}} f(t)$$

$$= \lim_{h \to 0} h^{-\mu} \sum_{j=0}^{h} (-1)^j \binom{\mu}{j} f(kh - jh) \tag{10}$$

Where h is a sample period, and coefficients

$$\omega_j^{\mu} = \binom{\mu}{j} = \frac{\Gamma(\mu + 1)}{\Gamma(j + 1)\Gamma(\mu - j + 1)} \tag{11}$$

With $\omega_0^{\mu} = \binom{\mu}{0} = 1$ are the following binomial coefficients:

$$\left(1 - z\right)^{\mu} = \sum_{j=0}^{\infty} (-1)^j \binom{\mu}{j} z^j = \sum_{j=0}^{\infty} \omega_j^{(\mu)} z^j \tag{12}$$

The fractional G-L integration is formulated as:

$$I_{GL}^{\lambda} f(t) = D_{GL}^{-\lambda} f(t)$$

$$= \lim_{h \to 0} h^{\lambda} \sum_{j=0}^{h} (-1)^{j} \binom{-\lambda}{j} f(kh - jh) \tag{13}$$

With $\omega_0^{(-\lambda)} = \binom{-\lambda}{0} = 1$ are the following binomial coefficients:

$$\left(1 - z\right)^{-\lambda} = \sum_{j=0}^{\infty} (-1)^{j} \binom{-\lambda}{j} z^{j} = \sum_{j=0}^{\infty} \omega_{j}^{(-\lambda)} z^{j} \tag{14}$$

Implementation of Fractional Operator

Generally, industrial control processes are sampled, so a numerical approximation of the fractional operator is indispensable. There exists several approximation approaches classes whether temporal or frequency domain. In the literature, the current used approaches in frequency domain are those of Charef (Ladaci &Bensafia, 2016) and Oustaloup (Oustaloup, 1991).In temporal domain, there is a lot of work about the numerical solution of the fractional differentials equations, Diethelm have propose an efficient method, based on a predictor-corrector Adams Algorithm(Diethelm, 2003).Definitions cited above have also numerical approximations:

1. Riemann-Liouville (R-L) Approximation

Numerical approximation of fractional Riemann-Liouville integral is based on rectangular method.
   Putting

$$t = k\Delta$$

Where t is current time, k integer and Δ is sample period.
We obtain:

$$I_{RL}^{\lambda} f(k\Delta) = \frac{\Delta}{\Gamma(\lambda)} \sum_{\tau=0}^{k-1} (k\Delta - \tau\Delta)^{\lambda-1} f(\tau\Delta)$$

$$= \frac{\Delta^{\lambda}}{\Gamma(\lambda)} \sum_{\tau=0}^{k-1} (k - \tau)^{\lambda-1} f(\tau\Delta) \tag{15}$$

2. Grünwald-Leitnikov (G-L) Approximation

For a causal function $f(t)$ and for $t = kh$, fractional derivative integral G-L approximation are given respectively by:

$$D^\mu f(kh) = \frac{d^\mu}{dt^\mu} f(t)$$
$$\cong h^{-\mu} \sum_{j=0}^{k} \omega_j^\mu f(kh - jh) \qquad (16)$$

$$I^\lambda f(kh) = D^{-\lambda} f(kh)$$
$$\cong h^\lambda \sum_{j=0}^{k} \omega_j^{-\lambda} f(kh - jh) \qquad (17)$$

Where ω_j^μ, $\omega_j^{-\lambda}$ are binomial coefficients of the equations 16 and 17 respectively, which can be calculated from the two following recurrent formula, for $j = 1, 2, ..., k$:

$$\omega_0^{(\mu)} = \omega_0^{(-\lambda)} = 1$$

$$\omega_j^{(\mu)} = \left(1 - \frac{1+\mu}{j}\right)\omega_{j-1}^{(\mu)}, \; \omega_j^{(-\lambda)} = \left(1 - \frac{1-\mu}{j}\right)\omega_{j-1}^{(-\lambda)}$$

STUDY OF THE DYNAMICAL BEHAVIOR OF THE FRACTIONAL CHAOTIC SYSTEM

Chaos is generally defined as a particular behavior of a dynamic system that includes non-linearity, determinism, unpredictability, irregularity plus sensitivity to initial conditions. Characterization of chaotic systems can be made from observations with graphical tools from the field of nonlinear dynamics such as the bifurcation diagram, the Poincaré section, phase space, or by numerical mathematical tools such as the Lyapunov exhibitors.

Bifurcation Diagram

Moving from a fixed point to a limit cycle of two periods and then to a limit cycle of four periods is an important event in the dynamics of a system. It is said that there is a bifurcation when such a qualitative change of solutions occurs when a parameter is changed. The graphs that explain these bifurcations are logically called bifurcation diagrams.

Bifurcation diagram is an effective tool for quickly evaluating all possible solutions of a system as a function of the variations of one of its parameters. It makes it possible to identify the particular values of the parameter which induce bifurcations. This notion is central to the study of chaos. When looking at such graphs, attention must be paid to the axes. On one axis we take the parameter, and on the other the state variable.

Identification Technique

Here, we study the behavior of the chaotic system in function of their fractional orders. So,the first use of the bifurcation diagram is to identify the suitable fractional order of the chaotic system. We begin by varying one order and fixing the others to 1, and then trace the evolution of the system in function of the varied one. From the obtained diagram, we extract the appropriate order and repeat the same procedure to the following orders. One we have the fractional orders we search for the new fractional order chaotic system by varying system parameters and trace the bifurcation diagram for each one.

Example

In this part two illustrative examples are proposed to well explain the technique used.

1. Lorenz System

The fractional chaotic Lorenz system is given by the following mathematical model (Lorenz, 1963):

$$\begin{cases} \dfrac{d^{q_1} x}{dt^{q1}} = \sigma\left(y - x\right) \\ \dfrac{d^{q_2} y}{dt^{q_2}} = \left(r - z\right)x - y \\ \dfrac{d^{q_3} z}{dt^{q_3}} = xy - bz \end{cases} \tag{18}$$

For $\left(\sigma, b, r\right) = \left(10, 8/3, 28\right)$ and $\left(q_1, q_2, q_3\right) = \left(1, 1, 1\right)$ the system present a chaotic behavior. With three fixed points;

$$xf_0 = \left(0, 0, 0\right), xf_1 = \left(\sqrt{b\left(r - 1\right)}, \sqrt{b\left(r - 1\right)}, r - 1\right)$$

and

$$xf_2 = \left(-\sqrt{b\left(r - 1\right)}, -\sqrt{b\left(r - 1\right)}, r - 1\right).$$

In the objective of generating a new fractional chaotic Lorenz system, we first search for adequate orders $\left(q_1, q_2, q_3\right)$ and then for the new parameters system $\left(\sigma^*, b^*, r^*\right)$ which prove the chaotic nature.

One can see that the variation of the derivate order causes a big change in a system behavior.

In the following, we take $\left(q_1, q_2, q_3\right) = \left(0.98, 0.98, 0.98\right)$ and with initial conditions $\left(x_0, y_0, z_0\right) = \left(-5, 5, 10\right)$, we get a fractional chaotic Lorenz system.

Figure 1. (a), (b) and (c): Bifurcation diagrams of the x state variable in function of q_1, q_2 and q_3 respectively

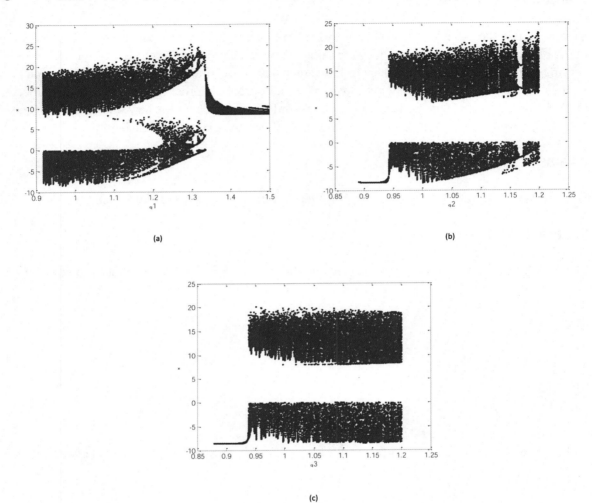

(a)

(b)

(c)

The second part consists of the determination of the new parameters $\left(\sigma^*, b^*, r^*\right)$. We begin by varying the parameter σ in the interval $[5, 15]$ with a steep $h = 0.005$. We choose $\sigma^* = 8$ from the chaotic interval we keep the old value of r and we change the value of b between 2 and 5. From the obtained bifurcation diagram we extract the suitable value $b^* = 2$ then we trace the evolution of the state variable x in function r varies between 15 and 30. To complete the identification phase of the parameters, the last appropriate parameter is chosen $r = 27$. The three bifurcation diagrams are gathered in Figure 2.

The attractor of the new fractional chaotic Lorenz system illustrated for $\left(\sigma^*, b^*, r^*\right) = \left(8, 2, 27\right)$ and can be presented in Figure 3.

Figure 2. (a), (b) and (c): Bifurcation diagram of the state variable x in function of σ, b, r parameters respectively

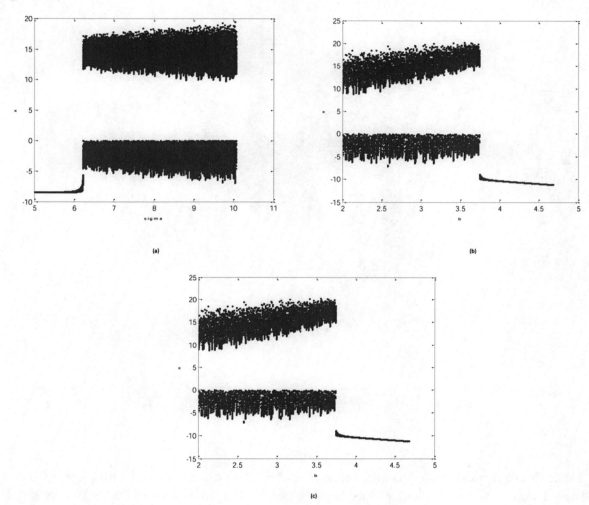

2. Rössler System

Chaos appears in Rössler system if the parameter of the mathematical model (19) (Rössler, 1976) takes these values $(a, b, c) = (0.38, 0.3, 4.82)$

$$
\begin{cases}
\dfrac{d^{q_1} x}{dt^{q1}} = -y - z \\[2mm]
\dfrac{d^{q2} y}{dt^{q_2}} = x + a\, y \\[2mm]
\dfrac{d^{q_3} z}{dt^{q_3}} = b\, x - c\, z + x\, z
\end{cases}
\tag{19}
$$

Figure 3. The attractor of the new fractional chaotic Lorenz system

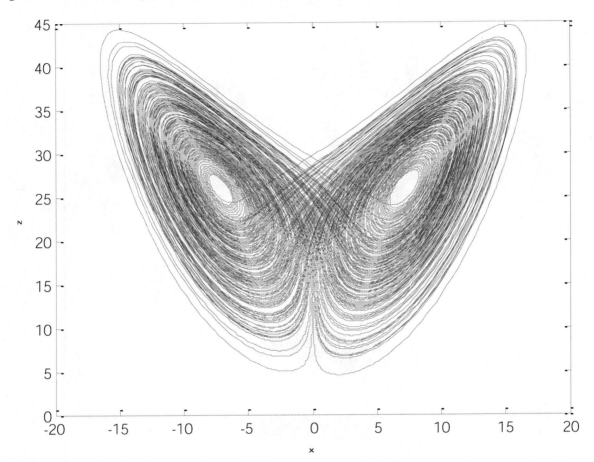

The simple particularity in the trace of the orders bifurcation diagrams of the Rössler system is that the evolution of the followed order depends on the choice of the previous one. So, the fractional orders choose for the next steps are: $\left(q_1, q_2, q_3\right) = \left(0.92, 1.05, 0.85\right)$.

Ones we have the fractional orders, we search for the new system parameters $\left(a^*, b^*, c^*\right)$ that ensures chaotic behavior. First, we keep $\left(b, c\right) = \left(0.3, 4.82\right)$ we trace the evolution of x in function of a parameter in the interval $\left[0.2, 0.6\right]$ with a step $h = 0.0002$. We select $a^* = 0.3$, keep $c = 4.82$ and varying b parameter between $\left[0.01, 3\right]$. finally we put $\left(a^*, b^*\right) = \left(0.3, 0.17\right)$ and we extract $c^* = 4.3$. The appropriate bifurcation diagrams in function of system parameters are given in Figure 5 and the attractor in Figure 6.

Figure 4. (a), (b) and (c): Bifurcation diagrams of the x state variable in function of q_1, q_2 and q_3 respectively

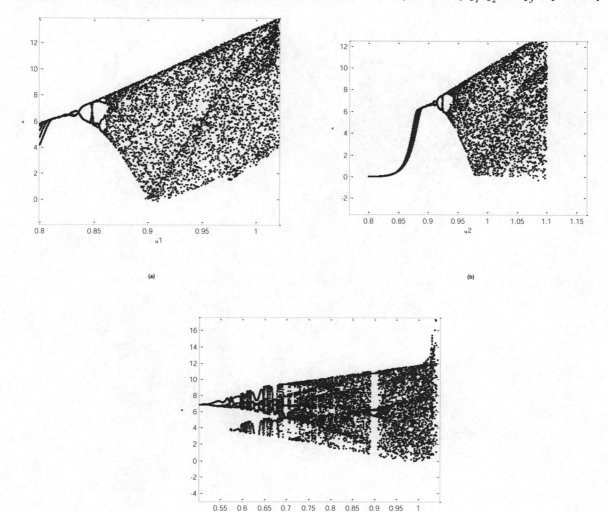

CONTROL OF THE FRACTIONAL CHAOTIC SYSTEM USING PI$^\lambda$D$^\mu$ CONTROLLER

In order to improve the performance of linear feedback systems, Podlubny (I. Podlubny, 1999)proposed a generalization of the classical PID controller to PI$^\lambda$D$^\mu$ form called the fractional PID, which has recently become very popular due to its additional flexibility to meet design specifications. Since, FOPID controllers have found application in several power systems.

Figure 5. (a), (b) and (c): Bifurcation diagram of the state variable x in function of a, b, c parameters respectively.

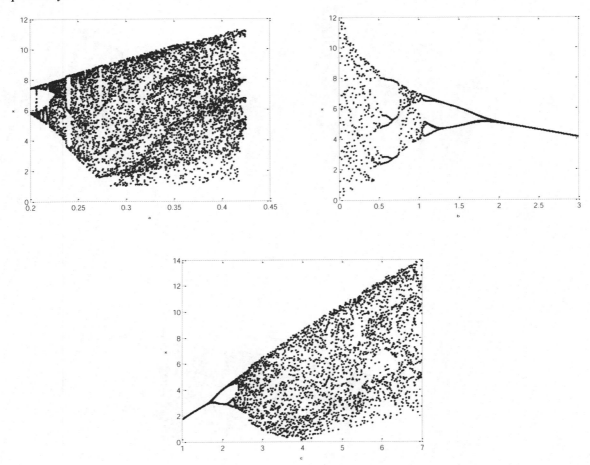

Definition of FOPID

The FOPID is a feedback mechanism from the control loop. It is widely used in industrial control systems. A $PI^\lambda D^\mu$ controller calculates an error value and tries to minimize it by adjusting the process using a manipulated variable (Rabahet al., 2016).

The control law of the FOPID controller is given by the following function.

$$u(t) = k_p X + k_I I^\lambda X + k_d D^\lambda X \tag{20}$$

The fractional proportional-integral-derivative controller applied on the new fractional Lorenz system can be schematized as in Figure 7.

Figure 6. The attractor of the new fractional chaotic Rössler

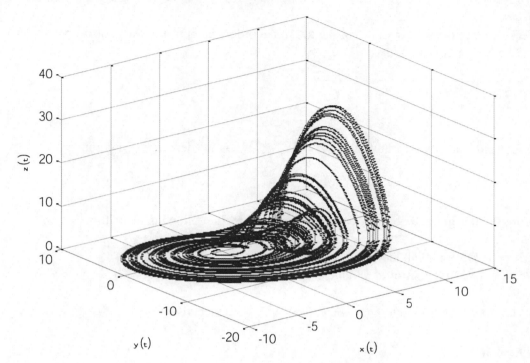

Figure 7. Controlled system using FOPID

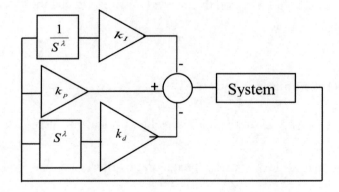

Design Construction

Bifurcation Diagram

The bifurcation diagram is an effective tool to quickly evaluate all possible solutions of the system based on the variation of one of its parameter. It enables to identify the particular values which introduce the stability area (L. Chen, Zhao, Li, & Zhao, 2015). Consequently, bifurcation control has attracted a great research effort in the last years (Colonius & Grne, 2002). In this chapter we will use this tool to identify k_p, k_i and k_d gains.

Optimization

In order to choose the proper values of the fractional order and optimize the controller gains, we use the quadratic criterion formulated as:

$$J = \sqrt{\sum \left(x - x_f\right)^2 + \left(y - y_f\right)^2 + \left(z - z_f\right)^2}$$
(21)

where x, y and z are state variables and $F = \left(x_f, y_f, z_f\right)$ is the desired fixed point.

Design Procedure

The proposed design methodology can be represented by the following algorithm.

Procedure 1: Design methodology
Step 1: Classical PID controller parameters

Let us denote the parameters $\left(k_P, k_I, k_D\right)$ by $\left(k_1, k_2, k_3\right)$ respectively.

- Initialise $\left(k_1^0, k_2^0, k_3^0\right)$.
- For i = 1:3: Trace the bifurcation diagram of the state $\left(x, y, z\right)$ in function of k_i
- Find out the interval I_i where the system stabilizes the desired fixed point for k_i
- Search for the optimal value k_{i-opt} on the interval I_i using the quadratic criteria J defined in (21).
- Update the k_i value, $k_i = k_{i-opt}$
  end.

Step 2: Fractional PI$^\lambda$D$^\mu$ controller parameters

- Fix the parameters $\left(k_P, k_I, k_D\right)$ to the optimal values obtained in step 1.
- Put $\mu = 1$
- Search for the optimal value λ_{opt} using the quadratic criteria J defined in (21)
- Put $\lambda = \lambda_{opt}$.
- Search for the optimal value μ_{opt}

Application Example

In this part, we applied the control strategy presented above to control the new fractional chaotic Lorenz System. The fractional Grünwald-Leitnikov method is used for numerical approximation of the control system.

The chaotic Lorenz system has three fixed point given by

$$xf_0 = \left(0,0,0\right), \ xf_1 = \left(\sqrt{b\left(r-1\right)}, \sqrt{b\left(r-1\right)}, r-1\right)$$

and

$$xf_2 = \left(-\sqrt{b\left(r-1\right)}, -\sqrt{b\left(r-1\right)}, r-1\right).$$

Replacing $\left(\sigma, b, r\right)$ by $\left(\sigma^*, b^*, r^*\right)$, fixed points are:

$$xf_0 = \left(0,0,0\right), xf_1 = \left(7.21, 7.21, 26\right)$$

and

$$xf_2 = \left(-7.21, -7.21, 26\right).$$

In order to control this system on its fixed point $xf_1 = \left(7.21, 7.21, 26\right)$, we use simultaneously a classical PID controller and a Fractional $PI^\lambda D^\mu$ one.

Classical PID Controller

In this section, $\left(k_P, k_I, k_D\right)$ parameters are identified using bifurcation diagrams and a quadratic criteria J. First, we fix the parameters $(k_I, k_D) = (0.2, 0.1)$ and we trace the bifurcation diagram which presents the evolution of the x state with the k_P gain showed in Figure 8. Then according to this one, we find out that the system stabilizes the desired fixed point for $k_P \in \left[0.4, 0.6\right]$. So, the search of the optimal values k_{P-opt} using the quadratic criteria J is limited on this interval as presented in Figure 9.

Once we have the optimal value k_{P-opt}, we fix it and keep $k_D = 0.1$, then trace the evolution of x state with k_I. This last is presented in Figure 10, in this case, the convergence is guaranteed for $k_I \in \left[0.01, 0.25\right]$, then the optimal value k_{I-opt} opt is pulled from Figure 11 that shows the evolution of the quadratic criterion J versus k_I.

From Figure 11 J is optimal for $k_D = 0.01$.

Now, we have the two optimal values $(k_{P-opt}, k_{I\_opt}) = (0.434, 0.01)$, and we look for the third parameter by the same procedure. For that the evolution of the x state and the quadratic criterion J versus k_D are represented in Figure 12 and Figure 13 respectively.

Thesystem reaches the desired fixed point for $k_D = 0.29$.

Figure 8. Bifurcation diagram x=f(kp)

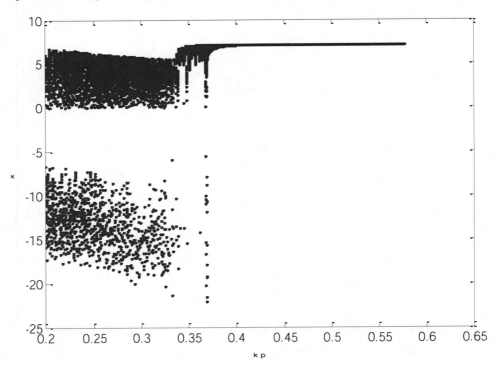

Figure 9. Quadratic criterion J=f (kp)

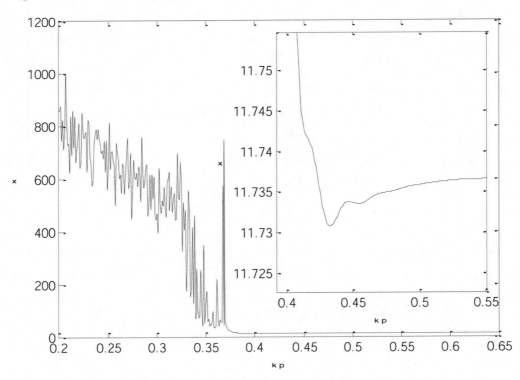

Figure 10. Bifurcation diagram x=f(k_I)

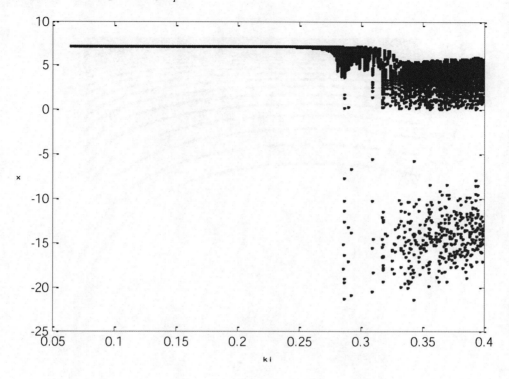

Figure 11. Quadratic criterion J=f (k_I)

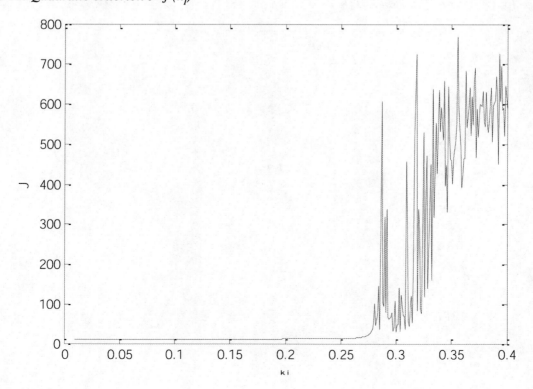

Figure 12. Bifurcation diagram x=f(k_D)

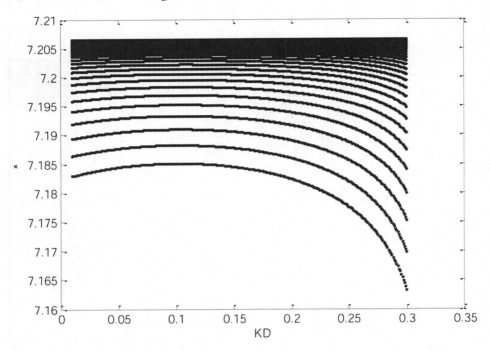

Figure 13. Quadratic criterion J=f (k_D)

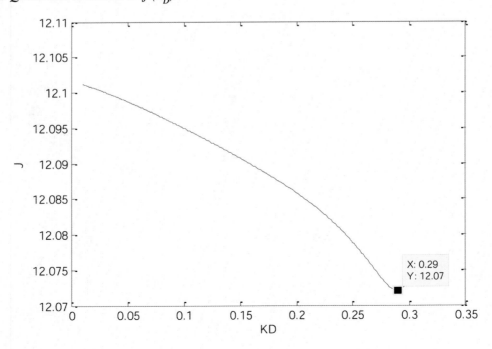

Fractional PI$^\lambda$D$^\mu$ Controller

In this step, we have the three optimal parameters $(k_{P-opt}, k_{I\_opt}, k_{D-opt}) = (0.434, 0.01, 0.29)$ and we need to get the optimal values λ_{opt} and μ_{opt} to tender system to the desired fixed point. For that, we use the quadratic criterion defined above.

Putting $\mu = 1$ and varying λ between 0.8 and 1.1. Obtained bifurcation diagram and quadratic criterion are presented in Figure 14 and Figure 15 respectively.

From the obtained result, J is optimal for $\lambda_{opt} = 0.965$.

We set $\lambda_{opt} = 0.965$ and we seek the optimal value μ_{opt} by calculating the J criterion for different values.

We have finally defined the five optimal values of the controller.

Applying the identified controller to the fractional chaotic Lorenz system we obtain the following simulation results.

From Figure 16, one can notice that control objective is reached and simulations results show the effectiveness of the proposed design approach (Rabah et al. 2017).

Figure 14. Bifurcation diagram x=f (λ)

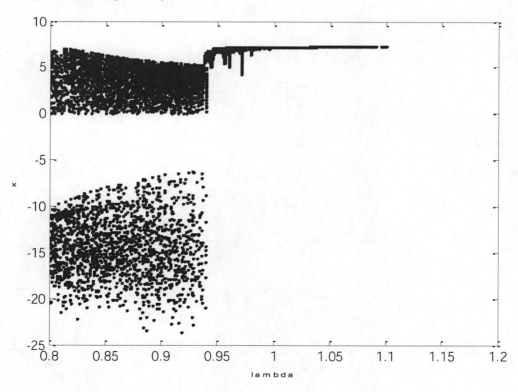

Figure 15. Quadratic criterion J=f (λ)

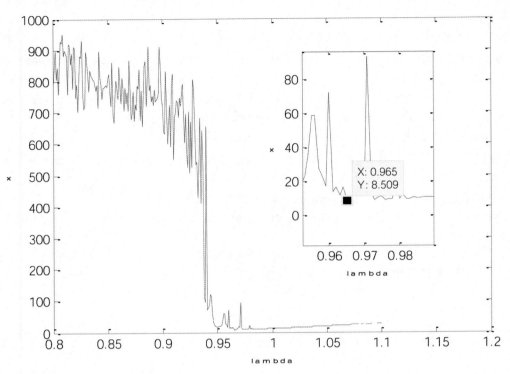

Figure 16. Controlled response system

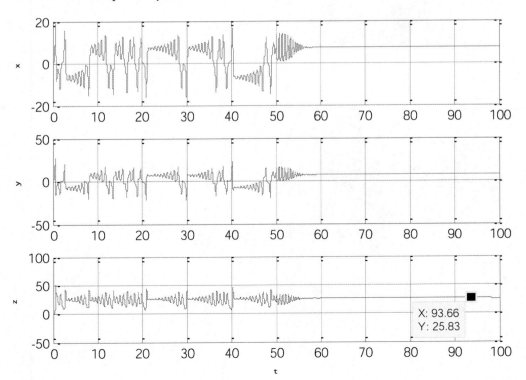

Figure 17. $PI^\lambda D^\mu$ controller signal

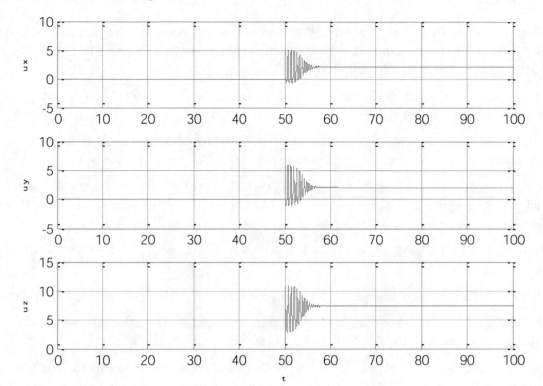

CONCLUSION

In this chapter, a technique based on bifurcation diagram is first proposed to identify the derivative order of the chaotic fractional-order system and its owner parameters, and then used to the selection of controller parameters. Bifurcation diagrams have proven to be a very efficient tool for identifying the stable points and limit cycles.

The fractional order proportional integral derivative (FOPID) controller is proposed to stabilize the chaotic system on one of its fixed points. The three parameters, k_P, k_I and k_D are also optimized by mean of a quadratic criterion, including the fractional orders. It is noticed that the state variables of the controlled system are asymptotically stabilized on the desired fixed point with some error which may be due to the approximation method used. We show by numerical simulations the effectiveness of the proposed design approach.

ACKNOWLEDGMENT

The author would like to thank Prof. Samir Ladaci for his valuable comments which have helped her to improve this chapter.

REFERENCES

Bouafoura, M. K., & Braiek, N. B. (2010). PIλDμ controller design for integer and fractional plants using piecewise orthogonal functions. *Communications in Nonlinear Science and Numerical Simulation*, *15*(5), 1267–1278. doi:10.1016/j.cnsns.2009.05.047

Charef, A., Sun, H., Tsao, Y., & Onaral, B. (1992). Fractal system as presented by singularity function. IEEE Trans. Autom. Control, 1465-1470.

Chen, L., Zhao, T., Li, W., & Zhao, J. (2015). bifurcation control of bounded noise excited duffing oscillator by a weakly fractional-order PIλDμfeedback controller. *Nonlinear Dynamics*.

Chen, Z., Yuan, X., Ji, B., Wang, P., & Tian, H. (2014). Design of a fractional order PID controller for hydraulic turbine regulating system using chaotic non-dominated sorting genetic algorithm II. *Energy Conversion and Management*, *84*, 390–404. doi:10.1016/j.enconman.2014.04.052

Colonius, F., & Grne, L. (2002). *Dynamics,bifurcationsand control*. New York: Springer. doi:10.1007/3-540-45606-6

Das, S. (2008). *Functional fractional calculus for system identification and controls*. Berlin: Springer.

Diethelm, K. (2003). Efficient Solution of Multi-Term Fractional Differential Equations Using P(EC) m E Methods. *Computing*, *71*(4), 305–319. doi:10.100700607-003-0033-3

Faieghi, M. R., Naderi, M., & Jalali, A. A. (2011). Design of fractional-order PID for ship roll motion control using chaos embedded PSO algorithm. In *Control, Instrumentation and Automation (ICCIA), 2011 2nd International Conference on Control, Instrumentation and Automation* (pp. 606–610). IEEE. Retrieved from http://ieeexplore.ieee.org/abstract/document/6356727/

Kilbas, A. A., Srivastava, H. M., & Trujillo, J. J. (2006). *Theory and applications of fractional differential equations* (1st ed.). Amsterdam: Elsevier.

Ladaci, S., Assabaa, M., & Charef, A. (2009).Fractional Order Integro-differential Adaptive Control. *10th Int. Conf. on Sciences and Techniques of Automatic Control and Computer Engineering, STA'2009*, 181–188.

Ladaci, S., & Bensafia, Y. (2016). Indirect fractional order pole assignment based adaptive control. *Engineering Science and Technology, an International Journal*, *19*(1), 518–530.

Ladaci, S., & Charef, A. (2006). On Fractional Adaptive Control. *Nonlinear Dynamics*, *43*(4), 365–378. doi:10.100711071-006-0159-x

Lorenz, E. (1963). Deterministic Nonperiodic Flow. *Journal of the Atmospheric Sciences*, *20*(2), 130–141. doi:10.1175/1520-0469(1963)020<0130:DNF2.0.CO;2

Miller, K., & Ross, B. (1993). *An Introduction to the Fractional Calculus and Fractional Differential Equations*. New York: Wiley.

Oldham, K. B., & Spanier, J. (2006). The Fractional Calculus: Theory and Applications of Differentiation and Integration to Arbitrary Order (mathematics in science and engineering, Vol. 111). Richard Bellman.

Oustaloup, A. (1991). *The CRONE control (La commande CRONE)*. Paris: Hermès.

Pan, I., & Das, S. (2012). Chaotic multi-objective optimization based design of fractional order PIλDμ controller in AVR system. *International Journal of Electrical Power & Energy Systems, 43*(1), 393–407. doi:10.1016/j.ijepes.2012.06.034

Podlubny, I. (1999). Fractional order systems and PIλDμ controllers. *Trans. Automatic Control, 44*(1), 208–214. doi:10.1109/9.739144

Rabah, K., Ladaci, S., & Lashab, M. (2016). Stabilization of a Genesio-Tesi Chaotic System Using a Fractional Order PIλDμ. *International Journal of Sciences and Techniques of Automatic Control & Computer Engineering, IJ-STA, 10*(1), 2085–2090.

Rabah, K., Ladaci, S., &Lashab, M. (2017). Bifurcation-based Fractional Order PI$^\Lambda$D$^\mu$ Controller Design Approach for Nonlinear Chaotic. *Frontiers of Information Technology & Electronic Engineering*.

Rabah, K., Ladaci, S., & Lashab, M. (2017b). A novel fractional sliding mode control configuration for synchronizing disturbed fractional-order chaotic systems. *Pramana, 89*(46).

Rabah, K., Ladaci, S., & Lashab, M. (2015). Stabilization of Fractional Chen Chaotic System by Linear Feedback Control. In *Proceedings of the 3rd Int. IEEE Conf. on Control, Engineering & Information Technology (CEIT2015)*. Tlemcen, Algeria: IEEE. 10.1109/CEIT.2015.7232990

Rössler, O. E. (1976). An equation for continuous Chaos. *Physics Letters, 5*(5), 397–397. doi:10.1016/0375-9601(76)90101-8

Sabatier, J., Agrawal, O. P., & Tenreiro Machado, J. A. (Eds.). (2007). *Advances in fractional calculus: theoretical developments and applications in physics and engineering*. Dordrecht: Springer. doi:10.1007/978-1-4020-6042-7

Tang, Y., Cui, M., Hua, C., Li, L., & Yang, Y. (2012). Optimum design of fractional order PIλDμ controller for AVR system using chaotic ant swarm. *Expert Systems with Applications, 39*(8), 6887–6896. doi:10.1016/j.eswa.2012.01.007

Chapter 7
Fuzzy Adaptive Controller for Synchronization of Uncertain Fractional–Order Chaotic Systems

Amel Bouzeriba
University of Jijel, Algeria

ABSTRACT

In this chapter, the projective synchronization problem of different multivariable fractional-order chaotic systems with both uncertain dynamics and external disturbances is studied. More specifically, a fuzzy adaptive controller is investigated for achieving a projective synchronization of uncertain fractional-order chaotic systems. The adaptive fuzzy-logic system is used to online estimate the uncertain nonlinear functions. The latter is augmented by a robust control term to efficiently compensate for the unavoidable fuzzy approximation errors, external disturbances as well as residual error due to the use of the so-called e-modification in the adaptive laws. A Lyapunov approach is employed to derive the parameter adaptation laws and to prove the boundedness of all signals of the closed-loop system. Numerical simulations are performed to verify the effectiveness of the proposed synchronization scheme.

INTRODUCTION

Fractional calculus is a mathematical topic with more than three centuries old history and can be considered as a natural generalization of ordinary differentiation and integration to arbitrary (non-integer) order. During the last 3 decades, it has attracted increasing attentions of physicists as well as engineers from an application point of view. In fact, it has been found that many systems in interdisciplinary fields can be accurately modeled by fractional-order differential equations, such as heat diffusion systems, batteries, neurons, viscoelastic systems (Bagley and Calico, 1991), dielectric polarization (Sun et al., 1984), electrode-electrolyte polarization (Ichise et al., 1971), some finance systems, electromagnetic waves (Heaviside, 1971), and so on.

DOI: 10.4018/978-1-5225-5418-9.ch007

Chaos (or hyperchaos) is a nonlinear phenomenon which has been observed in physical, mechanical, medical, biological, economical and electrical systems to name a few. Chaotic systems are nonlinear and deterministic rather than probabilistic (Yin-He et al., 2012; Ginarsa et al., 2013). They have some important characteristics such that: 1) they have an unusual sensitivity to initial states (therefore they are not predictable in the long run). 2)They are not periodic. 3) They have fractal structures, 4) Such systems are governed by one or more control parameters. The principal feature used to identify a chaotic behaviour is the well-known Lyapunov exponent criteria. In fact, a system that has one positive Lyapunov exponent is known as a chaotic system. However, a hyperchaotic circuit, which is usually a 4-dimensional system, is characterised by more than one positive Lyapunov exponent. It is worth mentioning that higher dimensional chaotic systems with more than one positive Lyapunov exponent can indeed show more complex dynamics. It has been recently demonstrated that many fractional-order systems can display chaotic (or heperchaotic) behaviours such that: fractional-order Duffing system (Gao and Yu, 2005), fractional-order Chua's system (Hartley et al., 1995), fractional-order Lorenz system (Yu et al., 2009), fractional-order Chen system (Li and Peng, 2004), fractional-order Rössler system (Li and Chen, 2004), fractional-order Liu system (Daftardar-Gejji and Bhalekar, 2010), fractional-order Arneodo system (Lu, 2005) to name a few.

The synchronization is defined as a problem that consists in designing a system (slave or response system) whose behaviour mimics another one (drive or master system). In the literature, several synchronization techniques have been already developed, namely: complete synchronization (Carroll et al., 1996; Sun and Zhang, 2004; Bowonga et al., 2006), phase synchronization (Rosenblum et al., 1996; Pikovsky et al., 1997), lag synchronization (Cailian et al., 2005), generalized synchronization (Morgul and Solak, 1996; Morgul and Solak, 1997), generalized projective synchronization (Li and Xu, 2004; Yan and Li, 2005; Li, 2006), and so on. However, all these synchronization methods focus on integer-order chaotic systems that represent a very special case of the non-integer (fractional-order) chaotic systems. In addition, it has been assumed in (Carroll et al., 1996; Sun and Zhang., 2004; Bowonga et al., 2006; Rosenblum et al., 1996; Pikovsky et al., 1997; Cailian et al., 2005; Morgul and Solak, 1996; Morgul and Solak, 1997; Li and Xu, 2004; Yan and Li, 2005; Li, 2006) that models of the chaotic systems are almost known. Therefore, it is very interesting to extend these fundamental results to uncertain fractional-order chaotic systems and to incorporate an online function approximator (such as a fuzzy system) to deal with model uncertainties.

A fuzzy adaptive controller is a fuzzy system equipped with an appropriate adaptation law which can estimate online the unknown fuzzy parameters. Based on the universal approximation capability of the fuzzy systems (Wang, 1994), numerous adaptive fuzzy control schemes (Wang et al., 2008; Roopaei and Jahromi, 2008; Poursamad and Davaie-Markazi, 2009; Chen and Chen, 2009; Hwang et al., 2009; Wang et al., 2009; Liu and Zheng, 2009; Lin et al., 2011; Precup et al., 2014; Jing et al., 2015; Precup and Tomescu, 2015) have been developed for a class of uncertain chaotic systems but with integer-order. In these schemes, the adaptive fuzzy systems are used to estimate the model uncertainties. The associated stability analysis as well as the adaptation law design has been carried out using a Lyapunov-based method. The robustness issues with respect to the inevitable fuzzy approximation error and the possible external disturbances have been improved by properly adding a robust control term to a dominant adaptive fuzzy controller. Such a robust control term can be conceived using a sliding mode control (Roopaei and Jahromi, 2008; Poursamad and Davaie-Markazi, 2009; Chen and Chen, 2009; Lin et al., 2011), an H∞ based robust control (Wang et al., 2008; Hwang et al., 2009; Wang et al., 2009) and a quasi-sliding mode control (Liu and Zheng, 2009). However, it is should be mentioned that the above results (Wang et al., 2008; Roopaei and Jahromi, 2008; Poursamad and Davaie-Markazi, 2009; Chen and Chen, 2009; Hwang et al., 2009; Wang et al., 2009; Liu and Zheng, 2009; Lin et al., 2011; Precup et al., 2014; Jing et al., 2015; Precup and Tomescu, 2015) are only applicable to chaotic systems with integer-order.

The chaos synchronization of fractional-order chaotic (or hyperchaotic) systems is yet considered as a challenging research topic (Peng, 2007; Wang and Zhang, 2009; Pan et al., 2010; Hosseinnia et al., 2010; Lin and Lee, 2011; Lin and Kuo, 2011; Chen et al., 2013). In (Chen et al., 2013), the authors have researched the synchronization for a class of fractional-order chaotic neural networks. In (Wang and Zhang, 2009), a local stability criterion for synchronization of incommensurate fractional-order chaotic systems has been derived based on the stability theory of linear incommensurate fractional-order differential equations. An active pinning control for synchronization and anti-synchronization of uncertain unified chaotic systems with fractional-order has been reported in (Pan et al., 2010). In addition, the author of (Peng, 2007) has designed a synchronization system of two identical fractional-order chaotic systems using a linear error feedback control. (Hosseinnia et al., 2010) have designed a linear sliding surface with its corresponding switching control law for synchronization of two identical uncertain fractional-order chaotic systems. In Lin and Lee (2011), an adaptive fuzzy sliding mode control for synchronization of uncertain fractional-order chaotic systems with time delay has been proposed. In Lin & Kuo (2011), an adaptive fuzzy logic controller has been designed for achieving an H_∞ synchronizing for a class of uncertain fractional-order chaotic systems. However, the fundamental results of Lin & Lee (2011) and Lin & Kuo (2011) are already questionable, because the stability analysis has not been derived rigorously in mathematics (Tavazoei, 2012; Aghababa, 2012).

Motivated by the above considerations, in this chapter, a novel projective synchronization scheme is investigated for two different uncertain chaotic systems with fractional-order by designing an appropriate fuzzy adaptive controller. In order to facilitate the controller design and stability analysis, a fractional integral type sliding surface is introduced. In other words, this fractional integral sliding surface allows us to transform a system with fractional-order into another system with integer-order. A Lyapunov approach is adopted to carry out the design of the adaptation laws and the stability analysis of the closed-loop system. The applicability and effectiveness of the presented synchronization system will be illustrated through two simulations examples. Compared to the existing works, Peng (2007), Wang & Zhang (2009), Pan et al. (2010), Hosseinnia et al. (2010), Lin & Lee (2011), Lin & Kuo (2011), Chen et al. (2013), the principal contributions of this study can be summarized as:

1. A projective synchronization scheme based on fuzzy control is proposed for a class of fractional-order chaotic systems.
2. Unlike the previous works, Peng, (2007), Wang & Zhang (2009), Pan et al. (2010), Hosseinnia et al. (2010), and Chen et al. (2013), the slave chaotic system is assumed to be subject to unknown dynamic disturbances. In addition, the model of this master-slave structure is assumed to be completely unknown (i.e. the controller designed here is free of the model). In fact, adaptive fuzzy systems are utilized to estimate the uncertain functions of this master-slave structure.
3. Unlike the closely related works, the stability analysis of the closed-loop system is rigorously established in this chapter, Lin & Lee (2011) and Lin & Kuo (2011). Recall that the work in Lin & Lee (2011) and Lin & Kuo (2011) are questionable, as stated in Tavazoei (2012) and Aghababa (2012).

4.   In order to conjointly compensate for the fuzzy approximation errors as well as the residual errors due to the incorporation of the so-called e-modification in the adaptive laws, the proposed fuzzy adaptive controller is appropriately augmented by a robust control term.

The rest of this chapter is organized as follows. Some basic definitions for fractional-order systems are given in Section 2. The problem statement and preliminaries, and the description of the used fuzzy logic system are presented in Section 3. The fuzzy adaptive control design and stability analysis are discussed in Section 4. Two simulation examples are given in section 5 to evaluate the effectiveness of the proposed control system.

BASIC DEFINITIONS FOR FRACTIONAL-ORDER SYSTEMS

Some fundamental definitions regarding the fractional-order integrals and derivatives are reviewed in this section. Also, one states a useful stability lemma from the fractional calculus.

Definition 1

The q th-order Riemann–Liouville (RL) fractional integration of a function $f(t)$ is defined as follows (Podlubny, 1999):

$$_{t_0}I_t^q f(t) = {}_{t_0}D_t^{-q} f(t) = \frac{1}{\Gamma(q)} \int_{t_0}^{t} \frac{f(\tau)}{(t-\tau)^{1-q}} d\tau, \tag{1}$$

where $\Gamma(.)$ is the Gamma function which is defined by $\Gamma(q) = \int_0^{\infty} t^{q-1} e^{-t} dt$. The latter can be seen as an extension of the factorial to real number arguments.

Definition 2

Let $m - 1 < q \le m$, with $m \epsilon N$, the RL fractional derivative of order q of a function $f(t)$ is defined as follows (Podlubny, 1999):

$$_{t_0}D_t^q f(t) = \frac{1}{\Gamma(m-q)} \frac{d^m}{dt^m} \int_{t_0}^{t} \frac{f(\tau)}{(t-\tau)^{q-m+1}} d\tau, \tag{2}$$

Definition 3

The q th-order Caputo fractional derivative of a continuous function $f(t): R^+ \to R$ is defined as follows (Podlubny, 1999):

$$
{}_{t_0}D_t^q f(t) = \begin{cases} \dfrac{1}{\Gamma(m-q)} \displaystyle\int_{t_0}^{t} \dfrac{f^{(m)}(\tau)}{(t-\tau)^{q-m+1}} \, d\tau, m-1 < q < m, \\[2em] \dfrac{d^m}{dt^m} f(t), q = m, \end{cases} \tag{3}
$$

with m is the smallest integer number that is larger than q.

Remark 1

1. It is worth noting that the definition of Caputo fractional integration is similar to that of RL fractional integration.
2. The major advantage of the Caputo definition is that the initial conditions for fractional-order differential equations take on a similar form as for integer-order differential equations.
3. In the literature, the Caputo definition is sometimes referred as a smooth fractional derivative.
4. As the Caputo fractional operator is more consistent than that of RL, then this operator will be employed in the rest of this chapter. Also, a modified version of Adams-Bashforth-Moulton algorithm proposed in Diethelm & Ford (2002) will be used for computer numerical simulation of the Caputo fractional-order differential equations.

Lemma 1 (Matignon, 1996)

Consider a linear system with inner dimension n, given by the following state space form:

$$
\begin{cases} {}_{t_0}D_t^q x = Ax + Bu \\ \qquad y = Cx \end{cases} \sqrt{a^2 + b^2}, x(0) = x_0
$$

With $0 < q < 1$, $x \in R^n$, $y \in R^p and A \in R^{n \times n}$. One assumes that the triplet (A,B,C) is minimal. This above system is bounded-input bounded-output (BIBO) stable if $\left| \arg(eig(A)) \right| > q\pi / 2$. When this linear system is externally stable, each part of its impulse response behaves as t^{-1-q} at infinity.

Remark 2

Lemma 1 states the principal difference between ordinary and fractional-order differential equations. It is worth noticing that the stability of fractional-order differential equations is not of exponential type. In fact, for a linear fractional-order system, when all the eigen values are situated outside the sector defined by $\left| \arg(eig(A)) \right| \leq \dfrac{q\pi}{2}$, the response of the initial conditions decays as t^{-q} but he impulse response decays as t^{-1-q}. This behavior does not take place in the linear system described by ordinary differential systems (Podlubny, 1999).

PROBLEM STATEMENT, PRELIMINARIES, AND FUZZY LOGIC SYSTEMS

Problem Statement and Preliminaries

As already mentioned in Introduction, the main motivation of this chapter consists in designing a novel projective synchronization system for a class of master-slave fractional-order chaotic multivariable systems. The projective synchronization between the master system and the slave system will be achieved by designing an adequate fuzzy adaptive controller, as shown in Figure 1.

Consider the following class of uncertain fractional-order chaotic systems as the master system:

$$D_t^q X = F_1(X), \tag{4}$$

In the above, $D_t^q = \dfrac{d^q}{dt^q}, 0 < q < 1$ is the fractional derivative order, with

$$X = [x_1, \ldots, x_n]^T \in R^n$$

is the state vector of the master system that is assumed to be completely measurable, and

$$F_1(X) = [f_{11}(X), \ldots, f_{1n}(X)]^T \in R^n$$

is a vector of smooth unknown nonlinear functions.

The uncertain fractional-order chaotic multivariable slave system can be described by:

$$D_t^q Y = F_2(Y) + u + D(t, Y), \tag{5}$$

With $Y = [y_1, \ldots, y_n]^T \in R^n$ is its state vector that is assumed to be measurable.

$$F_2(Y) = [f_{21}(Y), \ldots, f_{2n}(Y)]^T \in R^n$$

is a vector of smooth unknown nonlinear functions, $u = [u_1, \ldots, u_n]^T \in R^n$ denotes the control input vector and

$$D(t, Y) = [D_1(t, Y), \ldots, D_n(t, Y)] \in R^n$$

stands for the unknown external disturbance vector.

Remark 3

The systems (4) and (5) considered in this chapter represent a relatively large class of uncertain fractional-order chaotic systems. Note that many chaotic systems can be described in this considered form, such as: fractional-order Lu system, fractional-order Lorenz system, fractional-order unified chaotic system, fractional-order Chen system, so on.

Our main objective consists in designing a fuzzy adaptive control law u_i (for all $i = 1, \ldots, n$) achieving an appropriate synchronization between the master system (4) and the slave system (5), while assuring the boundedness of all variables involved in the closed-loop system as well as the asymptotical convergence of the associated synchronization errors to zero.

In order to quantify this objective, one defines the synchronization errors as follows:

$$e_1 = y_1 - \lambda x_1,$$

$$\begin{matrix} \cdot \\ \cdot \\ \cdot \end{matrix} \qquad (6)$$

$$e_n = y_n - \lambda x_n.$$

Where λ is a scaling factor that defines a proportional relation between the synchronized systems. Therefore, the complete synchronization and anti-synchronization are the special cases of a projective synchronization when λ takes the values $+1$ and -1, respectively.

The vector of the synchronization errors can be expressed as follows:

$$E = [e_1, \ldots, e_n]^T = Y - \lambda X. \qquad (7)$$

In order to facilitate the design of the control system and the stability analysis, a new variable (which is a fractional integral type sliding mode surface) is introduced:

$$S = D_t^{q-1} E + \int_0^t CE(\tau) d\tau, \qquad (8)$$

Where $C = Diag[c_1, \ldots, c_n]$ is a positive-define design matrix chosen such as the dynamics given by (11) are stable.

Once the system operates in the sliding mode, it satisfies the following expressions (Utkin, 1992):

$$S = D_t^{q-1} E + \int_0^t CE(\tau) d\tau = 0, \qquad (9)$$

and

$$\dot{S} = D_t^q E + CE = 0. \tag{10}$$

Consequently, the sliding mode dynamics can be written as follows:

$$D_t^q E = -CE. \tag{11}$$

Remark 4

According to the stability condition (given by Lemma 1), for fractional-order linear systems (Podlubny, 1999; Matignon, 1996), the dynamics (9) or (11) are already asymptotically stable. In fact, all eigenvalues of the fractional-order dynamics (11) are equal to $-c_i$, with $c_i > 0$. Thus, the order $0 < q < 1$ satisfies the stability condition, as $\left| \arg\left(-c_i\right) \right| = \pi > q\pi / 2$.

DYNAMICS OF THE SYNCHRONIZATION ERRORS

From (8), one can rewrite the dynamics of S as follows:

$$\dot{S} = \left[F_2\left(Y\right) - \lambda F_1\left(X\right) \right] + u + D\left(t, Y\right) + CE. \tag{12}$$

or equivalently,

$$\dot{S} = F_3\left(X, Y\right) + u + D\left(t, Y\right) + CE = \alpha\left(X, Y, D\right) + u, \tag{13}$$

with

$$F_3\left(X, Y\right) = \left[F_2\left(Y\right) - \lambda F_1\left(X\right) \right], \tag{14}$$

where

$$\alpha\left(X, Y, D\right) = [\alpha_1\left(X, Y, D\right), \dots, \alpha_n\left(X, Y, D\right)]^T = F_3\left(X, Y\right) + D\left(t, Y\right) + CE. \tag{15}$$

Since the nonlinear function $\alpha\left(X, Y, D\right)$ is unknown, one will use later an adaptive fuzzy system to approximate the functional upper-bound of $\alpha\left(X, Y, D\right)$.

Description of the Used Fuzzy Logic System

The configuration of a fuzzy logic system basically consists of a fuzzifier, a fuzzy knowledge-base, an inference engine and a defuzzifier, as shown in Figure 2. The fuzzy inference engine, being considered

Figure 1. Proposed projective synchronization system

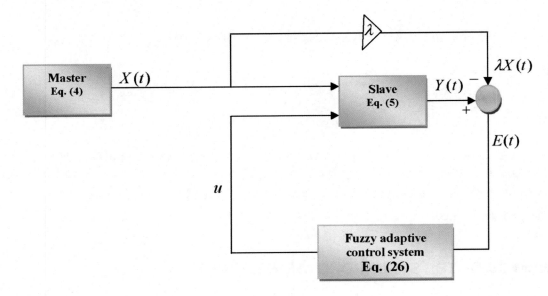

as an important part in this reasoning system, uses a set of fuzzy If–Then rules to perform a mapping from an input $\underline{x}^T = [x_1, \ldots, x_n] \in R^n$ to an output $\hat{f} \in R$. The ith fuzzy rule is in following form:

$$R^{(i)} : if \quad x_1 \quad is \quad A_1^i \quad and \ldots and \quad x_n \quad is \quad A_n^i \quad then \quad \hat{f} \quad is \quad f^i, \tag{16}$$

Where $A_1^i, A_2^i, \ldots,$ and A_n^i are fuzzy sets and f^i is a fuzzy singleton.

If one uses a singleton fuzzifier, product inference, and center-average defuzzifier, the output of this fuzzy logic system can be expressed as

$$\hat{f}(\underline{x}) = \frac{\sum_{i=1}^{m} f^i \left(\prod_{j=1}^{n} \mu_{A_j^i}(x_j) \right)}{\sum_{i=1}^{m} \left(\prod_{j=1}^{n} \mu_{A_j^i}(x_j) \right)} = \theta^T \psi(\underline{x}), \tag{17}$$

Where $\mu_{A_j^i}(x_j)$ is the membership function of the fuzzy set A_j^i, m is the number of fuzzy rules, $\theta^T = [f^1, \ldots, f^m]$ is the adjustable parameter (consequent parameters) vector, and $\psi^T = [\psi^1 \psi^2 \ldots \psi^m]$ with

$$\psi^i(\underline{x}) = \frac{\prod_{j=1}^{n} \mu_{A_j^i}(x_j)}{\sum_{i=1}^{m} \left(\prod_{j=1}^{n} \mu_{A_j^i}(x_j) \right)}. \tag{18}$$

being the fuzzy basis function (FBF).

Throughout the chapter (Wang, 1994; Tong et al., 2011; Tong et al., 2012; Tong et al., 2014; Li et al., 2014; Tong and Li, 2013; Li et al., 2013), it is assumed that the FBFs are appropriately selected so that:

$$\sum_{i=1}^{m}(\prod_{j=1}^{n}\mu_{A_j^i}(x_j)) > 0. \tag{19}$$

The fuzzy logic system (17) can approximate any nonlinear continuous function $f(\underline{x})$ defined on a compact operating space to an arbitrary accuracy (Wang, 1994; Tong et al., 2011; Tong et al., 2012; Tong et al., 2014; Li et al., 2014; Tong and Li, 2013; Li et al., 2013). Of particular importance, one assumes that the FBFs, i.e. $\psi(\underline{x})$, are properly specified in advance by designer. However, the consequent parameters, i.e. θ, are determined by some adequate estimation algorithms.

DESIGN OF FUZZY ADAPTIVE CONTROLLER

In the sequel, the following mild assumptions are required:

Assumption 1

The unknown external disturbance vector satisfies:

$$\left| D(t, Y) \right| \le \bar{D}(Y), \tag{20}$$

where $\bar{D}(Y)$ is a vector of unknown continuous positive functions.

Assumption 2

There exists a vector $\bar{\alpha}(Y)$ of unknown continuous positive functions such that:

$$\left| \alpha(X, Y, D) \right| \le \bar{\alpha}(Y), \tag{21}$$

where $\bar{\alpha}(Y) = [\bar{\alpha}_1(Y), \ldots, \bar{\alpha}_n(Y)]^T$.

Remark 5

Assumptions 1 and 2 are not restrictive, as the upper bounds $\bar{\alpha}(Y)$ and $\bar{D}(Y)$ are already assumed to be unknown and the state vector X of the master system is always bounded (an intrinsic property of the non-controlled chaotic systems). In addition, these assumptions are commonly used in the open control literature (Boulkroune et al. 2014a; 2014b).

Figure 2. The used fuzzy logic system

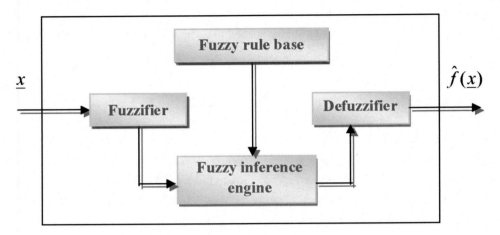

The unknown function $\bar{\alpha}_i(Y)$ can be approximated, on a compact set Ω_Y, by the linearly parameterized fuzzy systems (17) as follows:

$$\hat{\bar{\alpha}}_i\left(Y, \theta_i\right) = \theta_i^T \psi_i\left(Y\right), \text{with } i = 1, \ldots, n \tag{22}$$

where $\psi_i\left(Y\right)$ is the FBF vector, which is determined a priori by the designer, and θ_i is the vector of the adjustable parameters of this fuzzy system.

The optimal value of θ_i can be defined as:

$$\theta_i^* = \arg \min_{\theta_i} \left[\sup_{Y \in \Omega_Y} \left| \bar{\alpha}_i\left(Y\right) - \hat{\bar{\alpha}}_i\left(Y, \theta_i\right) \right| \right] \tag{23}$$

Note that the vector θ_i^* will be only used for analysis purposes and its value is not needed in the controller implementation.

Let us define $\tilde{\theta}_i = \theta_i - \theta_i^*$ and

$$\varepsilon_i\left(Y\right) = \bar{\alpha}_i\left(Y\right) - \hat{\bar{\alpha}}_i\left(Y, \theta_i^*\right) = \bar{\alpha}_i\left(Y\right) - \theta_i^{*T} \psi_i\left(Y\right) \tag{24}$$

as the parameter estimation errors and the fuzzy approximation errors, respectively.

As in Wang (1994), Boulkroune et al. (2008), Boulkroune & M'saad (2012), Boulkroune et al., (2012a; 2012b), and Boulkroune et al. (2014a; 2014b), one assumes that the fuzzy approximation error is upperly bounded for all $Y \in \Omega_Y$, i.e. $\left| \varepsilon_i\left(Y\right) \right| \leq \bar{\varepsilon}_i, \forall Y \in \Omega_Y$, where $\bar{\varepsilon}_i$ is an unknown positive constant. Now, let us denote

$$\hat{\alpha}\left(Y,\theta^*\right) = \left[\hat{\alpha}_1\left(Y,\theta_1^*\right),\ldots,\hat{\alpha}_n\left(Y,\theta_n^*\right)\right]^T = \theta^{*T}\psi\left(Y\right) = \left[\theta_1^{*T}\psi_1\left(Y\right),\ldots,\theta_n^{*T}\psi_n\left(Y\right)\right]^T,$$

$$\hat{\alpha}\left(Y,\theta\right) = \left[\hat{\alpha}_1\left(Y,\theta_1\right),\ldots,\hat{\alpha}_n\left(Y,\theta_n\right)\right]^T = \theta^T\psi\left(Y\right) = \left[\theta_1^T\psi_1\left(Y\right),\ldots,\theta_n^T\psi_n\left(Y\right)\right]^T$$

$$\varepsilon\left(Y\right) = \left[\varepsilon_1\left(Y\right),\ldots,\varepsilon_n\left(Y\right)\right]^T, \overline{\varepsilon} = \left[\overline{\varepsilon}_1,\ldots,\overline{\varepsilon}_n\right]^T.$$

From (24) and (22) and the previous notations, one can get the following expression:

$$\hat{\alpha}\left(Y,\theta\right) - \overline{\alpha}\left(Y\right) = \hat{\alpha}\left(Y,\theta\right) - \hat{\alpha}\left(Y,\theta^*\right) + \hat{\alpha}\left(Y,\theta^*\right) - \overline{\alpha}\left(Y\right),$$

$$= \theta^T\psi\left(Y\right) - \theta^{*T}\psi\left(Y\right) + \theta^{*T}\psi\left(Y\right) - \overline{\alpha}\left(Y\right),$$

$$= \tilde{\theta}^T\psi\left(Y\right) - \varepsilon\left(Y\right).$$

with $\tilde{\theta}^T\psi\left(Y\right) = \theta^T\psi\left(Y\right) - \theta^{*T}\psi\left(Y\right) = [\tilde{\theta}_1^T\psi_1\left(Y\right),\ldots,\tilde{\theta}_n^T\psi_n\left(Y\right)]^T$ (25)

and $\tilde{\theta}_i = \theta_i - \theta_i^*$, for $i = 1,\ldots,n$.

Our proposed fuzzy adaptive controller, given below, consists of three parts, namely an adaptive fuzzy control term to approximate the unknown nonlinear functions $\overline{\alpha}_i\left(Y\right)$, a robust control to deal with the fuzzy approximation errors and a linear control term for stability analysis purposes.

$$u = -\left(u_{fuzzy} + K_0\right)sign\left(S\right) - K_1 S,$$ (26)

where

$$u_{fuzzy} = Diag\left(\theta_1^T\psi_1\left(Y\right),\ldots,\theta_n^T\psi_n\left(Y\right)\right), K_0 = Diag\left(k_{01},\ldots,k_{0n}\right)$$

and $K_1 = Diag\left(k_{11},\ldots,k_{1n}\right)$ are positive-definite diagonal design matrices.

Equation (13) can be expressed as follows:

$$S^T\dot{S} = S^T\alpha\left(X,Y,D\right) + S^T u \le \left|S^T\right|\overline{\alpha}\left(Y\right) + S^T u$$ (27)

Using (25), Assumption 2 and the control law (26), (27) becomes:

$$S^T \dot{S} \leq -\left|S^T\right|\tilde{\theta}^T \psi\left(Y\right) + \left|S^T\right|\left|\varepsilon\left(Y\right)\right| - \sum_{i=1}^{n} k_{0i}\left|S_i\right| - S^T K_1 S \qquad (28)$$

The adaptation law associated to the proposed controller (26) can be designed as

$$\dot{\theta}_i = \gamma_{\theta i}\left(\left|S_i\right|\psi_i\left(Y\right) - \sigma_{\theta_i}\left|S_i\right|\theta_i\right), \qquad (29)$$

where γ_{θ_i} and σ_{θ_i} are positive design constants.

Remark 6

The term $\sigma_{\theta_i}\left|S_i\right|\theta_i$ in (29) borrowed from the well-known e-modification concept, is principally motivated by parameter boundedness purposes. Unlike $\sigma -$ modification concept, the combination of e-modification concept with the robust term $K_0 sign\left(S\right)$ in the proposed adaptive control scheme can ensure a convergence of the synchronization errors to zero.

On the basis of the previous discussions, the following theorem can be got.

Theorem 1

For the master-slave system (4) and (5), if Assumptions 1 and 2 are satisfied, the control law (26) together with adaptation laws (29) can ensure the following properties:

- All the signals in the closed-loop system are bounded.
- Signal S converges to zero in finite time.
- Synchronization error E asymptotically converges to zero.

Proof of Theorem 1

Let us consider the following Lyapunov function candidate:

$$V_1 = \frac{1}{2}S^T S + \sum_{i=1}^{n}\frac{1}{2\gamma_{\theta_i}}\tilde{\theta}_i^T \tilde{\theta}_i. \qquad (30)$$

The time derivative of V_1 is

$$\dot{V}_1 = S^T \dot{S} + \sum_{i=1}^{n}\frac{1}{\gamma_{\theta_i}}\tilde{\theta}_i^T \dot{\theta}_i. \qquad (31)$$

Substituting (28) and (29) into (31) results in

$$\dot{V}_1 \leq \sum_{i=1}^{n} \overline{\varepsilon}_i \left| S_i \right| - \sum_{i=1}^{n} k_{0i} \left| S_i \right| - \sum_{i=1}^{n} k_{1i} S_i^2 - \sum_{i=1}^{n} \sigma_{\theta_i} \left| S_i \right| \tilde{\theta}_i^T \theta_i \tag{32}$$

By completion of squares, one obtains

$$-\sigma_{\theta_i} \tilde{\theta}_i^T \theta_i \leq -\frac{\sigma_{\theta_i}}{2} \left\| \tilde{\theta}_i \right\|^2 + \frac{\sigma_{\theta_i}}{2} \left\| \theta_i^* \right\|^2 . \tag{33}$$

Using (33), (32) can be rewritten as follows:

$$\dot{V}_1 \leq -\sum_{i=1}^{n} k_{1i} S_i^2 - \sum_{i=1}^{n} k_{0i} \left| S_i \right| + \sum_{i=1}^{n} \overline{\varepsilon}_i \left| S_i \right| + \sum_{i=1}^{n} \frac{\sigma_{\theta_i}}{2} \left| S_i \right| \left\| \theta_i^* \right\|^2 - \sum_{i=1}^{n} \frac{\sigma_{\theta_i}}{2} \left| S_i \right| \left\| \tilde{\theta}_i \right\|^2 \tag{34}$$

If the constant k_{0i} is selected such as

$$k_{0i} \geq \alpha + \overline{\varepsilon}_i + \frac{\sigma_{\theta_i}}{2} \left\| \theta_i^* \right\|^2 . \tag{35}$$

where α is a positive design constant, then Equation (34) can be expressed as follows:

$$\dot{V}_1 \leq -\sum_{i=1}^{n} k_{1i} S_i^2 - \sum_{i=1}^{n} \alpha \left| S_i \right| \tag{36}$$

Therefore, all signals (i.e. $S_i, u_i, , \tilde{\theta}_i, \theta_i$) in the closed-loop control system remain bounded. From (13), (21) and (25), one can write the dynamics of S as follows:

$$\left| \dot{S} \right| \leq \left| \alpha \left(X, Y, D \right) \right| + \left| u \right| \leq \left| \tilde{\theta}^T \psi \left(Y \right) \right| + \left| \varepsilon \left(Y \right) \right| + \left| u \right| \tag{37}$$

From (37), it is clear that $\dot{S}_i \in L_\infty$. Equation (36) can be written as:

$$\dot{V}_1 \leq -\sum_{i=1}^{n} k_{1i} S_i^2 \tag{38}$$

By integrating (38) from 0 to ∞, one has

$$\int_0^\infty \sum_{i=1}^{n} k_{1i} S_i^2 \left(t \right) dt \leq V \left(0 \right) - V \left(\infty \right) < \infty \tag{39}$$

which implies that $S_i \in L_2$. Since $S_i \in L_\infty \cap L_2$ and $\dot{S} \in L_\infty$, by using Barbalat's lemma, one concludes the asymptotic convergence of the signal S_i towards zero.

a. Convergence in finite time of S_i

Now, one will show that the signal S_i can also converge to zero in finite time under some additional condition on the gains k_{0i}. To this end, let us consider the following Lyapunov function.

$$V_2 = \frac{1}{2}S^T S \tag{40}$$

Using (28), one can bound the time derivative of V_2 as follows:

$$\dot{V}_2 = S^T \dot{S} \leq -\left|S^T\right|\left|\tilde{\theta}^T \psi(Y)\right| + \left|S^T\right|\left\|\varepsilon(Y)\right\| - \sum_{i=1}^{n} k_{0i}\left|S_i\right| - S^T K_1 S$$

$$\leq \sum_{i=1}^{n}\left|S_i\right|\left\|\tilde{\theta}_i^T \psi_i(Y)\right\| + \sum_{i=1}^{n}\overline{\varepsilon}_i\left|S_i\right| - \sum_{i=1}^{n} k_{0i}\left|S_i\right| - S^T K_1 S$$

$$= -\sum_{i=1}^{n}\left(k_{0i} - \left|\tilde{\theta}_i^T \psi_i(Y)\right| - \overline{\varepsilon}_i\right)\left|S_i\right| - S^T K_1 S$$

$$\leq -\sum_{i=1}^{n}\left(k_{0i} - \overline{E}_{\tilde{\theta}i} - \overline{\varepsilon}_i\right)\left|S_i\right| - S^T K_1 S \tag{41}$$

where $\overline{E}_{\tilde{\theta}i}$ is the upper bound of the signal $\left|\tilde{\theta}_i^T \psi_i(Y)\right|$. Note that the existence of $\overline{E}_{\tilde{\theta}i}$ is already ensured by using the *e-modification* in the adaptive law (29).

From (35) and (41), one can select the constant k_{0i} as follows:

$$k_{0i} \geq \alpha + \max\left\{\overline{\varepsilon}_i + \frac{\sigma_{\theta_i}}{2}\left\|\theta_i^*\right\|^2, \overline{\varepsilon}_i + \overline{E}_{\tilde{\theta}i}\right\}, \tag{42}$$

Then, Equation (41) becomes

$$\dot{V}_2 \leq \sum_{i=1}^{n}\alpha\left|S_i\right| \leq -\alpha\left\|S\right\| = -2\alpha V_2^{1/2} \tag{43}$$

From (43) and (40), it is clear that the sliding motion can happen in finite time (Utkin, 1992), .i.e. all trajectories of the synchronization error E will converge to the sliding surface $S(t) = 0$ in a finite time.

b. Convergence of the synchronization error

When the sliding mode occurs on the sliding surface (9), $i.e. S(t) = \dot{S}(t) = 0$, the dynamics of the synchronization errors become:

$$D_t^q E + CE = \dot{S} = 0 \tag{44}$$

According to (Podlubny, 1999; Matignon, 1996), one can regard (44) as a linear fractional-order system with bound and convergent input $\dot{S}$. In addition, by Lemma 1, the system (44) is stable if

$$\left| \arg(-c_i) \right| > q\pi / 2 \tag{45}$$

Since $0 < q < 1$, (45) is always satisfied. Then, the synchronization errors are asymptotically stable when

$$S(t) = \dot{S}(t) = 0.$$

Remark 7

It is worth noting that the synchronization of the fractional-order chaotic systems with known and partially known dynamics have been comprehensively studied in many literatures (Peng, 2007; Wang and Zhang, 2009; Pan et al., 2010; Hosseinnia et al., 2010; Lin and Lee, 2011; Lin and Kuo, 2011; Chen et al., 2013; Tavazoei and Haeri, 2008; Agrawal and Das, 2013). But, to the best of authors knowledge, there are no theoretical or applied works in the literature on the synchronization of fractional chaotic systems with completely unknown dynamics and dynamic disturbances, except the works of (Lin and Lee, 2011, Lin and Kuo, 2011) which are already questionable, as stated recently in (Tavazoei, 2012; Aghababa, 2012).

Remark 8

Due to chattering problem caused by the discontinuous function (sign), our control law (26) can be smoothed as follows: $u = -\left(u_{fuzzy} + K_0 \right) \tan h \left(k_s S \right) - K_1 S$, where $\tan h(.)$ denotes the usual hyperbolic tangent function and k_s is a strictly positive real number.

Remark 9

From (43) and (36), it is clear that the synchronization error $\left| S_i \right|$ can be decreased and its rate convergence can be enhanced by increasing the design parameters k_{0i} and k_{1i}. As for the effect of the design parameters σ_{θ_i} and γ_{θ_i}, because the adaptive fuzzy system $\theta_i^T \psi_i(Y)$ is positive and added to k_{0i} in the control law (26), the effect of $\theta_i^T \psi_i(Y)$ on the synchronization performances is the same as that of k_{0i}. Thus, by increasing of γ_{θ_i} (i.e. increasing $\theta_i^T \psi_i(Y)$) and decreasing σ_{θ_i}, one can accelerate the convergence rate of the signal $|S_i|$. However, it is noted that if σ_{θ_i} is chosen too small, one cannot prevent the estimated fuzzy parameters (*i.e.* θ_i) from drifting. If k_{0i}, k_{1i} and γ_{θ_i} are big, the control signal is also large and the undesirable chattering problem becomes more noticeable. Therefore, in the practice, these design parameters should be carefully adjusted for achieving suitable synchronization performances and an admissible control action.

SIMULATION RESULTS

In order to show the effectiveness of the proposed scheme, two simulation examples are provided in this section.

Example 1

In this example, one will verify the effectiveness of the proposed scheme for the synchronization of two identical fractional-order Chua's systems (Hartley et al., 1995). The equations of these systems are given below.

The master system:

$$\begin{cases} D_t^q x_1 = 12\left(x_2 + \frac{1}{7}\left(x_1 - 2x_1^3\right)\right), \\ \quad D_t^q x_2 = x_1 - x_2 + x_3, \\ \quad\quad D_t^q x_3 = -\frac{100}{7}x_2, \end{cases} \tag{46}$$

The slave system:

$$\begin{cases} D_t^q y_1 = 12\left(y_2 + \frac{1}{7}\left(y_1 - 2y_1^3\right)\right) + u_1 + d_1(t), \\ \quad D_t^q y_2 = y_1 - y_2 + y_3 + u_2 + d_2(t), \\ \quad\quad D_t^q y_3 = -\frac{100}{7}y_2 + u_3 + d_3(t), \end{cases} \tag{47}$$

In the simulation, when $q = 0.9$, the external dynamic disturbances are selected as follows:

$$d_1(t) = d_2(t) = d_3(t) = 0.1\cos(3t) - 0.25\sin(2t).$$

The initial conditions of the master and slave systems are randomly selected as:

$$X(0) = \left[x_1(0), x_2(0), x_3(0)\right]^T = \left[0.2, -0.2, 0.3\right]^T,$$

$$Y(0) = \left[y_1(0), y_2(0), y_3(0)\right]^T, = \left[-0.1, 0.1, -1\right]^T.$$

The adaptive fuzzy systems, $\theta_i^T \psi_i(Y)$, with $i = 1, 2, 3,$ have the vector $Y = [y_1, y_2, y_3]^T$ as input. For each entry variable of these fuzzy systems, as in Boulkroune et al. (2008), one defines three triangular membership functions uniformly distributed on the intervals [-2, 2].

The controller parameters are selected as follows:

$$k_{01} = k_{02} = k_{03} = 2,$$

$$k_{11} = k_{12} = k_{13} = 10, \; \gamma_{\theta_1} = \gamma_{\theta_2} = \gamma_{\theta_3} = 4000,,$$

$$\sigma_{\theta_1} = \sigma_{\theta_2} = \sigma_{\theta_3} = 0.0005, c_1 = 25, c_2 = 5 \text{ and } c_3 = 1.$$

The initial conditions of the adaptive laws are selected as follows:

$$k_{01}(0) = k_{02}(0) = k_{03}(0) = 0, \theta_1(0) = \theta_2(0) = \theta_3(0) = 0.$$

Note that, in this simulation, the discontinuous function $sign(S_i)$ has been replaced by a smooth function $\tan h(k_{si} S_i)$, with $k_{0si} = 5$, $k_{\theta si} = 5, i = 1, 2, 3.$

The simulation results of a complete synchronization (i.e. with a scaling factor $\lambda = 1$) and the corresponding control signals are depicted in Figures 3(a) - 3(c) and Figure 3(d), respectively. It is clear from those figures that the synchronization errors converge towards small values and the control signals are smooth and bounded.

Figures 4(a)-4(c) and Figure 4(d) respectively illustrate the simulation results of an anti-phase synchronization (i.e. with a scaling factor $\lambda = -1$) and the associated control signals. Simulation results show that a fast synchronization of master and slave can be achieved.

Example 2

This example confirms the effectiveness of the proposed scheme for the synchronization between two distinct fractional-order chaotic systems.

The fractional-order Chen chaotic system is considered as a master system. It is described by the following dynamics Li & Chen (2004):

Figure 3. Complete synchronization (example 1): (a) x_1 (solid line) and y_1 (dotted line). (b) x_2 (solid line) and y_2 (dotted line). (c) x_3 (solid line) and y_3 (dotted line). (d) u_1 (solid line), u_2 (dotted line) and u_3 (dashed line).

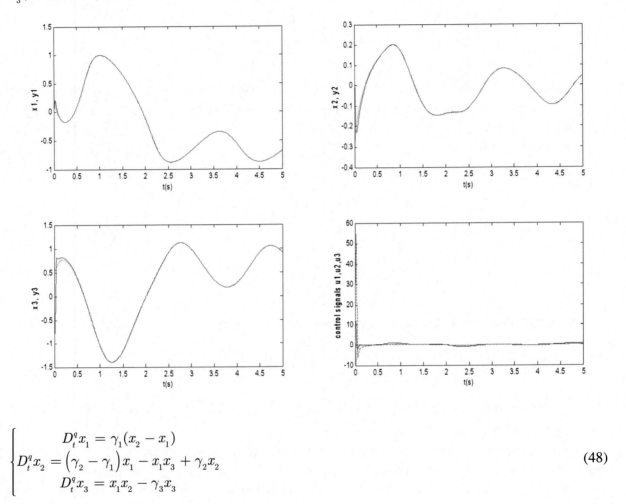

$$\begin{cases} D_t^q x_1 = \gamma_1(x_2 - x_1) \\ D_t^q x_2 = \left(\gamma_2 - \gamma_1\right)x_1 - x_1 x_3 + \gamma_2 x_2 \\ D_t^q x_3 = x_1 x_2 - \gamma_3 x_3 \end{cases} \tag{48}$$

The fractional-order Lorenz chaotic system is selected as a master system. It is described by (Caponetto et al., 2010):

$$\begin{cases} D_t^q y_1 = -\omega_1 y_1 + \omega_1 y_2 + u_1 + d_1(t) \\ D_t^q y_2 = -y_1 y_3 + \omega_2 y_1 - y_2 + u_2 + d_2(t) \\ D_t^q y_3 = y_1 y_2 - \omega_3 y_3 + u_3 + d_3(t) \end{cases} \tag{49}$$

In the simulation, the parameters of both systems are selected as: $q = 0.98$, $\gamma_1 = 35$, $\gamma_2 = 28$, $\gamma_3 = 3$, $\omega_1 = 10$, $\omega_2 = 28$ and $\omega_3 = 8/3$.

Figure 4. Anti-phase synchronization (example 1): (a) x_1 (solid line) and y_1 (dotted line). (b) x_2 (solid line) and y_2 (dotted line). (c) x_3 (solid line) and y_3 (dotted line). (d) u_1 (solid line), u_2 (dotted line) and u_3 (dashed line).

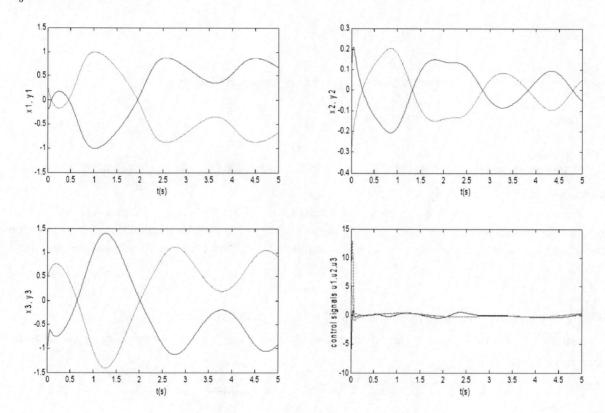

The external dynamic disturbances are chosen as:

$$d_1(t) = d_2(t) = d_3(t) = 0.35\cos(2t) + 0.1\sin(\pi t).$$

The initial conditions of the master and slave systems are randomly selected as:

$$X(0) = [x_1(0), x_2(0), x_3(0)]^T = [16, 15, -5]^T$$

and $Y(0) = [y_1(0), y_2(0), y_3(0)]^T = [1, 2, 2]^T$.

The adaptive fuzzy systems, $\theta_i^T \psi_i(Y)$, with $i = 1, 2, 3$, have the vector $Y = [y_1, y_2, y_3]^T$ as input. For each entry variable of these fuzzy systems, as in Boulkroune et al. (2008), one defines three triangular membership functions uniformly distributed on the interval [-50, 50].

The design parameters are chosen as follows:

$$k_{11} = k_{12} = k_{13} = 10 \; \gamma_{\theta_1} = \gamma_{\theta_2} = \gamma_{\theta_3} = 4000,$$

$$\sigma_{\theta_1} = \sigma_{\theta_2} = \sigma_{\theta_3} = 0.0005, \, c_1 = 25, c_2 = 5 \, ,$$

and $c_3 = 1$. The initial conditions of the adaptive laws are selected as follows:

$$k_{01}(0) = k_{02}(0) = k_{03}(0) = 0, \theta_1(0) = \theta_2(0) = \theta_3(0) = 0 \, .$$

Note that, in the simulation, the discontinuous function $sign(S_i)$ has been replaced by a smooth function $\tan h(k_{si} S_i)$, with $k_{0si} = 25$, $k_{\theta si} = 5, i = 1, 2, 3$.

The simulation results of a complete synchronization (i.e. with a scaling factor $\lambda = 1$) and the corresponding control signals are depicted in Figures 5(a)-5(c) and Figure 5(d), respectively. It is clear from those figures that the synchronization errors are small and the control signals are admissible and bounded.

Figure 5. Complete synchronization (example 2): (a) x_1 (solid line) and y_1 (dotted line). (b) x_2 (solid line) and y_2 (dotted line). (c) x_3 (solid line) and y_3 (dotted line). (d) u_1 (solid line), u_2 (dotted line) and u_3 (dashed line).

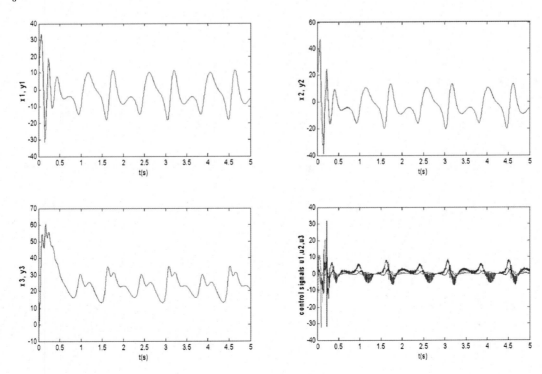

Figures 6(a)-6(c) and Figure 6(d) respectively illustrate the simulation results of an anti-phase synchronization (i.e. with a scaling factor $\lambda = -1$) and the associated control signals.

CONCLUSION

In this chapter, the problem of projective synchronization of fractional-order chaotic systems with both uncertain dynamics and external additive disturbances has been investigated. This synchronization has been achieved by a fuzzy adaptive controller. Of fundamental interest, a suitable Lyapunov based analysis has been carried out to conclude about the stability as well as the synchronization error convergence. Simulation results have been given to emphasize the effectiveness of the proposed synchronization system.

Figure 6. Anti-phase synchronization (example 2): (a) x_1 (solid line) and y_1 (dotted line). (b) x_2 (solid line) and y_2 (dotted line). (c) x_3 (solid line) and y_3 (dotted line). (d) u_1 (solid line), u_2 (dotted line) and u_3 (dashed line)

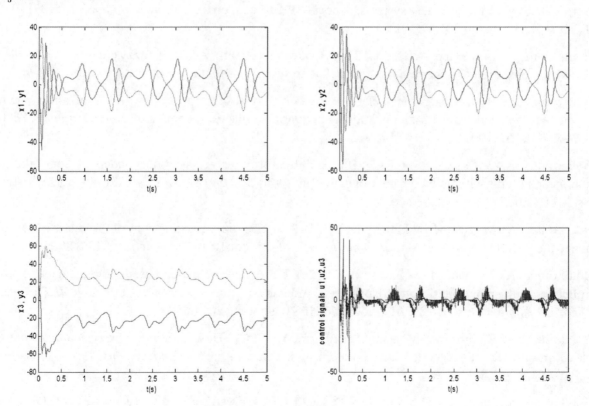

ACKNOWLEDGMENT

The author would like to thank Prof. Abdesselem Boulkroune for his valuable comments which have helped to improve this chapter.

REFERENCES

Aghababa, M. P. (2012). Comments on "H∞ synchronization of uncertain fractional order chaotic systems: Adaptive fuzzy approach". *ISA Transactions*, *51*(1), 11–12. doi:10.1016/j.isatra.2011.10.011 PMID:22075386

Agrawal, S. K., & Das, S. (2013). A modified adaptive control method for synchronization of some fractional chaotic systems with unknown parameters. *Nonlinear Dynamics*, *73*(1-2), 907–919. doi:10.100711071-013-0842-7

Bagley, R. L., & Calico, R. A. (1991). Fractional order state equations for the control of viscoelastically damped structures. *Journal of Guidance, Control, and Dynamics*, *14*(5), 304–311. doi:10.2514/3.20641

Boulkroune, A., Bounar, N., Msaad, M., & Farza, M. (2014a). Indirect adaptive fuzzy control scheme based on observer for nonlinear systems: A novel SPR-filter approach. *Neurocomputing*, *135*, 378–387. doi:10.1016/j.neucom.2013.12.011

Boulkroune, A., Bouzeriba, A., Hamel, S., & Bouden, T. (2014b). Adaptive fuzzy control-based projective synchronization of uncertain nonaffine chaotic systems. *Complexity*. doi:10.1002/cplx.21596

Boulkroune, A., Bouzeriba, A., Hamel, S., & Bouden, T. (2014c). A projective synchronization scheme based on fuzzy adaptive control for unknown multivariable chaotic systems. *Nonlinear Dynamics*, *78*(1), 433–447. doi:10.100711071-014-1450-x

Boulkroune, A., & M'saad, M. (2012). On the design of observer-based fuzzy adaptive controller for nonlinear systems with unknown control gain sign. *Fuzzy Sets and Systems*, *201*, 71–85. doi:10.1016/j.fss.2011.12.005

Boulkroune, A., M'saad, M., & Farza, M. (2012a). Adaptive fuzzy tracking control for a class of MIMO nonaffine uncertain systems. *Neurocomputing*, *93*, 48–55. doi:10.1016/j.neucom.2012.04.006

Boulkroune, A., M'saad, M., & Farza, M. (2012b). Fuzzy approximation-based indirect adaptive controller for multi-input multi-output Non-affine systems with unknown control direction. *IET Control Theory & Applications*, *6*(17), 2619–2629. doi:10.1049/iet-cta.2012.0565

Boulkroune, A., Tadjine, M., M'saad, M., & Farza, M. (2008). How to design a fuzzy adaptive control based on observers for uncertain affine nonlinear systems. *Fuzzy Sets and Systems*, *159*(8), 926–948. doi:10.1016/j.fss.2007.08.015

Boulkroune, A., Tadjine, M., Msaad, M., & Farza, M. (2014). Design of a unified adaptive fuzzy Observer for uncertain nonlinear systems. *Information Sciences*, *265*, 139–153. doi:10.1016/j.ins.2013.12.026

Bowonga, S., Kakmenib, M., & Koinac, R. (2006). Chaos synchronization and duration time of a class of uncertain systems. *Mathematics and Computers in Simulation, 71*(3), 212–228. doi:10.1016/j.matcom.2006.01.006

Cailian, C., Gang, F., & Xinping, G. (2005). An adaptive lag-synchronization method for time-delay chaotic systems. *Proceedings of the IEEE American Control Conference.* 10.1109/ACC.2005.1470651

Caponetto, R., Dongola, G., & Fortuna, L. (2010). *Fractional Order Systems: Modeling and Control Applications.* World Scientific. doi:10.1142/7709

Carroll, T. L., Heagy, J. F., & Pecora, L. M. (1996). Transforming signals with chaotic synchronization. *Physical Review E: Statistical Physics, Plasmas, Fluids, and Related Interdisciplinary Topics, 54*(5), 4676–4680. doi:10.1103/PhysRevE.54.4676 PMID:9965645

Chen, C., & Chen, H. (2009). Robust adaptive neural-fuzzy-network control for the synchronization of uncertain chaotic systems. *Nonlinear Analysis Real World Applications, 10*(3), 1466–1479. doi:10.1016/j.nonrwa.2008.01.016

Chen, L. P., Qu, J. F., Chai, Y., Wu, R. C., & Qi, G. Y. (2013). Synchronization of a class of fractional-order chaotic neural networks. *Entropy (Basel, Switzerland), 15*(8), 3265–3276. doi:10.3390/e15083355

Daftardar-Gejji, V., & Bhalekar, S. (2010). Chaos in fractional ordered Liu system. *Computers & Mathematics with Applications (Oxford, England), 59*(3), 1117–1127. doi:10.1016/j.camwa.2009.07.003

Diethelm, K., & Ford, N. J. (2002). Analysis of fractional differential equations. *Journal of Mathematical Analysis and Applications, 265*(2), 229–248. doi:10.1006/jmaa.2000.7194

Gao, X., & Yu, J. (2005). Chaos in the fractional order periodically forced complex Duffing's oscillators. *Chaos, Solitons, and Fractals, 24*(4), 1097–1104. doi:10.1016/j.chaos.2004.09.090

Ginarsa, I. M., Soeprijanto, A., & Purnomo, M. H. (2013). Controlling chaos and voltage collapse using an ANFIS-based composite controller-static var compensator in power systems. *International Journal of Electrical Power & Energy Systems, 46*, 79–88. doi:10.1016/j.ijepes.2012.10.005

Hartley, T. T., Lorenzo, C. F., & Qammer, H. K. (1995). Chaos in a fractional order Chua's system. *IEEE Transactions on Circuits and Systems. I, Fundamental Theory and Applications, 42*(8), 485–490. doi:10.1109/81.404062

Hartley, T. T., Lorenzo, C. F., & Qammer, H. K. (1995). Chaos in a fractional order Chua's system. *IEEE Transactions on Circuits and Systems. I, Fundamental Theory and Applications, 42*(8), 485–490. doi:10.1109/81.404062

Heaviside, O. (1971). *Electromagnetic Theory.* New York: Chelsea Pub. Co.

Hosseinnia, S., Ghaderi, R., Mahmoudian, M., & Momani, S. (2010). Sliding mode synchronization of an uncertain fractional order chaotic system. *Computers & Mathematics with Applications (Oxford, England), 59*(5), 1637–1643. doi:10.1016/j.camwa.2009.08.021

Hwang, E., Hyun, C., Kim, E., & Park, M. (2009). Fuzzy model based adaptive synchronization of uncertain chaotic systems: Robust tracking control approach. *Physics Letters. [Part A]*, *373*(22), 1935–1939. doi:10.1016/j.physleta.2009.03.057

Ichise, M., Nagayanagi, Y., & Kojima, T. (1971). An analog simulation of non-integer order transfer functions for analysis of electrode process. *Journal of Electroanalytical Chemistry and Interfacial Electrochemistry*, *33*(2), 253–265. doi:10.1016/S0022-0728(71)80115-8

Jing, C. G., He, P., Fan, T., Li, Y., Chen, C., & Song, X. (2015). Single state feedback stabilization of unified chaotic systems and circuit implementation. *Open Physics*, *13*, 111–122.

Li, C., & Chen, G. (2004a). Chaos and hyperchaos in the fractional-order Rössler equations. *Physica A*, *341*, 55–61. doi:10.1016/j.physa.2004.04.113

Li, C., & Chen, G. (2004b). Chaos in the fractional order Chen system and its control. *Chaos, Solitons, and Fractals*, *22*(3), 549–554. doi:10.1016/j.chaos.2004.02.035

Li, C., & Peng, G. (2004). Chaos in Chen's system with a fractional order. *Chaos, Solitons, and Fractals*, *22*(2), 443–450. doi:10.1016/j.chaos.2004.02.013

Li, G. H. (2006). Projective synchronization of chaotic system using backstepping control. *Chaos, Solitons, and Fractals*, *29*(2), 490–598. doi:10.1016/j.chaos.2005.08.029

Li, Y., Tong, S., & Li, T. (2013). Direct adaptive fuzzy backstepping control of uncertain nonlinear systems in the presence of input saturation. *Neural Computing & Applications*, *23*(5), 1207–1216. doi:10.100700521-012-0993-3

Li, Y., Tong, S., & Li, T. (2015). Observer-based adaptive fuzzy tracking control of MIMO stochastic nonlinear systems with unknown control direction and unknown dead-zones. *IEEE Transactions on Fuzzy Systems*, *23*(4), 1228–1241. doi:10.1109/TFUZZ.2014.2348017

Li, Z., & Xu, D. (2004). A secure communication scheme using projective chaos synchronization. *Chaos, Solitons, and Fractals*, *22*(2), 477–481. doi:10.1016/j.chaos.2004.02.019

Lin, T. C., & Kuo, C. H. (2011). synchronization of uncertain fractional order chaotic systems: Adaptive fuzzy approach. *ISA Transactions*, *50*(4), 548–556. doi:10.1016/j.isatra.2011.06.001 PMID:21741648

Lin, T. C., & Lee, T. Y. (2011). Chaos synchronization of uncertain fractional-order chaotic systems with time delay based on adaptive fuzzy sliding mode control. *IEEE Transactions on Fuzzy Systems*, *19*(4), 623–635. doi:10.1109/TFUZZ.2011.2127482

Lin, T. C., Lee, T. Y., & Balas, V. E. (2011). Adaptive fuzzy sliding mode control for synchronization of uncertain fractional order chaotic systems. *Chaos, Solitons, and Fractals*, *44*(10), 791–801. doi:10.1016/j.chaos.2011.04.005

Liu, Y. J., & Zheng, Y. Q. (2009). Adaptive robust fuzzy control for a class of uncertain chaotic systems. *Nonlinear Dynamics*, *57*(3), 431–439. doi:10.100711071-008-9453-0

Lu, J. G. (2005). Chaotic dynamics and synchronization of fractional order Arneodo's systems. *Chaos, Solitons, and Fractals*, *26*(4), 1125–1133. doi:10.1016/j.chaos.2005.02.023

Matignon, D. (1996, July). Stability results for fractional differential equations with applications to control processing. In Proceeding of Computational engineering in systems applications (vol. 2, pp. 963-968). Lille, France: IMACS, IEEE-SMC.

Morgül, Ö., & Solak, E. (1996). Observer based synchronization of chaotic systems. *Physical Review. E*, *54*(5), 4803–4811. doi:10.1103/PhysRevE.54.4803 PMID:9965660

Morgul, Ö., & Solak, E. (1997). On the synchronization of chaotic systems by using state observers. *International Journal of Bifurcation and Chaos in Applied Sciences and Engineering*, *7*(6), 1307–1322. doi:10.1142/S0218127497001047

Pan, L., Zhou, W., Fang, J., & Li, D. (2010). Synchronization and anti-synchronization of new uncertain fractional-order modified unified chaotic systems via novel active pinning control. *Communications in Nonlinear Science and Numerical Simulation*, *15*(12), 3754–3762. doi:10.1016/j.cnsns.2010.01.025

Peng, G. (2007). Synchronization of fractional order chaotic systems. *Physics Letters. [Part A]*, *363*(5-6), 426–432. doi:10.1016/j.physleta.2006.11.053

Pikovsky, A. S., Rosenblum, M. G., Osipov, G. V., & Kurths, J. (1997). Phase synchronization of chaotic oscillators by external driving. *Physica D. Nonlinear Phenomena*, *104*(3-4), 219–238. doi:10.1016/S0167-2789(96)00301-6

Podlubny, I. (1999). *Fractional Differential Equations*. New York: Academic Press.

Poursamad, A., & Davaie-Markazi, A. H. (2009). Robust adaptive fuzzy control of unknown chaotic systems. *Applied Soft Computing*, *9*(3), 970–976. doi:10.1016/j.asoc.2008.11.014

Precup, R. E., & Tomescu, M. L. (2015). Stable fuzzy logic control of a general class of chaotic systems. *Neural Computing & Applications*, *26*(3), 541–550. doi:10.100700521-014-1644-7

Precup, R. E., Tomescu, M. L., & Dragos, C. A. (2014). Stabilization of Rössler chaotic dynamical system using fuzzy logic control algorithm. *International Journal of General Systems*, *43*(5), 413–433. doi:10.1080/03081079.2014.893299

Roopaei, M., & Jahromi, M. Z. (2008). Synchronization of two different chaotic systems using novel adaptive fuzzy sliding mode control. *Chaos (Woodbury, N.Y.)*, *18*(3), 033133. doi:10.1063/1.2980046 PMID:19045471

Rosenblum, M. G., Pikovsky, A. S., & Kurths, J. (1996). Phase synchronization of chaotic oscillators. *Physical Review Letters*, *76*(11), 1804–1807. doi:10.1103/PhysRevLett.76.1804 PMID:10060525

Sun, H., Abdelwahad, A., & Onaral, B. (1984). Linear approximation of transfer function with a pole of fractional power. *IEEE Transactions on Automatic Control*, *29*(5), 441–444. doi:10.1109/TAC.1984.1103551

Sun, J., & Zhang, Y. (2004). Impulsive control and synchronization of Chua's oscillators. *Mathematics and Computers in Simulation*, *66*(6), 499–508. doi:10.1016/j.matcom.2004.03.004

Tavazoei, M. S. (2012). Comments on "Chaos Synchronization of Uncertain Fractional-Order Chaotic Systems With Time Delay Based on Adaptive Fuzzy Sliding Mode Control". *IEEE Transactions on Fuzzy Systems*, *20*(5), 993–995. doi:10.1109/TFUZZ.2012.2188637

Tavazoei, M. S., & Haeri, M. (2008). Synchronization of chaotic fractional-order systems via active sliding mode controller. *Physica A*, *387*(1), 57–70. doi:10.1016/j.physa.2007.08.039

Tong, S., & Li, Y. (2013). Adaptive fuzzy output feedback control of MIMO nonlinear systems with unknown dead-zone input. *IEEE Transactions on Fuzzy Systems*, *21*(1), 134–146. doi:10.1109/TFUZZ.2012.2204065

Tong, S., Li, Y., & Shi, P. (2012). Observer-based adaptive fuzzy backstepping output feedback control of uncertain MIMO pure-feedback nonlinear systems. *IEEE Transactions on Fuzzy Systems*, *20*(4), 771–785. doi:10.1109/TFUZZ.2012.2183604

Tong, S., Sui, S., & Li, Y. (2015). Fuzzy adaptive output feedback control of MIMO nonlinear systems with partial tracking errors constrained. *IEEE Transactions on Fuzzy Systems*, *23*(4), 729–742. doi:10.1109/TFUZZ.2014.2327987

Tong, S. C., Li, Y. M., Feng, G., & Li, T. S. (2011). Observer-based adaptive fuzzy backstepping dynamic surface control for a class of MIMO nonlinear systems. *IEEE Transactions on Systems, Man, and Cybernetics. Part B, Cybernetics*, *41*(4), 1124–1135. doi:10.1109/TSMCB.2011.2108283 PMID:21317084

Utkin, V. I. (1992). *Sliding modes in control optimization*. Berlin: Springer-Verlag. doi:10.1007/978-3-642-84379-2

Wang, J., Chen, L., & Deng, B. (2009). Synchronization of Ghostburster neuron in external electrical stimulation via H∞ variable universe fuzzy adaptive control. *Chaos, Solitons, and Fractals*, *39*(5), 2076–2085. doi:10.1016/j.chaos.2007.06.070

Wang, J., Zhang, Z., & Li, H. (2008). Synchronization of FitzHugh–Nagumo systems in EES via H∞ variable universe adaptive fuzzy control. *Chaos, Solitons, and Fractals*, *36*(5), 1332–1339. doi:10.1016/j.chaos.2006.08.012

Wang, J. W., & Zhang, Y. B. (2009). Synchronization in coupled non identical incommensurate fractional-order systems. *Physics Letters. [Part A]*, *374*(2), 202–207. doi:10.1016/j.physleta.2009.10.051

Wang, L. X. (1994). *Adaptive fuzzy systems and control: design and stability analysis*. Englewood Cliffs, NJ: Prentice-Hall.

Yan, J., & Li, C. (2005). Generalized projective synchronization of a unified chaotic system. *Chaos, Solitons, and Fractals*, *26*(4), 1119–1124. doi:10.1016/j.chaos.2005.02.034

Yin-He, W., Yong-Qing, F., Qing-Yun, W., & Yun, Z. (2012). Adaptive feedback stabilization with quantized state measurements for a class of chaotic systems. *Communications in Theoretical Physics*, *57*(5), 808–816. doi:10.1088/0253-6102/57/5/11

Yu, Y., Li, H., Wang, S., & Yu, J. (2009). Dynamic analysis of a fractional-order Lorenz chaotic system. *Chaos, Solitons, and Fractals*, *42*(2), 1181–1189. doi:10.1016/j.chaos.2009.03.016

KEY TERMS AND DEFINITIONS

Adaptive Control: A control methodology in which one or more parameters are used to vary the feedback control signals in order to satisfy some required performance criteria.

Chaos Synchronization: Synchronization of two chaotic dynamical systems implies tracking the trajectories of the slave system with that of its master system.

Chaotic Behavior: The behavior of a system whose final state depends so sensitively on the initial conditions. Its behavior is also unpredictable and cannot be distinguished from a random process, even though it is strictly determinate by a mathematical model.

Fractional-Order Control: A field of control theory that uses the fractional-order integrator and derivative as parts of the control system design toolkit.

Fuzzy Control System: An automatic control system in which the relation between the state variables of the system under control and the action variables is given as a set of fuzzy implications or as a fuzzy relation.

Nonlinear System: A system which can be modelled by a nonlinear differential equation.

Chapter 8

Chaos Synchronization of Optical Systems via a Fractional–Order Sliding Mode Controller

Abdesselem Boulkroune
University of Jijel, Algeria

Amina Boubellouta
University of Jijel, Algeria

ABSTRACT

In this chapter, one investigates the chaos synchronization of a class of uncertain optical chaotic systems. More precisely, one also presents a systematic approach for designing a fractional-order (FO) sliding mode controller to achieve a rapid, robust, and perfect chaos synchronization. By this robust controller, it is rigorously proven that the associated synchronization error is Mittag-Leffler (or asymptotically) stable. In a numerical simulation framework, this synchronization scheme is tested on many chaotic optical systems taken from the open literature. The obtained results clearly show that the proposed chaos synchronization controller is not only strongly robust with respect to the unavoidable system's uncertainties (as unmodeled dynamics, and parameters' variation and uncertainty) and eventual dynamical external disturbances, but also can significantly reduce the chattering effect.

INTRODUCTION

There are many practical reasons for *controlling and synchronizing of chaotic systems* (Chen & Dong, 1998; Li et al.,2016; Ahmad et al., 2016; Othman et al., 2016; Pham et al., 2016; Li et al., 2014 ; Li et al., 2013). This is why people get more and more attention in the research of the chaotic system theory and its applications. Chaotic systems are nonlinear and deterministic yet long-term unpredictable. This impossibility of predicting the future state of a deterministic system is due to the sensitivity of chaotic

DOI: 10.4018/978-1-5225-5418-9.ch008

orbits (Li & Chen, 2004). A chaotic behavior is characterized by the exponential divergence of initially nearby trajectories, or equivalendy, by sensitive dependence on initial conditions. Exponential divergence is quantified by Lyapunov exponents. Note that the chaotic comportment can appear in both dissipative systems and conservative systems. In recent literature, it also was revealed that many fractional-order (FO) systems can chaotically behave, for instance: FO Rössler system (Li & Chen, 2004), FO Arneodo system (Lu, 2005), FO Lü system (Deng & Li, 2005), FO Lorenz system (Grigorenko & Grigorenko, 2003).

After the finding of *master-slave synchronization* by Pecora and Carroll in 1990, the study of chaotic synchronization became popular (Hasler et al., 1998). The potential applications of chaos synchronization in secure communication systems, which were experimentally established in 1991, engaged the interest of the physician and engineer communities, and it has become an active topic of research since. Many different aspects of chaos synchronization were studied: synchronization in unidirectionally and bidirectionally coupled systems (Hale, 1997), (Ushio, 1995), anti-phase synchronization (Ushio, 1995; Rosenblum et al., 1996), partial synchronization (Hasler et al., 1998) and generalized synchronization (Abarbanel et al., 1996; Kocarev & Parlitz, 1996), and so on. This phenomenon has been observed in several physical systems, e.g. electrical and mechanical systems (Chua & Itoh, 1993), optical and laser systems (Terry & Thornburg Jr, 2009; Behnia et al., 2013), biological systems (Vaidyanathan, 2015) and Josephson junctions (Shahverdiev et al., 2014). Chaos synchronization has also found a number of applications in control theory (Pyragas, 1992), parameter estimation from time series (Maybhate & Amritkar, 1999), secret communication, information sciences, optimization problems, and in some connected nonlinear areas (Zhang et al.,2016a). A good review of developments in the theoretical and experimental study of synchronized chaotic systems can be found in (Aziz-Alaoui, 2005).

The sliding-mode control (SMC, or variable structure control) methodology is a powerful instrument for designing robust controllers for nonlinear uncertain systems subject to unknown bounded disturbances. The salient features of this methodology are for instance: robustness regarding to system parameter variations and possible external disturbances, reduced order comportment of the system in the sliding-mode, decoupling of the sliding-mode dynamic equations, fast and finite-time convergence. In addition to these attractive features, the SMC is applicable to a large variety of plants: including linear, nonlinear, uncertain, discrete, switched, hybrid, and distributed parameter systems. The principal of the SMC methodology is very straightforward: it consists to drive the nonlinear system's states to onto a suitably prespecified sliding surface in the state space and to keep the system's state trajectory on this sliding surface (also called switching surface) for subsequent time. Recently, the fractional-order calculus is used within the sliding mode control methodologies, in order to enhance the control performances. Several works dealt with the fractional-order sliding mode control (FO-SMC) of nonlinear or linear systems with fractional-orders (Calderón et al., 2006; Efe & Kasnakoğlu, 2008a; Si-Ammour et al., 2009; Pisano et al., 2010). It is worth noting that in general the choice of the sliding surface for this class of systems is not an easy task.

Fractional calculus (FC), which can be seen as a generalization of derivation and integration to non-integer (arbitrary) order operators, was born 300 years ago. The research on FC knew its boom only in the past decades, particularly in the field of chaos synchronization and control (Podlubny, 1999 ; Bou-zeriba et al., 2016, 2016b; Boulkroune et al., 2016 ; Zouari et al., 2017 ; Zouari et al., 2016). While the applications of fractional-order control (FOC) enjoyed a broad popularity, it spawned two main branches: FO modeling and FO control, which therefore formed three combinations in academic research and practical implementations, namely:

- Integer-order control of FO systems,
- FO control of integer-order systems, and
- FO control of FO systems.

About these topics, many existing methodologies and principles are waiting to be improved; meantime, dedicated new theoretical results and methodologies need to be developed in order to deal with the sprouting circumstances. Moreover, the fractional-order calculus is an incredible tool that can explain many physics phenomenon which classical math could not. It is particularly good at depicting precisely of long memory and heredity features of many substances and processes. Many authors have tried to integrate the FO calculus into sliding mode control (via the switching surface or sliding motion) to enhance performances and robustness. The first work on FO sliding mode control has been proposed in Calderón et al. (2006), for a power electronic buck converter. In Delavari et al. (2010), a fuzzy sliding-mode control methodology with a FO sliding motion has been presented for a class of uncertain nonlinear systems. In Efe, (2008), To enhance the robustness as well as performance of a fuzzy sliding-mode controller, a new parameter tuning scheme employing fractional-integration has been proposed.

Motivated by the aforementioned discussions, this chapter concerns the design problem of a FO sliding-mode control to asymptotically projective-synchronize of uncertain chaotic optical systems. First, a stable FO sliding surface of integral type is properly designed, and it allows to significantly diminish the chattering effect. Next, via a constructive use of FO Lyapunov stability theory, a FO sliding-mode control is proposed to guarantee a projective synchronization. The main contributions of this paper, from the methodological point of view, are twofold.

1. First, one proposes a robust FO sliding mode-control for projective-synchronizing a class of uncertain chaotic optical systems. To authors' best knowledge, chaos synchronization via FO sliding-mode control of uncertain optical systems has not been already reported in the literature.
2. Second, compared to the traditional sliding mode control, the proposed fractional-order sliding mode control incorporates a FO integral term which can alleviate efficiently the chattering effect.

SOME CONCEPTS RELATED TO THE FRACTIONAL CALCULUS

One first examines some indispensable concepts of fractional calculus. Up to now, to authors' best knowledge, there more than 10 types of definitions for FO integrals and derivatives. For readers convenience, only Riemann–Liouville (RL) definition and its properties, which will be used in the reminder of this paper, are listed below (Podlubny, 1999).

Definition 1 (Podlubny, 1999): The β th-order RL fractional integration of a function $g(t)$ is defined as

$$_0D_t^{-\beta}g(t) = \frac{1}{\Gamma(\beta)} \int_0^t \frac{g(\tau)}{(t-\tau)^{1-\beta}} \, d\tau \tag{1}$$

where $\Gamma(x)$ is the so-called Gamma function $\Gamma(x) = \int\limits_{0}^{\infty} t^{x-1}e^{-t}dt$. When the initial integral limit changes from 0 to any arbitrary point a, this definition can be generalize to that of Weyl:

$$_aD_t^{-\beta}g(t) = \frac{1}{\Gamma(\beta)} \int\limits_{a}^{t} \frac{g(\tau)}{(t-\tau)^{1-\beta}}\, d\tau \tag{2}$$

Definition 2 (Podlubny, 1999): The RL definition of FO derivative is based on that of fractional integral and the integer derivative:

$$_0D_t^{\beta}g(t) = \frac{d}{dt}\left[_0D_t^{-(1-\beta)}g(t) \right] \tag{3}$$

In the rest of this paper, for convenience, the simple and short notation D^{β} will be used for indicating the RL fractional derivative.

Property 1 (Podlubny, 1999): The RL fractional derivative D^{β} commutes with the integer derivative d^n / dt^n, i.e.:

$$\frac{d^n}{dt^n}(D^{\beta}g(t)) = D^{\beta}(\frac{d^n g(t)}{dt^n}) = D^{\beta+n}g(t) \tag{4}$$

Definition 3 (Li et al., 2010): The Mittag-Leffler (ML) function can be seen as a generalization of the usual exponential function which plays an essential role in the solution of fractional-order differential equations just like the exponential function does in the integer-order (ordinary) differential equations. It has four forms, and the most used forms are the one-parameter and two-parameter representations (Li et al., 2010).

$$E_{\alpha}(x) = \sum_{k=0}^{\infty} \frac{x^k}{\Gamma(\alpha k + 1)} \qquad (\alpha > 0); \tag{5}$$

$$E_{\alpha,\beta}(x) = \sum_{k=0}^{\infty} \frac{x^k}{\Gamma(\alpha k + \beta)} \qquad (\alpha > 0, \beta > 0); \tag{6}$$

Some of the nice properties of M-L function are: $E_{1,1}(x) = e^x$, $E_{1,2}(x) = \dfrac{e^x - 1}{x}$.

Definition 4 (Li et al., 2010): The solution of the system $D^{\alpha}x = g(x,t)$ is ML stable if

$$\left\| x(t) \right\| \leq \left\{ k \left[x(t_0) \right] E_\alpha \left(-\lambda (t - t_0)^\alpha \right) \right\}^b \tag{7}$$

where t_0 is the initial time $\lambda > 0, \quad b > 0, \quad k(0) = 0$,and $k(x) \geq 0$ is locally Lipschitz.

Theorem 1 (Li et al., 2010): Let $x = 0$ be an equilibrium point for the non-autonomous fractional-order system

$$D^\beta x = g(x, t) \tag{8}$$

where $g(x, t)$ is a Lipschitzian function and $\beta \in (0, 1)$. Suppose that there exists a Lyapunov function $V(t, x)$ fulfilling the following conditions:

$$\beta_1 \left\| x \right\|^a \leq V(t, x) \leq \beta_2 \left\| x \right\| \tag{9}$$

$$\dot{V}(t, x) \leq -\beta_3 \left\| x \right\| \tag{10}$$

with $\beta_1, \beta_2, \beta_3$ and a being positive constants. Hence, the equilibrium point of (8) is asymptotically (or ML) stable.

Theorem 2 (Zhang & Li, 2011): Consider a linear FO system: $D^{\alpha+1} e_1 + \lambda_1 e_1 = 0$, with $\alpha \in (0, 1)$. This system with RL derivative is asymptotically (or ML) stable if $\arg(-\lambda_n) > (\alpha + 1)\pi / 2$. In this case, the components of the state vanish at the origin like $t^{-\alpha-2}$.

FO SLIDING MODE CONTROL DESIGN

Consider two n–dimensional master and slave chaotic systems with uncertainties and external disturbances:

Master system:

$$\begin{cases} \dot{x}_1 = f_1(x, t) \\ \dot{x}_2 = f_2(x, t) \\ \vdots \\ \dot{x}_n = f_n(x, t) \end{cases} \tag{11}$$

Slave system:

$$\begin{cases} \dot{y}_1 = f_1(y,t) + \Delta f_1(y,t) + d_1(t) + u_1(t) \\ \dot{y}_2 = f_2(y,t) + \Delta f_2(y,t) + d_2(t) + u_2(t) \\ \vdots \\ \dot{y}_n = f_n(y,t) + \Delta f_n(y,t) + d_n(t) + u_n(t) \end{cases} \tag{12}$$

where $x(t) = [x_1, x_2, \ldots\ldots, x_n]^T \in R^n$ and $y(t) = [y_1, y_2, \ldots\ldots, y_n]^T \in R^n$ are the respective state vectors of the master and slave systems, $f_i(x,t)$ and $f_i(y,t) \in R, \quad i = 1,2,\ldots..n$ are known nonlinear functions of x and the time $t, \Delta f_i(y,t) \in R$ and $d_i(t) \in R, i = 1,2,\ldots.n$ represent respectively uncertainties and possible external disturbances and $u_i(t) \in R, \quad i = 1,2,\ldots., n$ is the input.

The projective-synchronization errors are defined as follows:

$$e_i(t) = y_i(t) - \kappa_i x_i(t), \quad \text{for } i=1,2,\ldots,\text{n} \tag{13}$$

where κ_i is a real constant.

From (11) and (12), the synchronization error dynamics can be given as:

$$\begin{cases} \dot{e}_1 = f_1(y,t) + \Delta f_1(y,t) + d_1(t) - \kappa_1 f_1(x,t) + u_1 \\ \dot{e}_2 = f_2(y,t) + \Delta f_2(y,t) + d_2(t) - \kappa_2 f_2(x,t) + u_2 \\ \vdots \\ \dot{e}_n = f_n(y,t) + \Delta f_n(y,t) + d_n(t) - \kappa_n f_n(x,t) + u_n \end{cases} \tag{14}$$

The next assumptions will be helpful to design our FO sliding-mode control based synchronization scheme.

Assumption 1: *The state variables of the master-slave system (11) and (12) are available for measurement.*
Assumption 2: *The uncertainties and possible external disturbances fulfill the following boundedness properties:*

$$\begin{aligned} \left\| D^{\alpha}\left(\Delta f_1(y,t) + d_1(t)\right) \right\| &\leq \delta_1 \left\| e \right\|_1 + \sigma_1 \\ \left\| D^{\alpha}\left(\Delta f_2(y,t) + d_2(t)\right) \right\| &\leq \delta_2 \left\| e \right\|_1 + \sigma_2 \\ \vdots \\ \left\| D^{\alpha}\left(\Delta f_n(y,t) + d_n(t)\right) \right\| &\leq \delta_n \left\| e \right\|_1 + \sigma_n \end{aligned} \tag{15}$$

where δ_n and σ_n are given positive constants and $e = [e_1, e_2, \ldots, e_n]^T$.

Now, one defines a novel error form as follows:

$$\begin{cases}
\overline{e}_1 = \int_0^t e_1 d\tau \\
\overline{e}_2 = \dot{\overline{e}}_1 = e_1 \\
\overline{e}_3 = \int_0^t e_2 d\tau \\
\overline{e}_4 = \dot{\overline{e}}_3 = e_2 \\
\vdots \\
\overline{e}_{2n-1} = \int_0^t e_n d\tau \\
\overline{e}_{2n} = \dot{\overline{e}}_{n-1} = e_n
\end{cases} \tag{16}$$

Then, the dynamics (14) become

$$\begin{cases}
\dot{\overline{e}}_1 = \overline{e}_2 \\
\dot{\overline{e}}_2 = f_1(y,t) + \Delta f_1(y,t) + d_1(t) - f_1(x,t) + u_1 \\
\dot{\overline{e}}_3 = \overline{e}_4 \\
\dot{\overline{e}}_4 = f_2(y,t) + \Delta f_2(y,t) + d_2(t) - f_2(x,t) + u_2 \\
\vdots \\
\dot{\overline{e}}_{2n-1} = \overline{e}_{2n} \\
\dot{\overline{e}}_{2n} = f_n(y,t) + \Delta f_n(y,t) + d_n(t) - f_n(x,t) + u_n
\end{cases} \tag{17}$$

One designs the FO sliding surfaces as:

$$\begin{cases}
s_1(t) = D^{\alpha+1}\overline{e}_1 + \lambda_1 \overline{e}_1 \\
s_2(t) = D^{\alpha+1}\overline{e}_3 + \lambda_2 \overline{e}_3 \\
\vdots \\
s_n(t) = D^{\alpha+1}\overline{e}_{2n-1} + \lambda_n \overline{e}_{2n-1}
\end{cases} \tag{18}$$

with $\lambda_i > 0$, $i = 1, 2, ..., n$, are design parameters chosen, according to Theorem 2, such as the dynamics $s_1(t) = s_2(t) = ... = s_n(t) = 0$ is asymptotically stable.

Note that once the system states operate in the sliding mode, one has $s_1(t) = s_2(t) = ... = s_n(t) = 0$, i.e.

$$\begin{cases} s_1(t) = D^{\alpha+1}\overline{e}_1 + \lambda_1\overline{e}_1 = 0 \\ s_2(t) = D^{\alpha+1}\overline{e}_3 + \lambda_2\overline{e}_3 = 0 \\ \vdots \\ s_n(t) = D^{\alpha+1}\overline{e}_{2n-1} + \lambda_n\overline{e}_{2n-1} = 0 \end{cases} \tag{19}$$

Taking the derivative of the switching surfaces $s_i(t)$ and using Property 1, one can rewrite (18) as:

$$\begin{cases} \dot{s}_1(t) = D^{\alpha}\dot{\overline{e}}_2 + \lambda_1\overline{e}_2 \\ \dot{s}_2(t) = D^{\alpha}\dot{\overline{e}}_4 + \lambda_2\overline{e}_4 \\ \vdots \\ \dot{s}_n(t) = D^{\alpha}\dot{\overline{e}}_{2n} + \lambda_n\overline{e}_{2n} \end{cases} \tag{20}$$

Our FO sliding-mode control can be designed as follows:

$$\begin{cases} u_1 = -D^{-\alpha}\left[(\rho_{11}s_1 Tanh(s_1/\varepsilon_1) + \rho_{12}\left(s_1 Tanh(s_1/\varepsilon_1)\right)^\eta)Tanh(s_1/\varepsilon_1) + \lambda_1\overline{e}_2 + (\delta_1\|e\|_1 + \sigma_1 + \sigma_0)sign(s_1)\right] - f_1(y,t) + \kappa_1 f_1(x,t) \\ u_2 = -D^{-\alpha}\left[(\rho_{21}s_2 Tanh(s_2/\varepsilon_2) + \rho_{22}\left(s_2 Tanh(s_2/\varepsilon_2)\right)^\eta)Tanh(s_2/\varepsilon_2) + \lambda_2\overline{e}_4 + (\delta_2\|e\|_1 + \sigma_2 + \sigma_0)sign(s_2)\right] - f_2(y,t) + \kappa_2 f_2(x,t) \\ \vdots \\ u_n = -D^{-\alpha}\left[(\rho_{n1}s_n Tanh(s_n/\varepsilon_n) + \rho_{n2}\left(s_n Tanh(s_n/\varepsilon_n)\right)^\eta)Tanh(s_n/\varepsilon_n) + \lambda_n\overline{e}_{2n} + (\delta_n\|e\|_1 + \sigma_n + \sigma_0)sign(s_n)\right] - f_n(y,t) + \kappa_n f_n(x,t) \end{cases} \tag{21}$$

where ρ_{11}, ρ_{12}, ρ_{21}, $\rho_{22}, \ldots, \rho_{n1}$, ρ_{n2} and η are positive design constants, δ_1, σ_1, δ_2, $\sigma_2, \ldots, \delta_n$ and σ_n have been previously defined in (12), and $\varepsilon_1, \varepsilon_2, \ldots, \varepsilon_n$ are small strictly positive design constants. $Tanh(.)$ and $sign(.)$ stand respectively for the usual *hyperbolic tangent* function and the *signum* function.

Theorem 3: Consider the slave system (11) and its master system (12) subject to Assumptions 1 et 2, and with the FO sliding-mode control law (21). Then, the corresponding closed-loop systems ensures the asymptotic convergence of sliding surfaces $s_i(t)$, for i=1,2,...,n, to zero.

Proof: Consider the following Lyapunov function:

$$V(t) = \left\|s_1(t)\right\|_1 + \left\|s_2(t)\right\|_1 + \ldots + \left\|s_n(t)\right\|_1 \tag{22}$$

where $\left\|s_i(t)\right\|_1$ stands for $L_1 - norm$.

The derivative of $V(t)$ is

$$\dot{V}(t) = \dot{s}_1\ sign(s_1) + \dot{s}_2\ sign(s_2) + \ldots + \dot{s}_n\ sign(s_n) \tag{23}$$

Considering (20), (23) becomes

$$\dot{V}(t) = (D^\alpha \ \dot{\bar{e}}_2 + \lambda_1 \bar{e}_2)sign(s_1) + (D^\alpha \ \dot{\bar{e}}_4 + \lambda_2 \bar{e}_4)sign(s_2) + \ldots + (D^\alpha \ \dot{\bar{e}}_{2n} + \lambda_n \bar{e}_{2n})sign(s_n) \tag{24}$$

Using (17) (i.e. the expressions of $\dot{\bar{e}}_2, \dot{\bar{e}}_4, \ldots, \dot{\bar{e}}_n$), (24) becomes:

$$\dot{V}(t) = \left(D^\alpha \left(f_1(y,t) + \Delta f_1(y,t) + u_1 + d_1(t) - \kappa_1 f_1(x,t)\right) + \lambda_1 \bar{e}_2\right)sign(s_1)$$
$$+ \left(D^\alpha \left(f_2(y,t) + \Delta f_2(y,t) + u_2 + d_2(t) - \kappa_2 f_2(x,t)\right) + \lambda_2 \bar{e}_4\right)sign(s_2) \tag{25}$$
$$+ \ldots + \left(D^\alpha \left(f_n(y,t) + \Delta f_n(y,t) + u_n + d_n(t) - \kappa_n f_n(x,t)\right) + \lambda_n \bar{e}_{2n}\right)sign(s_n)$$

Substituting the control expression (21) into (25) yields

$$\dot{V}(t) = -(\rho_{11}s_1 Tanh(s_1/\varepsilon_1) + \rho_{12}\left(s_1 Tanh(s_1/\varepsilon_1)\right)^\eta)\left|Tanh(s_1/\varepsilon_1)\right| - (\rho_{21}s_2 Tanh(s_2/\varepsilon_2) +$$
$$\rho_{22}\left(s_2 Tanh(s_2/\varepsilon_2)\right)^\eta)\left|Tanh(s_2/\varepsilon_2)\right| - (\rho_{31}s_3 Tanh(s_3/\varepsilon_3) + \rho_{32}\left(s_3 Tanh(s_3/\varepsilon_3)\right)^\eta)$$
$$\left|Tanh(s_3/\varepsilon_3)\right| - \ldots - (\rho_{n1}s_n Tanh(s_n/\varepsilon_n) + \rho_{n2}\left(s_n Tanh(s_n/\varepsilon_n)\right)^\eta)\left|Tanh(s_n/\varepsilon_n)\right| -$$
$$(\delta_1 \|e\| + \sigma_1 + \sigma_0) + D^\alpha \left(\Delta f_1(y,t) + d_1(t)\right) sign(s_1) - (\delta_2 \|e\| + \sigma_2 + \sigma_0) + \tag{26}$$
$$D^\alpha \left(\Delta f_2(y,t) + d_2(t)\right) sign(s_2) - (\delta_3 \|e\| + \sigma_3 + \sigma_0) + D^\alpha \left(\Delta f_3(y,t) + d_3(t)\right) sign(s_3) -$$
$$\ldots - (\delta_n \|e\| + \sigma_n + \sigma_0) + D^\alpha \left(\Delta f_n(y,t) + d_n(t)\right) sign(s_n)$$

Exploiting Assumption 2, $\dot{V}(t)$ becomes

$$\dot{V}(t) \leq -\sigma_0 \|s_1(t)\|_1 - \ldots - \sigma_0 \|s_n(t)\|_1 = -\sigma_0 V(t) \tag{27}$$

By using Theorem 1, from (27), it is clear that the sliding surfaces will asymptotically converge to $s_1(t) = s_2(t) = \ldots = s_n(t) = 0$. This ends the proof of this theorem.

Remark 2: Choice of a non-smooth Lyapunov function $V(t) = \|s_1(t)\|_1 + \|s_2(t)\|_1 + \ldots + \|s_n(t)\|_1$ is frequent in the control literature (Aghababa, 2013), in particularly, to prove the finite-time convergence of a system.

Remark 3: Following are some important characteristics of the proposed FO sliding mode control:

1. The motion in a sliding mode in general is independent of the master-salve system parameters and possible external disturbances., and the motion only depends on the sliding surface parameters λ_i. This important insensitivity feature of this proposed FO sliding mode control makes it possible to overcome the uncertainties and disturbances in control of nonlinear systems without requiring accurate modeling; it is sufficient to know only the bounds of the system parameters and these of disturbances.

2. Due the presence of the FO integral $D^{-\alpha}$ in the proposed control law (21), unlike the classic sliding mode control, the proposed fractional-order sliding mode controller can considerably reduce the chattering effect.

SIMULATION RESULTS

To illustrate the effectiveness of the proposed FO sliding-mode control based synchronization scheme, four simulation examples are presented in details and the results obtained by this proposed controller are compared with that of the classical sliding-mode control.

Classical Sliding Mode Controller

In order to compare our proposed controller with the classical sliding mode controller, one recalls now its principal.

Consider again the master-slave system given by (11) and (12), with the assumption 1 and the following assumption.

Assumption 3: *The uncertainties and possible external disturbances fulfill the following boundedness properties:*

$$
\begin{aligned}
&\left\| \Delta f_1(y,t) + d_1(t) \right\| \le k_{11} \left\| e \right\|_1 + k_{12} \\
&\left\| \Delta f_2(y,t) + d_2(t) \right\| \le k_{21} \left\| e \right\|_1 + k_{22} \\
&\vdots \\
&\left\| \Delta f_n(y,t) + d_n(t) \right\| \le k_{n1} \left\| e \right\|_1 + k_{n2}
\end{aligned}
\tag{28}
$$

with k_{i1} and $k_{j2} > 0$, for $i = 1,...,n$, $j = 1,...,n$, are given positive constants and $e = \left[e_1, e_2,..., e_n \right]^T$.

As in the previous controller, the sliding surfaces are selected as follows:

$$
\begin{cases}
s_1(t) = \dot{\bar{e}}_1 + \lambda_1 \bar{e}_1 = \bar{e}_2 + \lambda_1 \bar{e}_1 \\
s_2(t) = \dot{\bar{e}}_3 + \lambda_2 \bar{e}_3 = \bar{e}_4 + \lambda_2 \bar{e}_3 \\
\vdots \\
s_n(t) = \dot{\bar{e}}_{2n-1} + \lambda_n \bar{e}_{2n-1} = \bar{e}_{2n} + \lambda_n \bar{e}_{2n-1}
\end{cases}
\tag{29}
$$

with $\lambda_i > 0$, $i = 1,2,...,n$, are design parameters.

The classical sliding mode control associated to these sliding surfaces can be given by

$$\begin{cases} u_1 = -f_1(y,t) + f_1(x,t) - \lambda_1 \overline{e}_2 - (k_{11}\|e\|_1 + k_{12} + \chi_1)sign(s_1) \\ u_2 = -f_2(y,t) + f_2(x,t) - \lambda_2 \overline{e}_4 - (k_{21}\|e\|_1 + k_{22} + \chi_2)sign(s_2) \\ \vdots \\ u_n = -f_n(y,t) + f_n(x,t) - \lambda_3 \overline{e}_{2n} - (k_{n1}\|e\|_1 + k_{n2} + \chi_n)sign(s_n) \end{cases} \tag{30}$$

with $\chi_i > 0$ are design parameter.

Theorem 4: Consider the slave system (11) and its master system (12) subject to Assumptions 1 et 3, and with the classical sliding-mode control law (30). Then, the corresponding closed-loop systems ensures the asymptotic convergence of errors $s_i(t)$, for i=1,2,...,n, to zero.

SIMULATION STUDIES

Example 1 (BEC in a Moving Optical Lattice)

The dynamical equations of a Bose-Einstein condensate (BEC) system in a moving optical lattice can be quantitatively described by the nonlinear Schrödinger equation with a nonlinear term representing interactions, besides so-called the Gross- Pitaevskii (GP) equation (Zhang et al., 2016b; Chong et al., 2004):

$$\frac{\hbar^2}{2m}\frac{d^2\varphi}{d\zeta^2} + i(\frac{\hbar^2 \alpha_2}{m} + \hbar v_L - i\hbar\gamma v_L)\frac{d\varphi}{d\zeta} - (\hbar\beta + \frac{\hbar^2 \alpha_2^2}{2m} - i\hbar\beta\gamma)\varphi - g_0|\varphi|^2\varphi = V_1\cos^2(k\zeta)\varphi \tag{31}$$

where m stands for atomic mass, φ is the macroscopic quantum wave function and $v_L = \delta/2k$ is the optical lattice velocity. $\zeta = x + v_L t$ stands for the system' space-time variable, $g_0 = 4\pi\hbar^2 a/m$ is the nonlinear term in the Gross- Pitaevskii equation, representing the force of the atomic interaction and a is the S-wave scattering length. The case $a > 0$ represents repulsive interatomic interactions and $a < 0$ attractive interatomic interactions. This term nonlinear (this nonlinearity) makes generating chaos into the quantum system. α_2 and β are two undetermined constants and the term proportional to γ denotes the damping coefficient. One uses the following set of parameters and dimensionless variables to simplify Eq. (31).
    Put

$$\varphi = R(\eta)e^{i\theta(\eta)}, \quad \frac{d\theta}{d\eta} = -\frac{\beta_1}{v} = -(\frac{v}{2} + \alpha_1),$$

$$\eta = k\zeta, \quad v = \frac{2mv_L}{\hbar k}, \quad \beta_1 = \frac{\hbar\beta}{E_r}, \quad \alpha_1 = \frac{\alpha_2}{k}, \quad I_0 = \frac{V_1}{E_r} \quad E_r = \frac{\hbar^2 k^2}{2m}$$

In that case, Eq. (31) can be expressed as:

$$\frac{d^2R}{d\eta^2} - \frac{1}{4}v^2R - gR^3 = I_0\cos^2(\eta)R - \gamma v\frac{dR}{d\eta}. \tag{32}$$

Let $R = x_1$ and $\frac{dR}{d\eta} = x_2$, i.e.

$$Master \quad \begin{cases} \dfrac{dx_1}{dt} = x_2 \\[2mm] \dfrac{dx_2}{dt} = 0.25v^2x_1 + gx_1^3 + I_0\cos^2(\eta)x_1 - \gamma vx_2 \end{cases} \tag{33}$$

with $t = \eta$, I_0 being the intensity of the optical lattice potential. The square of the amplitude R is the particle number density because $|R| = |\varphi|$ and θ is the phase of φ. Equation (33) gives us a nonlinear quantum system. It has been proven in Zhang et al. (2016b) that the system (33) can chaotically behave. The system (33) here is used as a master system. Its controlled slave system is given by

$$Salve \quad \begin{cases} \dfrac{d^2y_1}{dt} = y_2 + \Delta f_1(y,t) + d_1(t) + u_1(t) \\[2mm] \dfrac{dy_2}{dt} = 0.25v^2y_1 + gy_1^3 + I_0\cos^2(t)y_1 - \gamma vy_2 + \Delta f_2(y,t) + d_2(t) + u_2(t) \end{cases} \tag{34}$$

Without lost of generality, the uncertainties and the external dynamic disturbances are chosen as:

$$\Delta f_1(y,t) = f_2(y,t) = 0.5\cos(6t) + 0.4\sin(t) \text{ and } d_1(t) = d_2(t) = 1.$$

The design parameters of the proposed controller are:

$$\rho_{11} = 10, \rho_{12} = 9.5, \ \rho_{21} = 1, \rho_{22} = 5, \varepsilon_1 = 0.1, \ \varepsilon_2 = 0.1,$$

$$\sigma_1 = 0.75, \sigma_2 = 0.98, \sigma_0 = 0.64, \delta_1 = 1.3, \delta_2 = 1.5, \ \alpha = 0.7,$$

$$\rho_{21} = 9.85, \rho_{22} = 10.5, \ \lambda_1 = \lambda_2 = 2, \eta = 0.9.$$

When the parameters of the system (33) are selected as:

$$v = 2.05, \ g = -0.75, \ I_0 = 5.5 \text{ and } \gamma = 0.05,$$

this system shows a chaotic behavior.

To numerically simulate the above master-slave equations, the fourth-order RK method is used with a fixed-step size of 0.001. One chooses the initial conditions of the master and slave system as $(x_1(0), x_2(0)) = (1.5, 0.5)$, and $(y_1(0), y_2(0)) = (2.5, 1.2)$.

The Lyapunov exponents of the master system (33) are depicted in Figure 1. From this figure, It is clear that the sum of these three Lyapunov exponents is positive. This confirms that the system (1) is dissipative. Figure 2 shows the chaotic attractor projections on $x_1 - x_2$ plan. The phase plan orbit is irregular and the chaos exists in the BEC system (33).

To test our FO sliding-mode controller and the classical sliding-mode controller for the master-slave system (33) and (34), four cases are considered here:

Figure 1. Lyapunov exponents

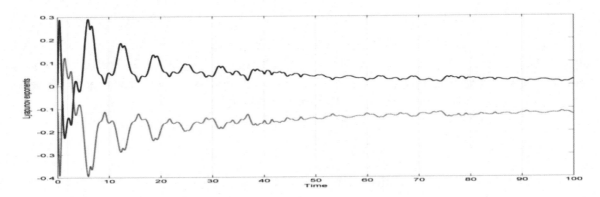

Figure 2. Chaotic attractor on plane $x_1 - x_2$

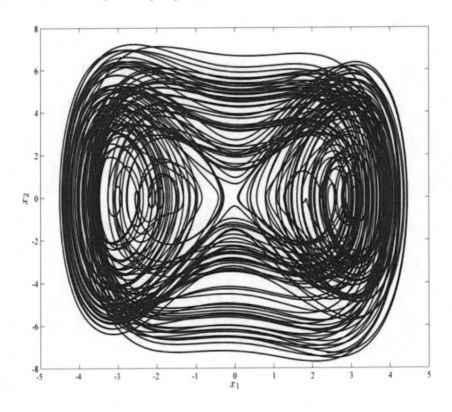

Case 1: Complete Synchronization Without Uncertainties and External Disturbances

For the case without uncertainties and external disturbances, the simulation results are depicted respectively in Figures 3 and 4 for both controllers. It can be seen that both controllers effectively synchronize the slave system with the master one. But, unlike the classical sliding mode control, the chattering effect is considerably reduced in the results obtained by applying the proposed FO sliding mode controller.

Case 2: Complete Synchronization With Uncertainties and External Disturbances

For the case with uncertainties and external disturbances, the obtained simulation results for both controllers are depicted respectively in Figures 5 and 6. From these results, it is clear that the state trajectories of the controlled system (slave system) are quickly synchronized with that of the master system, despite the presence of uncertainties and unknown external disturbances. In addition, unlike the classical sliding mode control, the chattering effect is significantly reduced by the proposed FO controller.

Figure 3. Synchronization trajectories of master-slave system and control signals of the conventional SMC method (without uncertainties)

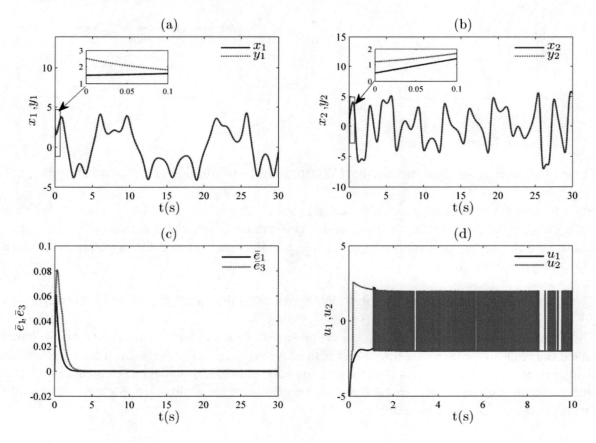

Figure 4. Synchronization trajectories of master-slave system and control signals of the proposed FOSMC method (without uncertainties)

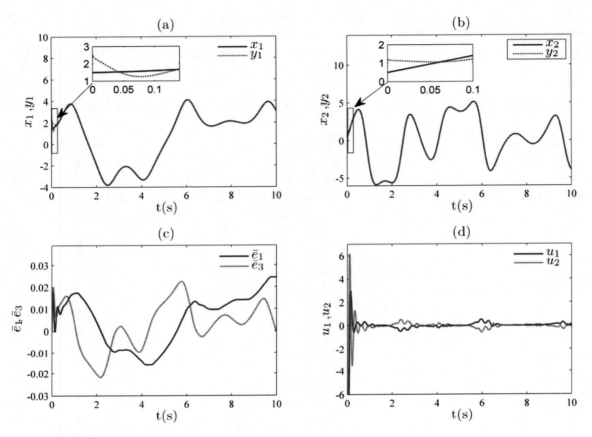

Case 3: Anti-Phase Synchronization Without Uncertainties and External Disturbances

For this case, the simulation results obtained are shown respectively in Figures 7 and 8 for both controllers. These figures show that both controllers perform well. But, unlike the classical sliding mode control, the chattering effect is considerably reduced in the results obtained by applying the proposed FO sliding mode controller.

Case 4: Anti-Phase Synchronization With Uncertainties and External Disturbances

The obtained simulation results for this case are given in Figures 9 and 10, respectively for both controllers. It can be clearly seen that the trajectories of the slave system are effectively anti-phase-synchronized with these of the master system, despite the presence of bounded uncertainties and external disturbances. In addition, in contrast to the classical sliding-mode controller, the control signals generated by our FO controller are free of chattering effect.

Figure 5. Synchronization trajectories of master-slave system and control signals of the conventional SMC method (with uncertainties)

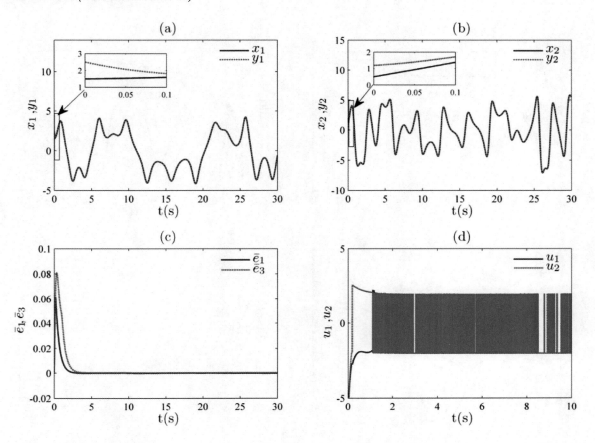

Example 2 (Electro-Optical Hybrid System)

An electro-optical hybrid system without time-delay has been described in (Mitschke & Flüggen, 1984; Korsch et al., 2008). The later exhibits a typical chaotic behavior. Its electronic realization has been also investigated, given in Figure 11. The simplified dynamics of this system can be described by (Abdel-ouahab & Hamri, 2012):

$$\dddot{U} = -\ddot{U}\left(\frac{L}{R} + R_m C\right) - \dot{U}\left(\frac{R_m}{R} + \frac{C}{C_m} + 1\right) - \frac{1}{RC_m}U + \frac{v^2}{RC_m}(U - \mu)^2 \tag{35}$$

where U is the voltage in the capacitor, R_m is the variable resistance, R is the resistance, C_m, C are the capacitors, L is the inductivity, μ is the bias, and v is the gain.

The system (35) can be represented in the state space as:

Figure 6. Synchronization trajectories of master-slave system and control signals of the proposed FOSMC method (with uncertainties)

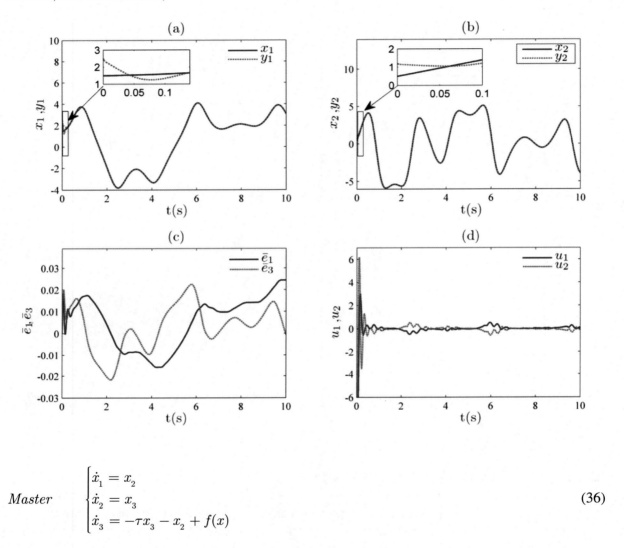

$$
Master \quad \begin{cases} \dot{x}_1 = x_2 \\ \dot{x}_2 = x_3 \\ \dot{x}_3 = -\tau x_3 - x_2 + f(x) \end{cases} \tag{36}
$$

with $f(x)$ being the so-called logistic function, given by $f(x) = \beta x_1 (1 - x_1^2)$, τ and β are some positive real constants (Abdelouahab & Hamri, 2012).

This system only has two equilibrium points $P_{e1} = (0,0,0)$ and $P_{e2} = (1,0,0)$. For certain values of parameters (τ and β), this system behaves chaotically. For example, for $\tau = 0.5$ and $\beta = 0.64$, the system (36) shows a chaotic attractor being represented in Figure 13.

The Lyapunov exponents of the master system (36) are depicted in Figure 12. From this figure, it is clear that the maximal Lyapunov exponent criterion shows that the nonlinear behaviors of the master system (36) are of chaotic nature. On the other hand, even when there is a positive Lyapunov exponent the sum over the entire spectrum is negative.

Figure 7. Anti-phase synchronization trajectories of master-slave system and control signals of the conventional SMC method (without uncertainties)

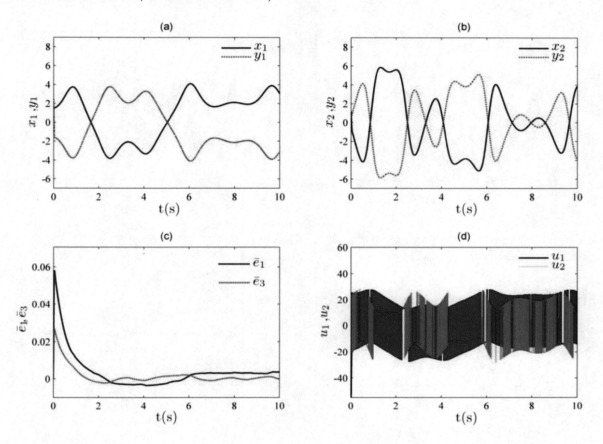

The slave system associated to the master system is given by:

$$Slave \begin{cases} \dot{y}_1 = y_2 + \Delta f_1(y,t) + d_1(t) + u_1(t) \\ \dot{y}_2 = y_3 + \Delta f_2(y,t) + d_2(t) + u_2(t) \\ \dot{y}_3 = -\tau y_3 - y_2 + f(y) + \Delta f_3(y,t) + d_3(t) + u_3(t) \end{cases} \qquad (37)$$

where $f(y) = \beta y_1(1 - y_1^2)$, τ and β are positive real numbers.

Without loss of generality, the uncertainties and the external dynamic disturbances are chosen as:

$$\Delta f_i(y,t) = 0.7\cos(t) + 0.5\sin(t) \text{ and } d_1(t) = d_2(t) = d_3(t) = 1.8.$$

Figure 8. Anti-phase synchronization trajectories of master-slave system and control signals of the proposed FOSMC method (without uncertainties)

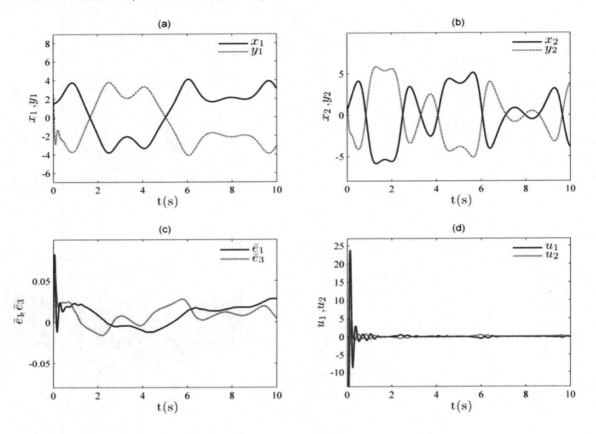

The design parameters of the proposed controller are:

$$\rho_{11} = 5.8, \quad \rho_{12} = 6, \rho_{21} = 6.5, \quad \rho_{22} = 7.6, \rho_{31} = 6.3, \rho_{32} = 8.5,$$

$$\lambda_1 = \lambda_2 = \lambda_3 = 2, \eta = 0.9, \alpha = 0.7 \ \sigma_1 = 0.1, \sigma_2 = 0.15, \quad \sigma_3 = 0.23,$$

$$\sigma_0 = 0.01, \quad \delta_1 = 1.3, \delta_2 = 1.5, \delta_3 = 1, \varepsilon_1 = 0.1, \varepsilon_3 = 0.1 \ \varepsilon_2 = 0.1$$

To numerically simulate the above master-slave equations, the 4th-order RK method is used with a fixed-step size of 0.005. One chooses the initial conditions of the master and slave system as

$$(x_1(0), x_2(0), x_3(0)) = (1.5, 0.1, 0.2), \quad (y_1(0), y_2(0), y_3(0)) = (-1.6, -0.5, 2).$$

Figure 9. Anti-phase synchronization trajectories of master-slave system and control signals of the conventional SMC method (with uncertainties)

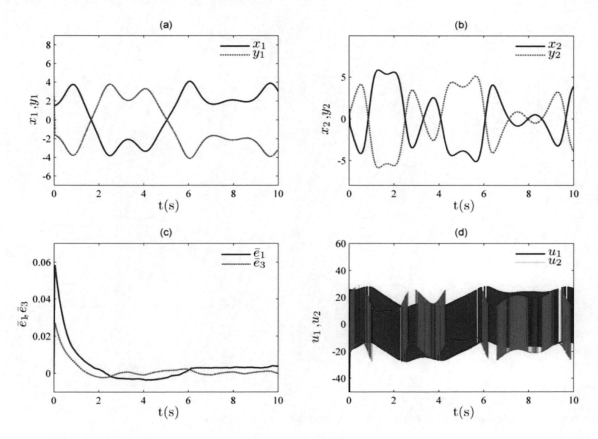

To test our FO sliding-mode controller and the classical sliding-mode controller for the master-slave system (36) and (37), four cases are considered here:

Case 1: Complete Synchronization Without Uncertainties and External Disturbances

For this case, the simulation results for both controllers are given respectively in Figures 14 and 15. It can be seen that both controllers efficiently synchronize the slave system with the master one. But, unlike the classical sliding mode control, the chattering effect is significantly attenuated in the results obtained by applying the proposed FO controller.

Case 2: Complete Synchronization With Uncertainties and External Disturbances

For the case with uncertainties and external disturbances, the simulation results for both controllers are represented respectively in Figures 16 and 17. From these figures, it can be seen that the state trajectories

Figure 10. Anti-phase synchronization trajectories of master-slave system and control signals of the proposed FOSMC method (with uncertainties)

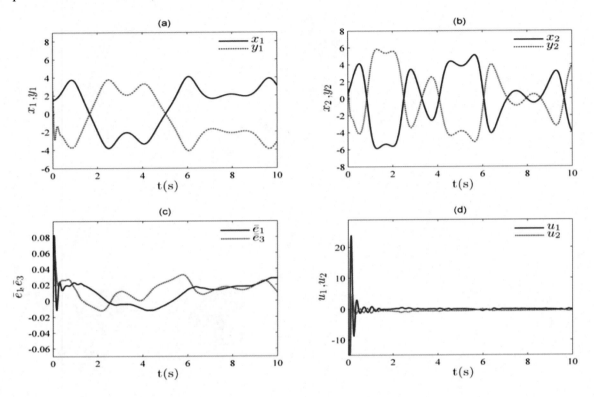

Figure 11. (a) Set-up of the hybrid optical device. (b) The electronic model

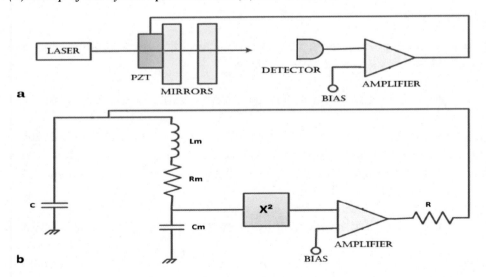

Figure 12. Lyapunov exponents

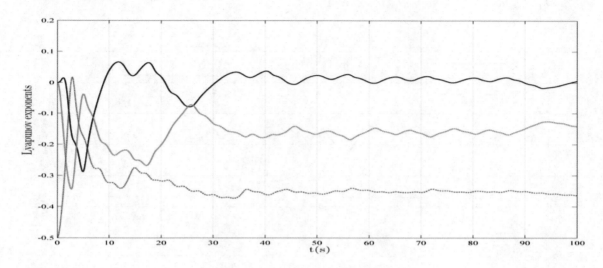

Figure 13. Chaotic attractors with $\tau = 0.5$ *and* $\beta = 0.64$

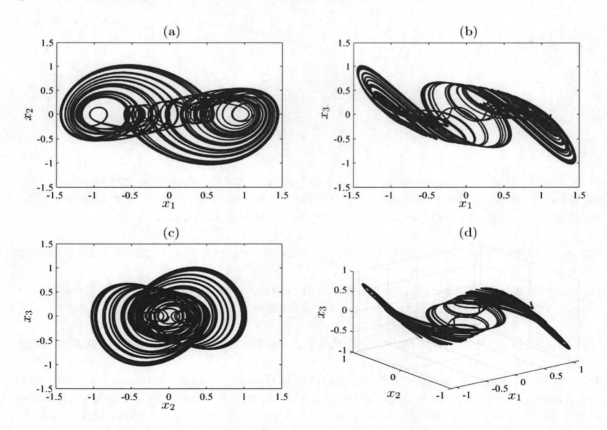

Figure 14. Synchronization trajectories of drive and response systems and control signals of the conventional SMC method (without uncertainties)

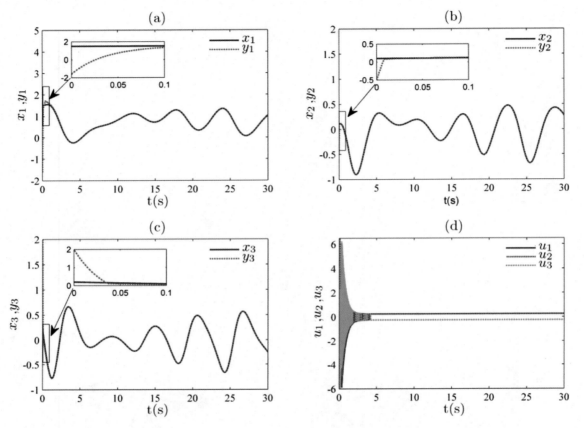

of the controlled system (slave system) are rapidly synchronized with that of the master system, despite the presence of uncertainties and unknown external disturbances. In addition, the chattering effect is considerably eliminated in the results obtained by the proposed FO controller.

Case 3: Anti-Phase Synchronization Without Uncertainties and External Disturbances

For this case, the simulation results obtained are shown respectively in Figures 18 and 19 for both controllers. These figures show that both controllers perform well.

Case 4: Anti-Phase Synchronization With Uncertainties and External Disturbances

The obtained simulation results for this case are given in Figures 20 and 21, respectively for both controllers. It can be clearly seen that the trajectories of the slave system are effectively anti-phase-synchronized with these of the master system, despite the presence of bounded uncertainties and external disturbances. In addition, in contrast to the classical sliding-mode controller, the control signals generated by our FO controller are free of chattering effect.

Figure 15. Synchronization trajectories of drive and response systems and control signals of the proposed FOSMC method (without uncertainties)

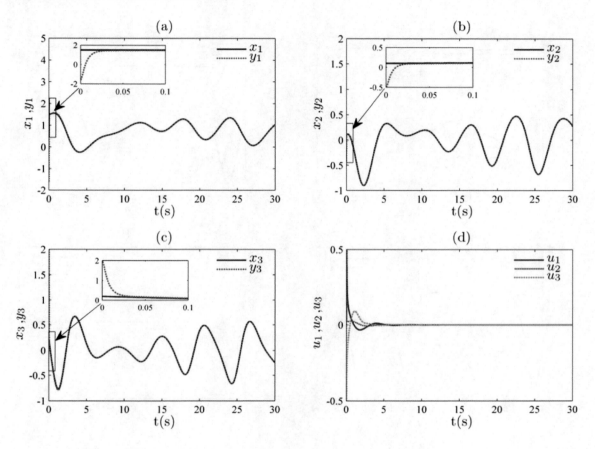

Example 3 (a Single Mode Two Level Laser)

Consider a single mode, homogeneously broadened, resonant, two level laser whose dynamics is given by the following dimensionless equations (Illing et al., 2007):

$$\begin{cases} \dfrac{dE}{dt} = -k(E + v + E_{ing}) \\ \dfrac{dv}{dt} = -(v - Ew) \\ \dfrac{dw}{dt} = -\gamma(w + Ev - w_p) \end{cases} \tag{38}$$

with E being the laser field strength inside the cavity, $v(w)$ atomic polarization (i.e. population inversion), $k(\gamma)$ cavity (i.e. atomic inversion) decay rate, w_p inversion due to the pumping process in the

Figure 16. Synchronization trajectories of drive and response systems and control signals of the conventional SMC method (with uncertainties)

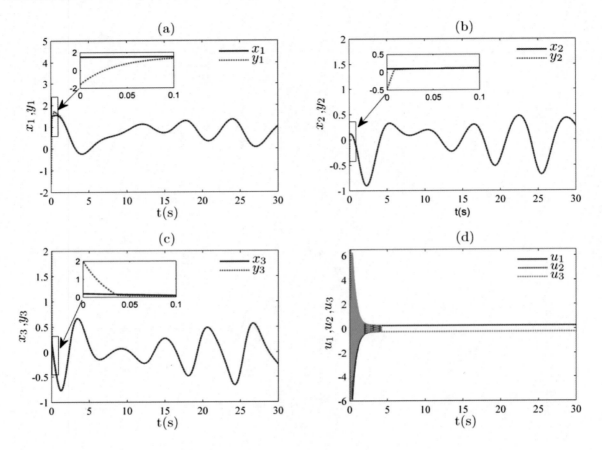

absence of a field, and E_{inj} accounts for the possibility of injecting a field into the cavity. The dynamical state vector is noted by $x = [x_1, x_2, x_3] = [E, v, w]$.

Then, the system (38) is chosen as a master system.

$$Master \quad \begin{cases} \dot{x}_1 = -k(x_1 + x_2 + E_{ing}) \\ \dot{x}_2 = -(x_2 - x_1 x_3) \\ \dot{x}_3 = -\gamma(x_3 + x_1 x_2 - w_p) \end{cases} \tag{39}$$

For some values of parameters (w_p, k, and γ), this system behave chaotically. For example, for $w_p = 16.8$, $k = 3.9$, and $\gamma = 0.53$, the system (39) shows a chaotic attractor being represented in Figure 23. The Lyapunov exponents of the master system (39) are depicted in Figure 22. From this figure, it is clear that the presence of a Lyapunov exponent confirm well the chaotic behavior of this system.

Figure 17. Synchronization trajectories of drive and response systems and control signals of the proposed FOSMC method (with uncertainties)

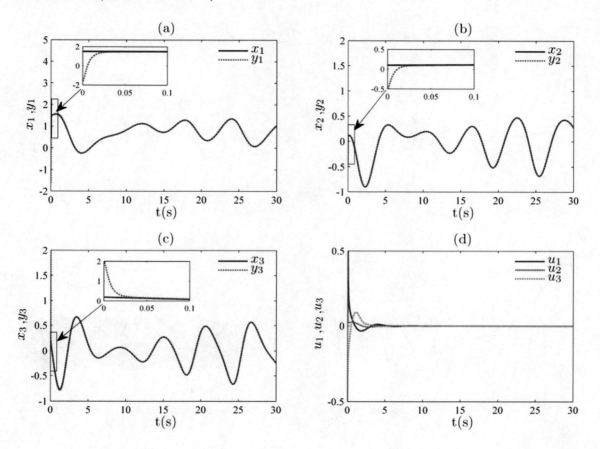

Its corresponding slave system can be given by:

$$Slave \quad \begin{cases} \dot{y}_1 = -k(y_1 + y_2 + E_{ing}) + \Delta f_1(y,t) + d_1 t) + u_1(t) \\ \dot{y}_2 = -(y_2 - y_1 y_3) + \Delta f_2(y,t) + d_2(t) + u_2(t) \\ \dot{y}_3 = -\gamma(y_3 + y_1 y_2 - w_p) + \Delta f_3(y,t) + d_3(t) + u_3(t) \end{cases} \quad (40)$$

Without loss of generality, the uncertainties and the external dynamic disturbances are chosen as:

$$\Delta f_i(y,t) = \cos(4t) + 0.5\sin(t) \text{ and } d_1(t) = d_2(t) = d_3(t) = 1.8.$$

The design parameters of the proposed controller are:

Figure 18. Anti-phase synchronization trajectories of drive and response systems and control signals of the conventional SMC method (without uncertainties)

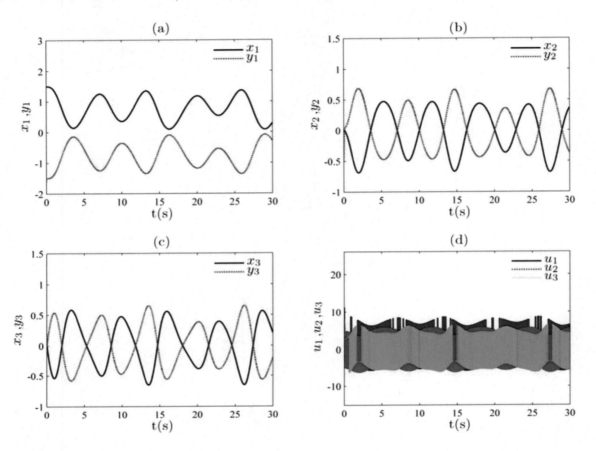

$$\rho_{11} = 1, \rho_{12} = 9.5, \; \rho_{21} = 1.2, \; \rho_{22} = 9.1, \rho_{31} = 1.1, \; \rho_{32} = 9.98,$$

$$\lambda_1 = \lambda_2 = \lambda_3 = 2, \eta = 0.9, \alpha = 0.7, \; \varepsilon_1 = 0.1, \; \varepsilon_3 = 0.1,$$

$$\varepsilon_2 = 0.1, \; \sigma_1 = 0.1, \sigma_2 = 0.21, \sigma_3 = 0.5, \quad \sigma_0 = 1, \delta_1 = 1..01, \delta_2 = 1.45, \delta_3 = 1, \quad ,$$

To numerically simulate the above master-slave equations, the 4th-order RK method is used with a fixed-step size of 0.001. One chooses the initial conditions of the master and slave system as

$$(x_1(0), x_2(0), x_3(0)) = (0.2, -2, 4), \; (y_1(0), y_2(0), y_3(0)) = (1.2, -3, 9).$$

Figure 19. Anti-phase synchronization trajectories of drive and response systems and control signals of the proposed FOSMC method (without uncertainties)

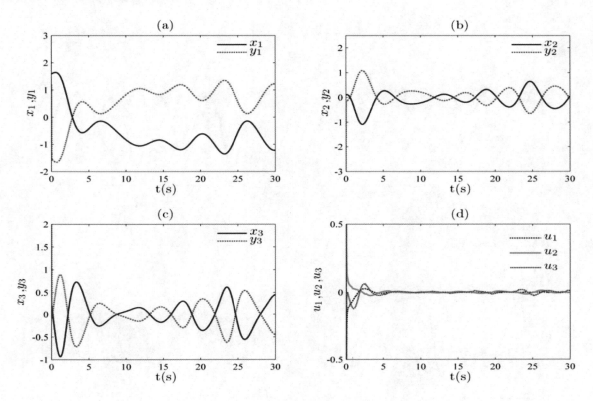

To test our FO sliding-mode controller and the classical sliding-mode controller for the master-slave system (39) and (40), two cases are considered here:

Case 1: Complete Synchronization With Uncertainties and External Disturbances

Simulation results for both controllers are represented respectively in Figures 24 and 25. From these figures, it can be seen that the state trajectories of the controlled system (slave system) are rapidly synchronized with that of the master system, despite the presence of uncertainties and unknown external disturbances. In addition, the chattering effect is considerably eliminated in the results obtained by the proposed FO controller.

Case 2: Anti-Phase Synchronization With Uncertainties and External Disturbances

Figures 26 and 27 respectively display the simulation results of an anti-phase synchronization for both controllers. It can be clearly seen that the trajectories of the slave system are effectively anti-phase-synchronized with these of the master system, despite the presence of bounded uncertainties and external disturbances. The control signals generated by our FO controller are not only admissible and bounded, but also smooth and free of chattering.

Figure 20. Anti-phase synchronization trajectories of drive and response systems and control signals of the conventional SMC method (with uncertainties)

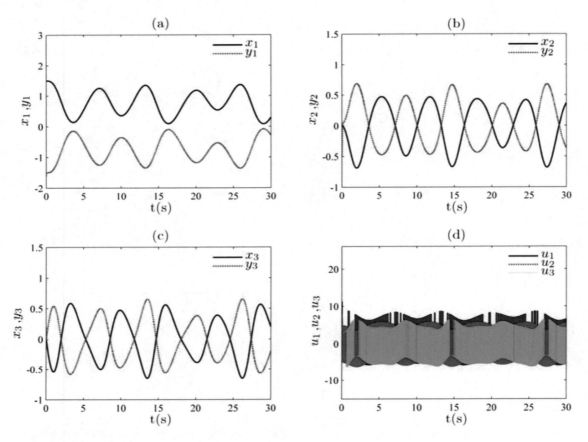

Example 4 (Degenerate Optical Parametric Oscillator (DOPO)

The mathematical model of DOPO is given by (Pettiaux et al., 1989; Oppo et al., 1994; Staliunas & Sanchez-Morcillo, 1998; Wang et al., 2010):

$$\begin{cases} \dot{A_1} = -(1 + i\Delta_1)A_1 + A_1^* A_0 \\ \dot{A_0} = -(\gamma + i\Delta_0)A_0 + E_A + A_1^2 \end{cases} \tag{41}$$

where A_1, A_0 describes the complex amplitude of the sub-harmonic mode and fundamental model, respectively. γ stands for the reduced decay rate of the fundamental model, Δ_1 and Δ_0 denote detuning parameters. E_A describes the input filed amplitude and is often selected with some positive values. The chaotic or hyperchaotic parameter regions can be found completely by calculating the Lyapunov exponents.

Figure 21. Anti-phase synchronization trajectories of drive and response systems and control signals of the proposed FOSMC method (with uncertainties)

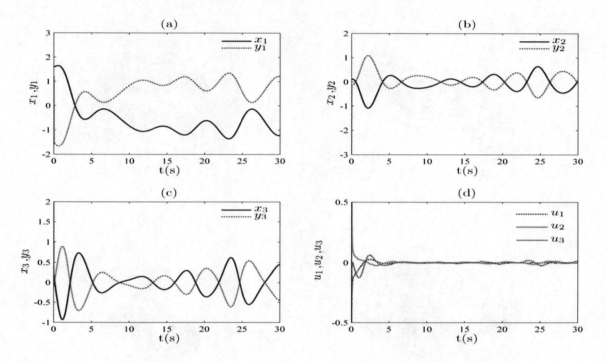

Figure 22. Lyapunov exponents

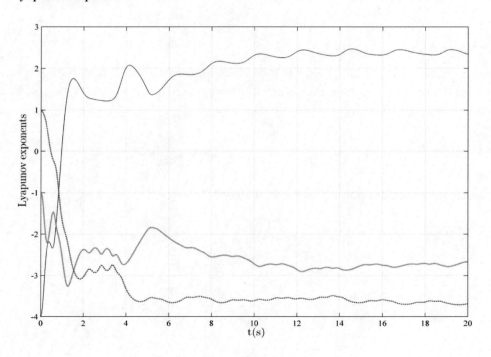

Figure 23. Chaotic attractors with $w_p = 16.8, k = 3.9,$ *and* $\gamma = 0.5.3.$

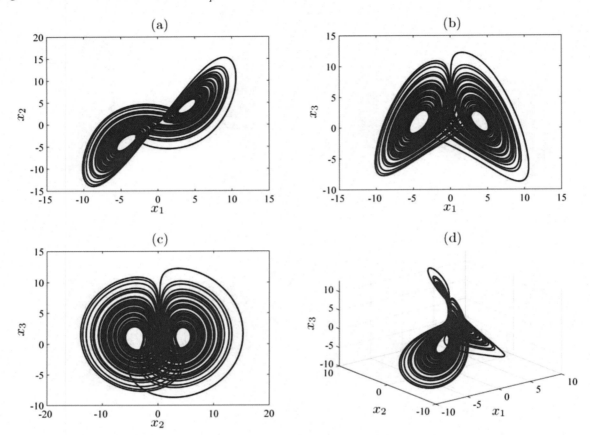

For sake simplicity, the complex field equations are transformed into differential equations with real numbers in simulating and analyzing. Four real variables are used to replace the two complex amplitudes by defining

$$A_1 = x + iy , A_0 = z + iw \tag{42}$$

The following equation is approached by inputting (42) into (41).

$$Master \quad \begin{cases} \dot{x}_1 = -x_1 + \Delta_1 x_2 + x_1 x_3 + x_2 x_4 \\ \dot{x}_2 = -\Delta_1 x_1 - x_2 - x_2 x_3 + x_1 x_4 \\ \dot{x}_3 = -\gamma x_3 + \Delta_0 x_4 + x_1^2 + x_2^2 + E_A \\ \dot{x}_4 = -\gamma x_4 - \Delta_0 x_3 + 2 x_1 x_2 \end{cases} \tag{43}$$

Figure 24. Synchronization trajectories of master-slave system and control signals of the conventional SMC method (with uncertainties)

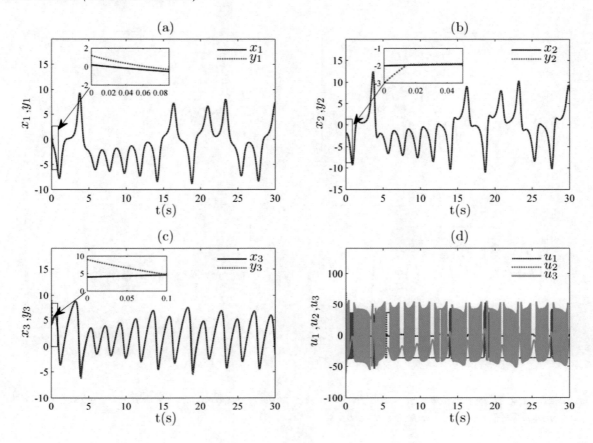

The system (43) is considered here as a master system. Its corresponding slave system is given by:

$$Slave \begin{cases} \dot{y}_1 = -y_1 + \Delta_1 y_2 + y_1 y_3 + y_2 y_4 + \Delta f_1(x_s, t) + D_1(t) + u_1(t) \\ \dot{y}_2 = -\Delta_1 y_1 - y_2 - y_2 y_3 + y_1 y_4 + \Delta f_2(x_s, t) + D_2(t) + u_2(t) \\ \dot{y}_3 = -\gamma y_3 + \Delta_0 y_4 + y_1^2 + y_2^2 + E_A + \Delta f_3(x_s, t) + D_3(t) + u_3(t) \\ \dot{y}_4 = -\gamma y_4 - \Delta_0 y_3 + 2 y_1 y_2 + \Delta f_4(x_s, t) + D_4(t) + u_4(t) \end{cases} \quad (44)$$

For some values of parameters (γ, Δ_0, Δ_1, E_A.), this system behaves chaotically. For example, for $\gamma = \Delta_0 = 1.0$, $\Delta_1 = -5$, $E_A = 10.8$, the system (43) shows a chaotic attractor being represented in Figure 33. The Lyapunov exponents of the master system (43) are depicted in Figure 32. From this figure, it is clear that the presence of a Lyapunov exponent confirm well the chaotic behavior of this system.

Figure 25. Synchronization trajectories of master-slave system and control signals of the proposed FOSMC method (with uncertainties)

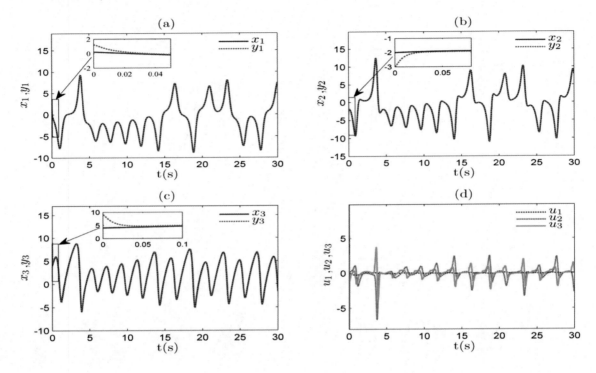

Figure 26. Anti-phase synchronization trajectories of master-slave system and control signals of the conventional SMC method (with uncertainties)

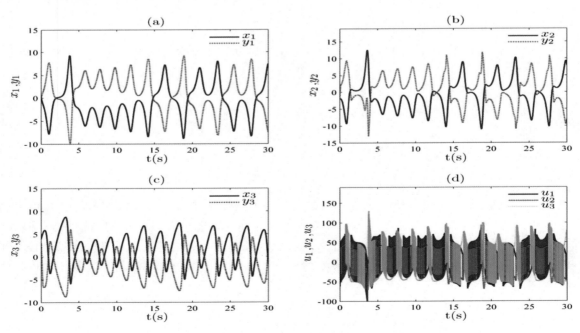

Figure 27. Anti-phase synchronization trajectories of drive and response systems and control signals of the proposed FOSMC method (with uncertainties)

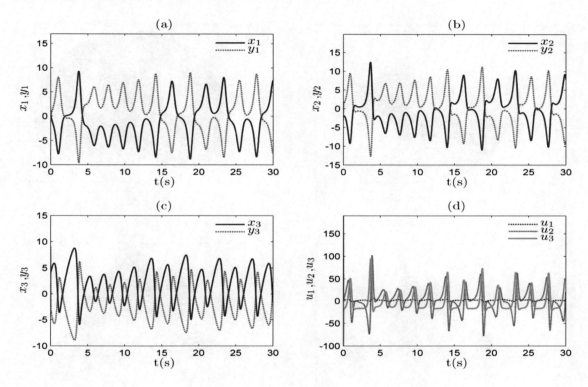

Figure 28. Lyapunov exponents

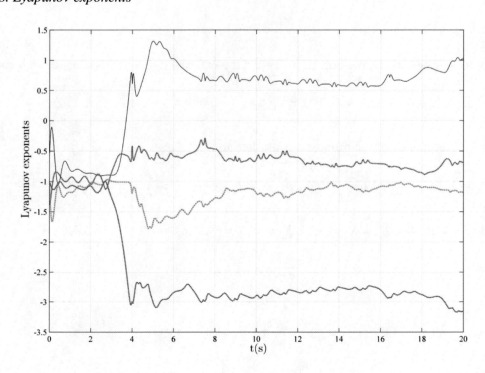

Figure 29. Chaotic attractors with $\gamma = \Delta_0 = 1, \Delta_1 = -5, E_A = 10.8$

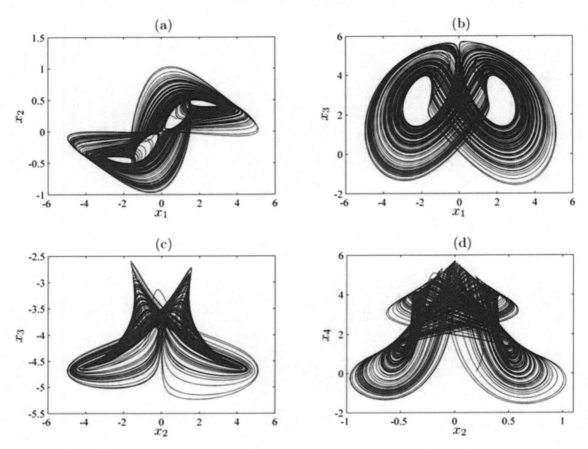

Without loss of generality, the uncertainties and the external dynamic disturbances are chosen as:

$$\Delta f_i(y, t) = \cos(6t) + 0.5\sin(t) \text{ and } d_1(t) = d_2(t) = d_3(t) = d_4(t) = 2.$$

The design parameters of the proposed controller are:

$$\rho_{11} = 8, \rho_{12} = 11, \rho_{21} = 7.89, \rho_{22} = 11.4, \ \rho_{31} = 7.9, \ \ \rho_{32} = 10.97,$$

$$\rho_{41} = 8.21, \rho_{42} = 10.45, \ \lambda_1 = \lambda_2 = \lambda_3 = \lambda_4 = 2, \ \delta_3 = 1.3, \delta_4 = 1, \ \ \sigma_1 = 0.124,$$

Figure 30. Synchronization trajectories of master-slave system and control signals of the conventional SMC method (with uncertainties)

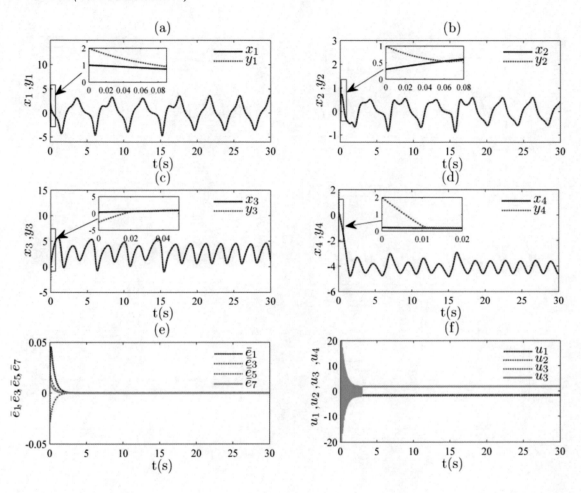

$\sigma_2 = 0.23, \quad \sigma_3 = 0.65, \sigma_4 = 0.897, \sigma_0 = 1, \delta_1 = 0.125, \delta_2 = 0.7, \alpha = 0.7,$

$\eta = 0.9, \varepsilon_1 = \varepsilon_2 = \varepsilon_3 = \varepsilon_4 = 0.1.$

To numerically simulate the above master-slave equations, the 4th-order RK method is used with a fixed-step size of 0.001. One chooses the initial conditions of the master and slave system as

$(x_1(0), x_2(0), x_3(0), x_4(0)) = (1, 0.3, 0.4, 0.2), (y_1(0), y_2(0), y_3(0), y_4(0)) = (2, 1, -2.6, 2).$

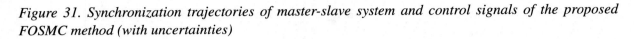

Figure 31. Synchronization trajectories of master-slave system and control signals of the proposed FOSMC method (with uncertainties)

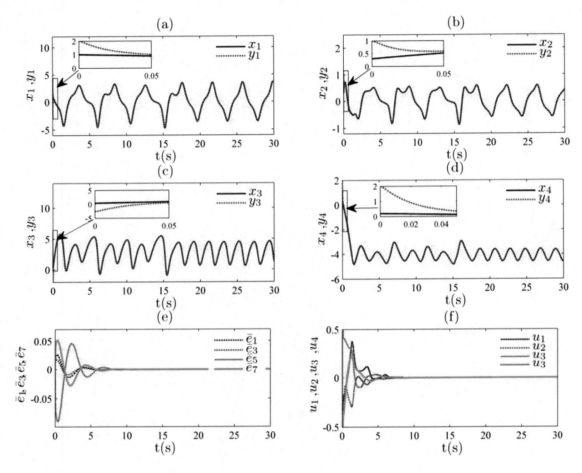

To test our FO sliding-mode controller and the classical sliding-mode controller for the master-slave system, equations (43) and (44), two cases are considered here:

Case 1: Complete Synchronization With Uncertainties and External Disturbances

For this case, the simulation results for both controllers are given respectively in Figures 30 and 31. It can be seen that both controllers efficiently synchronize the slave system with the master one, despite the presence of uncertainties and unknown external disturbances. But, unlike the classical sliding mode control, the chattering effect is significantly attenuated in the results obtained by applying the proposed FO controller.

Figure 32. Anti-phase synchronization trajectories of master-slave system and control signals of the conventional SMC method (with uncertainties)

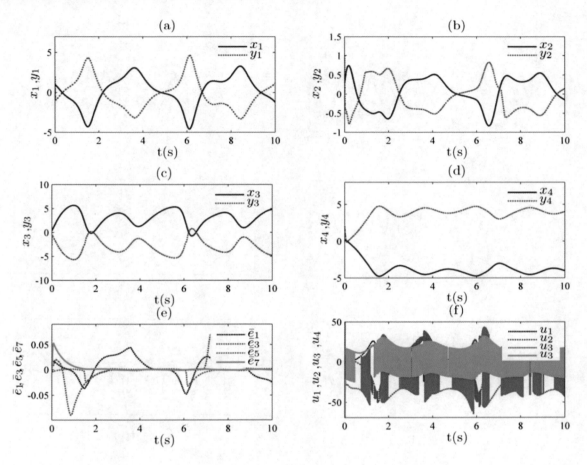

Case 2: Anti-Phase Synchronization With Uncertainties and External Disturbances

For this case, the simulation results obtained are shown respectively in Figures 32 and 33 for both controllers. These figures show that both controllers performs well. In addition, the chattering effect is considerably eliminated in the results obtained by the proposed FO controller.

CONCLUSION

In this study, a FO sliding mode control-based chaos synchronization for a class of uncertain optical systems exhibiting a chaotic behavior has been investigated. The stability associated to the correspond-

Figure 33. Anti-phase synchronization trajectories of master-slave system and control signals of the proposed FOSMC method (with uncertainties)

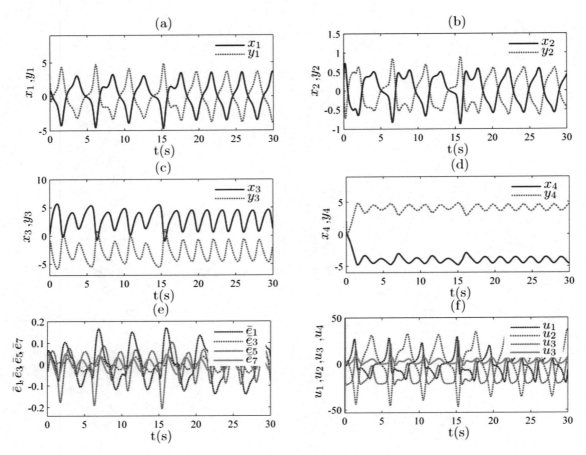

ing closed-loop control system has been analyzed via a FO Lyapunov stability theory. The simulation results obtained reveal that the proposed FO sliding mode controller is able to robustly and accurately synchronize the optical chaotic systems in spite of the presence the modeling uncertainties, parametric variations and unknown external disturbances, and also can significantly diminish the chattering effect.

REFERENCES

Abarbanel, H. D., Rulkov, N. F., & Sushchik, M. M. (1996). Generalized synchronization of chaos: The auxiliary system approach. *Physical Review. E*, *53*(5), 4528–4535. doi:10.1103/PhysRevE.53.4528 PMID:9964787

Abdelouahab, M. S., & Hamri, N. E. (2012). A new chaotic attractor from hybrid optical bistable system. *Nonlinear Dynamics*, *67*(1), 457–463. doi:10.100711071-011-9994-5

Aghababa, M. P. (2013). A fractional-order controller for vibration suppression of uncertain structures. *ISA Transactions*, *52*(6), 881–887. doi:10.1016/j.isatra.2013.07.010 PMID:23932858

Ahmad, I., Shafiq, M., Saaban, A. B., Ibrahim, A. B., & Shahzad, M. (2016). Robust finite-time global synchronization of chaotic systems with different orders. *Optik-International Journal for Light and Electron Optics*, *127*(19), 8172–8185. doi:10.1016/j.ijleo.2016.05.065

Aziz-Alaoui, M. A. (2005). A survey on chaos synchronization. *12th IEEE-ICECS*, 523-527.

Behnia, S., Afrang, S., Akhshani, A., & Mabhouti, K. (2013). A novel method for controlling chaos in external cavity semiconductor laser. *Optik-International Journal for Light and Electron Optics*, *124*(8), 757–764. doi:10.1016/j.ijleo.2012.01.013

Boulkroune, A., Bouzeriba, A., & Bouden, T. (2016). Fuzzy generalized projective synchronization of incommensurate fractional-order chaotic systems. *Neurocomputing*, *173*, 606–614. doi:10.1016/j.neucom.2015.08.003

Bouzeriba, A., Boulkroune, A., & Bouden, T. (2016a). Projective synchronization of two different fractional-order chaotic systems via adaptive fuzzy control. *Neural Computing & Applications*, *27*(5), 1349–1360. doi:10.100700521-015-1938-4

Bouzeriba, A., Boulkroune, A., & Bouden, T. (2016b). Fuzzy adaptive synchronization of uncertain fractional-order chaotic systems. *International Journal of Machine Learning and Cybernetics*, *7*(5), 893–908. doi:10.100713042-015-0425-7

Calderón, A. J., Vinagre, B. M., & Feliu, V. (2006). Fractional order control strategies for power electronic buck converters. *Signal Processing*, *86*(10), 2803–2819. doi:10.1016/j.sigpro.2006.02.022

Chen, G., & Dong, X. (1998). *From Chaos to Order: Perspective, Methodologies and Applications*. World Scientific Singapore. doi:10.1142/3033

Chong, G., Hai, W., & Xie, Q. (2004). Transient and stationary chaos of a Bose-Einstein condensate loaded into a moving optical lattice potential. *Physical Review. E*, *70*(3), 036213. doi:10.1103/PhysRevE.70.036213 PMID:15524618

Chua, L. O., Itoh, M., Kocarev, L., & Eckert, K. (1993). Chaos synchronization in Chua's circuit. *Journal of Circuits, Systems, and Computers*, *3*(01), 93–108. doi:10.1142/S0218126693000071

Delavari, H., Ghaderi, R., Ranjbar, A., & Momani, S. (2010). Fuzzy fractional order sliding mode controller for nonlinear systems. *Communications in Nonlinear Science and Numerical Simulation*, *15*(4), 963–978. doi:10.1016/j.cnsns.2009.05.025

Deng, W. H., & Li, C. P. (2005). Chaos synchronization of the fractional Lü system. *Physica A*, *353*, 61–72. doi:10.1016/j.physa.2005.01.021

Efe, M. Ö. (2008). Fractional fuzzy adaptive sliding-mode control of a 2-DOF direct-drive robot arm. *IEEE Transactions on Systems, Man, and Cybernetics. Part B, Cybernetics*, *38*(6), 1561–1570.

Efe, M. Ö., & Kasnakoğlu, C. (2008). A fractional adaptation law for sliding mode control. *International Journal of Adaptive Control and Signal Processing*, *22*(10), 968–986. doi:10.1002/acs.1062

Grigorenko, I., & Grigorenko, E. (2003). Chaotic Dynamics of the Fractional Lorenz System. *Physical Review Letters*, *91*(3), 034101. doi:10.1103/PhysRevLett.91.034101 PMID:12906418

Hale, J. K. (1997). Diffusive coupling, dissipation, and synchronization. *Journal of Dynamics and Differential Equations*, *9*(1), 1–52. doi:10.1007/BF02219051

Hasler, M., Maistrenko, Y., & Popovych, O. (1998). Simple example of partial synchronization of chaotic systems. *Physical Review. E*, *58*(5), 6843–6846. doi:10.1103/PhysRevE.58.6843

Illing, L., Gauthier, D. J., & Roy, R. (2007). Controlling optical chaos, spatio-temporal dynamics, and patterns. *Advances in Atomic, Molecular, and Optical Physics*, *54*, 615–697. doi:10.1016/S1049-250X(06)54010-8

Kocarev, L., & Parlitz, U. (1996). Generalized synchronization, predictability, and equivalence of unidirectionally coupled dynamical systems. *Physical Review Letters*, *76*(11), 1816–1819. doi:10.1103/PhysRevLett.76.1816 PMID:10060528

Korsch, H. J., Jodl, H. J., & Hartmann, T. (2008). Chaos A Program Collection for the PC (3rd ed.). Academic Press.

Li, C., & Chen, G. (2004). Chaos and hyperchaos in the fractional-order Rössler equations. *Physica A*, *341*, 55–61. doi:10.1016/j.physa.2004.04.113

Li, C., Su, K., Zhang, J., & Wei, D. (2013). Robust control for fractional-order four-wing hyperchaotic system using LMI. *Optik-International Journal for Light and Electron Optics*, *124*(22), 5807–5810. doi:10.1016/j.ijleo.2013.04.054

Li, C. L., Han, Q. T., & Xiong, J. B. (2016). Linear control for mixed synchronization of a fractional-order chaotic system. *Optik-International Journal for Light and Electron Optics*, *127*(15), 6129–6133. doi:10.1016/j.ijleo.2016.04.105

Li, C. L., Xiong, J. B., & Li, W. (2014). A new hyperchaotic system and its generalized synchronization. *Optik-International Journal for Light and Electron Optics*, *125*(1), 575–579. doi:10.1016/j.ijleo.2013.07.013

Li, Y., Chen, Y., & Podlubny, I. (2010). Stability of fractional-order nonlinear dynamic systems: Lyapunov direct method and generalized Mittag–Leffler stability. *Computers & Mathematics with Applications (Oxford, England)*, *59*(5), 1810–1821. doi:10.1016/j.camwa.2009.08.019

Lu, J. G. (2005). Chaotic dynamics and synchronization of fractional-order Arneodo's systems. *Chaos, Solitons, and Fractals*, *26*(4), 1125–1133. doi:10.1016/j.chaos.2005.02.023

Maybhate, A., & Amritkar, R. E. (1999). Use of synchronization and adaptive control in parameter estimation from a time series. *Physical Review. E*, *59*(1), 284–293. doi:10.1103/PhysRevE.59.284

Mitschke, F., & Flüggen, N. (1984). Chaotic behavior of a hybrid optical bistable system without a time delay. *Applied Physics. B, Lasers and Optics*, *35*(2), 59–64. doi:10.1007/BF00697423

Oppo, G. L., Brambilla, M., & Lugiato, L. A. (1994). Formation and evolution of roll patterns in optical parametric oscillators. *Physical Review A.*, *49*(3), 2028–2032. doi:10.1103/PhysRevA.49.2028 PMID:9910454

Othman, A. A., Noorani, M. S. M., & Al-Sawalha, M. M. (2016). Adaptive dual synchronization of chaotic and hyperchaotic systems with fully uncertain parameters. *Optik-International Journal for Light and Electron Optics*, *127*(19), 7852–7864. doi:10.1016/j.ijleo.2016.05.139

Pettiaux, N. P., Ruo-Ding, L., & Mandel, P. (1989). Instabilities of the degenerate optical parametric oscillator. *Optics Communications*, *72*(3-4), 256–260. doi:10.1016/0030-4018(89)90407-0

Pham, V. T., Vaidyanathan, S., Volos, C., Jafari, S., & Kingni, S. T. (2016). A no-equilibrium hyperchaotic system with a cubic nonlinear term. *Optik-International Journal for Light and Electron Optics*, *127*(6), 3259–3265. doi:10.1016/j.ijleo.2015.12.048

Pisano, A., Rapaić, M. R., Jeličić, Z. D., & Usai, E. (2010). Sliding mode control approaches to the robust regulation of linear multivariable fractional-order dynamics. *International Journal of Robust and Nonlinear Control*, *20*(18), 2045–2056. doi:10.1002/rnc.1565

Podlubny, I. (1999). *Fractional Differential Equations*. San Diego, CA: Academic Press.

Pyragas, K. (1992). Continuous control of chaos by self-controlling feedback. *Physics Letters. [Part A]*, *170*(6), 421–428. doi:10.1016/0375-9601(92)90745-8

Rosenblum, M. G., Pikovsky, A. S., & Kurths, J. (1996). Phase synchronization of chaotic oscillators. *Physical Review Letters*, *76*(11), 1804–1807. doi:10.1103/PhysRevLett.76.1804 PMID:10060525

Shahverdiev, E. M., Hashimova, L. H., Bayramov, P. A., & Nuriev, R. A. (2014). Chaos synchronization between Josephson junctions coupled with time delays. *Journal of Superconductivity and Novel Magnetism*, *27*(10), 2225–2229. doi:10.100710948-014-2599-8

Si-Ammour, A., Djennoune, S., & Bettayeb, M. (2009). A sliding mode control for linear fractional systems with input and state delays. *Communications in Nonlinear Science and Numerical Simulation*, *14*(5), 2310–2318. doi:10.1016/j.cnsns.2008.05.011

Staliunas, K., & Sanchez-Morcillo, V. J. (1998). Spatial-localized structures in degenerate optical parametric oscillators. *Physical Review A.*, *57*(2), 1454–1457. doi:10.1103/PhysRevA.57.1454

Terry, J. R., & Thornburg, K. S., Jr. (2009). Experimental synchronization of chaotic lasers. *Physical Review Let, 72.*

Ushio, T. (1995). Chaotic synchronization and controlling chaos based on contraction mappings. *Physics Letters. [Part A]*, *198*(1), 14–22. doi:10.1016/0375-9601(94)01015-M

Vaidyanathan, S. (2015). Global chaos synchronization of the Lotka-Volterra biological systems with four competitive species via active control. *International Journal of Pharm Tech Research*, *8*(6), 206–217.

Wang, C. N., Li, S. R., Ma, J., & Jin, W. Y. (2010). Synchronization transition in degenerate optical parametric oscillators induced by nonlinear coupling. *Applied Mathematics and Computation*, *216*(2), 647–654. doi:10.1016/j.amc.2010.01.101

Zhang, F., & Li, C. (2011). Stability analysis of fractional differential systems with order lying in (1, 2). *Advances in Difference Equations*, *1*, 213–485.

Zhang, W., Li, J., & Ding, C. (2016a). Anti-synchronization control for delayed memristor-based distributed parameter NNs with mixed boundary conditions. *Advances in Difference Equations*, *1*(1), 320. doi:10.118613662-016-1017-x

Zhang, Z., Feng, X., & Yao, Z. (2016b). Chaos control of a Bose–Einstein condensate in a moving optical lattice. *Modern Physics Letters B*, *30*(19), 165–238. doi:10.1142/S0217984916502389

Zouari, F., Boulkroune, A., & Ibeas, A. (2017). Neural adaptive quantized output-feedback control-based synchronization of uncertain time-delay incommensurate fractional-order chaotic systems with input nonlinearities. *Neurocomputing*, *237*, 200–225. doi:10.1016/j.neucom.2016.11.036

Zouari, F., Boulkroune, A., Ibeas, A., & Arefi, M. M. (2016). Observer-based adaptive neural network control for a class of MIMO uncertain nonlinear time-delay non-integer-order systems with asymmetric actuator saturation. *Neural Computing & Applications*, 1–18.

KEY TERMS AND DEFINITIONS

Chaos Synchronization: It is a technique wherein chaotic systems are coupled to asymptotically achieve identical dynamics.

Chaotic System: A deterministic system which is characterized by an erratic and unpredictable dynamic behavior. Necessary conditions for a system exhibiting such behavior are that it be nonlinear and have at least three independent state variables.

Fractional-Order Control: A control theory which employs the fractional-order integrators and derivatives.

Fractional-Order Sliding Surface: A sliding surface which employs the fractional-order integrators and derivatives.

Optics: The branch of science involving the behavior and properties of light, including its interactions with matter and the production of instruments that use or detect it.

Sliding Surface: A surface in the state space determined by a designer of a variable-structure (sliding-mode) controller. The role of a sliding-mode controller is to drive the system's states to this surface. The system then remains on this switching surface for all subsequent time to reduce disturbances and modelling uncertainties.

Sliding-Mode Control: A discontinuous control in which a sliding-mode is deliberately induced. The sliding mode control law synthesis entails two phases. In the first phase, a sliding surface is defined by a designer. Next, in the second phase, feedback gains are chosen so that the system's trajectories are driven toward the sliding surface. The main features of this control methodology are for instance: robustness regarding to parameters' variations and unknown external disturbances, reduced order comportment of the system in the sliding-mode, and fast and finite-time convergence.

Chapter 9
Fuzzy Control–Based Synchronization of Fractional–Order Chaotic Systems With Input Nonlinearities

Abdesselem Boulkroune
University of Jijel, Algeria

Amina Boubellouta
University of Jijel, Algeria

ABSTRACT

This chapter addresses the fuzzy adaptive controller design for the generalized projective synchronization (GPS) of incommensurate fractional-order chaotic systems with actuator nonlinearities. The considered master-slave systems are with different fractional-orders, uncertain models, unknown bounded disturbances, and non-identical form. The suggested controller includes two keys terms, namely a fuzzy adaptive control and a fractional-order variable structure control. The fuzzy logic systems are exploited for approximating the system uncertainties. A Lyapunov approach is employed for determining the parameter adaptation laws and proving the stability of the closed-loop system. At last, simulation results are given to demonstrate the validity of the proposed synchronization approach.

INTRODUCTION

Throughout the last decades, *fractional-order* (nonlinear or linear) plants (i.e. the systems with fractional integrals or derivatives) have been studied by several works in many branches of engineering and sciences (Podlubny,1999; Hilfer,2000). It turned out that several plants, in interdisciplinary research areas, may present fractional-order dynamics including: fluid mechanics, spectral densities of music, transmission lines, cardiac rhythm, electromagnetic waves, viscoelastic systems, dielectric polarization, heat diffusion systems, electrode-electrolyte polarization, and many others (Baleanu et al., 2010; Sabatier et al., 2007; Bouzeriba et al.,2016a; Boulkroune et al.,2016).

DOI: 10.4018/978-1-5225-5418-9.ch009

Chaotic systems are deterministic and nonlinear dynamical plants. They are also characterized by the self similarity of the strange attractor and extreme sensitivity to initial conditions (IC) quantified respectively by fractal dimension and the existence of a positive Lyapunov exponent (Bouzeriba et al.,2016a ; Boulkroune et al.,2016). In recent works, it was made known that several fractional-order systems may perform chaotically, e.g. fractional-order Lü system (Deng & Li, 2005), fractional-order Arneodo system (Lu,2005), fractional-order Lorenz system (Grigorenk & Grigorenko,2003), fractional-order Rössler system (Li & Chen,2004), and so on.

The sliding mode control technique is an effective tool to construct robust adaptive controllers for nonlinear systems with bounded external disturbances and uncertainties. The later has several attractive features, including finite and fast time convergence, strong robustness with respect to unmodelled dynamics, parameters variations and external disturbances. The purpose of the sliding mode is extremely simple: *it consists to oblige the system states to arrive at a suitably desired sliding surface based on a discontinuous control.* Recently, the fractional-order calculus is employed within the sliding mode control methodologies, in order to seek better performances. Many works have coped with control problems of nonlinear systems with fractional-orders (Calderon et al.,2006; Efe & Kasnakoglu,2008; Si-Ammour et al.,2009; Pisano et al.,2010). It is worthy to note that the selection of the sliding surface for this class of systems is not an easy task in general. In numerous recent researches, the fuzzy logic system is combined with the sliding mode control in order to remove the main issues of the sliding mode control, including the high-gain authority and chattering in the system. This hybridization can smoothen the sliding mode control in diverse ways, and can also successfully approximate online the model, uncertainties and disturbances present in the system (Bouzeriba et al.,2016a; Boulkroune et al.,2016a).

In recent years, *the synchronization and control* of the fractional-order systems is also one of the most attractive topics. Various researcher works have made great contributions in this research topic (Bouzeriba et al.,2016a; Boulkroune et al.,2016; Wang et al.,2012; Li-Ming et al.,2014 ; Lin et al.,2011 ; Lin & Lee, 2011; Lin & Kuo,2011; Tavazoei,2012; Aghababa,2012; Bouzeriba et al.,2016b ; Bouzeriba et al.,2016c). In (Wang et al.,2012), a modified projective synchronization of different fractional-order systems has been developed through active sliding mode control. By using a fuzzy adaptive sliding mode control strategy, a generalized projective synchronization of fractional order chaotic systems has been proposed in (Li-Ming et al.,2014). Chaos synchronization between two different uncertain fractional order chaotic systems has been studied based on a fuzzy adaptive sliding mode control in (Lin et al.,2011). In (Lin & Lee, 2011), a fuzzy adaptive control has been proposed for the synchronization of uncertain fractional-order chaotic delayed systems involving time delays. In (Lin & Kuo,2011), a fuzzy adaptive controller has been constructed to realize an H_∞ synchronizing for uncertain fractional-order chaotic systems. Nevertheless, the fundamental results of (Lin et al.,2011; Lin & Lee, 2011; Lin & Kuo,2011) are already questionable, because the stability analysis has not been derived rigorously in mathematics, as stated in (Tavazoei,2012; Aghababa,2012). In (Bouzeriba et al.,2016a; 2016b, 2016c, Boulkroune et al., 2016) some adaptive fuzzy controllers have been designed in a sliding mode framework for realizing an appropriate synchronization of fractional-order chaotic master-slave systems. In these synchronization approaches, the fuzzy systems have been employed to online estimate the unknown nonlinear functions. Although these schemes can guarantee the satisfactory performances, the issue of the input dead-zone (input nonlinearities) has not yet been considered in the synchronization control design of the fractional-order chaotic systems. This is by no means the case in the real world life as the physical systems commonly involve quantization, dead-zone, input saturations, backlash, and so on. It is worth pointing out that the input nonlinearities can guide to poor performances or even instability of the synchronization control system, if they are not taken into account into the control design. It is thereby more advisable to consider the effects of these input nonlinearities in one way or another when implementing and designing a synchronization control system.

In this research, a fuzzy adaptive variable-structure controller is constructed to correctly realize a generalized projective synchronization (GPS) of incommensurate fractional-order chaotic systems in which external disturbances and input nonlinearities are present. A fuzzy system is incorporate to estimate the uncertain dynamics and a fractional-order sliding surface is designed. The Lyapunov stability theorem is employed to determine the associated adaptive laws and to bear out the stability of the corresponding closed-loop system. The validity of the proposed synchronization scheme is confirmed by means of simulation results. Compared to the closely-related previous works (Bouzeriba et al.,2016a, 2016c,2016c; Boulkroune et al.,2016; Deng & Li,2005; Lu,2005; Si-Ammour et al.,2009; Pisano et al.,2010; Wang et al.,2012; Li-Ming et al.,2014; Lin et al.,2011; Lin & Lee, 2011; Lin & Kuo,2011; Tavazoei,2012; Aghababa,2012), the main contributions of this work lie in the following:

1. The design of a novel adaptive fuzzy variable-structure control based chaos synchronization of fractional-order chaotic systems with uncertain model, input dead-zone, distinct incommensurate fractional-orders, unknown dynamical disturbances and non-identical structures. To the best of our knowledge, the problem of the input dead-zone (input nonlinearities) has been seldom considered in the synchronization control design of the incommensurate fractional-order chaotic systems.
2. Unlike the previous literatures, the synchronization control system does not depend on the master-slave model. In fact, the adaptive fuzzy systems are adopted here to handle the dynamical disturbances and model uncertainties (Deng & Li,2005; Lu,2005; Si-Ammour et al.,2009; Pisano et al.,2010 ; Wang et al.,2012),.
3. Compared with the recent researches in Lin et al. (2011), Lin & Lee (2011), Lin & Kuo (2011), the stability analysis of the closed-loop system is rigorously established in this work.

BASIC CONCEPTS

There exist many definitions for fractional derivatives, namely: Caputo, Grünwald-Letnikov, Riemann-Liouville definitions, and so on (Podlubny,1999). Due to the meaning of the initial conditions (IC) for the systems described using the Caputo fractional operator is the same as for integer-order systems (Podlubny,1999; Li et al.,2010), one will employ this operator in the remainder of this work. Moreover, a modification of Adams-Bashforth-Moulton algorithm will be used for numerical simulation of the Caputo fractional-order differential equations (Diethelm et al., 2002; Diethelm & Ford, 2002). The Caputo fractional derivative of order α of a smooth function $x(t)$ with respect to time is defined as (Podlubny,1999):

$$D_t^\alpha x(t) = \frac{1}{\Gamma(m-\alpha)} \int_0^t (t-\tau)^{-\alpha+m-1} x^{(m)}(\tau) d\tau, \tag{1}$$

with $m = \lceil \alpha \rceil + 1$, $\lceil \alpha \rceil$ being the integer part of α, D_t^α being called the $\alpha - order$ Caputo differential operator, and $\Gamma(.)$ being the gamma function which is given by:

$$\Gamma(P) = \int_0^\infty t^{P-1} e^{-t} dt \; ; \text{ with } \Gamma(P+1) = P\Gamma(P) \tag{2}$$

The following basics properties of the Caputo fractional-order derivative operator will be useful in deriving our main results (Podlubny,1999):

Property 1: Let $0 < q < 1$ be a constant, afterward

$$Dx(t) = \frac{dx(t)}{dt} = D_t^{1-q} D_t^q x(t) \tag{3}$$

Property 2: The Caputo's fractional derivative is linear, i.e.:

$$D_t^q \left(\nu x(t) + \mu y(t) \right) = \nu D_t^q x(t) + \mu D_t^q y(t), \tag{4}$$

with ν and μ being real constants. Particularly, one has

$$D_t^q x(t) = D_t^q \left(x(t) + 0 \right) = D_t^q x(t) + D_t^q 0,$$

then $D_t^q 0 = 0$.

PROBLEM STATEMENT AND FUZZY APPROXIMATION

Problem Statement

Consider the following class of uncertain fractional-order chaotic master systems

$$D_t^{\alpha_i} x_i = f_{mi}(x), \text{ for } i = 1, \ldots, n \tag{5}$$

where $D_t^{\alpha_i} = \frac{d^{\alpha_i}}{dt^{\alpha_i}}, 0 < \alpha_i < 1$ is the fractional-order of the system, $x = [x_1, \ldots, x_n]^T \in R^n$ is the measurable pseudo-state vector, and $f_{mi}(x)$ is an unknown smooth function.

Its slave system with input nonlinearity is given by

$$D_t^{\beta_i} y_i = f_{si}\left(y\right) + \varphi_i\left(u_i\right) + d_i\left(t, y\right), \text{for } i = 1, \ldots, n \tag{6}$$

where $0 < \beta_i < 1$ is the fractional-order of the slave system, $f_{si}\left(y\right)$ is an unknown smooth function, $y = [y_1, \ldots, y_n]^T \in R^n$ is its measurable pseudo-state vector. u_i represents the control input which will be determined later, $\varphi_i\left(u_i\right)$ is the input nonlinearity (i.e. sector nonlinearities with dead-zone) and $d_i\left(t, y\right)$ is the external disturbance.

Remark 1: *Various fractional-order chaotic systems can be modeled as (5) or (6), like: fractional-order unified chaotic system, fractional-order Lorenz system, fractional-order Lu system, fractional-order Chen system, and so on.*

The objective of this paper is to design a continuous adaptive fuzzy variable-structure control law u_i (for all $i = 1, \ldots, n$) such that a GPS between the master system (5) and the slave system (6) is practically realized, while guaranteeing the boundedness of all closed-loop signals and despite the attendance of dynamical external disturbances, uncertainties, together with input (actuator) nonlinearities. Figure 1 demonstrates the proposed synchronization scheme.

For quantifying our purpose, the synchronization error variables between the systems (5) and (6) are defined as follows:

$$e_i = y_i - \lambda_i x_i, \text{for } i = 1, \ldots, n \tag{7}$$

where λ_i is the scaling factor that defines a proportional relation between the synchronized systems.

Now, one introduces a fractional-order sliding surface as

$$S_i = D_t^{\beta_i - 1} e_i + k_{0i} \int_0^t e_i d\tau, \text{for } i = 1, 2, \ldots, n \tag{8}$$

where $k_{0i} > 0$ is a stable feedback gain, which will be determined later. When the system operates in the sliding mode, one has $S_i = \dot{S}_i = 0$. Consequently, the equivalent fractional-order sliding mode dynamics can be obtained from $\dot{S}_i = 0$ as follows:

$$D_t^{\beta_i} e_i + k_{0i} e_i = 0, \text{for } i = 1, 2, \ldots, n \tag{9}$$

The sliding mode dynamics (9) are stable, if the constant k_{0i} is selected such as

$$\left|\arg\left(-k_{0i}\right)\right| > \beta_i \pi / 2, \text{for } i = 1, \ldots, n \tag{10}$$

Based on (5)-(8), one can write the dynamics of the fractional-order sliding mode surface as follows:

$$\dot{S}_i = D_t^{\beta_i} e_i + k_{0i} e_i = k_{0i} e_i + f_{si}\left(y\right) + \varphi_i\left(u_i\right) - \lambda_i D_t^{\beta_i} x_i + d_i\left(t, y\right). \tag{11}$$

or equivalently

$$\dot{S}_i = H_i\left(x, y, d_i\right) + \varphi_i\left(u_i\right), \tag{12}$$

with

$$H_i\left(x, y, d_i\right) = k_{0i} e_i + f_{si}\left(y\right) - \lambda_i D_t^{\beta_i} x_i + d_i\left(t, y\right) \tag{13}$$

Input Nonlinearity

In this work, the considered model of the actuator (input) nonlinearity includes dead-zones and sector nonlinearities (Shyu et al.,2005; Boulkroune et al.,2011):

$$\varphi_i\left(u_i\right) = \begin{cases} \varphi_{i+}\left(u_i\right)\left(u_i - u_{i+}\right), u_i > u_{i+} \\ 0, -u_{i-} \le u_i \le u_{i+} \\ \varphi_{i-}\left(u_i\right)\left(u_i + u_{i-}\right), u_i < -u_{i-} \end{cases} \tag{14}$$

Figure 1. Proposed synchronization scheme

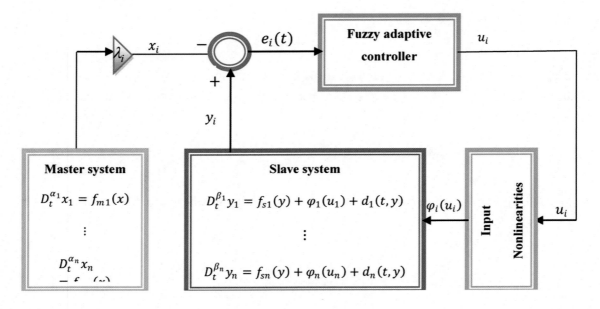

with $\varphi_{i+}\left(u_i\right) > 0$ and $\varphi_{i-}\left(u_i\right) > 0$ being nonlinear functions of u_i, and $u_{i+} > 0$ and $u_{i-} > 0$.

The nonlinearity $\varphi_i\left(u_i\right)$ satisfies the following properties:

$$\left(u_i - u_{i+}\right)\varphi_i\left(u_i\right) \geq m_{i+}^*\left(u_i - u_{i+}\right)^2, u_i > u_{i+}$$

$$\left(u_i + u_{i-}\right)\varphi_i\left(u_i\right) \geq m_{i-}^*\left(u_i + u_{i-}\right)^2, u_i < -u_{i-}, \tag{15}$$

with the gain reduction tolerances m_{i+}^* and m_{i-}^* being strictly positive constants (Shyu et al., 2005; Boulkroune et al., 2011).

Assumption 1: *The constants m_{i+}^* and m_{i-}^* and the functions $\varphi_{i+}\left(u_i\right)$ and $\varphi_{i-}\left(u_i\right)$ are unknown. But, the constants u_{i+} and u_{i-} are known and strictly positive.*

Fuzzy Approximation

The configuration of a fuzzy logic system is basically composed of a defuzzifier, a fuzzy inference engine, some fuzzy IF–THEN rules and a fuzzifier, as given in Figure 2.

The fuzzy inference engine is employed to represent a non-linear relationship between an output $\hat{f} \in R$ and an input vector $\overline{x}^T = \left[x_1, x_2, \ldots, x_n\right] \in R^n$, this relationship is described by a set of fuzzy rules of the form:

$$\text{if } x_1 \text{ is } A_1^i \text{ and} \ldots \text{and } x_n \text{ is } A_n^i \text{ then } \hat{f} \text{ is } f^i \tag{16}$$

Figure 2. Basic configuration of a fuzzy logic system

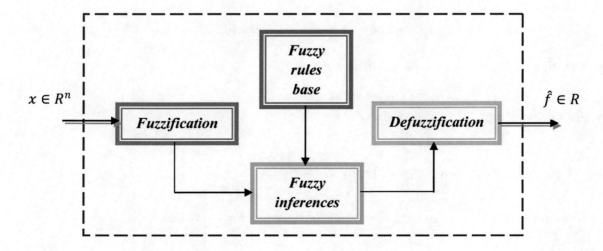

where $A_1^i, A_2^i, \ldots, A_n^i$ are fuzzy sets and f^i is the fuzzy singleton for the output in the *i*th rule.

By using the center-average defuzzifier, product inference, and singleton fuzzifier, the output of the fuzzy system can be simply expressed as follows:

$$\hat{f}(\overline{x}) = \frac{\sum_{i=1}^{m} f^i \left(\prod_{j=1}^{n} \mu_{A_j^i}(x_j) \right)}{\sum_{i=1}^{m} \left(\prod_{j=1}^{n} \mu_{A_j^i}(x_j) \right)} = \theta^T \psi(\overline{x}) \tag{17}$$

where $\mu_{A_j^i}(x_j)$ is the degree of membership of x_j to A_j^i, m is the number of fuzzy rules, $\theta^T = \left[f^1, f^2, \ldots, f^m \right]$ is the adjustable parameter vector (which are the consequent parameters), and $\psi^T = \left[\psi^1 \psi^2 \ldots \psi^m \right]$ with

$$\psi^i(\overline{x}) = \frac{\left(\prod_{j=1}^{n} \mu_{A_j^i}(x_j) \right)}{\sum_{i=1}^{m} \left(\prod_{j=1}^{n} \mu_{A_j^i}(x_j) \right)} \tag{18}$$

which is the fuzzy basis function (FBF).

Following the universal approximation results (Wang,1994), the fuzzy system (17) can approximate any smooth function $f(\overline{x})$ defined on a compact operating space to a given accuracy. It ought to be noted that the membership function parameters and the structure of the fuzzy systems are properly specified beforehand by designer. But, the vector of consequent parameters θ will be estimated online based on appropriate adaptations laws which will be determined later.

DESIGN OF FUZZY ADAPTIVE CONTROLLER

In this section, the following assumptions are necessary to develop the main result:

Assumption 2: *The unknown external disturbance satisfies:*

$$\left| d_i(t, y) \right| \le \overline{d}_i(y), \tag{19}$$

with $\overline{d}_i(y)$ being an unknown smooth positive function.

Assumption 3: *There exists an unknown smooth positive function* $\overline{h}_i(y)$ *such that:*

$$\left| H_i\left(x, y, d_i\right)\right| \leq \eta\, \overline{h}_i\left(y\right), \text{for } i = 1, \ldots, n \tag{20}$$

with $\eta = \min_i \left\{ m_{i+}^*, m_{i-}^* \right\}$, *for* $i = 1, \ldots, n$.

Remark 2: *Assumptions 2 and 3 are not strong, because the state vector of the master system is always bounded and the bounds $\overline{d}_i\left(y\right)$ and $\overline{h}_i\left(y\right)$ are unknown (for a non-controlled chaotic system). These assumptions are habitually employed in the literature, e.g.* (Bouzeriba et al.,2016a; Boulkroune et al.,2016).

Over a compact set Ω_y , the unknown function $\overline{h}_i\left(y\right)$ can be approximated by the linearly parameterized fuzzy systems (17) as follows:

$$\overline{h}_i\left(y, \theta_i\right) = \theta_i^T \psi_i\left(y\right), \text{with } i = 1, \ldots, n \tag{21}$$

where θ_i is the vector of the adjustable parameters of this fuzzy system, and the FBF vector $\psi_i\left(y\right)$ is determined a priori by the designer.

Without loss of generality, one assumes that there exists an optimal fuzzy approximator with m^* fuzzy rules that can identify the nonlinear function $\overline{h}_i\left(y\right)$ with a minimal approximation error, i.e.

$$\overline{h}_i\left(y\right) = \overline{h}_i\left(y, \theta_i^*\right) + \delta_i\left(y\right) = \theta_i^{*T} \psi_i\left(y\right) + \delta_i\left(y\right) \tag{22}$$

where the minimal approximation error $\delta_i\left(y\right)$ is usually assumed to be bounded for all $y \in \Omega_y$, i.e.

$\left| \delta_i\left(y\right)\right| \leq \overline{\delta}_i$, with $\overline{\delta}_i$ is an unknown constant (Wang, 1994; Benzaoui,2016; Hamel & Boulkroune, 2016; Zouari et al., 2016; Rigatos et al., 2016; Boulkroune, 2016; Boulkroune et al., 2015; Boulkroune et al., 2008), and

$$\theta_i^* = \arg \min_{\theta_i} \left[\sup_{y \in \mathbb{C}_y} \left| \overline{h}_i\left(y\right) - \hat{\overline{h}}_i\left(y, \theta_i\right)\right| \right] \tag{23}$$

Notice that θ_i^* is the optimal value of θ_i [29-36] and mainly introduced for analysis purposes (i.e. its value is not needed when implementing the control system), (Wang, 1994; Benzaoui,2016; Hamel & Boulkroune et al., 2016; Zouari et al., 2016; Rigatos et al., 2016; Boulkroune, 2016; Boulkroune et al., 2015; Boulkroune et al., 2008):

From the previous analysis, one can write:

$$\hat{\bar{h}}_i(y,\theta_i) - \bar{h}_i(y) = \hat{\bar{h}}_i(y,\theta_i) - \hat{\bar{h}}(y,\theta_i^*) + \hat{\bar{h}}(y,\theta_i^*) - \bar{h}_i(y),$$

$$= \theta_i^T \psi_i(y) - \theta_i^{*T} \psi_i(y) - \delta_i(y),$$

$$= \tilde{\theta}_i^T \psi_i(y) - \delta_i(y). \tag{24}$$

with $\tilde{\theta}_i = \theta_i - \theta_i^*$, for $i = 1, \ldots, n$.

To attain our objective, one can construct the following fuzzy adaptive variable-structure controller as follows:

$$u_i = \begin{cases} -\rho_i(t)\,sign(S_i) - u_{i-}, & S_i > 0 \\ 0, & S_i = 0 \\ -\rho_i(t)\,sign(S_i) + u_{i+}, & S_i < 0 \end{cases} \tag{25}$$

with

$$\rho_i(t) = k_{1i} + k_{2i} + k_{3i}|S_i| +, \forall i = 1, \ldots, n \tag{26}$$

The adaptation laws related to the proposed controller (25) can be expressed in the following form:

$$\dot{\theta}_i = \gamma_{\theta i}\left(|S_i|\psi_i(y) - \sigma_{\theta i}|S_i|\theta_i\right), \text{with} \theta_{ij}(0) > 0 \tag{27}$$

$$\dot{k}_{1i} = \gamma_{ki}\left(|S_i| - \sigma_{ki}|S_i|k_{1i}\right), \text{ with } k_{1i}(0) > 0 \tag{28}$$

with $\gamma_{\theta i}, \sigma_{\theta i}, \sigma_{ki}, \gamma_{ki}, k_{1i}, k_{2i}$ and k_{3i} being strictly positive design parameters.

According to (12), one has

$$\frac{1}{\eta}S_i\dot{S}_i = \frac{1}{\eta}S_iH_i(x,y,d_i) + \frac{1}{\eta}S_i\varphi_i(u_i) \leq |S_i|\bar{h}_i(y) + \frac{1}{\eta}S_i\varphi_i(u_i) + \rho_i|S_i| - \rho_i|S_i| \tag{29}$$

Using (24) and substituting the control law (26) into (29) leads to

$$\frac{1}{\eta}S_i\dot{S}_i \leq \frac{1}{\eta}S_i\varphi_i(u_i) + \rho_i|S_i| - \left(k_{1i} + k_{2i} + k_{3i}|S_i| +\right)|S_i| + \delta_i(y)S_i \tag{30}$$

According to (15) and (25), one obtains

$$u_i < -u_{i-} \text{ for } S_i > 0 \Rightarrow (u_i + u_{i-})\varphi_i(u_i) \geq m_{i-}^*(u_i + u_{i-})^2 \geq \eta(u_i + u_{i-})^2 \tag{31}$$

$$u_i > u_{i+} \text{ for } S_i < 0 \Rightarrow (u_i - u_{i+})\varphi_i(u_i) \geq m_{i+}^*(u_i - u_{i+})^2 \geq \eta(u_i - u_{i+})^2 \tag{32}$$

By considering (25) again, one can establish

$$S_i > 0 \Rightarrow (u_i + u_{i-})\varphi_i(u_i) = -\rho_i(t)\,sign(S_i)\varphi_i(u_i) \geq m_{i-}^*\rho_i^2(t)\left[sign(S_i)\right]^2 \geq \eta\rho_i^2(t) \tag{33}$$

$$S_i < 0 \Rightarrow (u_i - u_{i+})\varphi_i(u_i) = -\rho_i(t)\,sign(S_i)\varphi_i(u_i) \geq m_{i+}^*\rho_i^2(t)\left[sign(S_i)\right]^2 \geq \eta\rho_i^2(t) \tag{34}$$

Then, for $S_i > 0$ and $S_i < 0$, one has

$$-\rho_i(t)\,sign(S_i)\varphi_i(u_i) \geq \eta\rho_i^2(t) \tag{35}$$

Using the fact that $S_i\,sign(S_i) = |S_i|$, (35) can be rewritten as

$$-\rho_i(t)S_i^2\,sign(S_i)\varphi_i(u_i) \geq \eta\rho_i^2(t)S_i^2 = \eta\rho_i^2(t)|S_i|^2 \tag{36}$$

Finally, because $\rho_i(t) > 0$, for all S_i, one has

$$\frac{S_i\varphi_i(u_i)}{\eta} \leq -\rho_i(t)|S_i| \tag{37}$$

By considering (37), equation (30) can be rewritten as:

$$\frac{1}{\eta}S_i\dot{S}_i \leq -\left(k_{1i} + k_{2i} + k_{3i}|S_i|+\right)|S_i| + \delta_i(y)S_i \tag{38}$$

From the concepts mentioned above, one can state the following theorem.

Theorem 1: For the master-slave systems (5) and (6), if Assumptions 1-3 hold, the control law (25) together with its adaptation laws (27) and (28) can guarantee the following properties:

- All signals involved in the closed-loop system remain uniformly bounded.
- Signals S_i asymptotically converge to zero.

Proof: Consider the following continuous differentiable function as a Lyapunov function candidate for the subsystem i:

$$V_i = \frac{1}{2}S_i^2 + \frac{1}{2\gamma_{\theta i}}\tilde{\theta}_i^2 + \frac{1}{2\gamma_{ki}}\tilde{k}_{1i}^2. \text{ for } i=1,...,n \tag{39}$$

with $\tilde{k}_{1i} = k_{1i} - k_{1i}^*$, where. $k_{1i}^* = \overline{\delta}_i + \frac{\sigma_{\theta_i}}{2}\left\|\theta_i^*\right\|^2$

Differentiating V_i with respect to time yields

$$\dot{V}_i = S_i\dot{S}_i + \frac{1}{\gamma_{\theta i}}\tilde{\theta}_i^T\dot{\theta}_i + \frac{1}{\gamma_{ki}}\dot{k}_{1i}\tilde{k}_{1i} \tag{40}$$

Using (25)-(27), $\dot{V}_i$ becomes

$$\dot{V}_i \le -k_{3i}S_i^2 - k_{2i}\left|S_i\right| + \overline{\delta}_i\left|S_i\right| - \sigma_{\theta_i}\left|S_i\right|\tilde{\theta}_i^T\theta_i + \frac{1}{\gamma_{ki}}\dot{k}_{1i}\tilde{k}_{1i}. \tag{41}$$

It is obvious that

$$-\sigma_{\theta_i}\left|S_i\right|\tilde{\theta}_i^T\theta_i \le -\frac{\sigma_{\theta_i}}{2}\left|S_i\right|\left\|\tilde{\theta}_i\right\|^2 + \frac{\sigma_{\theta_i}}{2}\left|S_i\right|\left\|\theta_i^*\right\|^2 \tag{42}$$

$$-\sigma_{\theta_i}\left|S_i\right|k_{1i}\tilde{k}_{1i} \le -\frac{\sigma_{\theta_i}}{2}\left|S_i\right|k_{1i}^2 + \frac{\sigma_{\theta_i}}{2}\left|S_i\right|k_{1i}^{*2} \tag{43}$$

Substituting (42) and (43) into (41), one gets

$$\dot{V}_i \le -k_{3i}S_i^2 \tag{44}$$

where k_{2i} should be selected as $k_{1i}^* = \frac{\sigma_{\theta_i}}{2}k_{1i}^{*2}$.

Let $V(t) = \sum_1^n V_i(t)$ be the Lyapunov candidate function of the all subsystems.

Differentiating $V(t)$ with respect to time yields

$$\dot{V} = \sum_{1}^{n}\dot{V}_i \le -\sum_{1}^{n}k_{3i}S_i^2 \tag{45}$$

Therefore, all signals in the closed-loop control system are bounded. And hence the input u_i is bounded. By using the Barbalat's lemma, one can deduce the asymptotic convergence of the signal S_i towards zero.

Remark 3: *In the case where $u_{i+} = u_{i-} = u_{i0}$, (25) can be simplified to the following:*

$$u_i = -\left(\rho_i(t) + u_{i0}\right)\text{sgn}\left(S_i\right) \tag{46}$$

with $\rho_i(t) = k_{1i} + k_{2i} + k_{3i}\left|S_i\right| +, \forall i = 1, \ldots, n$.

By replacing the Sign function by tangent hyperbolic function (Tanh; an equivalent smooth function) to cope with the chattering effects, the expression (46) becomes:

$$u_i = -\left(\rho_i(t) + u_{i0}\right)\tanh\left(S_i / \varepsilon_i\right) \tag{47}$$

with ε_i being a small positive constant.

SIMULATION RESULTS

Two simulation examples are given in this section to illustrate the applicability and effectiveness of the proposed synchronization scheme.

Example 1

In this subsection, one will consider the synchronization of two fractional-order modified coupled dynamos systems, (Wang, 2009):

The master system:

$$\begin{cases} D_t^\alpha x_1 = -\mu x_1 + x_2\left(x_3 + \gamma\right), \\ D_t^\alpha x_2 = -\mu x_2 + x_1\left(x_3 - \gamma\right), \\ \quad D_t^\alpha x_3 = x_3 - x_1 x_2, \end{cases} \tag{48}$$

The slave system:

$$\begin{cases} D_t^{\beta} y_1 = -\mu y_1 + y_2 \left(y_3 + \gamma \right) + \varphi_1 \left(u_1 \right) + d_1 \left(t \right), \\ D_t^{\beta} y_1 = -\mu y_1 + y_2 \left(y_3 + \gamma \right) + \varphi_1 \left(u_1 \right) + d_1 \left(t \right), \\ D_t^{\beta} y_3 = y_3 - y_1 y_2 + \varphi_3 \left(u_3 \right) + d_3 \left(t \right), \end{cases} \tag{49}$$

The system (48) behave chaotically when the fractional order $\alpha \geq 0.87$ and for the parameters $\mu = 2$ and $\gamma = 1$, (Wang, 2009).

The simulation was performed suing the following initial conditions are

$$y\left(0\right) = \left[y_1\left(0\right), y_2\left(0\right), y_3\left(0\right) \right]^T = \left[-1, -2, 0 \right]^T$$

and

$$x\left(0\right) = \left[x_1\left(0\right), x_2\left(0\right), x_3\left(0\right) \right]^T = \left[1, 2, -3 \right].$$

The actuator nonlinearities $\varphi_i \left(u_i \right)$, for $i = 1, 2, 3,$ are chosen as:

$$\varphi_i \left(u_i \right) = \begin{cases} \left(u_i - 2 \right) \left(1.5 - 0.3e^{0.3|\sin \sin \left(u_i \right)|} \right), u_i > 2 \\ 0, -2 \leq u_i \leq 2 \\ \left(u_i + 2 \right) \left(1.5 - 0.3e^{0.3|\sin \sin \left(u_i \right)|} \right), u_i < -2 \end{cases}$$

The dynamical disturbances are chosen as follows:

$$d_1\left(t\right) = d_2\left(t\right) = d_3\left(t\right) = 0.25 \cos\left(6t\right) - 0.15 \sin\left(t\right).$$

The adaptive fuzzy systems, $\theta_i^T \psi_i \left(y \right)$, with $i = 1, 2, 3$, have the vector $y = \left[y_1, y_2, y_3 \right]^T$ as input. For each input variable of these fuzzy systems, as in (Boulkroune et al., 2008), one defines three (one triangular and two trapezoidal) membership functions uniformly distributed on the intervals [-10, 10].

The design parameters are selected as follows:

$$k_{21} = k_{22} = k_{23} = 0.5, \; k_{31} = k_{32} = k_{33} = 2, \gamma_{\theta 1} = \gamma_{\theta 2} = \gamma_{\theta 3} = 50,$$

$$\sigma_{\theta 1} = \sigma_{\theta 2} = \sigma_{\theta 3} = 0.001, \; \gamma_{k1} = \gamma_{k2} = \gamma_{k3} = 5, \; \sigma_{k1} = \sigma_{k2} = \sigma_{k3} = 0.005.$$

The initial conditions for the adaptive parameters are chosen as:

$\theta_{1j}\left(0\right) = \theta_{2j}\left(0\right) = \theta_{3j}\left(0\right) = 0.0$ and $k_{11}\left(0\right) = k_{12}\left(0\right) = k_{13}\left(0\right) = 0.1$.

Six simulation cases are considered here, for $\lambda_1 = \lambda_2 = \ldots = \lambda_n = \lambda = 1$.

Case 1: *Complete Synchronization of Two Chaotic Systems With Identical Fractional Orders by Applying the No-Smooth Controller (i.e. With Sign Function)*

When $\alpha = \beta = 0.97$ and when the controller (46) is employed, the simulation results of this complete synchronization are shown in Figure 3. From this figure, despite the attendance of both external disturbances and uncertainties, a satisfactory complete synchronization between both systems (48) and (49) can be seen. Nevertheless, one can clearly observe the non-smoothness of the control signals and the chattering phenomenon.

Case 2: *Complete Synchronization of Two Chaotic Systems With Identical Fractional Orders by Applying the Smooth Controller (i.e. with Tanh function)*

When $\alpha = \beta = 0.97$ and when the controller (47) is applied, the simulation results of this complete synchronization are depicted in Figure 4. One can see from this figure that the slave system effectively follows its master system and the control inputs are smooth.

Figure 3. Simulation results with SIGN function for example 1 (when $\alpha_i = \beta_i = 0.97, \lambda_i = 1$): (a) $\lambda_1 x_1$ (solid line) and y_1 (dashed line). (b) $\lambda_2 x_2$ (solid line) and y_2 (dashed line). (c) $\lambda_3 x_3$ (solid line) and y_3 (dashed line). (d) u_1 (solid line), u_2 (dotted line) and u_3 (dashed line.

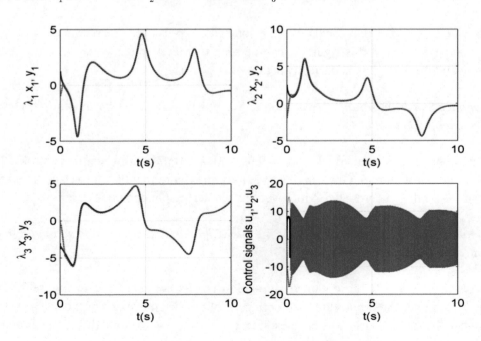

Figure 4. Simulation results with TANH function for example 1 (when $\alpha_i = \beta_i = 0.97, \lambda_i = 1$): (a) $\lambda_1 x_1$ (solid line) and y_1 (dashed line). (b) $\lambda_2 x_2$ (solid line) and y_2 (dashed line). (c) $\lambda_3 x_3$ (solid line) and y_3 (dashed line). (d) u_1 (solid line), u_2 (dotted line) and u_3 (dashed line).

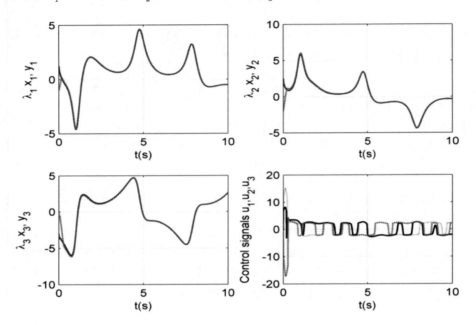

Case 3: *Complete Synchronization of Two Chaotic Systems With Different Fractional Orders by Applying the No-Smooth Controller (46)*

When $\alpha = 0.91$ and $\beta = 0.97$, and when the controller (46) is used, the obtained simulation results are shown in Figure 5. From this figure, it can be seen that a complete synchronization between the master system and the slave one is basically achieved.

Case 4: *Complete Synchronization of Two Chaotic Systems With Different Fractional-Orders by Applying the Smooth Controller (47)*

The simulation results, obtained when $\alpha = 0.91$ and $\beta = 0.97$, and when the controller (47) is applied, are presented in Figure 6. One can observe from this figure that the slave system and the master system are successfully synchronized. Moreover, the chattering phenomenon is removed.

Case 5: *Complete Synchronization of an Integer Order Chaotic System With a Fractional Order One by Applying the No-Smooth Controller (46)*

For $\alpha = 1$ and $\beta = 0.97$, the obtained simulation results are presented in Figure 7. This figure demonstrates that under the proposed no-smooth controller (46), the states of the slave system practically converge to that of the master system, despite the attendance of external disturbances and uncertain dynamics. However, the chattering phenomenon is clearly present in the control signals.

Figure 5. Simulation results with SIGN function for example 1 ($\alpha_i = 0.91$, $\beta_i = 0.97$ and $\lambda_i = 1$): (a) $\lambda_1 x_1$ (solid line) and y_1 (dashed line). (b) $\lambda_2 x_2$ (solid line) and y_2 (dashed line). (c) $\lambda_3 x_3$ (solid line) and y_3 (dashed line). (d) u_1 (solid line), u_2 (dotted line) and u_3 (dashed line).

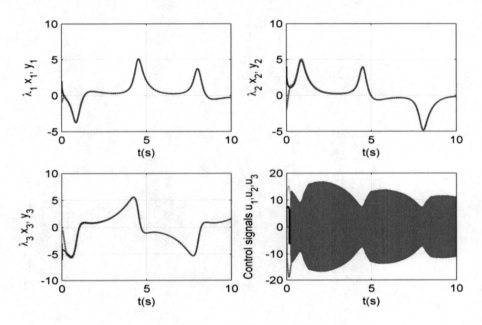

Figure 6. Simulation results with TANH function for example 1 ($\alpha_i = 0.91$, $\beta_i = 0.97$ and $\lambda_i = 1$): (a) $\lambda_1 x_1$ (solid line) and y_1 (dashed line). (b) $\lambda_2 x_2$ (solid line) and y_2 (dashed line). (c) $\lambda_3 x_3$ (solid line) and y_3 (dashed line). (d) u_1 (solid line), u_2 (dotted line) and u_3 (dashed line).

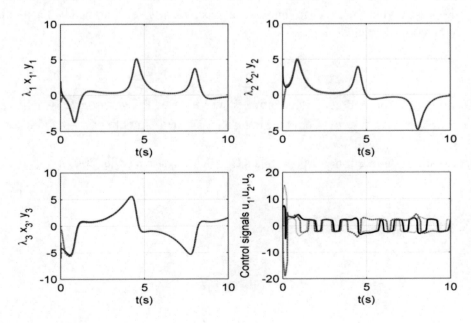

Figure 7. Simulation results with SIGN function for example 1 (when $\alpha_i = 1$, $\beta_i = 0.91$ and $\lambda_i = 1$):
(a) $\lambda_1 x_1$ (solid line) and y_1 (dashed line). (b) $\lambda_2 x_2$ (solid line) and y_2 (dashed line). (c) $\lambda_3 x_3$ (solid line)
and y_3 (dashed line). (d) u_1 (solid line), u_2 (dotted line) and u_3 (dashed line).

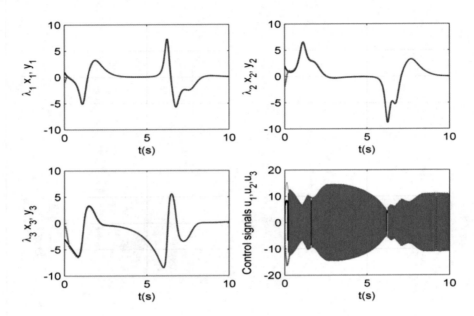

Case 6: *Synchronization of an Integer Order Chaotic System With a Fractional Order One by Applying*
the Smooth Controller (47)

The simulation results, obtained when $\alpha = 1$ and $\beta = 0.97$, and when the non-smooth controller (47) is used, are presented in Figure 8. In this case, one can clearly see that the chattering phenomenon is mitigated in the control signals.

Example 2

In this subsection, our proposed adaptive controller will be used to synchronize two different chaotic systems. According to the values of λ_i and the controller applied (smooth or no-smooth controller), six simulation cases will be considered here.

The master system is a fractional-order Chua's Oscillator system, (Zhu, 2009):

$$\begin{cases} D_t^{\alpha_1} x_1 = a\left(x_2 - x_1 - f\left(x_1\right)\right), \\ D_t^{\alpha_2} x_2 = x_1 - x_2 + x_3, \\ D_t^{\alpha_3} x_3 = -bx_2 - cx_3, \end{cases} \tag{50}$$

Figure 8. Simulation results with TANH function for example 1 (when $\alpha_i = 1$, $\beta_i = 0.91$ and $\lambda_i = 1$): (a) $\lambda_1 x_1$ (solid line) and y_1 (dashed line). (b) $\lambda_2 x_2$ (solid line) and y_2 (dashed line). (c) $\lambda_3 x_3$ (solid line) and y_3 (dashed line). (d) u_1 (solid line), u_2 (dotted line) and u_3 (dashed line).

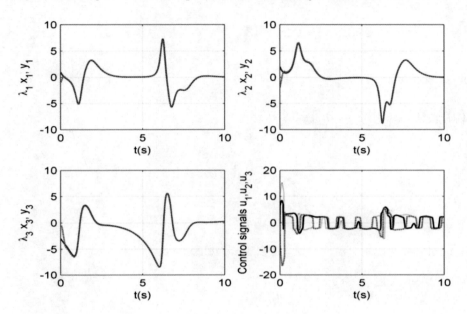

with

$$m_0 = -1.1726, m_1 = -0.7872,$$

$$a = 10, 725, b = 10.593, c = 0.268.$$

According to (Zhu, 2009), the system (50) can behave chaotically for $\alpha_1 = 0.93$, $\alpha_2 = 0.99$ and $\alpha_3 = 0.92$.

The slave system is a controlled fractional-order financial system (Chen, 2008; Bhalekar, 2014), which is described by:

$$\begin{cases} D_t^{\beta_1} y_1 = y_3 + \left(y_2 - a_1\right) y_1 + \varphi_1 \left(u_1\right) + d_1 \left(t\right), \\ D_t^{\beta_2} y_2 = 1 - b_1 y_2 - y_1^2 + \varphi_2 \left(u_2\right) + d_2 \left(t\right), \\ D_t^{\beta_3} y_3 = -y_1 - c_1 y_3 + \varphi_3 \left(u_3\right) + d_3 \left(t\right), \end{cases} \tag{51}$$

where $c_1 = 1$ is the elasticity of demand of commercial markets, $b_1 = 0.1$ is the cost per investment and $a_1 = 3$ is the saving amount, (Chen, 2008; Bhalekar, 2014). For $u_i = 0$ and $d_i\left(.\right) = 0$, the system (51) can behave chaotically for

$\beta_1 = 0.97, \beta_2 = 0.90$ and $\beta_3 = 0.96$.

The disturbances are chosen as:

$$d_1(t) = d_2(t) = d_3(t) = 0.2\sin(3t) + 0.2\cos(3t).$$

The initial conditions are:

$$x(0) = [x_1(0), x_2(0), x_3(0)]^T = [0.2, -0.1, 0.1]$$

and

$$y(0) = [y_1(0), y_2(0), y_3(0)]^T = [2, 1, 2]^T.$$

The input nonlinearities $\varphi_i(u_i)$ for $i = 1, 2, 3$ are selected as:

$$\varphi_i(u_i) = \begin{cases} (u_i - 3)\left(1.5 - 0.3e^{0.3|\sin\sin(u_i)|}\right), u_i > 3 \\ 0, -3 \le u_i \le 3 \\ (u_i + 3)\left(1.5 - 0.3e^{0.3|\sin\sin(u_i)|}\right), u_i < -3 \end{cases}$$

The used fuzzy logic systems, $\theta_i^T \psi_i(y)$, with $i = 1, 2, 3$, have the vector $y = [y_1, y_2, y_3]^T$ as an input. For each input variable of these fuzzy systems, as in Boulkroune et al. (2008), one defines three (one triangular and two trapezoidal) membership functions uniformly distributed on the intervals [-2, 2].

The design parameters are selected as follows:

$$k_{21} = k_{22} = k_{23} = 2,\ k_{31} = k_{32} = k_{33} = 10, \gamma_{\theta1} = \gamma_{\theta2} = \gamma_{\theta3} = 500,$$

$$\sigma_{\theta1} = \sigma_{\theta2} = \sigma_{\theta3} = 0.001,\ \gamma_{k1} = \gamma_{k2} = \gamma_{k3} = 5,\ \sigma_{k1} = \sigma_{k2} = \sigma_{k3} = 0.005.$$

The initial conditions for the adaptive parameters are chosen as:

$$\theta_{1j}(0) = \theta_{2j}(0) = \theta_{3j}(0) = 0.0 \text{ and } k_{11}(0) = k_{12}(0) = k_{13}(0) = 0.1.$$

According to the values of λ_i and the controller applied (smooth or no-smooth controller), one can distinguish six simulation cases.

Case 1: *Anti-Phase Projective Synchronization ($\lambda_i = -0.55$) by Applying the No-Smooth Controller (46)*

The obtained results are given in Figure 9. It is clear that the trajectories of slave system (y_1, y_2, y_3) quickly and practically converge to that of the master system $\left(\lambda_1 x_1, \lambda_2 x_2, \lambda_3 x_3 \right)$. Therefore, the projective anti-phase synchronization between the master and slave systems is effectively achieved. Nevertheless, one can clearly observe the chattering phenomenon and the non-smoothness of the control signals.

Case 2: *Anti-Phase Projective Synchronization ($\lambda_i = -0.55$) by Applying the Smooth Controller (47)*

The simulation results, obtained when $\lambda_i = -0.5$ and this smooth controller is used, are depicted in Figure 10. From this figure, one can see that the trajectories of slave system (y_1, y_2, y_3) effectively track that of its master system $\left(\lambda_1 x_1, \lambda_2 x_2, \lambda_3 x_3 \right)$ and the control inputs are smooth.

Case 3: *Complete Projective Synchronization ($\lambda_i = 0.2$) by Applying the No-Smooth Controller (46)*

The obtained simulation results for this complete projective synchronization are depicted in Figure 11. It is seen from this figure that the trajectories of slave system (y_1, y_2, y_3) effectively follow to that of the master system $\left(\lambda_1 x_1, \lambda_2 x_2, \lambda_3 x_3 \right)$. In addition, the corresponding control signals are admissible and bounded but with chattering.

Figure 9. Simulation results with SIGN function for example 2 (when $\lambda_i = -0.55$): (a) $\lambda_1 x_1$ (solid line) and y_1 (dashed line). (b) $\lambda_2 x_2$ (solid line) and y_2 (dashed line). (c) $\lambda_3 x_3$ (solid line) and y_3 (dashed line). (d) u_1 (solid line), u_2 (dotted line) and u_3 (dashed line).

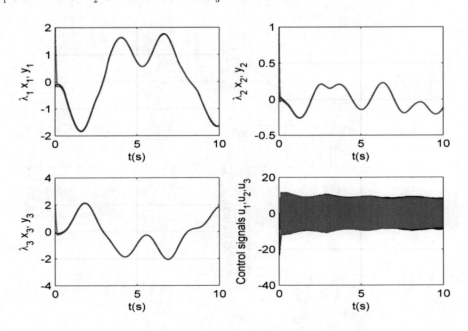

Figure 10. Simulation results with TANH function for example 2 (when $\lambda_i = -0.55$): (a) $\lambda_1 x_1$ (solid line) and y_1 (dashed line). (b) $\lambda_2 x_2$ (solid line) and y_2 (dashed line). (c) $\lambda_3 x_3$ (solid line) and y_3 (dashed line). (d) u_1 (solid line), u_2 (dotted line) and u_3 (dashed line).

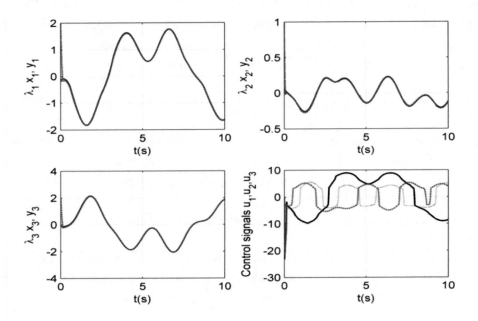

Figure 11. Simulation results with SIGN function for example 2 (when $\lambda_i = 0.2$): (a) $\lambda_1 x_1$ (solid line) and y_1 (dashed line). (b) $\lambda_2 x_2$ (solid line) and y_2 (dashed line). (c) $\lambda_3 x_3$ (solid line) and y_3 (dashed line). (d) u_1 (solid line), u_2 (dotted line) and u_3 (dashed line).

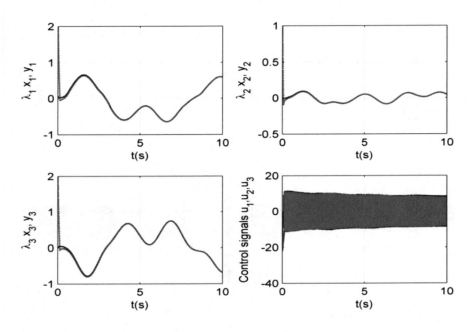

Case 4: *Complete Projective Synchronization ($\lambda_i = 0.2$) by Applying the Smooth Controller (47)*

The simulation results obtained when ($\lambda_i = 0.2$) and when the controller (47) is applied, are presented in Figure 12. From this figure, one can observe that the master system and the slave system are successfully projective synchronized. Moreover, the chattering phenomenon is removed.

Case 5: *Generalized Projective Synchronization ($\lambda_1 = 1, \lambda_2 = -1, \lambda_3 = 0.1$), by Applying the No-Smooth Controller (46)*

Figure 13 depicts the generalized projective synchronization between the master system (50) and the slave system (51) when the no-smooth controller (46) is employed.

Case 6: *Generalized Projective Synchronization ($\lambda_1 = 1, \lambda_2 = -1, \lambda_3 = 0.1$), by Applying the Smooth Controller (47)*

The simulation results, obtained when the smooth controller (47) is used and when ($\lambda_1 = 1, \lambda_2 = -1, \lambda_3 = 0.1$), are presented in Figure 14. In this case, one can obviously see that the chattering phenomenon is mitigated in the control signals.

Figure 12. Simulation results with TANH function for example 2 (when $\lambda_i = 0.2$): (a) $\lambda_1 x_1$ (solid line) and y_1 (dashed line). (b) $\lambda_2 x_2$ (solid line) and y_2 (dashed line). (c) $\lambda_3 x_3$ (solid line) and y_3 (dashed line). (d) u_1 (solid line), u_2 (dotted line) and u_3 (dashed line).

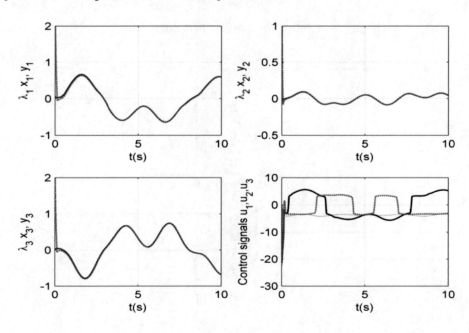

Figure 13. Simulation results with SIGN function for example 2 ($\lambda_1 = 1, \lambda_2 = -1, \lambda_3 = 0.1$): (a) $\lambda_1 x_1$ (solid line) and y_1 (dashed line). (b) $\lambda_2 x_2$ (solid line) and y_2 (dashed line). (c) $\lambda_3 x_3$ (solid line) and y_3 (dashed line). (d) u_1 (solid line), u_2 (dotted line) and u_3 (dashed line).

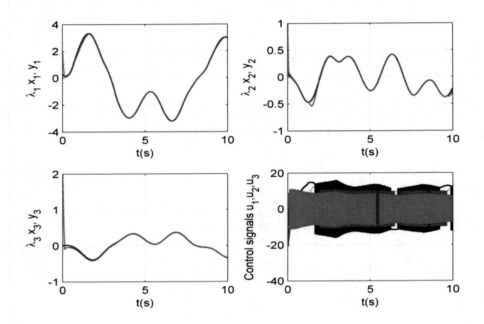

Figure 14. Simulation results with TANH function for example 2 ($\lambda_1 = 1, \lambda_2 = -1, \lambda_3 = 0.1$): (a) $\lambda_1 x_1$ (solid line) and y_1 (dashed line). (b) $\lambda_2 x_2$ (solid line) and y_2 (dashed line). (c) $\lambda_3 x_3$ (solid line) and y_3 (dashed line). (d) u_1 (solid line), u_2 (dotted line) and u_3 (dashed line).

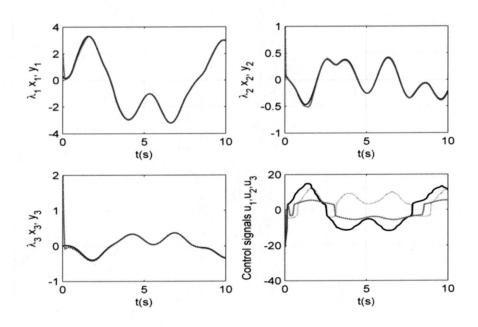

CONCLUSION

The issue of GPS of incommensurate fractional-order chaotic systems with dead-zone input has been investigated in this work. This GPS has been successfully accomplished by the conception of an adaptive fuzzy variable-structure controller. Of fundamental interest, a Lyapunov based analysis has been carried out to conclude about the asymptotical stability as well as the convergence of the fractional-order sliding surfaces towards zero. Computer simulation results have been provided to confirm the validity of the proposed GPS system based on adaptive fuzzy control for the synchronization of incommensurate fractional-order chaotic systems with unknown bounded disturbances, uncertain dynamics, and input nonlinearities.

REFERENCES

Aghababa, M. P. (2012). Comments on:H∞ synchronization of uncertain fractional order chaotic systems: Adaptive fuzzy approach. *ISA Transactions*, *51*(1), 11–12. doi:10.1016/j.isatra.2011.10.011 PMID:22075386

Baleanu, D., Güvenç, Z. B., & Tenreiro Machado, J. A. (2010). *New Trends in Nanotechnology and Fractional Calculus Applications*. Springer. doi:10.1007/978-90-481-3293-5

Benzaoui, M., Chekireb, H., Tadjine, M., & Boulkroune, A. (2016). Trajectory tracking with obstacle avoidance of redundant manipulator based on fuzzy inference systems. *Neurocomputing*, *196*, 23–30. doi:10.1016/j.neucom.2016.02.037

Bhalekar, S. (2014). Synchronization of incommensurate non-identical fractional order chaotic systems using active control. *The European Physical Journal. Special Topics*, *223*(8), 1495–1508. doi:10.1140/epjst/e2014-02184-0

Boulkroune, A. (2016). A fuzzy adaptive control approach for nonlinear systems with unknown control gain sign. *Neurocomputing*, *179*, 318–325. doi:10.1016/j.neucom.2015.12.010

Boulkroune, A., Bouzeriba, A., & Bouden, T. (2016). Fuzzy generalized projective synchronization of incommensurate fractional-order chaotic systems. *Neurocomputing*, *173*, 606–614. doi:10.1016/j.neucom.2015.08.003

Boulkroune, A., Bouzeriba, A., Hamel, S., & Bouden, T. (2015). Adaptive fuzzy control-based projective synchronization of uncertain nonaffine chaotic systems. *Complexity*, *21*(2), 180–192. doi:10.1002/cplx.21596

Boulkroune, A., M'Saad, M., & Farza, M. (2011). Adaptive fuzzy controller for multivariable nonlinear state time-varying delay systems subject to input nonlinearities. *Fuzzy Sets and Systems*, *164*(1), 45–65. doi:10.1016/j.fss.2010.09.001

Boulkroune, A., Tadjine, M., M'Saad, M., & Farza, M. (2008). How to design a fuzzy adaptive controller based on observers for uncertain affine nonlinear systems. *Fuzzy Sets and Systems*, *159*(8), 926–948. doi:10.1016/j.fss.2007.08.015

Bouzeriba, A., Boulkroune, A., & Bouden, T. (2016b). Fuzzy adaptive synchronization of uncertain fractional-order chaotic systems. *International Journal of Machine Learning and Cybernetics*, 1–16.

Bouzeriba, A., Boulkroune, A., & Bouden, T. (2016c). Projective synchronization of two different fractional-order chaotic systems via adaptive fuzzy control. *Neural Computing & Applications*, 27(5), 1349–1360. doi:10.100700521-015-1938-4

Bouzeriba, A., Boulkroune, A., Bouden, T., & Vaidyanathan, S. (2016a). Fuzzy Adaptive Synchronization of Incommensurate Fractional-Order Chaotic Systems. In *Advances and Applications in Chaotic Systems* (pp. 363–378). Springer International Publishing. doi:10.1007/978-3-319-30279-9_15

Calderon, A. J., Vinagre, B. M., & Feliu, V. (2006). Fractional-order control strategies for power electronic buck converters. *Signal Processing*, 86(10), 2803–2819. doi:10.1016/j.sigpro.2006.02.022

Chen, W. C. (2008). Nonlinear dynamics and chaos in a fractional-order financial system. *Chaos, Solitons, and Fractals*, 36(5), 1305–1314. doi:10.1016/j.chaos.2006.07.051

Deng, W., & Li, C. (2005). Chaos synchronization of the fractional Lü system. *Physica A*, 353, 61–72. doi:10.1016/j.physa.2005.01.021

Diethelm, K., & Ford, N. J. (2002). Analysis of fractional differential equations. *Journal of Mathematical Analysis and Applications*, 265(2), 229–248. doi:10.1006/jmaa.2000.7194

Diethelm, K., Ford, N. J., & Freed, A. D. (2002). A predictor-corrector approach for the numerical solution of fractional differential equations. *Nonlinear Dynamics*, 29(1/4), 3–22. doi:10.1023/A:1016592219341

Efe, M. O., & Kasnakoglu, C. A. (2008). Fractional adaptation law for sliding mode control. *International Journal of Adaptive Control and Signal Processing*, 22(10), 968–986. doi:10.1002/acs.1062

Grigorenko, I., & Grigorenko, E. (2003). Chaotic dynamics of the fractional Lorenz system. *Physical Review Letters*, 91(3), 034101. doi:10.1103/PhysRevLett.91.034101 PMID:12906418

Hamel, S., & Boulkroune, A. (2016). A generalized function projective synchronization scheme for uncertain chaotic systems subject to input nonlinearities. *International Journal of General Systems*, 45(6), 689–710. doi:10.1080/03081079.2015.1118094

Hilfer, R. (2000). *Applications of Fractional Calculus in Physics*. Singapore: World Scientific Publishing. doi:10.1142/3779

Li, C., & Chen, G. (2004). Chaos and hyperchaos in the fractional-order Rössler equations. *Physica A*, 34(1), 55–61. doi:10.1016/j.physa.2004.04.113

Li, Y., Chen, Y. Q., & Podlubny, I. (2010). Stability of fractional-order nonlinear dynamic systems: Lyapunov direct method and generalized Mittag--Leffler stability. *Computers & Mathematics with Applications (Oxford, England)*, 59(5), 1810–1821. doi:10.1016/j.camwa.2009.08.019

Li-Ming, W., Yong-Guang, T., Yong-Quan, C., & Feng, W. (2014). Generalized projective synchronization of the fractional-order chaotic system using adaptive fuzzy sliding mode control. *Chinese Physics B*, 23(10), 100501. doi:10.1088/1674-1056/23/10/100501

Lin, T. C., & Kuo, C. H. (2011). H∞ synchronization of uncertain fractional order chaotic systems: Adaptive fuzzy approach. *ISA Transactions*, *50*(4), 548–556. doi:10.1016/j.isatra.2011.06.001 PMID:21741648

Lin, T. C., & Lee, T. Y. (2011). Chaos synchronization of uncertain fractional-order chaotic systems with time delay based on adaptive fuzzy sliding mode control. *IEEE Transactions on Fuzzy Systems*, *19*(4), 623–635. doi:10.1109/TFUZZ.2011.2127482

Lin, T. C., Lee, T. Y., & Balas, V. E. (2011). Adaptive fuzzy sliding mode control for synchronization of uncertain fractional order chaotic systems. *Chaos, Solitons, and Fractals*, *44*(10), 791–801. doi:10.1016/j.chaos.2011.04.005

Lu, J. (2005). Chaotic dynamics and synchronization of fractional order Arneodo's systems. *Chaos, Solitons, and Fractals*, *26*(4), 1125–1133. doi:10.1016/j.chaos.2005.02.023

Pisano, A., Jelicic, Z., & Usai, E. (2010). Sliding mode control approaches to the robust regulation of linear multivariable fractional-order dynamics. *International Journal of Robust and Nonlinear Control*, *20*(18), 2021–2044. doi:10.1002/rnc.1565

Podlubny, I. (1999). *Fractional Differential Equations*. New York: Academic.

Rigatos, G., Zhu, G., Yousef, H., & Boulkroune, A. (2016). Flatness-based adaptive fuzzy control of electrostatically actuated MEMS using output feedback. *Fuzzy Sets and Systems*, *290*, 138–157. doi:10.1016/j.fss.2015.08.027

Sabatier, J., Agrawal, O. P., & Machado, J. A. T. (2007). *Advances in Fractional calculus*. London: Springer. doi:10.1007/978-1-4020-6042-7

Shyu, K. K., Liu, W. J., & Hsu, K. C. (2005). Design of large-scale time-delayed systems with dead-zone input via variable structure control. *Automatica*, *41*(7), 1239–1246. doi:10.1016/j.automatica.2005.03.004

Si-Ammour, A., Djennoune, S., & Bettayeb, M. (2009). A sliding mode control for linear fractional systems with input and state delays. *Communications in Nonlinear Science and Numerical Simulation*, *14*(5), 2310–2318. doi:10.1016/j.cnsns.2008.05.011

Tavazoei, M. S. (2012). Comments on: Chaos Synchronization of Uncertain Fractional-Order Chaotic Systems With Time Delay Based on Adaptive Fuzzy Sliding Mode Control. *IEEE Transactions on Fuzzy Systems*, *20*(5), 993–995. doi:10.1109/TFUZZ.2012.2188637

Wang, L. X. (1994). *Adaptive Fuzzy Systems and Control: Design and Stability Analysis*. Englewood Cliffs, NJ: Prentice-Hall.

Wang, X., He, Y., & Wang, M. (2009). Chaos control of a fractional order modified coupled dynamos system. *Nonlinear Analysis: Theory*. *Methods & Applications*, *71*(12), 6126–6134.

Wang, X., Zhang, X., & Ma, C. (2012). Modified projective synchronization of fractional order chaotic systems via active sliding mode control. *Nonlinear Dynamics*, *69*(1-2), 511–517. doi:10.100711071-011-0282-1

Zhu, H., Zhou, S., & Zhang, J. (2009). Chaos and synchronization of the fractional order Chua's system. *Chaos, Solitons, and Fractals*, *39*(4), 1595–1603. doi:10.1016/j.chaos.2007.06.082

Zouari, F., Boulkroune, A., Ibeas, A., & Arefi, M. M. (2016). Observer-based adaptive neural network control for a class of MIMO uncertain nonlinear time-delay non-integer-order systems with asymmetric actuator saturation. *Neural Computing & Applications*, 1–18.

KEY TERMS AND DEFINITIONS

Chaos Synchronization: A phenomenon that may occur, when two or more chaotic systems are coupled.

Chaotic Systems: Dissipative nonlinear dynamical systems having at least one positive Lyapunov exponent. Such systems are highly sensitive to initial conditions and system parameter variations, and also characterized by unpredictable and irregular motions exhibiting strange attractors in phase space.

Dead Zone: The portion of the operating range of a control device or transducer over which there is no change in output. This dead-zone nonlinearity is common in mechanical connections, hydraulic servovalves, piezoelectric translators, and electric servomotors.

Fractional-Order System: A dynamical system modeled by a fractional differential equation which contains derivatives of non-integer order.

Fuzzy Control: A control system that incorporates fuzzy logic and fuzzy inference rules.

Fuzzy System: A fuzzy system is a set of IF-THEN rules that maps the input space into the output space.

Nonlinear Dynamical System: A system described by a nonlinear differential equation.

Variable Structure Control: A discontinuous nonlinear control methodology. By application of a high-frequency switching control, this methodology alters the dynamics of a nonlinear system.

Chapter 10
Stabilization of a Class of Fractional-Order Chaotic Systems via Direct Adaptive Fuzzy Optimal Sliding Mode Control

Bachir Bourouba
Setif-1 University, Algeria

ABSTRACT

In this chapter a new direct adaptive fuzzy optimal sliding mode control approach is proposed for the stabilization of fractional chaotic systems with different initial conditions of the state under the presence of uncertainties and external disturbances. Using Lyapunov analysis, the direct adaptive fuzzy optimal sliding mode control approach illustrates asymptotic convergence of error to zero as well as good robustness against external disturbances and uncertainties. The authors present a method for optimum tuning of sliding mode control system parameter using particle swarm optimization (PSO) algorithm. PSO is a robust stochastic optimization technique based on the movement and intelligence of swarm, applying the concept of social interaction to problem solving. Simulation examples for the control of nonlinear fractional-order systems are given to illustrate the effectiveness of the proposed fractional adaptive fuzzy control strategy.

INTRODUCTION

Chaos is a complex nonlinear phenomenon which is frequently observed in physical, biological, electrical, mechanical, economical, and chemical systems. A chaotic system is a nonlinear deterministic dynamical system that exhibits special attributes including extraordinary sensitivity to system initial conditions, broad band Fourier spectrum, strange attractor, and fractal properties of the motion in phase space. Due to the existence of chaos in real world systems and many valuable applications in engineering and sci-

DOI: 10.4018/978-1-5225-5418-9.ch010

ence, synchronization and stabilization of chaotic systems have attracted significant interests among the researchers in the last decades (Rabah et al., 2017). The control of chaotic systems has been focused on more attentions in nonlinear science due to its potential applications in science and engineering such as circuit, mathematics, power systems, medicine, biology, chemical reactors, and so on. Many researchers have made great contributions. Chaotic behaviors can be a troublemaker when it causes undesired irregularity in dynamical systems. Due to troubles that may arise from unusual behaviors of a chaotic system, chaos control has gained increasing attention in the past few decades. In chaos control, an important objective is to suppress the chaotic oscillations completely or reduce them to the regular oscillations. Nowadays, many control techniques have been implemented in the control of chaotic systems (Tavazoei et al., 2009; Hamamci, 2012; Rabah et al., 2017b).

Chaotic dynamic of fractional order systems starts to attract increasing attention due to its potential applications in secure communication and control processing. An important challenge in chaos theory is the control, including stabilization of fractional order chaotic systems to steady states or regular behavior. Some approaches have been proposed to achieve chaos stabilization in fractional-order chaotic systems.

On the other hand, Fractional calculus is an area of mathematics that handles with differentiation and integration of arbitrary (non-integer) orders. It is a generalization of the ordinary differentiation and integration to non-integer (arbitrary) order. The subject is as old as the calculus of differentiation and goes back to times when Leibniz, Gauss, and Newton invented this kind of calculation. a fractional derivative was an ongoing topic in the last 300 years (Bouzeriba et al., 2015), but its application to physics and engineering has been reported only in the recent years (Hamamci, 2012). It has been found that many systems in interdisciplinary fields can be described by fractional differential equations, such as viscoelastic systems, dielectric polarization, electrode–electrolyte polarization, some finance systems, and electromagnetic wave systems, Moreover, applications of fractional calculus have been reported in many areas such as signal processing, image processing, automatic control, and robotics. These examples and many other similar samples perfectly clarify the importance of consideration and analysis of dynamical systems with fractional order models (Zamani et al., 2011; Bourouba et al., 2016).

The sliding mode control methodology is one such robust control technique which has its roots in the relay control. One of the most intriguing aspects of sliding mode is the discontinuous nature of the control action whose primary function is to switch between two distinctively different structures about some predefined manifold such that a new type of system motion called sliding mode exists in a manifold. This peculiar system characteristic is claimed to result in a superb system performance which includes insensitivity to parameter variations and complete rejection of certain class of disturbances. Furthermore, the system possesses new properties which are not present in original system. Sliding mode contains two phases (a) reaching phase in which the system states are driven from any initial state to reach the switching manifolds (the anticipated sliding modes) in finite time and (b) sliding phase in which the system is induced into the sliding motion on the switching manifolds, i.e., the switching manifolds become attractors. The robustness and order reduction property of sliding mode control comes into picture only after the occurrence of sliding mode.

Based on the universal approximation feature of the fuzzy systems some adaptive fuzzy control schemes have been designed for a class of unknown chaotic systems with integer-order. In these control schemes, the fuzzy systems are used to approximate the unknown nonlinear functions.

In this chapter, a class of fractional-order chaotic systems is introduced. To control chaos in these systems, a direct adaptive fuzzy optimal sliding mode controller is proposed. The sliding mode control law is derived to make the states of the fractional-order chaotic systems asymptotically stable. The direct adaptive fuzzy is used to commence uncertainty and the optimization PSO is used estimate the gains parameters of sliding mode controller.

BASIC DEFINITIONS AND PRELIMINARIES FOR FRACTIONAL-ORDER SYSTEMS

Fractional calculus (integration and differentiation of arbitrary (fractional) order) is an old concept which dates back to Cauchy, Riemann Liouville and Leitnikov in the 19th century. It has been used in mechanics since at least the 1930s and in electrochemistry since the 1960s. In control field, interesting works have been achieved in the Soviet Union, a later, several theoretical physicists and mathematicians have studied fractional differential operators and systems (Ladaci &Bensafia,2016).

In a general way, fractional order calculus refers that orders of differentials and integrals can be arbitrary or fractional (Ladaci & Charef,2006),(Liu, 2016).

$$
{}_aD_t^q = \begin{cases} \dfrac{d^q}{dt^q} & q > 0 \\ 1 & q = 0 \\ \displaystyle\int_a^t (d\tau)^{-q} & q < 0 \end{cases} \tag{1}
$$

Here, b is the initial value, q is the fractional order which can also be complex, and $R(q)$ is the real part of the fractional order.

There are two commonly used definitions for the general fractional differentiation and integration, i.e., the Grünwald–Letnikov (GL) and the Riemann–Liouville (RL) (Delavari et al., 2010).

The Grünwald–Letnikov (GL) fractional derivative of a function $f(t)$ with respect to t is defined as follows (Wang & Qi, 2016; Khettab et al., 2016):

$$
D_t^q f(t) = \lim_{h \to 0} \frac{1}{h^q} \sum_{j=0}^{[(t-q)/h]} (-1)^j \binom{q}{j} . f(t - jh) \tag{2}
$$

where $[\cdot]$ indicates the integer part, $\binom{q}{j} = \dfrac{n!}{j!(n-j)!}$ and $n - 1 < q < n$, j is an integer and h is the sampling period.

The Riemann-Liouville fractional derivative of order is defined as (Khettab et al., 2016; Lin & Kuo, 2011):

$$
D_t^q f(t) = \frac{1}{\Gamma(n - \alpha)} . \frac{d^n}{dt^n} \int_0^t (t - \tau)^{n-\alpha-1} f(\tau) \, d\tau \tag{3}
$$

where $n - 1 < \alpha < n$ and $\Gamma(\cdot)$ is the Gamma function. In this paper we employ D for representing the fractional differential.

Moreover, there are some properties for the fractional calculus (Khettab et al., 2016).

Property 1: The additive index law

$$D_t^\alpha D_t^\beta f(t) = D_t^\beta D_t^\alpha f(t) = D_t^{\alpha+\beta} f(t) \tag{4}$$

Property 2: Caputo fractional derivative operator is a linear operator

$$D_t^\alpha (af(t) + bg(x)) = a.D_t^\alpha f(t) + b.D_t^\alpha g(t) \tag{5}$$

(a,b are real constants).

Property 3: When $\alpha = 0$, it appears as the identity operator, i.e.,

$$D_t^\alpha f(t) = D_t^\alpha D_t^{-\alpha} f(t) = D_t^0 f(t) \tag{6}$$

BRIEF OVERVIEW OF THE FUZZY ADAPTIVE CONTROL

Fuzzy logic systems address the imprecision of the input and output variables directly by defining them with fuzzy numbers (and fuzzy sets) that can be expressed in linguistic terms (e.g., small, medium and large). A fuzzy logic system (FLS) consists of four parts: the knowledge base, the fuzzifier, the fuzzy inference engine working on fuzzy rules, and the defuzzifier. The knowledge base for FLS is comprised of a collection of fuzzy If-then rules of the following form (Khettab et al., 2017; Wang, 1993, Chen & Lee, 1996):

$$R^l : \quad if \quad x_1 \ is \ F_1^l \ and \ x_2 \ is \ F_2^l \ and....and \ x_n \ is \ F_n^l \ Then \ y_l \ is \ f_l(x) \quad where \ l = 1...N \tag{8}$$

where $x^T = (x_1, x_2, ..., x_N)$ and y_l are the fuzzy logic system input and output, respectively. N is the number of fuzzy IF–THEN rules.

The output of the fuzzy logic systems with central average defuzzifier, product inference and singleton fuzzifier can be expressed as

$$f(x) = \sum_{j=1}^{N} y_j \cdot \frac{\prod_{i=1}^{n} \mu_{F_i^j}(x_i)}{\sum_{j=1}^{N} (\prod_{i=1}^{n} \mu_{F_i^j}(x_i))} = \theta^T \xi(x) \tag{9}$$

where $\theta = \left[y_1, y_2, ..., y_N\right]^T$ is a vector of the consequence part of the fuzzy rule and $\xi(x) = \left[\xi_1(x), \xi_2(x), ..., \xi_N(x)\right]^T$;

$$\xi_j(x) = \frac{\prod\limits_{i=1}^{n} \mu_{F_i^j}(x_i)}{\sum\limits_{j=1}^{N}(\prod\limits_{i=1}^{n} \mu_{F_i^j}(x_i))} \tag{10}$$

Fuzzy controllers are supposed to work in situations where there is a large uncertainty or unknown variation in plant parameters and structures. Generally, the basic objective of adaptive control is to maintain consistent performance of a system in the presence of these uncertainties. Therefore, advanced fuzzy control should be adaptive (Wang, 1993).

What is adaptive fuzzy control? Roughly speaking, if a controller is constructed from adaptive fuzzy systems (an adaptive fuzzy system is a fuzzy logic system equipped with a training (adaptation) algorithm), it is called an adaptive fuzzy controller. An adaptive fuzzy controller can be a single adaptive fuzzy system or can be constructed from several adaptive fuzzy systems.

How does an adaptive fuzzy controller compare with a conventional adaptive controller? The most important advantage of adaptive fuzzy control over conventional adaptive control is that adaptive fuzzy controllers are capable of incorporating linguistic fuzzy information from human operators, whereas conventional adaptive controllers are not. This is especially important for the systems with a high degree of uncertainty, e.g., in chemical processes and in aircraft, because although these systems are difficult to control from a control theory point of view, they are often successfully controlled by human operators. How can human operators successfully control such complex systems without a mathematical model in their minds? If we ask the human operators what control strategies they follow, they may just tell us a few control rules in fuzzy terms and some linguistic descriptions about the behavior of the system under various conditions which are, of course, also in fuzzy terms. Although these fuzzy control rules and descriptions are not precise and may not be sufficient for constructing a successful controller, they provide very important information about how to control the. System and how the system behaves. Adaptive fuzzy control provides a tool for making use of the fuzzy information in a systematic and efficient manner. How are adaptive fuzzy controllers classified? We classify adaptive fuzzy controllers according to whether the adaptive fuzzy controller can incorporate fuzzy control rules or fuzzy descriptions about the system (Chen, 1993; Wang, 1993).

OPTIMIZATION ALGORITHM WITH PARTICLE SWARM

Particle swarm optimizer is based on the social behavior of animals such as fish schooling, insect swarming, and birds flocking (Yang &Bekdaş, 2015). The method considers an artificial swarm which consists of particles. The behavior of each particle in the swarm is simulated according to three rules. The first is separation where each particle tries to move away from its neighbors if they are too close. The second is alignment where each particle steers toward the average heading of its neighbors. The third is cohesion where each particle tries to go toward the average position of its neighbors. This simulation is extended to amend the above three rules as follows: each agent is attracted toward the location of roost; each agent remembers where it was closer to the roost and each agent shared information with all other agents about its closest location to the roost.

The particle swarm optimizer selects a number of particles to represent a swarm. Each particle in the swarm is a potential solution to the optimization problem under consideration. A particle explores the search domain by moving around. This move is decided by making use of its own experience and the collective experience of the swarm. Each particle has three main parameters: position, velocity, and fitness. Position represents the decision variables of the optimization problem, velocity determines the rate of change of the position, and fitness is the value of the objective function at the particle's current position. The fitness value is a measure of how good the solution is it represents for the optimization problem (Yang & Bekdaş, 2015; Kaveh, 2014).

Numerically, the position *x* of a particle *i* at iteration *k + 1* is updated as shown in Equation (11) and illustrated in Figure 1 (Perez & Behdinan, 2007).

$$x_{k+1}^i = x_k^i + v_{k+1}^i . \Delta t \tag{11}$$

where v_{k+1}^i is the corresponding updated velocity vector, and Δt is the time step value (Perez & Behdinan, 2007; Liu, 2006). The velocity vector of each particle is calculated as shown in Equation (12)

$$v_{k+1}^i = w.v_k^i + c_1 r_1 \frac{(p_k^i - x_k^i)}{\Delta t} + c_2 r_2 \frac{(p_k^g - x_k^i)}{\Delta t} \tag{12}$$

Figure 1. PSO position and velocity update

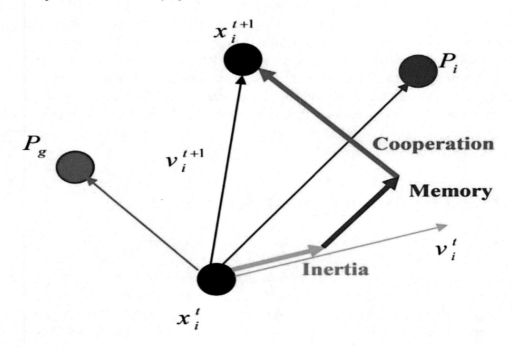

where r_1 and r_2 are the random numbers between 0 and 1, p_k^i is the best position found by particle i so far, and p_k^g is the best position in the swarm at time **k**. *w* is the inertia of the particle which controls the exploration properties of the algorithm. c_1 and c_2 are the trust parameters that indicate how much confidence the particle has in itself and in the swarm, respectively (Kevah, 2014; Perez & Behdinan, 2007; Liu, 2006).

Based on the particle and velocity updates as explained above,the steps of the standard algorithm are outlined in the following:

1. Initialize swarm of particles with positions x_0^i and initial velocities v_0^i randomly distributed throughout the design space.
2. Evaluate the objective function values $f(x_k^i)$ using the design space positions x_k^i.
3. Update the optimum particle position p_k^i at the current iteration k and the global optimum particle position p_k^i.
4. Update the position of each particle using its previous position (Equation 11.) and updated velocity vector as specified in Equation 12.
5. Repeat steps 2–4 until the stopping criteria is met. For the current implementation the stopping criteria is defined based on the number of iterations.

General Fractional-Order Chaotic System Description

Chaos is a very interesting nonlinear phenomenon and has been intensively investigated during the last decades. The first chaotic attractor was found by the American mathematical meteorologist Lorenz. In 1963, he discovered chaos in a simple systemof three autonomous ordinary differential equations, called the Lorenz system, in order to describe the simplified Rayleigh–Benard problem. The nonlinear characteristics and basic dynamic properties of the Lorenz system are well studied by many papers and monographs (Denga & Lib, 2005). As the first chaotic model, the Lorenz system has become a paradigm of chaos research. In 1976, Rössler constructed several three-dimensional quadratic autonomous chaotic systems. Sprott (1994) found 19 algebraically simple chaotic systems by exhaustive computer searching. It was noticed that the Rössler attractors and some of Sprott's attractors are all topologically simpler than the 2-scroll Lorenz attractor. Furthermore, Sprott's attractors behave similarly in that they all tend to resemble the single-fold band structure of the Rössler attractor. In 1999, Chen found another similar but topologically not equivalent chaotic attractor, as the dual of the Lorenz system. Lü et al. (2002) found a new chaotic system, bearing the name of the Lü system, which bridges the gap between the Lorenz and Chen attractors. The fractional version of Lu's system is described as (Chen et al., 2012; Yin et al., 2012):

$$\begin{cases} D_t^{q_1} x(t) = a.(y(t) - x(t)) \\ D_t^{q_2} y(t) = -x(t).y(t) - c.y(t) \\ D_t^{q_3} z(t) = x(t).y(t) - b.z(t) \end{cases} \tag{13}$$

Where $x(t), y(t), z(t)$ are state variables and $0 < q_1, q_2, q_3 < 1$ is fractional order.

Figure 2. The chaotic trajectories of the fractional-order Lu system

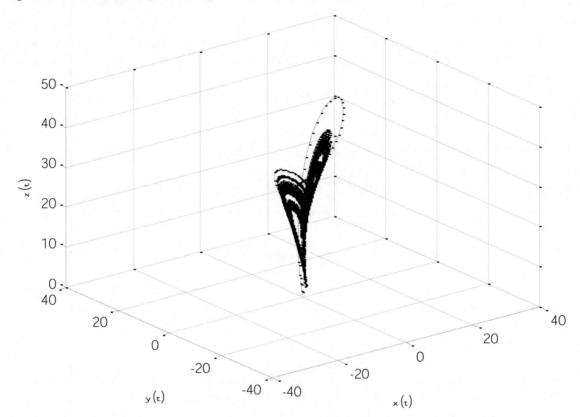

Let us consider the fractional-order chaotic system (13) with uncertainties in the presence of an external disturbance. It will be illustrated that the system can be stabilized under the sliding mode and fuzzy adaptive control.

$$\begin{cases} D_t^{q_1} x(t) = a.(y(t) - x(t)) \\ D_t^{q_2} y(t) = -x(t).y(t) - c.y(t) + \Delta(t) + d(t) + u(t) \\ D_t^{q_3} z(t) = x(t).y(t) - b.z(t) \end{cases} \tag{14}$$

The design procedure of sliding mode control has two steps: first, constructing a sliding surface that represents a desiredsystem dynamic. Second, developing a switching control law to make the sliding mode possible on every point in the slidingsurface. Any states outside the surface are driven to reach the surface in a finite time. To propose a sliding mode control scheme, we define the sliding surface as (Yang & Bekdaş, 2015; Yin et al., 2012);

$$S(t) = D^{q_2-1} y(t) + \int_0^t \psi(t) dt \tag{15}$$

Figure 3. Projection of the Lu's system onto corresponding plane

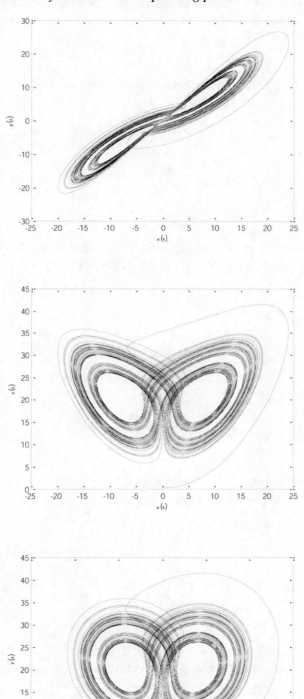

where $\psi(t)$ is a function described by (Yin et al., 2012; Bourouba & Ladaci, 2017)

$$\psi(t) = -a.y + k_1.x.y - (1 - k_2)x + \beta y \tag{16}$$

For the sliding mode method, the sliding surface and its derivative must satisfy

$$S(t) = 0 \tag{17}$$

and

$$\dot{S}(t) = 0 \Rightarrow D^{q_2}y(t) = -\psi(t) \tag{18}$$

To design the reaching mode control scheme, which drives states onto the sliding surface, a reaching law can be chosen as (Chen et al., 2012; Yin et al., 2012; Bourouba & Ladaci, 2017)

$$u_r(t) = -K_r.\text{sgn}(S(t)) \tag{19}$$

where

$$\text{sgn}(S(t)) \begin{cases} -1 \ if \ S(t) < 0 \\ 0 \ \ if \ S(t) = 0 \\ +1 \ if \ S(t) > 0 \end{cases} \tag{20}$$

And $u_{eq}(t) = -a.y + k_2.x.y - k_1.x$ (21)and the K is the reach gain of the controller, $K>0$. Finally, the total control law can be defined as

$$u_s(t) = u_{eq} + u_r(t) + u_{fuzzy}(t) \tag{22}$$

If we chose the followingfuzzy adaptive law:

$$u_{fuzzy}(t) = \theta^T \xi(x) \text{ with } \dot{\theta}(t) = -\eta.\xi(x).S(t) \tag{23}$$

where η is positive scalar value the fuzzy adaptive control $u_{fuzzy}(t)$ is employed to attenuate the error $\Delta(t)$ and external disturbance $d(t)$.

The Lyapunov candidate function is selected as:

$$V = \frac{1}{2}S^2 + \frac{1}{2\gamma}\phi^T\phi \tag{24}$$

where $\phi = \theta^* - \theta$ and θ^* is the optimal parameter vectors. The time derivative of the Lyapunov function is given by

$$\dot{V} = S\dot{S} + \frac{1}{\gamma}\phi^T\dot{\phi} \qquad (25)$$

Where

$$\dot{S}(t) = \frac{d}{dt}\{S(t)\} \text{ and } \dot{\phi} = -\dot{\theta} \qquad (26)$$

$$
\begin{aligned}
\dot{V} &= S(D^{q_2}y(t) + \psi(t)) + \frac{1}{\eta}\phi^T\dot{\phi} \\
&= S(-xy + \beta y + \Delta(t) + d(t) + u(t) + u_{fuzzy}(t) + a.y + k_1.x \\
&\quad + (1-k_2)xy + \beta y) - \frac{1}{\eta}\phi^T\dot{\theta} \\
&= (-xy + \Delta(t) + d(t) + u_{eq} + u_r(t) + u_{fuzzy}(t) + a.y) + k_1.x \\
&\quad + (1-k_2)x.y) - \frac{1}{\eta}\phi^T\dot{\theta} \\
&= S.\left[u_{fuzzy}(t) + \Delta(t) + d(t) - K_r.\mathrm{sgn}(S(t))\right] - \frac{1}{\eta}\phi^T\dot{\theta} \\
&= S.\left[\theta^T\xi(x) + \Delta(t) + d(t) - K_r.\mathrm{sgn}(S(t))\right] - \frac{1}{\eta}\phi^T\dot{\theta} \\
&= S.\left[\theta^T\xi(x) - \theta^{*T}\xi(x) + \theta^{*T}\xi(x) + \Delta(t) + d(t) - K_r.\mathrm{sgn}(S(t))\right] - \frac{1}{\eta}\phi^T\dot{\theta} \\
&= S\left[-\phi^T\xi(x) + \theta^{*T}\xi(x) + \Delta(t) + d(t) - K_r.\mathrm{sgn}(S(t))\right] - \frac{1}{\eta}\phi^T\dot{\theta} \\
&= S\left[-\phi^T\xi(x) + \theta^{*T}\xi(x) + \Delta(t) + d(t) - K_r.\mathrm{sgn}(S(t))\right] - \phi^T\left[\xi(x)S + \frac{1}{\eta}\dot{\theta}\right] \\
&= S.\left[\theta^{*T}\xi(x) + \sigma(t) - K_r.\mathrm{sgn}(S(t))\right]
\end{aligned}
\qquad (27)
$$

Where $\sigma(t) = \Delta(t) + d(t)$

Fuzzy logic systems are universal approximators, i.e., they can approximate any smooth function on a compact space, then the following result is obtained.

$$
\begin{aligned}
\dot{V} &= S.(-K_r.\mathrm{sgn}(S(t)) \\
&= -K_r|S| < 0
\end{aligned}
\qquad (28)
$$

Numerical Simulation

In this section, our goal is to stabilize of a class of fractional-order chaotic systems by applying the method direct adaptive fuzzy optimal sliding mode control on three different fractional-order chaotic system.

Consider the fractional-order Lu's system, which is expressed as

$$\begin{cases} D_t^{q_1} x(t) = a.(y(t) - x(t)) \\ D_t^{q_2} y(t) = -x(t).y(t) - c.y(t) + \Delta(t) + d(t) + u(t) \\ D_t^{q_3} z(t) = x(t).y(t) - b.z(t) \end{cases} \tag{29}$$

where the fractional-order $q_1 = 0.985$, $q_2 = 0.99$ and $q_3 = 0.98$, . The system (18) without the controller exhibits a chaotic behavior as shown in Figure 2 and Figure 3, when $(a, b, c) = (36, 3, 20)$ and the initial value $(x_0, y_0, z_0) = (12, -5, -7)$.

The control input *u(t)* to stabilized Lu's system is added to the second state equation in order to control chaos in the fractional order system (32).

For fuzzy adaptive controller we chose membership function for error and derivative of error as

$$\begin{aligned} \mu_{F_1^j}(e_i) &= \exp\left[-(e_i + 1.25) / 0.5)^2\right] \\ \mu_{F_2^j}(e_i) &= \exp\left[(-((e_i + 0.625) / 0.5)^2)\right] \\ \mu_{F_3^j}(e_i) &= \exp\left[-(e_i / 0.5)^2\right] \\ \mu_{F_4^j}(e_i) &= \exp\left[(-((e_i - 0.625) / 0.5)^2)\right] \\ \mu_{F_5^j}(e_i) &= \exp\left[-(e_i - 1.25) / 0.5)^2\right] \end{aligned} \tag{30}$$

Where i=1,2. And the adaptive gain is $\eta = 15$
The uncertainties term $\Delta(t)$, and the external disturbances $d(t)$ given by:

$$\Delta g(x, y, z) = 0.5 \sin\left(10x\left(t\right)\right). \cos\left(2.5.y(t)\right). \cos\left(3.z\left(t\right)\right)$$

and

$$d(t) = 0.65. \cos\left(2y\left(t\right).t\right) + 0.5. \sin\left(3t\right) \tag{31}$$

Tuning by Particle swarm optimization: setting the size of swarm is 30, the max-number of iteration is 100, the dimension of the problem is 3, the inertia weighting is 0.5 and accelerate coefficient are (c_1=1.5 and c_2=1.2). the parameters of controller (22) are given by; *k_1=0.8214, k_2= 0.0556 and k_r=0.0124*. The simulation results are given in Figure 4

Figure 4. State trajectories of stabilized fractional-order Lu system in the presence of uncertainty and external disturbance

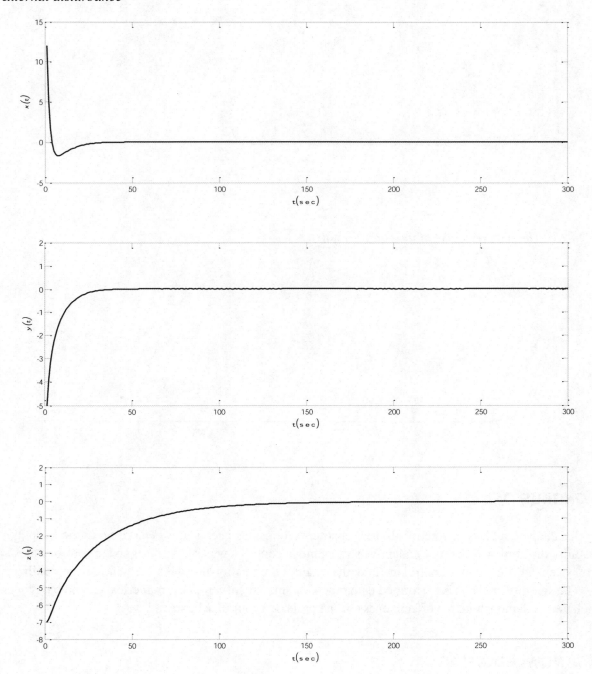

Figure 5. The time response of the surface S(t)

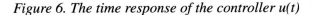

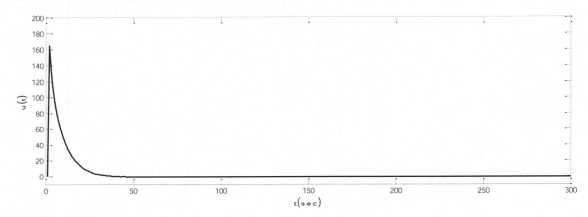

Figure 6. The time response of the controller u(t)

CONCLUSION

In this chapter, a class of fractional-order chaotic systems has been study. According to the Lyapunov stability theorem, a direct fuzzy adaptive sliding mode control law has been designed to control chaos in the systems. Based on this control method, the states of the fractional-order system have been stabilized.

The stability analysis is performed using the Lyapunov theory. Finally, numerical example has been included to demonstrate the effectiveness of the proposed control scheme.

ACKNOWLEDGMENT

The author is grateful to Professor Samir Ladaci for his contribution and helpful comments on an early version of this Chapter.

REFERENCES

Bourouba, B., & Ladaci, S. (2017). Stabilization of class of fractional-order chaotic system via new sliding mode control. *Proceeding 6th IEEE International Conference on Systems and Control, ICSC'2017,* 470-475. 10.1109/ICoSC.2017.7958681

Bourouba, B., Ladaci, S., & Chaabi, A. (2017). Moth-Flame optimization algorithm based fractional order $PI^\lambda D^\mu$ controller with MRAC tuning configuration. *International Journal of Systems, Control and Communications.*

Bouzeriba, A., Boulkroune, A., & Bouden T. (2015). Fuzzy adaptive synchronization of uncertain fractional-order chaotic systems. *International Journal of Machine Learning and Cybernetics.*

Chen, B.-S., Lee, C.-H., & Chang, Y.-C. (1996). H∞ tracking design of uncertain nonlinear SISO systems: Adaptive fuzzy approach. *IEEE Transactions on Fuzzy Systems, 4*(1), 32–42. doi:10.1109/91.481843

Chen, D.-y., Liu, Y.-X., Ma, X.-Y., & Zhang, R.-F. (2012). Control of a class of fractional-order chaotic systems via sliding mode. *Nonlinear Dynamics, 67*(1), 893–901. doi:10.100711071-011-0002-x PMID:22757537

Delavari, H., Ranjbar, A. N., Ghaderi, R., & Momani, S. (2010). Fractional order control of a coupled tank. *Nonlinear Dynamics, 61*(3), 383–397. doi:10.100711071-010-9656-z

Deng, W.-H., & Li, C.-P. (2005). Chaos synchronization of the fractional Lu system. *Physica A, 353*(1), 61–72. doi:10.1016/j.physa.2005.01.021

Hamamci, S.-E. (2012). Stabilization of fractional-order chaotic system via a single state adaptive-feedback controller. *Nonlinear Dynamics, 68*(1), 45–51.

Kaveh, A. (2014). *Advances in Metaheuristic Algorithms for Optimal Design of Structures.* Springer.

Khettab, K., Bensafia, Y., & Ladaci, S. (2017). Robust Adaptive Fuzzy Control for a Classof Uncertain Nonlinear Fractional Systems. In Recent Advances in Electrical Engineering and Control Applications. Springer.

Khettab, K., Ladaci, S., & Bensafia, Y.(2016) Fuzzy adaptive control of a fractional order chaotic system with unknown control gain sign using a fractional order nussbaum gain. *IEEE/CAA Journal of Automatica Sinica,* 1-8.

Ladaci, S., &Bensafia, Y. (2016). Indirect fractional order pole assignment based adaptive control. *Engineering Science and Technology, an International Journal, 19*(1), 518–530.

Ladaci, S., & Charef, A. (2006). On Fractional Adaptive Control. *Nonlinear Dynamics, 43*(4), 365–378. doi:10.100711071-006-0159-x

Lin, T.-C., & Kuo, C.-H. (2011). H∞ synchronization of uncertain fractional order chaotic systems: Adaptivefuzzy approach. *ISA Transactions, 50*(1), 548–556. doi:10.1016/j.isatra.2011.06.001 PMID:21741648

Liu, X. (2016). Optimization design on fractional order PID controllerbased on adaptive particle swarm optimization algorithm. *Nonlinear Dynamics, 84*(1), 379–386. doi:10.100711071-015-2553-8

Perez, R. E., & Behdinan, K. (2007). Particle swarm approach for structural design optimization. *Computers & Structures*, 85(1), 1579–1588. doi:10.1016/j.compstruc.2006.10.013

Rabah, K., Ladaci, S., & Lashab, M. (2017). A novel fractional sliding mode control configuration for synchronizing disturbed fractional-order chaotic systems. *Pramana*, 89(46).

Rabah, K., Ladaci, S., & Lashab, M. (2017b). (to appear). Bifurcation-based Fractional Order PI$^\Lambda$D$^\mu$ Controller Design Approach for Nonlinear Chaotic Systems. *Frontiers of Information Technology & Electronic Engineering*.

Ren, C., Tong, S., & Li, Y. (2012). Fuzzy adaptive high-gain-based observer backstepping control for SISO nonlinear systems with dynamical uncertainties. *Nonlinear Dynamics*, 67(1), 941–955. doi:10.100711071-011-0036-0

Tavazoei, M. S., Haeri, M., Bolouki, S., & Siami, M. (2009). Using fractional-order integrator to control chaos in single-input chaotic systems. *Nonlinear Dynamics*, 55(1), 179–190. doi:10.100711071-008-9353-3

Wang, L. X. (1993). Stable Adaptive Fuzzy Control of Nonlinear Systems. *IEEE Transactions on Fuzzy Systems*, 1(1), 146–155. doi:10.1109/91.227383

Yang, X-S., & Bekdaş, G. (2015). *Metaheuristics and Optimization in Civil Engineering*. Springer.

Yin, C., Zhong, S.-M., & Chen, W.-F. (2012). Design of sliding mode controller for a class of fractional-order chaotic systems. *Communications in Nonlinear Science and Numerical Simulation*, 17(1), 356–366. doi:10.1016/j.cnsns.2011.04.024

Zamani, M., Karimi, M., Sadati, N., & Parniani, M. (2011). Adaptive synchronization of fractional-order chaotic systems via a single driving variable. *Nonlinear Dynamics*, 66(1), 831–837.

Chapter 11
Design and Optimization of Generalized PD–Based Control Scheme to Stabilize and to Synchronize Fractional–Order Hyperchaotic Systems

Ammar Soukkou
University of Jijel, Algeria

Abdelkrim Boukabou
University of Jijel, Algeria

ABSTRACT

This chapter will establish the importance and significance of studying the fractional-order control of nonlinear dynamical systems and emphasize the link between the factional calculus and famous PID control design. It will lay the foundation related to the research scope, problem formulation, objectives and contributions. As a case study, a fractional-order PD-based feedback (Fo-PDF) control scheme with optimal knowledge base is developed in this work for achieving stabilization and synchronization of a large class of fractional-order chaotic systems (FoCS). Based and derived on Lyapunov stabilization arguments of fractional-order systems, the stability analysis of the closed-loop control system is investigated. The design and multiobjective optimization of Fo-PDF control law is theoretically rigorous and presents a powerful and simple approach to provide a reasonable tradeoff between simplicity, numerical accuracy, and stability analysis in control and synchronization of FoCS. The feasibility and validity of this developed Fo-PDF scheme have been illustrated by numerical simulations using the fractional-order Mathieu-Van Der Pol hyperchaotic system.

DOI: 10.4018/978-1-5225-5418-9.ch011

1. INTRODUCTION

Fractional calculus, considered as the generalization of the conventional integer-order calculus, is a very useful tool in describing the evolution of systems with memory, which are typically dissipative and considered as complex systems. Therefore, in many cases, these properties make fractional-order systems more adequate than usually adopted integer-order one. Modeling and control topics of nonlinear dynamical systems using the concept of fractional-order of integral and derivative operators have recently attracting more attentions.

The fractional-order chaotic systems (FoCS), as a generalization of integer-order chaotic systems, can be considered as a new topic, where significant attention has been focused on developing powerful techniques for chaos control and of this new class of dynamical systems. As a consequence, many researchers in the fractional control community have made great contributions, based on different approaches (Chen, Liu, & Ma, 2012; Zhu, Zhou, & Zhang, 2009; Petráš, 2011; Chen, He, Chai, & Wu, 2014; Zhang, Tian, Yang, & Cao, 2015; Agrawal, & Das, 2014; Wang & Chen, 2015; Li, 2014; Kuntanapreeda, 2015;Ushio, & Yamamoto, 1999; Pyragas, 1992; Zheng, 2015 Ding, Qi, Peng, & Wang, 2015). As an illustration examples, Chen et al. in Chen, Liu, & Ma (2012) investigated the chaos control of a class of FoCS via sliding mode concept. Zhu et al. (2009) presented an algorithm for numerical solution of fractional-order differential equation. The synchronization of fractional-order Chua oscillator is discussed. A survey of fractional dynamical systems, modeling and stability analysis has been presented in Petráš (2011). In Chen, He, Chai, & Wu (2014), Zhang, Tian, Yang, & Cao (2015), the authors investigated the stability conditions of n-dimensional fractional-order nonlinear systems with commensurate-order lying in [0, 2]. The obtained results are applied to stabilizing a large class of FoCS via a linear state-feedback controller. In Agrawal, & Das (2014), the function projective synchronization between different FoCS with uncertain parameters using modified adaptive control method is studied. The adaptive function projective synchronization controller and identification parameter laws are developed on the basis of Lyapunov stability theory. A new mean-based adaptive fuzzy neural network sliding mode control is developed by Wang & Chen (2015) to perform the chaos synchronization process of fractional-order uncertain systems. In Li (2014), problems of robust stability and stabilization of fractional order chaotic systems based on uncertain Takagi-Sugeno fuzzy model are studied. The tensor product model transformation-based controller design for control and synchronization of a class of FoCS is investigated in (Kuntanapreeda, 2015). The prediction-based control, has been introduced by Ushio and Yamamoto (1999) in order to overcome some limitations of the so-called delayed-time feedback control derived by Pyragas (1992). In particular, Zheng (2015) proposed the fuzzy prediction-based feedback control model using the Takagi–Sugeno (T-S) reasoning to stabilize a fractional-order chaotic system on its original equilibrium point. Therefore, a sufficient condition of asymptotical stability of fuzzy prediction model has been derived and based on direct Lyapunov stability theory. In Ding, Qi, Peng, & Wang (2015), the authors presented an adaptive fractional-order backstepping control design for a class of fractional-order nonlinear systems with additive disturbance. The proposed control laws do not require the specific knowledge on the disturbance and the system parameters. The asymptotic pseudo-state stability of the closed-loop system is guaranteed in terms of fractional Lyapunov stability.

Fractional-order Control (FoC) approach as an advanced technique, introduced firstly by Oustaloup (1999) is a trend that exploits the concepts of physical operators involved in the modeling of natural phenomena. These new concepts are aimed to improve the performance required in the analysis and control of nonlinear dynamical systems. The idea of using FoC technique is well addressed in Oustaloup (1991) and Podlubny (1999). Subsequently, Podlubny (1999) proposed a generalized form of the ordinary PID controller, namely $\mathrm{PI}^{\lambda}\mathrm{D}^{\mu}$, involving an integrator of constant-order $\lambda \in \mathbb{R}^{+}$ and a differentiator of constant-order $\mu \in \mathbb{R}^{+}$. More recently, many variants of FoC have been developed and used in different theoretical and practical applications. The most common is the family of the Fo-PID controllers.

The topic of FoC is well adopted in control and synchronization processes of FoCS (Sadeghian, Salarieh, Alasty, & Meghdari, 2011; Zhou, & Ding, 2012; Li, Wang, & Yang, 2014; Si, Sun, Zhang, & Chen, 2012; Tavazoei, & Haeri, 2008; Das, Pan, Das, & Gupta, 2012; Li, & Chen, 2014; Soukkou, Boukabou, & Leulmi, 2016). In particular, in Sadeghian, Salarieh, Alasty, & Meghdari (2011), the problem of controlling unstable equilibrium points and periodic orbits is investigated via the fractional-order delayed feedback of the measured states. In Zhou & Ding (2012), the control and synchronization of the fractional-order Lorenz chaotic system have been adressed via the fractional-order derivative approach. The single state FoC for chaos synchronization process based on the Lyapunov stability theory is presented by Li et al. (2014). In Si, Sun, Zhang, & Chen (2012), the fractional operators are introduced to develop a general form for synchronizing a class of FoCS. The authors, adopted the CRONE-Oustaloup method to simulate the fractional-order systems and the fractional calculus operators. Fractional-order PI controller to locally stabilize unstable equilibrium points of a class of fractional-order chaotic systems is proposed by Tavazoei and Haeri in 2008. The fractional-order PID controller has been designed by an intelligent bacterial foraging optimization algorithm to synchronize two chaotic systems (Das, Pan, Das, & Gupta, 2012). Oustaloup's band-limited frequency domain rational approximation technique is adopted by the authors. In Li & Chen (2014), an adaptive fractional-order feedback controller is developed by extending an adaptive integer-order feedback controller. Through rigorous theoretical proof by means of the Lyapunov stability theorem and Barbalat lemma, sufficient conditions are derived to guarantee chaos synchronization. A Generalized (fractional-order) Prediction-based Control law is developed by Soukkou et al. in 2016. Based on Lyapunov stabilization arguments and a recent stability theorem of fractional-order systems, stability analysis of the closed-loop control system is investigated. The design and multiobjective optimization of the proposed scheme offers some superior properties such as faster finite-time convergence, higher control precision which very low energy consumption and stability conditions guarantee in control and synchronization of a class of fractional-order hyperchaotic systems.

A view of the works carried out in the field of control and synchronization of FoCS, we can notice that most researches are, mainly, concentrated around four main important issues as summarized by Figure 1. The discretization 'approximation' process of fractional operators $D_{t}^{\pm\alpha}$, $\alpha \in \Re$ (resp. $s^{\pm\alpha}$) based on the analysis field under study (time or frequency-domain), the stability analysis criterions, the learning and the implementation processes analyze the tradeoff between the degree of complexity, accuracy, stability and the ability of real-time implementation of the closed loop control system (Soukkou, Boukabou, & Leulmi, 2016).

The stability analysis of the nonlinear FoCS as an open problem. A review of stability analysis methods used in field of Fractional-order systems is given in Soukkou, Boukabou, & Leulmi (2016) and Soukkou, & Leulmi (2017).

However, designing high-performance and cost-effective controllers (accuracy, reduced control cost, easy to implement and satisfying stability conditions) for nonlinear dynamical systems, especially FoCS, is relatively a difficult task. There are several open problems in fractional modeling and frac-

Figure 1. Search area of fractional-order systems field

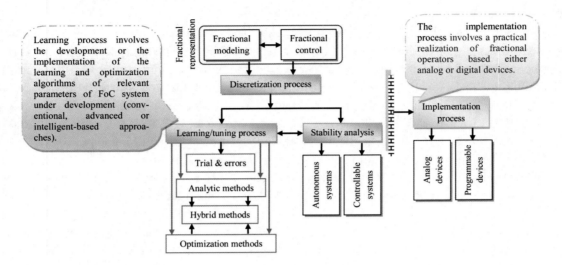

tional control areas. The elaboration of control law, the discretization process of fractional operators, the stability analysis of the closed-loop system and the practical implementation are the most fundamental and important issues.

Taking into consideration the previous discussion, we employ in this chapter the FoC approach to elaborate a generalized form of PD-based control law assigned to control and to synchronize a large class of FoCS. The design and optimization of the proposed fractional-order PD-based feedback controller (Fo-PDF) are derived and based on Lyapunov stabilization arguments and multiobjective genetic learning. Finally, numerical simulations are given to show the effectiveness of the proposed scheme by taking a class of fractional-order hyperchaotic systems as illustrative examples.

The rest of this chapter is organized as follows. In Section 2, basic definitions and some preliminaries of fractional calculus and fractional-order chaotic systems are introduced. Based on fractional-order approach, a new alternative of fractional model to control and to synchronize a large class of FoCS is proposed in Section 3. The design and optimization tools of the proposed scheme are also discussed. Some numerical simulations presented to confirm the validity of the analytical results are given in Section 4. Finally, conclusion is drawn in Section 5.

2. BRIEF INTRODUCTION TO FRACTIONAL-ORDER CALCULUS AND SYSTEMS

In this section, we will recall some basic Definitions, Remarks and Lemmas of the fractional-order calculus and FoCS systems (Petráš, 2011; Kilbas, Srivastava, & Trujillo, 2006).

2.1. Mathematics Background

Fractional calculus is a generalization of integration and differentiation to non-integer order fundamental operator $_cD_t^\alpha$. The generalized differ-integrator may be put forward as (Kilbas, Srivastava, & Trujillo, 2006) ${}_{c}D_t^{\alpha} f(t) = {}_{c}I_t^{-\alpha} f(t) = D_{t-c}^{\alpha} f(t) = d^{\alpha} f(t) \big/ \big[d(t-c) \big]^{\alpha}$, where $\alpha \in \mathbb{R}^+$ is the constant-order of operation, t is the limits and c is the initial time instance, often assumed to be zero.

Definition 1: Let us consider the following representation of large class of a continuous, nonlinear, complex and fractional-order chaotic dynamical systems

$$\begin{cases} {}_{0}D_t^{q} x(t) = F\big(x(t), t\big), & q \in \mathbb{R}^+, \quad t > 0 \\ x(t)\big|_{t=0} = x_0, \end{cases} \tag{1}$$

where $x(t) \in \mathbb{R}^n$ are the vector state, n is called the inner dimension of system, $q = \big[q_1, \cdots, q_n \big]^T$ are the differentiation vector order and $F\big(x(t), t\big) \mapsto [0, \infty) \times \mathbb{R} \to \mathbb{R}$ is the nonlinear vector field satisfies the Lipschitz condition with respect to $x(t)$, and $x_0 \in \mathbb{R}$ is the initial condition. If $\big(q_1 = q_2 = \cdots = q_n = \tilde{q}\big) \in \mathbb{R}$, we call Equation (1) the commensurate fractional-order dynamical system. Otherwise, we call it incommensurate one. Moreover, the effective dimension of the system (1) is measured by the sum of all involved derivatives $\sum_{i=1}^{n} q_i$.

Lemma 1: For the fractional-order uncontrolled nonlinear system (1), the function $F\big(x(t), t\big)$ satisfies the Lipschitz condition with respect to $x(t)$, *i.e.*,

$$\Big\| F\big(x_1(t), t\big) - F\big(x_2(t), t\big) \Big\| \leq \ell \big\| x_1(t) - x_2(t) \big\| \tag{2}$$

where $\| \bullet \|$ is the 1-norm and ℓ is a positive constant. we assume that $F\big(x(t), t\big)$ satisfies $F\big(x(t), t\big) = 0$ at $x(0) = 0$. Then,

$$\Big\| F\big(x(t), t\big) \Big\| \leq \ell \big\| x(t) \big\| \leq M < \infty \text{ for all } t \in \mathbb{R}. \tag{3}$$

That is,

$$\Big\| {}_{0}D_t^{q} x_1(t) \Big\| \leq \ell \big\| x_1(t) \big\| \tag{4}$$

Then, there exists a unique function $x(t) \in \mathbb{R}$ satisfying the system (1).

Several alternative definitions of the fractional-order integrals and derivatives exist. The three most common known definitions of fractional operators are Grünwald-Letnikov definition, Riemann–Liouville definition and Caputo definition.

Definition 2: The Riemann–Liouville (RL) fractional derivative of order $q > 0$ of a function $x(t)$ defined on the interval $[a,\ b]$ is given by

$$
{}^{RL}_{\ a}D^q_t x(t) = \frac{1}{\Gamma(n-a)} \left(\frac{d}{dt} \right)^n \int_a^t (t-\tau)^{n-q-1} \cdot x(\tau) d\tau \tag{5}
$$

where n is the first integer larger than q, *i.e*, $0 < (n-1) < q < n$ and $\Gamma(\bullet)$ is the Euler Gamma function.

Definition 3: The Caputo (C) fractional derivative of order $q > 0$ of a function $x(t)$ defined on the interval $[a,\ b]$ is given by

$$
{}^{C}_{a}D^q_t x(t) = \frac{1}{\Gamma(n-a)} \int_a^t (t-\tau)^{n-q-1} \cdot x(\tau) d\tau \tag{6}
$$

where n is the first integer larger than q.

Definition 4: The Grünwald-Letnikov (GL) approach is the most suitable method for the realization of discrete-control algorithms. The GL fractional derivative of order $q > 0$ of a function $x(t)$ is given by

$$
{}^{GL}_{\ a}D^q_t x(t) = \lim_{h \to 0} h^{-q} \cdot \sum_{i=0}^{N} c_i^q \cdot x(t - i \cdot h) \tag{7}
$$

where $N = \lfloor (t-a)/h \rfloor$ is the upper limit of the computational universe, $\lfloor \bullet \rfloor$ means the integer part and h is the step-time increment. $c_{i \geq 0}^q$ represents the binomial coefficients calculated according to the relation

$$
c_{i \geq 0}^q = (-1)^i \cdot \binom{q}{i} = \begin{cases} 1, & i = 0 \\ \left(1 - \frac{1+q}{i} \right) \cdot c_{i-1}^q, & \forall i > 0 \end{cases} \tag{8}
$$

As shown by GL definition, the fractional-order derivatives are global operators having a memory of all past events. This property is used to model hereditary and memory effects in most materials and systems (Barbosa, Machado, & Jesus, 2010).

Recently, many researchers have made large number of contributions for numerical solutions of fractional-order differential equations (Zhu, Zhou, & Zhang, 2009; Diethelm, Ford, Freed, 2002; Demirci, & Ozalp, 2012). Zhu et al. (2009) presented an iterative algorithm for numerical simulations of FoCS. Diethelm et al. (2002) proposed a predictor-corrector approach. The authors in Demirci, &

Ozalp (2012) proposed a method for solving differential equations of fractional-order systems. One of the main results is as follows.

Lemma 2 (Demirci, & Ozalp, 2012): Consider the fractional-order system (1). Let

$$g\big(\nu, x_*(\nu)\big) = F\left[x\left[t - \big(t^q - \nu\Gamma(q+1)\big)^{1/q}\right], \ t - \big(t^q - \nu\Gamma(q+1)\big)^{1/q}\right] \tag{9}$$

and assume that the conditions of Lemma 1 hold. Then, the solution $x(t)$ for the fractional-order system (1) is given by

$$x(t) = x_*\big(t^q/\Gamma(q+1)\big) \tag{10}$$

where $x_*(\nu)$ is the solution of the integer-order differential equation

$$\begin{cases} \dfrac{dx_*(\nu)}{d\nu} = g\big(\nu, x_*(\nu)\big), \\ x_*(0) = x_0 \end{cases} \tag{11}$$

Some examples are also given in Demirci, & Ozalp (2012) to show that this technique works properly.

Definition 5 (Zhu, Zhou, & Zhang, 2009): The GL definition (7) is used to numerically simulate the controlled FoCS with left side derivative in the following form $D_t^q x(t) = \tilde{F}\big(x(t)\big) + B \cdot u(t)$ and can be expressed for discrete-time $\big(t_k = k \cdot h \mapsto k\big)$ as follows:

$$x(k) = \hbar^q \cdot \tilde{F}\big(x(k)\big) - \sum_{i=1}^{n} \tilde{C}_i \cdot x(k-i) + \hbar q \cdot B \cdot u(k),$$

where $\tilde{C}_i = \text{diag}\big(c_j^{q_1}, \ \cdots, \ c_j^{q_n}\big)$ is a diagonal binomial matrix, $c_j^{q_i}$ is the j-th coefficient computed from Equation (5) and $\hbar q = \text{diag}\big(h^{q_1}, \ \cdots, \ h^{q_n}\big)$ is a diagonal sampling time matrix. Equation (8) is an implicit nonlinear algebraic equation with respect to $x(k) = \big(x_1(k) \quad x_2(k) \quad \cdots\big)^T$. Algorithm 1 shows the main steps to simulate the behavior of the FoCS with initial conditions $x(0) = x_0$.

Definition 6 (Scherer, Kalla, Tang, & Huang, 2011; Podlubny, 1998): A direct definition of the fractional derivative $D_t^q x(t)$ is based on finite difference of an equidistant grid in $[0, \ 1]$. Assume that the function $x(\tau)$ satisfies some smoothness conditions in every finite interval $[0, \ t], \ t \leq T$. Choosing the grid

Algorithm 1. Different steps to simulate behavior of the controlled FoCS

```
1. Begin
2. Set x₁[0], x₂[0], ⋯ ; // Initial conditions of systems
3. k = 0 ;
4. while (k ≤ Max-Sampling Time) do //Max-Sampling Time is the stopping crite-
ria or the evolution time of the FoCS to be controlled.
```
$\quad$ 4.1. $u[k] = \text{Control\_law}\left(x_1[k], x_2[k], x_3[k], \cdots, x_n[k]\right)$; // *Update the controller*

outputs

$\quad$ 4.2. $\Phi\left(x[k+1], x[k]\right) = \begin{pmatrix} \tilde{F}_1\left(x_1(k), x_2[k], x_3[k], \cdots, x_n[k]\right) \\ \tilde{F}_2\left(x_1[k+1], x_2[k], x_3[k], \cdots\cdots, x_n[k]\right) \\ \tilde{F}_3\left(x_1[k+1], x_2[k+1], x_3[k], \cdots\cdots\cdots, x_n[k]\right) \\ \cdots \\ \tilde{F}_n\left(x_1[k+1], x_2[k+1], x_3[k+1], \cdots, x_{n-1}[k+1], x_n[k]\right) \end{pmatrix}$;

$\quad$ 4.3. $x[k+1] = \hbar^q \cdot \Phi\left(x[k+1], x[k+1]\right) - \sum_{i=1}^{n} \tilde{C}_i \cdot x[k+1-i] + \hbar^q \cdot B \cdot u[k]$;

$\quad$ 4.4. $k := k+1$;

5. end.

$$\left(0 = \tau_0\right) < \tau_1 < \cdots < \left(\tau_{n+1} = t = (n+1) \cdot h\right), \ \left(\tau_{n+1} - \tau_n = h\right) \tag{12}$$

and using the notation of finite differences

$$\frac{1}{h^q} \cdot \Delta_h^q x(t) = \frac{1}{h^q} \cdot \left(x(\tau_{n+1}) - \sum_{v=1}^{n+1} c_v^q \cdot x(\tau_{n+1-v})\right) \tag{13}$$

where $c_v^q = (-1)^{v-1} \begin{pmatrix} q \\ v \end{pmatrix}$. The GL definition becomes

$$D_R^q x(t) = \lim_{h \to 0} \frac{1}{h^q} \cdot \Delta_h^q x(t) \tag{14}$$

Lemma 3 (Scherer et al., 2011; Podlubny, 1998): (Order of approximation). Let the function $x(\tau)$ be smooth in $[0, \ T]$. Then, the GL approximation satisfies for each $0 < t < T$ and a series of step sizes h with $t/h \in \mathbb{N}$ and $t = (n+1) \cdot h$ the following formula

$$D_R^q x(t) = \frac{1}{h^q} \cdot \Delta_h^q x(t) + o(h), \quad (h \mapsto 0) \tag{15}$$

where $o(h)$ is the truncated error. In the case of q a positive integer, the well known finite backward differences are given. If $q \in \mathbb{N}^+$, the well known finite backward differences are given. If $q = 1$, then the first-order finite difference $\left(x(\tau_{n+1}) - x(\tau_n)\right)/h$ follows. If $q = 2$, then the second-order finite difference $\left(x(\tau_{n+1}) - 2 \cdot x(\tau_n) + x(\tau_{n-1})\right)/h^2$, and so on.

3. FRACTIONAL-ORDER PD-BASED FEEDBACK CONTROL

In this section, we mainly consider the fractional-order PD-based feedback approach to stabilize and to synchronize a large class of FoCS (identical or non identical, commensurate or incommensurate). Most of the works in the field of stabilization and synchronization processes of FoCS are based on linearizing the nonlinear model of FoCS (9) around equilibrium points and applying the methods of linear systems.

Definition 7: The equilibrium points $x_e = \left(x_e^1, \ldots, x_e^n\right)^T$ of the autonomous system (1) are calculated via solving $F\left(x_e(t), t\right) = 0$, which is assumed to be stable or unstable. Then, we have the following Lemma for the stability of these equilibrium points.

Definition 8: Consider the generalized form of FoCS (1), the linearized form around the equilibrium points is given by

$$\begin{cases} D_t^q x(t) = A_e \cdot \left(x(t) - x_e\right) + F\left(x_e, t\right) \\ D_t^q x_e = F\left(x_e, t\right) \end{cases} \tag{16}$$

where x_e is the equilibrium point (stable or unstable $\left(x_e = x^*\right)$) or any trajectory of the uncontrolled system $\left(x_e \mapsto x_e(t)\right)$ and $A_e = \partial F(x,t)/\partial x(t)\big|_{x=x_e} = \left(a_{ij}^*\right) \in \mathbb{R}^{n \times n}$ is the Jacobian matrix of the free-running system (1) evaluated at x_e. Let $\tilde{x}(t) = x(t) - x_e$, the transformed coordinate vector in which the equilibrium point is at the origin, Equation (16) can be rewritten in the following form

$$D_t^q \tilde{x}(t) = A_e \cdot \tilde{x}(t) \tag{17}$$

Lemma 4 (Petráš, 2011): All the equilibrium points x_e of the autonomous system (1) are stable if all the eigenvalues of the Jacobian matrix A_e, evaluated at the equilibrium points x_e, satisfy the condition $\left|\arg\left(\text{eig}\left(A_e\right)\right)\right| > 0.5 \cdot q \cdot \pi$, where $q = \max\left(q_i\right)$, $\left(i = 1, 2, \ldots, n\right)$ and $\arg\left(\text{eig}\left(A_e\right)\right)$ denotes the argument of the eigenvalue of the matrix A_e.

The objective is to design a stabilizing model based on the generalized PD-based approach for system (17) that ensures Lyapunov stability of the closed-loop system. Next, fractional-order PD-based feedback control approach is briefly reviewed.

Definition 9: The purpose of a generalized PD-based control algorithm is to assure that the system (1) asymptotically converges towards the equilibrium point by adding an external control signal to the original uncontrolled system. Introducing the control input $u(t) \in \mathbb{R}^n$ into (17), we get

$$D_t^q \tilde{x}(t) = A_e \cdot \tilde{x}(t) + B \cdot u(t) \tag{18}$$

where $B = \mathrm{diag}(b_1, \cdots, b_n) \in \mathbb{R}^{n \times n}$ is a switch diagonal matrix ($b_{i=1 \sim n} = \{0,1\}$) used to designate the elementary control law to be applied. Fractional-order PD-based control with order q of a continuous-time FoCS (17) is determined as

$$u(t) = \tilde{K}_P \cdot \tilde{e}(t) + \tilde{K}_D \cdot D_t^q \tilde{e}(t) \tag{19}$$

where $\tilde{e}(t) = \tilde{x}(t) - \tilde{x}_e(t)$ is the error signal,

$$\tilde{K}_P = \mathrm{diag}(\tilde{k}_{p1}, \cdots, \tilde{k}_{pn}) \in \mathbb{R}^{n \times n}$$

and

$$\tilde{K}_D = \mathrm{diag}(\tilde{k}_{d1}, \cdots, \tilde{k}_{dn}) \in \mathbb{R}^{n \times n}$$

are the proportional state feedback and the fractional derivative gain matrices to be designed, respectively. Figure 2 shows the block diagram of the generalized PD-based feedback control. Usually, the elementary feedback gains are uniformly bounded.

Figure 2. Block diagram of the fractional-order PD-based feedback control

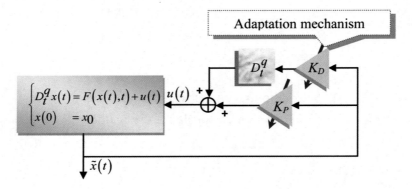

3.1 Fo-PDF Stabilization of FoCS

In this section, the key of PD-based feedback control is how to design the control law, which is able to stabilize the states of the chaotic trajectory on the equilibrium point.

Definition 10: Let $\tilde{F}\left(\tilde{x}\left(t\right)\right) \mapsto \tilde{F}\left(t\right) = \left(\tilde{F}_1\left(t\right), \; \cdots, \; \tilde{F}_n\left(t\right)\right)^T$ be the fractional-order PD-based vector component of the control force in the new coordinates, *i.e.*,

$$\tilde{F}\left(t\right) = \tilde{\Phi}_c \cdot \tilde{x}\left(t\right) \tag{20}$$

where $\tilde{\Phi}_c = -B \cdot \left(\tilde{K}_P + \tilde{K}_D \cdot A_e\right)$. So, the linearized feedback controlled system (17) will be described by

$$D_t^q \tilde{x}\left(t\right) = \tilde{\mathfrak{A}} \cdot \tilde{x}\left(t\right) \tag{21}$$

where $\tilde{\mathfrak{A}} = \left(A_e + \tilde{\Phi}_c\right)$. Based on Lemma 2, the solution of FoCS (21) is given by

$$\tilde{x}\left(t\right) = \tilde{x}_*\left(t^q / \Gamma\left(q + 1\right)\right) \tag{22}$$

where $\tilde{x}_*\left(\nu\right)$ is the solution of the integer-order differential equation

$$\begin{cases} \dfrac{d\tilde{x}_*\left(\nu\right)}{d\nu} = \tilde{\mathfrak{A}} \cdot \tilde{x}\left(\nu\right), \\ \tilde{x}_*\left(0\right) = \tilde{x}_0 \end{cases} \tag{23}$$

with

$$\tilde{x}_*\left(\nu\right) = \tilde{x}\left(t - \left(t^q - \nu\Gamma\left(q + 1\right)\right)^{1/q}\right) \tag{24}$$

Remark 1: The necessary and sufficient condition for the existence of the developed control law is

$$\det\left(\tilde{K}_P + \tilde{K}_D \cdot A_e\right) \neq 0 \tag{25}$$

Note that the origin is the equilibrium point of system (21), and our aim is to stabilize the system (21) at the equilibrium point $x_e = 0$, by designing the control gain matrices $\tilde{K}_P$ and $\tilde{K}_D$. Sufficient conditions derived and based on Lyapunov stabilization arguments are used to study the stability of the proposed scheme.

Theorem 1: *Consider the FoCS (21) of order* q, $0 < q < 1$. *Assume that the solution of system (21) is given by (22). The equilibrium point* $x_e = 0$ *is globally and exponentially stable if and only if there exist a positive definite matrices P and* $\tilde{\mathbb{Q}}$ *and a diagonal matrices* $\tilde{K}_P$ *and* $\tilde{K}_D$, *such that*

$$\lambda_{\min}\left(\tilde{\mathbb{Q}}\right)/\lambda_{\max}\left(P\right) > 0 \tag{26}$$

where $\lambda_{\min}\left(\tilde{\mathbb{Q}}\right)$ *and* $\lambda_{\max}\left(P\right)$ *to denote the minimum and maximum eigenvalues of a positive definite matrices* $\tilde{\mathbb{Q}}$ *and P, respectively.*

$$\tilde{\mathbb{Q}} = \left(\tilde{A}^T \cdot P + P \cdot \tilde{A}\right), \ \tilde{A} = \frac{1}{h} \cdot \left(\phi_q + H \cdot \tilde{\mathfrak{A}} - I\right),$$

$$\tilde{\mathfrak{A}} = A_e - B \cdot \left(\tilde{K}_P + \tilde{K}_D \cdot A_e\right), \ \phi_q = -\mathrm{diag}\left(q_1, \ \cdots, q_n\right)$$

and $H = \mathrm{diag}\left(h^{q_1}, \ \cdots, \ h^{q_n}\right)$.

Proof: The conditions of stability and stabilization of linearized FoCS are generally based on Lyapunov functions.

The most common choice consists in selecting a Lyapunov function candidate $V\left(x\left(t\right),t\right) : \left[t_0,\infty\right) \times \mathbb{R}^n \to \mathbb{R}^n$ which must satisfy the conditions

$$\begin{cases} V\left(x\left(t\right),t\right) > 0, & \forall \ x\left(t\right) \neq 0 \\ V\left(x\left(t\right),t_0\right) = 0, & \forall \ x\left(t\right) = 0 \\ V\left(x\left(t\right),t\right) \to \infty, & \left\|x\left(t\right)\right\|_i \to \infty, \ i = 1, 2, \infty \end{cases} . \tag{27}$$

Obviously, $V\left(x\left(t\right),t\right)$ is positive under any circumstances. The next Lemma represent the main tool of the proof of Theorem 1.

Lemma 5 (Haddad, & Chellaboina, 2007): Under the conditions (27), $x_e = 0$ is an equilibrium point, globally and exponentially stable for the closed-loop system if

$$\alpha\left(\left\|x\left(t\right)\right\|^b\right) \leq V\left(x\left(t\right),t\right) \leq \beta\left(\left\|x\left(t\right)\right\|^b\right) \tag{28}$$

$$D_t^+ V\left(x\left(t\right),t\right) \leq -\gamma\left(\left\|x\left(t\right)\right\|^2\right) \tag{29}$$

where α, β and γ are positive real constants. $D_t^+ V\left(x\left(t\right), t\right)$ represents the derivative with respect to time of the Lyapunov function along the trajectory of the variable $\tilde{x}\left(t\right)$.

Construct a positive definite, radially unbounded vector Lyapunov function for system (21) as

$$V\left(\tilde{x}_*\left(v\right)\right) = \tilde{x}_*^T\left(v\right) \cdot P \cdot \tilde{x}_*\left(v\right) \tag{30}$$

where P is a positive definite constant matrix. Starting from any initial states, it can be proved that $D_+ V\left(\tilde{x}_*\left(v\right)\right) = dV\left(\tilde{x}_*\left(v\right)\right)/d\tilde{x}_*\left(v\right)$ is always negative, $V\left(\tilde{x}_*\left(v\right)\right)$ in (30) decreases and $\tilde{x}_*\left(v\right)$ reaches the origin.

The derivative of V belongs to the variable $\tilde{x}_*\left(v\right)$ is given by

$$D_+ V\left(\tilde{x}_*\left(t\right)\right) = \dot{\tilde{x}}_*\left(t\right)^T \cdot P \cdot \tilde{x}_*\left(t\right) + \tilde{x}_*\left(t\right)^T \cdot P \cdot \dot{\tilde{x}}_*\left(t\right) \tag{31}$$

Along the solution of system (21), evaluating the Dini derivative of $\tilde{x}\left(t\right)$ yields

$$\dot{\tilde{x}}_*\left(v\right) = D_+ \tilde{x}_*\left(v\right) \cong \lim_{h \to 0^+} \frac{\tilde{x}_*\left(v+h\right) - \tilde{x}_*\left(v\right)}{h} \tag{32}$$

By using the Definition 5 and Lemma 3, the derivative operator can be approached by

$$^{\mathrm{GL}}D_+^q \tilde{x}_*\left(v\right) \cong h^{-q} \cdot \left(\tilde{x}_*\left(v+h\right) - c_1^q \cdot \tilde{x}_*\left(v\right)\right) + o\left(h\right) = \tilde{\mathfrak{A}} \cdot \tilde{x}_*\left(v\right) \tag{33}$$

where $o\left(h\right)$ is the truncated error ($o\left(h\right) \mapsto 0$). Thus, we obtain

$$\tilde{x}_*\left(v+h\right) \cong \left(\phi_q + H \cdot \tilde{\mathfrak{A}}\right) \cdot \tilde{x}_*\left(v\right) \tag{34}$$

where

$$H = \mathrm{diag}\left(h^{-q_1}, \cdots, h^{-q_n}\right), \tilde{C}_i = \mathrm{diag}\left(c_i^{q_1}, \cdots, c_i^{q_n}\right), c_0^q = \mathrm{I}^{n \times n},$$

and $c_1^q = \phi_q = -\mathrm{diag}\left(q_1, \cdots, q_n\right)$. Equation (32) becomes

$$\dot{\tilde{x}}_*\left(v\right) \cong \lim_{h \to 0^+} \frac{\left(\phi_q + H \cdot \tilde{\mathfrak{A}} - \mathrm{I}\right)}{h} \cdot \tilde{x}_*\left(v\right) \tag{35}$$

Substituting (35) into (31) gives

$$\dot{V}\left(\tilde{x}_*\left(v\right)\right) = -\tilde{x}_*^T\left(v\right)\cdot\tilde{\mathbb{Q}}\cdot\tilde{x}_*\left(v\right) \tag{36}$$

where $\tilde{\mathbb{Q}} = \left(\tilde{A}^T\cdot P + P\cdot\tilde{A}\right)$ and $\tilde{A} = \dfrac{1}{h}\cdot\left(\phi_q + H\cdot\tilde{\mathfrak{A}} - I\right)$. Let use $\lambda_{\min}\left(\cdot\right)$ and $\lambda_{\max}\left(\cdot\right)$ to denote the minimum and maximum eigenvalues of a positive definite matrix. From (30), we have

$$\lambda_{\min}\left(P\right)\cdot\left\|\tilde{x}_*\left(v\right)\right\|^2 \leq V\left(\tilde{x}_*\left(v\right)\right) \leq \lambda_{\max}\left(P\right)\cdot\left\|\tilde{x}_*\left(v\right)\right\|^2 \tag{37}$$

From (36) and (37), we obtain

$$\begin{aligned}\dot{V}\left(\tilde{x}_*\left(v\right)\right) &\leq \lambda_{\min}\left(\tilde{\mathbb{Q}}\right)\cdot\left\|\tilde{x}_*\left(v\right)\right\|^2 \\ &\leq -\left[\lambda_{\min}\left(\tilde{\mathbb{Q}}\right)/\lambda_{\max}\left(P\right)\right]\cdot\left\|\tilde{x}_*\left(v\right)\right\|^2 \\ &< 0 \end{aligned} \tag{38}$$

Which implies that

$$\lambda_{\min}\left(\tilde{\mathbb{Q}}\right)/\lambda_{\max}\left(P\right) > 0 \tag{39}$$

Now, we apply Lemma 5 with (37) and (38) to conclude that the equilibrium point is globally and exponentially stable. Furthermore, we can identify $\alpha = \lambda_{\min}\left(P\right)$, $\beta = \lambda_{\max}\left(P\right)$, $\gamma = \lambda_{\min}\left(\tilde{\mathbb{Q}}\right)$ and $b = 2$. Following the proof of Lemma 5 (Haddad, & Chellaboina, 2007), we have

$$\left\|\tilde{x}_*\left(v\right)\right\| \leq a\cdot\left\|\tilde{x}_*\left(0\right)\right\|\cdot e^{-\lambda\cdot t} \tag{40}$$

where $a = \sqrt{\lambda_{\max}\left(P\right)/\lambda_{\min}\left(P\right)}$ and $-\lambda = \lambda_{\min}\left(\tilde{\mathbb{Q}}\right)/\lambda_{\max}\left(P\right)$. For the necessary part, we have

$$\left\|\tilde{x}_*\left(v\right)\right\| \leq a\cdot\left\|\tilde{x}_*\left(0\right)\right\|\cdot e^{-\lambda\cdot t} \tag{41}$$

For some positive real constant a and λ, which implies that $\lim_{t\to\infty}\tilde{x}_*\left(v\right) = 0$. Since

$$\left\|\tilde{x}\left(t\right)\right\| = \exp\left(\tilde{\mathfrak{A}}\cdot t\right)\cdot\tilde{x}\left(0\right) \tag{42}$$

We can conclude that $\lim_{t\to\infty}\exp\left(\tilde{\mathfrak{A}}\cdot t\right) = 0$. In such case, for a positive definite matrix $\tilde{\mathbb{Q}}$, we can write

$$\int_0^\infty d\left[\exp\left(\tilde{\mathfrak{A}}^T \cdot t\right) \cdot \tilde{\mathbb{Q}} \cdot \exp\left(\tilde{\mathfrak{A}} \cdot t\right)\right] = -\tilde{\mathbb{Q}} \qquad (43)$$

For the left-hand side, we can obtain

$$\int_0^\infty d\left[\exp\left(\tilde{\mathfrak{A}}^T \cdot t\right) \cdot \tilde{\mathbb{Q}} \cdot \exp\left(\tilde{\mathfrak{A}} \cdot t\right)\right] =$$

$$\tilde{\mathfrak{A}}^T \cdot \int_0^\infty \exp\left(\tilde{\mathfrak{A}}^T \cdot t\right) \cdot \tilde{\mathbb{Q}} \cdot \exp\left(\tilde{\mathfrak{A}} \cdot t\right) \cdot t + \int_0^\infty \exp\left(\tilde{\mathfrak{A}}^T \cdot t\right) \cdot \tilde{\mathbb{Q}} \cdot \exp\left(\tilde{\mathfrak{A}} \cdot t\right) \cdot t \cdot \tilde{\mathfrak{A}} \qquad (44)$$

Let

$$P = \int_0^\infty \exp\left(\tilde{\mathfrak{A}}^T \cdot t\right) \cdot \tilde{\mathbb{Q}} \cdot \exp\left(\tilde{\mathfrak{A}} \cdot t\right) \cdot t \qquad (45)$$

and if we can show that P is positive definite, then we obtain $\tilde{\mathbb{Q}} = \left(\tilde{A}^T \cdot P + P \cdot \tilde{A}\right)$, and hence complete the proof. Indeed, for any $z \in \mathbb{R}^n \neq 0$, we have

$$z^T \cdot P \cdot z = \int_0^\infty z^T \cdot \exp\left(\tilde{\mathfrak{A}}^T \cdot t\right) \cdot \tilde{\mathbb{Q}} \cdot \exp\left(\tilde{\mathfrak{A}} \cdot t\right) \cdot zdt \qquad (46)$$

Since $\tilde{\mathbb{Q}}$ is positive definite, and $\exp\left(\tilde{\mathfrak{A}} \cdot t\right)$ is non-singular for any t, we have $z^T \cdot P \cdot z > 0$, and therefor P is positive definite.

3.2 Fo-PDF Synchronization of Two Identical FoCS

Consider a fractional-order drive (D) and response (R) systems of order $q \in [0,1]$, described by

$$\text{D:} \quad \begin{cases} D_t^q x\left(t\right) = f\left(x\left(t\right)\right) \\ x\left(0\right) \quad = x_0 \end{cases} \qquad (47)$$

$$\text{R:} \quad \begin{cases} D_t^q y\left(t\right) = g\left(y\left(t\right)\right) + \Theta\left(x,y\right) \\ y\left(0\right) \quad = y_0 \end{cases} \qquad (48)$$

where $x(t) \in \mathbb{R}^n$ and denotes the system's *n*-dimensional state vector and $f(x(t)): \mathbb{R}^n \mapsto \mathbb{R}^n$ is the nonlinear function of the system. $y(t)$ and $g(y(t))$ imply the same roles as $x(t)$ and $f(x(t))$ in the response system, respectively. $\Theta(\bullet) \in \mathbb{R}^n$ is the controller to be designed.

If there exists a suitable controller $\Theta(\bullet)$ such that

$$\lim_{t \to \infty} \left\| e(t) \right\| = \lim_{t \to \infty} \left\| y(t) - x(t) \right\| \mapsto 0 \tag{49}$$

then, the chaotic synchronization between the drive system (47) and the response system (48) belongs to the problem of tracking control, *i.e.*, the output signal $y(t)$ of system (48) follows the reference signal $x(t)$ ultimately.

Definition 11: Applying the same procedure of linearization used in the previous section, the linearized form of the drive system is given by

$$D_t^q \tilde{x}(t) = A_x^* \cdot \tilde{x}(t) \tag{50}$$

where $\tilde{x}(t) = x(t) - x_e$ and $A_x^* = \partial f(x(t)) / \partial x(t) \big|_{x=x_e}$. So, the linearized controlled response system will be described by

$$D_t^q \tilde{y}(t) = A_y^* \cdot \tilde{y}(t) + \Theta(\tilde{x}, \tilde{y}) \tag{51}$$

where $\tilde{y}(t) = y(t) - y_e$ and $A_y^* = \partial g(y(t)) / \partial y(t) \big|_{y=y_e}$.

Define the synchronization error system $\tilde{e}(t) = \tilde{y}(t) - \tilde{x}(t)$. Then, subtracting system (51) from system (50), and if the chaotic drive and response systems are identical, *i.e.*, $A_y^* = A_x^*$, then the synchronization error dynamics for two identical FoCS is designed as

$$D_t^q \tilde{e}(t) = A_x^* \cdot \tilde{e}(t) + \Theta(\tilde{x}, \tilde{y}) \tag{52}$$

Definition 12: By applying the linear control law similar to the previous section (19), the error dynamics (52) becomes

$$D_t^q \tilde{e}(t) = \tilde{\mathfrak{A}}_e \cdot \tilde{e}(t) \tag{53}$$

where $\tilde{\mathfrak{A}}_e = \left(I - B \cdot \tilde{K}_D \right)^{-1} \cdot \left(A_x^* + B \cdot \tilde{K}_P \right)$. The design procedure consists of choosing $\tilde{K}_P$ and $\tilde{K}_D$ to stabilize the error dynamics (53) at the origin point. Based on Lemma 2, the solution of FoCS (53) is given by

$$\tilde{e}\left(t\right) = \tilde{e}_{*}\left(t^{q}\big/\Gamma\left(q+1\right)\right) \tag{54}$$

where $\tilde{e}_{*}\left(\nu\right)$ is the solution of the integer-order differential equation.

$$\frac{d\tilde{e}_{*}\left(\nu\right)}{d\nu} = \tilde{\mathfrak{A}}_{e} \cdot \tilde{e}\left(\nu\right), \quad \tilde{e}_{*}\left(0\right) = \tilde{e}_{0} \tag{55}$$

With

$$\tilde{e}_{*}\left(\nu\right) = \tilde{e}\left[t - \left(t^{q} - \nu\Gamma\left(q+1\right)\right)^{1/q}\right] \tag{56}$$

Our goal is to design an appropriate feedback controller, such that the trajectory of the response system with initial condition $y\left(0\right)$ asymptotically approaches the trajectory of the drive system with initial condition $x\left(0\right)$ and, finally, implement synchronization condition (49).

Theorem 2: *Given the fractional-order drive system (50) and the fractional-order response system (51). Assume that the solution of system (53) is given by (54), there exists a Fo-PDF control law such that the equilibrium point of (53) is globally and exponentially stable, i.e., the synchronization between the response system and the drive system can be achieved. If and only if there exist a positive definite matrices P and $\tilde{\mathbb{Q}}_{s}$ and diagonal matrices $\tilde{K}_{P}$ and $\tilde{K}_{D}$, such that*

$$\lambda_{\min}\left(\tilde{\mathbb{Q}}_{s}\right)\big/\lambda_{\max}\left(P\right) > 0 \tag{57}$$

where

$$-\tilde{\mathbb{Q}}_{s} = \tilde{A}_{s}^{T} \cdot P + P \cdot \tilde{A}_{s},$$

$$\tilde{A}_{s} = \frac{1}{h} \cdot \left(\phi_{q} + H \cdot \tilde{\mathfrak{A}}_{e} - I\right)$$

and $\tilde{\mathfrak{A}}_{e} = \left(I - B \cdot \tilde{K}_{D}\right)^{-1} \cdot \left(A_{x}^{*} + B \cdot \tilde{K}_{P}\right)$, *then the controlled system is globally and exponentially stable, i.e., the equilibrium point will be globally and exponentially stabilized.*

Proof: The proof is similar to that developed in previous section, but the state vector $-\tilde{x}\left(t\right)$ is replaced by the error vector $\tilde{e}\left(t\right)$.

3.3 Multiobjective Optimization of the Proposed Fo-PDF Scheme

The design process consists to find the optimal knowledge base of the Fo-PDF scheme, while satisfying the objectives and constraints specified by the designer. In this work, genetic algorithms have been proposed as a learning method that allows automatic generation of optimal parameters of the proposed Fo-PDF control scheme, which can be represented as an extremum problem of optimization index. So, the parameters set to be optimized may be such that

$$\theta = \left\{ \left[\left(\tilde{K}_P, \tilde{K}_D \right) \right]_{\in \mathbb{R}^{n \times n}}, \left(\underset{\in \mathbb{R}^{n \times n}}{P} \right), \left(\underset{\in \{0,1\}}{B} \right) \right\} \tag{58}$$

Remark 2: To simplify the optimization task, the elementary control laws to be applied must be defined beforehand. In addition, the matrix P should be equal to the weighted identity matrix, *i.e.*, $P = q.\mathrm{I}$, where $q = \sum_{i=1}^{n} q_i$ is the effective dimension of the FoCS.

Definition 13: The general design procedure consists to find the optimal knowledge base (58) that minimize the objectives J and satisfying the design constraints. The multiobjective optimization process can be pronounced as follows

$$\text{Minimize } J = \min_{\theta} \left\{ w_1 \cdot \sum_{k=0}^{N-1} \tilde{x}^T(k) \cdot P \cdot \tilde{x}(k) + w_1 \cdot \max_{k} \left(\tilde{x}^T(k) \cdot P \cdot \tilde{x}(k) \right) \right. $$
$$\left. + w_2 \cdot \sum_{k=0}^{N-1} u^T(k) \cdot Q \cdot u(k) \right\} \tag{59}$$

Subject to

$$\lambda_{\min}(\tilde{\mathbb{Q}}) / \lambda_{\max}(P) > 0$$
$$\theta_{\min} \leq \theta \leq \theta_{\max} \tag{60}$$

where $\tilde{\mathbb{Q}}$ is derived from (36), $\theta_{\min}$ and $\theta_{\max}$ are the lower and the upper bounds in the decision space for θ parameter. w_1 and w_2 are non-negative weights and $w_1 + w_2 = 1$. These weights can be either fixed or adapted dynamically during the design process. $P = \tilde{q} \cdot \mathrm{I}_{n \times n}$ and $Q = \tilde{q} \cdot \mathrm{I}_{m \times m}$, where $\tilde{q} = \sum_{i=1}^{n} q_i$ is the effective order of FoCS and N represents the running time.

In the rest of the algorithm, the constrained problem (59)-(60) can be transformed to an unconstrained optimization problem via the Quadratic Extended Interior Penalty Function (QEIPF) method described in Isermann & Münchhof (2011) to construct the objective function of the genetic algorithm. The idea consists on adding a constraint (60) to the design problem (59) that ensures Lyapunov stabilization arguments of the closed-loop system. Next, we propose a simplified form of developed control law in its incremental form.

3.4. Numerical Implementation of the Fo-PDF Control Law

In practical implementation of the Fo-PFD controller, real-time realization problems arise due to linearly growing processed samples (known as 'the growing calculation tail') and finite microprocessor memory. In order to reduce the amount of historical data and finite microprocessor memory (Podlubny, 1999), improve the accuracy of the numerical solution and derive the recursive control algorithm in its simplified well suited for practical implementation, an optimal structure and parameters of the fractional-order PD-based feedback control law is proposed.

Proposition 1: By using the Definition 4 and Lemma 3, the i-th active control law, $b_i = 1$, in its incremental form is obtained as

$$
\begin{aligned}
\tilde{F}_i\left(\tilde{e}_i\left(k\right)\right) &= \left(\tilde{k}_{pi} \cdot \tilde{e}_i\left(k\right) + \tilde{k}_{di} \cdot \Delta_k^q \tilde{e}_i\left(k\right)\right), \ i = 1 \sim n \\
&= \left(\tilde{k}_{pi} + \tilde{k}_{di} \cdot h^{-q_i}\right) \cdot \tilde{e}_i\left(k\right) + \tilde{k}_{di} \cdot h^{-q_i} \cdot c_1^{q_i} \cdot \tilde{e}_i\left(k-1\right) + \tilde{k}_{di} \cdot h^{-q_i} \cdot \sum_{l=2}^{N} c_j^{q_i} \cdot \tilde{e}_i\left(k-l\right) \\
&\cong - \odot_{1i}\left(k\right) - \sum_{l=1}^{\mathrm{nbr\_reg}_i} \left\{\sum_{j=2 \cdot l}^{2 \cdot l + 1} \tilde{K}_j \cdot \tilde{e}_i\left(k-j\right)\right\}
\end{aligned}
\tag{61}
$$

where,

$$
\odot_{1i}\left(k\right) = \tilde{K}_0 \cdot \tilde{e}_i\left(k\right) + \tilde{K}_1 \cdot \tilde{e}_i\left(k-1\right), \ i = 1 \sim n
\tag{62}
$$

is the i-th zero-order subsystem with gains $\tilde{K}_0 = \left[K_{Pi} + K_{Ii} \cdot h^{q_i}\right]$ and $\tilde{K}_1 = \left[-K_{Ii} \cdot h^{q_i} \cdot q_i\right]$, respectively. $\mathrm{nbr\_reg} \in \mathbb{N}$ is the number of regulators (subsystems) included in formulation of the Fo-PDF control law.

The elementary active control law (61) of a single state variable, $x\left(t\right)$, to be controlled is schematized by the Figure 3. Obviously, the control law (61) can be viewed as a combination of a large set of linear integer-order PD-based feedback subsystems, (Subsys_i, $\left(i = 1, 2, \ldots\right)$), temporarily shifted with moderate gains

$$
\tilde{K}_j = \left[\tilde{K}_{Ij} \cdot h^{q_i} \cdot c_j^{q_i}\right], \ \left(j = 1 \sim \mathrm{nbr\_reg}_i\right)
$$

and $c_i^{q_i}$ is the binomial coefficient computed from Equation (8).

Proposition 2: The number of PD-based feedback subsystems, $\mathrm{nbr\_reg} \in \mathbb{N}$, is the chosen function $\left\{\Psi\left(\bullet\right)\right\}$ of the desired performances, such as the accuracy (measured by the precision $\left\{\zeta_d\right\}$), the computation steps $\left\{h\right\}$ and the memory storage requirements $\left\{\mathrm{M}_s\right\}$, as

Figure 3. Equivalent model of the proposed Fo-PDF control scheme

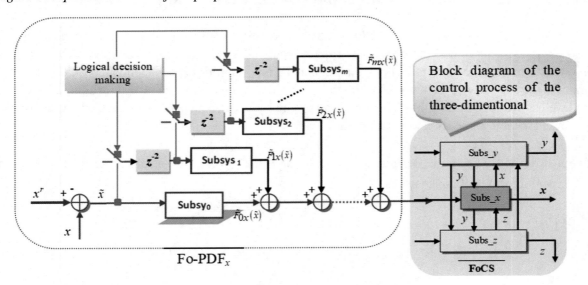

$$0 \leq \text{nbr\_reg} \leq \left[\Psi \left(h, \text{M}_s, \zeta_d \right) \right] \tag{63}$$

where $\left[\bullet \right]$ is the integer part. If $\text{nbr\_reg} = 0$, Equation (61) is similar to control by the integer-order PD-based feedback approach (zero-order regulator). To simplify the dimensioning problem encountered in the design of the control law (61), two approaches can be proposed and exploited.

- The first so-called constructive (or destructive) process. It consists in building a simplest (or complex) possible model, and then adding (or to reduce) the elementary regulators during the test phase (creation of dynamic regulators).
- The second approach, the so-called the automatic learning, is based on the application of optimization techniques, especially metaheuristics to define an optimal number of regulators included in modeling of control law (61). So, The parameters set to be optimized may be such that

$$\theta = \left\{ \left(\underset{\in \mathbb{R}^{n \times n}}{\left(\tilde{K}_P, \tilde{K}_D \right)}, \; \underset{\in \mathbb{R}^{n \times n}}{\left(P \right)}, \; \underset{\in \{0,1\}}{\left(B \right)}, \; \underset{\in \mathbb{N}}{\left(\text{nbr\_reg}_1, \; \dots, \; \text{nbr\_reg}_n \right)} \right) \right\} \tag{64}$$

The proposed optimal fractional-order PD-based feedback control law (46) in its simplified (optimal structure and parameters) is well suited for practical implementation of the control law.

4. SIMULATION RESULTS

In this section, the goal is to achieve the chaos control and synchronization between two identical fractional-order hyperchaotic systems. The fractional-order Mathieu-Van Der Pol hyperchaotic system is considered as illustrative example. Specifications of the multiobjective genetic algorithm (MGA) used here are summarized in Table 1. The knowledge base to be optimized has the dimension of four, *i.e*, $n = 4$.

4.1 Stabilization of Fractional-Order Mathieu-Van Der Pol Hyperchaotic System

The fractional-order Mathieu-Van Der Pol hyperchaotic system is defined as (Vishal, Agrawal, & Das, 2016)

$$\begin{cases} D_t^q x = y \\ D_t^q y = -\left(a + bz\right)x - \left(a + bz\right)x^3 - cy + dz \\ D_t^q z = w \\ D_t^q w = -ez + f\left(1 - z^2\right)w + gx \end{cases} \tag{65}$$

where x, y, z and w are the state variables and a, b, c, d, e and f are the system parameters. To show that the system (65) has chaotic behavior, we solve it using the algorithm presented by Demirci, & Ozalp (2012). The commensurate fractional-order Mathieu-Van Der Pol hyperchaotic system with orders $q_{i=1\sim4} = 0.95$ and the parameters

$$a = 10.0, \ b = 3.0, \ c = 0.4, \ d = 70.0, \ e = 1.0, \ f = 5.0$$

and $g = 0.1$ can exhibit chaotic attractors, under initial conditions $\begin{bmatrix} 0.1, & -0.5, & 0.1, & -0.5 \end{bmatrix}$. In Figure 4, we plot the chaotic attractor in $\left(x, \ y, \ z\right)$ space and time series of the fractional-order chaotic system. The other spaces can be similarly plotted.

A feasible solutions of matrices $\tilde{K}_p$ and $\tilde{K}_D$ are obtained after around 120 generations number, such that

Table 1. Specifications of the MGA

Mechanism / Parameter	Value / Type
Coding mode	Real
Initialization process	Random
Selection process	Tournament
Crossover operator	Single-point ($P_c = 0.8$)
Mutation operator	Nonuniform ($P_m = 0.08$)
Replacement-mode	Elitism strategy
Population Size	50
Max generation	1-500

Figure 4. Chaotic attractor in $\left(x, \; y, \; w\right)$ space (a) and time series of the fractional-order Mathieu-Van Der Pol hyperchaotic system (b)

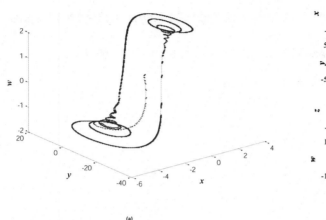

(a)

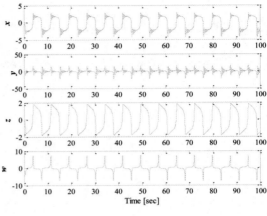

(b)

$$\tilde{K}_p = \mathrm{diag}\left\{0.4274, 0.5932, 0.4307, 0.9400\right\}$$

and

$$\tilde{K}_D = \mathrm{diag}\left\{0.0695, 0.9362, 0.044, 0.9855\right\}.$$

In addition, the matrices P and B are fixed as

$$P = q \cdot \mathrm{I}^{4\times 4}, \quad \left(q = \sum_{i=1}^{4} q_i = 3.8\right)$$

and $\left(B\right) = \mathrm{I}^{4\times 4}$, respectively.

By assuming that the condition in Theorem 1 is fulfilled, then the equilibrium point $x_e = 0$ is globally and exponentially stable. The corresponding system states of the fractional-order Mathieu-Van Der Pol hyperchaotic are depicted by Figure 5. It can be remarked that the controller is switched ON for $t \geq 20\left[\mathrm{sec}\right]$, and the fractional-order Mathieu-Van Der Pol states converge towards the equilibrium point, *i.e.*, the dynamic of system states are stabilized to the equilibrium point.

Simulation results show the controllers are switched ON when the controlled fractional-order Mathieu-Van Der Pol hyperchaotic system is closed to the equilibrium point. It can be observed that the controlled fractional-order Mathieu-Van Der Pol hyperchaotic is asymptotically stable at the origin. Then, the Fo-PDF was able to ensure convergence with relatively short transient responses.

Figure 5. Stabilizing the fractional-order Mathieu-Van Der Pol hyperchaotic system on the equilibrium point (origin)

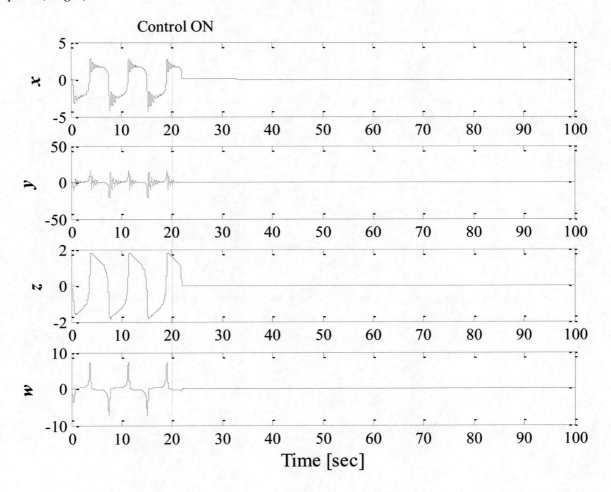

4.2 Fo-PDF Synchronization of Two Identical Fractional-Order Mathieu-Van Der Pol Hyperchaotic Systems

In order to observe the synchronization behavior in two identical commensurate fractional-order Mathieu-Van Der Pol hyperchaotic systems, we construct a drive-response configuration described by the following differential equations.

$$
\text{D:} \quad
\begin{cases}
D_t^q x_1 = x_2 \\
D_t^q x_2 = -\left(a + bx_3\right)x_1 - \left(a + bx_3\right)x_1^3 - cx_2 + dx_3 \\
D_t^q x_3 = x_4 \\
D_t^q x_4 = -ex_3 + f\left(1 - x_3^2\right)x_4 + gx_1
\end{cases}
\tag{66}
$$

$$\text{R:} \begin{cases} D_t^q y_1 = y_2 + b_1 \cdot u_1 \\ D_t^q y_2 = -\left(a + by_3\right)y_1 - \left(a + by_3\right)y_1^3 - cy_2 + dy_3 + b_2 \cdot u_2 \\ D_t^q y_3 = y_4 + b_3 \cdot u_3 \\ D_t^q y_4 = -ey_3 + f\left(1 - y_3^2\right)y_4 + gy_1 + b_4 \cdot u_4 \end{cases} \tag{67}$$

Numerical simulations are performed by choosing the values of the parameters of the drive and the response systems as given in previous section. The initial conditions of the drive system is

$$x_m(0) = \left(0.1, \ -0.5, \ 0.1, \ -0.5\right)^T$$

and the response system is chosen as

$$y_s(0) = \left(0.2, \ -0.6, \ 0.2, \ -0.4\right)^T.$$

A feasible solutions of matrices $\tilde{K}_p$ and $\tilde{K}_D$ are obtained after around 100 generations number, such that

$$\tilde{K}_p = \text{diag}\left\{0.8597, 0.7341, 0.8216, 0.8849\right\}$$

and $\tilde{K}_D = \text{diag}\left\{0.9570, 0.6699, 0.6906, 0.7795\right\}$.

In addition, the matrices P and B are fixed as

$$P = q \cdot I^{4 \times 4}, \quad \left(q = \sum_{i=1}^{4} q_i = 3.8\right)$$

and $\left(B\right) = I^{4 \times 4}$, respectively.

By assuming that the condition in Theorem 2 is fulfilled, then the equilibrium point is globally and exponentially stable, *i.e.*, the synchronization between the response and the drive systems can be achieved.

As soon as the Fo-PDF control law is applied for $t \geq 1.25\left[\text{sec}\right]$, the synchronization between the drive and the response systems is achieved. In Figure 6 (a), we plot $\left(x_1 - y_1, \ x_2 - y_2, \ x_3 - y_3\right)$ space, and the other spaces can be similarly plotted. One can observe from Figure 6 (a) that the trajectories of the response system, asymptotically, synchronizes the one of the drive system. The numerical results, illustrated in Figure 6 (b), shows that the error system is driven to the original point fast, *i.e.*, the systems (66) and (67) are synchronized.

Figure 6. Phase diagram for drive and response fractional-order Mathieu-Van Der Pol hyperchaotic systems (a) and Synchronization errors (b)

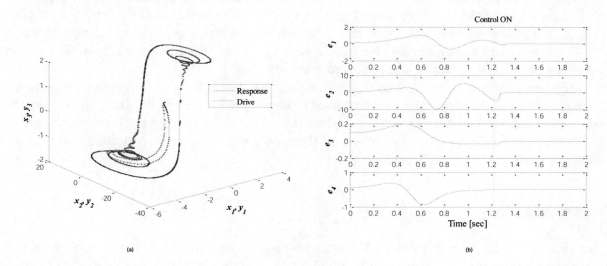

(a)   (b)

From Figure 6 (b), in point of reference signal transitions, we can observe that the effect of coupling between the four controlled variables was reduced. This is a good compensation of the interactions between the state variables. The controller was able to ensure convergence with relatively short transient responses.

Simulation results on stabilizing and synchronizing a class of factional-order hyperchaotic systems show the good performance of the developed algorithm and confirm the universality and the effectiveness of the proposed approach.

5. CONCLUSION

In this chapter, we offer a tutorial on fractional calculus in modeling and control systems. Basic definitions of fractional calculus, fractional order dynamic systems and control systems are presented. Numerical methods for simulating fractional-order systems and discretization techniques for fractional order operators are introduced in some details in the first part of this chapter. After introducing the fundamental definitions of the fractional calculus, starting from the mathematical foundations of the fractional integral and differential operators, we have presented in the second part of this paper, the generalization to non-integer orders of the basic control actions, their effects on the controlled system behavior, and the possible advantages of combining them in a closed-form controller. Some ideas and examples for the controller tuning and implementation in the time-domain, as well as computational tools for the controller design and the fractional-order systems simulation, have been reviewed.

As a study case, a fractional-order PD-based feedback controller has been proposed in this chapter for stabilizing and synchronizing a large class of fractional-order chaotic and hyperchaotic systems. The proposed controller combines the fractional-order control and the PD-based control approaches. Analysis of the stability for the proposed method is provided based on the Lyapunov stability theory and a recent stability theorem of fractional-order systems. The proposed design and optimization processes offer a practical and systematic way of the controllers design for the considered class of factional-order chaotic systems. Simulation results on stabilizing and synchronizing the factional-order chaotic systems, by taking the fractional-order Mathieu-Van Der Pol hyperchaotic system as an illustrative example, demonstrate the universality and the effectiveness of the proposed strategy.

The study covers the general modeling techniques, the system analysis, the optimization design methods as well as the performance evaluations. The techniques involved in this study are transferable into similar applications and the results generated from this work could bring valuable contributions to manufacturing industry. Therefore, this study brings significant original contributions to both the academia world and the manufacturing industry.

REFERENCES

Agrawal, S. K., & Das, S. (2014). Function projective synchronization between four dimensional chaotic systems with uncertain parameters using modified adaptive control method. *Journal of Process Control*, *24*(5), 517–530. doi:10.1016/j.jprocont.2014.02.013

Barbosa, R. S., Machado, T. J. A., & Jesus, I. S. (2010). Effect of fractional-orders in the velocity control of a servo system. *Computers & Mathematics with Applications (Oxford, England)*, *59*(5), 1679–1686. doi:10.1016/j.camwa.2009.08.009

Chen, D. Y., Liu, Y. X., Ma, X. Y., & Zhang, R. (2012). Control of a class of fractional-order chaotic systems via sliding mode. *Nonlinear Dynamics*, *67*(1), 893–901. doi:10.100711071-011-0002-x PMID:22757537

Chen, L., He, Y., Chai, Y., & Wu, R. (2014). New results on stability and stabilization of a class on nonlinear fractional-order systems. *Nonlinear Dynamics*, *75*(4), 633–641. doi:10.100711071-013-1091-5

Das, S., Pan, I., Das, S., & Gupta, A. (2012). Master-slave chaos synchronization via optimal fractional-order $PI^{\lambda}D^{\mu}$. *Nonlinear Dynamics*, *69*(4), 2193–2206. doi:10.100711071-012-0419-x

Demirci, E., & Ozalp, N. (2012). A method for solving differential equations of fractional order. *Journal of Computational and Applied Mathematics*, *236*(11), 2754–2762. doi:10.1016/j.cam.2012.01.005

Diethelm, K., Ford, N. J., & Freed, A. D. (2002). A predictor-corrector approach for the numerical solution of fractional differential equations. *Nonlinear Dynamics*, *29*(1), 3–22. doi:10.1023/A:1016592219341

Ding, D., Qi, D., Peng, J., & Wang, Q. (2015). Asymptotic pseudo-state stabilization of commensurate fractional-order nonlinear systems with additive disturbance. *Nonlinear Dynamics*, *81*(1-2), 667–677. doi:10.100711071-015-2018-0

Haddad, W. M., & Chellaboina, V. S. (2007). *Nonlinear dynamical systems and control: A Lyapunov-based approach*. Princeton University Press.

Isermann, R., & Münchhof, M. (2011). *Identification of dynamic systems: An introduction with applications*. Springer-Verlag Berlin Heidelberg. doi:10.1007/978-3-540-78879-9

Kilbas, A. A., Srivastava, H. M., & Trujillo, J. J. (2006). *Theory and applications of fractional differential equations*. Amsterdam: Elsevier.

Kuntanapreeda, S. (2015). Tensor product model transformation based control and synchronization of a class of fractional-order chaotic systems. *Asian Journal of Control, 17*(2), 371–38. doi:10.1002/asjc.839

Li, R., & Chen, W. (2014). Lyapunov-based fractional-order controller design to synchronize a class of fractional-order chaotic systems. *Nonlinear Dynamics, 76*(1), 785–795. doi:10.100711071-013-1169-0

Li, T., Wang, Y., & Yang, Y. (2014). Designing synchronization schemes for fractional-order chaotic system via a single state fractional-order controller. *International Journal for Light and Electron Optics, 125*(22), 6700–6705. doi:10.1016/j.ijleo.2014.07.087

Li, Y., & Li, J. (2014). Stability analysis of fractional order systems based on T-S fuzzy model with the fractional order α: $0 < \alpha < 1$. *Nonlinear Dynamics, 78*(4), 2909–2919. doi:10.100711071-014-1635-3

Oustaloup, A. (1991). *La Dérivation non entière*. Paris: Hermès.

Oustaloup, A. (1999). *La Commande CRONE: Commande Robuste d'Ordre Non Entier*. Paris: Editions Hermès.

Petráš, I. (2011). *Fractional-order nonlinear systems: Modeling, analysis and simulation*. Higher Education Press.

Podlubny, I. (1998). *Fractional differential equations: An introduction to fractional derivatives, fractional differential equations, some methods of their solution and some of their applications*. San Diego, CA: Academic Press.

Podlubny, I. (1999). *Fractional Differential Equations*. San Diego, CA: Academic Press.

Podlubny, I. (1999). Fractional-order systems and $PI^{\lambda}D^{\mu}$. *IEEE Transactions on Automatic Control, 44*(1), 208–214. doi:10.1109/9.739144

Pyragas, K. (1992). Continuous control of chaos by self-controlling feedback. *Physics Letters. [Part A], 170*(2), 421–428. doi:10.1016/0375-9601(92)90745-8

Sadeghian, H., Salarieh, H., Alasty, A., & Meghdari, A. (2011). On the control of chaos via fractional delayed feedback method. *Computers & Mathematics with Applications (Oxford, England), 62*(3), 1482–1491. doi:10.1016/j.camwa.2011.05.002

Scherer, R., Kalla, S. L., Tang, Y., & Huang, J. (2011). The Grünwald-Letnikov method for fractional differential equations. *Computers & Mathematics with Applications (Oxford, England), 62*(3), 902–917. doi:10.1016/j.camwa.2011.03.054

Si, G., Sun, Z., Zhang, Y., & Chen, W. (2012). Projective synchronization of different fractional-order chaotic systems with non-identical orders. *Nonlinear Analysis Real World Applications, 13*(4), 1761–1771. doi:10.1016/j.nonrwa.2011.12.006

Soukkou, A., Boukabou, A., & Leulmi, S. (2016). Prediction-based feedback control and synchronization algorithm of fractional-order chaotic systems. *Nonlinear Dynamics, 85*(4), 2183–2206. doi:10.100711071-016-2823-0

Soukkou, A., & Leulmi, S. (2017). Elaboration of a generalized approach to control and to synchronize the fractional-order chaotic systems. *International Journal of General Systems, 46*(8), 853–878. doi:10 .1080/03081079.2017.1324854

Tavazoei, M. S., & Haeri, M. (2008). Stabilization of unstable fixed points of chaotic fractional order systems by a state fractional PI controller. *European Journal of Control, 3*(3), 247–257. doi:10.3166/ ejc.14.247-257

Ushio, T., & Yamamoto, S. (1999). Prediction-based control of chaos. *Physics Letters. [Part A], 264*(1), 30–35. doi:10.1016/S0375-9601(99)00782-3

Vishal, K., Agrawal, S. K., & Das, S. (2016). Hyperchaos control and adaptive synchronization with uncertain parameter for fractional-order Mathieu–van der Pol systems. *Pramana-. Journal of Physics, 86*(1), 59–75.

Wang, C.H., & Chen, C.Y. (2015). Intelligent chaos synchronization of fractional order systems via mean-based slide mode controller. *International Journal of Fuzzy Systems, 17*(2), 144-157.

Zhang, R., Tian, G., Yang, S., & Cao, H. (2015). Stability analysis of a class of fractional order nonlinear systems with order lying in (0, 2). *ISA Transactions, 56*, 102–110. doi:10.1016/j.isatra.2014.12.006 PMID:25617942

Zheng, Y. (2015). Fuzzy prediction-based feedback control of fractional-order chaotic systems. *International Journal for Light and Electron Optics, 126*(24), 5645–5649. doi:10.1016/j.ijleo.2015.08.164

Zhou, P., & Ding, R. (2012). Control and synchronization of the fractional-order Lorenz chaotic system via fractional-order derivative. *Mathematical Problems in Engineering*. doi:.10.1155/2012/214169

Zhu, H., Zhou, S., & Zhang, J. (2009). Chaos and synchronization of the fractional-order Chua's system. *Chaos, Solitons, and Fractals, 39*(4), 1595–1603. doi:10.1016/j.chaos.2007.06.082

Chapter 12
Chaos in Nonlinear Fractional Systems

Nasr-eddine Hamri
University of Mila, Algeria

ABSTRACT

The first steps of the theory of fractional calculus and some applications traced back to the first half of the nineteenth century, the subject only really came to life over the last few decades. A particular feature is that fractional derivatives provide an excellent instrument for the description of memory and hereditary properties of various materials and processes. This is the main advantage of fractional models in comparison with classical integer-order models; another feature is that scientists have developed new models that involve fractional differential equations in mechanics, electrical engineering. Many scientists have become aware of the potential use of chaotic dynamics in engineering applications. With the development of the fractional-order algorithm, the dynamics of fractional order systems have received much attention. Chaos cannot occur in continuous integer order systems of total order less than three due to the Poincare-Bendixon theorem. It has been shown that many fractional-order dynamical systems behave chaotically with total order less than three.

INTRODUCTION

In this chapter, the dynamics of a fractional-order nonlinear system is studied. A simple system of three nonlinear ordinary differential equations is considered, which define a continuous-time dynamical system that exhibits chaotic dynamics associated with the fractal properties of the attractor.

We will focus on the dynamical behavior of both integer and fractional-order nonlinear systems. Experience of dynamical behavior will be considered. Bifurcation of the parameter-dependent system which provides a summary of essential dynamics is investigated. Period-3 windows, coexisting limit cycles and chaotic zones are found. The occurrence and the nature of chaotic attractors are verified by evaluating the largest Lyapunov exponents.

This chapter is organized as follows. Some preliminary concepts are introduced, including the Laplace transform and their basic properties, special functions (the gamma and the beta function, the

DOI: 10.4018/978-1-5225-5418-9.ch012

Mitag-Leffler function) which play the most important role in the theory of fractional derivatives and fractional differential equations. Three approaches (Riemann-Liouville, Grünwald-Letnikov and Caputo approaches) to the generalization of the notions of derivation and integration are considered. In the end of this chapter some methods of treatment of the fractional differential equations are introduced including numerical algorithm. The second part is devoted to the concept of fractional-order dynamical systems and applications, a generalization of notion of dynamical systems (Fractional-order dynamical systems) is considered including stability theory, periodic solutions, bifurcations and chaos, it is shown that all most classical criterion and tools for the study of dynamical systems have been reformulated in a general sitting and used for the study of fractional-order dynamical systems. A method for solving fractional-order differential equation and some stability results are introduced. Additionally, the fractional-order nonlinear Bloch system is presented based on the integer-order system. Bifurcation and the largest Lyapunov exponents of the fractional-order nonlinear system are also studied in this chapter and some concluding remarks are given at the end of the chapter.

FRACTIONAL CALCULUS FUNDAMENTALS

We introduce some necessary mathematical tools that will arise in the study of the concepts of fractional calculus. These are the Laplace transform, the Gamma function, the Beta function and the Mittag-Leffler Function.

The Laplace Transform

The Laplace transform is a powerful tool that we shall exploit in investigation of fractional differential equations. We denote the Laplace transform of a function $f(t)$ by the symbol $\mathsf{L}\{f(t)\}$, or when convenient, by $F(s)$. More detailed information may be found in (Ditkin, 1966; Doetsch, 1974).

The Laplace transform of a function $f(t)$ of a real variable $t \in \mathbb{R}^+$ is formally defined by

$$\mathsf{L}\{f(t)\}(s) = F(s) = \int_0^\infty e^{-st} f(t) dt, \quad s \in \mathbb{C} \tag{1}$$

If the integral in (1) is convergent at $s_0 \in \mathbb{C}$, then it converges absolutely for $s \in \mathbb{C}$ such that $Re(s) > Re(s_0)$. The inverse Laplace transform is given for $t \in \mathbb{R}^+$ by the formula

$$\mathsf{L}^{-1}\{g(s)\}(t) = \frac{1}{2\pi i} \int_{\gamma-i\infty}^{\gamma+i\infty} e^{st} g(s) ds, \quad (\gamma = Re(s_0)). \tag{2}$$

Obviously, L and L^{-1} are linear integral operators. The direct and the inverse Laplace transforms are inverse to each other for "sufficiently good" functions f and g

$$\mathsf{L}^{-1}\mathsf{L}\{f\} = f \text{ and } \mathsf{L}\mathsf{L}^{-1}\{g\} = g.$$

Existence Conditions for the Laplace Transform

Theorem 1: *Let f be a continuous or piecewise continuous function in every finite interval $(0, T)$. If $f(t)$ is of exponential order e^{at}, then the Laplace transform of $f(t)$ exists for all s such that $Re(s) > a$.*

Proof: Suppose that f, is of exponential order e^{at}, then there exists a positive constant K such that for all $t > T$

$$\left| f(t) \right| \leq K e^{at}.$$

We have

$$\left| \int_0^\infty e^{-st} f(t) dt \right| \leq \int_0^\infty e^{-st} \mid f(t) \mid dt,$$

$$\leq K \int_0^\infty e^{-t(s-a)} dt = \frac{K}{s-a},$$

for $Re(s) > a$.

This complete the proof.

Basic Properties of the Laplace Transform

Heavisides First Shifting Property

Theorem 2: *For a real constant a we have*

$$\mathsf{L}\{e^{-at} f(t)\}(s) = F(s + a)$$

where $F(s) = \mathsf{L}\{f(t)\}(s)$.

Proof: By definition we have

$$\mathsf{L}\{e^{-at} f(t)\}(s) = \int_0^\infty e^{-(s+a)t} f(t) dt = F(s + a).$$

Scaling Property

For a constant $a \neq 0$, we have

$$\mathsf{L}\{f(at)\}(s) = \frac{1}{\mid a \mid} F\left(\frac{s}{a}\right).$$

The Laplace Transform of Derivatives

To find the Laplace transform of a derivative, we integrate the expression (1) by parts. Then, we obtain

$$\int_0^\infty e^{-st} f(t)dt = \left[\frac{-f(t)e^{-st}}{s}\right]_0^\infty + \frac{1}{s}\int_0^\infty e^{-st} f'(t)dt.$$

Evaluating the limits and multiplying by s gives the following

$$s\mathsf{L}\{f(t)\}(s) = f(0) + \mathsf{L}\{f'(t)\}(s).$$

This gives the Laplace transform of $f'(t)$ as follows

$$\mathsf{L}\{f'(t)\}(s) = s\mathsf{L}\{f(t)\}(s) - f(0).$$

This can be continued for higher order derivatives (replacing $f(t)$ by $f'(t)$ in the above equation) and gives the following expression for the Laplace transform of the nth derivative of $f(t)$.

$$\mathsf{L}\{f^{(n)}(t)\}(s) = s^n\mathsf{L}\{f(t)\}(s) - \sum_{k=1}^{n} s^{n-k} f^{(k-1)}(0). \tag{3}$$

Convolution Property

If $\mathsf{L}\{f(t)\}(s) = F(s)$ and $\mathsf{L}\{g(t)\}(s) = G(s)$, then

$$\mathsf{L}\{f(t) * g(t)\}(s) = F(s)G(s). \tag{4}$$

Or, equivalently,

$$\mathsf{L}^{-1}\{F(s)G(s)\} = f(t) * g(t),$$

where $f(t) * g(t)$ is the convolution of $f(t)$ and $g(t)$ defined by the integral

$$f(t) * g(t) = \int_0^t f(t - \tau)g(\tau)d\tau.$$

The Laplace Transform of Some Usual Functions

1.　$\mathsf{L}\{1\}(s) = \int_0^\infty e^{-st}dt = \dfrac{1}{s},$

2.　$\mathsf{L}\{e^{at}\}(s) = \int_0^\infty e^{-(s-a)t}dt = \dfrac{1}{s-a},$ for $s > a$

3. $\mathsf{L}\{\sin(at)\}(s) = \int_0^\infty e^{-st} \sin(at) dt = \dfrac{a}{s^2 + a^2}$,

4. $\mathsf{L}\{\cos(at)\}(s) = \int_0^\infty e^{-st} \cos(at) dt = \dfrac{s}{s^2 + a^2}$,

5. $\mathsf{L}\{t^n\}(s) = \int_0^\infty t^n e^{-st} dt = \dfrac{n!}{s^{n+1}}$.

SPECIAL FUNCTIONS

This section deals with definitions and some basic properties of the special functions (Gamma, Beta and Mittag-Leffler) these later are essential elements in our coming study.

Gamma Function

One of the important basic functions of the fractional calculus is the Euler's Gamma function, which generalizes the factorial *n!*, and allows *n* to take also non-integer and even complex values.

This function plays an important role in the theory of differ-integration. A comprehensive definition of $\Gamma(x)$ is that provided by the Euler limit (Eckmann, 1985)

$$\Gamma(x) = Lim_{N \to \infty} [\frac{N!N^x}{x[x+1][x+2]...[x+N]}],$$

But the so-called Euler integral definition:

$$\Gamma(x) = \int_0^\infty t^{x-1} e^{-t} dt \quad (x > 0), \tag{5}$$

is often more useful, although it is restricted to positive values of x. An integration by parts applied to the definition (5) leads to the recurrence relationship

$$\Gamma(x+1) = x\Gamma(x).$$

Since $\Gamma(1) = 1$, this recurrence shows that for a positive integer *n*, we have

$$\Gamma(n+1) = n\Gamma(n) = n[n-1]\Gamma(n-1) = ... = n[n-1]...2.1.\Gamma(1) = n!.$$

Rewritten as

$$\Gamma(x-1) = \frac{\Gamma(x)}{x-1}. \quad x-1 > 0$$

Using this relation, the Euler Gamma function is extended to negative arguments for which definition (5) is inapplicable. The graph of the gamma function is shown in Figure 1.

Beta Function

The function that is closely related to the gamma function is the complete beta function $B(x, y)$. For positive values of the two parameters, x and y, this function is defined by the Beta integral:

$$B(x,y) = \int_0^1 t^{x-1}[1-t]^{y-1}dt. \quad (x > 0, \, y > 0) \tag{6}$$

The beta function $B(x, y)$ is symmetric with respect to its arguments x and y, that is, $B(x, y) = B(y, x)$. This follows from (6) by the change of variables $1 - t = u$, that is

$$B(x,y) = \int_0^1 u^{y-1}[1-u]^{x-1}du = B(y,x).$$

Using the Laplace transform, we can prove that this function is connected with the Gamma function by the relation

$$B(x,y) = \frac{\Gamma(x)\Gamma(y)}{\Gamma(x+y)}. \quad (x, y \notin \mathbf{Z}_0^-)$$

Figure 1. Graphical representation of Euler Gamma function

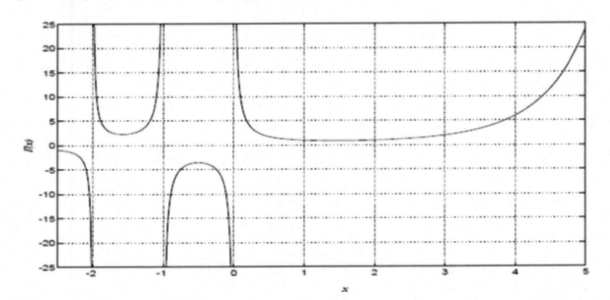

Clearly this relationship extended the beta function to negative non-integer arguments for which the definition (6) is inapplicable.

With help of the Beta function we can establish the following two important relationships for the Gamma function. The first one is

$$\Gamma(x)\Gamma(1-x) = \frac{\pi}{\sin(\pi x)}, \quad (0 < x < 1),$$

for example $\Gamma(\frac{1}{2}) = \sqrt{\pi}$.

The second one is the Legendre formula

$$\Gamma(x)\Gamma(x + \frac{1}{2}) = \sqrt{\pi} 2^{2x-1} \Gamma(2x), \quad (2x \notin \mathbb{Z}_0^-).$$

Mittag-Leffler Function

The exponential function e^z , plays a very important role in the theory of integer-order differential equations. Its one-parameter generalization, is the Mittag-Leffler function defined by

$$E_\alpha(z) = \sum_{k=0}^{\infty} \frac{z^k}{\Gamma(\alpha k + 1)}, \quad z \in \mathbb{C}; \alpha > 0 \tag{7}$$

This function was introduced by Mittag-Leffler (Grunwald, 1867; Grigorenko, 2003). $E_\alpha(z)$ is an entire function of z. In particular we have

$$E_1(z) = e^z \text{ and } E_2(z) = \cosh(\sqrt{z}).$$

Graphical representations of this function for some values of α are shown in Figure 2.

Now we shall give some information about the asymptotic behavior of this function (Oustaloup, 2008).

Theorem 3: Let $\alpha > 0$, $r > 0$, $\phi \in [-\pi, \pi]$, then the following statements hold

1. $\lim_{r \to \infty} E_\alpha(re^{i\phi}) = 0$ if $|\phi| > \alpha\pi / 2$.
2. $\lim_{r \to \infty} |E_\alpha(re^{i\phi})| = \infty \ |\phi| < \alpha\pi / 2$.
3. $E_\alpha(re^{i\phi})$ remains bounded for $r \to \infty$ if $|\phi| = \alpha\pi / 2$.

The following theorem describe the interconnection between the one-parameter Mittag-Leffler function and the Laplace transform operation.

Figure 2. Graphical representation of the one parameter Mittag-Leffler function for some value of α

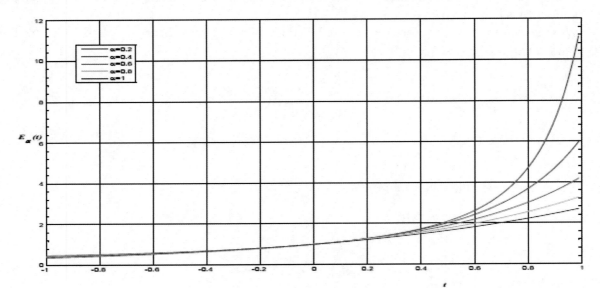

Theorem 4: Let $\alpha > 0$, $\lambda \in C$ and define $x(t) = E_{-\alpha}(\lambda t^{\alpha})$, then the Laplace transform of x is given by

$$\mathsf{L}x(s) = \frac{s^{\alpha-1}}{s^{\alpha}+\lambda} \quad (\lambda \in C; \, Re(s) > 0; \, |\lambda s^{-\alpha}| < 1). \tag{8}$$

Proof: Writing down the series expansion of $x(t)$ in powers of t^{α} gives

$$x(t) = E_{\alpha}(-\lambda t^{\alpha}) = \sum_{k=0}^{\infty} \frac{(-\lambda t^{\alpha})^{k}}{\Gamma(\alpha k + 1)}.$$

Applying the Laplace transform in a term-wise manner yields

$$\mathsf{L}x(s) = \sum_{k=0}^{\infty} \frac{\mathsf{L}\left(-\lambda t^{\alpha}\right)^{k}}{\Gamma(\alpha k + 1)},$$

$$= \frac{1}{s}\sum_{k=0}^{\infty}\left(-\lambda s^{-\alpha}\right)^{k},$$

$$= \frac{s^{\alpha-1}}{s^{\alpha}+\lambda}.$$

Differentiating (8) n times with respect to λ leads to the following relation

$$\mathsf{L}[t^{\alpha n} E^{(n)}(-\lambda t^{\alpha})](s) = \frac{n! s^{\alpha-1}}{(s^{\alpha}+\lambda)^{n+1}}, \quad (\lambda \in C; \, Re(s) > 0; |\lambda s^{-\alpha}| < 1). \tag{9}$$

Now, let us introduce an important theorem called "Final value theorem" which gives information about the asymptotic behavior of the function $f(t)$ directly from his Laplace's transform $F(s)$.

Theorem 5 (Final Value Theorem): *Let $F(s)$ be the Laplace transform of the function $f(t)$. If all poles of $sF(s)$ are in the open left-half plane, then*

$$\lim_{t \to \infty} f(t) = \lim_{s \to 0} sF(s).$$

Using theorems 4 and 5 we obtain a statement on the asymptotic behavior of the function $x(t) = E_{\alpha}(-\lambda t^{\alpha})$ as its argument tends to infinity:

Theorem 6: *Let $\alpha > 0$, $r > 0$, $\phi \in [-\pi, \pi]$ and $\lambda = r \exp(i\phi)$. Define $x(t) = E_{\alpha}(-\lambda t^{\alpha})$. Then, the following two statements hold*

1. $\lim_{t \to \infty} x(t) = 0$ *if* $|\phi| < \alpha \pi / 2$,
2. $x(t)$ *is unbounded as* $t \to \infty$ *if* $|\phi| > \alpha \pi / 2$.

The two-parameter Mittag-Leffler function $E_{\alpha,\beta}(z)$, generalizing the one in (7), is defined by the series expansion (Cafagna D. &., Grassi, G., 2009)

$$E_{\alpha,\beta}(z) = \sum_{k=0}^{\infty} \frac{z^k}{\Gamma(\alpha k + \beta)}, \quad (z \in C; \alpha > 0, \beta > 0). \tag{10}$$

When $\beta = 1$, $E_{\alpha,\beta}(z)$ coincides with $E_{\alpha}(z)$

$$E_{\alpha,1}(z) = E_{\alpha}(z).$$

From the definition (10) we can get

$$E_{1,1}(z) = \sum_{k=0}^{\infty} \frac{z^k}{\Gamma(k+1)} = \sum_{k=0}^{\infty} \frac{z^k}{k!} = e^z,$$

$$E_{1,2}(z) = \sum_{k=0}^{\infty} \frac{z^k}{\Gamma(k+2)} = \sum_{k=0}^{\infty} \frac{z^k}{(k+1)!} = \frac{1}{z} \sum_{k=0}^{\infty} \frac{z^{k+1}}{(k+1)!} = \frac{e^z - 1}{z}.$$

The hyperbolic sine and cosine are also particular cases of the two-parameter Mittag-Leffler function:

$$E_{2,1}(z^2) = \sum_{k=0}^{\infty} \frac{z^{2k}}{\Gamma(2k+1)} = \sum_{k=0}^{\infty} \frac{z^{2k}}{(2k)!} = \cosh(z),$$

$$E_{2,2}(z^2) = \sum_{k=0}^{\infty} \frac{z^{2k}}{\Gamma(2k+2)} = \frac{1}{z} \sum_{k=0}^{\infty} \frac{z^{2k+1}}{(2k+1)!} = \frac{\sinh(z)}{z}.$$

The Mittag-Leffler function satisfies the following differentiation formulas

$$\left(\frac{d}{dz}\right)^n [z^{\beta-1} E_{n,\beta}(\lambda z^n)] = z^{\beta-n-1} E_{n,\beta-n}(\lambda z^n) \quad (n \in \mathsf{N}; \lambda \in \mathsf{C}).$$

FRACTIONAL INTEGRALS AND FRACTIONAL DERIVATIVES

We can say that fractional calculus grows out of the classical definitions of the integral and derivative operators; in much the same way fractional exponents is an outgrowth of exponents with integer value.

The meaning of integer exponents is a repeated multiplication of a numerical value; this concept can clearly become confused when considering exponents of non-integer value, it is the notation that makes the jump seems obvious. While one cannot imagine the multiplication of a quantity a fractional number of times, there seems no practical restriction to placing a non-integer into the exponential position. Similarly, the common formulation for the fractional derivative (integral) can be derived directly from a traditional expression of the repeated differentiation (integration) of a function, and provides an interpolation between integer-order derivatives (integrals).

There are several types of fractional derivatives and fractional integrals. In this section we give definitions and some basic properties of three different types (the choice has been reduced to those definitions which are related to applications).

Riemann-Liouville Fractional Integral

Definition

According to Riemann-Liouville approach the notion of fractional integral of order $\alpha (\alpha > 0)$ is a natural consequence of the well known formula (usually attributed to Cauchy) that reduces the calculation of the n-fold integral of a function $f(t)$ to a single integral of convolution type.

We begin by a review of the n-fold integral of a function f assumed to be continuous on the interval $[a,b]$, where $b > x$.

First recalling that if $G(x,t)$ is jointly continuous on $[a,b] \times [a,b]$, then we have

$$\int_a^x dx_1 \int_a^{x_1} G(x_1,t)dt = \int_a^x dt \int_t^x G(x_1,t)dx_1. \tag{11}$$

In particular when $G(x,t)$ is a function of a variable t only, that is if $G(x,t) \equiv f(t)$ then (1) can be written as

$$\int_a^x dx_1 \int_a^{x_1} f(t)dt = \int_a^x f(t)dt \int_t^x dx_1,$$

$$= \int_a^x (x-t)f(t)dt,$$

This is the formula of two-fold integral reduced to a single integral. Similar computation gives the following formula of 3-fold integral reduced to a single integral

$$\int_a^x dx_1 \int_a^{x_1} dx_2 \int_a^{x_2} f(t)dt = \int_a^x \frac{(x-t)^2}{2} f(t)dt.$$

By induction we deduce the Cauchy formula of n-fold integral

$$J_a^n f(x) = {}_aD_x^{-n} f(x) = \int_a^x dx_1 \int_a^{x_1} dx_2 ... \int_a^{x_{n-1}} f(t)dt,$$

$$= \frac{1}{(n-1)!} \int_a^x (x-t)^{n-1} f(t)dt. \quad x > a, n \in \mathbb{N}^*$$

Using the Gamma function this formula can be rewritten as

$$J_a^n f(x) = {}_aD_x^{-n} f(x) = \frac{1}{\Gamma(n)} \int_a^x (x-t)^{n-1} f(t)dt. \quad x > a, n \in \mathbb{N}^* \tag{12}$$

Since the gamma function is an analytic expansion of the factorial for all positive real values, one can replace n by a real positive number α, in (11), then one defines the Riemann-Liouville fractional integral of order $\alpha > 0$ as follows

$$J_a^\alpha f(x) = {}_a^{RL}D_x^{-\alpha} f(x) = \frac{1}{\Gamma(\alpha)} \int_a^x (x-t)^{\alpha-1} f(t)dt, \quad x > a, \alpha > 0. \tag{13}$$

Example

Let $f(x) = (x-a)^\beta$ for a fixed $\beta > -1$ and $\alpha > 0$, we have

$$J_a^\alpha f(x) = \frac{1}{\Gamma(\alpha)} \int_a^x (x-a)^\beta (x-t)^{\alpha-1} dt.$$

Using the substitution $t = a + s(x-a)$ and the Beta function we get

$$J_a^\alpha f(x) = \frac{1}{\Gamma(\alpha)} (x-a)^{\alpha+\beta} \int_0^1 s^\beta (1-s)^{\alpha-1} ds$$

$$= \frac{\Gamma(\beta+1)}{\Gamma(\alpha+\beta+1)} (x-a)^{\alpha+\beta}.$$

Theorem 7: *Let $f \in L_1[a,b]$ and $\alpha > 0$, then the integral $J_a^\alpha f(x)$ exists for almost every $x \in [a,b]$. Moreover, the function $J_a^\alpha f$ itself is also an element of $L_1[a,b]$.*

Proof: *We have*

$$J_a^\alpha f(x) = \frac{1}{\Gamma(\alpha)} \int_a^x (x-t)^{\alpha-1} f(t) dt = \int_{-\infty}^{+\infty} \Phi_1(x-t)\Phi_2(t) dt.$$

where

$$\Phi_1(u) = \begin{cases} u^{\alpha-1} & \text{for } 0 < u \le b-a, \\ 0 & \text{else,} \end{cases}$$

and

$$\Phi_2(u) = \begin{cases} f(u) & \text{for } a \le u \le b, \\ 0 & \text{else.} \end{cases}$$

Clearly $\Phi_1, \Phi_2 \in L_1(\mathbb{R})$, and thus the desired result follows.

Some Basic Properties

- If f is a continuous function for $x \ge a$ then, we have (Cafagna D. &., Grassi, G., 2009)

$$\lim_{\alpha \to 0} J_a^\alpha f(x) = f(x), \tag{14}$$

so we can put

$$J_a^0 f(x) = f(x).$$

- Let f be a continuous function for $x \geq a$, we have

$$J_a^\alpha \left(J_a^\beta f(x) \right) = J_a^{\alpha+\beta} f(x). \tag{15}$$

In fact we have

$$J_a^\alpha \left(J_a^\beta f(x) \right) = \frac{1}{\Gamma(\alpha)} \int_a^x (x-t)^{\alpha-1} J_a^\beta f(t) dt,$$

$$= \frac{1}{\Gamma(\alpha)\Gamma(\beta)} \int_a^x (x-t)^{\alpha-1} dt \int_a^t (t-s)^{\beta-1} f(s) ds,$$

$$= \frac{1}{\Gamma(\alpha)\Gamma(\beta)} \int_a^x f(s) ds \int_s^x (x-t)^{\alpha-1} (t-s)^{\beta-1} dt,$$

$$= \frac{1}{\Gamma(\alpha+\beta)} \int_a^x (x-s)^{\alpha+\beta-1} f(s) ds,$$

$$= J_a^{\alpha+\beta} \left(f(x) \right).$$

where the integral

$$\int_s^x (x-t)^{\alpha-1} (t-s)^{\beta-1} dt = (x-s)^{\alpha+\beta-1} \int_0^1 (1-y)^{\alpha-1} y^{\beta-1} dy,$$

$$= B(\alpha,\beta)((x-s)^{\alpha+\beta-1},$$

$$= \frac{\Gamma(\alpha)\Gamma(\beta)}{\Gamma(\alpha+\beta)} (x-s)^{\alpha+\beta-1},$$

is evaluated using the substitution

$$t = s + y(x-s),$$

and the definition of the beta function.

- If $F(s)$ is the Laplace transform of the function $f(x)$ then the Laplace transform of the Riemann-Liouville fractional integral $J_a^\alpha f(x)$ is given by

$$\mathsf{L}(J_a^\alpha f(x))(s) = \frac{F(s)}{s^\alpha}. \tag{16}$$

For the proof of (16) we introduce the following causal function

$$\Phi_\alpha(t) = \frac{t_+^{\alpha-1}}{\Gamma(\alpha)}, \ \alpha > 0,$$

where the suffix $+$ is just denoting that the function is vanishing for $t < 0$. Clearly this function is locally absolutely integrable in $\mathbb{R}^+$ and the Laplace transform of $\Phi_\alpha(t)$ is given by

$$\mathsf{L}(\Phi_\alpha(t)) = \frac{1}{s^\alpha}.$$

Notice that the Riemann-Liouville fractional integral of $f(t)$ could be expressed as the convolution of the two functions $\Phi_\alpha(t)$ and $f(t)$ namely

$$J_a^\alpha f(x) = \int_a^x \frac{(x-t)^{\alpha-1}}{\Gamma(\alpha)} f(t)dt,$$

$$= \int_a^x \Phi_\alpha(x-t)f(t)dt,$$

$$= \Phi_\alpha(t) * f(t).$$

Based on the convolution property of the Laplace transform (4), one deduces that

$$\mathsf{L}(J_a^\alpha f(x)) = \mathsf{L}(\Phi_\alpha(t))\mathsf{L}(f(t)) = \frac{F(s)}{s^\alpha}. \tag{17}$$

Riemann-Liouville Fractional Derivatives

Now we come to the corresponding differential operators. First, we recall the following identity which holds for a function f having a continuous n^{th} derivative on the interval $[a,b]$

$$D^n f = D^m J^{m-n} f, \tag{18}$$

where $n, m \in \mathbb{N}$, such that $m > n$.

Suppose that n is not an integer. In light of previous sections, the right-hand side of 18 is meaningful. Hence, we come to the following definition of the Riemann-Liouville fractional differential operator.

Definition

Let $\alpha \in \mathbb{R}^+$ and $m = [\alpha]$ (the smallest integer that exceeds α). The operator $\,_a^{RL}D_t^\alpha$ defined by

$$_a^{RL}D_t^\alpha f = D^m J_a^{m-\alpha} f, \tag{19}$$

is called the Riemann-Liouville fractional differential operator of order α.

Equivalently, we have

$$_a^{RL}D_t^\alpha f(t) = \begin{cases} \dfrac{1}{\Gamma(m-\alpha)} \dfrac{d^m}{dt^m} \displaystyle\int_a^t (t-s)^{m-\alpha-1} f(s)\,ds, & m-1 < \alpha < m \\[3mm] \dfrac{d^m}{dt^m} f(t). & \alpha = m \end{cases}$$

For $\alpha = 0$ we set $\,_a^{RL}D_t^0 = I$, the identity operator, and whenever $\alpha \in \mathbb{N}$ the new operator $\,_a^{RL}D_t^\alpha$ coincides with the classical differential operator D^α.

Remark

The Riemann-Liouville fractional operator, is not local.

Example 1

Let $f(t) = c$, then

$$_a^{RL}D_t^\alpha f(t) = D^m(J_a^{m-\alpha} f(t)),$$

$$= \frac{c}{\Gamma(m-\alpha)} D^m(\int_a^t (t-s)^{m-\alpha-1} ds),$$

$$= \frac{c(t-a)^{-\alpha}}{\Gamma(1-\alpha)}.$$

Example 2

Let $f(t) = (t-a)^\beta$ for a fixed $\beta > -1$ and $\alpha > 0$. Then, in view of example (11), we have

$$_{a}^{RL}D_{t}^{\alpha}f(t) = D^{m}(J_{a}^{m-\alpha}f(t)), \quad m=\lceil\alpha\rceil$$

$$= \frac{\Gamma(\beta+1)}{\Gamma(m-\alpha+\beta+1)}D^{m}(x-t)^{m-\alpha+\beta}.$$

One can distinguish two cases. Namely:

If $(\alpha-\beta)\in\mathbf{N}$, then the right-hand side is the mth derivative of a polynomial of degree $m-(\alpha-\beta)$, this implies that

$$_{a}^{RL}D_{t}^{\alpha}f(t) = 0.$$

But if $(\alpha-\beta)\notin\mathbf{N}$, then

$$_{a}^{RL}D_{t}^{\alpha}f(t) = \frac{\Gamma(\beta+1)}{\Gamma(\beta-\alpha+1)}(t-s)^{\beta-\alpha}.$$

Some Basic Properties

The Law of Exponents

We have proved the rule of composition for Riemann-Liouville fractional integrals. That is if f is a continuous function for $x\geq a$ and $\alpha>0$, $\beta>0$, then

$$J_{a}^{\alpha}\left(J_{a}^{\beta}f(x)\right) = J_{a}^{\alpha+\beta}f(x). \tag{20}$$

However, this rule may not be generalized to the case of fractional derivatives without imposing some additional restrictions on f. To show that (20) does not necessarily hold for all α and β when replacing J_{a}^{α} and J_{a}^{β} by $_{a}^{RL}D_{t}^{\alpha}$ and $_{a}^{RL}D_{t}^{\beta}$, let introduce the following example

Let $f(t)=t^{\frac{1}{2}}$, $\alpha=\dfrac{1}{2}$ and $\beta=\dfrac{3}{2}$ then

$$_{0}^{RL}D_{t}^{\alpha}(f(t)) = \frac{1}{2}\sqrt{\pi},$$

$$_{0}^{RL}D_{t}^{\beta}(f(t)) = 0,$$

$$_{0}^{RL}D_{t}^{\alpha}(\,_{0}^{RL}D_{t}^{\beta}(f(t))) = 0,$$

$$\,^{RL}_0 D_t^{\beta} (\,^{RL}_0 D_t^{\alpha} (f(t))) = -\frac{1}{4} t^{-\frac{3}{2}},$$

$$\,^{RL}_0 D_t^{\alpha+\beta} (f(t)) = -\frac{1}{4} t^{-\frac{3}{2}}.$$

Obviously in this example we have

$$\,^{RL}_0 D_t^{\alpha} (\,^{RL}_0 D_t^{\beta} (f(t))) \neq \,^{RL}_0 D_t^{\alpha+\beta} (f(t)).$$

In the following we shall state, precisely, some conditions under which the law of exponents holds.

1.   Composition With Integer-Order Derivatives

The composition of Riemann-Liouville fractional derivatives with integer order derivatives appears in many applied problems, so it is convenient to introduce it here. Let us consider the nth derivative of the Riemann Liouville fractional derivative of real order α, we have

$$D^n (\,^{RL}_a D_t^{\alpha} f(t)) = \frac{1}{\Gamma(m-\alpha)} D^{n+m} \left(\int_a^t (t-s)^{m-\alpha-1} f(s) ds \right),$$

$$= \frac{1}{\Gamma(n+m-(n+\alpha))} D^{n+m} \left(\int_a^t (t-s)^{n+m-(n+\alpha)-1} f(s) ds \right),$$

$$= \,^{RL}_a D_t^{n+\alpha} f(t).$$

To consider the fractional derivatives of the nth integer derivative we recall the following relationships

$$\,_a D_t^{-n} f^{(n)}(t) = \frac{1}{(n-1)!} \int_a^t (t-s)^{n-1} f^{(n)}(s) ds,$$

$$= f(t) - \sum_{j=0}^{n-1} \frac{f^{(j)}(a)(x-a)^j}{\Gamma(j+1)},$$

and

$$\,^{RL}_a D_t^{\alpha} g(t) = \,^{RL}_a D_t^{\alpha+n} \left(\,_a D_t^{-n} g(t) \right).$$

Using the above relations we obtain

$$
{}_{a}^{RL}D_t^{\alpha}(f^{(n)}(t)) = {}_{a}^{RL}D_t^{\alpha+n}\left({}_aD_t^{-n}f^{(n)}(t)\right),
$$

$$
= {}_{a}^{RL}D_t^{\alpha+n}\left(f(t) - \sum_{j=0}^{n-1}\frac{f^{(j)}(a)(t-a)^j}{\Gamma(j+1)}\right),
$$

$$
= {}_{a}^{RL}D_t^{\alpha+n}f(t) - \sum_{j=0}^{n-1}\frac{f^{(j)}(a)(t-a)^{j-n-\alpha}}{\Gamma(j-n-\alpha+1)}.
$$

From this results we see that the Riemann-Liouville fractional operator ${}_{a}^{RL}D_t^{\alpha}$ commutes with the integer operator D^n only if f^j vanishes in the lower terminal α for all $j = 0,1,2,...,n-1$.

2.   Composition With Fractional-Order Derivatives

Now, let us consider the composition of two fractional Riemann-Liouville operators ${}_{a}^{RL}D_t^{\alpha}$ and ${}_{a}^{RL}D_t^{\beta}$, we put $m = [\alpha]$ and $n = [\beta]$ then

$$
{}_{a}^{RL}D_t^{\alpha}\left({}_{a}^{RL}D_t^{\beta}f(t)\right) = D^m\left({}_{a}^{RL}D_t^{-(m-\alpha)}\left({}_{a}^{RL}D_t^{\beta}f(t)\right)\right),
$$

$$
= D^m\left({}_{a}^{RL}D_t^{\alpha+\beta-m}f(t)\right.
$$

$$
\left. -\sum_{j=1}^{n}\left[{}_{a}^{RL}D_t^{\beta-j}f(t)\right]_{t=a}\frac{(t-a)^{m-\alpha-j}}{\Gamma(m-\alpha-j+1)}\right),
$$

$$
= {}_{a}^{RL}D_t^{\alpha+\beta}f(t) - \sum_{j=1}^{n}\left[{}_{a}^{RL}D_t^{\beta-j}f(t)\right]_{t=a}\frac{(t-a)^{-\alpha-j}}{\Gamma(-\alpha-j+1)}, \tag{21}
$$

and

$$
{}_{a}^{RL}D_t^{\beta}\left({}_{a}^{RL}D_t^{\alpha}f(t)\right) = {}_{a}^{RL}D_t^{\beta+\alpha}f(t) - \sum_{j=1}^{m}\left[{}_{a}^{RL}D_t^{\alpha-j}f(t)\right]_{t=a}\frac{(t-a)^{-\beta-j}}{\Gamma(-\beta-j+1)}. \tag{22}
$$

From this relationship we deduce that in general case the Riemann-Liouville fractional operators ${}_{a}^{RL}D_t^{\alpha}$ and ${}_{a}^{RL}D_t^{\beta}$ do not commute, except for the case $\alpha = \beta$. When $\alpha \neq \beta$ it commutes only if both sums in the right-hand sides of 21 and (22) vanish, that is if

$$f^{j}(a) = 0, \quad \text{for all} \quad j = 0,1,2,\dots, \quad \max(n-1, m-1).$$

3. The Laplace Transform

In order to evaluate the Laplace transform of the Riemann-Liouville fractional derivative $\,{}_{0}^{RL}D_{t}^{\alpha}f(t)$ we write it in the form:

$$\,{}_{0}^{RL}D_{t}^{\alpha}f(t) = g^{(m)}(t),$$

where

$$g(t) = \,{}_{0}^{RL}D_{t}^{-(m-\alpha)}f(x) = \frac{1}{\Gamma(m-\alpha)}\int_{0}^{t}(t-s)^{m-\alpha-1}f(s)ds. \quad m = \lceil \alpha \rceil$$

Using the notation $\mathsf{L}(f(x))(s) = F(s)$, $\mathsf{L}(g(x))(s) = G(s)$ and the formula for the Laplace transform of integer-order derivative (13) we get

$$\mathsf{L}\left\{ \,{}_{0}^{RL}D_{t}^{\alpha}f(x)\right\}(s) = s^{m}G(s) - \sum_{k=0}^{m-1}s^{k}g^{(m-k-1)}(0). \tag{23}$$

$G(s)$ can be evaluated by the formula of the Laplace transform of the Riemann-Liouville fractional integral (17) namely

$$G(s) = s^{-(m-\alpha)}F(s). \tag{24}$$

On the other hand, we have

$$g^{(m-k-1)}(t) = \frac{d^{m-k-1}}{dt^{m-k-1}}\,{}_{0}^{RL}D_{t}^{-(m-\alpha)}f(t) = \,{}_{0}^{RL}D_{t}^{\alpha-k-1}f(t). \tag{25}$$

Substituting (24) and (25) into (23), then we obtain the formula for the Laplace transform of the Riemann-Liouville fractional derivative

$$\mathsf{L}\left\{ \,{}_{0}^{RL}D_{t}^{\alpha}f(t)\right\}(s) = s^{\alpha}F(s) - \sum_{k=0}^{m-1}s^{k}\left[\,{}_{0}^{RL}D_{t}^{\alpha-k-1}f(t)\right]_{t=0}. \tag{26}$$

The practical application of this Laplace transform is limited by the absence of physical interpretation of the limit values of fractional derivative at the lower terminal $t = 0$, (Cafagna & Grassi, 2009).

Grünwald-Letnikov Fractional Derivative

Definition

As presented above, the Riemann-Liouville formulation approaches the problem of fractional calculus from the repeated integral, but the Grünwald-Letnikov formulation approaches the problem from the derivative side by observing that the derivative of integer order m and the m-fold integral are two notions closer to each other than one usually assumes, namely they are particular cases of the following general expression

$$
{}_aD_t^p f(t) = \lim_{\substack{h \to 0 \\ nh=t-a}} h^{-p} \sum_{k=0}^{n} (-1)^k \binom{p}{k} f(t-kh), \tag{27}
$$

where

$$
\binom{p}{k} = \frac{p(p-1)(p-2)...(p-k+1)}{k!},
$$

are the binomial coefficients.

The expression (27) represents the derivative of order m if $p = m$ and the m-fold integral if $p = -m$, this expression is used to define a fractional derivative and fractional integral by directly replacing $p \in \mathbb{N}$ in (27), by an arbitrary real α, provided that the binomial coefficient can be understood as using the Gamma function in place of the standard factorial. Also, the upper limit of the summation goes to infinity as $\frac{t-a}{h}$.

We end up with the generalized form of the Grünwald-Letnikov fractional derivative

$$
{}_a^{GL}D_t^\alpha f(t) = \lim_{h \to 0} h^{-\alpha} \sum_{k=0}^{\frac{t-a}{h}} (-1)^k \left(\frac{\Gamma(\alpha+1)}{k!\Gamma(\alpha-k+1)} \right) f(t-kh). \tag{28}
$$

It is conceivable, that like the definition of Riemann-Liouville for the fractional integral may be used to define the fractional derivative, the above form of the Grünwald-Letnikov derivative could be altered for use in an alternate definition of the fractional integral. The most natural alteration of this form is to consider the Grünwald-Letnikov derivative for negative α. But in (27), there is a problem that $\binom{-p}{k}$ is not defined using factorials. We have

$$
\binom{-p}{k} = \frac{-p(-p-1)(-p-2)...(-p-k+1)}{k!},
$$

$$= (-1)^k \frac{(p+k-1)!}{(p-1)!k!}. \tag{29}$$

The factorial in (29) may be generalized for negative real, using the Gamma function, thus

$$\binom{-p}{k} = (-1)^k \frac{\Gamma(p+k)}{\Gamma(p)k!}. \tag{30}$$

Now we can rewrite (18) for $-\alpha$, and this leads to the Grünwald-Letnikov fractional integral

$$_{a}^{GL}D_t^{-\alpha} f(t) = \lim_{h \to 0} h^{\alpha} \sum_{k=0}^{\frac{t-a}{h}} \left(\frac{\Gamma(\alpha+k)}{k!\Gamma(\alpha)} \right) f(t-kh). \tag{31}$$

Link to the Riemann-Liouville Approach

If we assume that the derivatives $f^{(k)}(t), (k=1,2,...,m)$ are continuous in the interval $[a,T]$ and m is an integer such that $m > \alpha$, we can rewrite (28) as follows

$$_{a}^{GL}D_t^{\alpha} f(t) = \sum_{k=0}^{m-1} \frac{f^{(k)}(a)(t-a)^{k-\alpha}}{\Gamma(k-\alpha+1)} + \frac{1}{\Gamma(m-\alpha)} \int_a^t (t-s)^{m-\alpha-1} f^{(m)}(s)ds. \tag{32}$$

Also, the right hand side of (32) can be written as

$$\frac{d^m}{dt^m} \left\{ \sum_{k=0}^{m-1} \frac{f^{(k)}(a)(t-a)^{m-\alpha+k}}{\Gamma(m-\alpha+k+1)} + \frac{1}{\Gamma(2m-\alpha)} \int_a^t (t-s)^{2m-\alpha-1} f^{(m)}(s)ds \right\}, \tag{33}$$

and after m integration by part, we obtain the expression of the Riemann-Liouville derivative

$$\frac{d^m}{dt^m} \left\{ \frac{1}{\Gamma(m-\alpha)} \int_a^t (t-s)^{m-\alpha-1} f(t)dt \right\} = \frac{d^m}{dt^m} \left\{ {}_{a}^{RL}D_t^{-(m-\alpha)} f(t) \right\},$$

$$= {}_{a}^{RL}D_t^{\alpha} f(t). \tag{34}$$

So, under the above assumptions we have

$$_{a}^{RL}D_t^{\alpha} f(t) = {}_{a}^{GL}D_t^{\alpha} f(t).$$

Therefore, the properties that we have seen in the Riemann-Liouville definition for the fractional derivative remain valid for the Grünwald-Letnikov definition, under a suitable assumptions.

The Riemann-Liouville definition of the fractional integral and derivative is suitable to find the analytic solution for relatively simple functions. Conversely, the Grünwald-Letnikov definition is adopted for numerical computations.

Caputo Fractional Derivative

As it is mentioned above, the Laplace transform of the Riemann-Liouville fractional derivative include the limit values of fractional derivative at the lower terminal $t = 0$, so the initial conditions required for the solution of fractional order differential equations are themselves of a non-integer order. Also, the fractional derivative of a constant is not a 0.

In the mathematical sense, when solving non-integer order differential equations, it is possible to use this definition given the proper initial conditions as it happens. However in the physical world, these properties of the Riemann-Liouville definition presents, a serious problem. Today, we are well versed with the interpretation of the physical world in the equations of integer order, and we do not have a practical knowledge of the world in a fractional order. Our mathematical tools go in excess of practical limitations of our comprehension.

The Italian mathematician Caputo proposed a solution to this conflict in 1967, (Caputo, 1967). By introducing a new definition, in which he attempts to find a link between what is possible and what is practical. The aim of the slight modification of the concept of fractional derivative is to allow the use of integer order initial conditions in the solution of fractional differential equations. In addition, the Caputo derivative of a constant is 0, as we will see below. In order to achieve this goal, Caputo proposes the same operations as in Riemann-Liouville definition but in the reverse order, namely to get the Riemann-Liouville derivative of order $\alpha > 0$, of a function f, first one must integrate f by the fractional order m-α, after that, differentiate the resulting function by the integer order m. While in the Caputo approach, first one must differentiate f by the integer order m, then integrate $f^{(m)}$ by the fractional order m-α.

Definition

Let $\alpha \geq 0$, and $m = \lceil \alpha \rceil$. Then, we define the Caputo's fractional operator $_{a}^{C}D_{t}^{\alpha}$ by

$$_{a}^{C}D_{t}^{\alpha} f(t) = J_{a}^{m-\alpha} \frac{d^{m}}{dt^{m}} f(t),$$

$$= \frac{1}{\Gamma(m-\alpha)} \int_{a}^{t} (t-s)^{m-\alpha-1} f^{(m)}(s)ds,$$

whenever $\dfrac{d^{m}}{ds^{m}} f \in L_{1}[a,b]$.

Remark

As in the case of the Riemann-Liouville operators, we see that the Caputo derivatives are not local either.

Some Basic Properties

1. Linearity

Let $\lambda, \gamma \in \mathbb{R}$, From the definition of $_a^C D_t^\alpha$ it follows directly that

$$_a^C D_t^\alpha (\lambda f(t) + \gamma g(t)) = \lambda \, _a^C D_t^\alpha (f(t)) + \gamma \, _a^C D_t^\alpha (g(t)).$$

2. Interpolation

When $\alpha \in \mathbb{N}$, we have m=α, then the definition above implies that

$$_a^C D_t^\alpha f = J_a^0 \frac{d^m}{dt^m} f = \frac{d^m}{dt^m} f.$$

This means that: similarly to the Riemann-Liouville and Grünwald-Letnikov approaches, the Caputo approach provides also an interpolation between integer-order derivatives.

3. Composition

Let $n \in \mathbb{N}$ and $m = [\alpha]$, we have

$$_a^c D_t^\alpha (_a^c D_t^m f(t)) = _a^c D_t^{\alpha+n} f(t).$$

Namely

$$_a^c D_t^\alpha (_a D_t^n f(t)) = _a D_t^{-(m-\alpha)} \, _a D_t^m (_a D_t^n f(t)),$$

$$= _a D_t^{-(m-\alpha)} \, _a D_t^{m+n} f(t),$$

$$= _a D_t^{-(m+n-(\alpha+n))} \, _a D_t^{m+n} f(t),$$

$$= _a^c D_t^{\alpha+n} f(t).$$

4.   Laplace transform

We begin by writing the derivative in the form:

$$^C_0D^\alpha_t f(t) = J^{m-\alpha} g(t),$$

where

$$g(x) = f^{(m)}(x), \quad m = [\alpha].$$

Using the formula for the Laplace transform of Riemann-Liouville fractional integral (17), and the formula for the Laplace transform of integer-order derivative (3) we get

$$\mathsf{L}\left\{ {}^C_0D^\alpha_t f(t)\right\}(s) = S^{-(m-\alpha)}G(s) = s^\alpha F(s) - \sum_{k=0}^{m-1} s^{\alpha-k-1} f^{(k)}(0). \tag{35}$$

Clearly, the Laplace transform of the Caputo fractional derivative involves the values of $f(x)$ and its derivatives at the lower terminal $x = 0$, for which a certain physical interpretation exists, so we expect that the fractional Caputo derivative can be useful for solving applied problems.

Link to the Riemann-Liouville Approach

Let $\alpha > 0$ and f a function having a continuous derivatives $f^{(k)}(t)$, $(k = 1, 2, ..., m)$ in the interval $[a, T]$, where $m = [\alpha]$, then from (34) we have

$$^{RL}_{a}D^\alpha_t f(t) = \sum_{k=0}^{m-1} \frac{f^{(k)}(a)(t-a)^{k-\alpha}}{\Gamma(k-\alpha+1)} + \frac{1}{\Gamma(m-\alpha)} \int_a^t (t-s)^{m-\alpha-1} f^{(m)}(s)ds,$$

$$= \sum_{k=0}^{m-1} \frac{f^{(k)}(a)(t-a)^{k-\alpha}}{\Gamma(k-\alpha+1)} + {}^C_aD^\alpha_t f(t). \tag{36}$$

Clearly if $f^{(k)}(a) = 0$, $(k = 0, 1, 2, ..., m-1)$ then

$$^{RL}_{a}D^\alpha_t f(t) = {}^C_aD^\alpha_t f(t).$$

FRACTIONAL DIFFERENTIAL EQUATIONS

This section will be devoted to the study of Caputo's fractional differential equations. In the first subsection we aboard the existence and uniqueness questions for the initial value problems with a most general class of fractional equations, then in the second subsection we move to the analytical resolution of linear equations. Whereas in the third subsection we shall deal with numerical resolution.

Initial Value Problems

We begin with initial value problem of the form

$$\begin{cases} {}_0^c D_t^\alpha x(t) = f(t,x), \\ x^k(0) = x_0^{(k)}, \ \ k = 0,1,2,...,m-1 \end{cases} \tag{37}$$

where as usual we have set $m = \lceil \alpha \rceil$.

The existence and uniqueness theory for such equations have been presented in (Diethelm, 2010).

Theorem 8: Let $\alpha > 0$ and $m = \lceil \alpha \rceil$. Moreover, let $x_0^0, x_0^1, ..., x_0^{m-1} \in \mathbb{R}, K > 0$ and $T^* > 0$.

Define

$$G = \left\{ (t,x) : t \in \left[0, T^* \right], |\, x - \sum_{k=0}^{m-1} t^k x_0^{(k)} / k! \,| \leq K \right\},$$

and let the function $f : G \to \mathbb{R}$ be continuous.

Furthermore, define $M = sup_{(t,z) \in G} |\, f(t,z)\,|$ and

$$T = \begin{cases} T^* & \text{if} \ \ M = 0, \\ \min \left\{ T^*, (K\Gamma(\alpha+1)/M)^{1/\alpha} \right\} & \text{else.} \end{cases} \tag{38}$$

Then, there exists a function $x \in C\left[0, T \right]$ solving the initial value problem (37).

Theorem 9: *Let $\alpha > 0$ and $m = \lceil \alpha \rceil$. Moreover, let $x_0^0, x_0^1, ..., x_0^{m-1} \in \mathbb{R}, \ \ K > 0$ and $T^* > 0$.*

Define G as in Theorem 8, and let the function $f : G \to \mathbb{R}$ be continuous and satisfying a Lipschitz condition with respect to the second variable, i.e;

$$|\, f(t, x_1) - f(t, x_2) \,| \leq L \,|\, x_1 - x_2 \,|, \tag{39}$$

with some constant $L > 0$. Then define T as in Theorem 8, there exists a uniquely defined function $x \in C\left[0, T \right]$ solving the initial value problem (37).

Corollary

Assumes the hypotheses of the Theorems 8 and 9, except that the set G, i.e; the domain of definition of the function f is now taken to be $G = \mathsf{R}^2$.

Moreover, we assume that f is continuous and that there exist constants $c_1 \geq 0$, $c_2 \geq 0$ and $0 \leq \mu < 1$ such that

$$|f(t,x)| \leq c_1 + c_2 |x|^\mu \quad \text{for all } (t,x) \in G.$$

Then, there exists a uniquely function $x \in C[0,\infty)$, solving the initial value problem (27). For the proof of theorem 8 and 9 one can refer to (Diethelm, 2010).

Remark

- In real applications, we have usually $0 < \alpha \leq 1$. In this case, the set G is just the simple rectangle

$$G = [0,T] \times \left[x_0^{(0)} - K, x_0^{(0)} + K \right]$$

- For simplicity of the presentation we only treat the scalar case here. However, all the results in this section can be extended to vector-valued functions x (i.e. systems of equations) without any problems.

It is well know that if $f : [0,a] \times [b,c] \to \mathsf{R}$, is a continuous function and satisfy a Lipschitz condition with respect to the second variable and y, z are two solutions of the differential equation of order 1.

$$\frac{dx(t)}{dt} = f(t,x),$$

subject to the initial conditions $y(0) = y_0$, $z(0) = z_0$ where $y_0 \neq z_0$. Then, for all t where both $y(t)$ and $z(t)$ exist, we have $y(t) \neq z(t)$. But a similar statement does not hold for equations of higher order, for example the equation

$$\frac{d^2 x}{dt^2} = -x(t),$$

has solutions $x_1(t) = 0$, $x_2(t) = \cos t$ and $x_3(t) = \sin t$ clearly the graphs of these solutions cross each other. Similar effects arise for fractional equations and we have the following result

Theorem 10: *Let* $0 < \alpha < 1$ *and assume that* $f : [0,a] \times [b,c] \to \mathbb{R}$, *is a continuous function and satisfy the Lipschitz condition (39) with respect to the second variable and* y, z *are two solutions of the fractional differential equation of order* α

$$_0^C D_t^\alpha x(t) = f(t,x),$$

subject to the initial conditions $y(0) = y_0$, $z(0) = z_0$ *where* $y_0 \neq z_0$. *Then, for all* t *where both* $y(t)$ *and* $z(t)$ *exist, we have* $y(t) \neq z(t)$.

INITIAL VALUE PROBLEMS FOR LINEAR EQUATIONS

It is a common observation in many areas of mathematics that the linearity assumption allows to derive more precise statements. So, we'll restrict our attention to linear fractional differential equations which are very important in many applications. Explicit expressions for solutions of such equations can be obtained and used for the study of stability property.

One Dimensional Case

For simplicity, we begin by the scalar (one dimensional) case

Theorem 11: Let $\alpha > 0$ and $m = [\alpha]$, $\lambda \in \mathbb{R}$ and $q \in C[0,T]$. The solution of the initial value problem

$$\begin{cases} _0^C D_t^\alpha x(t) = \lambda x(t) + q(t), \\ x^{(k)}(0) = x_0^{(k)}, \quad k = 0,1,...m-1, \end{cases} \tag{40}$$

is given by

$$x(t) = \sum_{k=0}^{m-1} x_0^{(k)} u_k(t) + \tilde{x}(t), \tag{41}$$

with

$$\tilde{x}(t) = \begin{cases} J_0^\alpha q(t), & if \lambda = 0, \\ \dfrac{1}{\lambda} \displaystyle\int_0^t q(t-\tau) u_0'(\tau) d\tau & if \lambda \neq 0, \end{cases} \tag{42}$$

where $u_k(t) = J_0^k e_\alpha(t)$, $k = 0,1,...m-1$ and $e_\alpha(t) = E_\alpha(\lambda t^\alpha)$.

Remark

In the special case $0 < \alpha < 1$, the solution is given by

$$x(t) = x_0^{(0)} E_\alpha(\lambda t^\alpha) + \alpha \int_0^t q(t-\tau)\tau^{\alpha-1} E_\alpha'(\lambda \tau^\alpha)d\tau,$$

$$= x_0^{(0)} E_\alpha(\lambda t^\alpha) + \alpha \int_0^t (t-\tau)^{\alpha-1} E_\alpha'(\lambda(t-\tau)^\alpha)q(\tau)d\tau.$$

In the limit case $\alpha \to 1^-$ we obtain the classical formula

$$x(t) = x_0^{(0)} e^{\lambda t} + \int_0^t e^{\lambda(t-\tau)}q(\tau)d\tau.$$

Proof (Theorem 11): In the case $\lambda = 0$, we have $e_\alpha(t) = E_\alpha(0) = 1$. Then, $u_k(t) = t^k / k!$, for every k. Thus, the direct differentiation of a given $x(t)$ affirms the claim. In the case $\lambda \neq 0$, the proof will be divided into two facts:

The first is that the functions u_k satisfy the homogeneous differential equation

$$_0^C D_t^\alpha u_k = \lambda u_k \quad (k = 0,1,...,m-1),$$

with initial conditions $u_k^{(j)}(0) = \delta_{kj}$ (Kronecker's delta) for $j,k = 0,1,...,m-1$.

The second fact is that the function $\tilde{x}$ is a solution of (40). Then the proof will be achieved by the superposition principal.

1.   We have

$$e_\alpha(t) = \sum_{j=0}^\infty \frac{\lambda^j t^{\alpha j}}{\Gamma(1+j\alpha)}.$$

Then

$$u_k(t) = J_0^k e_\alpha(t) = \sum_{j=0}^\infty \frac{\lambda^j t^{\alpha j + k}}{\Gamma(1+j\alpha+k)}, \tag{43}$$

applying the operator $_0^C D_t^\alpha$ to both sides of (43) yields

$$_0^C D_t^\alpha u_k(t) = \sum_{j=1}^{\infty} \frac{\lambda^j t^{\alpha(j-1)+k}}{\Gamma(1+(j-1)\alpha+k)},$$

$$= \sum_{j=0}^{\infty} \frac{\lambda^{j+1} t^{\alpha j+k}}{\Gamma(1+j\alpha+k)},$$

$$= \lambda \sum_{j=0}^{\infty} \frac{\lambda^j t^{\alpha j+k}}{\Gamma(1+j\alpha+k)},$$

$$= \lambda u_k(t).$$

Moreover, for $j = k$, we have

$$u_k^{(k)}(0) = D^k J_0^k e_\alpha(0) = 1.$$

For $j < k$, we have

$$u_k^{(j)}(0) = D^j J_0^k e_\alpha(0) = J_0^{k-j} e_\alpha(0) = \frac{1}{\Gamma(k-j)} \int_0^0 (0-\tau)^{k-j-1} e_\alpha(\tau) d\tau = 0.$$

And for $j > k$, we have

$$u_k^{(j)}(0) = D^j J_0^k e_\alpha(0) = D_0^{j-k} e_\alpha(0) = 0,$$

since

$$D_0^{j-k} e_\alpha(t) = D_0^{j-k} \sum_{l=0}^{\infty} \frac{\lambda^l t^{l\alpha}}{\Gamma(1+l\alpha)},$$

$$= \sum_{l=1}^{\infty} \frac{\lambda^l t^{l\alpha+k-j}}{\Gamma(1+l\alpha+k-j)}.$$

2.   We have

$$\tilde{x}(t) = \frac{1}{\lambda} \int_0^t q(t-\tau) u_0'(\tau) d\tau = \frac{1}{\lambda} \int_0^t q(t-\tau) e_\alpha'(\tau) d\tau = \frac{1}{\lambda} \int_0^t q(\tau) e_\alpha'(t-\tau) d\tau.$$

Since q is continuous and e'_α is at least improperly integrable, then the integral exists and it is a continuous function of t, thus $\tilde{x}(0) = 0$. Using the well know rules for differentiation of parameter integrals we obtain

$$D\tilde{x}(t) = \frac{1}{\lambda}\int_0^t q(\tau)e''_\alpha(t-\tau)d\tau + \frac{1}{\lambda}q(t)e'_\alpha(0) = \frac{1}{\lambda}\int_0^t q(\tau)e''_\alpha(t-\tau)d\tau$$

because $e'_\alpha(0) = 0$, this formula can be generalized for $(k = 0,1,...,m-1)$ as follows

$$D^k\tilde{x}(t) = \frac{1}{\lambda}\int_0^t q(\tau)e^{(k+1)}_\alpha(t-\tau)d\tau,$$

then $D^k\tilde{x}(0) = 0$ for $(k = 0,1,...,m-1)$. Thus $\tilde{x}$ Fulfills the required homogeneous initial conditions. Now, it remains to show that $\tilde{x}$ solves the non-homogeneous differential equation. We have

$$e'_\alpha(t) = \lambda\alpha t^{\alpha-1}E'_\alpha(\lambda t^\alpha) = \lambda\alpha t^{\alpha-1}\sum_{j=1}^\infty \frac{j(\lambda t^\alpha)^{j-1}}{\Gamma(1+j\alpha)},$$

$$= \lambda t^{\alpha-1}\sum_{j=1}^\infty \frac{(\lambda t^\alpha)^{j-1}}{\Gamma(j\alpha)} = \sum_{j=1}^\infty \frac{\lambda^j t^{j\alpha-1}}{\Gamma(j\alpha)},$$

then

$$\tilde{x}(t) = \frac{1}{\lambda}\int_0^t q(\tau)e'_\alpha(t-\tau)d\tau = \frac{1}{\lambda}\int_0^t q(\tau)\sum_{j=1}^\infty \frac{\lambda^j(t-\tau)^{j\alpha-1}}{\Gamma(j\alpha)}d\tau,$$

$$= \sum_{j=1}^\infty \frac{\lambda^{j-1}}{\Gamma(j\alpha)}\int_0^t q(\tau)(t-\tau)^{j\alpha-1}d\tau = \sum_{j=1}^\infty \lambda^{j-1}J_0^{j\alpha}q(t) \quad .$$

Thus

$$^C_0D^\alpha_t\tilde{x}(t) = \sum_{j=1}^\infty \lambda^{j-1}\,^C_0D^\alpha_t J_0^{j\alpha}q(t) = \sum_{j=1}^\infty \lambda^{j-1}J_0^{(j-1)\alpha}q(t),$$

$$= \sum_{j=0}^\infty \lambda^j J_0^{(j)\alpha}q(t) = q(t) + \sum_{j=1}^\infty \lambda^j J_0^{j\alpha}q(t) = q(t) + \lambda\tilde{x}(t).$$

Notice here that in view of the convergence property of the series expansion for e'_α and the continuity of q, the interchange between summation and integration is possible.

Multidimensional Case

First, let us give the general solution for the commensurate fractional order linear homogeneous system

$$_0^C D_t^\alpha X(t) = AX(t), \quad 0 < t \le a, \tag{44}$$

where $X \in \mathbb{R}^n$, $a > 0$, and $A \in \mathbb{R}^n \times \mathbb{R}^n$. To derive this general solution the author of (Odibat Z., 2010), proceeds by analogy with treatment of homogeneous integer order linear systems with constant coefficients where the exponential function $Exp(t)$ is replaced by the Mittag-Leffler function $E_\alpha(t^\alpha)$. Hence, we seek solutions of the form

$$X(t) = u E_\alpha(\lambda t^\alpha), \tag{45}$$

the constant λ and the vector u are to be determined. Substituting (45) in (44) gives

$$u \lambda E_\alpha(\lambda t^\alpha) = Au E_\alpha(\lambda t^\alpha). \tag{46}$$

Thus

$$(A - \lambda I)u = 0, \tag{47}$$

because $E_\alpha(\lambda t^\alpha) \ne 0$. Therefore, the vector X in (45) is a solution of the system (44) on condition that λ is an eigenvalue and u an associated eigenvector of the matrix A. Now, if all k-fold eigenvalues of A have k eigenvectors, then we know that the set of all these eigenvectors is linearly independent and thus it forms a basis of C^n. Hence, the following result holds.

Theorem 12: Let $\lambda_1, ..., \lambda_n$ be the eigenvalues of the matrix A and $u^{(1)}, ..., u^{(n)}$ be the corresponding eigenvectors. Then, the general solution of the fractional differential equation (44) is given by

$$X(t) = \sum_{k=1}^{n} C_k u^{(k)} E_\alpha(\lambda_k t^\alpha), \tag{48}$$

with certain constants $C_k \in C$.

Example

Let us consider the system

$$_0^C D_t^\alpha X(t) = AX(t),$$

where $0 < \alpha < 1$ and $A = \begin{pmatrix} 2 & -1 \\ 4 & -3 \end{pmatrix}$.

The eigenvalues of the matrix A are $\lambda_1 = 1$ and $\lambda_2 = -2$ and their corresponding eigenvectors are $u^{(1)} = [1,1]^T$ and $u^{(2)} = [1,4]^T$ respectively. Thus, the general solution of the given system is

$$X(t) = c_1 \begin{pmatrix} 1 \\ 1 \end{pmatrix} E_\alpha(t^\alpha) + c_2 \begin{pmatrix} 1 \\ 4 \end{pmatrix} E_\alpha(-2t^\alpha),$$

where c_1 and c_2 are arbitrary constants.

Remark

If the matrix A has a repeated eigenvalue λ, of algebraic multiplicity k and geometric multiplicity m (i.e.: with m linearly independent eigenvectors $u^{(1)}, ..., u^{(m)}$), then we envisage two cases.

1. *If $m = k$, then*

$$X^{(1)} = u^{(1)} E_\alpha(\lambda t^\alpha), ..., X^{(k)} = u^{(k)} E_\alpha(\lambda t^\alpha),$$

are k linearly independent solutions of the homogeneous system (44).

2. *If $m < k$, then, the theorem (12) is not applicable and we must resort to a different representation of the general solution.*

Definition

Let λ be an eigenvalue of multiplicity k, of the $n \times n$ matrix A. Then for $i = 1, ..., k$, any nonzero solution v of

$$(A - \lambda I)^i v = 0 \quad with \quad (A - \lambda I)^{i-1} v \neq 0,$$

is called a generalized eigenvector of order i, of the matrix A. The set of generalized eigenvectors $v^{(1)}, ..., v^{(k)}$ is linearly independent and is called a Jordan chain.

Notice that an ordinary eigenvector u can be considered as a generalised eigenvector of order 1. The generalized eigenvectors $v^{(1)}, ..., v^{(k)}$ can be determined by solving the following successive sequence of linear equations, in which $v^{(r)}$ is known and $v^{(r+1)}$ is unknown:

$$(A - \lambda I) v^{(1)} = 0,$$

$$(A - \lambda I)v^{(2)} = v^{(1)},$$

$$(A - \lambda I)v^{(3)} = v^{(2)},$$

. . .

$$(A - \lambda I)v^{(k)} = v^{(k-1)}.$$

In the case (b), the generalized eigenvalues will be useful for creating the fundamental set of solutions of the homogeneous system (44) as shown in the following theorem.

Theorem 13: For each k-fold eigenvalue λ, of the matrix A we have k linearly independent solutions $X^{(1)}, ..., X^{(k)}$ of the homogeneous linear system (44) which can be represented in the form

$$X^{(l)}(t) = \sum_{s=0}^{l-1} v^{(s+1)} t^{(l-1-s)\alpha} E_\alpha^{(l-1-s)}(\lambda t^\alpha), \quad l = 1, ..., k. \tag{49}$$

The combination of these solutions for all eigenvalues leads to n linearly independent solutions of the system (44).

Remark

Let $X(t) = [x_1(t), x_2(t), ..., x_n(t)]^T$ be the solution of the initial value problem, consisting of the homogeneous system (34) and the initial condition $X(0) = X_0$. Then, the initial value problem for the non-homogeneous fractional order system

$$\begin{cases} {}_0^C D_t^\alpha X(t) = AX(t) + B(t), & 0 < t \le a, \\ X(0) = X_0, \end{cases}$$

where

$$B(t) = [b_1(t), b_2(t), ..., b_n(t)]^T,$$

has the solution

$$Y(t) = [y_1(t), y_2(t), ..., y_n(t)]^T,$$

such that

$$y_i(t) = x_i(t) + \int_0^t x_i(\tau - t) b_i(\tau) d\tau.$$

NUMERICAL ALGORITHMS FOR FRACTIONAL EQUATIONS

Two sets of the numerical methods have been mainly used in the literature, to solve fractional-order differential equations, namely, the frequency-domain methods (Sun,1984) and the time-domain methods (Deng, 2007b; Deng, 2007c; Diethelm et al., 2002).

The frequency-domain methods have been primarily most frequently used to investigate chaos in fractional order systems (Hartley, 1995; Li, 2004). Unfortunately, it has been shown that these approaches are not always reliable for detecting chaos in such systems (Tavazoei, 2007) (Tavazoei, 2008). Therefore, a great deal of effort has been recently expended over the last years in attempting to find robust and stable numerical as well as analytical time-domain methods for solving fractional differential equations of physical interest. The Adomian decomposition method (Abdulaziz, 2008), homotopy perturbation method (Odibat, 2008), homotopy analysis method (Cang, 2009), differential transform method (Momani, 2008) and variational iteration method (Odibat, 2006) are relatively new approaches to provide an analytical approximate solution to linear and nonlinear fractional differential equations.

An efficient method for solving fractional differential equations in term of Caputo type fractional derivative, is the predictor-corrector scheme or more precisely, PECE (Predict, Evaluate, Correct, Evaluate) (Diethelm et al., 2002; Diethelm, 1999), which represents a generalization of Adams-Bashforth-Moulton algorithm. This method is described as follows.

Let us consider the following fractional order initial value problem

$$\begin{cases} {}_0^C D_t^\alpha x = f(t,x), \ 0 \le t \le T, \\ x^{(k)}(0) = x_0^k, \ k = 0,1,2,...,[\alpha]-1 \end{cases} \tag{50}$$

which is equivalent to the Volterra integral equation

$$x(t) = \sum_{k=0}^{n-1} x_0^k \frac{t^k}{k!} + \frac{1}{\Gamma(\alpha)} \int_0^t (t-\tau)^{(\alpha-1)} f(\tau,x(\tau)) d\tau. \tag{51}$$

Set $h = T/N$ and $t_j = jh, \ (j = 0,1,2,...,N)$ with T being the upper bound of the interval on which we are looking for the solution. Then, the corrector formula for equation (51) is given by

$$x_h(t_{n+1}) = \sum_{k=0}^{[\alpha]-1} x_0^k \frac{t_{n+1}^k}{k!} + \frac{h^\alpha}{\Gamma(\alpha+2)} f(t_{n+1}, x_h^p(t_{n+1})) + \frac{h^\alpha}{\Gamma(\alpha+2)} \sum_{j=0}^n a_{j,n+1} f(t_j, x_h(t_j)), \tag{52}$$

where

$$a_{j,n+1} = \begin{cases} n^{\alpha+1} - (n-\alpha)(n+1)^{\alpha}, & j = 0 \\ (n-j+2)^{\alpha+1} + (n-j)^{\alpha+1} - 2(n-j+1)^{\alpha+1}, & 1 \le j \le n. \end{cases} \tag{53}$$

By using a one-step Adams-Bashforth rule instead of a one-step Adams-Moulton rule, the predictor $x_h^p(t_{n+1})$ is given by

$$x_h^p(t_{n+1}) = \sum_{k=0}^{n-1} x_0^k \frac{t_{n+1}^k}{k!} + \frac{1}{\Gamma(\alpha)} \sum_{j=0}^{n} b_{j,n+1} f(t_j, x_h(t_j)), \tag{54}$$

where

$$b_{j,n+1} = \frac{h^{\alpha}}{\alpha}((n-j+1)^{\alpha} - (n-j)^{\alpha}), \ 0 \le j \le n. \tag{55}$$

The error estimate of this method is

$$\varepsilon = \max_{0 \le j \le n} |x(t_j) - x_h(t_j)| = O(h^p), \tag{56}$$

where $p = \min(2, 1+\alpha)$.

Now, the basic algorithm for the fractional Adams-Bashforth-Moulton method is completely described.

For numerical resolution of fractional differential equations in term of Riemann-Liouville derivative we adopt the algorithm derived from the Grünwald-Letnikov definition (28). This approach is based on the fact that for a wide class of functions, two definitions Grünwald-Letnikov (28) and Riemann-Liouville (19) are equivalent. The relation for the explicit numerical approximation of the αth derivative at the points kh ($k = 1, 2, ...$) has the following form

$$_{0}^{RL}D_t^{\alpha} x(kh) \approx \frac{1}{h^{\alpha}} \sum_{j=0}^{k} (-1)^j \binom{\alpha}{j} x((k-j)h), \tag{57}$$

where h is the time step of the calculation and $(-1)^j \binom{\alpha}{j} = C_j^{\alpha}$, ($j = 0, 1, ...$) are binomial coefficients.

For their calculation we can use the following expression

$$C_0^{\alpha} = 1, \ C_j^{\alpha} = (\frac{j-\alpha-1}{j})C_{j-1}^{\alpha}. \tag{58}$$

The described numerical method is a so-called Power Series Expansion (PSE) of a generating function.

For $t >> a$ the number of addends in the fractional-derivative approximation (52) (57) becomes enormously large. However, it follows from the expression for the coefficients in the Grünwald-Letnikov definition (27) that for large t the role of the history of behaviour of the function $f(t)$ near the lower terminal $t = a$ can be neglected under certain assumption. Those observations lead Podlubny (Podlubny, 1999), to the formulation of the short memory principle which mean taking into account the behaviour of $f(t)$ only in the short interval $[t - L, t]$, where L is the memory length

$$_aD_t^\alpha f(t) \approx {}_{t-L}D_t^\alpha f(t), \quad (t > a + L).$$ (59)

Clearly, the fractional derivative with lower limit a is approximated by the fractional derivative with moving lower limit $t - L$, therefore the number of addends in (59) is always less than L / h.

If $f(t) \le M$ for all $t \in [a, b]$ then the error of approximation is given by (Podlubny, 1999)

$$\Delta(t) =| \ _aD_t^\alpha f(t) - {}_{t-L}D_t^\alpha f(t) | \le \frac{M}{L^\alpha \, |\Gamma(1-\alpha)|}, \quad (a + L \le t).$$ (60)

Thus, in order to obtain a good approximation (i.e.; $\Delta(t) \le \varepsilon$) we must choose the memory length L which satisfies

$$L \ge \left(\frac{M}{\varepsilon \, |\Gamma(1-\alpha)|} \right)^{1/\alpha}.$$ (61)

FRACTIONAL-ORDER DYNAMICAL SYSTEMS

Fractional-order dynamical systems, can be considered as a generalization of integer order systems (Miller, 1993; Oldham, 1974). In this chapter we will focus our attention on the qualitative study (stability theory, periodic behavior, bifurcation and chaos) of a fractional-order dynamical system given in the following form

$$_0^C D_t^\alpha x = f(t, x),$$ (62)

where $x \in \mathbb{R}^n$, f is defined on a suitable subset $U \subset \mathbb{R}^{n+1}$ and $\alpha = [\alpha_1, \alpha_2, ..., \alpha_n]^T$ are the fractional orders, $0 \le \alpha_i \le 1$, $(i = 1, 2, ..., n)$ (we adopt this restriction of fractional order α because fractional equations in this range require only one initial condition to guarantee the uniqueness of the solution). When $\alpha_1 = \alpha_2 = ... = \alpha_n$, the system (1) is called a commensurate order system, otherwise it is an incommensurate order system. If f depends explicitly on t then (62) is called non-autonomous system otherwise it is called autonomous system. The constant a is an equilibrium point of the Caputo fractional dynamical system (62), if and only if $f(t, a) = 0$, for all t.

Stability Theory of Fractional Systems

A well known and important area of research in theory of dynamical system is the stability theory, the stability of fractional system is different from that in the integer one. When talking about stability, one is interested in the behaviour of solutions of (62) for $t \to \infty$. Therefore we will only consider problems whose solutions x exist on $[0, \infty)$. Moreover, some additional assumptions are required in this section. The first assumption is that f is defined on a set $G = [0, \infty) \times \{w \in \mathbf{R}^n : \|w\| < W\}$ with some $0 < W \leq \infty$ The norm of G may be an arbitrary norm on $\mathbb{R}^n$. The second assumption is that f is continuous on its domain of definition and that it satisfies a Lipschitz condition there. This asserts that the initial value problem consisting of (1) and the initial condition $x(0) = x_0$ has a unique solution on the interval $[0, b)$ with some $b \leq \infty$ if $\|x_0\| \leq W$. And finally we assume that the function $x(t) = 0$ is a solution of (62) for $t \geq 0$. Under these assumptions we may formulate the followings main concepts.

Definition

Under the hypothesis mentioned above, the solution $x(t) = 0$ of the system (62) is said to be

- **Stable if:** *For any $\varepsilon > 0$ there exists some $\delta > 0$ such that the solution of the initial value problem consisting of (62) and the initial condition $x(0) = x_0$ satisfies $\|x(t)\| < \varepsilon$ for all $t \geq 0$ whenever $\|x_0\| < \delta$.*
- **Asymptotically stable if:** *It is stable and there exists some $\gamma > 0$ such that $\lim_{t \to \infty} x(t) = 0$ whenever $\|x_0\| < \gamma$.*

Remark

A solution y of the differential equation ${}_0^C D_t^\alpha x = g(t, x)$ is said to be (asymptotically) stable if and only if the zero solution of ${}_0^C D_t^\alpha z = f(t, z)$ with $f(t, z) = g(t, z + y(t)) - g(t, y(t))$ is (asymptotically) stable.

Definition (Exponential Stability)

The solution $x(t) = 0$ of the system (1) is said to be (locally) exponentially stable if there exist two real constants $\alpha, \lambda > 0$ such that

$$\|x(t)\| \leq \alpha \|x(t_0)\| e^{-\lambda t} \quad \text{for all } t > t_0, \tag{63}$$

whenever $\|x(t_0)\| < \delta$. It is said to be globally exponentially stable if (63) holds for any $x(t_0) \in \mathbf{R}^n$.

A generalization of exponential stability is the Mittag-Leffler stability which is more useful for fractional system.

Definition (Mittag-Leffler Stability)

The solution $x(t) = 0$ of (1) is said to be Mittag-Leffler stable if

$$\|x(t)\| \leq \{m[x(t_0)]E_\alpha(-\lambda(t-t_0)^\alpha)\}^b,$$

where t_0 is the initial time, $\alpha \in (0,1)$ the fractional order, $\lambda \geq 0$, $b > 0$, $m(0) = 0$, $m(x) > 0$ and $m(x)$ is locally Lipschitz on $x \in B \subset \mathbf{R}^n$ with constant Lipschitz m_0.

Definition (Generalized Mittag-Leffler Stability)

The solution $x(t) = 0$ of (62) is said to be generalized Mittag-Leffler stable if

$$\|x(t)\| \leq \{m[x(t_0)](t-t_0)^{-\gamma}E_{\alpha,1-\gamma}(-\lambda(t-t_0)^\alpha)\}^b,$$

where t_0 is the initial time, $\alpha \in (0,1)$ the fractional order, $-\alpha < \gamma \leq 1-\alpha$, $\lambda \geq 0$, $b > 0$, $m(0) = 0$, $m(x) \geq 0$ and $m(x)$ is locally Lipschitz on $x \in B \subset \mathbf{R}^n$ with constant Lipschitz m_0.

Notice here that the Mittag-Leffler stability and Generalized Mittag-Leffler stability implies asymptotic stability.

As mentioned in (Matignon, 1996), the stabilities of fractional-order systems are not of exponential type. Thus, a new definition called power law stability $t^{-\beta}$ was introduced in (Oustaloup, 2008), which is a special case of the Mittag-Leffler stability (Li et al., 2008) and it is defined as follows.

Definition (Power Law Stability $t^{-\beta}$).

The trajectory $x(t) = 0$ of the system (1) is $t^{-\beta}$ asymptotically stable if there is a positive real β such that:

$$\forall \|x(t)\| \text{ with } t \leq t_0, \exists N(x(t)), \text{ such that } \forall t \geq t_0, \|x(t)\| \leq Nt^{-\beta}.$$

Stability of Fractional LTI Systems

Stability of linear fractional order systems, which is of main interest in control theory, has been thoroughly investigated where necessary and sufficient conditions have been derived. In 1996, Matignon (Matignon, 1996), have been introduced the stability properties of n-dimension a linear fractional order systems from a point of view of control. In Deng (2007d), Deng studied the stability of n-dimensional linear fractional differential equation with time delays. An interesting difference between stable integer-order system and a stable fractional-order system is that the last one may have roots in right half of the complex plane.

Theorem 14: Consider the N-dimensional linear differential system with fractional commensurate order α

$$_0^C D_t^\alpha X = AX,$$ (64)

where A is an arbitrary constant $N \times N$ matrix.

1. The system (64) is asymptotically stable if and only if $|\arg(spec(A))| > \alpha\pi/2$. In this case the components of the state decay towards 0 like $t^{-\alpha}$.

2. The system (64) is stable if and only if $|\arg(spec(A))| \geq \alpha\pi/2$ and all eigenvalues with $|\arg(\lambda)| = \alpha\pi/2$ have a geometric multiplicity that coincides with their algebraic multiplicity.

The fact that the components of $x(t)$ slowly decay towards 0 following $t^{-\alpha}$ leads to fractional systems, sometimes, being called long memory systems.

In the limit case $\alpha \to 1$ we recover the well known classical result (Corduneanu, 1977), that the eigenvalues must have negative real parts in case (a) and non-positive real parts and a full set of eigenvectors if the real parts are zero for case (b).

Proof: If the matrix A is diagonalisable then according to theorem (14), the general solution is given by

$$X(t) = \sum_{k=1}^{n} C_k u^{(k)} E_\alpha(\lambda_k t^\alpha),$$ (65)

and by theorem (13) its Laplace transform is

$$X(s) = \sum_{k=1}^{n} C_k u^{(k)} \frac{s^{\alpha-1}}{s^\alpha - \lambda_k}.$$ (66)

If A is not diagonalisable then according to theorem (17), the general solution can be given by a linear combination of a fundamental solutions given by

$$X^{(j,l)}(t) = \sum_{i=0}^{l-1} v^{(j,i+1)} t^{(l-1-i)\alpha} E_\alpha^{(l-1-i)}(\lambda_j t^\alpha), \quad l = 1, \ldots, k_j \quad j = 1, \ldots, m.$$ (67)

where k_j is the multiplicity of eigenvalue λ_j and $\sum_{j=1}^{m} k_j = n$.

Taking into account the relation (27) and applying Laplace transform to both sides of (67) yields

$$X^{(j,l)}(s) = \sum_{i=0}^{l-1} v^{(j,i+1)} \frac{(l-i-1)! s^{\alpha-1}}{(s^\alpha - \lambda_j)^{l-i}}, \quad l = 1, \ldots, k_j \quad j = 1, \ldots, m.$$ (68)

Now, if all eigenvalues lie in the region $|\arg(\lambda^{\frac{1}{\alpha}})| > \dfrac{\pi}{2}$; (i.e $|\arg(\lambda)| > \alpha\pi/2$), then using (66), (67) and the final value theorem we get

$$\lim_{t\to\infty} X(t) = \lim_{s\to 0} sX(s) = 0.$$

If there is some eigenvalues lie in the region $|\arg(\lambda)| < \alpha\pi/2$, then from theorem (7) we have

$$\lim_{t\to\infty} |E_\alpha(\lambda t^\alpha)| = \infty$$

Thus from (65) and (66), $X(t)$ is unbounded.

Therefore, the system (64) is asymptotically stable if and only if all eigenvalues lie in the region $|\arg(\lambda)| > \alpha\pi/2$.

Next we consider the stability of incommensurate rational order system (Deng, 2007d).

Corollary

Suppose that $\alpha_1 \neq \alpha_2 \neq ... \neq \alpha_n$ and all α_i's are rational numbers between 0 and 1, and suppose that m is the lowest common multiple of the denominators u_i of α_i, $(i = 1,...,n)$ where $\alpha_i = \dfrac{v_i}{u_i}$, for , and setting then system (3) is asymptotically stable if:

$$|\arg(\lambda)| > \gamma \frac{\pi}{2} \tag{69}$$

for all roots λ of the following characteristic equation

$$det(diag([\lambda^{m\alpha_1},...,\lambda^{m\alpha_n}]) - A) = 0. \tag{70}$$

The characteristic equation of (64) is of fractional powers of s, this corollary tells that in case of rational orders the characteristics equation can be transformed to an integer-order polynomial equation.

Proof: The application of the Laplace transform to both sides of (64) gives the equation

$$(diag([s^{\alpha_1},...,s^{\alpha_n}]) - A)X(s) = (s^{\alpha_1-1}x_1(0),...,s^{\alpha_n-1}x_n(0))^T, \tag{71}$$

multiplying s on both sides of (10) gives

$$(diag([s^{\alpha_1},...,s^{\alpha_n}]) - A)sX(s) = (s^{\alpha_1}x_1(0),...,s^{\alpha_n}x_n(0))^T, \tag{72}$$

which does not have an unique solution $sX(s)$ only when

$$det(diag([s^{\alpha_1},...,s^{\alpha_n}]) - A) = 0. \tag{73}$$

Denoting $s = \lambda^{\frac{1}{\gamma}} = \lambda^m$ and subtracting in (12) yields the equation (19). If all roots of the equation (73) lie in open left half complex plane, $Re(s) < 0$ (i.e. $|arg(s)| > \dfrac{\pi}{2}$ which imply $|arg(\lambda)| > \gamma\dfrac{\pi}{2}$), then we consider (21) in $Re(s) \geq 0$. In this restricted area, (21) has a unique solution $sX(s) = (sX_1(s),...,sX_n(s))$. So, we have

$$\lim_{s \to 0, Re(s) \geq 0} sX_i(s) = 0, i = 1,...,n.$$

Using the final-value theorem of Laplace transform, we get

$$\lim_{t \to \infty} x_i(t) = \lim_{s \to 0, Re(s) \geq 0} sX_i(s) = 0, i = 1,...,n.$$

This complete the proof.

Theorem 14, remain valid (Moze, 2005), in the case $1 < \alpha < 2$.

Stability of Fractional Nonlinear Systems

Let consider the commensurate fractional-order nonlinear autonomous system given by

$$^C_0 D^\alpha_t x = f(x) \tag{74}$$

where $x \in \mathsf{R}^n$, f is defined on a suitable subset $U \subset \mathsf{R}^n$. According to stability theorem defined in Tavazoei (2008) and Abdelouahab (2010), an equilibrium point $\tilde{x}$ of system (23) is locally asymptotically stable for a given α in $(0,2)$ if all the eigenvalues $\lambda_i, (i = 1, 2,...,n)$ of the Jacobian matrix $J = \dfrac{\partial f}{\partial x}|_{x=\tilde{x}}$ satisfy the condition

$$|\arg(\lambda_i)| > \alpha\frac{\pi}{2}, \ i = 1, 2,...,n. \tag{75}$$

Remark

The given theoretical results make clear that the stability condition for fractional-order systems differs from the well-known condition for integer order systems. In particular, the left half-plane (stable region) for integer-order systems maps into the angular sector $|\arg(spec(J))| > \alpha\pi / 2$ in the case of fractional-order systems, indicating that the stable region becomes larger and larger when the value of fractional-order α is decreased. Figure 3 shows stable and unstable regions of the complex plane, for $0 < \alpha < 2$.

Now, let consider the incommensurate fractional order system $\alpha_1 \neq \alpha_2 \neq ... \neq \alpha_n$ and suppose that m is the LCM of the denominators u_i of α_i, ($i = 1,...,n$) where $\alpha_i = \dfrac{v_i}{u_i}$, $v_i, u_i \in Z^+$ for $i = 1,...,n$, then the system (23) is asymptotically stable if:

$$|arg(\lambda)| > \frac{\pi}{2m},$$

for all roots λ of the following equation

$$det(diag([\lambda^{m\alpha_1},...,\lambda^{m\alpha_n}]) - J) = 0.$$

Some Routh-Hurwitz Conditions for Fractional Systems

Routh-Hurwitz criterion is a powerful tool used for the stability analysis of some parameter dynamical systems, because it provides an opportunity to study the stability of such parameter system without the need to set its control parameters, therefore we can identify the stability region in the parameter space, this technique is extensively used in the area of control and synchronization. Some Routh-Hurwitz stability conditions are generalized to the fractional order case in (Ahmed, 2006), and largely used in field of control and synchronization (Abdelouahab, 2012; Matouk, 2009). Consider the commensurate system

$$_{0}^{C}D_{t}^{\alpha}x = f(x, \mu), \tag{76}$$

Figure 3. Stability region for fractional-order systems

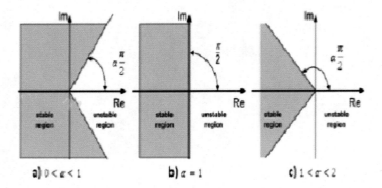

where $x \in \mathbb{R}^n$ is the state space vector, $\mu \in \mathbb{R}^m$ is the parameter vector and f is defined on a suitable subset $U \subset \mathbb{R}^n \times \mathbb{R}^m$. An interesting question arises when analysing the condition (75), namely, what are the conditions on μ, that all the roots of the polynomial equation

$$P(\lambda) = \lambda^n + a_1(\mu)\lambda^{n-1} + \ldots + a_{n-1}(\mu)\lambda + a_n(\mu) = 0, \tag{77}$$

satisfy (75) where all the coefficients in (77) are real?

For $\alpha = 1$ the answer is given by the classical Routh-Hurwitz criterion (Mishina, 1965) that is

$$a_1 > 0,$$

$$\begin{vmatrix} a_1 & 1 \\ a_3 & a_2 \end{vmatrix} > 0,$$

$$\begin{vmatrix} a_1 & 1 & 0 \\ a_3 & a_2 & a_1 \\ a_5 & a_4 & a_3 \end{vmatrix} > 0,$$

$$\ldots$$

$$\begin{vmatrix} a_1 & 1 & 0 & \ldots & & 0 \\ a_3 & a_2 & a_1 & 1 & & 0\ldots0 \\ a_5 & a_4 & a_3 \ldots & & 1 & 0\ldots0 \\ \cdot & \cdot & \cdot & \cdot & \cdot & \\ 0 & 0 & 0 & \ldots & & a_n \end{vmatrix} > 0.$$

For $\alpha \in (0,1)$ the classical Routh-Hurwitz conditions are sufficient but not necessary, therefore we need a new version of this criterion that will be adopted in the last case.

Definition

The discriminant $D(P)$ of a polynomial $P(\lambda)$ is defined by

$$D(P) = (-1)^{n(n-1)/2} R(P, P'),$$

where P' is the derivative of P and $R(P, P')$ is the $(2n-1) \times (2n-1)$ resultant of $P(\lambda)$ and its derivative $P'(\lambda)$, given as follows

$$R(P,P') = \begin{vmatrix} 1 & a_1 & \cdots & a_n & 0 & \cdots & 0 \\ 0 & 1 & a_1 & \cdots & a_n & 0\cdots & 0 \\ \cdot & \cdot & \cdot & \cdot & \cdot & \cdot & \cdot \\ 0 & \cdots & 0 & 1 & a_1 & \cdots & a_n \\ n & (n-1)a_1 & \cdots & a_{n-1} & 0 & \cdots & 0 \\ 0 & n & (n-1)a_1 & \cdots & a_{n-1} & 0\cdots & 0 \\ \cdot & \cdot & \cdot & \cdot & \cdot & \cdot & \cdot \\ 0 & \cdots & 0 & n & (n-1)a_1 & \cdots & a_{n-1} \end{vmatrix}$$

For $n = 3$, we have

$$D(p) = 18a_1 a_2 a_3 + (a_1 a_2)^2 - 4a_3(a_1)^3 - 4(a_2)^3 - 27(a_3)^2.$$

Noting that if $D(P) > 0$ (< 0), there is an even (odd) number of pairs of complex roots for the equation $P(\lambda) = 0$.

For $n = 3$, $D(P) > 0$ implies that all the roots are real, and $D(P) < 0$ implies that there is only one real root and one pair of complex conjugate roots.

Proposition

1. *For $n = 1$, the condition for (75) is $a_1 > 0$.*
2. *For $n = 2$:*
   a. *If $D(p) \geq 0$, the condition for (75) is $a_1 > 0$ and $a_2 > 0$.*
   b. *If $D(p) < 0$, the condition for (75) is $\left| \tan^{-1}\left(\dfrac{\sqrt{4a_2 - (a_1)^2}}{a_1} \right) \right| > \alpha \dfrac{\pi}{2}$.*
3. *For $n = 3$:*
   a. *When $D(p) > 0$, the necessary and sufficient conditions of (75) are the classical Routh-Hurwitz conditions given by $a_1 > 0$, $a_3 > 0$ and $a_1 a_2 > a_3$.*
   b. *When $D(p) < 0$, we distinct the three following cases*
      i. *If $a_1 > 0$, $a_2 > 0$, $a_3 > 0$ and $\alpha < \dfrac{2}{3}$ then (75) is satisfied.*
      ii. *If $a_1 < 0$, $a_2 < 0$ and $\alpha > \dfrac{2}{3}$ then all roots of $P(\lambda) = 0$ satisfies $|\arg(\lambda)| < \alpha \dfrac{\pi}{2}$.*
      iii. *If $a_1 > 0$, $a_2 > 0$ and $a_1 a_2 = a_3$ then (75) is satisfied for all $\alpha \in [0,1)$.*
4. *For general $n > 1$, the necessary and sufficient condition for (14) is*

$$\int_0^\infty \frac{dz}{P(z)}\bigg|_{C_2} + \int_{-\infty}^0 \frac{dz}{P(z)}\bigg|_{C_1} = 0,$$

where C_1 is the curve

$$z = x(1 - i\tan\alpha\pi / 2),$$

and C_2 is the curve

$$z = x(1 + i\tan\alpha\pi / 2).$$

Proof

1. For $n = 1$, we have $P(\lambda) = \lambda + a_1$ which posses a single real root $\lambda = -a_1$ then (75) is satisfied if and only if $a_1 > 0$.
2. For $n = 2$, we have

$$P(\lambda) = \lambda^2 + a_1\lambda + a_2,$$

its roots are given by

$$\lambda_\pm = \frac{-a_1 \pm \sqrt{(a_1)^2 - 4a_2}}{2}.$$

  a. If $D(p) \geq 0$, $\lambda_\pm$ are real and (75) will be converted to classical Routh-Hurwitz conditions, namely $a_1 > 0$, $a_2 > 0$.

  b. If $D(p) < 0$, $\lambda_\pm$ are complex conjugates and the condition (75) is equivalent to

$$\left| \tan^{-1}\left(\frac{\sqrt{4a_2 - (a_1)^2}}{a_1} \right) \right| > \alpha\frac{\pi}{2}.$$

3. For $n = 3$, we have:
  a. When $D(p) > 0$ then all the roots of $P(\lambda) = 0$ are real. Thus, the classical Routh-Hurwitz conditions are equivalents to (75).

  b. When $D(p) < 0$, the roots of $P(\lambda) = 0$ are one real $\lambda_0 = -b$ and a complex conjugate pair $\lambda_\pm = \beta \pm i\gamma$. Hence,

$$P(\lambda) = (\lambda + b)(\lambda - \beta - i\gamma)(\lambda - \beta + i\gamma),$$

and its coefficients are

$$a_1 = b - 2\beta, a_2 = \beta^2 + \gamma^2 - 2b\beta, a_3 = b(\beta^2 + \gamma^2).$$

      i. $a_3 > 0$ imply $b > 0$, $a_1 > 0$ imply $b > 2\beta$, and

$$a_2 > 0 \text{ imply } \frac{\beta^2}{\cos^2(\theta)} > 2b\beta > 4\beta^2$$

thus

$$\theta > \frac{\pi}{3}$$

where $\theta = |\arg(\lambda)|$, so if $\alpha < \dfrac{2}{3}$ then (75) is satisfied.

      ii. $a_1 < 0$ imply $b < 2\beta$ and

$$a_2 < 0 \text{ imply } \frac{\beta^2}{\cos^2(\theta)} < 2b\beta < 4\beta^2$$

thus

$$\theta < \frac{\pi}{3}$$

so if $\alpha > \dfrac{2}{3}$ then

$$|\arg(\lambda)| < \alpha \frac{\pi}{2}.$$

      iii. $a_1 a_2 = a_3$ imply $\beta(\beta^2 + \gamma^2) + b^2\beta = 2b\beta^2$ thus

$$\beta = 0 \text{ } or \text{ } \beta^2 + \gamma^2 + b^2 = 2b\beta.$$

The last equality is not valid if both $a_1 > 0$ and $a_2 > 0$ thus

$$\min_\lambda |\arg(\lambda)| = \frac{\pi}{2}.$$

Therefore (75) is satisfied for all $\alpha \in [0,1)$.

4. For general $n > 1$ if $P(z)$ has no roots in the region

$$|\arg(\lambda)| < \alpha \frac{\pi}{2},$$

then the function $\dfrac{1}{P(z)}$ will be analytic in this region. Using Cauchy theorem

$$\oint_C f(z)dz = 0,$$

for all $f(z)$ analytic within and on C, and the fact that $P(z)$ is polynomial of degree > 1 this completes the proof.

Corollary

For general $n > 1$, a necessary condition for (75) is $a_n > 0$.

Proof: For general $n > 1$, we have

$$P(\lambda) = [\prod_i (\lambda + b_i)][\prod_j (\lambda^2 - 2\beta_j \lambda + \beta_j^2 + \gamma_j^2)]$$

then

$$a_n = [\prod_i b_i][\prod_j (\beta_j^2 + \gamma_j^2)].$$

So if $a_n \leq 0$, there exists at last i_0 such that $(b_{i_0} \leq 0)$. Hence, there exists at last a positive real rout $(-b_{i_0} \geq 0)$ of $P(\lambda) = 0$. Thus, $\min_\lambda |\arg(\lambda)| = 0$. Therefore, for all $\alpha \in [0,1)$ (75) is not satisfied. Hence, the necessary condition for (75) is $a_n > 0$.

LYAPUNOV DIRECT METHOD FOR FRACTIONAL SYSTEM

Lyapunov direct method is used for studying both local and global stability of the corresponding systems. In this section we discuss the extension of Lyapunov direct method for fractional-order nonlinear systems which leads to the Mittag-Leffler stability (Delavari et al., 2012; Li, 2010).

Theorem 15: *Let $x = 0$ be an equilibrium point for the system*

$$\,_{0}^{C}D_{t}^{\alpha}x(t) = f(t,x), \ \alpha \in [0,1), \tag{78}$$

and $D \subset \mathbf{R}^{n}$ be a domain containing the origin.

Let $V(t,x(t)) : [0,\infty) \times D \to \mathbf{R}$ be a continuously differentiable function and locally Lipschitz with respect to x such that

$$\alpha_{1}\|x\|^{a} \le V(t,x(t)) \le \alpha_{2}\|x\|^{ab}, \tag{79}$$

$$\,_{0}^{C}D_{t}^{\beta}V(t,x(t)) \le -\alpha_{3}\|x\|^{ab}, \tag{80}$$

where $t \ge 0, x \in D, \beta \in [0,1), \alpha_{1},\alpha_{2},\alpha_{3}, a$ and b are arbitrary positive constants.

Then, $x = 0$ is Mittag-Leffler stable.

If the assumptions hold globally on $\mathbf{R}^{n}$. Then, $x = 0$ is globally Mittag-Leffler stable.

The following theorem gives a generalized fractional Lyapunov direct method.

Theorem 16: *Let $x = 0$ be an equilibrium point for the system (78) and $D \subset \mathbf{R}^{n}$ be a domain containing the origin.*

Let $V(t,x(t)) : [0,\infty) \times D \to \mathbf{R}$ be a continuously differentiable function and locally Lipschitz with respect to x such that

$$\alpha_{1}\|x\|^{a} \le V(t,x(t)) \le \alpha_{2}\,_{0}^{C}D_{t}^{-\eta}\|x\|^{ab}, \tag{81}$$

$$\,_{0}^{C}D_{t}^{\beta}V(t,x(t)) \le -\alpha_{3}\|x\|^{ab}, \tag{82}$$

where

$$t \ge 0, x \in D, \beta \in [0,1), \eta \ne \beta, \eta > 0, |\beta - \eta| < 1, \alpha_{1},\alpha_{2},\alpha_{3}, a$$

and b are arbitrary positive constants. Then, $x = 0$ is asymptotically stable.

Now we apply the class-K functions to the analysis of fractional Lyapunov direct method.

Definition

A continuous function $\alpha : [0,t) \to [0,\infty)$ is said to belong to class-K if it is strictly increasing and $\alpha(0) = 0$.

Lemma (Fractional Comparison Principle): Assume that $_0^C D_t^\alpha x(t) \geq _0^C D_t^\alpha y(t)$ and $x(0) = y(0)$, for $\alpha \in (0,1)$. So $x(t) \geq y(t)$.

Theorem 17: *Let* $x = 0$ *be an equilibrium point for the system (78). Assume that there exists a Lyapunov function* $V(t,x(t))$. *and a class-K functions* $\alpha_i (i = 1,2,3$ *satisfying*

$$\alpha_1(\|x\|) \leq V(t,x(t)) \leq \alpha_2(\|x\|), \tag{83}$$

$$_0^C D_t^\beta V(t,x(t)) \leq -\alpha_3(\|x\|), \tag{84}$$

where $\beta \in [0,1)$. *Then* $x = 0$ *is asymptotically stable.*

Example

Let consider the fractional system

$$_0^C D_t^\alpha \mid x(t) \mid = - \mid x(t) \mid, \tag{85}$$

where $\alpha \in (0,1)$. We choose the Lipschitz function $V(t,x) = \mid x \mid$ as a Lyapunov candidate and $\alpha_1 = \alpha_2 = a = b = 1, \alpha_3 = -1$. Then,

$$\alpha_1 \mid x(t) \mid^a \leq V(t,x) \leq \alpha_2 \mid x(t) \mid^{ab}$$

and $_0^C D_t^\alpha V(t,x) \leq - \mid x(t) \mid$. Applying theorem (15) gives the Mittag-Leffler stability of the equilibrium point $x = 0$.

PERIODIC SOLUTIONS

Much attention has been focused on the existence of periodic solutions in fractional-order systems (Travazoei, 2010; Travazoei & Haeri, 2009; Travazoei, 2008; Wang & Li, 2007; Yazdani & Salarieh, 2011). The aim of this section is to highlight on one of the basic differences between fractional order and integer order systems. It is analytically shown that a time invariant fractional order system contrary to its integer order counterpart cannot generate exactly periodic signals. As a result, a limit cycle cannot be expected in the solution of these systems.

Fractional-Order Derivatives of Periodic Functions

Suppose that $x(t)$ is a non-constant periodic function with a specific period T, i.e.

$$x(t+T) = x(t), \text{ for all } t \geq 0. \tag{86}$$

Taking the derivative of both sides of (25) we obtain

$$\frac{dx}{dt}(t+T) = \frac{dx}{dt}(t), \text{ for all } t \geq 0. \tag{87}$$

Hence, the derivative of a non-constant periodic function $x(t)$ with period T is a periodic function with the same period T. Now we ask the following reasonable question. is there a similar result for the fractional derivative of a non-constant periodic function? A negative answer for this question is claimed in (Travazoei, 2010).

Theorem 18: *Suppose that $x(t)$ is a non-constant periodic function with a specific period T and m -times differentiable. The fractional-order derivative function ${}_0D_t^\alpha x(t)$ (symbol ${}_0D_t^\alpha$ denote the Riemann-Liouville, Grünwald-Litnikov or Caputo fractional-order derivative operator) where $0 < \alpha \notin N$ and m is the first integer greater than α, cannot be a periodic function with period T .*

Proof: The proof of this theorem can be found in (Travazoei, 2010)

Example

Consider the function $x(t) = sin(t)$, the Laplace transform of fractional-order derivative of $x(t)$ is given as

$$L({}_0D_t^\alpha x(t)) = s^\alpha X(s) = \frac{s^\alpha}{1+s^2} \tag{88}$$

where $0 < \alpha < 1$. The inverse Laplace transform of (27) is obtained as

$${}_0D_t^\alpha x(t) = t^{1-\alpha} E_{2,2-\alpha}(-t^2). \tag{89}$$

For $\alpha = 1$ the function $t^{1-\alpha} E_{2,2-\alpha}(-t^2)$ is a non-constant periodic function and for $0 < \alpha < 1$ this function is not periodic, but it asymptotic converges to the periodic function $sin(t + \alpha\pi / 2)$ as shown in Figure 4.

Non-Existence of Periodic Solutions in a Class of Fractional-Order Systems

Given a fractional-order time-invariant system based on the Caputo derivative and a vector of continuous functions f in the form

$${}_0^C D_t^\alpha x(t) = f(x), \ \alpha \in (0,1) \tag{90}$$

Figure 4. Graphical representation of the fractional derivative ${}_0D_t^{0.5}\sin(t)$ *and the function* $\sin(t + 0.5\dfrac{\pi}{2})$

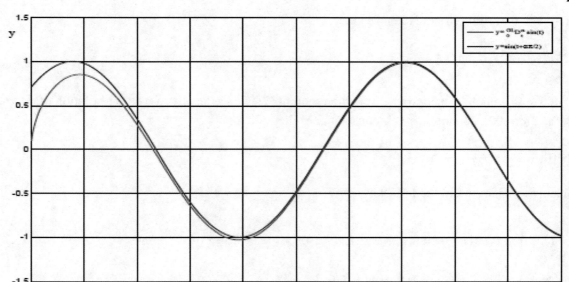

a non-constant solution

$$x(t) = (x_1(t), x_2(t), ..., x_n(t))^T,$$

of the system (90) is said to be a periodic solution if there exists a constant $T > 0$ such that:

$$x(t + T) = x(t), \tag{91}$$

for all $t \geq 0$. The minimum of such T is called period of this solution. The periodic orbit or cycle is the image of the interval $[0, T]$ under

$$x(t) = (x_1(t), x_2(t), ..., x_n(t))^T,$$

in the state space $\mathbb{R}^n$ (Wiggins, 2003).

The main outcome of this section is summarized in the following theorem:

Theorem 19: *The fractional-order time-invariant system (90) defined via the Caputo derivative cannot have any non-constant smooth periodic solution. This result has been extended in (Travazoei, 2010), by analytically proving that fractional-order system (90) based on Grünwald-Letnikov derivative or Riemann-Liouville derivative cannot generate exact periodic solutions.*

Proof: Suppose that $\tilde{x}(t)$ is a solution for differential equation (90). If $\tilde{x}(t)$ is a non-constant periodic function with periodic T, then

$$f(\tilde{x}(t)) = f(\tilde{x}(t+T)),\tag{92}$$

for all $t > 0$. From (90) and (92) we get

$$_0 D_t^\alpha \tilde{x}(t+T) =_0 D_t^\alpha \tilde{x}(t),$$

for all $t > 0$, which is in contradiction with theorem (7). Consequently, $\tilde{x}(t)$, as a solution of differential equation (90), cannot be a non-constant periodic function.

Example

Consider the marginally stable LTI system

$$\begin{cases} {}_0^C D_t^\alpha x = k\,\cos(\alpha\tfrac{\pi}{2})x + k\,\sin(\alpha\tfrac{\pi}{2})y \\ {}_0^C D_t^\alpha y(t) = -k\,\sin(\alpha\tfrac{\pi}{2})x + k\,\cos(\alpha\tfrac{\pi}{2})y. \end{cases}\tag{93}$$

System (32) can be written in matricial form as follows

$$_0^C D_t^\alpha X = AX\tag{94}$$

where

$$A = \begin{pmatrix} k\,\cos(\alpha\tfrac{\pi}{2}) & k\,\sin(\alpha\tfrac{\pi}{2}) \\ -k\,\sin(\alpha\tfrac{\pi}{2}) & k\,\cos(\alpha\tfrac{\pi}{2}) \end{pmatrix},$$

and

$$X = \begin{pmatrix} x \\ y \end{pmatrix}.$$

The matrix A has two complex conjugate eigenvalues

$$\lambda_{1,2} = k(\,\cos(\alpha\tfrac{\pi}{2}) \pm i\sin(\alpha\tfrac{\pi}{2})),$$

and its corresponding eigenvectors are

$$v_1 = \begin{pmatrix} 1 \\ i \end{pmatrix},$$

and

$$v_2 = \begin{pmatrix} 1 \\ -i \end{pmatrix}.$$

Hence, the general solution of (32) is given by

$$X(t) = \frac{1}{2}\left[c_1 \begin{pmatrix} 1 \\ 0 \end{pmatrix} + c_2 \begin{pmatrix} 0 \\ 1 \end{pmatrix} \right]\left[E_\alpha(\lambda_1 t^\alpha) + E_\alpha(\lambda_2 t^\alpha) \right]$$

$$-\frac{1}{2i}\left[c_1 \begin{pmatrix} 1 \\ 0 \end{pmatrix} - c_2 \begin{pmatrix} 0 \\ 1 \end{pmatrix} \right]\left[E_\alpha(\lambda_1 t^\alpha) - E_\alpha(\lambda_2 t^\alpha) \right], \tag{95}$$

where c_1, c_2 are arbitrary real numbers.

For special case $\alpha = 1$ the solution can be rewritten as

$$X(t) = \begin{pmatrix} c_1(cos(kt) - sin(kt)) \\ c_2(cos(kt) + sin(kt)) \end{pmatrix}. \tag{96}$$

If $(x_0, y_0) \neq (0,0)$, then all solutions of system (32) are periodic of period $\frac{2\pi}{k}$. But, for case $0 < \alpha < 1$, non-zero solutions of (93) are not periodic, although they converge to periodic signals (Travazoei M. S., 2008).

Remark

The fractional order system with lower terminal of $a = \pm\infty$ could have periodic solutions (Yazdani & Salarieh, 2011).

BIFURCATION AND CHAOS IN FRACTIONAL NONLINEAR SYSTEMS

Chaotic systems have been a focal point of renewed interest for many researchers in the past few decades. Such non-linear systems can occur in various natural and man-made systems, and are known to have great sensitivity to initial conditions. Thus, two trajectories starting at arbitrarily nearby initial conditions in such systems could evolve in drastically different fashions, and soon become totally uncorrelated. At first glance, chaotic time trajectories look very much like noise. In fact, chaotic signals and noise have similar broad-band frequency spectrum characteristics. However, there is a fundamental difference between noise and chaos, which is determinism. Chaos can be classified as deterministic but unpredictable. Whereas noise is neither deterministic nor predictable. This unpredictability of chaotic time signals has been utilized for secure communication applications (Ahmed, 2003). Basically, the useful signal is encapsulated in a chaotic envelope (produced by a chaotic oscillator) at the transmitter end, and is transmitted over the communication channel as a chaotic signal. At the receiver end, the information-bearing signal is recovered using various techniques (Bai, 2002). It has been shown that fractional-order systems, as generalizations of many well-known systems, can also behave chaotically, such as the fractional order systems of Lorenz Grigorenko (2003), Chua Hartley (1995), Chen Li (2004), Rössler Li (2004), Coullet Shahiri (2010), modified Van der Pol-Duffing (Matouk, 2011; Wang & Wang, 2007).

It has been shown that, chaos in fractional order autonomous systems can occur for orders less than three and this cannot happen in their integer order counterparts according to the Poincaré-Bendixon theorem (Hirsch, 1974).

Various scenarios of transition to chaos have been detected in fractional order systems. A well know one of them is the period doubling to chaos which is initialized in general by a Hopf bifurcation (Abdelouahab, 2012; Hamri, 2011; Sun, 2009).

Hopf Bifurcation

Different from integer order systems, there exist less theoretical tools to study dynamics of fractional-order systems. Recall that Hopf bifurcation in integer order systems can be investigated in detail by means of normal form theory and center manifold theorem (Hassard, 1982), while similar tools have not yet developed for fractional systems. So detailed results about fractional Hopf bifurcation are few. Only through stability theory of equilibrium points and numerical simulations, we have analyzed Hopf bifurcation of 3-dimensional fractional-order systems in (Abdelouahab, 2012; Hamri, 2011).

Let consider the following three-dimensional fractional-order commensurate system:

$$D^q x = f(\beta, x) \tag{97}$$

where $q \in]0, 2[$, $x \in \mathsf{R}^3$, and suppose that E is an equilibrium point of this system. In the integer case (when $q = 1$) the stability of E is related to the sign of $Re(\lambda_i), i = 1, 2, 3$ where λ_i are the eigenvalues of the jacobian matrix $\dfrac{\partial f}{\partial x}|_E$.

If $Re(\lambda_i) < 0$ for all $i = 1, 2, 3$ then E is locally asymptotically stable. If there exist i such that $Re(\lambda_i) > 0$ then E is unstable.

The conditions of system (36) with $q = 1$, to undergo a Hopf bifurcation at the equilibrium point E when $\beta = \beta^*$, are:

- The jacobian matrix has two complex-conjugate eigenvalues $\lambda_{1,2}(\beta) = \theta(\beta) \pm i\omega(\beta)$, and one real $\lambda_3(\beta)$ (this can be expressed by $D(P_E(\beta)) < 0$),
- $\theta(\beta^*) = 0$, and $\lambda_3(\beta^*) \neq 0$,
- $\omega(\beta^*) \neq 0$,
- $\left. \dfrac{d\theta}{d\beta} \right|_{\beta=\beta^*} \neq 0$.

But in the fractional case the stability of E is related to the sign of

$$m_i(q,\beta) = q\frac{\pi}{2} - \left| \arg(\lambda_i(\beta)) \right|, \quad i = 1,2,3.$$

If $m_i(q,\beta) < 0$ for all $i = 1,2,3$, then E is locally asymptotically stable.

If there exist i such that $m_i(q,\beta) > 0$, then E is unstable.

So the function $m_i(q,\beta)$ has a similar effect as the real part of eigenvalue in integer systems, therefore we extend the Hopf bifurcation conditions to the fractional systems by replacing $Re(\lambda_i)$ with $m_i(q,\beta)$ as follows

- $D(P_E(\beta)) < 0$,
- $m_{1,2}(q,\beta^*) = 0$, and $\lambda_3(\beta^*) \neq 0$,
- $\left. \dfrac{\partial m}{\partial \beta} \right|_{\beta=\beta^*} \neq 0$.

Remark

The limit cycle which appear through a Hopf bifurcation is not a solution for a fractional system but it attracts a nearby solutions.

A Necessary Condition to Have Chaos in Fractional-Order Systems

A saddle point in a 3-D nonlinear integer order system, is an equilibrium point on which the equivalent linearized model, has at least, one eigenvalue in the stable region and one in the unstable region. A saddle point is of index 1 if one of the eigenvalues is in the unstable region and others are in the stable region. A saddle point is of index 2 if two eigenvalues are in the unstable region and one is in the stable region. In chaotic systems, it is found that scrolls are generated only around the saddle points of index 2. The saddle points of index 1 are responsible only for connecting the scrolls (Cafagna, 2003, Chua, 1986; Lu, 2004; Silva, 1993). In the 3-D commensurate fractional order systems like their ordinary counterparts, the saddle points of index 2 play a key role in generation of scrolls (Deng, 2006; Deng, 2007a). Assume that a 3-D chaotic system

$$\dot{x} = f(x),$$

displays a chaotic attractor. For every scroll existing in the chaotic attractor, this system has a saddle point of index 2 encircled by its respective scroll. Suppose that Ω is the set of equilibrium points of the system surrounded by scrolls. The corresponding fractional system

$$D^{\alpha} x = f(x),$$

possesses the same equilibriums points. Hence, a necessary condition for fractional order system to exhibit the chaotic attractor similar to its integer order counterpart is instability of the equilibrium points in Ω. Otherwise, one of these equilibrium points becomes asymptotically stable and attracts the nearby trajectories. According to (75), this necessary condition is mathematically equivalent to (Tavazoei, 2008)

$$\alpha \frac{\pi}{2} - \min_{i}(|\arg(\lambda_i)|) \geq 0.$$

However, referring to 3-D integer-order systems, recent findings have shown that in general case the local instability of the equilibrium points cannot be considered as a necessary condition to generate chaos. For example, in (Yang et al., 2010), a simple 3-D autonomous system displays a chaotic attractor located around two stable node-type of foci as its only equilibrium points. Additionally, in (Wang & Chen, 2012), it has been reported a 3-D autonomous chaotic system that has only one equilibrium and furthermore, this equilibrium is a stable node-focus. these recent findings make clear that in general case a necessary condition to generate chaos is the global instability of the equilibrium points. In order to confirm the existence or no-existence of chaotic behaviors in a fractional-order system, two useful tools are a valuable, namely the bifurcation diagram and the Lyapunov exponents.

Lyapunov Exponents

Lyapunov exponents were first introduced by Lyapunov in order to study the stability of non-stationary solutions of ordinary differential equations. These exponents provide a meaningful way to categorize steady-state behavior of dynamical systems, determine instability in the system, classify invariant sets, and approximate the dimension of strange attractors or other non-trivial invariant sets. Lyapunov exponents

$$\lambda_i \ (i = 1, \ldots, n),$$

are the average exponential rates of divergence or convergence of nearby orbits in the state space. The signs of Lyapunov exponents indicate the stability property of the dynamic system. For example, when all Lyapunov exponents are negative, trajectories from all directions in the state space converge to the equilibrium point. In this case, the system is exponentially stable about the equilibrium point and the attractor of the system is a fixed point. If one exponent is zero while others are negative, trajectories converge from all and the attractor in the state space is a one-dimensional curve. If the trajectory is further bounded and forms a closed loop, the system performs a periodic motion and has a stable limit cycle. Two zero Lyapunov exponents mean that the attractor is a two-dimensional torus in the state space, indicating quasi-periodic motion. If at least one Lyapunov exponent is positive, two initially nearby trajectories separate at an exponential rate and the system is chaotic. The computation of Lyapunov characteristic exponents (LCE) for nonlinear dynamical systems is a fundamental problem for understanding the dynamical behaviour of nonlinear systems, and can be classified on two set (analytical methods based on the mathematical model and numerical methods based on an observed time series). Many researches works have been devoted to this end, including (Benettin, 1980; Bremen, 1997; Brown, 1991; Eckmann, 1985; Holzfuss, 1989; Wolf et al., 1985; Zeng et al., 1992).

Although an autonomous fractional system cannot define a dynamical system in the sense of semi-group because of the memory property determined by the fractional derivative, we can't use directly classical analytical methods for computation of Lyapunov exponents in fractional systems based on the knowledge of Jacobian matrix, but we can still estimating Lyapunov exponents from time series data after performing a phase-space reconstruction. A time series is a sequence of observations which are ordered in time. Since a single experimental time series is affected by all of the relevant dynamical variables, it contains a relatively complete historical record of the dynamics. The procedure of calculating Lyapunov exponents from a time series can be summarized in the following steps (Wolf et al., 1985; Zeng et al., 1992):

1. Reconstructing the dynamics in a finite-dimensional space. Choose an embedding dimension d_E and construct a d_E-dimensional orbit representing the time evolution of the system by the time-lag method. This means that we define

$$y_i = (x_i, x_{i+T_{lag}}, ..., x_{i+(d_E-1)T_{lag}}), \qquad (98)$$

where T_{lag} is the time lag. Equation (98) provides the fiducial trajectory for the analysis of Lyapunov exponents.

2. Determining the neighbors y_j of y_i, i.e., the point of the orbit which are contained in a shell of suitable radius r, and centered at y_i

$$r_{min} \leq \|y_j - y_i\| \leq r. \qquad (99)$$

3. Determining the $d_E \times d_E$ matrix J_i which describes how the time evolution sends small vectors around y_i to small vectors around y_{i+1}. The matrix J_i is obtained by looking for neighbors y_j of y_i, and imposing

$$J_i(y_j - y_i) \approx y_{j+1} - y_{i+1}. \qquad (100)$$

The elements of J_i are obtained by a least-squares method then we obtain a sequence of matrices $J_1, J_2, J_3....$

4.   Using QR decomposition, one determines successively orthogonal matrices $Q_{(j)}$ and upper tri-angular matrices $R_{(j)}$ with positive diagonal elements such that $Q_{(0)}$ is the unit matrix and

$$J_1 Q_{(0)} = Q_{(1)} R_{(1)},$$

$$J_2 Q_{(1)} = Q_{(2)} R_{(2)},$$

...

$$J_{j+1} Q_{(j)} = Q_{(j+1)} R_{(j+1)}.$$

This decomposition is unique except in the case of zero diagonal elements. Then Lyapunov exponents λ_K^i are given by

$$\lambda_K^i = \frac{1}{TK} \sum_{j=0}^{K-1} \ln R_{(j)ii}, \qquad\qquad (101)$$

where K is the available number of matrices, T is sampling time step, and $i = 1, 2, ..., d_E$.

5.   Repeating Step 2 through Step 4 along the fiducial trajectory until the convergent Lyapunov exponents are achieved.

Another approach for estimating Lyapunov exponents in fractional-order systems recently introduced is the semi-analytical method in (Caponetto, 2013).

The 0-1 Test for Validating Chaos

An efficient binary test for chaos called the $0-1$ test has been recently proposed and applied to fractional systems in (Cafagna & Grassi, 2009; Cafagna, 2010). The idea underlying the test is to construct a random walk-type process from the data and then to examine how the variance of the random walk scales with time. Specifically, consider a set of discrete data, sampled at times $n = 1, 2, 3, ...$, representing a one-dimensional observable data set obtained from the system dynamics. Consider the real valued function $p(n)$, as defined in (Cafagna D. &., An Effective Method for Detecting Chaos in fractional-Order systems, 2010). On the basis of the function $p(n)$, define the mean square displacement $M(n)$. In particular:

•   If the behavior of $p(n)$ is Brownian (i.e., the underlying dynamics is chaotic), then $M(n)$ grows linearly in time.
•   If the behavior of $p(n)$ is bounded (i.e., the underlying dynamics is nonchaotic), then $M(n)$ is bounded.

Thus it should be examined whether the asymptotic growth rate

$$K = \lim_{n \to \infty} \frac{log M(n)}{log n},$$

approaches 0 or 1.

When K is close to 0, the motion is classified as regular (i.e. periodic or quasi-periodic); when K is close to 1, the motion is classified as chaotic.

APPLICATION: THE CASE OF NONLINEAR BLOCH SYSTEM

Numerical Methods for Calculation of the Fractional Order Derivatives

A suitable numerical method needs to be selected. Among the literature of fractional order field, two approximation methods have been proposed in order to obtain response of a fractional order system, one of which is the Adams-Bashforth-Moulton predictor-corrector scheme (Diethelm, 1997; Diethelm & Freed, 1999), while the other one is the frequency domain approximation (Charef, 1992). Due to the specificity of the error estimation bound, simulation results obtained by the former method are more reliable than those of the latter (Tavazoei, 2008b). As a result, the former method is used because of its efficiency and reliability. The method is based on the fact that fractional differential equation is equivalent to the Volterra integral equation.

Example 1: Integer-Order Nonlinear Bloch System

The dynamics of an ensemble of spins usually described by the nonlinear Bloch equation is very important for the understanding of the underlying physical process of nuclear magnetic resonance. The basic process can be viewed as the combination of a precession about a magnetic field and of a relaxation process, which gives rise to the damping of the transverse component of the magnetization with a different time constant. The basic model is derived from a magnetization M processing in the magnetic induction field B_0 in the presence of a constant radiofrequency field B_1 with intensity $B_1 = \omega_1 \gamma$ and frequency ωrf. The following modified nonlinear Bloch equation govern the evolution of the magnetization,

$$\begin{cases} \dot{x} = \delta y + \gamma z \left(\sin(c) - y \cos(c) \right) - \dfrac{x}{\Gamma_2} \\ \dot{y} = -\delta x - z + \gamma z \left(x \cos(c) + y \sin(c) \right) - \dfrac{x}{\Gamma_2} \\ \dot{z} = y - \gamma \sin(c) \left(x^2 + y^2 \right) - \dfrac{z - 1}{\Gamma_1} \end{cases} \qquad (102)$$

Where the variables are properly scaled (Abergel, 2002). It is easy to visualize that fixed the point (x_0, y_0, z_0) of the above system is given as $x_0 = f(z_0, \gamma, c, \delta, \Gamma_2)$, $y_0 = f(z_0, \gamma, c, \delta, \Gamma_2)$ where z_0 is given by a cubic equation.

$$\gamma^2 z_0^3 - \gamma \left[\frac{2\sin(c)}{\Gamma_2} + 2\delta\cos(c) + \gamma \right] z_0^2 +$$

$$\left[\frac{1}{\Gamma_2^2} + \delta^2 + \frac{2\gamma\sin(c)}{\Gamma_2} + 2\gamma\cos(c) + \frac{\Gamma_1}{\Gamma_2} \right] z_0 - \left[\frac{1}{\Gamma_2^2} + \delta^2 \right] = 0$$

In particular for real root one can always get the restriction on the parameters. The jacobian matrix of system (102), evaluated at the equilibrium (x_0, y_0, z_0)

$$J = \begin{pmatrix} \gamma\sin(c)z_0 - \frac{1}{\Gamma_2} & \delta - \cos(c)z_0 & \gamma(\sin(c)x_0 - \cos(c)y_0) \\ -\delta + \gamma\cos(c)z_0 & \gamma\sin(c)z_0 - \frac{1}{\Gamma_2} & -1 + \gamma(\cos(c)x_0 + \sin(c)y_0) \\ -2\gamma\sin(c)x_0 & 1 - 2\gamma\sin(c)y_0 & -\frac{1}{\Gamma_1} \end{pmatrix}$$

The system (102) possess chaotic attractors for two different sets of parameters values, the first set of parameters is: $\gamma = 10$, $\delta = 1.26$, $c = 0.7764$, $\Gamma_1 = 0.5$, $\Gamma_2 = 0.25$ and the second set is: $\gamma = 35$, $\delta = -1.26$, $c = 0.173$, $\Gamma_1 = 5$, $\Gamma_2 = 2.5$

The form of attractors is given in Figure 5.

Figure 5. Chaotic attractors of system (102) for the parameters: (a) $\gamma = 10$, $\delta = 1.26$, $c = 0.7764$, $\Gamma1 = 0.5$, $\Gamma2 = 0.25$; (b) $\gamma = 35$, $\delta = -1.26$, $c = 0.173$, $\Gamma1 = 5$, $\Gamma2 = 2.5$

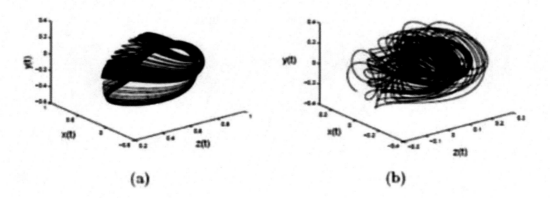

Example 2: Fractional-Order Nonlinear Bloch System

Here we consider the fractional system. The standard derivative is replaced by a fractional derivative as follows:

$$
\begin{cases}
\dfrac{d^q x}{dt} = \delta y + \gamma z \left(\sin(c) - y \cos(c) \right) - \dfrac{x}{\Gamma_2} \\[2mm]
\dfrac{d^q y}{dt} = -\delta x - z + \gamma z \left(x \cos(c) + y \sin(c) \right) - \dfrac{x}{\Gamma_2} \\[2mm]
\dfrac{d^q z}{dt} = y - \gamma \sin(c) \left(x^2 + y^2 \right) - \dfrac{z-1}{\Gamma_1}
\end{cases}
\tag{103}
$$

Our study will be for the two sets of parameters cited above, and using the fractional order q as a bifurcation parameter.

First Set of Parameters

System parameters are specified as:

$\gamma = 10$, $\delta = 1.26$, $c = 0.7764$, $\Gamma_1 = 0.5$, $\Gamma_2 = 0.25$,

for these system parameters, nonlinear Bloch system has one equilibrium and his corresponding eigenvalues are:

$E = (0.13985, 0.06727, 0.94926)$: $\lambda_1 = -1.8116$, $\lambda_{2,3} = 2.5574 \pm 5.5218j$.

Hence, the fixed point E is a saddle point of index 2. According to conditions cited above, for $q > 0.72$, the fractional order nonlinear Bloch system with this set of parameters has the necessary condition for remaining chaotic. Applying the predictor-corrector scheme and using phase diagrams, and the largest Lyapunov exponents, we find that chaos indeed exists in the fractional order system (103) with order less than 3. The system is calculated numerically with $q \in [0.7, 1]$, and the increment of q equals to 0.001. Bifurcation diagram is shown in Figure 6.

With growth of values of parameter q in the system (103), a cascade of period doubling bifurcations of an original cycle is observed. So for the value $q = 0.86$ a cycle of the period 2 is born, for the value $q = 0.93$ a cycle of the period 4 is born, for the value $q = 0.94$ a cycle of the period 8 is born, etc. Some cycles of the Feigenbaum cascade and a singular Feigenbaum attractor for the value of the parameter $q = 0.947$, as a result of the period doubling bifurcations, are shown in Figure 7.

The cascade of period doubling bifurcation is followed by the subharmonic cascade of bifurcations characterized by the birth of limit cycle of any period in compliance with the scenario established by Sharkovskii (Sharkowskii, 1964). So further increase in the value of the parameter q leads to realization of the Sharkovskii complete subharmonic cascade of bifurcations of stable cycle in accordance with the Sharkovskii order:

Figure 6. Bifurcation diagram with parameter q increasing from 0.7 to 1

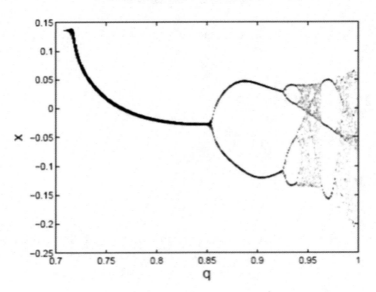

Figure 7. Projections of original cycle, period two cycle, period four cycle, period eight cycle and Feigenbaum attractor in the fractional order nonlinear Bloch system

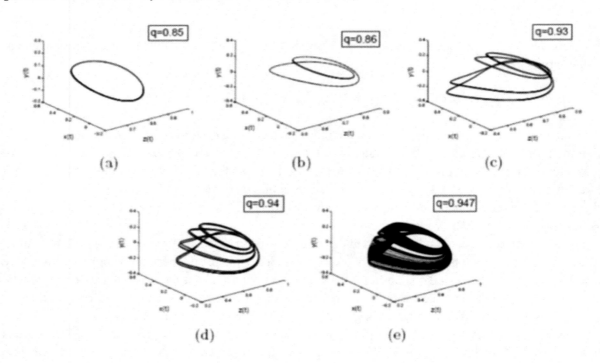

$$1 \lhd 2 \lhd 2^2 \lhd 2^3 \lhd \ldots 2^2.7 \lhd 2^2.5 \lhd 2^2.3 \lhd 2.7 \lhd 2.5 \lhd 2.3 \lhd \ldots \lhd 7 \lhd 5 \lhd 3 \qquad (104)$$

The ordering $n \lhd k$ in this equation means that the existence of a cycle of period k implies the existence of all cycles of period n. So, if the system (103) has a stable limit cycle of period three then it has also all unstable cycles of all periods in accordance with the Sharkovskii order (104).

The Sharkovskii complete subharmonic cascade of bifurcations of stable cycles is proved by existence of a limit cycle of period 6 for the parameter value $q = 0.948$, a limit cycle of period 5 for $q = 0.955$ and a limit cycle of period 3 lying in the interval [0.965, 0.979] which with further increase of the parameter q goes through a cascade of period doubling bifurcations.

Thus, for $q = 0.98$ we observe a doubled cycle of period 3. The subharmonic cascade also terminates with the formation of an irregular attractor.

Some cycles of this cascade and a subharmonic singular attractor are shown in Figure 8.

To demonstrate the chaotic dynamics, the largest Lyapunov exponent should be the first thing to be considered, because any system containing at least one positive Lyapunov exponent is defined to be chaotic (Shaw, 1981). Measuring the largest Lyapunov exponent (LLE) is always an important problem whatever in a fractional order system or in an integral-order system. Wolf and Jacobian algorithms are the most popular algorithm in calculating the largest Lyapunov exponent of integer-order system. However, Jacobian algorithm is not applicable for calculating LLE of a fractional order system, since the Jacobian matrix of fractional order system is hard to be obtained.

Figure 8. Projections of period six cycle, period five cycle, period three cycle, doubled period three cycle and more complex subharmonic singular attractor in the fractional order nonlinear Bloch system

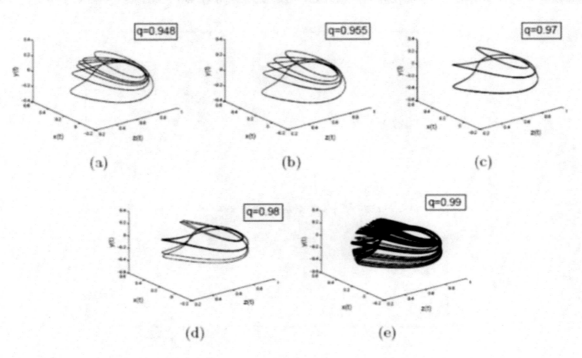

Wolf algorithm (Wolf et al., 1985) is relatively difficult to implement. Therefore, in this work, the small data sets algorithm developed by Michael T. Rosenstein et al. (Roseinstein et al., 1993) is chosen to calculate LLE of the Fractional order nonlinear Bloch system. The diagram is plotted in Figure 9.

Second Set of Parameters

System parameters are specified as:

$\gamma = 35.0$, $\delta = -1.26$, $c = 0.173$, $\Gamma 1 = 5.0$, $\Gamma 2 = 2.5$,

for these system parameters, nonlinear Bloch system has one equilibrium and his corresponding eigenvalues are:

$E = (0.02730, 0.00429, 0.99847)$: $\lambda_1 = -0.19971$, $\lambda_{2,3} = 5.6155 \pm 35.685 j$.

Hence, the fixed point E is a saddle point of index 2. The necessary condition to remain chaotic for the fractional order nonlinear Bloch system with this set of parameters is $q > 0.90$.

At $q \approx 0.90$ a Hopf bifurcation gives birth to a stable limit cycle. For certain parameter values, this limit cycle co-exists with another limit cycle with different period, each with its basin of attraction. Figure 10 shows the bifurcation diagram against the parameter q and the coexisting limit cycle for different initial conditions.

Figure 9. Maximal Lyapunov Exponents versus q form 0.7 to 1 step with 0.01

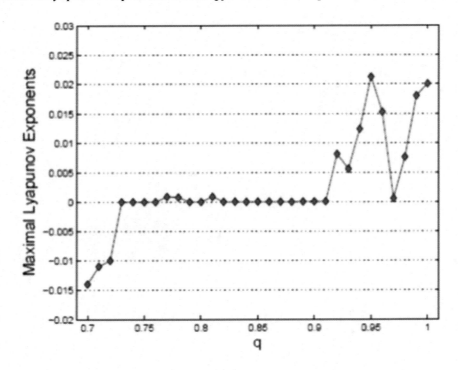

Figure 10. (a) bifurcation diagram vs. q, (b) coexisting limit cycle. Initial conditions: (0.1, 0.1, 0.1) for the thick line and (0.01, 0.01, 0.01) for the thin line

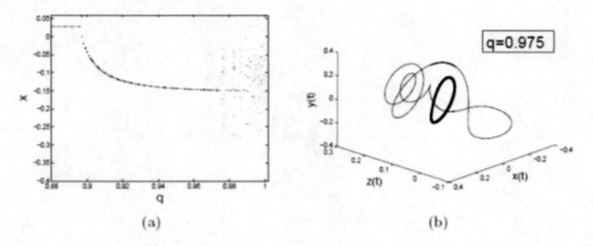

(a)   (b)

Fixing the initial conditions at (0.1, 0.1, 0.1) and increasing the parameter q, the initial period one limit cycle will disappear suddenly and is replaced by a period four limit cycle at $q = 0.99$, the two limit cycle goes through a cascade of period doubling bifurcations which terminates with the formation of irregular attractors as shown in Figure 11.

The largest Lyapunov exponents are calculated numerically with $q \in [0.85, 1]$ for an increment of 0.01 which are plotted in Figure 12.

Figure 11. Projections of the period doubling bifurcations and irregular attractors

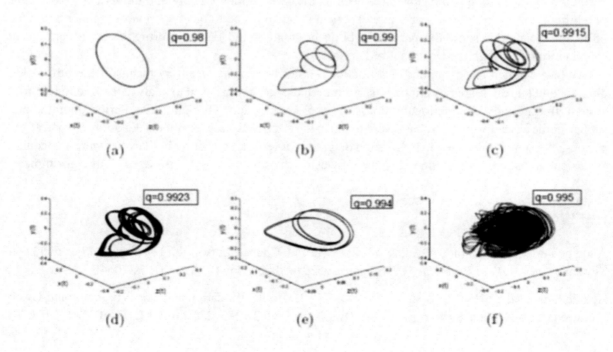

(a)   (b)   (c)

(d)   (e)   (f)

Figure 12. Maximal Lyapunov Exponents versus q form 0.85 to 1 step with 0.01

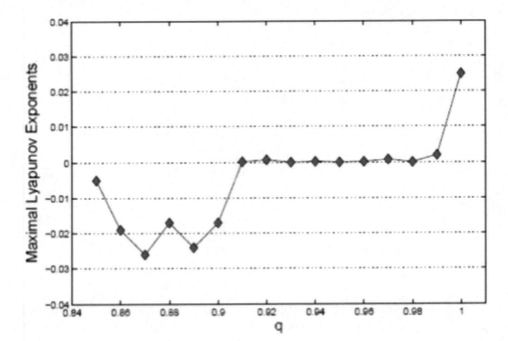

CONCLUSION

We have presented some necessary tools that are eventually used in study of fractional-order systems.

Dynamical behaviors of chaotic system, including some basic dynamical properties, bifurcations, periodic windows, routes to chaos, have been analyzed both theoretically and numerically, by means of a bifurcation diagram with Lyapunov exponent spectrum. The Largest Lyapunov exponents and the bifurcation diagrams show the period-doubling bifurcation and the transformation from periodic to chaotic motion through the fractional-order.

We have studied the dynamics of a fractional-order nonlinear system by means of the bifurcation diagram and largest Lyapunov exponents. A numerical algorithm is used to analyze the fractional-order system. In this study the fractional order is the explore direction. Through these, Period-doubling and subharmonic cascade routes to chaos were found in the fractional-order nonlinear equations. Especially, a period-3 window is presented in bifurcation diagram. Moreover, coexisting limit cycles were also found. We calculate the largest Lyapunov exponent by using the small data sets instead of Wolf algorithm.

REFERENCES

Abdelouahab, M. S., Hamri, N.-E., & Wang, J. (2010). Chaos Control of a Fractional Order Financial System. *Mathematical Problems in Engineering, 2010*, 1–18. doi:10.1155/2010/270646

Abdelouahab, M. S., Hamri, N.-E., & Wang, J. (2012). Hopf Bifurcation and Chaos in Fractional-Order Modified Hybrid Optical System. *Nonlinear Dynamics, 69*(1-2), 275–284. doi:10.100711071-011-0263-4

Abdulaziz, O. N., Noor, N. F. M., Hashim, I., & Noorani, M. S. M. (2008). Further Accuracy Tests on Adomian Decomposition Method for Chaotic Systems. *Chaos, Solitons, and Fractals*, *5*(36), 1405–1411. doi:10.1016/j.chaos.2006.09.007

Abergel, D. L.-Y., Louis-Joseph, A., & Lallemand, J.-Y. (2002). Self Sustained Maser Oscillations of a Large Magnetization Driven by a Radiation Damping-Based Electronic Feedback. *The Journal of Chemical Physics*, *16*(116), 7073–7080. doi:10.1063/1.1462583

Ahmed, E. E.-S., El-Sayed, A. M. A., & El-Saka, H. A. A. (2006). On Some Routh-Hurwitz conditions for Fractional-Order Differential Equations and their Applications in Lorentz, Rossler, Chua and Chen Systems. *Physics Letters. [Part A]*, *358*(1), 1–4. doi:10.1016/j.physleta.2006.04.087

Ahmed, W. M. (2003). Chaos in Fractional-Order Automous Nonlinear Systems. *Chaos, Solitons, and Fractals*, *16*(2), 339–351. doi:10.1016/S0960-0779(02)00438-1

Bai, E. L., Lonngren, K. E., & Sprott, J. C. (2002). On the Synchronization of a Class of Electronic Circuits that Exibit Chaos. *Chaos, Solitons, and Fractals*, *13*(7), 1515–1521. doi:10.1016/S0960-0779(01)00160-6

Benettin, G. G.-M. (1980). LyapunA Chaotic System with Only one Stable Equilibrium Characteristic Exponents for Smooth Dynamical systems and for hamiltonian Systems: a method for Computing all of them. Part 1: Theory. *Meccanica*, (15): 9–20. doi:10.1007/BF02128236

Bremen, H. F. (1997). An Efficient QR Based Method for the Computation of lyapunov Exponents. *Physica D. Nonlinear Phenomena*, *1*(15), 1–16. doi:10.1016/S0167-2789(96)00216-3

Brown, R. B., Bryant, P., & Abarbanel, H. D. I. (1991). Computing the Lyapunov Spectrum of a Dynamical System from an Observed Time Series. *Physical Review A.*, *43*(6), 2787–2806. doi:10.1103/PhysRevA.43.2787 PMID:9905344

Cafagna, D. (2010). An Effective Method for Detecting Chaos in fractional-Order systems. *International Journal of Bifurcation and Chaos in Applied Sciences and Engineering*, 20.

Cafagna, D., & Grassi, G. (2003). New 3-d Scroll Attractors in Hyperchaotic Chua's Circuit Forming a Ring. *International Journal of Bifurcation and Chaos in Applied Sciences and Engineering*, *13*(10), 2889–2903. doi:10.1142/S0218127403008284

Cafagna, D., & Grassi, G. (2009). Hyperchaos in the Fractional-Order Rossler System with Lowest-order. *International Journal of Bifurcation and Chaos in Applied Sciences and Engineering*, *19*(01), 339–347. doi:10.1142/S0218127409022890

Cang, J. T., Tan, Y., Xu, H., & Liao, S.-J. (2009). Series Solutions of Non-Linear Riccati Differential Equations with Fractional Order. *Chaos, Solitons, and Fractals*, *1*(40), 1–9. doi:10.1016/j.chaos.2007.04.018

Caponetto, M., & Fazzino, S. (2013). A Semi-analytical Method for the Computation of the Lyapinov Exponents of Fractional-Order Systems. *Communications in Nonlinear Science and Numerical Simulation*, *18*(1), 22–27. doi:10.1016/j.cnsns.2012.06.013

Caputo, M. (1967). Linear Models of Dissipation whosw q is Almost Freqency Independent-ii. *Geophysical Journal International*, *13*(5), 529–539. doi:10.1111/j.1365-246X.1967.tb02303.x

Charef, A. S., Sun, H. H., Tsao, Y. Y., & Onaral, B. (1992). Fractal System as Represented by singularity function. *IEEE Transactions on Automatic Control*, *37*(9), 1465–1470. doi:10.1109/9.159595

Chua, L. O., Komuro, M., & Matsumoto, T. (1986). The Double scroll Family. *IEEE Transactions on Circuits and Systems*, *33*(11), 1072–1118. doi:10.1109/TCS.1986.1085869

Corduneanu, C. (1977). Principles of Differential and Integral Equations (2nd ed.). New York: Chelsea Publishing Company.

Delavari, H., Baleanu, D., & Sadati, J. (2012). Stability Analysis of Caputo Fractional-Order Nonlinear Systems Revisited. *Nonlinear Dynamics*, *67*(4), 2433–2439. doi:10.100711071-011-0157-5

Deng, W. (2006). Design of Multidirectional Multi-Scroll Chaotic Attractors Based on Fractional Differential Systems via switching Control. *Chaos (Woodbury, N.Y.)*, *17*(4).

Deng, W., & Lü, J. (2007a). Generating Multidirectional Multi-Scroll Chaotic Attractors via a Fractional Differential Hysteresis System. *Physics Letters. [Part A]*, *369*(5-6), 438–443. doi:10.1016/j.physleta.2007.04.112

Deng, W. H. (2007b). Numerical Algorithm for Time Fractional Fokker-Planck Equation. *Journal of Computational Physics*, *227*(2), 1510–1522. doi:10.1016/j.jcp.2007.09.015

Deng, W. H. (2007c). Short Memory Principle and a Predictor-Corrector Approach for Fractional Differential Equations. *Journal of Computational and Applied Mathematics*, *206*(1), 174–188. doi:10.1016/j.cam.2006.06.008

Deng, W. L., Li, C., & Lü, J. (2007d). Stability Analysis of Linear Fractional Differential System with Multiple Time Delay. *Nonlinear Dynamics*, *48*(4), 409–416. doi:10.100711071-006-9094-0

Diethelm, K. (1997). An algorithm for the NumericalSolution of Differential Equations of Fractional-Order. *Electronic Transactions on Numerical Analysis*, *5*, 1–6.

Diethelm, K. (2010). *The Analysis of Fractional Differential Equations*. Heidelberg, Germany: Springer-Verlag. doi:10.1007/978-3-642-14574-2

Diethelm, K., Ford, N. J., & Freed, A. D. (2002). A Predictor-Corrector Approach for the Numerical Solution of Fractional Differential Equations. *Nonlinear Dynamics*, *29*(1-4), 3–22. doi:10.1023/A:1016592219341

Diethelm, K., &. Freed, A.D. (1999). The fracPECE subrutine for the Numerical Solution of Differential Equations of Fractional Order. *Heinzel S, Plesser T*, 57-71.

Ditkin, K. a. (1966). *Operational Calculus*. Moscow: Vysshaja Shlokola.

Doetsch, G. (1974). *Introduction to the theory and Application of the Laplace Transformation*. Berlin: Springer-Verlag. doi:10.1007/978-3-642-65690-3

Eckmann, J. P., & Ruelle, D. (1985). Ergodic Theory of chaos and strange Attractors. *Reviews of Modern Physics*, *57*(3), 617–656. doi:10.1103/RevModPhys.57.617

Grigorenko, I., & Grigorenko, E. (2003). Chaotic Dynamics of the Fractional Lorentz System. *Physical Review Letters*, *91*(3), 034101. doi:10.1103/PhysRevLett.91.034101 PMID:12906418

Grunwald, A. (1867). Ueber be grenz te Derivationen und deren Anwe dung. *Z. Math. Phys.*, *12*, 441–480.

Hamri, N. (2011). Chaotic Dynamics of the Fractional Order Nonlinear Bloch System. *Electronic Journal of Theoretical Physics*, *8*(25), 233–244.

Hartley, T. T., Lorenzo, C. F., & Killory Qammer, H. (1995). Chaos in a Fractional Order Chua's System. *IEEE Transactions on Circuits and Systems. I, Fundamental Theory and Applications*, *42*(8), 485–490. doi:10.1109/81.404062

Hassard, B. K. (1982). *Theory and Applications of Hopf Bifurcation*. Cambridge, UK: Cambridge University Press.

Hirsch, M. M. (1974). *Differential Equations: Dynamical Systems and Linear Algebra*. New York: Academic Press.

Holzfuss, J., & Lauterborn, W. (1989). Lyapunov Exponents from a Time Series of Acoustic Chaos. *Physical Review A.*, *39*(4), 2146–2152. doi:10.1103/PhysRevA.39.2146 PMID:9901470

Li, C., & Chen, G. (2004). Chaos in the Fractional Order Chen System and its Control. *Chaos, Solitons, and Fractals*, *22*(3), 549–554. doi:10.1016/j.chaos.2004.02.035

Li, C. G., & Chen, G. (2004). Chaos and Hyperchaos in the Fractional-Order Rossler Equations. *Physica A*, *341*, 55–61. doi:10.1016/j.physa.2004.04.113

Li, C. P., & Peng, G. (2004). Chaos in Chen's system with a Fractional order. *Chaos, Solitons, and Fractals*, *22*(2), 443–450. doi:10.1016/j.chaos.2004.02.013

Li, Y., Chen, Y., & Podlubny, I. (2008). Mittag-Leffler Stability of Fractional Order Nonlinear Dynamic System. *Automatica*, *45*(8), 1965–1969. doi:10.1016/j.automatica.2009.04.003

Li, Y. C., Chen, Y. Q., & Podlubny, I. (2010). Stability of fractional-Order Nonlinear Dynamic Systems: Lyapunov Direct Method and Generalized Mittag-Leffler Stability. *Computers & Mathematics with Applications (Oxford, England)*, *59*(5), 1810–1821. doi:10.1016/j.camwa.2009.08.019

Lu, J. C., Chen, G., Yu, X., & Leung, H. (2004). Design and Analysis of Multi-Scroll Chaotic Attractors from Saturated Function Series. *IEEE Transactions on Circuits and Systems*, *12*(51), 2476–2490. doi:10.1109/TCSI.2004.838151

Matignon, D. (1996). Stability result on fractional differential equations with applications to control processing. In IMACS-SMC proceedings (pp. 963-968). Lille.

Matouk, A. E. (2009). Stability Conditions, Hyperchaos and Control in a novel Fractional Order Hyperchaotic System. *Physics Letters. [Part A]*, *373*(25), 2166–2173. doi:10.1016/j.physleta.2009.04.032

Matouk, A. E. (2011). Chaos, Feedback Control and Synchronization of a Fractional-Order Modified autonomous Van Der Pol-Duffing Circuit. *Communications in Nonlinear Science and Numerical Simulation*, *16*(2), 975–986. doi:10.1016/j.cnsns.2010.04.027

Miller, K. S. (1993). *An Introduction to the Fractional Calculus and Fractional Differential Equations*. New York: Wiley and Sons.

Mishina, A. P. (1965). *Higher Algebra*. Moscow: Nauka.

Momani, S., & Odibat, Z. (2008). A Novel Method for Nonlinear Fractional Partial Differential Equations: Combination of DTM and Generalized Taylor's Formula. *Journal of Computational and Applied Mathematics, 1-2*(220), 85–95. doi:10.1016/j.cam.2007.07.033

Moze, M. &. (2005). Lmi Tools for Stabilty Analysis of Fractional Systems. *Proc. of ASME International Design Engineering Technical Conferences, Computers and and Information in Information in Engineering Conference.*

Odibat, Z. (2010). Analytic Study on linear Systems of Fractional Differential Equations. *Computers & Mathematics with Applications (Oxford, England), 59*(3), 1171–1183. doi:10.1016/j.camwa.2009.06.035

Odibat, Z., & Momani, S. (2006). Application of Variational Iteration Method to Nonlinear Differential Equations of Fractional Order. *International Journal of Nonlinear Sciences and Numerical Simulation, 7*(1), 27–34. doi:10.1515/IJNSNS.2006.7.1.27

Odibat, Z., & Momani, S. (2008). Modified Homotopy Perturbation Method: Application to Quadratic Riccati Differential Equation of Fractional Order. *Chaos, Solitons, and Fractals, 36*(1), 167–174. doi:10.1016/j.chaos.2006.06.041

Oldham, K. B. (1974). *The Fractional Calculus: Theory and applications of Differentiation and Integration to Arbitrary Order*. Academic Press.

Oustaloup, A. S. (2008). An Overview of the Crone Approach in System Analysis, Modelling and Identification, Observation and Control. 17th World Comgress IFAC, 14254-14265.

Podlubny, I. (1999). *Fractional differential Equations*. San Diego, CA: Academic Press.

Roseinstein, M. T., Collins, J. J., & De Luca, C. J. (1993). A Practical Method for Calculating Largest Lyapunov Exponents from Small Data Sets. *Physica D. Nonlinear Phenomena, 65*(1-2), 117–134. doi:10.1016/0167-2789(93)90009-P

Shahiri, M., Gharderi, R., Ranjbar, A. N., Hosseinnia, S. H., & Momani, S. (2010). Chaotic Fractional-Order Coullet System: Synchronization and Control Approach. *Communications in Nonlinear Science and Numerical Simulation, 15*(3), 665–674. doi:10.1016/j.cnsns.2009.05.054

Sharkowskii, A. (1964). Cycles Coexistence of Continuous Tranformation of Line in Itself. *Ukrainian Mathematical Journal, 1*(26), 61–71.

Shaw, R. (1981). Strange Attractors, Chaotic Behavior and Information Flow. *Zeitschrift fur Naturforschung. Section A. Physical Sciences, 36*(1), 80–112. doi:10.1515/zna-1981-0115

Silva, C. P. (1993). Shilnikov's Theorem - a Tutorial. *IEEE Transactions on Circuits and Systems, I*(40), 675–682. doi:10.1109/81.246142

Sun, H., Abdelwahab, A., & Onaral, B. (1984). Linear Approximation for Tranfer Function with a Pole of Fractional Order. *IEEE Transactions on Automatic Control, 29*(5), 441–444. doi:10.1109/TAC.1984.1103551

Sun, K., & Sprott, J. C. (2009). Bifrucations of Fractional-Order Diffusionless Lorenz System. *Electronic Journal of Theoretical Physics*, *6*(22), 123–134.

Tavazoei, M. S. (2008b). Limitations of Frequency Domain Approximation for Detecting Chaos in Fractional Order Systems. *Nonlinear Analysis - Theory Methods and Applications,* (69), 1299-1320.

Tavazoei, M. S., & Haeri, M. (2007). Unreability of Frequency Domain Approximation in Recognizing Chaos in fractional Order Systems. *IET Signal Processing*, *1*(4), 171–181. doi:10.1049/iet-spr:20070053

Tavazoei, M. S., & Haeri, M. (2008a). Chaotic Attractors in incommensurate Fractional Order Systems. *Physica D. Nonlinear Phenomena*, *237*(20), 2628–2637. doi:10.1016/j.physd.2008.03.037

Travazoei, M., & Haeri, M. (2009). A Proof for Non Existence of Periodic Solutions in Time invariant Fractional Order Systems. *Automatica*, *45*(8), 1886–1890. doi:10.1016/j.automatica.2009.04.001

Travazoei, M. S. (2010). A Note on Fractional-Order Derivatives of Periodic Functions. *Automatica*, *46*(5), 945–948. doi:10.1016/j.automatica.2010.02.023

Travazoei, M. S., Haeri, M., & Nazari, N. (2008). Analysis of Undamped Oscillations Generated by Marginally Stable Fractional Order Systems. *Signal Processing*, *88*(12), 2971–2978. doi:10.1016/j.sigpro.2008.07.002

Wang, X., & Chen, G. (2012). A Chaotic System with Only one Stable Equilibrium. *Communications in Nonlinear Science and Numerical Simulation*, *17*(3), 1264–1272. doi:10.1016/j.cnsns.2011.07.017

Wang, X. Y., & Wang, M. (2007). Dynamic Analysis of the Fractional- Order Liu System and its Synchronization. *Chaos (Woodbury, N.Y.)*, *17*(3), 033106. doi:10.1063/1.2755420 PMID:17902988

Wang, Y., & Li, C. (2007). Does the Fractional Brusselator with Efficient Dimension Less than 1 have a Limit Cycle. *Physics Letters. [Part A]*, *363*(5-6), 414–419. doi:10.1016/j.physleta.2006.11.038

Wiggins, S. (2003). *Introduction to Applied Nonlinear Dynamical Systems and Chaos*. New York: Springer-Verlag.

Wolf, A., Swift, J. B., Swinney, H. L., & Vastano, J. A. (1985). Determining Lyapunov Exponents from a Time Series. *Physica D. Nonlinear Phenomena*, *16*(3), 285–317. doi:10.1016/0167-2789(85)90011-9

Yang, Q., Wei, Z., & Chen, G. (2010). An unusual 3d Autonomous Quadratic Chaotic System with two Stable Node-Foci. *International Journal of Bifurification and Chaos*, *20*(4), 1061–1083. doi:10.1142/S0218127410026320

Yazdani, M., & Salarieh, H. (2011). On the Existence of Periodic Solutions in Time Invariant Fractional Order Systems. *Automatica*, *47*(8), 1834–1837. doi:10.1016/j.automatica.2011.04.013

Zeng, X., Pielke, R. A., & Eykholt, R. (1992). Extracting Lyapunov Exponents from Short Time Series of Low Precision. *Modern Physics Letters B*, *6*(2), 55–75. doi:10.1142/S0217984992000090

Chapter 13
Novel Cryptography Technique via Chaos Synchronization of Fractional-Order Derivative Systems

Alain Giresse Tene
University of Dschang, Cameroon

Timoleon Crépin Kofane
University of Yaounde I, Cameroon

ABSTRACT

Synchronization of fractional-order-derivative systems for cryptography purpose is still exploratory and despite an increase in cryptography research, several challenges remain in designing a powerful cryptosystem. This chapter addresses the problem of synchronization of fractional-order-derivative chaotic systems using random numbers generator for a novel technique to key distribution in cryptography. However, there is evidence that researchers have approached the problem using integer order derivative chaotic systems. Consequently, the aim of the chapter lies in coding and decoding a text via chaos synchronization of fractional-order derivative, the performance analysis and the key establishment scheme following an application on a text encryption using the chaotic Mathieu-Van Der Pol fractional system. In order to improve the level of the key security, the Fibonacci Q-matrix is used in the key generation process and the initial condition; the order of the derivative of the responder system secretly shared between the responder and the receiver are also involved. It followed from this study that compared to the existing cryptography techniques, this proposed method is found to be very efficient due to the fact that, it improves the key security.

DOI: 10.4018/978-1-5225-5418-9.ch013

INTRODUCTION

Nowadays, developing new strategies to protect sensitive information from eavesdropping has attracted significant attention in the worldwide communication networks. That is, wide investigations have been made to implement an effective cryptosystem to ensure information encryption and decryption. These include the algorithmic key based encryption systems which usually consider a digital stream and convolute it with a given binary pattern using as the key. This encryption method can be denoted as the Vernam Cipher method (Bloisi and Iocchi 2007). In this method, the message is transformed to a binary string (a sequence of 0 and 1), and the key is a randomly generated sequence of 0 and 1 having the same length as the message. The encryption is done by adding the key to the message modulo 2 bit by bit, this includes the symmetric key encryption such as the Data Encryption Standard (DES) cryptosystem (Standard 1977), the Advanced Encryption Standard (AES) (Standard 2001) cryptosystems, etc. Even though this encryption method has been used for long times and is still used today, it presents some lacks in the key security and the key distribution. The drawback of this encryption technique comes from the fact that, it is easily breakable even if the key can be used only one time (one time-pad key). However, this drawback has been avoided by developing other software cryptosystems that use asymmetric algorithms key distribution which is called a public key cryptography such as the Rivest Shamir Adleman (RSA), the Elliptic Curve Cryptography (ECC) cryptosystems just to name a few (Bleichenbacher 1998, Habib 2009). Such cryptosystems usually use several computational resources and compare them with their counterparts but they are not generally used to encrypt bulk data stream and are computationally hard. Although this encryption technique is not yet broken, further investigations have been made to develop another encryption method that is based on chaos. Chaos theory has simulated increasing attentions of scientists since the work of Lorenz (1963). Due to their random-like behavior, their unpredictability character and their high degree of nonlinearity, chaotic signals have been proven to be very efficient for information security then, in the recent few decades, chaos based cryptosystems which consists of masking an information to be transmitted through a chaotic signal have received a great deal of interest. Here one denotes the chaos masking (CMA) which consists of masking the plaintext through a chaotic signal, the chaos shift keying (CSK), the chaos modulation (CMO), etc (Annovazzi-Lodi *et al.* 2005, Dedieu *et al.* 1993, Tang *et al.* 2002). However, particular attentions have been given to the encryption technique based on chaos synchronization between distant elements in large networks in order to improve the effectiveness of information security. This encryption technique has been developed by several authors (Alvarez 2006) and has even been implemented in the real experiment. These authors demonstrated that a cryptosystem based on this encryption is highly efficient, although it is difficult to synchronize two chaotic systems. Therefore, this method consists of generating an encryption key by synchronizing two chaotic signals (driver and responder systems). Thus, the aim of this chapter is to develop new strategy of key encryption based on chaos synchronization of two chaotic systems with fractional order derivative in order to improve the information security.

The main motivation behind such an idea includes the fact that, the fractional order derivative chaotic system is geometrically complex and its high nonlinearity degree makes such a system an efficient tool to encrypt message. Furthermore, the order of the derivative might be used as the secret key as well as other parameters of the system enhancing the effectiveness of the encryption method. In addition, it was shown by Tene & Kofane (2017) that the fractional order of the derivative can induce quick synchronization of chaotic systems which can highly improve the encryption and decryption speed. Such encryption method successfully realized in photonics will have significant impact in physical larger based encryption techniques and will offer high confidentiality in real-time encryption and decryption.

In this chapter, the authors focus on one hand on the synchronization of fractional order chaotic systems in general, where the condition of synchronization of the fractional Mathieu-Van der Pol system will be approached in Section 1. In this work, since this cryptosystem involves the synchronization of fractional order derivative chaotic systems, in order to improve the efficiency of this cryptosystem one of the best method will be chosen to perform the synchronization. That is, the synchronization will be approached by the Ge-Yao-Chen (GYC) partial region stability theory (2011). Compared to other techniques of synchronization which include the back stepping method, the adaptive design method, the linear and nonlinear feedback method, sampled-data feedback synchronization, time-delay feedback, etc. (Karthikeyan & Sundarapandian 2014, Yang *et al.* 2004, Rodríguez *et al.* 2008), the GYC partial region stability theory techniques is very appropriate due to the fact that, it minimizes the simulation error, also from the fact that using this theory, it is possible to construct the Lyapunov function as a simple linear-function from where the control parameters are easily designed, following by the synchronization based key encryption via fractional order chaotic systems in Section 2. Moreover, the authors consider a practical example where the Mathieu-Van der Pol chaotic system with fractional order derivative will be used for random numbers generator in the key distribution process in Section 3. One refers to the scheme of key distribution based on synchronized random numbers generation. In this section, a plaintext will be encrypted as concrete example and the sensitivity attack of the key will be provided. By this novel cryptosystem, authors are expecting to improve the level of confidentiality in the key exchange process and increase the speed of the encryption/decryption procedure.

CHAOS SYNCHRONIZATION BASED CRYPTOGRAPHY WITH FRACTIONAL ORDER DERIVATIVE SYSTEMS

The chaos theory is the best mechanism for signal design with potential application in telecommunication and coding systems (Bleichenbacher 1998). Chaotic phenomena are very difficult to control. However, it has been shown that a chaotic motion can be controlled under certain given conditions. Then, synchronization of chaotic phenomena became a big challenge and has been successfully realized either theoretically or experimentally. That is, the main interest in this section includes the study of the synchronization of chaotic or hyper-chaotic systems described by fractional order-derivative systems applied for the cryptography purpose. It is known that as chaotic phenomena are unpredictable, sensitive to initial conditions and has a random-like behavior, they can be a necessary tool to generate pseudo random numbers very useful in the theory of cryptography. In the present section, one is interested on a particular case where chaotic systems have been used to encode a message. Here, one refers to the chaos masking (CMA) method, the chaos shift keying (CSK), etc. However, a novel method based on chaos synchronization will be developed in this section. Generally, chaos synchronization implies making two chaotic systems with different initial conditions oscillate in the same way by using an active control parameter. Then, the main preoccupation in this section is to describe in detail how can the synchronization of chaotic systems with fractional order derivative be used in the cryptography processes.

Synchronization of Chaotic Systems With Fractional Order Derivative

Generally as one defines above, chaos synchronization implies making two chaotic systems with different initial conditions oscillate in the same way by using an active control parameter. Consider the following coupled chaotic systems.

$$D_*^{\alpha_i} x_i(t) = f(t, x_1(t), x_2(t), \cdots, x_n(t)), \tag{1.1}$$

and

$$D_*^{\alpha_i} y_i(t) = g(t, y_1(t), y_2(t), \cdots, y_n(t)) + u(t, x, y), \tag{1.2}$$

where $D_*^{\alpha_i}$, denotes the *Caputo* (Ishteva *et al.* 2005) derivative of order α_i, $i = 1, 2, \cdots, n$. The variables $x = \begin{bmatrix} x_1, x_2, \cdots x_n \end{bmatrix}^T \in \mathbb{R}^n$ and $y = \begin{bmatrix} y_1, y_2, \cdots y_n \end{bmatrix}^T \in \mathbb{R}^n$, denote the master (or driver) and the slave (or response) equations, respectively, while f and g are two vector functions so that $f : \mathbb{R}^n \mapsto \mathbb{R}^n$, consequently, $g : \mathbb{R}^n \mapsto \mathbb{R}^n$. It is important to notice that f and g are two continuous nonlinear functions. Finally, $u(t, x, y)$ denotes the control parameter vector and is defined such that $u = \begin{bmatrix} u_1, u_2, \cdots u_n \end{bmatrix}^T \in \mathbb{R}^n$.

One defines the error vector function as follows: $e(t) = \begin{bmatrix} e_1(t), e_2(t), \cdots e_n(t) \end{bmatrix}^T \in \mathbb{R}^n$, with $e_i(t) = x_i(t) - y_i(t)$. The synchronization can be achieved when

$$\lim_{t \to \infty} e(t) \mapsto \|x(t) - y(t)\| \mapsto 0, \tag{1.3}$$

where $\|\bullet\|$ denotes the Euclidean norm. The error dynamics corresponding to Equations (1.1) and (1.2) is defined as follows:

$$D_*^{\alpha_i} e_i(t) = D_*^{\alpha_i}(x_i - y_i)$$

$$= D_*^{\alpha_i} x_i - D_*^{\alpha_i} y_i$$

$$= f_i(t, x_1, x_2, \cdots x_n) - g_i(t, y_1, y_2, \cdots y_n) - u_i. \tag{1.4}$$

In order to easily control the system one can choose the control parameter so that the error dynamics is described by a linear function. For this purpose, one redefines the control function such that the nonlinear term in $e_i(t)$, $\forall i = 1, 2, \cdots, n$ cancels. Furthermore, synchronization implies also stabilization of the system. So, from the partial region stability theory (Ge & Li 2011), one can construct the Lyapunov function from where the controller can be designed.

In fact, if one considers a function $V : \mathbb{R}^n \mapsto \mathbb{R}^n$ so that, the following conditions:

- $V(x)$ is positive definite function ($V(x) \geq 0$ with equality if and only if $x = 0$),

- The derivative of $V(x)$ is negative semi-definite function $\left(\dfrac{d^{\alpha}}{dt^{\alpha}} V(x) \leq 0 \right)$ with additional property like boundedness, are fulfilled, then $V(x)$ is a good Lyapunov function candidate.

In these conditions, the system is stable in the sense of Lyapunov. This stability condition might be verified by evaluating the largest Lyapunov exponent. For this reason, the following definition provides how the largest Lyapunov exponent for fractional order derivative systems might be evaluated.

Definition (Tene & Kofane 2017)

Let $f : \mathbb{R}^n \to \mathbb{R}^n$ be an arbitrary function, the largest Lyapunov exponent of fractional order derivative systems is given by:

$$\lambda_{\alpha}(f) = \underset{t \to \infty}{Lim} \left[Sup \left(\frac{1}{t^{\alpha}} \log_{\alpha}^{N} \left\| f(t) \right\| \right)^{\alpha} \right],$$

where in this relation, $\left\| \bullet \right\|$ defines an arbitrary norm in $\mathbb{R}^n$.

The theorem below states clearly the practical formulation of this definition of λ_{α}.

Theorem

Let $f : \mathbb{R}^n_+ \to \mathbb{R}^n$ be an arbitrary function, one has:

- $\lambda_{\alpha}(f) \succ 0$ if and only if the ordinary Lyapunov exponent $\lambda(f) \succ 0$. In that condition,

$$\lambda_{\alpha}(f) = \underset{t \to \infty}{Lim} \left[Sup \left(\frac{1}{t^{\alpha}} \log_{\alpha}^{N} \left\| f(t) \right\| \right) \right]$$

- If $\underset{t \to \infty}{Lim} \left[Sup \left(t^{\alpha} \left\| f(t) \right\| \right) \right]$ is finite then, $\lambda_{\alpha}(f) \prec 0$. In this case,

$$\lambda_{\alpha}(f) = \frac{1}{\Gamma(1 - \alpha) \underset{t \to \infty}{Lim} \left[Sup \left(t^{\alpha} \left\| f(t) \right\| \right) \right]},$$

- $\lambda_{\alpha}(f) = 0$ if and only if $\lambda(f) \leq 0$ and $\underset{t \to \infty}{Lim} \left[Sup \left(t^{\alpha} \left\| f(t) \right\| \right) \right]$ is finite.

This theorem has been well proved by Cong *et al.* in 2014. Using this theorem the largest Lyapunov exponent was simulated in (Tene & Kofane 2017) for the fractional Mathieu-Van Der Pol systems, and it is observed from this graph that, the system moves quickly from non chaotic to hyper-chaotic state.

A concrete example is studied in section **(3.e)**, where the master and the slave equations to be synchronized are both Mathieu-Van der Pol fractional order-derivative. As it is shown how to synchronize fractional order chaotic systems, one can use this procedure to generate pseudo-random numbers and use them to encrypt a message.

Classical Encryption Based on Chaos Theory

Chaos based cryptography emerged in 1990's as an innovative application of nonlinear dynamical systems in the chaotic regime. Since the earlier work of Pecora and Caroll (1990) on chaos synchronization, using chaos for communication purpose has attracted the attention of several physicists and computer scientists this by the generation of the Cipher keys for pseudo random chaotic systems in cryptography. Therefore, wide interests have been given to the chaos based systems as an alternative to the existing schemes such as the Rivest Shami Adleman (RSA) scheme, the Digital Encryption Standard (DES) scheme, etc (Gura et al. 2014). In the last decade, a chaotic behavior has been simulated from the simplest one or two dimensional discreet maps or has been derived from higher dimensional physical systems described by autonomous or non autonomous differential equation. Several chaos based cryptosystems have been proposed theoretically as well as practically and are nowadays used in the worldwide communication networks. These include the chaos masking cryptosystem (CMA), the chaos shift keying (CSK), etc.

Chaos Masking (CMA) Cryptosystems

This is the simplest encryption method, where the analog message m(t) is masked with a chaotic signal $x(t)$ at the transmitter side following the scheme depicted by Figure 1.

In this cryptography scheme, an analogue message is encrypted at the transmitter side and sent to the receiver. Upon receiving the encrypted signal S(t) at the receiver side, the synchronization is performed and the chaotic component is subtracted from the receiving encryption signal leading to the message recovering $m(t)$. This message at the transmitter side is encrypted using the following relation:

$$S(t) = m(t) + y(t), \tag{1.5}$$

Figure 1. Chaos masking cryptosystem scheme

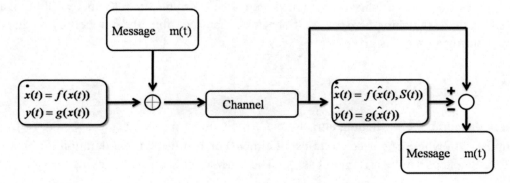

where $y(t)$ defines the output of the chaotic signal. At the receiver side, the dynamics driven by $S(t)$ is given by the state space representation,

$$\begin{cases} \hat{x}(t) = f(\hat{x}(t), S(t)) \\ \hat{y}(t) = g(\hat{x}(t)) \end{cases} \tag{1.6}$$

Once the synchronization is achieved, which implies that

$$\lim_{t \to \infty} \left\| \hat{x}(t) - x(t) \right\| \to 0, \tag{1.7}$$

Then, the estimated message $x(t)$ can be done by simply subtracting the estimated $\hat{y}(t)$ from $S(t)$ as follows:

$$\widehat{m}(t) = S(t) - \hat{y}(t). \tag{1.8}$$

In the CMA scheme, the message signal extraction is generally possible if $m(t)$ consists of periodic frames within a sufficiently long duration of times and this is accomplished by using different methods such as auto-correlation, cross-correlation, etc. The CMA cryptosystem presents an advantage of simplicity and can be easily implemented in electronics circuit (Cuomo & Oppenheim 1993). However, as it needs long times to be achieved, another method to encrypt a message still by using chaotic systems has been developed, here one refers to the CSK cryptosystem.

Chaos Switching or Chaos Shift Keying (CSK) Cryptosystems

In the chaos shift keying (CSK) cryptosystem, a binary message signal is used to choose the carrier signal from two or more different chaotic attractors. These attractors are generated by two chaotic systems that have slightly difference in their initial condition but with the same structure. In this cryptosystem, the direct extraction of the message signal is possible using returns maps, correlation analysis or short-time period (Alvarez & Li 2006). The message could be recovered via non-coherent detection scheme where synchronization is not required. The bits are extracted by looking at the statistical attributes such as bit energy distribution, variance of the transmitted signal (Kolumban & Kennedy 2000). In addition, in the CSK method, switching between multiple attractors is possible; the number of bits that could be transmitted during a time T is given by:

$$N_b = \log_2 M, \tag{1.9}$$

where M is the number of switching attractors, N_b the number of bits, then the required attractor will be two in the case where one needs to transmit either 0 or 1 in the symbol duration for binary signal. Log_2 defines the neperian logarithm in basis 2. The scheme for chaos shift keying encryption is given in Figure 2.

Figure 2. Chaos shift keying scheme

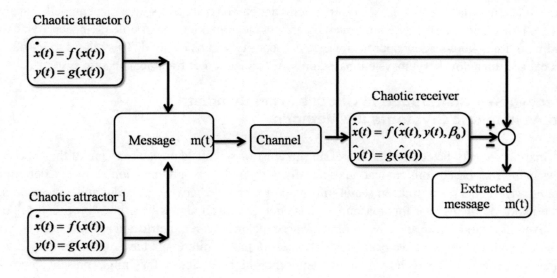

In this scheme, the transmitter is given by:

$$\begin{cases} \dot{x}(t) = f(x(t), \beta(m(t))) \\ y(t) = g(x(t)) \end{cases}, \qquad\qquad\qquad (1.10)$$

where $\beta(m(t))$ defined the two parameter 0 and 1 so that,

$$\beta\big(m(t)\big) = \begin{cases} \beta_0 & if & m(t) = 0 \\ \beta_1 & if & m(t) = 1 \end{cases} \qquad\qquad (1.11)$$

and $y(t)$ is the output transmitted chaotic signal. The receiver signal is given by:

$$\begin{cases} \hat{x}(t) = f(\hat{x}(t)) \\ \hat{y}(t) = g(\hat{x}(t)). \end{cases} \qquad\qquad\qquad (1.12)$$

Although the CSK cryptosystem is found to be more robust against noise and parametric mishmashes, it has been found to present some lacks in security as well as the CMA encryption (Rubezic & Ostojic 2000). Even though these two encryption techniques based on chaos are most used and robust against cryptography attack and noisy channel, other methods have been developed such as the chaotic cipher based on searching plain-bits in a chaotic pseudo random sequence (Rubezic & Ostojic 2000), the block cipher based on forward or backward chaotic iteration (Kocarev *et al.* 2004), the stream cipher based on chaos pseudo random number generator (Bhasin *et al.* 2013). These encryption techniques do not usually use chaos synchronization and they usually use one or more chaotic maps in which the initial condition are used as the secret key due to their sensitivity to initial conditions. However, the drawback of most of them comes from the fact that, these cryptosystems are based on some mathematical models that are not well explained and the key generation method are not clear, making impossible their security analysis, yielding to think about a new approach where the security will be ensured. This allows to introduce in the next section a novel cryptosystem based on synchronization of fractional chaotic systems.

Effective Key Distribution to Choose From Symmetric and Asymmetric Cryptography Methods

Information security has gained an increasing interest of scientists nowadays. Due to the exponential grows in internet-based communication especially with modern communication networks, determining a better way to encrypt or to keep secret information exchange between a sender and a receiver is one of the major problems. For this reason, various encryption techniques have been proposed to protect sensitive information from any eavesdropper. These include the symmetric and asymmetric encryption methods. Both techniques have been well discussed in the literature and have even been implemented in practice. However, it was shown that no matter their high efficiency, they might present some lacks.

Up to now, both the symmetric and asymmetric cryptosystems have been found to be very efficient for data encryption. However, they present serious drawbacks, for example the asymmetric key encryption cannot be used for bulk data encryption while the symmetric key encryption is very fit for the purpose. Moreover, the asymmetric key encryption requires too large CPU space compared to the symmetric key encryption and is slightly slow. But due to the fact that the secret key must be shared between the sender and the receiver, the symmetric key encryption is not secured since as it is known there is no a perfect secret channel in real life for such secret communication. It has also been found to present more weakness compared to the asymmetric key encryption and has even been broken as one mentioned above. Therefore, although both cryptosystems present each other some lacks they have been widely used and are still used nowadays in the worldwide communication network. In case one may need to look at the speed during the communication process the symmetric key encryption might be extremely recommend, while the asymmetric key encryption technique should be very recommend for high security compared to the previous one. However, due to these weaknesses that present cryptosystems using these encryption techniques, computer scientists have looked forward to develop some other encryption techniques which may not use symmetric or asymmetric encryption methods but that may be seen as the combination of both encryption techniques. Here, authors refer to cryptosystems from chaos synchronization point of view.

ENCRYPTION KEY DISTRIBUTION VIA CHAOS SYNCHRONIZATION OF SYSTEMS WITH FRACTIONAL ORDER DERIVATIVE

Chaos synchronization was proven to be a great technique to generate a key for message encryption by forcing two chaotic systems using a driver into synchronization. In this section, the authors focus on a novel technique, where the key is generated by synchronizing two fractional chaotic or hyper chaotic systems. In reality, consider two persons (usually called Alice and Bob) that wish to communicate between them secret messages using this technique. How does it work actually? First of all, they must share between them an identical fractional chaotic system called Responder. Having done that, the transmitter (Alice) can now generate another chaotic signal called driver and then, force it into synchronization with the responder signal previously shared afterward random numbers are generated by converting digital signal into numerical signal. These numbers are generated by considering the synchronization time and the critical values of the corresponding variable as shown in the next section. When it is the case, she might now use that encryption key to encode a message to be sent. Then, both the encrypted message and the driver signal are sent to a receiver (Bob) through a public channel. Once these are received, Bob can force the driver signal into synchronization with the responder signal previously shared to generate the key needed to decrypt the message. That means Bob should perform the same operations as Alice upon receiving the driver signal to generate the decryption key. The effectiveness of this method comes from the fact that, if an eavesdropper intercepts the message and the driver signal, he doesn't have in his possession the responder signal previously shared between the transmitter (Alice) and the receiver (Bob) in order to generate the key then, cannot generate any useful information. This is because of the unpredictability character of chaotic signals, the high ergodicity that presents the trajectory of chaotic signals and finally because chaotic signals are wideband and pseudo-random. Important information to be noticed is that the fractional order of the derivative used here improves the effectiveness of the key distribution process because it has complex geometry interpretation and will be involved in the secret key generation. After this description, it is clear that further development is required in this section concerning the possible algorithm of encryption and the key establishment on one hand and the sensitivity, the speed and the key space analysis on the other hand.

Encryption Protocol via Synchronization of Fractional Order Derivative Chaotic Systems

Description of the Proposed Technique

In Figure 3, the overall architecture of this secure communication scheme with a public transmission channel is presented. In the encryption step, both the sender (Alice) and the receiver (Bob) secretly shared two identical chaotic signals (responder signal). The encryption technique is the following:

Alice first generates via a driver a fractional chaotic signal (driver signal) and forces it into synchronization with the previously shared signal called responder. Once the synchronization is completed, the critical value of time for which both signals go into synchronization and the corresponding critical values of the chaotic variables are reported. Having these values that can be considered as random, the secret key is generated using the procedure described below. Therefore, the message itself is also transformed into digital signal and using the Boolean Exclusive OR (XOR) function, the secret key is added to the message.

The encryption of the message is, then described as follows: if one reconsiders the fractional order derivative chaotic system as described by Equation (1.27) in the previous section,

$$D_*^\alpha x(t) = f(t, x), \tag{2.1}$$

with the initial condition $x_0 = \left[x_{01}, x_{02}, x_{03} \cdots, x_{0N} \right]^T$ and $\alpha_i, \ \forall \ i = 1, 2, \cdots, N$ defines the order of the derivative taking in the interval $\left[0, 1 \right]$ then, this equation is used as the driver system. Consequently, the

Figure 3. Encryption Protocol

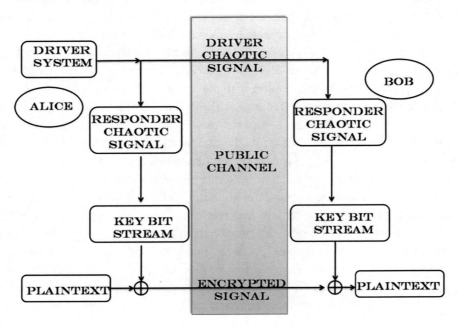

responder system is given by Equation (1.28) with initial condition $y_0 = \left[y_{01}, y_{02}, y_{03} \cdots, y_{0N} \right]^T$. Since x is defined in vector space $\mathbb{R}^N$, one first chooses the variables x_k and y_k. The author's purpose for instance consists of determining the critical value of time τ_c for which the synchronization is achieved and the corresponding critical values. The encryption of characters in the message consists of running the dynamical systems from their initial conditions until the tolerance ν is reached, i.e. the difference $x_k - y_k$ is equal to some given number μ, since this difference cannot reach exactly zero. One notices that this tolerance should also be shared between Alice and Bob. Therefore, the corresponding time is the so-called critical time for synchronization. Then, for this value of time, the corresponding critical values of the variable x_k and y_k are derived with a precision corresponding to that of the critical time. The process is repeated for each variable and three vectors τ, χ and η are derived so that:

$$
\begin{cases}
\tau = \left[\tau_1, \tau_2, \tau_3 \cdots, \tau_N \right]^T, \\
\chi = \left[\chi_1, \chi_2, \chi_3 \cdots, \chi_N \right]^T, \\
\eta = \left[\eta_1, \eta_2, \eta_3 \cdots, \eta_N \right]^T.
\end{cases}
\tag{2.2}
$$

To get the secret keys, the elements of the Fibonacci Q-matrices are used. The Fibonacci Q-matrix is one of the most popular and recurrent method used. It is the continuation of the study of Fibonacci sequence in the last few decades. This theory has been well studied in (Hoggat 2011, Gould1981). The Fibonacci Q-matrix is defined by:

$$Q^k = \begin{bmatrix} F_{k+1} & F_k \\ F_k & F_{k-1} \end{bmatrix}, \ \forall \ k \in \mathbb{N}, \tag{2.3}$$

where F_k, $\forall \ k \in \mathbb{N}$, are the Fibonacci sequence defined by the following recurrence relation:

$$F_{k+1} = F_k + F_{k-1} \tag{2.4}$$

with the conditions $F_0 = 0$, $F_1 = F_2 = 1$, Q^k denotes the kth Fibonacci Q-matrix so that $Det\left(Q^k\right) = F_{k+1}F_{k-1} - F_k^2 = (-1)^k \ \forall \ k \in \mathbb{N}$. This relation represents the so called Cassini formula which has been kindly demonstrated in (Hoggat 2011, Gould1981). One has:

$$Q^k = \begin{bmatrix} F_2 & F_1 \\ F_1 & F_0 \end{bmatrix} = \begin{bmatrix} 1 & 1 \\ 1 & 0 \end{bmatrix}, \tag{2.5}$$

where the eigenvalues of this matrix are given by $\lambda_1 = \dfrac{1 + \sqrt{5}}{2}$ and $\lambda_2 = \dfrac{1 - \sqrt{5}}{2}$. One realizes that the positive one corresponds to the famous golden number very useful in number theory. As the Fibonacci Q-matrix define a 2×2 matrix, the plaintext is then divided into blocks of four terms including every characters and a number is assigned to each character following Table 1.

It is noticed that, this procedure can be extended to other characters such as parenthesis, brackets etc., this is the reason why in the present chapter, one considers a number of M characters. This implies at this level that, the plaintext is transformed into a sequence of numbers divided into blocks of four terms, each block made of numbers between 0 and M. Then, the cipher text is obtained as follows:

$$C = P + K \bmod(M), \tag{2.6}$$

where P represents the plaintext and K the secret key. This procedure requires a key length of dimension N, where N denotes the length of the plaintext.

Table 1. ASCII table

Characters	0	1	...	8	9	A	B	...	Y	Z	Blank space	.	-	...
Assigned numbers	0	1	...	8	9	10	11	...	34	35	36	37	38	...

Key Establishment Scheme Via Chaos Synchronization of Fractional Order Derivative Systems

As it has been mentioned in the above section, a secret key for the message encryption can be derived by synchronizing fractional order derivative chaotic systems. The procedure in this work is described as follows:

Alice forces the driver and the responder systems into synchronization. Once the chosen variable of the driver x_k is synchronized with the responder variable y_k so that the difference $x_k - y_k$ reaches some fixed value (with a tolerance), the corresponding time τ_k which is called the critical synchronization time and for this value of time, the corresponding value of the variable x_k denoted χ_k of the driver signal and that of the responder y_k signal denoted η_k are reported. Having these values, the following product is evaluated:

$$R_k = round\left[\left|\alpha_k \tau_k \chi_k \eta_k y_{k0} \, \Pi(param)\right|\right] \forall \; k = 1, 2, \cdots, N, \tag{2.7}$$

where in this relation, α_k represents the order of the derivative of the variable y_k and must be taken between 0 and 1, τ_k represents the critical synchronization time. y_{k0} the initial condition of the variable y_k, $\Pi(param)$ represents the product of all the system's parameters for which the responder system exhibits chaotic behavior. The symbol $round\left[\bullet\right]$ denotes the nearest integer. Therefore, Alice can now construct a secret key following the relation:

$$K_k = K_1\left[\mod(M)\right]. \tag{2.8}$$

The process is repeated for each system's variable to get a series of secret keys as given by:

$$K_s = \left[K_{s_1} K_{s_2} K_{s_3} \cdots K_{s_N}\right], \tag{2.9}$$

where N denotes the number of variables in the dynamical system. The high secrecy of the key is due to the fact that, each parameter in the key generation process is secret. Moreover, the parameter τ_k is extremely important and cannot be guess due to the random-like behavior, the high nonlinearity degree and the complex geometry of fractional chaotic systems. However, one notices that the response system is pre-shared before the communication even starts making impossible an eavesdropper to generate the exact value of τ_k. In addition, the initial conditions of the responder system are involved in the key generation process which greatly improves the level of security of the key since chaotic systems are extremely sensitive to initial condition. So, a small difference in that value makes the system behaves in a very different way so that an eavesdropper without the exact value of these initial conditions will never be able to generate the value of τ_k and consequently that of χ_k and η_k. In the decryption process,

Bob must perform the same operation after getting the driver signal from Alice in order to generate the decryption key. That means the driver and responder systems are forced into synchronization running the system from the initial conditions until the same tolerance as that of Alice is reached afterward the corresponding time is taken. In the following section the algorithm of this encryption technique is provided in detail.

Encryption and Decryption Schemes

The Algorithm

In the previous section, it was seen that, two systems in a state of high dimensional chaos can be synchronized by a responder system being exchanged between both the sender and the receiver. Suppose a sender (Alice) wishing to transmit an encrypted message to a receiver (Bob), so that any other person (eavesdropper) intercepting the encrypted text should not be able to generate any useful information or decrypt the message. How does she proceed? Based on synchronization of fractional order derivative chaotic systems, the encryption technique is then described step by step as follows:

Step 1: Rearrange the plaintext P into a sequence of integers as follows:

$$P = \{p_1, p_2, \cdots, p_N\}. \tag{2.10}$$

One notices that an integer should be assigned to a character following the procedure described in table 1.

Step 2: Divide the set P into a series of blocks, each block containing a series of four characters substituted with their corresponding numbers obtained using the above table.

$$P' = \{\{p_1, p_2, p_3, p_4\}, \{p_5, p_6, p_7, p_8\}, \cdots, \{p_{N-3}, p_{N-2}, p_{N-1}, p_N\}\}. \tag{2.11}$$

Step 3: Check if the number of blocks in the set $\{P'\}$ is not a multiple of four, then include the necessary blank space corresponding number at the end of the sequence to complete the number of block into a multiple of four.

Step 4: From each block in the set $\{P'\}$ form a 2×2 square matrix as follows:

$$P_1 = \begin{bmatrix} p_{11} & p_{12} \\ p_{13} & p_{14} \end{bmatrix}, P_2 = \begin{bmatrix} p_{21} & p_{22} \\ p_{23} & p_{24} \end{bmatrix}, \cdots, P_l = \begin{bmatrix} p_{l-3N} & p_{l-2N} \\ p_{l-1N} & p_{lN} \end{bmatrix}, \tag{2.12}$$

with $l = \dfrac{N}{4}$.

Step 5: Run the dynamical system with the corresponding parameters and initial conditions for which the system exhibits chaotic behavior until the required tolerance is reached in order to evaluate the critical synchronization times τ_k and the corresponding critical value χ_k of the variable x_k and η_k of the variable y_k. Therefore, find the secret key using the relations (2.7) and (2.8) given as follows:

$$R_k = round\left[\left|\alpha_k \tau_k \chi_k \eta_k y_{k0} \prod(param)\right|\right], \ \forall \ k = 1, 2, \cdots, N, \tag{2.13}$$

and

$$K_k = R_k\left[\mod(M)\right]. \tag{2.14}$$

Step 6: For the first variables x_1 and y_1, compute the first four keys using the following procedure:

$$Q^{k_1} = \begin{bmatrix} F_{k_1+1} & F_{k_1} \\ F_{k_1} & F_{k_1-1} \end{bmatrix} = \begin{bmatrix} \tilde{k}_{11} & \tilde{k}_{12} \\ \tilde{k}_{13} & \tilde{k}_{14} \end{bmatrix}, \tag{2.15}$$

Using this relation, determine the four corresponding keys:

$$\begin{cases} k_{11} = \tilde{k}_{11} \mod(M), \\ k_{12} = \tilde{k}_{12} \mod(M), \\ k_{13} = \tilde{k}_{13} \mod(M), \\ k_{14} = \tilde{k}_{14} \mod(M). \end{cases} \tag{2.16}$$

Step 7: The ciphertext is obtained using the relation given by:

$$c_{ij} = p_{ij} + k_{ij}, \ \forall \ i = 1, 2, \cdots, N \ \text{and} \ j = 1, 2, \cdots, 4. \tag{2.17}$$

Step 8: Repeat the process until the full text is recovered. To recover the encrypted message, the receiver must perform the same steps and the decipher text is obtained as follows:

$$d_{ij} = c_{ij} - k_{ij}. \ \forall \ i = 1, 2, \cdots, N \ \text{and} \ j = 1, 2, \cdots, 4. \tag{2.18}$$

For an illustration and a well understanding of this technique, a plaintext will be encrypted considering as a chaotic system the fractional order derivative Mathieu-Van der Pol system, which is a system with high degree of nonlinearity and that has been proven to exhibit chaotic behavior when the parameters and initial conditions are well selected.

The Encryption and Decryption Speed Analyses

The performance of an encryption algorithm might also be measured in terms of the speed. Here, one means by the number of steps (or complexity) required in the procedure of encryption/decryption. Thus, the speed of an algorithm may be characterized by measuring the time required for the encryption and decryption key generation. Compared to the traditional ciphers such as DES, AES, etc., the proposed chaotic based cryptosystem presents some distinct properties. On one hand, the plaintext size of chaotic systems is not fixed. With this advantage, the chaotic system is suitable for large volume data encryption. On the other hand, the confusion and diffusion process that are well known from users are completely controlled via the user keys. In (2005), Lian *et al.* have shown that the encryption speed of the chaotic cryptosystem is high compared to the DES algorithm. They found that the speed of the encryption increases with the size of the plaintext.

Sensitivity and Key Space Analyses

The size of the key space is the number of encryption/decryption key pair available in the cryptosystem. In the present cryptosystem, the encryption method, the sequences $x_1(t)$, $x_2(t)$, $x_3(t)$ and $x_4(t)$ are generated using the Mathieu-Van der Pol chaotic system with fractional order derivative $(\alpha_1, \alpha_2, \alpha_3, \alpha_4)$. However, the parameters (a, b, c, d, e, f, g) and the responder's initial conditions $(y_{10}, y_{20}, y_{30}, y_{40})$ are involved in the key generation. Furthermore, the critical values $\tau_c, \chi_c,$ and η_c are also used for the key generation. Therefore, the key size is high enough making the encryption technique extremely robust from brute force attack. The size of the key space might also be seen as the total number of different keys that can be used in encryption/decryption process. From cryptography point of view, the key space size should not be less than 2^{100}, to ensure high cryptography security. In the present cryptosystem, since the secret key is generated by considering the initial conditions of the responder system, the system's parameters, the order of the derivative, and the critical values for which the systems inter into synchronization, the secret key can then be written as follows: $K = \left[k_1 k_2 k_3 \cdots k_N \right]$. Thus, the key size here is $2^{N'}$. In the present cryptosystem, one denotes 12 parameters involved in the key generation. Therefore, $N' = 4N = 12 \times 8 \times 4 = 384$, since each parameter represents 2^8 bits, and one has 4 different variables. This implies that the key space dimension is $2^{384} = 10^{116}$. One realizes that the key size is large enough compared to the existing cryptosystems and one can conclude that the key is highly secured and robust against brute force attack.

RACTICAL EXAMPLE ON A MESSAGE ENCRYPTION WITH THE MATHIEU-VAN DER POL FRACTIONAL SYSTEM

The Mathieu-Van der Pol system is a perfect nonlinear equation described by numerous parameters and which can be obtained by combining the Mathieu and the Van der Pol equations. The first can be derived from a simple parametric oscillator while the second can be derived from an electrical circuit both coupling can then, be easily implemented as a simple electrical circuit. It was shown that this system exhibits chaotic behavior for some given parameters and even with fractional order derivative

(Petras, 2011). The complexity and the high nonlinearity character of such a system can make it an important tool in the cryptography process. The author's focus in this section includes but not limited to the chaotic behavior via the phase portrait analysis of this system following by its synchronization conditions on one hand and on the other hand, a key for message encryption is provided by forcing this system into synchronization following by the key distribution via the synchronization of this system. Finally, a possible procedure of coding and decoding secret message from chaos synchronization point of view will be provided.

The Van der Pol Equation

This equation was first introduced by Balthazar Van der Pol in 1927 when describing a triode oscillation in electrical circuits. It can be derived from the simple electrical circuit as shown in figure 4.

On this circuit R represents the resistance, C the capacitor, $V_g(t)$ an external source and then, D the diode. In order to determine the equation which governs the voltage in the capacitor, consider the Kirchhoff's laws:

$$\textbf{Node A: } i_R = i_L, \; i_R = \frac{V_A - V_g}{R}, \tag{3.1a}$$

$$\textbf{Node B: } i_L = i_C + i_D \; i_C = C \frac{d}{dt} V_C, \tag{3.1b}$$

Combining these equations, one gets:

Figure 4. Electronic Circuit of the Van der Pol equation

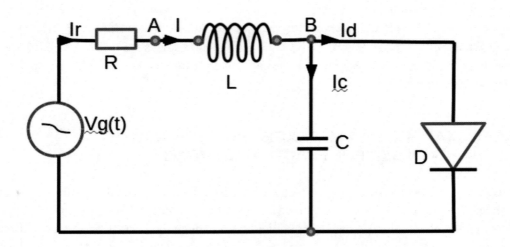

$$i_L = C\frac{d}{dt}V_C + i_D = \frac{V_A - V_g}{R}, \tag{3.1c}$$

with

$$V_A = RC\frac{d}{dt}V_C + Ri_D + V_g. \tag{3.1d}$$

The derivative of Equation (3.1d) with respect to time leads to:

$$\frac{d}{dt}V_A = RC\frac{d^2}{dt^2}V_C + R\frac{d}{dt}i_D + \frac{d}{dt}V_g,$$

and one also has:

$$V_C - V_A = \frac{L}{R}\left(\frac{d}{dt}V_A - \frac{d}{dt}V_g\right) \quad implying \quad that, \quad V_C = V_A + \frac{L}{R}\left(\frac{d}{dt}V_A - \frac{d}{dt}V_g\right). \tag{3.1e}$$

From where one finally gets:

$$V_C = RC\frac{d}{dt}V_C + Ri_D + V_g + LC\frac{d^2}{dt^2}V_C + L\frac{d}{dt}i_D. \tag{3.1f}$$

Simplifying Equation (3.1), considering $i_D = -a_1 V_C + a_3 V_C^3$, and setting

$$-3a_3 = RC, -a_1 = aC, Ra_1 - 1 = kLC, \frac{1}{LC} = b,$$

one obtains:

$$\frac{d^2}{dt^2}V_C(t) - a\left(1 - V_C^2(t)\right)\frac{d}{dt}V_C(t) + kV_C(t) = bV_g(t). \tag{3.2}$$

Equation (3.2) is well known mathematically as a second order differential equation and defines the forced and damped Van der Pol equation. In the more general form, it is defined by:

$$\frac{d^2}{dt^2}x - \mu\left(1 - x^2\right)\frac{d}{dt}x + \varepsilon x = f_1 \sin(\omega t). \tag{3.3}$$

Equation (3.3) can be written in the form of two first order differential equations. Taking $x_1 = x$ and $x_2 = \frac{d}{dt} x$, one has:

$$\begin{cases} \frac{d}{dt} x_1 = x_2, \\ \frac{d}{dt} x_2 = f_1 \sin(\omega t) - \varepsilon x_1 + \mu \left(1 - x_1^2\right) x_2. \end{cases} \tag{3.4}$$

Equation (3.4) is the non-autonomous Van der Pol equation. It is very useful in modeling oscillatory process in Electronics, Physics, Biology, Neurology, Economics, etc. In Biology for example, the Van der Pol is used as the basis of a model of coupled neurons in the gastric mill circuit. Some extended Van der Pol systems such as the Fitzhugh-Nagumo equation have been used for action potential of neurons. In seismology, it is used to develop a model of the interaction of two plates.

The Mathieu Equation

First discovered by Mathieu when solving the wave equation for an elliptical membrane moving through fluids, the Mathieu equation can be derived from a simple parametric oscillator and it is a second order differential equation given by:

$$\frac{d^2}{dt^2} x + \delta \frac{d}{dt} x + (a + b \sin(\omega t)) x + (a + b \sin(\omega t)) x^3 = \gamma \sin(\omega t), \tag{3.5}$$

where δ is the damped coefficient, γ the amplitude of the external force. Equation (3.5) can be also written in two first order differential equations. If one considers:

$x_3 = x$ and $x_4 = \frac{d}{dt} x$, then:

$$\begin{cases} \frac{d}{dt} x_3 = x_4, \\ \frac{d}{dt} x_4 = \gamma \sin(\omega t) - \delta x_4 - \alpha x_3 - \beta x_3^3. \end{cases} \tag{3.6}$$

With $\alpha = \beta = a + b \sin(\omega t)$, the parameter β introduces the amount of nonlinearity and α the stiffness in the system. Equation (3.6) is the non-autonomous Mathieu equation and presents also several applications in Physics where it is used in the study of elastic oscillations of a ferromagnetic substance, to describe the motion of particles vibrating in an elliptic drum, to study the inverted pendulum, and also in engineering, etc.

The Coupled Mathieu-Van der Pol Equations

Coupling the Mathieu and Van der Pol equations, one gets the Mathieu-Van der Pol equation (Ge & Chen 2004). For the Van der Pol equation, one takes $x_3 = \sin(\omega t)$ while for the Mathieu equation one takes $x_1 = \sin(\omega t)$. Doing so, both equations are transformed from non-autonomous to autonomous equation given by:

$$\begin{cases} \dfrac{d}{dt}x_1 = x_2, \\ \dfrac{d}{dt}x_2 = -\left(a + bx_3\right)\left(x_1 + x_1^3\right) - cx_2 + dx_3, \\ \dfrac{d}{dt}x_3 = x_4, \\ \dfrac{d}{dt}x_4 = ex_3 + f\left(1 - x_3^2\right)x_4 + gx_1. \end{cases} \tag{3.7}$$

Equation **(3.7)** is the so-called coupled Mathieu-Van der Pol equation with parameters a, b, c, d, e, f, g and initial conditions well known, it is a first order differential system and provides the evolution in times of the system. Knowing that the fractional order derivative is the generalization of ordinary differentiation, one can consider the previous system with order α which is a real between 0 and 1. From the definition of fractional order derivative, the variation of α does not affect the right hand side of system (3.7) so, one has:

$$\begin{cases} D_*^{\alpha_1}x_1 = x_2, \\ D_*^{\alpha_2}x_2 = -\left(a + bx_3\right)\left(x_1 + x_1^3\right) - cx_2 + dx_3, \\ D_*^{\alpha_3}x_3 = x_4, \\ D_*^{\alpha_4}x_4 = ex_3 + f\left(1 - x_3^2\right)x_4 + gx_1. \end{cases} \tag{3.8}$$

This equation will be used in this chapter as the driver signal; the corresponding responder signal is defined by:

$$\begin{cases} D_*^{\alpha_1}y_1 = y_2 + u_1(t), \\ D_*^{\alpha_2}y_2 = -\left(a + by_3\right)\left(y_1 + y_1^3\right) - cy_2 + dy_3 + u_2(t), \\ D_*^{\alpha_3}y_3 = y_4 + u_3(t), \\ D_*^{\alpha_4}y_4 = ey_3 + f\left(1 - y_3^2\right)y_4 + gy_1 + u_4(t). \end{cases} \tag{3.9}$$

where $u_i(t) \; \forall \; i = 1, \cdots, 4$ are the control parameters to be designed so that the system **(3.8)** synchronize with (3.9).These equations present high degree of non linearity and have a random-like behavior in their dynamics, therefore well fit to be used as the chaotic signals in this cryptosystem. $D_*^{\alpha_i} x$, $\forall$ $i = 1, \cdots, 4$ denote the Caputo derivative of the variable x defined by:

$$D_*^{\alpha} f(t) = \frac{1}{\Gamma(n - \alpha)} \int_a^t (t - s)^{n-\alpha-1} f^n(s) ds,$$

where f^n denotes the ordinary derivative of order n ($n \in \mathbb{N}$), D_*^{α} the Caputo operator, and one has $n - 1 \prec \alpha \prec n$, $\alpha, a, t \in \mathbb{R}$. The use of this order of the derivative as fractional is to improve the level of security in the key distribution process due to its high complex geometry. The synchronization problem of this equation is addressed in the following section.

Synchronization Problem of Chaotic Mathieu-Van der Pol Fractional System

The Mathieu-Van der Pol equation with fractional order derivative is a perfect nonlinear equation. Ge and Li *(2011)* showed that, for the initial conditions $x_{10}, x_{20}, x_{30}, x_{40} = \left(0.1, -0.5, 0.1, -0.5\right)$ and the parameters a, b, c, d, e, f, g=(10,3,0.4,70,1,5,0.1), the system exhibits chaotic behavior. Figure 5 plots the phase portrait of the system and represents the proof that the system effectively depicts chaotic behavior during its times evolution for different values of the order of the derivative so that: $\alpha_1 = 0.97999$, $\alpha_2 = 0.98999$, $\alpha_3 = 0.96999$, $\alpha_4 = 0.99111$. Therefore, due to this chaotic behavior, and the high degree of nonlinearity that presents this system, it is a perfect candidate to perform this cryptosystem. Thus, it will be used as both the driver and responder systems during the communication process between Alice and Bob. The problem that remains is how to synchronize both systems. However, it was seen in section (1.a) that the condition for synchronization is that if one considers $e(t) = x(t) - y(t)$, where $x(t)$ and $y(t)$ are the driver and responder signals respectively, one has: $\lim_{t \to \infty} e(t) \to 0$, which implies that $x(t) \to y(t)$ as the time becomes large. But, this condition is fulfilled if the control parameter is kindly designed. In that case, it is seen that if a function $V(t)$ is chosen so that, it is a positive semi-definite function with its derivative a negative semi-definite function, then $V(t)$ is a good Lyapunov function

Figure 5. Phase portrait for chaotic Mathieu-Van der Pol error dynamical system with fractional order derivative

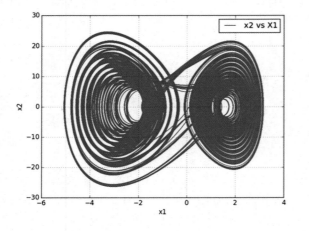
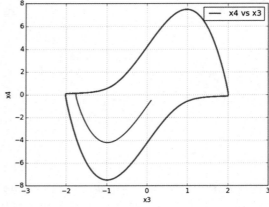

candidate. In this condition, the system is stable in the sense of Lyapunov. So, in this section, the purpose is to show how the control parameter should be designed so that the system initially unstable and uncontrollable becomes stable or goes to synchronization.

Let $e(t) = x(t) - y(t)$, then $D_*^\alpha e(t) = D_*^\alpha(x(t) - y(t))$, this implies that:

$$\begin{cases} D_*^{\alpha_1} e_1(t) = D_*^{\alpha_1} x_1(t) - D_*^{\alpha_1} y_1(t), \\ D_*^{\alpha_2} e_2(t) = D_*^{\alpha_2} x_2(t) - D_*^{\alpha_2} y_2(t), \\ D_*^{\alpha_3} e_3(t) = D_*^{\alpha_3} x_3(t) - D_*^{\alpha_3} y_3(t), \\ D_*^{\alpha_4} e_4(t) = D_*^{\alpha_1} x_4(t) - D_*^{\alpha_1} y_4(t). \end{cases} \tag{3.10}$$

Which implies that,

$$\begin{cases} D_*^{\alpha_1} e_1(t) = x_2(t) - y_2(t) - u_1(t), \\ D_*^{\alpha_2} e_2(t) = -\left(a + bx_3\right)\left(x_1 + x_1^3\right) - cx_2 + dx_3 - \left[-\left(a + by_3\right)\left(y_1 + y_1^3\right) - cy_2 + dy_3\right] - u_2(t), \\ D_*^{\alpha_3} e_3(t) = x_4(t) - y_4(t) - u_3(t), \\ D_*^{\alpha_4} e_4(t) = -e(x_3 - y_3) + \left[f\left(1 - x_3^2\right)x_4 - f\left(1 - y_3^2\right)y_4\right] + g(x_1 - y_1) - u_4(t). \end{cases} \tag{3.11}$$

System (3.11) depicts the error dynamics and from Figure 7 plotting its behavior, as the time increases one can easily realize that the error goes to zero as the time become large which is the proof that the system becomes stable. From the condition $D_*^\alpha V(t) \leq 0$ one has $V(t) = e_1(t) + e_2(t) + e_3(t) + e_4(t)$ and it is noticed that $V(t)$ in this form is a positive definite function due to the assumption that the authors are working in the partial region where $e_i(t) \ \forall \ i = 1, \cdots, 4$ are positive, this by the Ge-Yao-Chen partial region stability theory (Ge & Li 2011) which states that one should make sure that all errors always happen in the first quadrant. In order to make this happens the errors have been chosen so that

$$e_i(t) = x_i(t) - y_i(t) + 100 \quad \forall \ i = 1, \ldots, n.$$

Taking the derivative of this Lyapunov function, one gets:

$$D_*^\alpha V(t) = D_*^{\alpha_1} e_1(t) + D_*^{\alpha_2} e_2(t) + D_*^{\alpha_3} e_3(t) + D_*^{\alpha_4} e_4(t),$$

$$D_*^\alpha V(t) = \left(x_2(t) - y_2(t) - u_1(t)\right) - \left(a + bx_3\right)\left(x_1 + x_1^3\right) - cx_2 + dx_3$$
$$- \left[-\left(a + by_3\right)\left(y_1 + y_1^3\right) - cy_2 + dy_3\right] - u_2(t) + \left(x_4(t) - y_4(t) - u_3(t)\right)$$

$$+ \left(-e(x_3 - y_3) + \left[f\left(1 - x_3^2\right)x_4 - f\left(1 - y_3^2\right)y_4\right] + g(x_1 - y_1) - u_4(t)\right). \tag{3.12}$$

In order to have $D_*^\alpha V(t)$ as a negative semi-definite function, one may choose the control parameters as follows:

$$\begin{cases} u_1(t) = x_2(t) - y_2(t) + e_1(t), \\ u_2(t) = -\left(a + bx_3\right)\left(x_1 + x_1^3\right) - cx_2 + dx_3 - \left[-\left(a + by_3\right)\left(y_1 + y_1^3\right) - cy_2 + dy_3\right] + e_2(t), \\ u_3(t) = x_4(t) - y_4(t) + e_3(t), \\ u_4(t) = -e(x_3 - y_3) + \left[f\left(1 - x_3^2\right)x_4 - f\left(1 - y_3^2\right)y_4\right] + g(x_1 - y_1) + e_4(t). \end{cases} \quad (3.13)$$

Then, from system (3.11), one has:

$$D_*^\alpha V(t) = -e_1(t) - e_2(t) - e_3(t) - e_4(t) \prec 0,$$

since $e_i(t), \forall \ i = 1, \cdots, 4$, is positive definite-function in the first quadrant. So, in order to force this system into synchronization, one should choose the control parameters as given by Equation (3.13). After synchronizing these systems, it can then be used in cryptography. In the following section, a practical example will be developed using as the driver and the responder systems the fractional Mathieu-Van der Pol system.

Figures 6 and 7 depict the synchronization of systems (3.8) and its error dynamics respectively. One easily realizes that after some time, the error goes quick to zero and then the systems inter to a perfect synchronization. However, authors are highly interested on the time where this happens (called critical synchronization time) since its value and the corresponding critical values of the driver and the responder systems will be very important parameters involved in the key generation for this cryptosystem.

Application to Plaintext Encryption

Encryption

This section is deserved to a practical example where a plaintext is encrypted using a cryptography technique based on synchronization of fractional order derivative chaotic systems. In fact, as two identical responder signals are shared between the sender (Alice) and the receiver (Bob), a driver signal needs to be generated from Alice side so that she must follow the encryption steps mentioned in section (2.b.i) above. First, the driver signal generated is forced into synchronization with the responder signal and then, the time where the signals $x(t)$ and $y(t)$ must undergo to synchronization is reported. Secondly, the critical values of the variables $x(t)$ and $y(t)$ for which the systems inter into synchronization are also reported. Having these values, the secret key is then, generated following the steps as described in section (2.b.i). In this example, it is assumed that the responder and driver signals are both the Mathieu-Van der Pol systems with fractional order derivative as defined by Equations (3.8) and (3.9). The condition for synchronization has been studied and it is sure that with the control parameter kindly designed this system is synchronized so that the desired parameters can be reported. One mentions that these values are pseudo-random and very sensitive due to the random-like behavior of the chaotic signal, so that it is not possible to guess their exact values without the exact chaotic signals used.

Figure 6. Synchronization of chaotic Mathieu-Van der Pol system with fractional order-derivative via active control

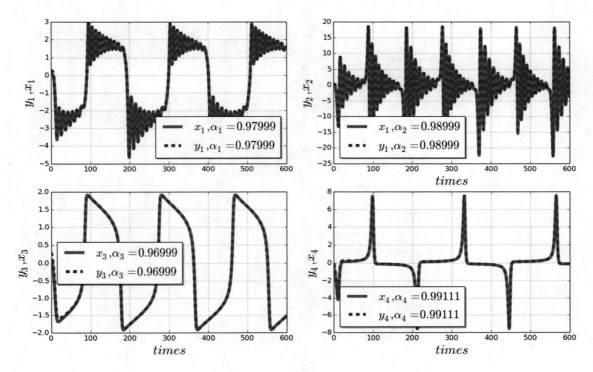

Figures 6 and 7 depict the synchronization of the Mathieu-Van der pol chaotic system with fractional order derivative to be used in this cryptosystem and its error dynamics. It is clear from these curves that the systems inter into synchronization after some time. However, one notices that a particular interest is given to the time where the systems inter to a perfect synchronization. This is the reason to consider the difference $x(t) - y(t)$ with a tolerance of 10^{-9}. Once the critical synchronization time is obtained, the next operation is to determine the corresponding critical values of the driver and responder signals, respectively and repeat the process for each variable in the system from where a series of secret keys for message encryption is generated.

Consider that the message Alice wishes to send to Bob is "I LOVE CRYPTOGRAPHY." one can easily see that, this message contains 20 characters, which is a multiple of 4. This includes the full stop and blank space. Assuming that after synchronizing the driver and responder signal given by Equations (3.8) and (3.9) as shown on Figure 6, over a range of time of 600 milliseconds, the following critical values are reported:

$$\left(x_1(t), y_1(t) \right) \mapsto \begin{cases} \tau_1 = 311.1111 \\ \chi_1 = 1.7228 \\ \eta_1 = 1.7235 \\ \alpha_1 = 0.97999 \end{cases} ; \left(x_2(t), y_2(t) \right) \mapsto \begin{cases} \tau_2 = 178.8789 \\ \chi_2 = 2.29936 \\ \eta_2 = 2.9944 \\ \alpha_2 = 0.98999, \end{cases} \tag{3.14}$$

Figure 7. Time evolution of the error of chaotic Mathieu-Van der Pol system with different order of the derivative when the control is introduced

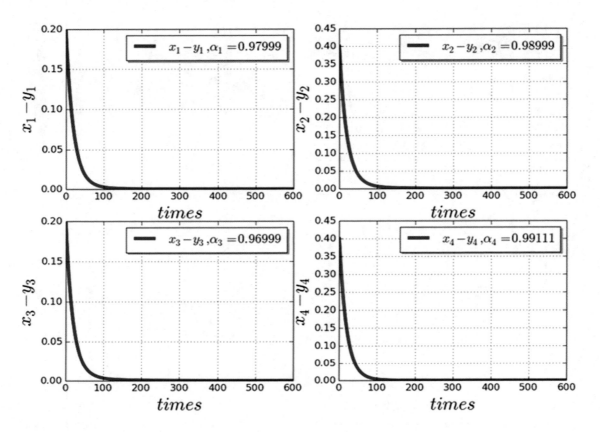

$$\left(x_3(t), y_3(t)\right) \mapsto \begin{cases} \tau_3 = 434.23 \\ \chi_3 = -1.3538 \\ \eta_3 = -1.3531 \\ \alpha_3 = 0.96999 \end{cases}; \left(x_4(t), y_4(t)\right) \mapsto \begin{cases} \tau_4 = 171.7111 \\ \chi_4 = 2.2179 \\ \eta_4 = 1.4219 \\ \alpha_4 = 0.99111, \end{cases} \tag{3.15}$$

where in relations (3.14) and (3.15), τ_i ($i = 1, \cdots, N$) corresponds to the critical values of time for which the variables x_i and y_i undergo into synchronization. That means x_i tends to y_i with a tolerance of 10^{-9}, χ_i and η_i for ($i = 1, \cdots, N$) define the corresponding critical values of x_i and y_i respectively where both variables enter into synchronization, α_i defines the order of the derivative. Having these values one can now determine the series of keys needed to encrypt a plaintext using Equation (2.13) as follows:

$$\wp_i = \left[\tau_i \chi_i \eta_i \alpha_i y_{0i} \left(abcdefg\right)\right] \forall i = 1, 2, \cdots, N, \tag{3.16}$$

where a,b,c,d,e,f,g are the parameters of the system for which the responder system exhibits chaotic behavior and y_{0i} the responders system's initial values. Having this value, one considers $\beta_i = round\left[\left\|\wp_i\right\|\right]$ where $round\left[\left\|\wp_i\right\|\right]$ define the nearest integer of $\left|\wp_i\right|$. In this example, one got after evaluation:

$$
\begin{cases} \wp_1 = 15.37863468 \\ \wp_2 = 21.89482008 \\ \wp_3 = 16.95867126 \\ \wp_4 = 14.12531629 \end{cases} \longmapsto \begin{cases} \beta_1 = 15 \\ \beta_2 = 22 \\ \beta_3 = 17 \\ \beta_4 = 14 \end{cases} \tag{3.17}
$$

Therefore, one can now construct the keys following the procedure given in section (2.b.i) above as follows:

$$
\left(x_1(t), y_1(t)\right) \longmapsto Q^{15} = \begin{bmatrix} F_{16} & F_{15} \\ F_{15} & F_{14} \end{bmatrix} = \begin{bmatrix} \tilde{k}_{11} & \tilde{k}_{12} \\ \tilde{k}_{13} & \tilde{k}_{14} \end{bmatrix} = \begin{bmatrix} 987 & 610 \\ 610 & 377 \end{bmatrix}, \tag{3.18}
$$

$$
\left(x_2(t), y_2(t)\right) \longmapsto Q^{22} = \begin{bmatrix} F_{23} & F_{22} \\ F_{22} & F_{21} \end{bmatrix} = \begin{bmatrix} \tilde{k}_{21} & \tilde{k}_{22} \\ \tilde{k}_{23} & \tilde{k}_{24} \end{bmatrix} = \begin{bmatrix} 28657 & 17711 \\ 17711 & 10946 \end{bmatrix}, \tag{3.19}
$$

$$
\left(x_3(t), y_3(t)\right) \longmapsto Q^{17} = \begin{bmatrix} F_{18} & F_{17} \\ F_{17} & F_{16} \end{bmatrix} = \begin{bmatrix} \tilde{k}_{31} & \tilde{k}_{32} \\ \tilde{k}_{33} & \tilde{k}_{34} \end{bmatrix} = \begin{bmatrix} 2584 & 1597 \\ 1597 & 987 \end{bmatrix}, \tag{3.20}
$$

$$
\left(x_4(t), y_4(t)\right) \longmapsto Q^{14} = \begin{bmatrix} F_{15} & F_{14} \\ F_{14} & F_{13} \end{bmatrix} = \begin{bmatrix} \tilde{k}_{41} & \tilde{k}_{42} \\ \tilde{k}_{43} & \tilde{k}_{44} \end{bmatrix} = \begin{bmatrix} 610 & 377 \\ 377 & 233 \end{bmatrix}, \tag{3.21}
$$

Finally, the secret key K_s can be constructed for this example considering that 50 characters are used following the table above. Therefore, one gets:

$$
k_{s_{ij}} = \tilde{k}_{ij}\left[\mathrm{mod}(50)\right] \forall \ i = 1, \cdots, 4 \ \text{and} \ j = 1, 2, \cdots, N. \tag{3.22}
$$

The modulus 50 is considered because one needs to reduce the size of numbers to be used in the encryption. That means for this example, the series of key will be random numbers between 0 and 50 in order to increase the speed in the encryption/decryption process. One recalls that, $a\left\lceil\text{mod}(b)\right\rfloor$ is the reminder of a divided by b. In this example, the blocks of keys obtained are the following:

$$K_s = \begin{cases} k_{s_1} = \begin{bmatrix} k_{11} & k_{12} \\ k_{13} & k_{14} \end{bmatrix} = \begin{bmatrix} 37 & 10 \\ 10 & 27 \end{bmatrix}, \\ k_{s_2} = \begin{bmatrix} k_{21} & k_{22} \\ k_{23} & k_{24} \end{bmatrix} = \begin{bmatrix} 7 & 11 \\ 11 & 46 \end{bmatrix}, \\ k_{s_3} = \begin{bmatrix} k_{31} & k_{32} \\ k_{33} & k_{34} \end{bmatrix} = \begin{bmatrix} 34 & 47 \\ 47 & 37 \end{bmatrix}, \\ k_{s_4} = \begin{bmatrix} k_{41} & k_{42} \\ k_{43} & k_{44} \end{bmatrix} = \begin{bmatrix} 10 & 27 \\ 27 & 33 \end{bmatrix}. \end{cases} \tag{3.23}$$

Having the secret key, the plaintext can now be encrypted following the procedure described in section (2.b.i), where the plaintext has to be divided into block of 4 including each character and making sure that the number of characters should be a multiple of 4. If it is not the case one completes with the necessary blank spaces. Thus, the plaintext "I LOVE CRYPTOGRAPHY." is divided as follows:

$$\text{Message} = \underbrace{I\ LO}_{1^{st}\ Block}\underbrace{VE\ C}_{2^{nd}\ Block}\underbrace{RYPT}_{3^{rd}\ Block}\underbrace{OGRA}_{4^{th}\ Block}\underbrace{PHY.}_{5^{th}\ Block} \tag{3.24}$$

Therefore, the blocks of matrices are formed by assigning to each character, a number following the rule given in the table above. For this particular example, the above plaintext becomes:

$$\text{Plaintext} = P = \underbrace{\begin{bmatrix} 18 & 38 \\ 21 & 24 \end{bmatrix}}_{1^{st}\ Block}\underbrace{\begin{bmatrix} 31 & 14 \\ 38 & 12 \end{bmatrix}}_{2^{nd}\ Block}\underbrace{\begin{bmatrix} 31 & 14 \\ 38 & 29 \end{bmatrix}}_{3^{rd}\ Block}\underbrace{\begin{bmatrix} 27 & 34 \\ 25 & 29 \end{bmatrix}}_{4^{th}\ Block}\underbrace{\begin{bmatrix} 25 & 17 \\ 34 & 37 \end{bmatrix}}_{5^{th}\ Block}, \tag{3.25}$$

the encrypted text (Ciphertext) can then be derived as follows:

$$\text{Ciphertext} = C = P + K_s, \tag{3.26}$$

which implies that,

$$\text{Ciphertext} = C = \underbrace{\begin{bmatrix} 55 & 48 \\ 31 & 51 \end{bmatrix}}_{1^{st}\ Block}\underbrace{\begin{bmatrix} 38 & 25 \\ 49 & 58 \end{bmatrix}}_{2^{nd}\ Block}\underbrace{\begin{bmatrix} 65 & 61 \\ 85 & 66 \end{bmatrix}}_{3^{rd}\ Block}\underbrace{\begin{bmatrix} 37 & 61 \\ 52 & 62 \end{bmatrix}}_{4^{th}\ Block}\underbrace{\begin{bmatrix} 62 & 27 \\ 44 & 70 \end{bmatrix}}_{5^{th}\ Block}, \tag{3.27}$$

So, relation (3.27) gives the ciphertext of the message and can now be sent through a public channel. It is clear that if this ciphertext is intercepted by an eavesdropper during the transmission process, he could not derive any useful information from it, since each number appears as random and due also to the fact that during the communication, the key is not sent at any time no matter if the channel is secured or not. This technique is very efficient and is impossible to be broken, and compared to the existing chaotic cryptosystems, this is highly secured from the fact that, the critical values here are extremely secured while in other cryptosystems, these values need most of the time to be shared between the sender and the receiver, making them vulnerable. Moreover, the use of critical values of the chaotic variables for which the systems inter into synchronization still increase the level of security of this cryptosystem.

As the communication was performed between Alice and Bob, at the Bop side (receiver), from the block of numbers received, he can now generate the decryption key by forcing the driver signal received from Alice into synchronization with the responder one previously shared (secretly). Therefore, he can now perform the same operations as Alice to generate the decryption key and once the key is obtained, he can decipher the message he received as follows:

$$D = C - K_d, \tag{3.28}$$

so, performing this operation in that example, the decipher text he got is:

$$\text{Deciphertext} = D = \underbrace{\begin{bmatrix} 18 & 38 \\ 21 & 24 \end{bmatrix}}_{1^{st}\ Block} \underbrace{\begin{bmatrix} 31 & 14 \\ 38 & 12 \end{bmatrix}}_{2^{nd}\ Block} \underbrace{\begin{bmatrix} 31 & 14 \\ 38 & 29 \end{bmatrix}}_{3^{rd}\ Block} \underbrace{\begin{bmatrix} 27 & 34 \\ 25 & 29 \end{bmatrix}}_{4^{th}\ Block} \underbrace{\begin{bmatrix} 25 & 17 \\ 34 & 37 \end{bmatrix}}_{5^{th}\ Block},$$

$$= \underbrace{\begin{bmatrix} I & \\ L & O \end{bmatrix}}_{1^{st}\ Block} \underbrace{\begin{bmatrix} V & E \\ & C \end{bmatrix}}_{2^{nd}\ Block} \underbrace{\begin{bmatrix} R & Y \\ P & T \end{bmatrix}}_{3^{rd}\ Block} \underbrace{\begin{bmatrix} O & G \\ R & A \end{bmatrix}}_{4^{th}\ Block} \underbrace{\begin{bmatrix} P & H \\ Y & . \end{bmatrix}}_{5^{th}\ Block}. \tag{3.29}$$

It is clear that with this cryptography technique, Bob easily recovers the message. However, one notices that this cryptography technique is very efficient, easily implementable in electronics and it is hard enough to be hacked. Moreover, the only difficulty comes from chaos synchronization since it is not really possible to have $x(t) - y(t) = 0$, that means $x(t) \to y(t)$, but this drawback has been avoided by considering some tolerance notably 10^{-9}, which should be agreed between Alice and Bob before the communication process starts.

Key Sensitivity Attack

In this section, one assumes that there exists a third part usually called Eve (an eavesdropper) that is not officially involved in the communication process, but willing to be informed about the communication between Alice and Bob. In order to better analyze the resistance of this encryption technique from brute force attack, considering that Eve knows exactly what are the steps to be performed in order to get the decryption key. However, she has no idea about the whole parameters that intervenes in the key generation, although she has intercepted the driver signal and the ciphertext. Assuming that Eve has the exact information on both systems and considering that she wishes to decrypt the ciphertext intercepted then, one need to show that even if at any way she knows all the parameters that are involved in the decryption key generation, without the exact values that have been used she cannot derive any useful information. Therefore, it is considered that for each parameter involved in the key derivation, she simply makes an error in the order of $\pm 10^{-9}$. Therefore, one can demonstrate that with this error, even small as it is, the initial message cannot be recovered. For the example used above, an error of $\pm 10^{-9}$ is made in each value. That means instead of:

$$\begin{cases} y_{01} = 0.3, & \alpha_1 = 0.97999 \\ y_{02} = -0.1, & \alpha_2 = 0.98999 \\ y_{03} = 0.3, & \alpha_3 = 0.96999 \\ y_{04} = -0.1, & \alpha_4 = 0.99111 \end{cases}$$

one considers

$$\begin{cases} y_{01} = 0.3 \pm 10^{-9}, & \alpha_1 = 0.97999 \pm 10^{-9} \\ y_{02} = -0.1 \pm 10^{-9}, & \alpha_2 = 0.98999 \pm 10^{-9} \\ y_{03} = 0.3 \pm 10^{-9}, & \alpha_3 = 0.96999 \pm 10^{-9} \\ y_{04} = -0.1 \pm 10^{-9}, & \alpha_4 = 0.99111 \pm 10^{-9} \end{cases} \tag{3.30}$$

Considering this slight difference, the generated key is given as follows:

$$K_s^e = \begin{cases} k_{s_1}^e = \begin{bmatrix} k_{11}^e & k_{12}^e \\ k_{13}^e & k_{14}^e \end{bmatrix} = \begin{bmatrix} 27 & 33 \\ 33 & 44 \end{bmatrix}, \\ k_{s_2}^e = \begin{bmatrix} k_{21}^e & k_{22}^e \\ k_{23}^e & k_{24}^e \end{bmatrix} = \begin{bmatrix} 37 & 10 \\ 10 & 27 \end{bmatrix}, \\ k_{s_3}^e = \begin{bmatrix} k_{31}^e & k_{32}^e \\ k_{33}^e & k_{34}^e \end{bmatrix} = \begin{bmatrix} 11 & 46 \\ 46 & 15 \end{bmatrix}, \\ k_{s_4}^e = \begin{bmatrix} k_{41}^e & k_{42}^e \\ k_{13}^e & k_{44}^e \end{bmatrix} = \begin{bmatrix} 47 & 37 \\ 37 & 10 \end{bmatrix}. \end{cases} \tag{3.31}$$

Having this key, the deciphertext can then be derived as follows $D^e = C - K_s^e$. Considering this relation, the decipher text obtained by Eve is the following:

$$D^e = \begin{bmatrix} 28 & 15 \\ -2 & 7 \end{bmatrix} \underbrace{\begin{bmatrix} 1 & 15 \\ 39 & 31 \end{bmatrix}}_{} \begin{bmatrix} 54 & 15 \\ 39 & 51 \end{bmatrix} \begin{bmatrix} -10 & 24 \\ 15 & 52 \end{bmatrix} \begin{bmatrix} 35 & -6 \\ 15 & 26 \end{bmatrix} \neq P, \tag{3.32}$$

$\underbrace{\qquad}_{1^{st}\ Block} \quad \underbrace{\qquad}_{2^{nd}\ Block} \quad \underbrace{\qquad}_{3^{rd}\ Block} \quad \underbrace{\qquad}_{4^{th}\ Block} \quad \underbrace{\qquad}_{5^{th}\ Block}$

It is observed that with this error of $\pm 10^{-9}$ on the initial conditions, and on the order of the derivative of the responder signal only, even small as it is, make impossible the message decryption. In this example, it is just assumed the worst case where Eve knows all the system's parameters involved in the key generation, except the initial conditions and the order of the derivative used because it is known that the responder system was pre-shared between Alice and Bop, so that there is not any possibility to be intercepted. Therefore, one concludes that this encryption technique is very efficient and robust against brute force attack.

Performance Analysis

The most important element in a cryptosystem is its key. More the key is secret more the cryptosystem is powerful in the security point of view. The secrecy of the encryption and decryption key implies how it must be shared between the sender and the receiver in security, so that if there is another part that is not involved in the communication process, but which can intercept the ciphertext, he cannot have any idea about the key. However, most of the time, there is not exactly a method or such a secret channel throughout what the secret key could be shared, so that nobody can intercept it and this constitute the weakness in most of the existing encryption methods as mentioned above, since in most of them, the sender must used a key, encrypt a text and send both the key and the ciphertext. It has been shown that no matter the secrecy of the channel used to send the key, it is vulnerable from attack. Therefore, in this proposed encryption technique, and that one thinks if it is successfully implemented in photonics, will enhance the level of key security, the encryption key is not sent at all and even if the receiver has no idea about the encryption key. The only thing he has knowledge are the steps to generate the decryption key and the parameters that are involved. So, with this procedure it is impossible for any eavesdropper to generate any useful information from the ciphertext intercepted. This encryption technique might be seen as the asymmetric key encryption such as the RSA, ECC just to name a few. The difference comes from the fact that, the chaotic signal used in the key generation and the Fibonacci Q-matrix used makes the key robust against attack. Although the cryptosystem should be a little bit slow, it is highly secured and easily implementable. Furthermore, it is shown in the previous section that a so small error made in choosing the parameters involved in the key generation make impossible the message recoverage. One has also seen that in the same plaintext, different characters might be encoded with the same encryption code making hard to guess the key. Compared to the RSA that uses the factorization of large prime numbers which may take several times with the complexity in the polynomial order and some existing encryption methods, this encryption technique will be faster and more efficient, since it was observed that, at just t=2 milliseconds, the systems already go into synchronization, which is the slowest step in the encryption/decryption procedure.

CONCLUDING REMARKS AND FUTURE TRENDS

In the framework of this chapter, novel strategies, features and benefits to cryptography based on the synchronization of fractional order derivative chaotic systems are provided. For this purpose, the authors studied on one hand the synchronization of fractional order derivative chaotic systems. On the other hand, one studied the key distribution via chaos synchronization of fractional order derivative systems and the Fibonacci Q-matrix has been introduced in order to improve the level of the key security. It followed from this study that compared to the existing cryptography techniques such as CMA, CSK, RSA, etc.; this proposed method was found to be very efficient due to the fact that, it provides high level of security from the complex geometry and high nonlinearity degree of fractional order derivative chaotic systems. It turned out from the speed, performance and key space analysis that, the cryptosystem provided if successfully implemented in photonics might be very powerful and fast compared to the CMA and CSK based cryptosystem which are the most known in the nowadays communication networks. Moreover, it followed that the key space is of 2^{384} or 10^{116} order, which is very large compared to the existing cryptosystem's key space. Furthermore, in order to better understand the proposed crypto-technique, the authors provided a concrete example where the chaotic Mathieu-Van der Pol system with fractional order derivative has been used as the slave and responder signals. With this example, one has been able to show that the proposed cryptosystem works excellently. Finally, the sensitivity of the key to brute force attack has been studied and it followed that, considering the worth case where an eavesdropper has an idea on each parameter involved in the key derivation but not the exact values of at least the initial condition and the order of the derivative which are real numbers between 0 and 1, but wishes to decrypt the message, with an error of 10^{-9} in these parameters he might not be able to decrypt the ciphertext intercepted which demonstrates that the proposed cryptosystem is extremely efficient. However, this chapter does not content the electronics model, thus the authors are planning to implement a physical model in the next research work.

REFERENCES

Alvarez, G., & Li, S. (2006). Some basic cryptographic requirements for chaos-based cryptosystems. *International Journal of Bifurcation and Chaos in Applied Sciences and Engineering*, *16*(08), 2129–2151. doi:10.1142/S0218127406015970

Annovazzi-Lodi, V., Benedetti, M., Merlo, S., Norgia, M., & Provinzano, B. (2005). Optical chaos masking of video signals. *IEEE Photonics Technology Letters*, *17*(9), 1995–1997. doi:10.1109/LPT.2005.853267

Bhasin, H., Kumar, R., & Kathuria, N. (2013). Cryptography Using Cellular Automata. *International Journal of Computer Science and Information Technologies*, *4*(2), 355–357.

Bleichenbacher, D. (1998). Chosen ciphertext attacks against protocols based on the RSA encryption standard PKCS# 1. In Advances in Cryptology-CRYPTO'98 (pp. 1-12). Springer Berlin/Heidelberg.

Bloisi, D. D., & Iocchi, L. (2007, March). Image based steganography and cryptography. VISAPP, (1), 127-134.

Cong, N., Son, D., & Tuan, H. (2014). On fractional Lyapunov exponent for solutions of linear fractional differential equations. *Fractional Calculus & Applied Analysis*, *17*(2), 285–306. doi:10.247813540-014-0169-1

Cuomo, K. M., & Oppenheim, A. V. (1993). Circuit implementation of synchronized chaos with applications to communications. *Physical Review Letters*, *71*(1), 65–68. doi:10.1103/PhysRevLett.71.65 PMID:10054374

Dedieu, H., Kennedy, M. P., & Hasler, M. (1993). Chaos shift keying: Modulation and demodulation of a chaotic carrier using self-synchronizing Chua's circuits. *IEEE Transactions on Circuits and Systems. 2, Analog and Digital Signal Processing*, *40*(10), 634–642. doi:10.1109/82.246164

Ge, Z. M., & Chen, Y. S. (2004). Synchronization of unidirectional coupled chaotic systems via partial stability. *Chaos, Solitons, and Fractals*, *21*(1), 101–111. doi:10.1016/j.chaos.2003.10.004

Ge, Z.-M., & Li, S.-Y. (2011). Chaos generalized synchronization of new Mathieu–Vander Pol systems with new Duffing–Van der Pol systems as functional system by GYC partial region stability theory. *Applied Mathematical Modelling*, *35*(11), 5245–5264. doi:10.1016/j.apm.2011.03.022

Ghaderi, R., Hosseinnia, S. H., & Momani, S. (2012). *Control and Synchronization of Chaotic Fractional-Order Coullet System via Active Controller*. arXiv preprint arXiv:1206.2415

Giresse, T. A., & Crépin, K. T. (2017). Chaos generalized synchronization of coupled Mathieu-Van der Pol and coupled Duffing-Van der Pol systems using fractional order-derivative. *Chaos, Solitons, and Fractals*, *98*, 88–100. doi:10.1016/j.chaos.2017.03.012

Gould, H. W. (1981). A history of the Fibonacci Q-matrix and a higher-dimensional problem. *Fibonacci Quart*, *19*(3), 250–257.

Gura, N., Patel, A., Wander, A., Eberle, H., & Shantz, S. C. 2004, August. Comparing elliptic curve cryptography and RSA on 8-bit CPUs. CHES, 4, 119-132.

Habib, M., Mehmood, T., Ullah, F., & Ibrahim, M. 2009, November. Performance of wimax security algorithm (the comparative study of rsa encryption algorithm with ecc encryption algorithm). In *Computer Technology and Development, 2009. ICCTD'09. International Conference on* (vol. 2, pp. 108-112). IEEE.

Hoggat Koshy, T. (2011). *Fibonacci and Lucas numbers with applications*. John Wiley & Sons.

Ishteva, M., Boyadjiev, L., & Scherer, R. (2005). On the Caputo operator of fractional calculus and C-Laguerre functions. *Mathematical Sciences Research Journal*, *9*(6), 161.

Jafari, H., & Daftardar-Gejji, V. (2006). Positive solutions of nonlinear fractional boundary value problems using Adomian decomposition method. *Applied Mathematics and Computation*, *180*(2), 700–706. doi:10.1016/j.amc.2006.01.007

Jiang, J. A., Yang, J. Z., Lin, Y. H., Liu, C. W., & Ma, J. C. (2000). An adaptive PMU based fault detection/location technique for transmission lines. I. Theory and algorithms. *IEEE Transactions on Power Delivery*, *15*(2), 486–493. doi:10.1109/61.852973

Karthikeyan, R., & Sundarapandian, V. (2014). Hybrid Chaos Synchronization of Four–Scroll Systems via Active Control. *Journal of Electrical Engineering*, *65*(2), 97–103. doi:10.2478/jee-2014-0014

Kocarev, L., Amato, P., Ruggiero, D., & Pedaci, I. 2004. Discrete Lyapunov exponent for Rijndael block cipher. *Proc. 2004 International Symposium on Nonlinear Theory and its Applications (NOLTA 2004)*, 609-612.

Kolumban, G., & Kennedy, M. P. (2000). Communications using chaos/spl Gt/MINUS. III. Performance bounds for correlation receivers. *IEEE Transactions on Circuits and Systems. I, Fundamental Theory and Applications*, *47*(12), 1673–1683. doi:10.1109/81.899919

Lian, S., Sun, J., & Wang, Z. (2005). A block cipher based on a suitable use of the chaotic standard map. *Chaos, Solitons, and Fractals*, *26*(1), 117–129. doi:10.1016/j.chaos.2004.11.096

Lorenz, E. N. (1963). Deterministic nonperiodic flow. *Journal of the Atmospheric Sciences*, *20*(2), 130–141. doi:10.1175/1520-0469(1963)020<0130:DNF2.0.CO;2

Lu, J., Wu, X., Han, X., & Lü, J. (2004). Adaptive feedback synchronization of a unified chaotic system. *Physics Letters. [Part A]*, *329*(4), 327–333. doi:10.1016/j.physleta.2004.07.024

Ma, S., Xu, Y., & Yue, W. (2012). Numerical solutions of a variable-order fractional financial system. *Journal of Applied Mathematics*.

Pecora, L. M., & Carroll, T. L. (1990). Synchronization in chaotic systems. *Physical Review Letters*, *64*(8), 821–824. doi:10.1103/PhysRevLett.64.821 PMID:10042089

Petras, I. (2011). *Fractional-order nonlinear systems: modeling, analysis and simulation*. Springer Science & Business Media. doi:10.1007/978-3-642-18101-6

Rodríguez, A., De León, J., & Fridman, L. (2008). Quasi-continuous high-order sliding-mode controllers for reduced-order chaos synchronization. *International Journal of Non-linear Mechanics*, *43*(9), 948–961. doi:10.1016/j.ijnonlinmec.2008.07.007

Rubezic, V., & Ostojic, R. (2000). *Breaking chaotic switching using generalized synchronization*. Academic Press.

Standard, A. E. (2001). *Federal information processing standard (fips) publication 197*. Washington, DC: National Bureau of Standards, US Department of Commerce.

Standard, D. E. (1977). *Federal information processing standards publication 46*. National Bureau of Standards, US Department of Commerce.

Tang, S., Chen, H. F., Hwang, S. K., & Liu, J. M. (2002). Message encoding and decoding through chaos modulation in chaotic optical communications. *IEEE Transactions on Circuits and Systems. I, Fundamental Theory and Applications*, *49*(2), 163–169. doi:10.1109/81.983864

Wu, G. C., & Lee, E. W. M. (2010). Fractional variational iteration method and its application. *Physics Letters. [Part A]*, *374*(25), 2506–2509. doi:10.1016/j.physleta.2010.04.034

KEY TERMS AND DEFINITIONS

Chaos: A theory that describes erratic behavior occurring in some nonlinear dynamical systems.

Ciphertext: The coded message obtained after applying an algorithm to be sent through a public channel.

Cryptosystem: A physical system that can be used to encode/decode a message.

Deciphertext: The decoded message obtained after applying an algorithm on the ciphertext.

Decryption: Process of decoding a coded message.

Encryption: Process of coding a message or process of making a text unreadable from any person who does not have the key.

Fractional-Order Derivative: Derivative with respect to non-integer order.

Key: Variable value applied on the plaintext/ciphertext to get the encrypted/decrypted text.

Plaintext: The transformed message into blocks of numbers.

Synchronization: The fact of making two chaotic systems with different initial conditions behave in the same way using a controller.

438

Chapter 14
Secure Digital Data Communication Based on Fractional–Order Chaotic Maps

Hamid Hamiche
Mouloud Mammeri University, Algeria

Sarah Kassim
Mouloud Mammeri University, Algeria

Ouerdia Megherbi
Mouloud Mammeri University, Algeria

Said Djennoune
Mouloud Mammeri University, Algeria

Maamar Bettayeb
Sharjah University, UAE

ABSTRACT

The aim of the chapter is twofold. First, a literature review on synchronization methods of fractional-order discrete-time systems is exposed. Second, a secure digital data communication based on synchronization of fractional-order discrete-time chaotic systems is proposed. Two synchronization methods based on observers are proposed to synchronize two fractional-order discrete-time chaotic systems. The first method concerns the impulsive synchronization where sufficient conditions for the synchronization error of the states are given. The second method concerns the exact synchronization which is based on a step-by-step delayed observer. In the same way, conditions are provided in order to allow the reconstruction of the states and the unknown input which is the message in this case. The two synchronization methods are combined in order to design a novel robust secure digital data communication. The performance of the proposed communication system is illustrated in numerical simulations where digital image signal is considered.

DOI: 10.4018/978-1-5225-5418-9.ch014

1. INTRODUCTION

Fractional-order differentiation and integration operators become useful mathematical tools in many areas of science and engineering (Kilbas et al., 2006). In recent years, attention has been brought on the investigation of the chaotic behavior of fractional-order systems.

For continuous-time systems, the basic idea is to replace the integer-order derivative by a fractional-order derivative in some well-known nonlinear chaotic integer-order systems. Among the continuous-time fractional-order chaotic systems proposed in the literature, one can find the Chua's system, the Newton-Leipnik's system, the Lorenz system (Sabatier et al., 2007). Meanwhile, with the rapid growth of the fractional-order calculus, some researchers are devoted to practical applications, such as the fractional-order PID controllers (Podlubny, 1999), the fractional-order signal processing, (Sejdic et al., 2011), fractional calculus to fluid mechanics, (Kulish & Jose, 2002), fractional calculus to polymer science, (Douglas, 2007) etc. Recently, some works are devoted to the application of the fractional-order (discrete-time or continuous) chaotic systems in secure communication (Gao et al., 2011; Kiani et al., 2009; Odibat, 2010; Zhang and Yang, 2011; Zhou and Ding, 2012). Indeed, with the rapid progress of communication network and information technology, several standard encryption methods have been developed. In the early 1970, the Data Encryption Standard (DES) algorithm has been proposed (DES, 1977). Due to the short length of its key, this algorithm has been replaced by the Advanced Encryption Standard (AES) (Daemen and Rijmen, 2002). These algorithms belong to the symmetric encryption category. They are called so, because they require the same secrete key for both encryption and decryption. On the other hand, another algorithms category uses different keys for encryption and decryption. It is qualified as asymmetric encryption category. The RSA algorithm is the most known algorithm in this category (Rivest et al.,1978). Unfortunately, for complex data secure transmission especially images security, the cited methods may not be the most desired candidates because they suffer from many issues, such as bulk volume of data, high correlation among adjacent pixels, high redundancy and real time requirement. To overcome these limitations, chaos based cryptography has been considered. Since then, this field becomes a new interesting research topic and several new schemes have been established. The most recent chaotic cryptosystems use fractional-order chaotic systems instead of the integer order ones. The major advantage of using fractional-order chaotic systems in secure data transmission is the improved security. We can explain this by the fact that fractional order chaotic system based transmission scheme has supplementary secret keys which are its fractional orders (Hamiche et al., 2015b; Kassim et al., 2016; Kassim et al., 2017). Then, with the consideration of chaotic features and the performance of algorithms, lots of novel encryption algorithms based on fractional-order chaotic systems have been proposed (Gao et al., 2011; Xu et al., 2014; Zhen et al., 2013; Zhen et al., 2012). As for the integer-order case, the fractional-order chaotic systems used at the transmitter and receiver levels should be synchronized in order to retrieve the sent original message. This is why, many synchronization approaches already proposed to synchronize integer-order chaotic systems have been generalized for the fractional-order ones. For instance, we can mention the sliding mode synchronization (Muthukumar et al., 2015), the impulsive synchronization method (Andrew et al., 2015), the active synchronization method (Agrawal et al., 2012) and the adaptive synchronization method (Zhou and Bai, 2015). It should be noted that the search in secure digital data based on the synchronization of fractional order chaotic systems is focused on the continuous case. On the other hand, the search in the discrete case is very limited. Indeed, except some few works and synchronization methods, this topic has not been well addressed in the literature. This can be justified by the fact that this topic is recent (Huang et al., 2016; Wu and Baleanu, 2014; Xin et al., 2017).

In this paper, one of our main objectives is to design a new secured digital image transmission scheme based on fractional-order chaotic discrete-time systems. The proposed scheme is composed of two blocks which are the transmitter and the receiver and consists primarily, on separating synchronization and encryption operations. This is achieved by using two coupled fractional-order discrete-time chaotic systems in the transmitter: one used for encryption and the other for synchronization. The advantage of using this strategy has been explained in (Dimassi et al., 2012; Hamiche et al., 2013b) where the authors introduced the method of separating the encryption and synchronization tasks to design an amplitude-independent scheme based on nonlinear chaotic systems. Through the results obtained in (Dimassi et al.,2012), the proposed communication scheme withstands channel noise and other disturbances. In this chapter, the synchronization method adopted is the impulsive synchronization (Hamiche et al., 2013a; Hamiche et al., 2015a; Megherbi et al., 2013; Yang and Chua, 1997; Zheng et al., 2002; Zheng et al., 2003). This technique has many advantages where it showed great efficiency in chaos communication applications since it maintains synchronization by small synchronization impulses. Also, since these impulses are at discrete times, the redundancy of the synchronization information in the channel will be reduced and therefore the security of the chaos based communication system is increased (Yang and Chua, 1997). For the encryption method, in order to reconstruct the states and the encrypted message image, we have chosen a delayed step by step observer. The major advantage of this observer is the exact reconstruction of the states and messages after a short delay, without any error as explained in (Kassim et al., 2017; Sira-Ramirez and Rouchon, 2001). To highlight the effectiveness of our proposed communication scheme in terms of its high level of security as well as its robustness, we present some robustness tests by simulation.

This chapter is organized as follows. After some preliminaries and definitions of nonlinear discrete-time fractional-order systems, we will give some recall on the synchronization of this class of systems. Then, we discuss the practical aspects of security. To this end, an application on the secure digital data is given where a new robust transmission scheme is presented. Finally, we provide the simulation results illustrating the synchronization and the reconstruction of the transmitted information. We also give the security analysis. We conclude with some remarks and some perspectives to improve the proposed scheme.

2. PRELIMINARIES ON FRACTIONAL-ORDER DISCRETE-TIME CHAOTIC SYSTEMS

In this section, some definitions on the fractional-order discrete-time systems are given. Let us consider the discrete-time state-space model of integer order:

$$x(k + 1) = f(x(k)) + g(x(k))u(k) \tag{1}$$

where $x(k) \in \mathbb{R}^n$ is the n-dimensional state vector and $u(k) \in \mathbb{R}$ is the input control, $f(x)$ and $g(x)$ are smooth vector fields for $x \in \mathbb{R}^n$. The state vector is written as $x(k) = [x_1(k) \ x_2(k) \dots x_n(k)]^T$

The first-order difference for $x(k+1)$, which represents the Euler discrete approximation of the integer order derivative $\dfrac{dx(t)}{dt}$, can be defined as $\Delta^1 x(k+1) = x(k+1) - x(k)$. Therefore, using (1), we deduce that

$$\Delta^1 x(k+1) = f(x(k)) + g(x(k))u(k) - x(k) \tag{2}$$

In (Dzielinski and Sierociuk, 2005); Kilbas et al., 2006), the α order difference operation was specified using Grunwald-Letnikov definition as follows:

$$\Delta^\alpha x(k) = \frac{1}{h^\alpha} \sum_{j=0}^{k} (-1)^j \binom{\alpha}{j} x(k-j) \tag{3}$$

The equation (3) represents the Euler discrete approximation of the fractional-order derivative $\dfrac{d^\alpha x(t)}{dt^\alpha}$, where, $\alpha \in \mathbb{R}^{*+}$ i.e., the set of strictly positive real numbers, is the fractional order, $h \in \mathbb{R}^{*+}$ is a sampling period taken equal to unity in all that follows, and $k \in \mathbb{N}$ represents the discrete time. We define

$$\binom{\alpha}{j} = \begin{cases} 1 & \text{for } j = 0 \\ \dfrac{\alpha(\alpha-1)\dots(\alpha-j+1)}{j!} & \text{for } j > 0 \end{cases} \tag{4}$$

The α-order difference is indicated in the same way that the first-order difference as follows

$$\Delta^\alpha x(k+1) = f(x(k)) + g(x(k))u(k) - x(k) \tag{5}$$

Noting the α-order difference (3), we obtain

$$\Delta^\alpha x(k+1) = x(k+1) + \sum_{j=1}^{k+1} (-1)^j \binom{\alpha}{j} x(k+1-j) \tag{6}$$

Equation (6) can be rewritten as

$$\Delta^\alpha x(k+1) = x(k+1) - \alpha x(k) + \sum_{j=2}^{k+1} (-1)^j \binom{\alpha}{j} x(k+1-j) \tag{7}$$

Substituting (7) into (5), we obtain

$$x(k+1) = \quad f(x(k)) + g(x(k))u(k) + (\alpha - 1)x(k)$$
$$-\sum_{j=2}^{k+1} (-1)^j \begin{pmatrix} \alpha \\ j \end{pmatrix} x(k-j+1) \tag{8}$$

Introducing the new variables $C_p = (-1)^{p+1} \begin{pmatrix} \alpha \\ p+1 \end{pmatrix}$ and $p = j - 1$, it follows that

$$x(k+1) = \quad f(x(k)) + g(x(k))u(k) + (\alpha - 1)x(k)$$
$$-\sum_{p=1}^{k} C_p x(k-p) \tag{9}$$

Remark 1

Commonly, the differentiation order α may not be the same for all the state variables $x_i(k)$. Therefore, for each state variable $x_i(k)$, we denote by α_i its corresponding fractional-order. When all orders α_i are equal, then the system is called commensurate-order. Otherwise, the system is of incommensurate order.

The infinite long memory property is well presented in System (9). It is easy to verify that when the number of iterations p increases the coefficient C_p decreases. Then, truncation of the memory is a reasonable approach for practical use and for computation process. Therefore, we can use the short memory principle to specify a more exploitable fractional-order nonlinear system.

We denote by L the limited length of memory. Then, System (9) can be rewritten as follows

$$x(k+1) = \quad f(x(k)) + g(x(k))u(k) + (\alpha - 1)x(k)$$
$$-\sum_{p=1}^{L} C_p x(k-p) \tag{10}$$

Remark 2

The model described by (10) is similar to nonlinear time-delay state space model with a time-delay in the state, where the number of time-delay states is equal to L.

In the following, the observability and observability matching condition features for nonlinear discrete-time fractional-order systems are introduced.

3. SYNCHRONIZATION OF FRACTIONAL-ORDER DISCRETE-TIME CHAOTIC SYSTEMS

This part is devoted to the presentation of two synchronization methods based on the chaotic systems. The first concerns an exact synchronization method based on a step-by-step observer. The second method is based on an impulsive observer. A detailed study on the principle of the two methods will be given below.

3.1 Synchronization Method Based on a Step-By-Step Observer

In order to design a discrete observer, the observability and observability matching condition of nonlinear discrete-time fractional-order systems must be satisfied. The observability and the observability matching condition allow to reconstruct all states and the message of the fractional-order discrete-time system, respectively. Some results are given below:

3.1.1 Observability and Observability Matching Condition of Nonlinear Discrete-Time Fractional-Order Systems

Observability

In this part, we study the observability properties of nonlinear discrete-time fractional-order systems (Kassim et al., 2017). Firstly, we present some definitions on the observability of nonlinear discrete-time systems. Then, we aim to extend this concept to the fractional-order systems.

System (1) can be described: as follows:

$$\begin{cases} x(k+1) &= f(x(k)) + g(x(k))u(k) \\ y(k) &= h(x(k)) \end{cases} \tag{11}$$

where $x(k) \in D \subset \mathbb{R}^n$ is the state vector and $y(k) \in \mathbb{R}$ is the output vector, $h(x): \mathbb{R}^n \to \mathbb{R}$ is the output map of the system.

In Wu, Wang, & Lu (2012) some definitions of the notion of observability for this class of systems are presented:

- **Definition 1:** Indistinguishability. Two states $x^1, x^2 \in \mathbb{R}^n$, are said to be indistinguishable (denoted $x^1 I x^2$) for (11) if, for every admissible input function u, the output function $h(x^1(k)), k \geq 0$, of the system for initial state $x^1(0) = x_0^1$, and the output function $h(x^2(k)), k \geq 0$, of the system for initial state $x^2(0) = x_0^2$, such that $x_0^2 \neq x_0^1$ are identical on their common domain of definition.
- **Definition 2:** A state x^0 is said to be observable, if, for each $x^1 \in \mathbb{R}^n, x^0 I x^1$ implies $x^0 = x^1$.
- **Definition 3:** A state x^0 is said to be locally observable, if there exists a neighborhood W_{x^0} of x^0, such that, for each $x^1 \in W_{x^0}, x^0 I x^1$ implies $x^0 = x^1$.
- **Definition 4:** A System (11) is (locally) observable, if each state $x \in \mathbb{R}^n$ enjoys this property. The observation space will prove to be essential for local observability.
- **Definition 5:** Consider the nonlinear System (11). The observation space O of (11) is the linear space of functions on $\mathbb{R}^n$ given as follows

$$O = [h, h \circ f, \ldots, h \circ f^{(n-1)}]^T \tag{12}$$

where $"\circ"$ denotes the usual composition function, $"\circ f^{(j)}"$ denotes the function f composed j times.

The observability codistribution, denoted as dO, is defined by the observability space O as follows

$$dO = span\{dh, dh°f, \ldots, dh°f^{(n-1)}\} \tag{13}$$

- **Theorem 1:** Consider System (11). Assume that

$$dim\ dO = n \tag{14}$$

then the system is locally observable.

Now, let us consider the fractional-order discrete-time system defined as follows

$$\begin{cases} x(k+1) &= f(x(k)) + g(x(k))u(k) + (\alpha - 1)x(k) \\ & \qquad -\sum_{p=1}^{L} C_p x(k-p) \\ y(k) &= h(x(k)) \end{cases} \tag{15}$$

As mentioned in Remark 2, System (15) can be classified as a discrete-time system with time-delay in the state. To study the observability of this system, the augmented system obtained from the following change of coordinates is considered

$$\begin{cases} Z_1(k) &= x(k) \\ Z_2(k) &= x(k-1) \\ & \vdots \\ Z_{L+1}(k) &= x(k-L) \end{cases} \tag{16}$$

where $Z_1, Z_2, \ldots, Z_{L+1} \in \mathbb{R}^n$. Then, the augmented system in the new coordinates is obtained and presented as follows

$$\begin{cases} Z_1(k+1) = f(Z_1(k)) + g(Z_1(k))u(k) + (\alpha - 1)Z_1(k) - \sum_{p=1}^{L} C_p Z_{p+1}(k) \\ Z_2(k+1) = Z_1(k) \\ \qquad \vdots \\ Z_j(k+1) = Z_{j-1}(k) \\ \qquad \vdots \\ Z_{L+1}(k+1) = Z_L(k) \\ y(k) = h(Z_1(k)) \end{cases} \tag{17}$$

where $j = 2, \ldots, L+1$.

System (17) can be rewritten as follows

$$\begin{cases} Z(k+1) & = & F(Z(k)) + G(Z(k))u(k) \\ y(k) & = & H(Z(k)) \end{cases} \tag{18}$$

where $Z(k) = [Z_1, Z_2, \ldots, Z_{L+1}] \in \mathbb{R}^{n'}$ is the new state vector and $n' = n\left(L+1\right)$

- **Proposition 1:** The observation space O' of (15) is also given as the linear space of functions on $\mathbb{R}^{n'}$ given as follows.

$$O' = [H, H^{\circ}F, \ldots, H^{\circ}F^{(n'-1)}]^T \tag{19}$$

with F is the vector field of the augmented System (18) and H is the output function.

In this case, the observability codistribution is given as follows

$$dO' = span\{dH, dH^{\circ}F, \ldots, dH^{\circ}F^{(n'-1)}\} \tag{20}$$

The main theorem concerning local observability reads as follows

- **Theorem 2:** The nonlinear discrete-time fractional-order system modeled by (18) is locally observable if and only if

$$dim\ dO' = n' \tag{21}$$

- **Proof:** Assume $dim\ dO' = n'$. Then, there exists n' functions

$$\Gamma_i(.) = \Gamma_1, \ldots, \Gamma_{n'} \in O,$$

where

$$\Gamma_1 = H, \Gamma_2 = H^{\circ}F, \ldots, \Gamma_{n'} = H^{\circ}F^{(n'-1)},$$

whose differentials are linearly independent at Z^0. By continuity, they remain independent in a neighborhood W_{Z^0} of Z^0. Therefore, $\Gamma_i(.)$ define a smooth mapping from $\mathbb{R}^{n'}$ to $\mathbb{R}$, which, restricted to W_{Z^0} is injective. Let $Z^1 \in W_{Z^0}$, if $Z^1 I Z^0$, in particular, for all $i = 1, \ldots, n'$, it must hold $\Gamma_i(Z^0) = \Gamma_i(Z^1)$. By the injectivity of $\Gamma_i(.), i = 1, \ldots, n'$, it follows that $Z^0 = Z^1$. Thus Z^0 is a locally observable state.

Observability Matching Condition

In this part, a brief presentation of the property of observability matching condition of discrete-time nonlinear systems is given. Then, a new theorem, which concerns the observability matching condition of fractional-order discrete-time nonlinear systems, is proposed. To this end, we consider the nonlinear analytic system given by Equation (11). The observability matching condition of System (11) is defined, as given in (Perruquetti and Barbot, 2006), as follows

- **Definition 6:** The observability matching condition is:

$$\left((dh)\,(dh\circ f)\,\ldots(dh\circ f^{(n-1)})\right)^T g = (0\ldots0\ *)^T \tag{22}$$

where "* " means a non-null term almost everywhere in the neighborhood of $x = 0$.

To study the observability matching condition of the fractional-order discrete-time system defined by (15), the following theorem is given.

- **Theorem 3:** The observability matching condition of nonlinear fractional-order discrete-time systems modeled by (15) is

$$\left((dh)\,(dh\circ\tilde{f})\,\ldots(dh\circ\tilde{f}^{(n-1)})\right)^T g = (0\ldots0\ *)^T \tag{23}$$

where $\tilde{f} = f(x(k)) + (\alpha - 1)x(k) + \beta(x)$ and $\beta(x(k)) \in \mathbb{R}^n$ is the $n-$dimensional vector of linear functions with respect to the delayed state $x\left(k - j\right)$, with $j = 1\ldots, L$ given by

$$\beta(x(k)) = [\beta_1(x_1(k)), \beta_2(x_2(k)), \ldots, \beta_n(x_n(k))]^T$$

with

$$\beta_i(x_i(k)) = -\sum_{j=1}^{L} C_{ij} x_i(k - j)$$

with $i = 1, \ldots, n,$ and $C_{ij} = (-1)^{j+1}\begin{pmatrix} \alpha_i \\ j+1 \end{pmatrix}.$

- **Proof:** Let us consider System (15) which can be presented as follows:

$$\begin{cases} x(k+1) &= \quad f(x(k)) + g(x(k))u(k) \\ &\quad +(\alpha - 1)x(k) + \beta(x(k)) \\ y(k) &= \quad\quad\quad h(x(k)) \end{cases} \tag{24}$$

Define the derivative of $\beta_i(x_i)$ with respect to x_i as $\dfrac{d\beta_i(x_i)}{dx_i}$. As mentioned above, the function $\beta_i(x_i)$ is linear with respect to $x_i(k-j)$ and coefficients C_{ij} are constants, then we obtain

$$\frac{d\beta_i(x_i)}{dx_i} = -\sum_{j=1}^{L} C_{ij} \tag{25}$$

System (24) may be rewritten in the following form:

$$\begin{cases} x(k+1) &= \tilde{f}(x(k)) + g(x(k))u(k) \\ y(k) &= h(x(k)) \end{cases} \tag{26}$$

Then, applying Definition 6 completes the proof.

The observability and the observability matching conditions of System (15) guarantee the left invertibility property, i.e., the possibility of recovering all the states and the input u from the output $y(k)$ and its iterations.

3.2 Synchronization Method Based on an Impulsive Observer

The second observer considered in the proposed chapter is the impulsive observer. The advantage of using this observer has been explained above. In the following, some results on the impulsive synchronization of integer-order and fractional-order discrete-time chaotic systems are given.

3.2.1 Impulsive Synchronization of Integer-Order Discrete-Time Chaotic Systems

The impulsive synchronization method consists of using a pulse sequence in order to force the states of a dynamic chaotic system to have the same evolution as those of another system. In this part, we study, at first, this method on integer-order discrete maps. For this, we consider the following master chaotic discrete-time system (Zheng et al., 2002; Zheng et al., 2003):

$$x(k+1) = Ax(k) + \varphi(x(k)) \tag{27}$$

where $x \in \mathbb{R}^n$ is the state vector and k is the discrete-time. $A \in \mathbb{R}^{n \times n}$ and $\varphi(x(k))$ is a $n-$ dimensional nonlinear map satisfying the Lipschitz condition:

$$\| \varphi(x(k)) - \varphi(\hat{x}(k)) \| < l \| x(k) - \hat{x}(k) \| \tag{28}$$

where l denotes the Lipschitz constant and $\| \cdot \|$ refers to the standard Euclidian norm.

Let us define k_i as a subset of discrete-time k taken so that

$$0 < 1 = k_1 < k_2 < \cdots < k_i < \cdots, k_i \to \infty$$

as $i \to \infty$. It denotes, in fact, the instants at which the pulses occur. We assume that the pulses are equidistant and denote the distance between two successive pulses by d. k_i^+ and k_i^- are, respectively, defined as the instants just after k_i and just before k_i, namely:

$$k_i^+ = \lim_{\epsilon \to 0} k_i + \epsilon, \quad \epsilon > 0 \tag{29}$$

$$k_i^- = \lim_{\epsilon \to 0} k_i - \epsilon, \quad \epsilon > 0 \tag{30}$$

The response system of (27) is given by the following discrete-time impulsive observer:

$$\begin{cases} \hat{x}(k+1) = A\hat{x}(k) + \varphi(\hat{x}(k)) & for \ k \neq k_i \\ \hat{x}(k_i^+) = \hat{x}(k_i) - B(k_i)e(k_i) & for \ k = k_i, i = 1, 2, \cdots \end{cases} \tag{31}$$

where $\hat{x} \in \mathbb{R}^n$ is the estimated state vector and $B(k_i), i = 1, 2, \dots$ are a sequence of $n \times n$ diagonal matrices. They are considered as control parameters and should be chosen appropriately to achieve synchronization.

The term $\hat{x}(k_i^-)$ is defined as follows: $\hat{x}(k_i^-) = \hat{x}(k_i)$ and $e(k)$ is the synchronization error given by:

$$e(k) = x(k) - \hat{x}(k) \tag{32}$$

We define two further errors with respect to the instants k_i:

$$e(k_i^-) = x(k_i) - \hat{x}(k_i^-) = e(k_i) \tag{33}$$

$$e(k_i^+) = x(k_i) - \hat{x}(k_i^+) \tag{34}$$

The impulsive synchronization between Systems (27) and (31) depends on the asymptotic stability of the following synchronization error (Sejdic et al., 2011):

$$
\begin{cases}
\begin{aligned}
e(k+1) \quad &= A\,e(k) + \varphi(x(k)) - \varphi(\hat{x}(k)) \\
&\qquad\qquad\qquad\qquad\qquad for\ \ k \neq k_i \\
\Delta e(k) \quad &= e(k_i^{+}) - e(k_i^{-}) \\
&= B(k_i)e(k_i^{-}) = B(k_i)e(k) \\
&\qquad\qquad\qquad\qquad\qquad for\ \ k = k_i \\
&\qquad\qquad\qquad\qquad\qquad i = 1, 2, \cdots
\end{aligned}
\end{cases} \tag{35}
$$

3.2.2 Impulsive Synchronization of Fractional-Order Discrete-Time Chaotic Systems

Let us now apply the previous theory to impulsively synchronize two discrete-time fractional-order chaotic systems. The master system is defined as System (10) i.e.

$$
x(k+1) = f(x(k)) + (\alpha - 1)x(k) - \sum_{p=1}^{L} C_p x(k - p) \tag{36}
$$

For a non-commensurate system (the derivative orders are different), we can rewrite the previous fractional-order difference equation as follows (Kilbas et al., 2006; Zheng et al., 2002):

$$
x(k+1) = A x(k) + \varphi(x(k)) - \sum_{p=1}^{L} A_d(p)x(k - p) \tag{37}
$$

where the matrix A, of dimension $n \times n$, describes the linear non delayed part of the system and the vector $\varphi(x(k))$ denotes the nonlinear terms and satisfies the Lipchitz condition (28). $A_d(p)$ are diagonal $n \times n$ which contains the coefficients C_p presented previously with respect to the derivative orders, namely:

$$
A_d(p) = \begin{pmatrix}
C_{p1} & 0 & \ldots & 0 \\
0 & C_{p2} & \ldots & 0 \\
\vdots & \vdots & \ddots & \vdots \\
0 & 0 & \ldots & C_{pn}
\end{pmatrix}
$$

The impulsive observer for System (37) is given by:

$$
\begin{cases}
\begin{aligned}
\hat{x}(k+1) \quad &= \quad A\hat{x}(k) + \varphi(\hat{x}(k)) \\
&\quad - \sum_{p=1}^{L} A_d(p)\hat{x}(k - p), \quad for\ \ k \neq k_i \\
\hat{x}(k_i^{+}) \quad &= \quad \hat{x}(k_i) - B(k_i)e(k_i), \quad for\ \ k = k_i, i = 1, 2, \cdots
\end{aligned}
\end{cases} \tag{38}
$$

where $\hat{x} \in \mathbb{R}^n$ is the estimated state vector.

The synchronization error between the two systems is as follows:

$$
\begin{cases}
e(k+1) &= A\,e(k) + \tilde{\varphi}(x(k), \hat{x}(k)) \\
&\quad - \displaystyle\sum_{p=1}^{L} A_d(p)e(k-p), \\
&\qquad\qquad for \ \ k \neq k_i \\
\Delta e(k) &= B(k_i)e(k_i), \\
&\qquad\qquad for \ \ k = k_i, i = 1, 2, \cdots
\end{cases}
\tag{39}
$$

with $\tilde{\varphi}(x(k), \hat{x}(k)) = \varphi(x(k)) - \varphi(\hat{x}(k))$

To study the impulsive synchronization between Systems (37) and (38), we use the theorem presented in (Liu and Marquez, 2008). where the authors study the impulsive control of a delayed discrete system networks. Indeed, it has been shown in recent works (Megherbi et al., 2017a), that System (39) is asymptotically stable and Systems (37) and (38) achieve the impulsive synchronization.

Remark 3

Our main objective in this paper is to study the possibility of impulsive synchronization of two fractional-order discrete-time chaotic systems. This is why; we have not been interested in computing the maximum pulses period required to establish this synchronization.

4. PROPOSED SECURE IMAGE TRANSMISSION SCHEME

In this section, we aim to propose a robust image transmission scheme by using fractional-order chaotic systems. The global scheme is shown in Figure 1. It consists principally of two main blocks: The transmitter and the receiver. The transmitter is composed of two fractional-order discrete chaotic systems: The fractional-order Lozi and modified-Hénon maps. At the receiver level, two fractional-order observers are used. In order to estimate the states of the transmitter maps, two observers are used: an impulsive observer for the fractional-order Lozi map and a delayed step by step observer for the fractional-order modified Hénon map.

In the following, the different blocks of the proposed transmission scheme are described.

4.1 Transmitter Study

Two fractional-order discrete-time systems are used at the transmitter level, the first is the fractional-order Lozi map and the second is the fractional-order modified Hénon map. In this subsection, we develop each system in more details and explain the role it plays in the transmission process. We start with the

Figure 1. Block diagram of the proposed scheme

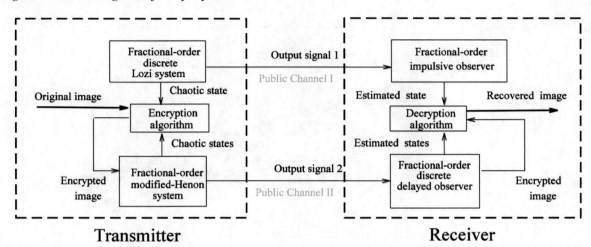

fractional-order chaotic Lozi system which is a two- dimensional nonlinear map described by the following state representation (Zheng et al., 2002).

$$
\begin{cases}
x_1(k+1) & = \quad 1 - a\hat{u}x_1(k)\hat{u} + bx_2(k) \\
& + \quad (\alpha_1 - 1)x_1(k) - \mu_1 \\
x_2(k+1) & = \quad x_1(k) + (\alpha_2 - 1)x_2(k) \\
& - \quad \mu_2 \\
y(k) = x_1(k)
\end{cases}
\tag{40}
$$

where $x = \begin{bmatrix} x_1 & x_2 \end{bmatrix}^T \in \mathbb{R}^2$ is the state vector, y is the output signal 1 and k denotes the discrete time. The coefficients μ_1 and μ_2 are defined as follows:

$$
\mu_1 = \sum_{p=1}^{L} C_{p1}x_1(k-p), \mu_2 = \sum_{p=1}^{L} C_{p2}x_2(k-p),
$$

α_1 and α_2 are the derivative orders satisfying relations $0 < \alpha_1 \leq 1, 0 < \alpha_2 \leq 1$.

We choose $a = 1.7$ and $b = 0.5$, so that the fractional-order Lozi map present a chaotic behavior. The obtained strange attractor for the derivative orders $\alpha_1 = \alpha_2 = 0.95$ and $L = 5$ is illustrated on Figure 2. Initial conditions are taken as follows: $x_1(0) = 0.1$ and $x_2(0) = 0.2$.

The second fractional-order map we used in our scheme is the fractional-order modified-Hénon map defined by the following system (Kassim et al., 2016; Kiani et al., 2009).

Figure 2. Chaotic attractor of the fractional-order Lozi map

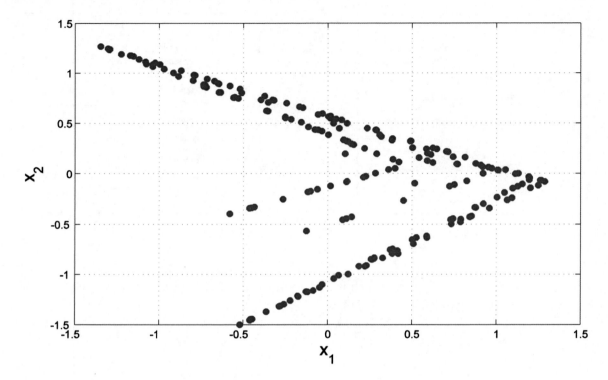

$$\begin{cases} z_1(k+1) &= \tilde{a} - z_2^2(k) - \tilde{b}z_3(k) \\ &+ (\tilde{\alpha}_1 - 1)z_1(k) - \nu_1 \\ z_2(k+1) &= z_1(k) + (\tilde{\alpha}_2 - 1)z_2(k) \\ &- \nu_2 \\ z_3(k+1) &= z_2(k) + (\tilde{\alpha}_3 - 1)z_3(k) \\ &- \nu_3 \\ \tilde{y}_{(k)} &= z_2(k) \end{cases} \qquad (41)$$

where $z = [z_1 \quad z_2 \quad z_3]^T \in \mathbb{R}^3$ is the state vector, $\tilde{y}$ is the output signal 2. The coefficients $\nu_i, \ i = 1, 2, 3$ are defined as follows:

$$\nu_1 = \sum_{p=1}^{L} \tilde{C}_{p1} z_1(k-p); \nu_2 = \sum_{p=1}^{L} \tilde{C}_{p2} z_2(k-p); \nu_3 = \sum_{p=1}^{L} \tilde{C}_{p3} z_3(k-p).$$

The Coefficients $\tilde{C}_{pi}, i = 1, 2, 3$ are computed in the same way as coefficients C_p of the fractional-order Lozi map. The derivative orders are:

$0 < \tilde{\alpha}_1 \leq 1, 0 < \tilde{\alpha}_2 \leq 1, 0 < \tilde{\alpha}_3 \leq 1.$

The different states present chaotic evolution for the following parameters values: $\tilde{a} = 1.5, \tilde{b} = 0.1$. Figure 3 shows the chaotic attractor got with $\tilde{\alpha}_1 = 0.85, \tilde{\alpha}_2 = 0.9, \tilde{\alpha}_3 = 0.75$ and memory length $L = 5$. The chosen initial conditions are $z_1(0) = -0.1$, $z_2(0) = 0.5$ and $z_3(0) = 0.1$.

In order to enhance the transmission security, the original image to send is encrypted in many steps. The different treatments brought to the original message before sending it on the public channel are described as follows.

Step 1: The original image is represented by matrix $A_{M \times N}$ (M and N are the rows and columns of the image). Then, we arrange, by order, the image pixels from left to right and from top to bottom so as to form first a decimal set $A = A_1, A_2, \cdots, A_{M \times N}$. The latter is subsequently transformed on a binary set, $B(k) = de2bi(A(k)) = B_1, B_2, \ldots, B_{M \times N \times 8}$.

Step 2: The fractional-order modified-Hénon system (51) is iterated for $N_f = M \times N \times 8$. Then, chaotic decimal sequences $z_1(k), z_3(k), k = 1, 2, \cdots, M \times N$ are obtained. These sequences are preprocessed as follows:

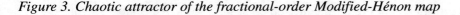

Figure 3. Chaotic attractor of the fractional-order Modified-Hénon map

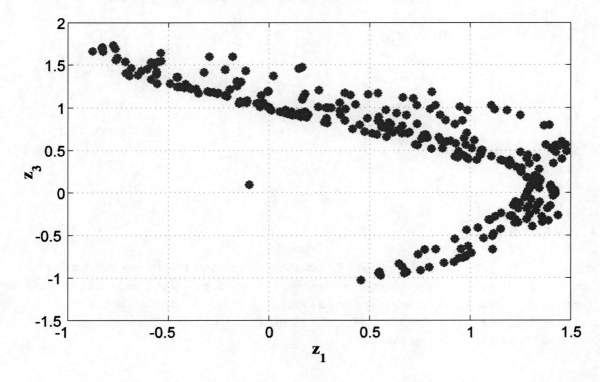

$$C(k) = cz_1(k) + dz_3(k)$$
$$D(k) = abs(C(k)) - floor(abs(C(k)))$$
$$E(k) = round(mod(D(k) \times 10^4, 255))$$
$$K(k) = de2bi(E(k))$$

c and d are considered as new secret keys.

Step 3: The XOR function is applied to the original image. Then, the cipher set $m_1 = m_{11}, m_{12}, \cdots, m_{1M \times N \times 8}$ is obtained as follows:

$$m_1(k) = B(k) \oplus K(k) \tag{42}$$

Step 4: The obtained message m_1 is combined with states z_1, z_3 of the fractional-order modified- Hénon map and the state x_2 of the fractional-order Lozi map. The chosen combination gives rise to a new encrypted message set we denote m_c and given by:

$$m_c(k) = m_1(k) + g_1 z_1(k) + g_2 z_3(k) + f_1 x_2(k) + f_2 x_2^2(k) \tag{43}$$

Step 5: The ciphered set is introduced in the third equation of System (51). We finally obtain

$$\begin{cases} z_1(k+1) & = \quad \tilde{a} - z_2^2(k) - \tilde{b} z_3(k) \\ & + \quad (\tilde{\alpha}_1 - 1)z_1(k) - \nu_1 \\ z_2(k+1) & = \quad z_1(k) + (\tilde{\alpha}_2 - 1)z_2(k) \\ & - \quad \nu_2 \\ z_3(k+1) & = \quad z_2(k) + (\tilde{\alpha}_3 - 1)z_3(k) \\ & - \quad \nu_3 + m_c(k) \\ \\ \tilde{y}(k) = z_2(k) \end{cases} \tag{44}$$

4.2 Receiver Study

In this part, we present the fractional-order observers used to recover the states of the fractional-order Lozi and modified-Hénon maps. In order to reconstruct the fractional-order Lozi system, an impulsive observer is proposed. Its role consists in using a train of pulses and to reproduce the states of a system at the arrival of each pulse (Hamiche et al., 2013a; Yang and Chua, 1997). The impulsive observer for system (40) can then be given as follows:

$$
\begin{cases}
\hat{x}_1(k+1) &= 1 - a\hat{u}\hat{x}_1(k)\hat{u} + b\hat{x}_2(k) \\
&+ (\alpha_1 - 1)\hat{x}_1(k) \\
&- \displaystyle\sum_{p=1}^{L} C_{p1}\hat{x}_1(k-p) \\
\hat{x}_2(k+1) &= \hat{x}_1(k) + (\alpha_2 - 1)\hat{x}_2(k) \\
&- \displaystyle\sum_{p=1}^{L} C_{p2}\hat{x}_2(k-p) \qquad for \ k \neq k_l \\
\hat{x}(k_{l+}) &= \hat{x}(k_l) - B(k_l)e(k_l) \qquad for \ k = k_l
\end{cases}
\tag{45}
$$

where $\hat{x} = [\hat{x}_1 \quad \hat{x}_2]^T \in \mathbb{R}^n$ is the estimated state vector. We define the instants k_l, $l = 1, 2, \cdots$, as the instants of pulses arrival. We define also k_{l+} and k_{l-} respectively as the instants which precedes or follows shortly the arrival of each pulse. $e(k)$ designate the synchronization error between systems namely

$$
e(k) = x(k) - \hat{x}(k) \text{ and } B(k_l) = \begin{pmatrix} b_1(k_l) & 0 \\ 0 & b_2(k_l) \end{pmatrix}
$$

is symmetric matrix containing control parameters acting when pulse k_l occurs.

Remark 4

The matrices $B(k_i)$ should be chosen appropriately so that they satisfy the conditions of Theorem 1 cited in (Megherbi et al., 2017a). Otherwise, the synchronization process can be affected and the original message cannot be recovered at the receiver end.

In our synchronization scheme, we have used only samples of the state x_1 for the impulsive control. Therefore, the control parameter consists of the parameter $b_1(k_l)$. In addition, it has been taken constant i. e.: $b_1(k_1) = b_1(k_2) = \cdots = b_1(k_i)$.

Now, we present the second fractional-order observer used in order to estimate the state of the fractional-order modified-Hénon map. This consists of a step by step delayed observer. It is called so, because delays are applied to the observer input in order to estimate each state step by step. Now, we develop at first, the recovering process of the states z_1 and z_3 of the fractional-order modified-Hénon map. It should be noted that the observability matching conditions presented in section 3.1 has been verified in our case.

To get $\hat{z}_1$, the estimate of state z_1, we apply one step delay to the second equation of System (51). Therefore, we deduce the state $zo_1 = \hat{z}_1$ as follows:

$$
zo_1(k-1) = \tilde{y}(k) - (\tilde{\alpha}_2 - 1)\tilde{y}(k) + v_{d2}
\tag{46}
$$

where $\nu_{d2} = \sum_{p=1}^{L} \tilde{C}_{p2} z_2(k-p-1)$

Once the state zo_1 is estimated, it is easy to reconstruct the state $zo_3 = \hat{z}_3$ from the first equation. In fact, by applying two steps delay to $\tilde{y}$, we obtain:

$$
\begin{aligned}
zo_3(k-2) &= \frac{1}{b}(\tilde{a} - \tilde{y}^2(k-2)) - zo_1(k-1) \\
&+ (\tilde{\alpha}_1 - 1)zo_1(k-2) - \nu_{d1})
\end{aligned}
\tag{47}
$$

where $\nu_{d1} = \sum_{p=1}^{L} \tilde{C}_{p1} zo_1(k-p-2)$

Now, one can deduce the message $m_c o$. For this, we consider the third equation of System (41) and by applying three steps delay, we can write:

$$
\begin{aligned}
m_c o(k-3) &= zo_3(k-2) - \tilde{y}(k-3) \\
&+ (\tilde{\alpha}_3 - 1)zo_3(k-3) + \nu_{d3})
\end{aligned}
\tag{48}
$$

where $\nu_{d3} = \sum_{p=1}^{L} \tilde{C}_{p3} zo_3(k-p-3)$.

Finally, to recover the original image, we should return to the previous encryption algorithm steps, except that the key is obtained from the delayed discrete-time observer with the same parameters. Then, the recovered image is obtained.

5. SIMULATION RESULTS

In this section, some simulation results of the proposed image cryptosystem are illustrated. Firstly, we present the simulation results on the synchronization of the transmitter and the receiver. Lastly, some analyses on the performance of the proposed transmission scheme are given.

5.1 Simulation Results on the Synchronization

In the following, Systems (50), (51) and their observers are considered. The chosen initial conditions for the impulsive observer are $x_1(0) = 3, x_2(0) = 2$ as mentioned before. Matrix B is chosen so as to verify the conditions for the impulsive synchronization. It is taken constant and equals to
$B = \begin{pmatrix} -0.95 & 0 \\ 0 & -0.95 \end{pmatrix}$.

As shown below, Figures 4, 5, 6 and 7 illustrate the simulation results for recovering the states $z_1(k), z_3(k), x_1(k)$ and the input $m(k)$, respectively. The reconstruction of these latter is done step by step and is perfect. The phase planes of the states $z_1(k), z_3(k)$ and the message $m(k)$, respectively, are

Figure 4. Phase plane $z_1(k)$ vs. $zo_1(k)$

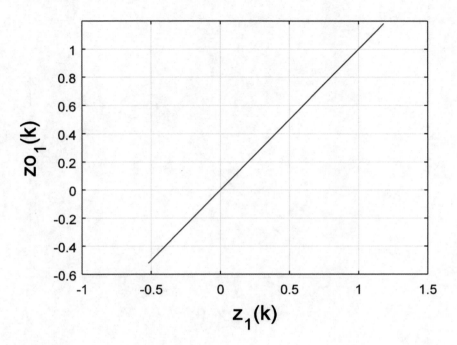

Figure 5. Phase plane $z_3(k)$ vs. $zo_3(k)$

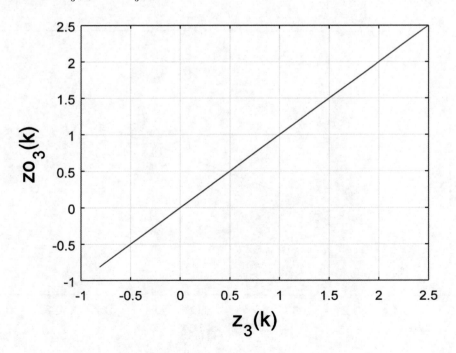

Figure 6. Phase plane $x_1(k)$ vs. $xo_1(k)$

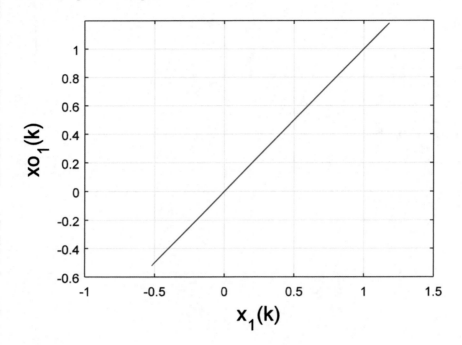

Figure 7. Phase plane $m(k)$ vs. $mo(k)$

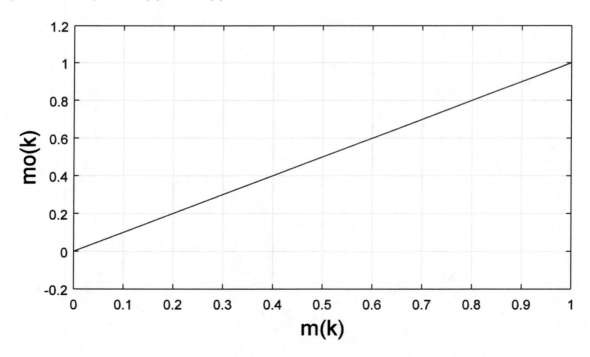

given in Figures 4, 5 and 7. The straight lines displayed on the three figures confirm that the synchronization is well established.

5.2 Robustness Analysis of the Proposed Transmission Scheme

In this subsection, we aim to prove the security of the proposed transmission scheme. To this end, different security measures are performed using original image of size 128×128. These measures consist of statistical analysis, information entropy analysis, sensibility analysis, and key space analysis. Each of these measures which are widely used in the literature in the field of chaos-based cryptography is described in what follows.

5.2.1 Statistical Analysis

According to Shannon (Shannon, 1949), two principles should be employed in a cryptosystem, which are diffusion and confusion, in order to resist the statistical analysis. In the following, we present two types of statistical analysis: histogram and correlation analysis.

Histogram analysis: From image histogram, one can see the frequency of each gray level which can leak image information. Indeed, in a good encryption algorithm the distribution of encrypted image should hide the redundancy of original one and not leak any information about it or the relationship between the original and the encrypted images (Megherbi, 2017b). Fig.8 displays the original, encrypted and decrypted Lena images and their histograms. From these figures, one can found that the histogram of the ciphered image has approximately a uniform distribution and is completely different from that of the original image.

To ensure the uniformity of encrypted image histogram, the chi-square test given below is used (Megherbi et al., 2017b):

$$\chi^2 = \sum_{i=0}^{255} \frac{(o_i - e_i)^2}{e_i} \tag{49}$$

where o_i are the observed frequencies of each gray level $(0 - 255)$ in the encrypted image histogram's, and e_i is the expected frequency of the uniform distribution, given here by $e_i = (n \times m) / 256$, where n and m present the image size's. The calculation result of the chi-square test of the encrypted image histogram's, with a significant level of 0.05 is $\chi^2 = 265.12$, which is lower than the critical value of $\chi^2_{255,0.05} = 293$.

Correlation analysis: In the ordinary image, each pixel with its adjacent pixels either in vertical, horizontal or diagonal directions is usually highly correlated. This correlation is determined by a value of the Pearson's Correlation Coefficient very close to 1. So, to analyze the encryption quality of the proposed algorithm, one can use the correlation coefficient to evaluate the correlations between adjacent pixels of the original and encrypted images in each direction. To this end, we calculate the correlation coefficient in each direction by the following equation:

Figure 8. The Lena gray original image, the encrypted image, the decrypted image and their corresponding gray histograms

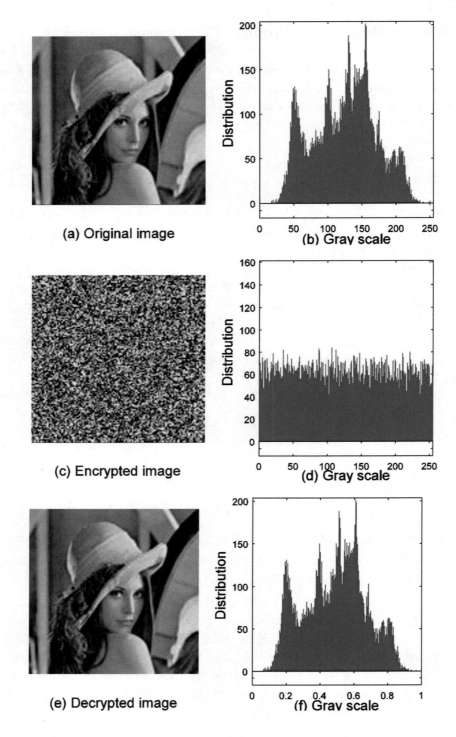

(a) Original image

(b) Gray scale

(c) Encrypted image

(d) Gray scale

(e) Decrypted image

(f) Gray scale

$$cov(x,y) = \frac{\frac{1}{N}\sum_{i=1}^{N}(x_i - \overline{x})(y_i - \overline{y})}{\sqrt{(\frac{1}{N}\sum_{i=1}^{N}(x_i - \overline{x})^2)(\frac{1}{N}\sum_{i=1}^{N}(y_i - \overline{y})^2)}} \tag{50}$$

where N in the total number of pixel pairs and $\overline{x} = \frac{1}{N}\sum_{i=1}^{N}x_i, \overline{y} = \frac{1}{N}\sum_{i=1}^{N}y_i, (x_i, y_i)$ is the ith pair of adjacent pixels in the same direction. As shown in Figure 9, the correlation distribution of two horizontally, vertically and diagonally neighboring pixels in the original and that in the encrypted Lena images is illustrated.

The detailed results of the correlation coefficients of Lena images are presented in Table 1. From this table, one can see that these results are far apart. Therefore, we conclude that the proposed cryptosystem is highly secure against statistical analysis.

5.2.2 Information Entropy Analysis

The information entropy, which was introduced by Shannon (Rivest et al., 1978), is calculated quantitatively for an image with n gray levels by the succeeding formula:

$$H(S) = \sum_{i=0}^{n} p(x_i) log_2 \frac{1}{p(x_i)} \tag{51}$$

where $p(x_i)$ denotes the probability of appearance of the information value x_i.

For a purely random source which produces 2^L symbols, the entropy is L. However, the entropy value of practical information is smaller than the ideal one. Therefore, after encryption, the ideal value of information entropy is as close as possible to L. In this work, we take a 256-gray-scale image in which the pixel data have 2^8 possible values. The information entropy of original Lena image is 7.4514. Nevertheless, the information entropy of encrypted Lena image is 7.9891. The obtained value, for the encrypted image, is very close to the theoretical maximum value $L = 8$, which indicates that the proposed transmission scheme is secure against an entropy attack.

Table 1. Correlation coefficients in the original and encrypted images

	Original Image	**Encrypted Image**
Horizontal	0.8939	0.0106
Vertical	0.9523	$-$ 0.0321
Diagonal	0.8550	$-$ 0.0023

Figure 9. Correlations of two horizontal, vertical and diagonal adjacent pixels in the Lena gray original image and encrypted image

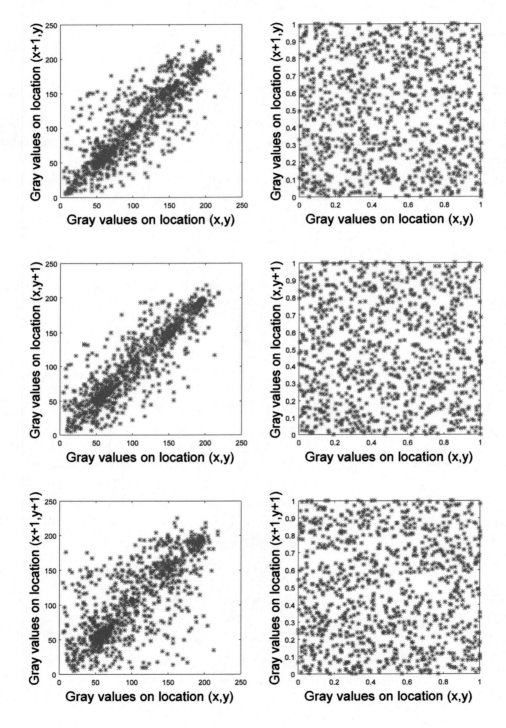

5.2.3 Sensitivity Analysis

A good cryptosystem should guarantee the security, of its algorithm, against the brute force attack. Then, high key sensitivity is an important characteristic for any robust secure image transmission scheme. This means that, a minor change in the input should cause a large change in the output. Indeed, chaotic systems are very sensitive to initial values and this guarantees the key sensitivity of the proposed scheme. In addition, security is improved by using the fractional-order chaotic systems by adding the fractional-orders derivative as new parameters to the security key. In our work, one can verify the key sensitivity of the proposed scheme by using decryption image obtained with key that is somewhat different from the original one. For this purpose, the number of pixels change rate (NPCR) can be used which is defined as follows:

$$NPCR = \frac{\sum_{i,j} D(i,j)}{M \times N} \times 100\% \tag{52}$$

where C_1 and C_2 are two images of the same size $M \times N$, the gray-scale values of the pixels at position (i,j) of C_1 and C_2 are denoted as $C_1(i,j)$ and $C_2(i,j)$, respectively. $D(i,j)$ is determined by $C_1(i,j)$ and $C_2(i,j)$, namely, if $C_1(i,j) = C_2(i,j)$ then $D(i,j) = 0$ otherwise $D(i,j) = 1$.

The *NPCR* of original and recovered images with different keys are presented in Table 2. From the latter, we finds that the *NPCR* under correct secret keys is quite small, however, under other a small difference with correct one the *NPCR* is close to 100%.

5.2.4 Key Space Analysis

The total number of various keys, which can be applied in the secure transmission scheme, is defined by the size of the key space. In fact, a robust encryption/decryption scheme must resist the brute force attack. To this end, the size of the key space should be large enough. In what follows, the level of security, produced by the secret key of the proposed scheme, is evaluated. Therefore, the fractional derivative orders $(\alpha_1, \alpha_2, \widetilde{\alpha_1}, \widetilde{\alpha_2})$ and the parameters $(a, \tilde{a}, b, \tilde{b}, c, d, f_1, f_2, g_1, g_2)$ are considered to construct the secrete key of the scheme. The precision is assumed to be at least 10^{10}, then the size of the key space is:

Table 2. NPCR of original image and recovered image with different keys

Secret Keys	*NPCR* $\left(100\%\right)$
Correct keys	8.86
Incorrect parameter $a + 10^{-14}$	99.69
Incorrect fractional-order $\alpha_1 + 10^{-14}$	99.72

$$N = \prod_{i=1}^{14} = 10^{(10 \times 14)} = 10^{140} \gg 2^{128}.$$

The obtained result satisfies the requirement of resisting the brute force attack.

6. CONCLUSION

In this chapter, we have proposed a novel image transmission scheme using synchronized fractional-order chaotic discrete-time systems. Two different observers have been used to achieve the synchronization: an impulsive observer and a step by step delayed observer. The message was encrypted by an encryption function before sending it by a chaotic carrier. Various methods for security analysis, such as statistical analysis and sensitivity analysis etc., are employed and illustrated by the simulation results. The latter show that the proposed transmission scheme can resist different attacks. Finally, many prospects can be considered for improving the presented work. The first one is to design an optimal protocol for real-time key transmission. In this case, an adaptation of the transmitted data in a given communication network, such as wireless networks, should be carried out. Another idea for enhancing the transmission scheme security is to use more complex encryption functions in the proposed algorithm and transmit more complex data, such as color images, speech or videos. Once these objectives are reached, practical implementation will be planned on programmable devices, such as Arduino-boards and FPGA circuits, etc.

REFERENCES

Agrawal, S. K., Srivastava, M., & Das, S. (2012). Synchronization of fractional order chaotic systems using active control method. *Chaos, Solitons, and Fractals, 45*(6), 737–752. doi:10.1016/j.chaos.2012.02.004

Andrew, L.Y.T., Li, X.F., Chu, Y.D., & Hui, Z. (2015). A novel adaptive-impulsive synchronization of fractional-order chaotic systems. *Chinese Phys. B, 24.*

Daemen, J., & Rijmen, V. (2002). *The Design of Rijndael: AES-The Advanced Encryption Standard.* Berlin: Springer. doi:10.1007/978-3-662-04722-4

Data Encryption Standard. (1977). *Federal Information Processing Standards Publication (FIPS PUB) 46.* Washington, DC: National Bureau of Standards.

Dimassi, H., Lorı́a, A., & Belghith, S. (2012). A new secured scheme based on chaotic synchronization via smooth adaptive unknown-input observer. *Communications in Nonlinear Science and Numerical Simulation, 17*(9), 3727–3739. doi:10.1016/j.cnsns.2012.01.024

Douglas, J. F. (2007). Some applications of fractional calculus to polymer science. *Advances in Chemical Physics, 102.*

Dzielinski, A., & Sierociuk, D. (2005). Adaptive feedback control of fractional order discrete state-space systems. *Proceedings of the 2005 International Conference on Computational Intelligence for Modelling, Control and Automation, and International Conference on Intelligent Agents, Web Technologies and Internet Commerce (CIMCA,IAWTIC,05),* 804-809. 10.1109/CIMCA.2005.1631363

Gao, Y., Zhang, X., Lu, G., & Zheng, Y. (2011). Impulsive synchronization of discrete-time chaotic systems under communication constraints. *Communications in Nonlinear Science and Numerical Simulation, 16*(3), 1580–1588. doi:10.1016/j.cnsns.2010.07.002

Guermah, S., Bettayeb, M., & Djennoune, S. (2008). Controllability and the observability of linear discrete-time fractional-order systems. *International Journal of Applied Mathematics and Computer Science, 18*(2), 213–222. doi:10.2478/v10006-008-0019-6

Guermah, S., Bettayeb, M., & Djennoune, S. (2009). A New Approach for Stability Analysis of Linear Discrete-Time Fractional-Order Systems. In New Trends in Nanotechnology and Fractional Calculus Applications (pp 151-162). Springer Netherlands.

Hamiche, H., Ghanes, M., Barbot, J. P., Kemih, K., & Djennoune, S. (2013b). Hybrid dynamical systems for private digital communications. *International Journal of Modeling, Identification and Control, 20*(2), 99–113. doi:10.1504/IJMIC.2013.056182

Hamiche, H., Guermah, S., Djennoune, S., Kemih, K., Ghanes, M., & Barbot, J. P. (2013a). Chaotic synchronization and securecommunication via sliding-mode and impulsive observers, *International Journal of Modeling, Identification and Control, 20*(4), 305–318. doi:10.1504/IJMIC.2013.057564

Hamiche, H., Guermah, S., Saddaoui, R., Hannoune, K., Laghrouche, M., & Djennoune, S. (2015a). Analysis and implementation of a novel robust transmission scheme for private digital communications using Arduino Uno board. *Nonlinear Dynamics, 81*(4), 1921–1932. doi:10.100711071-015-2116-z

Hamiche, H., Kassim, S., Djennoune, S., Guermah, S., Lahdir, M., & Bettayeb, M. (2015b). Secure data transmission schemebased on fractional-order discrete chaotic system. *International Conference on Control, Engineering and Information Technology (CEIT'2015).* 10.1109/CEIT.2015.7233065

Huang, L., Wang, L., & Shi, D. (2016). Discrete fractional order chaotic systems synchronization based on the variable structure control with a new discrete reaching-law. *IEEE/CAA Journal of Automatica Sinica.* doi: 10.1109/JAS.2016.7510148

Kassim, S., Hamiche, H., Djennoune, S., & Bettayeb, M. (2017). A novel secure image transmission scheme based on synchronization of fractional-order discrete-time hyperchaotic systems. *Nonlinear Dynamics, 88*(4), 2473–2489. doi:10.100711071-017-3390-8

Kassim, S., Hamiche, H., Djennoune, S., Megherbi, O., & Bettayeb, M. (2016). A novel robust image transmission scheme based on fractional-order discrete chaotic systems. *International Workshop on Cryptography and its Applications (IWCA).*

Kiani, B. A., Fallahi, K., Pariz, N., & Leung, H. (2009). A chaotic secure communication scheme using fractional chaotic systemsbased on an extended fractional Kalman filter. *Communications in Nonlinear Science and Numerical Simulation, 14*(3), 863–879. doi:10.1016/j.cnsns.2007.11.011

Kilbas, A. A., Srivastava, H. M., & Trujillo, J. J. (2006). *Theory and application of fractional differential equations.* Amsterdam: Editor Elsevier.

Kulish, V., & Jose, L. (2002). Lage application of fractional calculus to fluid mechanics. *Journal of Fluids Engineering, 124*(3), 803–806. doi:10.1115/1.1478062

Liu, B., & Marquez, H. J. (2008). Uniform stability of discrete delay systems and synchronization of discrete delay dynamical networks via Razumikhin Thechnique. *IEEE Transactions on Circuits and Systems. I, Regular Papers*, *55*(9), 2795–2805. doi:10.1109/TCSI.2008.923163

Megherbi, O., Guermah, S., Hamiche, H., Djennoune, S., & Ghanes, M. (2013). A novel transmission scheme based on impulsivesynchronization of two Colpittschaotic systems. *3rd International Conference on Systems and Control, ICSC'13*. 10.1109/ICoSC.2013.6750845

Megherbi, O., Hamiche, H., Djennoune, S., & Bettayeb, M. (2017). A new contribution for the impulsive synchronization of fractional-order discrete-time chaotic systems. *Nonlinear Dynamics*, *90*(3), 1519–1533. doi:10.100711071-017-3743-3

Megherbi, O., Kassim, S., Hamiche, H., Djennoune, S., Bettayeb, M., & Barbot, J-P. (2017). Robust image transmission scheme based on coupled fractional-order chaotic maps. *SIAM Conference on Control and its Application*. 10.1137/1.9781611975024.8

Muthukumar, P., Balasubramaniam, P., & Ratnavelu, K. (2015). Sliding mode control design for synchronization of fractionalorder chaotic systems and its application to a new cryptosystem. *International Journal of Dynamics and Control*, *5*(1), 115–123. doi:10.100740435-015-0169-y

Nijmeijer, H., & Van der Schaft, A. J. (1990). *Nonlinear dynamical control systems*. New York: Springer-Verglag. doi:10.1007/978-1-4757-2101-0

Odibat, Z. M. (2010). Adaptive feedback control and synchronization of non-identical chaotic fractional order systems. *Nonlinear Dynamics*, *60*(4), 479–487. doi:10.100711071-009-9609-6

Perruquetti, W., & Barbot, J.-P. (2006). *Chaos in Automatic Control*. CRC Press.

Podlubny, I. (1999). Fractional-order systems and PID controllers. *IEEE Transactions on Automatic Control*, *44*, 208–214. doi:10.1109/9.739144

Rivest, R. L., Shamir, A., & Adleman, L. (1978). A Method for Obtaining Digital Signatures and Public-Key Cryptosystems. *Communications of the ACM*, *21*(2), 120–126. doi:10.1145/359340.359342

Sabatier, J., Agrawal, O., & Machado, J. A. T. (2007). *Advances in fractional calculus: theoretical developments and applications. In physic and engineering*. Berlin, Germany: Editor Springer. doi:10.1007/978-1-4020-6042-7

Sejdic, E., Djurovic, I., & Stankovic, L. (2011). Fractional Fourier transform as a signal processing tool: An overview of recent developments. *Signal Processing*, *91*(6), 1351–1369. doi:10.1016/j.sigpro.2010.10.008

Shannon, C. E. (1949). Communication theory of secrecy systems. *The Bell System Technical Journal*, *28*(4), 656–715. doi:10.1002/j.1538-7305.1949.tb00928.x

Sira-Ramirez, H., & Rouchon, P. (2001). Exact delayed reconstruction in nonlinear discrete-time system. *European Union Nonlinear Control Network Workshop*.

Wu, G. C., & Baleanu, D. (2014). Chaos synchronization of the discrete fractional logistic map. *Signal Processing*, *102*, 96–99. doi:10.1016/j.sigpro.2014.02.022

Wu, X., Wang, H., & Lu, H. (2012). Modified generalized projective synchronization of a new fractional-order hyperchaotic system and its application to secure communication. *Nonlinear Analysis Real World Applications*, *13*(3), 1441–1450. doi:10.1016/j.nonrwa.2011.11.008

Xin, B., Liu, L., Hou, G., & Ma, Y. (2017). Chaos synchronization of nonlinear fractional discrete dynamical systems via linear control. *Entropy (Basel, Switzerland)*, *19*(7), 351. doi:10.3390/e19070351

Xu, Y., Wang, H., Li, Y., & Pei, B. (2014). Image encryption based on synchronization of fractional chaotic systems. *Communications in Nonlinear Science and Numerical Simulation*, *19*(10), 3735–3744. doi:10.1016/j.cnsns.2014.02.029

Yang, T., & Chua, L. O. (1997). Impulsive stabilization for control and synchronization of chaotic systems: Theory and application to secure communication'. *IEEE Transactions on Circuits and Systems. I, Fundamental Theory and Applications*, *44*(10), 976–978. doi:10.1109/81.633887

Zhang, R., & Yang, S. (2011). Adaptive synchronization of fractional-order chaotic systems via a single driving variable. *Nonlinear Dynamics*, *66*(4), 831–837. doi:10.100711071-011-9944-2

Zhen, W., Xia, H., Ning, L., & Xiao-Na, S. (2012). Image encryption based on a delayed fractional-order chaotic logisticsystem. *Chinese Physics B*, *21*(5).

Zhen, W., Xia, H., Yu-Xia, L., & Xiao-Na, S. (2013). A new image encryption algorithm based on the fractional-order hyperchaoticLorenz system. *Chinese Physics B*, *22*(1).

Zheng, Y. A., Nyan, Y. B., & Liu, Z. R. (2003). Impulsive synchronization of discrete chaotic systems. *Chinese Physics Letters*, *20*(2).

Zheng, Y. I., Nian, Y. B., & Liu, Z. R. (2002). Impulsive control for the stabilization of discrete chaotic system. *Chinese Physics B*, *19*(9), 251–1253.

Zhou, P., & Bai, R. (2015). The adaptive synchronization of fractional-order chaotic system with fractional-order 1<q <2 via linear parameter update law. *Nonlinear Dynamics*, *80*(1-2), 753–765. doi:10.100711071-015-1903-x

Zhou, P., & Ding, R. (2012). Modified function projective synchronization between different dimension fractional-order chaotic systems. Abstract and Applied Analysis, ID 862989.

Chapter 15

Neural Approximation–Based Adaptive Control for Pure–Feedback Fractional–Order Systems With Output Constraints and Actuator Nonlinearities

Farouk Zouari
Université de Tunis El Manar, Tunisia

Amina Boubellouta
University of Jijel, Algeria

ABSTRACT

In this chapter, an adaptive control approach-based neural approximation is developed for a category of uncertain fractional-order systems with actuator nonlinearities and output constraints. First, to overcome the difficulties arising from the actuator nonlinearities and nonaffine structures, the mean value theorem is introduced. Second, to deal with the uncertain nonlinear dynamics, the unknown control directions and the output constraints, neural networks, smooth Nussbaum-type functions, and asymmetric barrier Lyapunov functions are employed, respectively. Moreover, for satisfactorily designing the control updating laws and to carry out the stability analysis of the overall closed-loop system, the Backstepping technique is used. The main advantage about this research is that (1) the number of parameters to be adapted is much reduced, (2) the tracking errors converge to zero, and (3) the output constraints are not transgressed. At last, simulation results demonstrate the feasibility of the newly presented design techniques.

DOI: 10.4018/978-1-5225-5418-9.ch015

INTRODUCTION

Over the last few decades, fractional order calculus has attracted increasing attention from control community (Chen et al., 2014; Fu et al., 2016; Gao et al., 2017; Lin &Lee, 2011; Liu et al., 2017; Tarasov, 2016; Zouari et al., 2017a). There are two major factors account for this (Chen et al.,2014; Lin &Lee, 2011). On one hand, many engineering plants and processes cannot be described concisely and precisely without the introduction of fractional order calculus (Liu et al., 2017; Tarasov, 2016; Zouari et al., 2017b). On the other hand, it has been proved that fractional order controllers have more potential advantages and design freedom than integer order controllers (Zouari et al., 2017b). Due to the great efforts devoted by researchers, a large volume of outcomes have been obtained on fractional order systems (Lin &Lee, 2011; Liu et al., 2017; Tarasov, 2016; Zouari et al., 2017b). For the details of the most recent advance, one can refer to some excellent monographs i.e., (Chen et al.,2014; Lin &Lee, 2011; Liu et al., 2017; Tarasov, 2016; Zouari et al., 2017b), and the references therein as well.

The adaptive control for nonlinear systems have been an active topic in both academic and engineering fields because of its remarkable adapting ability to handle parametric and structural uncertainties, see typically (Achili et al., 2016; Bogkovic et al. 2001). Together with fuzzy logic systems or neural networks (NNs), tremendous advanced adaptive fuzzy/neural control schemes as in (Boulkroune et al., 2010; Boulkroune et al., 2012b, Boukezzoula et al. 2007 ; Chen et al., 2017) have been developed for nonlinear systems with nonparametric and nonstructural uncertainties. Particularly, the Radial basis function (RBF) based adaptive neural control approach in (Zouari et al., 2017a) ensures a good robustness to highly uncertain nonlinear systems. Moreover, the problem of curse of dimensionality resulting from the soaring fuzzy rules or NNs nodes has been overcome in (Boulkroune et al., 2010, Boulkroune et al., 2012a; Boulkroune et al., 2012b; Boulkroune et al. 2014a; Boulkroune et al. 2014b; Boukezzoula et al., 2007; Chang et al., 2016; Chen et al., 2017; Chen et al., 2016; Du & Chen, 2009; Fu et al., 2016; Gao et al., 2017; Guo et al., 2016; He et al., 2016; He et al., 2017; Hamel &Boulkroune, 2016; Jafrasteh &Fathianpour, 2017; Lai et al., 2017; Li et al., 2016; Li et al., 2017; Li et al., 2016). Although much progress has been made in adaptive control field, there still have many engineering problems which desiderate to be resolved (Liu et al., 2017; Na et al., 2012; Wen et al., 2011; Yu &Du, 2011; Zhang et al., 2017; Zhou et al., 2017). The most challenging one of which is that in practical implementation the actuator used to bridge the controller and the plant may suffer from output-to-input insensitivity which can be modeled as actuator nonlinearities, see in (Boulkroune et al. 2010; Chang et al., 2016; Gao et al., 2017; Lai et al., 2017; Yin et al., 2017; Zouari et al., 2017a; Zouari et al., 2017b). Without proper suppression, such actuator nonlinearities may cause performance degradation and even lead to instability of closed-loop systems (Yin et al., 2017; Zouari et al., 2017a; Zouari et al., 2017b). As a result, compensating for actuator nonlinearities is an important issue in adaptive control design (Gao et al., 2017; Lai et al., 2017; Yin et al., 2017; Zouari et al., 2017a; Zouari et al., 2017b). In (Gao et al., 2017; Lai et al., 2017; Zouari et al., 2017a; Zouari et al., 2017b), adaptive neural control schemes have been proposed for the uncertain nonlinear system that subject to actuator nonlinearities. The authors did not investigate the nonlinear systems with non-affine structures in some of the aforementioned works (Chang et al., 2016; Zhang et al., 2017).

In practice, there are many nonlinear systems with nonaffine structure, such as chemical reactors, biochemical process, some aircraft dynamics, dynamic model in pendulum control, and so on (Bogkovic et al., 2001; Boulkroune et al., 2012b; Du & Chen, 2009; ; Zouari et al., 2017a; Zouari et al., 2017b). Some remarkable results for nonaffine mono- variable systems have been obtained (Bogkovic et al.,

2001). It is worth noting that affine systems are a special case of the nonaffine systems (Boulkroune et al., 2012b; Du & Chen, 2009; ; Zouari et al., 2017a; Zouari et al., 2017b). Thus, all schemes in (Zouari et al., 2017a; Zouari et al., 2017b) can be applied directly to affine systems in which the control input appears in a linear fashion. In the literature, one can find five methods dealing with nonaffine problem (Boulkroune et al., 2012b; Zouari et al., 2017a; Zouari et al., 2017b), such as: (i) Method using Taylor series expansion in order to get an affine system. (ii) Method using implicit function theorem. (iii) Method exploit- ing the mean value theorem in order to obtain an affine form. (iv) By differentiating the original system equation so that, in the augmented resulting model, the time derivative of the control input appears linearly and the latter can be used as a new control variable. (v) By using a local inversion of the Takagi–Sugeno (TS) fuzzy affine model. Note that there are two common modeling assumptions in these above adaptive control schemes namely: the sign of the control-gain is known a priori, and the model is mono-variable. The sign of the control gain (i.e.,theso- called control direction) represents motion direction of the system under any control, and knowledge of this sign makes adaptive control design much easier (Boulkroune et al., 2012b; Zouari et al., 2017a).

In the adaptive control literature, the unknown control-direction problem has been addressed by many methods (Boulkroune et al., 2010; Oliveira et al., 2010; Zouari et al., 2017a; Zouari et al., 2017b): (i) By incorporating the Nussbaum-type function in the control law, (ii) By directly estimating unknown parameters involved in the control direction. (iii) By using the so-called correction-vector method for first order nonlinear systems. (iv) Via a switching scheme based on a monitoring function for variable structure model reference adaptive control for linear plants. (v) By incorporating a hysteresis-type function in adaptive fuzzy control. (vi) By using a hysteresis- dead-zone type function with the Nussbaum function in the adaptive control law. Other hand, few results are available in the literature on the design of the neural adaptive controllers for multivariable nonaffine nonlinear uncertain systems, (Zouari et al., 2017b) Note that it is difficult and complicated to control this class of systems due to the existence of unknown nonaffine functions and the coupling strength among subsystems (Oliveira et al., 2010; Zouari et al., 2017a). In (Chang et al., 2016), this difficulty has been overcome by introducing some special type Lyapunov functions and taking advantage of the backstepping design method and the approximation property of the fuzzy systems. In (Zouari et al., 2017a), the considered systems are a more general class of nonaffine MIMO systems. To facilitate the controller design, the mean value theory is used to transform unknown non-affine functions into a structure which is similar to affine form (Zouari et al., 2017b). This control scheme has two main advantages: (i) it does not require a priori knowledge of the signs of the control gains and (ii) only one parameter is needed to be adjusted online in controller design procedure for each subsystem. Nevertheless, the works (Achili, 2016; Fu et al., 2016; Chen et al., 2016) have not studied the effect of actuator nonlinearities in the control design and stability analysis.

The non-smooth input nonlinearity structures like the hysteresis, the quantization, the saturation, the backlash, the dead zone and the sector nonlinearities, are regularly involved in many practical systems, such as shape memory alloys, piezoceramics, mechanical connections, electric servomotors, and so on (Lin &Lee, 2011; Oliveira et al., 2010; Zouari et al., 2017a; Zouari et al., 2017b). It is well known that neglected actuator nonlinearities in order to facilitate the controller design may deteriorate system performance and cause system damage or even closed-loop instability throughout operation (Boulkroune & M'saad, 2012a; Boukezzoula, 2007; Chang, 2016; Fridman &Dambrine, 2009; He, 2016; Zouari et al., 2017a; Zouari et al., 2017b). Up to now, there exist results about the stability and control of uncertain systems with different kinds of input nonlinearities, see (Hamel &Boulkroune, 2016; Zouari et al., 2017a). For the sake of reliability and safety, the input nonlinearity compensation has been achieved by utilizing intelligent adaptive controllers (Boulkroune et al.,2010; Fridman &Dambrine, 2009). Roughly speaking, the direct decomposition and inverse compensation methods based on smooth functions are also useful approaches for suppressing nonsmooth input nonlinearities (Lai et al., 2017; Zouari et al., 2017a; Zouari et al., 2017b). Following the above mentioned researches, it is worth noticing that the strategies for handling input nonlinearities did not address the state and output constraint problems (Zhang et al., 2017; Zouari et al., 2017a; Zouari et al., 2017b).

In physical and practical plants, constraints on outputs, states and inputs are omnipresent, and usually manifest themselves as security specifications, physical limitations, nonlinear saturations, and performance requirements (Han et al., 2016; Chang et al., 2016). The violation of constraints akin to the time delays and the actuator nonlinearities also may degrade system performance and even lead to the system instability (Lai et al., 2017). To date, the symmetric and asymmetric barrier Lyapunov functions, which tend to infinity when its parameters (or arguments) approach some limits, are efficient techniques for resolving the control problems of nonlinear systems with state and output constraints (Zhang et al., 2017; He et al., 2016; Liu &Tong, 2016). It has to be noted that the majority of barrier Lyapunov functions possess logarithmic structure*s* and the symmetric barrier Lyapunov functions are very special cases of asymmetric barrier Lyapunov functions (He et al., 2017; Liu et al., 2016; Panagou et al., 2016). In the literature, survey papers on the utilization of asymmetric barrier Lyapunov functions to design the adaptive controllers of uncertain systems with constant and time-varying output constraints have been well established (He et al., 2017; Zhang et al., 2017). Also, in (Li et al., 2016; Liu et al., 2017), integral barrier Lyapunov functions have been developed for settling the uncertain systems with state constraints. In (Li et al., 2016; Panagou et al., 2016; Zhang et al., 2017), experimental and simulation results have shown that the maximum overshoots and convergence rates of tracking errors could be described by the barrier Lyapunov functions. It must be noted that the barrier Lyapunov functions ought to be bounded along the system trajectories in order to prevent the transgression of constraints (Panagou et al., 2016, He et al., 2017; Liu et al., 2017).

Motivated by the above discussion, an adaptive control technique is investigated in this work for a class of uncertain multi-input multi-output (MIMO) pure-feedback fractional-order systems with output constraints, unknown control directions, external dynamical disturbances and unknown actuator nonlinearities. Based on some assumptions and Caputo's definitions for fractional calculus (derivatives and integrals), the control design procedure is composed of a number of steps. First, the mean value theorem is utilized to eradicate the difficulties emerging from unknown actuator nonlinearities and nonaffine structures. Second, neural networks and smooth Nussbaum-type functions are also introduced for dealing with uncertain nonlinear dynamics, and unknown control directions, respectively. Then, thanks to a new Lemma on the Chain rule for fractional-order derivatives, a new class of Lyapunov-like asymmetric barrier functions is applied for tackling the output constraint problems. Furthermore, the backstepping technique is used to adequately determine the control updating laws, and to assess the stability of the overall closed-loop system. The foremost contributions of the current study include the following aspects.

1. Unlike the analogous literature (Chang et al., 2016; Han et al., 2016; He et al., 2016; He et al., 2017; Li &Yang, 2016; Liu &Tong, 2016; Xu et al., 2015; Zhang et al., 2017), the class of considered systems is quite large. Moreover, the structures of the actuator nonlinearities are more general than those in (Boulkroune et al. 2010; Chang et al., 2016; Gao et al., 2017).

2. In contrast to the research works in (Boulkroune et al.,2010; Liu et al., 2017; Zouari et al. 2017a, Zouari et al. 2017b), several assumptions regarding the estimation errors, actuator nonlinearities, uncertain nonlinear dynamics, and unknown control directions are not required in this paper.

3. Comparing to the previous works (He et al., 2016; Li et al., 2016; Liu &Tong, 2016; Zhang et al., 2017), the proposed controller design is incredibly simple, so that fewer parameters are adjustable and it does not require to compute the differentiations of some functions repetitively.

4. Different from the results in (Chen et al., 2016; Zouari et al., 2017a; Zouari et al., 2017b), the stability analysis of the closed-loop system is carried out in this work without its continuous frequency distributed equivalent model.

5. Unlike the works in (Boulkroune et al., 2012a; Boulkroune et al., 2014a; Chen et al., 2016; ; Du &Chen, 2009), our proposed control scheme, which is based on a new combination of existing methods and approaches along with new results from fractional calculus, solves a large variety of problems in practical systems and ensures that all closed-loop signals are semi-globally uniformly ultimately bounded and the tracking errors converge to zero, whereas the constraints are never transgressed.

Notation and Terminology

t stands for the time index. D^{δ} indicates the $\delta-$order Caputo differential operator. $\|\cdot\|$ refers to the usual Euclidean norm of a vector. $\exp(.)$ is the natural exponential function. $\ln(.)$ is the natural logarithm function. $|.|$ refers to the absolute value function. $\mathbb{R}^n$ represents the n-dimensional Euclidean space. C^1 denotes the set of continuously differentiable functions. L_2 represents the set of square-integrable functions. L_{∞} is the set of bounded functions. $\sin(.)$ and $\cos(.)$ are trigonometric functions.

PROBLEM STATEMENT AND PRELIMINARIES

Consider the following uncertain multi-input multi-output (MIMO) pure-feedback nonlinear incommensurate fractional-order system with output constraints and actuator nonlinearities

$$\begin{cases} D^{\delta_{i,j}} x_{i,j} = f_{i,j}\left(\overline{\mathrm{x}}_{i,j}, x_{i,j+1}, d_{i,j}\right), \text{ for } j=1,\ldots,n_i-1, \\ D^{\delta_{i,n_i}} x_{i,\mathrm{n}_i} = f_{i,\mathrm{n}_i}\left(\overline{x}_{i,n_i}, \nu_i, d_{i,n_i}\right), \\ \nu_i = \eta_i\left(u_i\right) \\ y_i = x_{i,1}, \text{ for } i=1,\ldots,\mathrm{p} \end{cases} \qquad (1)$$

where:

- The fractional orders $0 < \delta_{i,j} \le 1$, $j=1,\ldots,n_i$, $i=1,\ldots,\mathrm{p}$ are known constants.

- $x = \left[x_1^{\ T}, \ldots, x_p^{\ T} \right]^T \in \mathbb{R}^n$, $u = \left[u_1, \ldots, u_p \right]^T \in \mathbb{R}^p$ and $y = \left[y_1, \ldots, y_p \right]^T \in \mathbb{R}^p$ denote the pseudo-state vector, the control input vector and the output vector of the system, respectively, with $\overline{x}_{i,j} = \left[x_{i,1}, \ldots, x_{i,j} \right]^T \in \mathbb{R}^j$, $\overline{x}_{i,n_i} = x_i = \left[x_{i,1}, \ldots, x_{i,n_i} \right]^T \in \mathbb{R}^{n_i}$, $x_{i,j+1} \in \mathbb{R}$, $u_i \in \mathbb{R}$, $y_i \in \mathbb{R}$, $j = 1, \ldots, n_i - 1$, $i = 1, \ldots, \mathrm{p}$ and $n_1 + \cdots + n_p = n$.

- y_i is required to remain in the set $-\kappa_{1,i} < y_i < \kappa_{2,i}$ (Output Constraints) with $\kappa_{1,i}$ and $\kappa_{2,i}$ being known strictly positive constants, for $i = 1, \ldots, p$.

- $d_{i,j} \in \mathbb{R}$, $j = 1, \ldots, n_i$, $i = 1, \ldots, \mathrm{p}$, are bounded external disturbances.

- The functions $f_{i,j}\left(. \right)$, $j = 1, \ldots, n_i$, $i = 1, \ldots, \mathrm{p}$ are sufficiently smooth and unknown.

The actuator nonlinearity output $\nu = \left[\nu_1, \ldots, \nu_p \right]^T \in \mathbb{R}^p$ is described as follows (Boulkroune et al. 2010; Chang et al., 2016; Gao et al., 2017; Lai et al., 2017; Yin et al., 2017; Zouari et al., 2017a; Zouari et al., 2017b)

$$\nu_i = \eta_i\left(u_i \right) = \begin{cases} \eta_{1,i}\left(u_i \right) + \Delta_{1,i}, & \text{if } u_i \leq -u_{\min,i} \leq 0 \\ \eta_{2,i}\left(u_i \right), & \text{if } -u_{\min,i} \leq u_i \leq u_{\max,i} \\ \eta_{3,i}\left(u_i \right) + \Delta_{2,i}, & \text{if } u_i \geq u_{\max,i} \geq 0 \end{cases}, \quad \text{for } i = 1, \ldots, p \tag{2}$$

where the constants $u_{\min,i}$ and $u_{\max,i}$ are strictly positive and unknown, for $i = 1, \ldots, p$.

$\eta_i\left(u_i \right)$ is an unknown continuous function, such that:

- $\eta_{1,i}\left(u_i \right)$, $\eta_{2,i}\left(u_i \right)$ and $\eta_{3,i}\left(u_i \right)$ are continuously differentiable functions,

- $\eta_{1,i}\left(-u_{\min,i} \right) + \Delta_{1,i} = \eta_{2,i}\left(-u_{\min,i} \right)$ and $\eta_{2,i}\left(u_{\max,i} \right) = \eta_{3,i}\left(u_{\max,i} \right) + \Delta_{2,i}$,

- $\Delta_{1,i}$ and $\Delta_{2,i}$ are bounded.

- The functions $\left| \dfrac{\partial \eta_{1,i}\left(u_i \right)}{\partial u_i} \right|$ and $\left| \dfrac{\partial \eta_{3,i}\left(u_i \right)}{\partial u_i} \right|$ are strictly positive and bounded, for $i = 1, \ldots, p$.

- **Remark 1:** There are several kinds' definitions for fractional order derivatives, such as Caputo definition, Riemann–Liouville definition and Grünwald– Letnikov definition (Chen et al.,2014; Lin &Lee, 2011; Liu et al., 2017; Tarasov, 2016; Zouari et al., 2017a) . Compared to others definitions, the great advantage of the Caputo definition is that the initial conditions for fractional-order differential equations take on a similar form as for integer-order differential equations (Lin &Lee, 2011; Liu et al., 2017) . In the literature, such an operator is sometimes referred as a smooth fractional derivative (Tarasov, 2016; Zouari et al., 2017b).

- **Remark 2:** It is worth pointing out that the considered system (1) can be used to describe a relatively large class of uncertain nonlinear systems, such as communication networks, chemical processes, underwater vehicles, Duffing chaotic system, aircraft wing rock, induction servo motor drive, fractional-order Lü system, fractional-order Lorenz system, fractional-order unified chaotic system, and fractional-order Chen system, and so on (Chang et al., 2016; Chen et al., 2016; Gao et al., 2017; Guo &Chen, 2016; Han et al., 2016; He et al., 2016; He et al., 2017; Lai et al., 2017; Li et al., 2017; Lin &Lee, 2011) .

The objective of this chapter is to design a stable control system allowing the system output vector y to follow a specified desired trajectory $y_d = \left[y_{d1}, \ldots, y_{dp} \right]^T \in \mathbb{R}^p$.

Let us define the tracking error variables and the virtual control signals as follows

$$\begin{cases} \alpha_{i,0} = y_{di} \\ z_{i,j} = x_{i,j} - \alpha_{i,j-1} \\ \alpha_{i,n_i} = u_i, \text{ for } j = 1, \ldots, n_i, \quad i = 1, \ldots, p \end{cases} \tag{3}$$

where $\alpha_{i,j-1}$, $j = 1, \ldots, n_i$, $i = 1, \ldots, p$ are virtual control signals, which will be determined later. α_{i,n_i} , y_{di} and $z_{i,1}$ are the control input, the reference signal and the tracking error variable, respectively, for $i = 1, \ldots, p$.

Throughout this chapter, the following Assumptions 1-2 are imposed on the system (1) and the reference signals.

Assumption 1: For $j = 1, \ldots, n_i - 1$, $i = 1, \ldots, p$, the functions

$$\frac{\partial f_{i,n_i} \left(\overline{x}_{i,n_i}, \nu_i, d_{i,n_i} \right)}{\partial \nu_i} \text{ and } \frac{\partial f_{i,j} \left(\overline{x}_{i,j}, x_{i,j+1}, d_{i,j} \right)}{\partial x_{i,j+1}}$$

are bounded, unknown and sufficiently smooth, such that

$$\frac{\partial f_{i,n_i} \left(\overline{x}_{i,n_i}, \nu_i, d_{i,n_i} \right)}{\partial \nu_i} \neq 0 \text{ and } \frac{\partial f_{i,j} \left(\overline{x}_{i,j}, x_{i,j+1}, d_{i,j} \right)}{\partial x_{i,j+1}} \neq 0 .$$

Assumption 2: The functions y_{di} and $D^{\sum_{k=1}^{j} \delta_{i,k}} y_{di}$ are sufficiently smooth and bounded, such that $\left| y_{di} \right| \leq \kappa_{3,i}$ with $\kappa_{3,i} < \min\left\{ \kappa_{1,i}, \ \kappa_{2,i} \right\}$ being a known positive constant, for $j = 1, \ldots, n_i$, $i = 1, \ldots, \mathrm{p}$.

- **Remark 3:** Note that the Assumptions 1-2 are not restrictive as they are normally found in various research works related to real systems, such as chemical reactors, mobile robots, robotic manipulators, flexible crane system, mass–spring–damper systems, and so on (Boulkroune &M'saad, 2012a; Boulkroune et al., 2014b; Chang et al., 2016; Hamel & Boulkroune, 2016; Zouari et al., 2017a; Zouari et al., 2017b). Furthermore, Assumptions 1-2 may be viewed as a controllability condition (Hamel & Boulkroune, 2016; He et al., 2016 ; Zhang et al., 2017; Zouari et al., 2017a; Zouari et al., 2017b).

Controller Design and Main Results

Based on Assumptions 1-2, the following elements will be employed in the controller design for the system (1):

- The mean-value theorem to convert the system (1) into a new special form so that the control input appears linearly in the state-space system,
- Neural networks to approximate the uncertain nonlinear dynamics,
- A smooth Nussbaum-type function to solve the unknown control direction problem,
- New asymmetric barrier Lyapunov functions with the tracking error variables to deal with the output constraints,
- And the Backstepping technique to appropriately derive the control signals and the control updating laws.

System Transformation

As explained in (Zouari et al., 2017a; Zouari et al., 2017b; Liu &Tong, 2016), the continuous functions in the systems (1) and (2) can be rewritten by using the mean-value theorem as follows

$$
\begin{cases}
f_{i,j}\left(\overline{\mathrm{x}}_{i,j}, x_{i,j+1}, d_{i,j}\right) = f_{i,j}\left(\overline{\mathrm{x}}_{i,j}, 0, d_{i,j}\right) + g_{i,j} x_{i,j+1}, & \text{for } j = 1,\ldots, n_i - 1 \\
\eta_i\left(u_i\right) = \beta_i\left(t\right) u_i + \phi_{1,i} \\
f_{i,\mathrm{n}_i}\left(\overline{x}_{i,n_i}, \nu_i, d_{i,n_i}\right) = f_{i,\mathrm{n}_i}\left(\overline{x}_{i,n_i}, 0, d_{i,n_i}\right) + \phi_i + g_{i,n_i} u_i, & \text{for } i = 1,\ldots, p
\end{cases}
\tag{4}
$$

where

$$
g_{i,j} = \left. \frac{\partial f_{i,j}\left(\overline{\mathrm{x}}_{i,j}, x_{i,j+1}, d_{i,j}\right)}{\partial x_{i,j+1}} \right|_{x_{i,j+1} = x_{\lambda_{3,i,j+1}}},
$$

$$
\beta_i\left(t\right) = \begin{cases}
\left. \dfrac{\partial \eta_{3,i}\left(u_i\right)}{\partial u_i} \right|_{u_i = u_{\lambda_{1,i}}}, & \text{if } u_i \geq 0 \\[4mm]
\left. \dfrac{\partial \eta_{1,i}\left(u_i\right)}{\partial u_i} \right|_{u_i = u_{\lambda_{2,i}}}, & \text{if } u_i < 0
\end{cases}
$$

$$\phi_{1,i} = \begin{cases} \eta_{3,i}\left(u_{\max,i}\right) - \dfrac{\partial \eta_{3,i}\left(u_i\right)}{\partial u_i}\Bigg|_{u_i = u_{\lambda_{1,i}}} u_{\max,i} + \Delta_{2,i}, \text{ if } u_i \geq u_{\max,i} \\[1.5em] \eta_{2,i}\left(u_i\right) - \dfrac{\partial \eta_{3,i}\left(u_i\right)}{\partial u_i}\Bigg|_{u_i = u_{\lambda_{1,i}}} u_i, \text{ if } 0 \leq u_i < u_{\max,i} \\[1.5em] \eta_{2,i}\left(u_i\right) - \dfrac{\partial \eta_{1,i}\left(u_i\right)}{\partial u_i}\Bigg|_{u_i = u_{\lambda_{2,i}}} u_i, \text{ if } -u_{\min,i} \leq u_i < 0 \\[1.5em] \eta_{1,i}\left(-u_{\min,i}\right) + \dfrac{\partial \eta_{1,i}\left(u_i\right)}{\partial u_i}\Bigg|_{u_i = u_{\lambda_{2,i}}} u_{\min,i} + \Delta_{1,i}, \text{ if } -u_{\min,i} > u_i \end{cases},$$

$$\phi_i = \frac{\partial f_{i,n_i}\left(\overline{x}_{i,n_i}, \nu_i, d_{i,n_i}\right)}{\partial \nu_i}\Bigg|_{\nu_i = \nu_{\lambda_{4,i}}} \phi_{1,i},$$

$$g_{i,n_i} = \beta_i\left(t\right)\frac{\partial f_{i,n_i}\left(\overline{x}_{i,n_i}, \nu_i, d_{i,n_i}\right)}{\partial \nu_i}\Bigg|_{\nu_i = \nu_{\lambda_{4,i}}}$$

are bounded functions, with

$$u_{\lambda_{1,i}} = \lambda_{1,i}u_i + \left(1 - \lambda_{1,i}\right)u_{\max,i}, \ u_{\lambda_{2,i}} = \lambda_{2,i}u_i - \left(1 - \lambda_{2,i}\right)u_{\min,i},$$

$$x_{\lambda_{3,i,j+1}} = \lambda_{3,i,j+1}x_{i,j+1}, \ \nu_{\lambda_{4,i}} = \lambda_{4,i}\nu_i, \ 0 < \lambda_{1,i} < 1,$$

$$0 < \lambda_{2,i} < 1, \ 0 < \lambda_{3,i,j+1} < 1 \text{ and } 0 < \lambda_{4,i} < 1,$$

for $j = 1, \ldots, n_i - 1, \ i = 1, \ldots, p$.

By utilizing (3) and (4), the dynamics of the tracking errors can be represented as

$$\begin{cases} D^{\delta_{i,j}}z_{i,j} = F_{i,j}\left(Z_{i,j}\right) - g_{i,j-1}\mathrm{E}_{i,j-1} + g_{i,j}\alpha_{i,j} + g_{i,j}\mathrm{E}_{i,j+1}, \\[1em] u_i = \alpha_{i,n_i}, \text{ for } j = 1, \ldots, n_i, \ i = 1, \ldots, p \end{cases} \tag{5}$$

where:

- $F_{i,j}\left(Z_{i,j}\right) = f_{i,j}\left(\overline{\mathrm{x}}_{i,j}, 0, d_{i,j}\right) + g_{i,j-1}\mathrm{E}_{i,j-1} - D^{\delta_{i,j}}\alpha_{i,j-1}$,

and

$$F_{i,n_i}\left(Z_{i,n_i}\right) = f_{i,n_i}\left(\overline{x}_{i,n_i}, 0, d_{i,n_i}\right) + \phi_i + g_{i,n_i-1}\mathrm{E}_{i,n_i-1} - D^{\delta_{i,n_i}}\alpha_{i,n_i-1}$$

are smooth functions with

$$Z_{i,j} = \left[\mathrm{E}_{i,1}, \ldots, \mathrm{E}_{i,j}, \alpha_{i,0}, \ldots, \alpha_{i,j-1}\right]^T \in \mathbb{R}^{2j},$$

$$Z_{i,n_i} = \left[\mathrm{E}_{i,1}, \ldots, \mathrm{E}_{i,n_i}, \alpha_{i,0}, \ldots, \alpha_{i,n_i-1}\right]^T \in \mathbb{R}^{2n_i},$$

and $g_{i,0} = 0$, for $j = 1, \ldots, n_i - 1$, $i = 1, \ldots, p$.

- $$\begin{cases} \mathrm{E}_{i,0} = 0 \\ \mathrm{E}_{i,1} = \left|\left[\dfrac{H_i}{\left[\kappa_{4,i}^{\aleph_i} - z_{i,1}^{\aleph_i}\right]} + \dfrac{1 - H_i}{\left[\kappa_{5,i}^{\aleph_i} - z_{i,1}^{\aleph_i}\right]}\right] z_{i,1}^{\aleph_i-1}\right|, \\ \mathrm{E}_{i,j} = z_{i,j}, \text{ for } j = 2, \ldots, n_i \\ \mathrm{E}_{i,n_i+1} = 0 \end{cases}$$

$$H_i = \begin{cases} 1, \text{ if } z_{i,1} \le 0 \\ 0, \text{ if } z_{i,1} > 0 \end{cases}, \; \aleph_i = 2^{n_i}, \; \kappa_{4,i} = \kappa_{1,i} - \kappa_{3,i}$$

and $\kappa_{5,i} = \kappa_{2,i} - \kappa_{3,i}$, for $i = 1, \ldots, p$.

Neural Network for Approximating Uncertain Nonlinear Dynamics

Similar to (Zouari et al., 2017a; Zouari et al., 2017b; Yu & Du, 2011), based on the well-known universal approximation property, the unknown continuous function $F_{i,j}\left(Z_{i,j}\right)$, can be approximated over the sufficiently large compact set

$$\Omega_{i,j} = \left\{ Z_{i,j} \in \mathbb{R}^{2j}, \begin{aligned} &\|Z_{i,j}\| \le M_{i,j} \\ &\text{and} -\kappa_{4,i} < z_{i,1} < \kappa_{5,i} \end{aligned} \right\} \subset \mathbb{R}^{2j}$$

with arbitrary accuracies by three-layer neural network as follows

$$F_{i,j}\left(Z_{i,j}\right) = w_{i,j}^{*T}\xi_{i,j}\left(Z_{i,j}\right) + \varepsilon_{i,j}, \text{ for } j = 1,\ldots,n_i, \quad i = 1,\ldots,p \tag{6}$$

where the unknown constants $M_{i,j}$, $j = 1,\ldots,n_i$, $i = 1,\ldots,p$, are very large and strictly positive. $Z_{i,j} \in \mathbb{R}^{2j}$ and $\xi_{i,j}\left(Z_{i,j}\right) \in \mathbb{R}^{q_{i,j}}$, denote the input and the so-called hidden-layer activation functions of the neural network, respectively, with $q_{i,j} > 1$ being the neural network node number, for $j = 1,\ldots,n_i$, $i = 1,\ldots,p$.

The corresponding reconstruction error (the approximation error) $\varepsilon_{i,j} \in \mathbb{R}$, is bounded and unknown on the compact set $\Omega_{i,j}$, i.e., $\left|\varepsilon_{i,j}\right| \leq \varepsilon_{i,j}^{*}$, with the constant $\varepsilon_{i,j}^{*}$ being strictly positive and unknown, for $j = 1,\ldots,n_i$, $i = 1,\ldots,p$.

For analytical purposes, the optimal neural network parameters (the ideal constant weight vectors) are formulated as

$$w_{i,j}^{*} = \arg\min_{w_{i,j}^{*} \in \mathbb{R}^{q_{i,j}}}\left(\sup_{Z_{i,j} \in \Omega_{i,j}}\left|F_{i,j}\left(Z_{i,j}\right) - w_{i,j}^{T}\xi_{i,j}\left(Z_{i,j}\right)\right|\right), \quad j = 1,\ldots,n_i, \quad i = 1,\ldots,p.$$

From (Chen et al. 2016; Fu et al. 2016; He et al., 2016; He et al., 2017; Jafrasteh & Fathianpour, 2017; Li et al., 2017; Na et al., 2012; Xu et al., 2015; Yan et al. 2016; Yu &Du, 2011; Zouari et al., 2017a; Zouari et al., 2017b), $\left\|w_{i,j}^{*}\right\|$ is an unknown constant, while the known function $\left\|\xi_{i,j}\left(Z_{i,j}\right)\right\|$ is bounded, for $j = 1,\ldots,n_i$, $i = 1,\ldots,p$.

Adaptive Control Laws

Based on the Backstepping technique (Chang et al., 2016; He et al., 2017; Li et al.,2017; Li &Tong, 2017; Liu &Tong, 2016; Zhang et al., 2017; Zhou et al., 2017), the adaptive control laws can be designed as follows

$$\begin{cases} \alpha_{i,j} = N\left(\zeta_{i,j}\right)\left[\mathrm{K}_{i,j}\mathrm{E}_{i,j} + \hat{\theta}_{i,j}\Phi_{i,j}\mathrm{E}_{i,j} + \hat{w}_{i,j}^{T}\xi_{i,j}\left(\mathrm{Z}_{i,j}\right)\right], \\ u_i = \alpha_{i,n_i} \\ \dot{\zeta}_{i,j} = \left[\mathrm{K}_{i,j}\mathrm{E}_{i,j} + \hat{\theta}_{i,j}\Phi_{i,j}\mathrm{E}_{i,j} + \hat{w}_{i,j}^{T}\xi_{i,j}\left(\mathrm{Z}_{i,j}\right)\right]\mathrm{E}_{i,j}, \\ \dot{\hat{w}}_{i,j} = \chi_{1,i,j}\xi_{i,j}\left(\mathrm{Z}_{i,j}\right)\mathrm{E}_{i,j} - \left[\hat{w}_{i,j} - \hat{w}_{i,j}\left(0\right)\right]\chi_{1,i,j}\sigma, \\ \dot{\hat{\theta}}_{i,j} = \chi_{2,i,j}\Phi_{i,j}\mathrm{E}_{i,j}^{2} - \left[\hat{\theta}_{i,j} - \hat{\theta}_{i,j}\left(0\right)\right]\chi_{2,i,j}\sigma, \text{ for } j = 1,\ldots,n_i, \quad i = 1,\ldots,p \end{cases} \tag{7}$$

where the design parameters $\chi_{m,i,j}$ and $\mathrm{K}_{i,j}$, $m = 1,2$, $j = 1,\ldots,n_i$, $i = 1,\ldots,p$, are known strictly positive constants.

$$N\left(\zeta_{i,j}\right) = \left(\zeta_{i,j}^{\,2} + 2\right)\exp\left(\frac{\zeta_{i,j}^{\,2}}{2}\right)\sin\left(\zeta_{i,j}\right)$$

stands for a smooth Nussbaum-type function (Boulkroune et al., 2010; Oliveira et al., 2010; Zouari et al., 2017a; Zouari et al., 2017b). $\hat{\theta}_{i,j}$ and $\dot{\hat{w}}_{i,j}$ are the estimates of the unknown constants $\theta_{i,j}^{\,*} = \left\|w_{i,j}^{\,*}\right\| + \varepsilon_{i,j}^{\,*} + 1$ and $w_{i,j}^{\,*}$, respectively, for $j = 1,\ldots,n_i$, $i = 1,\ldots,p$.

$\Phi_{i,j} = \dfrac{\rho_{i,j}^{\,2}}{\sqrt{\rho_{i,j}^{\,2}\mathrm{E}_{i,j}^{\,2} + \sigma^2}}$ is a known positive function with $\rho_{i,j} = \left\|\xi_{i,j}\left(\mathrm{Z}_{i,j}\right)\right\| + \left\|\mathrm{Z}_{i,j}\right\| + q_{i,j}$ being a

known function, for $j = 1,\ldots,n_i$, $i = 1,\ldots,p$.

The function σ is strictly positive, known and sufficiently smooth such that $\int_0^t \sigma\left(\tau\right)d\tau$ is bounded.

- **Remark 4:** It is well known that the functions $\left(\zeta^2 + 2\right)\exp\left(\dfrac{\zeta^2}{2}\right)\sin\left(\zeta\right)$, $\cos\left(\dfrac{\pi}{2}\zeta\right)\exp\left(\zeta^2\right)$,

  $\zeta\cos\left(\sqrt{|\zeta|}\right)$, $\zeta^2\sin\left(\zeta\right)$ and $\zeta^2\cos\left(\zeta\right)$ are widely used in many research works as smooth Nussbaum functions (Zouari et al., 2017a; Zouari et al., 2017b) . As stated in [19, 22, 44], the Nussbaum function is characterized by $\lim\limits_{s\to\pm\infty}\sup\dfrac{1}{s}\int_0^s N\left(\zeta\right)d\zeta = +\infty$ and $\lim\limits_{s\to\pm\infty}\inf\dfrac{1}{s}\int_0^s N\left(\zeta\right)d\zeta = -\infty$. Moreover, the research work (Boulkroune et al., 2010; Oliveira et al., 2010) successfully proved that with the help of the Nussbaum function $\left(\zeta^2 + 2\right)\exp\left(\dfrac{\zeta^2}{2}\right)\sin\left(\zeta\right)$, the problems of input non-linearities, unknown identical control directions, and external disturbances could be solved simultaneously.

- **Remark 5:** Similar to (Boulkroune et al., 2014b; Yu &Du, 2011; Zouari et al., 2017a; Zouari et al., 2017b), it must be chosen $\hat{\theta}_{i,j}\left(0\right) \geq 0$ in order that the inequality $\hat{\theta}_{i,j} \geq 0$ holds for all $t \geq 0$, $j = 1,\ldots,n_i$, $i = 1,\ldots,p$. Furthermore, the sigma-modification terms $\left[\hat{w}_{i,j} - \hat{w}_{i,j}\left(0\right)\right]\chi_{1,i,j}\sigma$ and $\left[\hat{\theta}_{i,j} - \hat{\theta}_{i,j}\left(0\right)\right]\chi_{2,i,j}\sigma$, $j = 1,\ldots,n_i$, $i = 1,\ldots,p$, are used for making the adaptive laws robust in the attendance of external disturbances and neural network approximation errors (Yu &Du, 2011; Zouari et al., 2017a; Zouari et al., 2017b).

- **Remark 6:** From the equation (7), it is observed that the adaptive control laws are continuous on the set $-\kappa_{4,i} < z_{i,1} < \kappa_{5,i}$, $i = 1,\ldots,p$. Consequently, the possible chattering phenomena and control singularity problem in the controller design can be avoided.

Stability Analysis

At the present stage, the main results of the proposed controller are summarized in the following theorem 1. Furthermore, the following Lemmas 1-2 will be employed in the Proof of Theorem 1.

Lemma 1 (Vargas-De-León, 2015)

Let $\mu_1(t) > 0$ and $\mu_2(t) \in \mathbb{R}$ be smooth functions. Then, by using the Caputo definition of fractional derivatives, one can get:

$$D^\delta \ln\left(\frac{1}{\mu_1(t)}\right) \le -\frac{1}{\mu_1(t)} D^\delta \mu_1(t)$$

and

$$\frac{1}{2} D^\delta \mu_2^2(t) \le \mu_2(t) D^\delta \mu_2(t),$$

for any time instant $t \ge 0$ and constant $0 < \delta < 1$.

Lemma 2 (Boulkroune et al., 2010; Boulkroune et al., 2012a; Boulkroune et al., 2012b)

Let the functions $V(t)$ and $\zeta(t)$ be sufficiently smooth over the interval $\left[0, t_f\right]$, with $V(t) \ge 0$ and

$$N(\zeta) = \left(\zeta^2 + 2\right) \exp\left(\frac{\zeta^2}{2}\right) \sin(\zeta)$$

being a smooth Nussbaum-type function. If the inequality

$$V(t) \le \lambda_0 + \int_0^{t_f} \left(1 + g_\lambda(\tau) N(\zeta) + 1\right) \dot{\zeta}(\tau) d\tau$$

holds, where λ_0 is a constant and $g_\lambda(\tau)$ is a bounded function that never vanishes, then $V(t)$,

$$\int_0^{t_f} \left(1 + g_\lambda(\tau) N(\zeta) + 1\right) \dot{\zeta}(\tau) d\tau$$

and $\zeta(t)$ should be bounded over $[0, t_f]$. It is worth to mention that the above results are also correct for $t_f = +\infty$.

Theorem 1

Let us consider the system (1), subject to unknown actuator nonlinearities (2) and under Assumptions 1–2. Then, for any bounded initial condition satisfying $-\kappa_{1,i} < y_i(0) < \kappa_{2,i}$, and given bounded reference signals $|y_{di}| \leq \kappa_{3,i} < \min\{\kappa_{1,i}, \kappa_{2,i}\}$, $i = 1, \ldots, p$, the adaptive control laws (7) can guarantee the following properties:

- All signals in the closed-loop system are semi-globally uniformly ultimately bounded, i.e., $\hat{\theta}_{i,j}$, $\zeta_{i,j}$, $\alpha_{i,j}$, u_i, $E_{i,j}$, $\Phi_{i,j}$, and $\rho_{i,j} \in L_\infty$, for $j = 1, \ldots, n_i$, $i = 1 \ldots, p$.
- The tracking error constraints are never transgressed, i.e., $-\kappa_{4,i} < z_{i,1}(t) < \kappa_{5,i}$, for $i = 1, \ldots, p$.
- The tracking error converges asymptotically to zero, i.e., $z_{i,1} \to 0$, $i = 1 \ldots, p$ as $t \to +\infty$.

Proof of Theorem 1
Consider the following positive definite Lyapunov function

$$V = \sum_{i=1}^{p} \sum_{j=1}^{n_i} V_{1,i,j} + \sum_{i=1}^{p} \sum_{j=1}^{n_i} V_{2,i,j} + \sum_{i=1}^{p} \sum_{j=1}^{n_i} V_{3,i,j} \tag{8}$$

with

$$\begin{cases} V_{1,i,1} = \dfrac{H_i}{\aleph_i} D^{\delta_{i,1}-1} \left[\ln \left(\dfrac{\kappa_{4,i}^{\aleph_i}}{\kappa_{4,i}^{\aleph_i} - z_{i,1}^{\aleph_i}} \right) \right] + \dfrac{1-H_i}{\aleph_i} D^{\delta_{i,1}-1} \left[\ln \left(\dfrac{\kappa_{5,i}^{\aleph_i}}{\kappa_{5,i}^{\aleph_i} - z_{i,1}^{\aleph_i}} \right) \right]. \\ V_{1,i,j} = \dfrac{1}{2} D^{\delta_{i,j}-1} \left[E_{i,j}^{2} \right], \text{ for } j = 2, \ldots, n_i, \; i = 1, \ldots, p \end{cases}$$

$$\tilde{\theta}_{i,j} = \theta_{i,j}^{*} - \hat{\theta}_{i,j}, \; \tilde{w}_{i,j} = w_{i,j}^{*} - \hat{w}_{i,j}, \; V_{2,i,j} = \frac{\tilde{w}_{i,j}^{T} \tilde{w}_{i,j}}{2\chi_{1,i,j}}$$

and $V_{3,i,j} = \dfrac{\tilde{\theta}_{i,j}^{2}}{2\chi_{2,i,j}}$ for $j = 1, \ldots, n_i$, $i = 1, \ldots, p$.

By using the Lemma 1, the first time derivative of the function $V_{1,i,j}$, for $j = 1, \ldots, n_i$, $i = 1, \ldots, p$ is given by

$$\begin{cases} \dot{V}_{1,i,1} = \dfrac{H_i}{\aleph_i} D^{\delta_{i,1}}\left[\ln\left(\dfrac{\kappa_{4,i}{}^{\aleph_i}}{\kappa_{4,i}{}^{\aleph_i} - z_{i,1}{}^{\aleph_i}}\right)\right] + \dfrac{1-H_i}{\aleph_i} D^{\delta_{i,1}}\left[\ln\left(\dfrac{\kappa_{5,i}{}^{\aleph_i}}{\kappa_{5,i}{}^{\aleph_i} - z_{i,1}{}^{\aleph_i}}\right)\right] \\[4mm] \qquad \leq \left[\dfrac{H_i}{\left[\kappa_{4,i}{}^{\aleph_i} - z_{i,1}{}^{\aleph_i}\right]} + \dfrac{1-H_i}{\kappa_{5,i}{}^{\aleph_i} - z_{i,1}{}^{\aleph_i}}\right] z_{i,1}{}^{\aleph_i - 1} D^{\delta_{i,1}} z_{i,1} \\[4mm] \qquad \leq \mathrm{E}_{i,1} D^{\delta_{i,1}} z_{i,1} \\[6mm] \dot{V}_{1,i,j} = \dfrac{1}{2} D^{\delta_{i,j}}\left[\mathrm{E}_{i,j}{}^2\right] \\[4mm] \qquad \leq \mathrm{E}_{i,j} D^{\delta_{i,j}} z_{i,j}, \quad j = 2,\ldots,n_i, \ i = 1,\ldots,p \end{cases} \tag{9}$$

By utilizing the equation (9), the derivative of the Lyapunov function V with respect to time along the solutions of (5) can be written as follows

$$\begin{aligned} \dot{V} &\leq \sum_{i=1}^{p}\sum_{j=1}^{n_i} \mathrm{E}_{i,j} D^{\delta_{i,j}} z_{i,j} + \sum_{i=1}^{p}\sum_{j=1}^{n_i} \frac{\tilde{w}_{i,j}{}^T \dot{\tilde{w}}_{i,j}}{\chi_{1,i,j}} + \sum_{i=1}^{p}\sum_{j=1}^{n_i} \frac{\tilde{\theta}_{i,j}\dot{\tilde{\theta}}_{i,j}}{\chi_{2,i,j}} \\[2mm] &\leq \sum_{i=1}^{p}\sum_{j=1}^{n_i}\left[F_{i,j}\left(Z_{i,j}\right) - g_{i,j-1}\mathrm{E}_{i,j-1} + g_{i,j}\alpha_{i,j} + g_{i,j}\mathrm{E}_{i,j+1}\right]\mathrm{E}_{i,j} \\[2mm] &\quad + \sum_{i=1}^{p}\sum_{j=1}^{n_i} \frac{\tilde{w}_{i,j}{}^T \dot{\tilde{w}}_{i,j}}{\chi_{1,i,j}} + \sum_{i=1}^{p}\sum_{j=1}^{n_i} \frac{\tilde{\theta}_{i,j}\dot{\tilde{\theta}}_{i,j}}{\chi_{2,i,j}} \\[2mm] &\leq \sum_{i=1}^{p}\sum_{j=1}^{n_i}\left[F_{i,j}\left(Z_{i,j}\right) + g_{i,j}\alpha_{i,j}\right]\mathrm{E}_{i,j} + \sum_{i=1}^{p}\sum_{j=1}^{n_i} \frac{\tilde{w}_{i,j}{}^T \dot{\tilde{w}}_{i,j}}{\chi_{1,i,j}} + \sum_{i=1}^{p}\sum_{j=1}^{n_i} \frac{\tilde{\theta}_{i,j}\dot{\tilde{\theta}}_{i,j}}{\chi_{2,i,j}} \end{aligned} \tag{10}$$

According to (6) and (7), the above inequality (10) can be represented as

$$\begin{aligned} \dot{V} &\leq -\sum_{i=1}^{p}\sum_{j=1}^{n_i} \mathrm{K}_{i,j}\mathrm{E}_{i,j}{}^2 + \sum_{i=1}^{p}\sum_{j=1}^{n_i} \tilde{w}_{i,j}{}^T\left[\frac{\dot{\tilde{w}}_{i,j}}{\chi_{1,i,j}} + \xi_{i,j}\left(Z_{i,j}\right)\mathrm{E}_{i,j}\right] \\[2mm] &\quad + \sum_{i=1}^{p}\sum_{j=1}^{n_i} \tilde{\theta}_{i,j}\left[\frac{\dot{\tilde{\theta}}_{i,j}}{\chi_{2,i,j}} + \Phi_{i,j}\mathrm{E}_{i,j}{}^2\right] + \sum_{i=1}^{p}\sum_{j=1}^{n_i}\left[1 + g_{i,j}N\left(\zeta_{i,j}\right)\right]\dot{\zeta}_{i,j} \\[2mm] &\quad + \sum_{i=1}^{p}\sum_{j=1}^{n_i}\left|\varepsilon_{i,j}\mathrm{E}_{i,j}\right| - \sum_{i=1}^{p}\sum_{j=1}^{n_i} \theta_{i,j}{}^{*}\Phi_{i,j}\mathrm{E}_{i,j}{}^2 \end{aligned} \tag{11}$$

By using the Young's inequality (Zhou et al., 2017), one can establish that

$$\begin{cases} \sum_{i=1}^{p}\sum_{j=1}^{n_i}\left|\varepsilon_{i,j}\mathrm{E}_{i,j}\right| - \sum_{i=1}^{p}\sum_{j=1}^{n_i}\theta_{i,j}^{*}\Phi_{i,j}\mathrm{E}_{i,j}^{2} \leq \sigma\sum_{i=1}^{p}\sum_{j=1}^{n_i}\theta_{i,j}^{*} \\[2mm] \sum_{i=1}^{p}\sum_{j=1}^{n_i}\tilde{\theta}_{i,j}\left[\dfrac{\dot{\hat{\theta}}_{i,j}}{\chi_{2,i,j}}+\Phi_{i,j}\mathrm{E}_{i,j}^{2}\right] \leq -\dfrac{\sigma}{2}\sum_{i=1}^{p}\sum_{j=1}^{n_i}\tilde{\theta}_{i,j}^{2} \\[5mm] \qquad\qquad\qquad +\dfrac{\sigma}{2}\sum_{i=1}^{p}\sum_{j=1}^{n_i}\left[\theta_{i,j}^{*}-\hat{\theta}_{i,j}(0)\right]^{2} \\[5mm] \sum_{i=1}^{p}\sum_{j=1}^{n_i}\tilde{w}_{i,j}^{T}\left[\dfrac{\dot{\hat{w}}_{i,j}}{\chi_{1,i,j}}+\xi_{i,j}(Z_{i,j})\mathrm{E}_{i,j}\right] \leq -\dfrac{\sigma}{2}\sum_{i=1}^{p}\sum_{j=1}^{n_i}\left\|\tilde{w}_{i,j}\right\|^{2} \\[5mm] \qquad\qquad\qquad +\dfrac{\sigma}{2}\sum_{i=1}^{p}\sum_{j=1}^{n_i}\left\|w_{i,j}^{*}-\hat{w}_{i,j}(0)\right\|^{2} \end{cases} \tag{12}$$

From the above inequalities (11) and (12), it is easy to obtain

$$\begin{aligned} V(t)+\sum_{i=1}^{p}\sum_{j=1}^{n_i}\mathrm{K}_{i,j}\int_{0}^{t}\mathrm{E}_{i,j}^{2}(\tau)d\tau \leq\ & V(0)+\sum_{i=1}^{p}\sum_{j=1}^{n_i}\int_{0}^{t}\left[1+g_{i,j}N(\zeta_{i,j}(\tau))\right]\dot{\zeta}_{i,j}(\tau)d\tau \\ & +\frac{1}{2}\sum_{i=1}^{p}\sum_{j=1}^{n_i}\left[\theta_{i,j}^{*}-\hat{\theta}_{i,j}(0)\right]^{2}\int_{0}^{t}\sigma(\tau)d\tau \\ & +\sum_{i=1}^{p}\sum_{j=1}^{n_i}\theta_{i,j}^{*}\int_{0}^{t}\sigma(\tau)d\tau \\ & +\frac{1}{2}\sum_{i=1}^{p}\sum_{j=1}^{n_i}\left\|w_{i,j}^{*}-\hat{w}_{i,j}(0)\right\|^{2}\int_{0}^{t}\sigma(\tau)d\tau \end{aligned} \tag{13}$$

Based on the Lemma 2 and the equation (13), one can deduce that $V(t)$,

$$\sum_{i=1}^{p}\sum_{j=1}^{n_i}\mathrm{K}_{i,j}\int_{0}^{t}\mathrm{E}_{i,j}^{2}(\tau)d\tau,\ \sum_{i=1}^{p}\sum_{j=1}^{n_i}\int_{0}^{t}\left[1+g_{i,j}N(\zeta_{i,j}(\tau))\right]\dot{\zeta}_{i,j}(\tau)d\tau,$$

$$\sum_{i=1}^{p}\sum_{j=1}^{n_i}\theta_{i,j}^{*}\int_{0}^{t}\sigma(\tau)d\tau,\ \sum_{i=1}^{p}\sum_{j=1}^{n_i}\left[\theta_{i,j}^{*}-\hat{\theta}_{i,j}(0)\right]^{2}\int_{0}^{t}\sigma(\tau)d\tau$$

and $\sum_{i=1}^{p}\sum_{j=1}^{n_i}\left\|w_{i,j}^{*}-\hat{w}_{i,j}(0)\right\|^{2}\int_{0}^{t}\sigma(\tau)d\tau$ are bounded $\forall t\geq0$.

As a result, it is obvious that $z_{i,j}\in L_{2}$, for $j=1,\ldots,n_{i}$, $i=1,\ldots,p$.

Since the function $F_{i,j}(.)$ is sufficiently smooth and the variable $Z_{i,j}$ is bounded, afterward, one has $D^{\delta_{i,j}}z_{i,j}\in L_{\infty}$, for $j=1,\ldots,n_{i}$, $i=1,\ldots,p$.

In the end, by utilizing Barbalat's lemma (Zouari et al. 2017a; Zouari et al. 2017b), one can conclude that $\lim_{t\to+\infty}z_{i,1}(t)=0$ because $z_{i,1}\in L_{2}\cap L_{\infty}$, for $i=1,\ldots,p$, i.e., the tracking errors converge asymptotically to zero. This completes the proof.

- **Remark 7:** It is noticed that the Lyapunov function candidate V, which grows to infinity when $z_{i,1}$ approaches $-\kappa_{4,i}$ and $\kappa_{5,i}$, is C^{1} and positive definite on the compact sets $\Omega_{i,j}$, $j=1,\ldots,n_{i}$,

$i = 1,...,p$. On the other hand, the new barrier Lyapunov functions $V_{1,i,j}$, $j = 1,...,n_i$, $i = 1,...,p$, can be used for solving the output constraint problem of several fractional order systems.

- **Remark 8:** Almost all the existing adaptive intelligent control schemes can only guarantee the semi-global stability of the closed-loop system for the reason that the universal approximation property of fuzzy logic system or artificial neural network holds only over a compact set (Liu et al., 2017; Liu et al., 2017; Li &Tong, 2017; Na et al., 2012; Xu et al., 2015; Yan et al., 2016; Yu &Du, 2011; Zhou et al. 2017; Zouari et al. 2017b).

SIMULATION RESULTS

In this Section, Simulation studies are carried out to show the effectiveness of the proposed adaptive neural controllers.

Example 1: An Academic Fractional-Order System

Consider the following non-affine pure-feedback system with output constraints and actuator saturation

$$
\begin{cases}
D^{\delta_{i,1}} x_{i,1} = x_{i,1}\exp\left(-x_{i,1}^2\right) + \left(1 + \dfrac{i}{100i + 7x_{i,2}^2 + 8x_{i,1}^2}\right)x_{i,2} + d_{i,1} \\[2mm]
D^{\delta_{i,2}} x_{i,2} = (2-i)x_{i,1} - ix_{i,2}^2 + \left(1 + \exp\left(-6v_i^2 - 2ix_{i,2}^2\right)\right)v_i + d_{i,2}, \\[2mm]
v_i = \eta_i\left(u_i\right) \\[2mm]
y_i = x_{i,1}, \text{ for } i = 1,2
\end{cases}
\tag{14}
$$

where $\delta_{i,1} = 0.98$ and $\delta_{i,2} = 0.99$ are the fractional orders of the system (14), for $i = 1,2$.

$x = \left[x_1^T, x_2^T\right]^T \in \mathbb{R}^4$, $u = [u_1, u_2]^T \in \mathbb{R}^2$ and $y = [y_1, y_2]^T \in \mathbb{R}^2$ denote the state, the control input and the output of the system, respectively, with $x_i = \left[x_{i,1}, x_{i,2}\right]^T \in \mathbb{R}^2$, $x_{i,j} \in \mathbb{R}$, $u_i \in \mathbb{R}$ and $y_i \in \mathbb{R}$, for $j = 1,2$, $i = 1,2$. The outputs are constrained in $-8.1 < y_1 < 9.1$ and $-6 < y_2 < 8$. $d_{i,j} = \dfrac{0.5}{i+j}\sin(t)$, $j = 1,2$, $i = 1,2$ are external disturbances. The initial values of the states are $x_1(0) = [7.5, -0.3]^T$ and $x_2(0) = [-4, 0.1]^T$. The actuator nonlinearity output $v = [v_1, v_2]^T \in \mathbb{R}^{2\times 1}$ is described by

$$
v_i = \eta_i\left(u_i\right) =
\begin{cases}
-8, & \text{if } u_i < -8 \\[1mm]
u_i, & \text{if } -8 \le u_i \le 9i + (i-1)12 \\[1mm]
9i + (i-1)12, & \text{if } u_i > 9i + (i-1)12
\end{cases},
$$

for $i = 1,2$.

In this example, our objective is to make the system output y follows the reference signal

$$y_d = \begin{bmatrix} y_{d1} \\ y_{d2} \end{bmatrix} = \begin{bmatrix} 5\sin\left(\dfrac{t}{2}\right) \\ 3\cos\left(\dfrac{t}{3}\right) \end{bmatrix}$$

whilst preventing the constraint violation.

From section 3, to adequately achieve our goal, the proposed adaptive control design is based on the subsequent four steps:

Step 1: Pick up the design parameters and the initial conditions, which are used in the control laws (7), as follows, $\chi_{m,i,j} = 100$, $K_{i,j} = 10$, $\hat{\theta}_{i,j}(0) = 0$, $\hat{w}_{i,j}(0) = 0_{10\times1}$, and $\zeta_{i,j}(0) = 1.05$, for $m = 1,2$, $j = 1,2$, $i = 1,2$.

Step 2: By utilizing (3) and (5), determine the vectors $Z_{i,j} \in \mathbb{R}^{2j}$, $j = 1,2$, $i = 1,2$.

Step 3: For estimating the unknown dynamics of the system (14), select RBF neural networks $w_{i,j}^{*T}\xi_{i,j}(Z_{i,j})$, $j = 1,2$, $i = 1,2$, containing 70 nodes (i.e., $q_{i,j} = 70$, $j = 1,2$, $i = 1,2$) with, centers evenly spaced in the interval $\overbrace{[-6, \quad 6]\times\cdots\times[-6, \quad 6]}^{2j} \subset \mathbb{R}^{2j}$ and widths being equal to 12.

Step 4: By using (7), compute the control input u.

The Simulation results, which are obtained by using our proposed adaptive controller, are depicted in Figures 1-6. It can be seen from Figure 1-2 that the output system y adequately tracks the desired trajectory y_d. The actuator nonlinearity output v and the control input u are given in Figure 3-4. Inspecting Figure 5-6, we observe that the tracking errors ($z_{1,1}$ and $z_{2,1}$) rapidly converge to zero.

As can be seen from the Figures 1-6, our proposed adaptive control has a good tracking performance while the constraints are never violated. In addition, it is effortless to substantiate the robustness of the proposed neural adaptive control scheme in the presence of disturbances, actuator nonlinearities, and uncertain dynamics.

Example 2: A Practical Fractional-Order System (Liu & Tong, 2016)

By utilizing the properties of Caputo fractional-order derivatives ($D^\delta D^\delta x = D^{2\delta} x$ and $D^1 x = \dot{x}$), the dynamics of a single-link robot subject to output constraints and actuator dead zone, can be written as follows:

$$\begin{cases} D^{\delta_{1,j}} x_{1,j} = x_{1,j+1} + d_{1,j}, \text{ for } j = 1,\ldots,3, \quad \forall t \geq 0 \\ D^{\delta_{1,4}} x_{1,4} = 2v_1 - 9.8\sin(x_{1,1}) + d_{1,4}, \quad \forall t \geq 0 \\ v_1 = \eta(u_1) \\ y_1 = x_{1,1} \end{cases} \tag{15}$$

where $\delta_{1,j} = \dfrac{1}{2}$, $j = 1,\ldots,4$, are the fractional orders of the system.

Figure 1. Reference signal y_{d1} and system output y_1

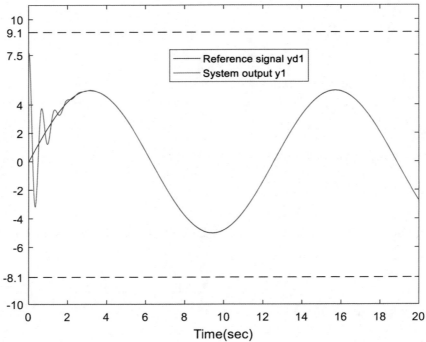

Figure 2. Reference signal y_{d2} and system output y_2

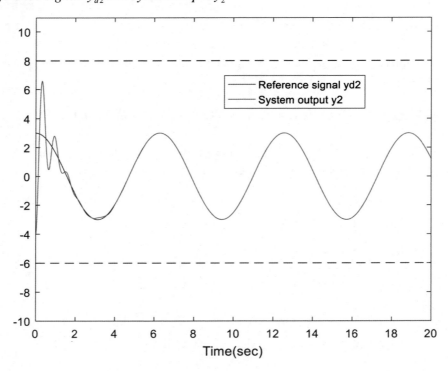

Figure 3. Actuator nonlinearity output v_1 and control input u_1

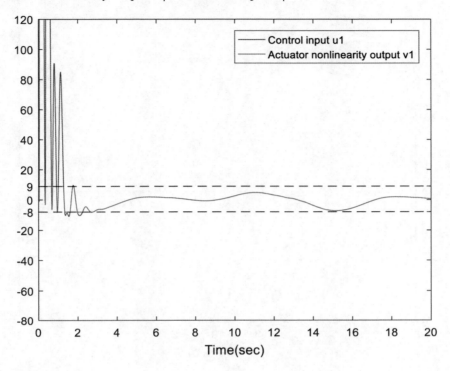

Figure 4. Actuator nonlinearity output v_2 and control input u_2

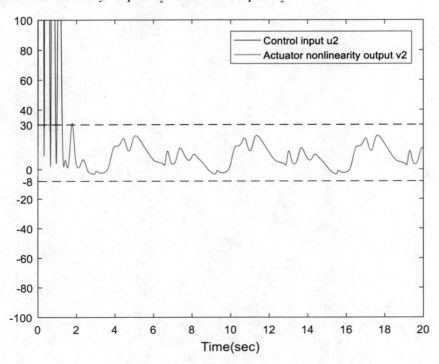

Figure 5. Tracking error $z_{1,1}$

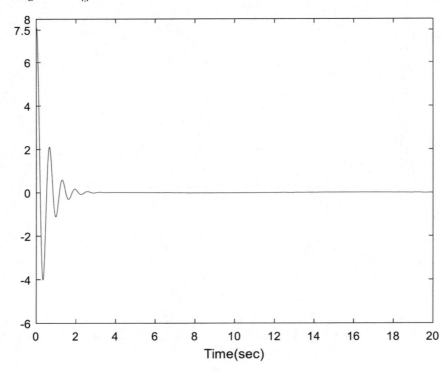

Figure 6. Tracking error $z_{2,1}$

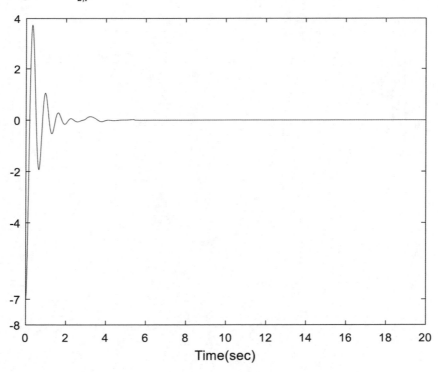

$x = x_1 = \begin{bmatrix} x_{1,1}, \ldots, x_{1,4} \end{bmatrix}^T \in \mathbb{R}^4$, $u = u_1 \in \mathbb{R}$ and $y = y_1 \in \mathbb{R}$ are the state, the control input (the input torque) and the output (the angle) of the system, respectively. The output y is constrained in $-0.7 < y < 1$.

$d_{1,j} = \dfrac{0.05}{1+j}\sin(t)$, $j = 1 \ldots, 4$, are external disturbances.

The actuator nonlinearity output is expressed by

$$v = v_1 = \eta_1(u_1) = \begin{cases} 2u_1 + 0.8, & \text{if } u_1 < -0.4 \\ 0, & \text{if } -0.4 \le u_1 \le 0.3 \\ 3u_1 - 0.9, & \text{if } u_1 > 0.3 \end{cases}.$$

Our purpose is to make the system output y follows the reference signal $y_d = 0.5\cos(t)$, whilst ensuring that all closed loop signals are bounded and the constraints are not transgressed.

From section 3, to satisfactorily accomplish our objective, the proposed adaptive controller is constructed based on the succeeding four steps:

Step 1: Select the design parameters and the initial conditions, which are used in the control laws (7), as follows $\chi_{m,1,j} = 100$, $\mathrm{K}_{1,j} = 10$, $\hat{\theta}_{1,j}(0) = 0$, $\hat{w}_{1,j}(0) = 0_{8 \times 1}$, and $\zeta_{1,j}(0) = 1.05$, for $m = 1, 2$, $j = 1, \ldots, 4$.

Step 2: By utilizing (3) and (5), determine the vectors $Z_{1,j} \in \mathbb{R}^{2j}$, $j = 1, \ldots, 4$.

Step 3: To estimate the unknown dynamics of the system (15), select RBF neural networks $w_{1,j}^{*T}\xi_{1,j}(Z_{1,j})$, $j = 1, \ldots, 4$, containing 50 nodes (i.e., $q_{1,j} = 50$, $j = 1, \ldots, 4$) with, centers evenly spaced in the interval $\overbrace{\begin{bmatrix} -0.8, & 0.8 \end{bmatrix} \times \cdots \times \begin{bmatrix} -0.8, & 0.8 \end{bmatrix}}^{2j} \subset \mathbb{R}^{2j}$ and widths being equal to 1.6.

Step 4: By using (7), compute the control input u.

The Simulation results, which are obtained by using our proposed controller, are illustrated in Figures 7-9. From Figure 7, we can observe that the system output y adequately tracks the desired trajectory y_d. The actuator nonlinearity output v and the control input u are exhibited in Figure 8. Inspecting Figure 9, it is palpable that the tracking error $z_{1,1}$ rapidly converges to zero.

Obviously, the Figures 7-9 revealed that the constraints are never violated and our proposed adaptive controller has the better tracking performance. Moreover, it is effortless to verify the robustness of the proposed neural adaptive control scheme in the presence of uncertain dynamics, actuator nonlinearities, and disturbances.

CONCLUSION

In this chapter, we have introduced an adaptive neural network to control an uncertain multi-input multi-output (MIMO) pure-feedback fractional-order system with output constraints and unknown actuator nonlinearities. In the control design process, the mean value theorem has been introduced to cope with the actuator nonlinearities and nonaffine structures. Furthermore, neural networks, and smooth Nussbaum-type functions and asymmetric Barrier Lyapunov Functions have been used to deal with the difficulties

Figure 7. Reference signal y_d and system output y

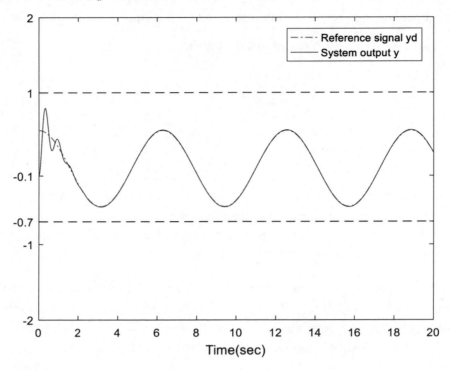

Figure 8. Actuator nonlinearity output v and control input u

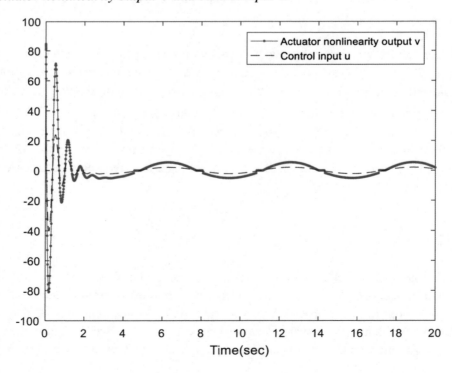

Figure 9. Tracking error $z_{1,1}$

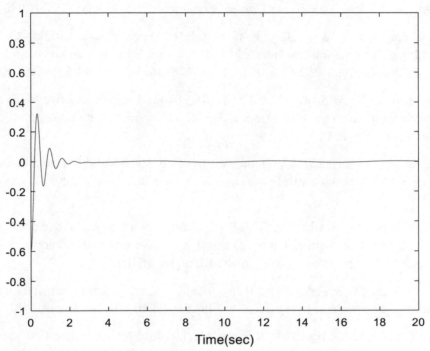

from uncertain nonlinear dynamics, unknown control directions and output constraints, respectively. Furthermore, the Backstepping technique has also been employed in order to satisfactorily determine the control updating laws and to prove the stability of the overall closed-loop system. The major advantages of our proposed control scheme are that: (1) the number of adaptive tuning parameters is reduced, (2) the signals of the closed loop system are semi-globally uniformly ultimately bounded and (3) the tracking errors converge asymptotically to zero without violation of any constraint. Finally, Simulation results have illustrated the effective performance of the designed control law.

ACKNOWLEDGMENT

The author would like to thank Prof. Abdesselem Boulkroune for his valuable comments, which have helped to improve this chapter.

REFERENCES

Achili, B., Madani, T., Daachi, B., & Djouani, K. (2016). Adaptive Observer Based on MLPNN and Sliding Mode for Wearable Robots: Application to an Active Joint Orthosis. *Neurocomputing*, *197*, 69–77. doi:10.1016/j.neucom.2016.01.065

Bogkovic, J. D., Chen, L., & Mehra, R. K. (2001). Adaptive tracking control of a class of non-affine plants using dynamic feedback. *American Control Conference*. 10.1109/ACC.2001.946120

Boukezzoula, R., Galichet, S., & Foulloy, L. (2007). Fuzzy Feedback Linearizing Controller and Its Equivalence With the Fuzzy Nonlinear Internal Model Control Structure. *International Journal of Applied Mathematics and Computer Science*, *17*(2), 233–248. doi:10.2478/v10006-007-0021-4

Boulkroune, A., Bounar, N., M'Saad, M., & Farza, M. (2014a). Indirect adaptive fuzzy control scheme based on observer for nonlinear systems: A novel SPR-filter approach. *Neurocomputing*, *135*, 378–387. doi:10.1016/j.neucom.2013.12.011

Boulkroune, A., & M'saad, M. (2012a). On the design of observer-based fuzzy adaptive controller for nonlinear systems with unknown control gain sign. *Fuzzy Sets and Systems*, *201*, 71–85. doi:10.1016/j.fss.2011.12.005

Boulkroune, A., M'Saad, M., & Chekireb, H. (2010). Design of a fuzzy adaptive controller for MIMO nonlinear time-delay systems with unknown actuator nonlinearities and unknown control direction. *Information Sciences*, *180*(24), 5041–5059. doi:10.1016/j.ins.2010.08.034

Boulkroune, A., M'Saad, M., & Farza, M. (2012b). Adaptive fuzzy tracking control for a class of MIMO nonaffine uncertain systems. *Neurocomputing*, *93*, 48–55. doi:10.1016/j.neucom.2012.04.006

Boulkroune, A., Tadjine, M., M'Saad, M., & Farza, M. (2014b). Design of a unified adaptive fuzzy observer for uncertain nonlinear systems. *Information Sciences*, *265*, 139–153. doi:10.1016/j.ins.2013.12.026

Chang, W., Tong, S., & Li, Y. (2016). Adaptive fuzzy backstepping output constraint control of flexible manipulator with actuator saturation. *Neural Computing & Applications*. doi:10.100700521-016-2425-2

Chen, B., Zhang, H., & Lin, C. (2016). Observer-Based Adaptive Neural Network Control for Nonlinear Systems in Nonstrict-Feedback Form. *IEEE Transactions on Neural Networks and Learning Systems*, *27*(1), 89–98. doi:10.1109/TNNLS.2015.2412121 PMID:25823044

Chen, C., Liu, Z., Xie, K., Liu, Y., Zhang, Y., & Chen, C. L. P. (2017). Adaptive Fuzzy Asymptotic Control of MIMO Systems with Unknown Input Coefficients Via a Robust Nussbaum Gain based Approach. *IEEE Transactions on Fuzzy Systems*, *25*(5), 1252–1263. doi:10.1109/TFUZZ.2016.2604848

Chen, L., He, Y., Chai, Y., & Wu, R. (2014). New results on stability and stabilization of a class of nonlinear fractional-order systems. *Nonlinear Dynamics*, *75*(4), 633–641. doi:10.100711071-013-1091-5

Chen, Y., Wei, Y., Liang, S., & Wang, Y. (2016). Indirect model reference adaptive control for a class of fractional order systems. *Communications in Nonlinear Science and Numerical Simulation*, *39*, 458–471. doi:10.1016/j.cnsns.2016.03.016

Du, H., & Chen, X. (2009). NN-based output feedback adaptive variable structure control for a class of non-affine nonlinear systems: A nonseparation principle design. *Neurocomputing*, *72*(7–9), 2009–2016. doi:10.1016/j.neucom.2008.12.015

Fridman, E., & Dambrine, M. (2009). Control under quantization, saturation and delay: An LMI approach. *Automatica*, *45*(10), 2258–2264. doi:10.1016/j.automatica.2009.05.020

Fu, Z.-J., Xie, W.-F., & Na, J. (2016). Robust adaptive nonlinear observer design via multi-time scales neural network. *Neurocomputing*, *190*, 217–225. doi:10.1016/j.neucom.2016.01.015

Gao, Y.-F., Sun, X.-M., Wen, C., & Wang, W. (2017). Observer-Based Adaptive NN Control for a Class of Uncertain Nonlinear Systems With Nonsymmetric Input Saturation. *IEEE Transactions on Neural Networks and Learning Systems*, *28*(7), 1520–1530. doi:10.1109/TNNLS.2016.2529843 PMID:28113478

Guo, T., & Chen, W. (2016). Adaptive Fuzzy Decentralized Fault-Tolerant Control for Uncertain Non-linear Large-Scale Systems with Unknown Time-Delay. *IET Control Theory & Applications*, *10*(18), 2437–2446. doi:10.1049/iet-cta.2016.0471

Hamel, S., & Boulkroune, A. (2016). A generalized function projective synchronization scheme for uncertain chaotic systems subject to input nonlinearities. *International Journal of General Systems*, *45*(6), 689–710. doi:10.1080/03081079.2015.1118094

Han, S., Ha, H., & Lee, J. (2016). Barrier Lyapunov function-based model-free constraint position control for mechanical systems. *Journal of Mechanical Science and Technology*, *30*(7), 3331–3338. doi:10.100712206-016-0642-3

He, W., David, A. O., Yin, Z., & Sun, C. (2016). Neural Network Control of a Robotic Manipulator With Input Deadzone and Output Constraint. *IEEE Transactions on Systems, Man, and Cybernetics. Systems*, *46*(6), 759–770. doi:10.1109/TSMC.2015.2466194

He, W., Yin, Z., & Sun, C. (2017). Adaptive Neural Network Control of a Marine Vessel With Constraints Using the Asymmetric Barrier Lyapunov Function. *IEEE Transactions on Cybernetics*, *47*(7), 1641–1651. doi:10.1109/TCYB.2016.2554621

Jafrasteh, B., & Fathianpour, N. (2017). A hybrid simultaneous perturbation artificial bee colony and back-propagation algorithm for training a local linear radial basis neural network on ore grade estimation. *Neurocomputing*, *235*, 217–227. doi:10.1016/j.neucom.2017.01.016

Lai, G., Liu, Z., Zhang, Y., Chen, C. L. P., Xie, S., & Liu, Y.-J. (2017). Fuzzy Adaptive Inverse Compensation Method to Tracking Control of Uncertain Nonlinear Systems With Generalized Actuator Dead Zone. *IEEE Transactions on Fuzzy Systems*, *25*(1), 191–204. doi:10.1109/TFUZZ.2016.2554152

Li, D.-J., Li, J., & Li, S. (2016). Adaptive control of nonlinear systems with full state constraints using Integral Barrier Lyapunov Functionals. *Neurocomputing*, *186*, 90–96. doi:10.1016/j.neucom.2015.12.075

Li, H., Bai, L., Wang, L., Zhou, Q., & Wang, H. (2017). Adaptive Neural Control of Uncertain Nonstrict-Feedback Stochastic Nonlinear Systems with Output Constraint and Unknown Dead Zone. *IEEE Transactions on Systems, Man, and Cybernetics. Systems*, *47*(8), 2048–2059. doi:10.1109/TSMC.2016.2605706

Li, X.-J., & Yang, G.-H. (2016). FLS-Based Adaptive Synchronization Control of Complex Dynamical Networks With Nonlinear Couplings and State-Dependent Uncertainties. *IEEE Transactions on Cybernetics*, *46*(1), 171–180. doi:10.1109/TCYB.2015.2399334 PMID:25720020

Li, Y., & Tong, S. (2017). Adaptive Fuzzy Output-Feedback Stabilization Control for a Class of Switched Nonstrict-Feedback Nonlinear Systems. *IEEE Transactions on Cybernetics*, *47*(4), 1007–1016. doi:10.1109/TCYB.2016.2536628 PMID:26992190

Lin, T.-C., & Lee, T.-Y. (2011). Chaos Synchronization of Uncertain Fractional-Order Chaotic Systems With Time Delay Based on Adaptive Fuzzy Sliding Mode Control. *IEEE Transactions on Fuzzy Systems*, *19*(4), 623–635. doi:10.1109/TFUZZ.2011.2127482

Liu, H., Li, S., Cao, J., Alsaedi, G., Li, A., & Alsaadi, F. E. (2017). Adaptive fuzzy prescribed performance controller design for a class of uncertain fractional-order nonlinear systems with external disturbances. *Neurocomputing*, *219*, 422–430. doi:10.1016/j.neucom.2016.09.050

Liu, Y. J., & Tong, S. (2016). Barrier Lyapunov Functions-based adaptive control for a class of nonlinear pure-feedback systems with full state constraints. *Automatica*, *64*, 70–75. doi:10.1016/j.automatica.2015.10.034

Liu, Y.-J., Tong, S., Chen, C. L. P., & Li, D.-J. (2017). Adaptive NN Control Using Integral Barrier Lyapunov Functionals for Uncertain Nonlinear Block-Triangular Constraint Systems. *IEEE Transactions on Cybernetics*, *47*(11), 3747–3757. doi:10.1109/TCYB.2016.2581173 PMID:27662691

Na, J., Ren, X., Shang, C., & Guo, Y. (2012). Adaptive neural network predictive control for nonlinear pure feedback systems with input delay. *Journal of Process Control*, *22*(1), 194–206. doi:10.1016/j.jprocont.2011.09.003

Oliveira, T. R., Peixoto, A. J., & Hsu, L. (2010). Sliding Mode Control of Uncertain Multivariable Nonlinear Systems With Unknown Control Direction via Switching and Monitoring Function. *IEEE Transactions on Automatic Control*, *55*(4), 1028–1034. doi:10.1109/TAC.2010.2041986

Panagou, D., & Stipanovi, D. M. (2016). Distributed coordination control for multi-robot networks using Lyapunov-like barrier functions. *IEEE Transactions on Automatic Control*, *61*(3), 617–632. doi:10.1109/TAC.2015.2444131

Tarasov, V. E. (2016). On chain rule for fractional derivatives. *Communications in Nonlinear Science and Numerical Simulation*, *30*(1–3), 1–4. doi:10.1016/j.cnsns.2015.06.007

Vargas-De-León, C. (2015). Volterra-type Lyapunov functions for fractional-order epidemic systems. *Communications in Nonlinear Science and Numerical Simulation*, *24*(1–3), 75–85. doi:10.1016/j.cnsns.2014.12.013

Wen, C., Zhou, J., Liu, Z., & Su, H. (2011). Robust Adaptive Control of Uncertain Nonlinear Systems in the Presence of Input Saturation and External Disturbance. *IEEE Transactions on Automatic Control*, *56*(7), 1672–1678. doi:10.1109/TAC.2011.2122730

Xu, B., Yang, C., & Pan, Y. (2015). Global Neural Dynamic Surface Tracking Control of Strict-Feedback Systems With Application to Hypersonic Flight Vehicle. *IEEE Transactions on Neural Networks and Learning Systems*, *26*(10), 2563–2575. doi:10.1109/TNNLS.2015.2456972 PMID:26259222

Yan, P., Liu, D., Wang, D., & Ma, H. (2016). Data-driven controller design for general MIMO nonlinear systems via virtual reference feedback tuning and neural networks. *Neurocomputing*, *171*, 815–825. doi:10.1016/j.neucom.2015.07.017

Yin, S., Gao, H., Qiu, J., & Kaynak, O. (2017). Descriptor reduced-order sliding mode observers design for switched systems with sensor and actuator faults. *Automatica*, *76*, 282–292. doi:10.1016/j.automatica.2016.10.025

Yu, Z., & Du, H. (2011). Adaptive neural control for uncertain stochastic nonlinear strict-feedback systems with time-varying delays: A Razumikhin functional method. *Neurocomputing*, *74*(12–13), 2072–2082. doi:10.1016/j.neucom.2010.12.030

Zhang, Z., Duan, G., & Hou, M. (2017). Robust adaptive dynamic surface control of uncertain non-linear systems with output constraints. *IET Control Theory & Applications*, *11*(1), 110–121. doi:10.1049/iet-cta.2016.0456

Zhou, Q., Wang, L., Wu, C., Li, H., & Du, H. (2017). Adaptive Fuzzy Control for Nonstrict-Feedback Systems With Input Saturation and Output Constraint. *IEEE Transactions on Systems, Man, and Cybernetics. Systems*, *47*(1), 1–12. doi:10.1109/TSMC.2016.2557222

Zouari, F., Boulkroune, A., & Ibeas, A. (2017b). Neural Adaptive quantized output-feedback control-based synchronization of uncertain time-delay incommensurate fractional-order chaotic systems with input nonlinearities. *Neurocomputing*, *237*, 200–225. doi:10.1016/j.neucom.2016.11.036

Zouari, F., Boulkroune, A., Ibeas, A., & Arefi, M. M. (2017a). Observer-based adaptive neural network control for a class of MIMO uncertain nonlinear time-delay non-integer-order systems with asymmetric actuator saturation. *Neural Computing & Applications*, *28*(S1), 993–1010. doi:10.100700521-016-2369-6

Compilation of References

Abarbanel, H. D., Rulkov, N. F., & Sushchik, M. M. (1996). Generalized synchronization of chaos: The auxiliary system approach. *Physical Review. E, 53*(5), 4528–4535. doi:10.1103/PhysRevE.53.4528 PMID:9964787

Abbaoui, K., & Cherruault, Y. (1994). Convergence of Adomian's method applied to differential equations. *Mathematical and Computer Modelling, 28*(5), 103–109.

Abdelouahab, M. S., & Hamri, N. (2014). Fractional-order hybrid optical system and its chaos control synchronization. *EJTP, 11*(30), 49–62.

Abdelouahab, M. S., & Hamri, N. E. (2012). A new chaotic attractor from hybrid optical bistable system. *Nonlinear Dynamics, 67*(1), 457–463. doi:10.100711071-011-9994-5

Abdelouahab, M. S., Hamri, N.-E., & Wang, J. (2010). Chaos Control of a Fractional Order Financial System. *Mathematical Problems in Engineering, 2010*, 1–18. doi:10.1155/2010/270646

Abdelouahab, M. S., Hamri, N.-E., & Wang, J. (2012). Hopf Bifurcation and Chaos in Fractional-Order Modified Hybrid Optical System. *Nonlinear Dynamics, 69*(1-2), 275–284. doi:10.100711071-011-0263-4

Abdulaziz, O. N., Noor, N. F. M., Hashim, I., & Noorani, M. S. M. (2008). Further Accuracy Tests on Adomian Decomposition Method for Chaotic Systems. *Chaos, Solitons, and Fractals, 5*(36), 1405–1411. doi:10.1016/j.chaos.2006.09.007

Abergel, D. L.-Y., Louis-Joseph, A., & Lallemand, J.-Y. (2002). Self Sustained Maser Oscillations of a Large Magnetization Driven by a Radiation Damping-Based Electronic Feedback. *The Journal of Chemical Physics, 16*(116), 7073–7080. doi:10.1063/1.1462583

Achili, B., Madani, T., Daachi, B., & Djouani, K. (2016). Adaptive Observer Based on MLPNN and Sliding Mode for Wearable Robots: Application to an Active Joint Orthosis. *Neurocomputing, 197*, 69–77. doi:10.1016/j.neucom.2016.01.065

Adomian, G. (1990). A Review of the decomposition method and some recent results for nonlinear equations. *Mathematical and Computer Modelling, 13*(7), 17–43. doi:10.1016/0895-7177(90)90125-7

Aghababa, M. P. (2012). Comments on "H∞ synchronization of uncertain fractional order chaotic systems: Adaptive fuzzy approach". *ISA Transactions, 51*(1), 11–12. doi:10.1016/j.isatra.2011.10.011 PMID:22075386

Aghababa, M. P. (2013). A fractional-order controller for vibration suppression of uncertain structures. *ISA Transactions, 52*(6), 881–887. doi:10.1016/j.isatra.2013.07.010 PMID:23932858

Agrawal, S. K., & Das, S. (2013). A modified adaptive control method for synchronization of some fractional chaotic systems with unknown parameters. *Nonlinear Dynamics, 73*(1-2), 907–919. doi:10.100711071-013-0842-7

Agrawal, S. K., & Das, S. (2014). Function projective synchronization between four dimensional chaotic systems with uncertain parameters using modified adaptive control method. *Journal of Process Control, 24*(5), 517–530. doi:10.1016/j.jprocont.2014.02.013

Agrawal, S. K., Srivastava, M., & Das, S. (2012). Synchronization of fractional order chaotic systems using active control method. *Chaos, Solitons, and Fractals, 45*(6), 737–752. doi:10.1016/j.chaos.2012.02.004

Aguila-Camacho, N., Duarte-Mermoud, M. A., & Delgado-Aguilera, E. (2016). Adaptive synchronization of fractional Lorenz systems using a re duce d number of control signals and parameters. *Chaos, Solitons, and Fractals, 87*, 1–11. doi:10.1016/j.chaos.2016.02.038

Aguila-Camacho, N., Duarte-Mermoud, M. A., & Gallegos, J. A. (2014). Lyapunov functions for fractional order systems. *Communications in Nonlinear Science and Numerical Simulation, 19*(9), 2951–2957. doi:10.1016/j.cnsns.2014.01.022

Ahmad, I., Shafiq, M., Saaban, A. B., Ibrahim, A. B., & Shahzad, M. (2016). Robust finite-time global synchronization of chaotic systems with different orders. *Optik-International Journal for Light and Electron Optics, 127*(19), 8172–8185. doi:10.1016/j.ijleo.2016.05.065

Ahmad, W. M., & Sprott, J. C. (2003). Chaos in fractional-order autonomous nonlinear systems. *Chaos, Solitons, and Fractals, 16*(2), 339–351. doi:10.1016/S0960-0779(02)00438-1

Ahmed, E. E.-S., El-Sayed, A. M. A., & El-Saka, H. A. A. (2006). On Some Routh-Hurwitz conditions for Fractional Order Differential Equations and their Applications in Lorentz, Rossler, Chua and Chen Systems. *Physics Letters. [Part A], 358*(1), 1–4. doi:10.1016/j.physleta.2006.04.087

Alexiadis, A., Vanni, M., & Gardin, P. (2004). Extension of the method of moments for population balances involving fractional moments and application to a typical agglomeration problem. *Journal of Colloid and Interface Science, 276*(1), 106–112. doi:10.1016/j.jcis.2004.03.052 PMID:15219436

Alvarez, G., & Li, S. (2006). Some basic cryptographic requirements for chaos-based cryptosystems. *International Journal of Bifurcation and Chaos in Applied Sciences and Engineering, 16*(08), 2129–2151. doi:10.1142/S0218127406015970

Andrew, L.Y.T., Li, X.F., Chu, Y.D., & Hui, Z. (2015). A novel adaptive-impulsive synchronization of fractional-order chaotic systems. *Chinese Phys. B, 24*.

Annovazzi-Lodi, V., Benedetti, M., Merlo, S., Norgia, M., & Provinzano, B. (2005). Optical chaos masking of video signals. *IEEE Photonics Technology Letters, 17*(9), 1995–1997. doi:10.1109/LPT.2005.853267

Arefi, M. M., Jahed-Motlagh, M. R., & Karimi, H. R. (2014a). Adaptive Neural Stabilizing Controller for a Class of Mismatched Uncertain Nonlinear Systems by State and Output Feedback. *IEEE Transactions on Cybernetics, 45*(8), 1587–1596. doi:10.1109/TCYB.2014.2356414 PMID:25265641

Arefi, M. M., Ramezani, Z., & Jahed-Motlagh, M. R. (2014b). Observer-based adaptive robust control of nonlinear nonaffine systems with unknown gain sign. *Nonlinear Dynamics, 78*(3), 2185–2194. doi:10.100711071-014-1573-0

Arena, F., Gatti, G., & Martra, G. (2012). Adaptation of differential transform method for the numeric-analytic solution of fractional-order Rössler chaotic and hyperchaotic systems. *Abstract & Applied Analysis,* (4), 305-309.

Arena, P., Caponetto, R., Fortuna, L., & Porto, D. (1997). Chaos in a fractional order duffing system. In *Proceedings of The International Conference of ECCTD* (pp. 1259-1262). Budapest: Academic Press.

Arena, P., Caponetto, R., Fortuna, L., & Porto, D. (1997). Chaos in a fractional order Duffing system. *Proc. Int. Conf. of ECCTD*, 1259-1262.

Azar, A. T. (2012). Overview of Type-2 Fuzzy logic systems. *International Journal of Fuzzy System Applications*, 2(4), 1–28. doi:10.4018/ijfsa.2012100101

Azar, A. T., & Vaidyanathan, S. (2015). *Chaos Modeling and Control Systems Design, Studies in Computational Intelligence* (Vol. 581). Springer-Verlag.

Aziz-Alaoui, M. A. (2005). A survey on chaos synchronization. *12th IEEE-ICECS*, 523-527.

Bagley, R. L., & Calico, R. A. (1991). Fractional order state equations for the control of viscoelastically damped structures. *Journal of Guidance, Control, and Dynamics*, 14(5), 304–311. doi:10.2514/3.20641

Bagley, R. L., & Torvik, P. J. (1984). On the appearance of the fractional derivative in the behavior of real materials. *Journal of Applied Mechanics*, 51(2), 294–298. doi:10.1115/1.3167615

Bai, E. L., Lonngren, K. E., & Sprott, J. C. (2002). On the Synchronization of a Class of Electronic Circuits that Exibit Chaos. *Chaos, Solitons, and Fractals*, 13(7), 1515–1521. doi:10.1016/S0960-0779(01)00160-6

Baleanu, D., Güvenç, Z. B., & Tenreiro Machado, J. A. (2010). *New Trends in Nanotechnology and Fractional Calculus Applications*. Springer. doi:10.1007/978-90-481-3293-5

Baleanu, D., Machado, J. A. T., & Luo, A. C. (Eds.). (2011). *Fractional dynamics and control*. New York: Springer.

Bandt, C., & Pompe, B. (2002). Permutation entropy: A natural complexity measure for time series. *Physical Review Letters*, 88(17), 174102. doi:10.1103/PhysRevLett.88.174102 PMID:12005759

Bao, H. B., & Cao, J. D. (2015). Projective synchronization of fractional-order memristor-based neural networks. *Neural Networks*, 63, 1–9. doi:10.1016/j.neunet.2014.10.007 PMID:25463390

Bao, H., Park, J. H., & Cao, J. (2015). Adaptive synchronization of fractional-order memristor-based neural networks with time delay. *Nonlinear Dynamics*, 82(3), 1343–1354. doi:10.100711071-015-2242-7

Barbosa, R. S., Machado, T. J. A., & Jesus, I. S. (2010). Effect of fractional-orders in the velocity control of a servo system. *Computers & Mathematics with Applications (Oxford, England)*, 59(5), 1679–1686. doi:10.1016/j.camwa.2009.08.009

Behnia, S., Afrang, S., Akhshani, A., & Mabhouti, K. (2013). A novel method for controlling chaos in external cavity semiconductor laser. *Optik-International Journal for Light and Electron Optics*, 124(8), 757–764. doi:10.1016/j.ijleo.2012.01.013

Benettin, G. G.-M. (1980). LyapunA Chaotic System with Only one Stable Equilibrium Characteristic Exponents for Smooth Dynamical systems and for hamiltonian Systems: a method for Computing all of them. Part 1: Theory. *Meccanica*, (15): 9–20. doi:10.1007/BF02128236

Benzaoui, M., Chekireb, H., Tadjine, M., & Boulkroune, A. (2016). Trajectory tracking with obstacle avoidance of redundant manipulator based on fuzzy inference systems. *Neurocomputing*, 196, 23–30. doi:10.1016/j.neucom.2016.02.037

Bettayeb, M., Al-Saggaf, U. M., & Djennoune, S. (2017). High gain observer design for fractional-order non-linear systems with delayed measurements: Application to synchronisation of fractional-order chaotic systems. *IET Control Theory & Applications*, 11(17), 3191–3178. doi:10.1049/iet-cta.2017.0396

Bhalekar, S. (2014). Synchronization of incommensurate non-identical fractional order chaotic systems using active control. *The European Physical Journal. Special Topics*, 223(8), 1495–1508. doi:10.1140/epjst/e2014-02184-0

Bhalekar, S., & Daftardar-Gejji, V. (2010). Synchronization of different fractional order chaotic systems using active control. *Communications in Nonlinear Science and Numerical Simulation*, 15(11), 3536–3546. doi:10.1016/j.cnsns.2009.12.016

Bhandari, A., & Marziliano, P. (2010). Fractional Delay Filters Based on Generalized Cardinal Exponential Splines. *IEEE Signal Processing Letters*, *17*(3), 225–228. doi:10.1109/LSP.2009.2036386

Bhasin, H., Kumar, R., & Kathuria, N. (2013). Cryptography Using Cellular Automata. *International Journal of Computer Science and Information Technologies*, *4*(2), 355–357.

Bigdeli, N., & Ziazi, H. A. (2017). Finite-time fractional-order adaptive intelligent backstepping sliding mode control of uncertain fractional-order chaotic systems. *Journal of the Franklin Institute*, *354*(1), 160–183. doi:10.1016/j.jfranklin.2016.10.004

Bleichenbacher, D. (1998). Chosen ciphertext attacks against protocols based on the RSA encryption standard PKCS# 1. In Advances in Cryptology-CRYPTO'98 (pp. 1-12). Springer Berlin/Heidelberg.

Bloisi, D. D., & Iocchi, L. (2007, March). Image based steganography and cryptography. VISAPP, (1), 127-134.

Blu, T., & Unse, M. (2007). Self-Similarity: Part II- Optimal Estimation of Fractal Processes. *IEEE Trans. On Signal Proc*, *55*(4), 1364–1378. doi:10.1109/TSP.2006.890845

Boeing, G. (2016). *Visual Analysis of Nonlinear Dynamical Systems: Chaos, Fractals, Self-Similarity and the Limits of Prediction. Systems, 4(4).* doi:10.3390ystems4040037

Bogkovic, J. D., Chen, L., & Mehra, R. K. (2001). Adaptive tracking control of a class of non-affine plants using dynamic feedback. *American Control Conference.* 10.1109/ACC.2001.946120

Boroujeni, E. A., & Momeni, H. R. (2012). Non-fragile nonlinear fractional order observer design for a class of nonlinear fractional order systems. *Signal Processing*, *92*(10), 2365–2370. doi:10.1016/j.sigpro.2012.02.009

Bouafoura, M. K., & Braiek, N. B. (2010). $PI\lambda D\mu$ controller design for integer and fractional plants using piecewise orthogonal functions. *Communications in Nonlinear Science and Numerical Simulation*, *15*(5), 1267–1278. doi:10.1016/j.cnsns.2009.05.047

Boubellouta, A., & Boulkroune, A. (2016). Chaos synchronization of two different PMSM using a fractional order sliding mode controller. In *Modelling, Identification and Control (ICMIC), 2016 8th International Conference on* (pp. 995-1001). IEEE. 10.1109/ICMIC.2016.7804259

Boukezzoula, R., Galichet, S., & Foulloy, L. (2007). Fuzzy Feedback Linearizing Controller and Its Equivalence With the Fuzzy Nonlinear Internal Model Control Structure. *International Journal of Applied Mathematics and Computer Science*, *17*(2), 233–248. doi:10.2478/v10006-007-0021-4

Boulkroune, A. (2016). A fuzzy adaptive control approach for nonlinear systems with unknown control gain sign. *Neurocomputing*, *179*, 318–325. doi:10.1016/j.neucom.2015.12.010

Boulkroune, A., Bounar, N., M'Saad, M., & Farza, M. (2014b). Indirect adaptive fuzzy control scheme based on observer for nonlinear systems: A novel SPR-filter approach. *Neurocomputing*, *135*, 378–387. doi:10.1016/j.neucom.2013.12.011

Boulkroune, A., Bouzeriba, A., & Bouden, T. (2016a). Fuzzy generalized projective synchronization of incommensurate fractional-order chaotic systems. *Neurocomputing*, *173*(3), 606–614. doi:10.1016/j.neucom.2015.08.003

Boulkroune, A., Bouzeriba, A., Bouden, T., & Azar, A. T. (2016). *Fuzzy Adaptive Synchronization of Uncertain Fractional-order Chaotic Systems. In Advances in Chaos Theory and Intelligent Control. Studies in Fuzziness and Soft Computing* (Vol. 337). Springer-Verlag.

Boulkroune, A., Bouzeriba, A., & Hamel, S. (2015a). Projective synchronization scheme based on Fuzzy controller for uncertain multivariable chaotic systems. In *Chaos Modeling and Control Systems Design* (pp. 73–93). Springer International Publishing. doi:10.1007/978-3-319-13132-0_5

Boulkroune, A., Bouzeriba, A., Hamel, S., & Bouden, T. (2014c). A projective synchronization scheme based on fuzzy adaptive control for unknown multivariable chaotic systems. *Nonlinear Dynamics*, *78*(1), 433–447. doi:10.100711071-014-1450-x

Boulkroune, A., Bouzeriba, A., Hamel, S., & Bouden, T. (2015b). Adaptive fuzzy control-based projective synchronization of uncertain nonaffine chaotic systems. *Complexity*, *21*(2), 180–192. doi:10.1002/cplx.21596

Boulkroune, A., Hamel, S., Zouari, F., Boukabou, A., & Ibeas, A. (2017). Output-Feedback Controller Based Projective Lag-Synchronization of Uncertain Chaotic Systems in the Presence of Input Nonlinearities. *Mathematical Problems in Engineering*.

Boulkroune, A., & M'Saad, M. (2011). A practical projective synchronization approach for uncertain chaotic systems with dead-zone input. *Communications in Nonlinear Science and Numerical Simulation*, *16*(11), 4487–4500. doi:10.1016/j.cnsns.2011.02.016

Boulkroune, A., & M'saad, M. (2012). On the design of observer-based fuzzy adaptive controller for nonlinear systems with unknown control gain sign. *Fuzzy Sets and Systems*, *201*, 71–85. doi:10.1016/j.fss.2011.12.005

Boulkroune, A., & M'Saad, M. (2012b). On the design of observer-based fuzzy adaptive controller for nonlinear systems with unknown control gain sign. *Neurocomputing*, *201*, 71–85.

Boulkroune, A., M'Saad, M., & Chekireb, H. (2010). Design of a fuzzy adaptive controller for MIMO nonlinear time-delay systems with unknown actuator nonlinearities and unknown control direction. *Information Sciences*, *180*(24), 5041–5059. doi:10.1016/j.ins.2010.08.034

Boulkroune, A., M'Saad, M., & Farza, M. (2011). Adaptive fuzzy controller for multivariable nonlinear state time-varying delay systems subject to input nonlinearities. *Fuzzy Sets and Systems*, *164*(1), 45–65. doi:10.1016/j.fss.2010.09.001

Boulkroune, A., M'Saad, M., & Farza, M. (2012a). Adaptive fuzzy tracking control for a class of MIMO nonaffine uncertain systems. *Neurocomputing*, *93*, 48–55. doi:10.1016/j.neucom.2012.04.006

Boulkroune, A., M'saad, M., & Farza, M. (2012b). Fuzzy approximation-based indirect adaptive controller for multi-input multi-output Non-affine systems with unknown control direction. *IET Control Theory & Applications*, *6*(17), 2619–2629. doi:10.1049/iet-cta.2012.0565

Boulkroune, A., M'saad, M., & Farza, M. (2016b). Adaptive fuzzy system-based variable-structure controller for multivariable nonaffine nonlinear uncertain systems subject to actuator nonlinearities. *Neural Computing & Applications*. doi:10.100700521-016-2241-8

Boulkroune, A., Tadjine, M., M'Saad, M., & Farza, M. (2008a). A unified approach for design of indirect adaptive output-feedback fuzzy controller. *International Journal of Intelligent Systems Technologies and Applications*, *5*(1-2), 83–103. doi:10.1504/IJISTA.2008.018168

Boulkroune, A., Tadjine, M., M'Saad, M., & Farza, M. (2008b). How to design a fuzzy adaptive controller based on observers for uncertain affine nonlinear systems. *Fuzzy Sets and Systems*, *159*(8), 926–948. doi:10.1016/j.fss.2007.08.015

Boulkroune, A., Tadjine, M., M'saad, M., & Farza, M. (2011). Adaptive fuzzy observer for uncertain nonlinear systems. *Control and Intelligent Systems*, *39*(3), 145–153. doi:10.2316/Journal.201.2011.3.201-1985

Boulkroune, A., Tadjine, M., M'Saad, M., & Farza, M. (2014a). Design of a unified adaptive fuzzy observer for uncertain nonlinear systems. *Information Sciences, 265*, 139–153. doi:10.1016/j.ins.2013.12.026

Bounar, N., Boulkroune, A., & Boudjema, F. (2014). Adaptive fuzzy control of doubly-fed induction machine. *Journal of Control Engineering and Applied Informatics, 16*(2), 98–110.

Bounar, N., Boulkroune, A., Boudjema, F., & Farza, M. (2015). Adaptive fuzzy vector control for a doubly-fed induction motor. *Neurocomputing, 151*, 756–769. doi:10.1016/j.neucom.2014.10.026

Bourouba, B., & Ladaci, S. (2017). Adaptive sliding mode control for the stabilization of a class of fractional-order Lü chaotic systems. In *Proceedings of the 5th IEEE International Conference on Electrical Engineering – (ICEE'2017)* (pp.1-5). Boumerdes, Algeria: IEEE.

Bourouba, B., & Ladaci, S. (2017). Stabilization of class of fractional-order chaotic system via new sliding mode control. *Proceeding 6th IEEE International Conference on Systems and Control, ICSC'2017*, 470-475. 10.1109/ICoSC.2017.7958681

Bourouba, B., Ladaci, S., & Chaabi, A. (2017). Reduced-Order Model Approximation of Fractional-Order Systems Using Differential Evolution Algorithm. *Journal of Control, Automation and Electrical Systems*. doi: 10.1007/s40313-017-0356-5

Bourouba, B., Ladaci, S., & Chaabi, A. (2017). Moth-Flame optimization algorithm based fractional order PI$^\lambda$D$^\mu$ controller with MRAC tuning configuration. *International Journal of Systems, Control and Communications*.

Bouzeriba, A., Boulkroune, A., & Bouden T. (2015). Fuzzy adaptive synchronization of uncertain fractional-order chaotic systems. *International Journal of Machine Learning and Cybernetics*.

Bouzeriba, A., Boulkroune, A., & Bouden, T. (2015). Fuzzy adaptive synchronization of a class of fractional-order chaotic systems. In *Control, Engineering & Information Technology (CEIT), 2015 3rd International Conference on* (pp. 1-6). IEEE. 10.1109/CEIT.2015.7233073

Bouzeriba, A., Boulkroune, A., & Bouden, T. (2016a). Fuzzy adaptive synchronization of a class of fractional-order chaotic systems. In *Advances and Applications in Chaotic Systems* (pp. 363–378). Springer International Publishing. doi:10.1007/978-3-319-30279-9_15

Bouzeriba, A., Boulkroune, A., & Bouden, T. (2016a). Fuzzy adaptive synchronization of uncertain fractional-order chaotic systems. *International Journal of Machine Learning and Cybernetics, 7*(5), 893–908. doi:10.100713042-015-0425-7

Bouzeriba, A., Boulkroune, A., & Bouden, T. (2016b). Projective synchronization of two different fractional-order chaotic systems via adaptive fuzzy control. *Neural Computing & Applications, 27*(5), 1349–1360. doi:10.100700521-015-1938-4

Bowonga, S., Kakmenib, M., & Koinac, R. (2006). Chaos synchronization and duration time of a class of uncertain systems. *Mathematics and Computers in Simulation, 71*(3), 212–228. doi:10.1016/j.matcom.2006.01.006

Bremen, H. F. (1997). An Efficient QR Based Method for the Computation of lyapunov Exponents. *Physica D. Nonlinear Phenomena, 1*(15), 1–16. doi:10.1016/S0167-2789(96)00216-3

Brown, R. B., Bryant, P., & Abarbanel, H. D. I. (1991). Computing the Lyapunov Spectrum of a Dynamical System from an Observed Time Series. *Physical Review A., 43*(6), 2787–2806. doi:10.1103/PhysRevA.43.2787 PMID:9905344

Cafagna, D. (2010). An Effective Method for Detecting Chaos in fractional-Order systems. *International Journal of Bifurcation and Chaos in Applied Sciences and Engineering*, 20.

Cafagna, D., & Grassi, G. (2003). New 3-d Scroll Attractors in Hyperchaotic Chua's Circuit Forming a Ring. *International Journal of Bifurcation and Chaos in Applied Sciences and Engineering, 13*(10), 2889–2903. doi:10.1142/S0218127403008284

Cafagna, D., & Grassi, G. (2008). Bifurcation and chaos in the fractional-order Chen system via a time-domain approach. *International Journal of Bifurcation and Chaos in Applied Sciences and Engineering, 18*(7), 1845–1863. doi:10.1142/S0218127408021415

Cafagna, D., & Grassi, G. (2009). Hyperchaos in the Fractional-Order Rossler System with Lowest-order. *International Journal of Bifurcation and Chaos in Applied Sciences and Engineering, 19*(01), 339–347. doi:10.1142/S0218127409022890

Cailian, C., Gang, F., & Xinping, G. (2005). An adaptive lag-synchronization method for time-delay chaotic systems. *Proceedings of the IEEE American Control Conference.* 10.1109/ACC.2005.1470651

Calderón, A. J., Vinagre, B. M., & Feliu, V. (2006). Fractional order control strategies for power electronic buck converters. *Signal Processing, 86*(10), 2803–2819. doi:10.1016/j.sigpro.2006.02.022

Cang, J. T., Tan, Y., Xu, H., & Liao, S.-J. (2009). Series Solutions of Non-Linear Riccati Differential Equations with Fractional Order. *Chaos, Solitons, and Fractals, 1*(40), 1–9. doi:10.1016/j.chaos.2007.04.018

Caponetto, M., & Fazzino, S. (2013). A Semi-analytical Method for the Computation of the Lyapinov Exponents of Fractional-Order Systems. *Communications in Nonlinear Science and Numerical Simulation, 18*(1), 22–27. doi:10.1016/j.cnsns.2012.06.013

Caponetto, R., Dongola, G., Fortina, L., & Petráš, I. (2010). *Fractional Order Systems: Modeling and control application.* World Scientific Publishing. doi:10.1142/7709

Caponetto, R., & Fazzino, S. (2013). An application of Adomian decomposition for analysis of fractional-order chaotic systems. *International Journal of Bifurcation and Chaos in Applied Sciences and Engineering, 23*(03), 1350050. doi:10.1142/S0218127413500508

Caputo, M. (1967). Linear Models of Dissipation whosw q is Almost Freqency Independent-ii. *Geophysical Journal International, 13*(5), 529–539. doi:10.1111/j.1365-246X.1967.tb02303.x

Carpinteri, A., & Mainardi, F. (1997). *Fractal and Fractional Calculus in Continuum Mechanics.* Wien: Springer-Verlag. doi:10.1007/978-3-7091-2664-6

Carroll, T. L., Heagy, J. F., & Pecora, L. M. (1996). Transforming signals with chaotic synchronization. *Physical Review E: Statistical Physics, Plasmas, Fluids, and Related Interdisciplinary Topics, 54*(5), 4676–4680. doi:10.1103/PhysRevE.54.4676 PMID:9965645

Castillo, O., & Melin, P. (2012). *Recent Advances in Interval Type-2 Fuzzy Systems.* Springer Briefs in Computational Intelligence; doi:10.1007/978-3-642-28956-9

Cazarez-Castro, N. R., Aguilar, L. T., & Castillo, O. (2012). Designing type-1 and type-2 fuzzy logic controllers via fuzzy Lyapunov synthesis for non-smooth mechanical systems. *Engineering Applications of Artificial Intelligence, 25*(5), 971–979. doi:10.1016/j.engappai.2012.03.003

Chang, W., Tong, S., & Li, Y. (2016). Adaptive fuzzy backstepping output constraint control of flexible manipulator with actuator saturation. *Neural Computing & Applications.* doi:10.100700521-016-2425-2

Charef, A., Sun, H., Tsao, Y., & Onaral, B. (1992). Fractal system as presented by singularity function. IEEE Trans. Autom. Control, 1465-1470.

Charef, A., Sun, H. H., Tsao, Y. Y., & Onaral, B. (1992). Fractal system as represented by singularity function. *IEEE Transactions on Automatic Control, 37*(9), 1465–1470. doi:10.1109/9.159595

Chen, B., & Chen, J. (2015). Razumikhin-type stability theorems for functional fractional-order differential systems and applications. *Applied Mathematics and Computation*, *254*, 63–69. doi:10.1016/j.amc.2014.12.010

Chen, B., Liu, X., Liu, K., Shi, P., & Lin, C. (2010). Direct adaptive fuzzy control for nonlinear systems with time-varying delays. *Information Sciences*, *180*(5), 776–792. doi:10.1016/j.ins.2009.11.004

Chen, B.-S., Lee, C.-H., & Chang, Y.-C. (1996). H∞ tracking design of uncertain nonlinear SISO systems: Adaptive fuzzy approach. *IEEE Transactions on Fuzzy Systems*, *4*(1), 32–42. doi:10.1109/91.481843

Chen, B., Zhang, H., & Lin, C. (2016). Observer-Based Adaptive Neural Network Control for Nonlinear Systems in Nonstrict-Feedback Form. *IEEE Transactions on Neural Networks and Learning Systems*, *27*(1), 89–98. doi:10.1109/TNNLS.2015.2412121 PMID:25823044

Chen, C., & Chen, H. (2009). Robust adaptive neural-fuzzy-network control for the synchronization of uncertain chaotic systems. *Nonlinear Analysis Real World Applications*, *10*(3), 1466–1479. doi:10.1016/j.nonrwa.2008.01.016

Chen, C., Liu, Z., Xie, K., Liu, Y., Zhang, Y., & Chen, C. L. P. (2017). Adaptive Fuzzy Asymptotic Control of MIMO Systems with Unknown Input Coefficients Via a Robust Nussbaum Gain based Approach. *IEEE Transactions on Fuzzy Systems*, *25*(5), 1252–1263. doi:10.1109/TFUZZ.2016.2604848

Chen, D., Liu, Y., Ma, X., & Zhang, R. (2012). Control of a class of fractional-order chaotic systems via sliding mode. *Nonlinear Dynamics*, *67*(1), 893–901. doi:10.100711071-011-0002-x PMID:22757537

Chen, D., Wu, C., Iu, H. H. C., & Ma, X. (2013). Circuit simulation for synchronization of a fractional-order and integer-order chaotic system. *Nonlinear Dynamics*, *73*(3), 1671–1686. doi:10.100711071-013-0894-8

Chen, D., Zhang, R., & Sprott, J. C. (2012). Synchronization between integer-order chaotic systems and a class of fractional-order chaotic systems via sliding mode control. *Chaos (Woodbury, N.Y.)*, *70*(2), 1549–1561. PMID:22757537

Chen, D., Zhao, W., Sprott, J. C., & Ma, X. (2013). Application of Takagi–Sugeno fuzzy model to a class of chaotic synchronization and anti-synchronization. *Nonlinear Dynamics*, *73*(3), 1495–1505. doi:10.100711071-013-0880-1

Chen, G., & Dong, X. (1998). *From Chaos to Order: Perspective, Methodologies and Applications*. World Scientific Singapore. doi:10.1142/3033

Chen, L. P., Qu, J. F., Chai, Y., Wu, R. C., & Qi, G. Y. (2013). Synchronization of a class of fractional-order chaotic neural networks. *Entropy (Basel, Switzerland)*, *15*(8), 3265–3276. doi:10.3390/e15083355

Chen, L., He, Y., Chai, Y., & Wu, R. (2014). New results on stability and stabilization of a class on nonlinear fractional-order systems. *Nonlinear Dynamics*, *75*(4), 633–641. doi:10.100711071-013-1091-5

Chen, L., Liu, C., Wu, R., He, Y., & Chai, Y. (2016). Finite-time stability criteria for a class of fractional-order neural networks with delay. *Neural Computing & Applications*, *27*(3), 549–556. doi:10.100700521-015-1876-1

Chen, L., Zhao, T., Li, W., & Zhao, J. (2015). bifurcation control of bounded noise excited duffing oscillator by a weakly fractional-order PIλDμfeedback controller. *Nonlinear Dynamics*.

Chen, W. C. (2008). Nonlinear dynamics and chaos in a fractional-order financial system. *Chaos, Solitons, and Fractals*, *36*(5), 1305–1314. doi:10.1016/j.chaos.2006.07.051

Chen, W. T., Zhuang, J., Yu, W. X., & Wang, Z. (2009). Measuring complexity using FuzzyEn, ApEn, and SampEn. *Medical Engineering & Physics*, *31*(1), 61–68. doi:10.1016/j.medengphy.2008.04.005 PMID:18538625

Chen, Y., Wei, Y., Liang, S., & Wang, Y. (2016). Indirect model reference adaptive control for a class of fractional order systems. *Communications in Nonlinear Science and Numerical Simulation*, *39*, 458–471. doi:10.1016/j.cnsns.2016.03.016

Chen, Z., Yuan, X., Ji, B., Wang, P., & Tian, H. (2014). Design of a fractional order PID controller for hydraulic turbine regulating system using chaotic non-dominated sorting genetic algorithm II. *Energy Conversion and Management*, *84*, 390–404. doi:10.1016/j.enconman.2014.04.052

Chong, G., Hai, W., & Xie, Q. (2004). Transient and stationary chaos of a Bose-Einstein condensate loaded into a moving optical lattice potential. *Physical Review. E*, *70*(3), 036213. doi:10.1103/PhysRevE.70.036213 PMID:15524618

Chua, L. O., Itoh, M., Kocarev, L., & Eckert, K. (1993). Chaos synchronization in Chua's circuit. *Journal of Circuits, Systems, and Computers*, *3*(01), 93–108. doi:10.1142/S0218126693000071

Chua, L. O., Komuro, M., & Matsumoto, T. (1986). The Double scroll Family. *IEEE Transactions on Circuits and Systems*, *33*(11), 1072–1118. doi:10.1109/TCS.1986.1085869

Colonius, F., & Grne, L. (2002). *Dynamics,bifurcationsand control*. New York: Springer. doi:10.1007/3-540-45606-6

Cong, N., Son, D., & Tuan, H. (2014). On fractional Lyapunov exponent for solutions of linear fractional differential equations. *Fractional Calculus & Applied Analysis*, *17*(2), 285–306. doi:10.247813540-014-0169-1

Corduneanu, C. (1977). Principles of Differential and Integral Equations (2nd ed.). New York: Chelsea Publishing Company.

Cui, G., Wang, Z., Zhuang, G., Li, Z., & Chu, Y. (2015). Adaptive decentralized NN control of large-scale stochastic nonlinear time-delay systems with unknown dead-zone inputs. *Neurocomputing*, *158*, 194–203. doi:10.1016/j.neucom.2015.01.048

Cuomo, K. M., & Oppenheim, A. V. (1993). Circuit implementation of synchronized chaos with applications to communications. *Physical Review Letters*, *71*(1), 65–68. doi:10.1103/PhysRevLett.71.65 PMID:10054374

Daemen, J., & Rijmen, V. (2002). *The Design of Rijndael: AES-The Advanced Encryption Standard*. Berlin: Springer. doi:10.1007/978-3-662-04722-4

Daftardar-Gejji, V., & Bhalekar, S. (2010). Chaos in fractional ordered Liu system. *Computers & Mathematics with Applications (Oxford, England)*, *59*(3), 1117–1127. doi:10.1016/j.camwa.2009.07.003

Das, S. (2008). *Functional fractional calculus for system identification and controls*. Berlin: Springer.

Das, S., Pan, I., Das, S., & Gupta, A. (2012). Master-slave chaos synchronization via optimal fractional-order $PI^\lambda D^\mu$. *Nonlinear Dynamics*, *69*(4), 2193–2206. doi:10.100711071-012-0419-x

Data Encryption Standard. (1977). *Federal Information Processing Standards Publication (FIPS PUB) 46*. Washington, DC: National Bureau of Standards.

Dedieu, H., Kennedy, M. P., & Hasler, M. (1993). Chaos shift keying: Modulation and demodulation of a chaotic carrier using self-synchronizing Chua's circuits. *IEEE Transactions on Circuits and Systems. 2, Analog and Digital Signal Processing*, *40*(10), 634–642. doi:10.1109/82.246164

Delavari, H., Baleanu, D., & Sadati, J. (2012). Stability Analysis of Caputo Fractional-Order Nonlinear Systems Revisited. *Nonlinear Dynamics*, *67*(4), 2433–2439. doi:10.100711071-011-0157-5

Delavari, H., Ghaderi, R., Ranjbar, A., & Momani, S. (2010). Fuzzy fractional order sliding mode controller for nonlinear systems. *Communications in Nonlinear Science and Numerical Simulation*, *15*(4), 963–978. doi:10.1016/j.cnsns.2009.05.025

Delavari, H., Ranjbar, A. N., Ghaderi, R., & Momani, S. (2010). Fractional order control of a coupled tank. *Nonlinear Dynamics*, *61*(3), 383–397. doi:10.100711071-010-9656-z

Demirci, E., & Ozalp, N. (2012). A method for solving differential equations of fractional order. *Journal of Computational and Applied Mathematics*, *236*(11), 2754–2762. doi:10.1016/j.cam.2012.01.005

Deng, W. (2006). Design of Multidirectional Multi-Scroll Chaotic Attractors Based on Fractional Differential Systems via switching Control. *Chaos (Woodbury, N.Y.)*, *17*(4).

Deng, W. H. (2007b). Numerical Algorithm for Time Fractional Fokker-Planck Equation. *Journal of Computational Physics*, *227*(2), 1510–1522. doi:10.1016/j.jcp.2007.09.015

Deng, W. H. (2007c). Short Memory Principle and a Predictor-Corrector Approach for Fractional Differential Equations. *Journal of Computational and Applied Mathematics*, *206*(1), 174–188. doi:10.1016/j.cam.2006.06.008

Deng, W. H., & Li, C. P. (2005). Chaos synchronization of the fractional Lü system. *Physica A*, *353*, 61–72. doi:10.1016/j.physa.2005.01.021

Deng, W. L., Li, C., & Lü, J. (2007d). Stability Analysis of Linear Fractional Differential System with Multiple Time Delay. *Nonlinear Dynamics*, *48*(4), 409–416. doi:10.100711071-006-9094-0

Deng, W., & Lü, J. (2007a). Generating Multidirectional Multi-Scroll Chaotic Attractors via a Fractional Differential Hysteresis System. *Physics Letters. [Part A]*, *369*(5-6), 438–443. doi:10.1016/j.physleta.2007.04.112

Diethelm, K., &. Freed, A.D. (1999). The fracPECE subrutine for the Numerical Solution of Differential Equations of Fractional Order. *Heinzel S, Plesser T*, 57-71.

Diethelm, K. (1997). An algorithm for the NumericalSolution of Differential Equations of Fractional-Order. *Electronic Transactions on Numerical Analysis*, *5*, 1–6.

Diethelm, K. (2003). Efficient Solution of Multi-Term Fractional Differential Equations Using P(EC)mE Methods. *Computing*, *71*(4), 305–319. doi:10.100700607-003-0033-3

Diethelm, K. (2010). *The Analysis of Fractional Differential Equations*. Heidelberg, Germany: Springer- Verlag. doi:10.1007/978-3-642-14574-2

Diethelm, K., & Ford, N. J. (2002). Analysis of fractional differential equations. *Journal of Mathematical Analysis and Applications*, *265*(2), 229–248. doi:10.1006/jmaa.2000.7194

Diethelm, K., Ford, N. J., & Freed, A. D. (2002). A predictor-corrector approach for the numerical solution of fractional differential equations. *Nonlinear Dynamics*, *29*(1/4), 3–22. doi:10.1023/A:1016592219341

Diethelm, K., Ford, N. J., Freed, A. D., & Luchko, Y. (2005). Algorithms for the fractional calculus: A selection of numerical methods. *Computer Methods in Applied Mechanics and Engineering*, *194*(6-8), 743–773. doi:10.1016/j.cma.2004.06.006

Dimassi, H., Lorı́a, A., & Belghith, S. (2012). A new secured scheme based on chaotic synchronization via smooth adaptive unknown-input observer. *Communications in Nonlinear Science and Numerical Simulation*, *17*(9), 3727–3739. doi:10.1016/j.cnsns.2012.01.024

Ding, D., Qi, D., Meng, Y., & Xu, L. (2014). Adaptive Mittag-Leffler stabilization of commensurate fractional-order nonlinear systems. *Decision and Control (CDC), 53rd Annual Conference on*, 6920-6926.

Ding, D., Qi, D., Peng, J., & Wang, Q. (2015). Asymptotic pseudo-state stabilization of commensurate fractional-order nonlinear systems with additive disturbance. *Nonlinear Dynamics*, *81*(1-2), 667–677. doi:10.100711071-015-2018-0

Ditkin, K. a. (1966). *Operational Calculus*. Moscow: Vysshaja Shlokola.

Doetsch, G. (1974). *Introduction to the theory and Application of the Laplace Transformation*. Berlin: Springer-Verlag. doi:10.1007/978-3-642-65690-3

Domek, S., & Dworak, P. (2016). Theoretical Developments and Applications of Non-Integer Order Systems. *Lecture Notes in Electrical Engineering, 357*.

Douglas, J. F. (2007). Some applications of fractional calculus to polymer science. *Advances in Chemical Physics*, 102.

Duarte, F. B. M., & Machado, J. A. T. (2002). Chaotic Phenomena and Fractional-Order Dynamics in the Trajectory Control of Redundant Manipulators. *Nonlinear Dynamics, 29*(1–4), 315–342. doi:10.1023/A:1016559314798

Duarte-Mermoud, M. A., Aguila-Camacho, N., Gallegos, J. A., & Castro-Linares, R. (2015). Using general quadratic Lyapunov functions to prove Lyapunov uniform stability for fractional order systems. *Communications in Nonlinear Science and Numerical Simulation, 22*(1-3), 650–659. doi:10.1016/j.cnsns.2014.10.008

Du, H., & Chen, X. (2009). NN-based output feedback adaptive variable structure control for a class of non-affine nonlinear systems: A nonseparation principle design. *Neurocomputing, 72*(7-9), 2009–2016. doi:10.1016/j.neucom.2008.12.015

Dzielinski, A., & Sierociuk, D. (2005). Adaptive feedback control of fractional order discrete state-space systems. *Proceedings of the 2005 International Conference on Computational Intelligence for Modelling, Control and Automation, and International Conference on Intelligent Agents, Web Technologies and Internet Commerce (CIMCA,IAWTIC,05)*, 804-809. 10.1109/CIMCA.2005.1631363

Eckmann, J. P., & Ruelle, D. (1985). Ergodic Theory of chaos and strange Attractors. *Reviews of Modern Physics, 57*(3), 617–656. doi:10.1103/RevModPhys.57.617

Efe, M. Ö. (2008). Fractional fuzzy adaptive sliding-mode control of a 2-DOF direct-drive robot arm. *IEEE Transactions on Systems, Man, and Cybernetics. Part B, Cybernetics, 38*(6), 1561–1570.

Efe, M. O. (2008). Fractional Fuzzy Adaptive Sliding-Mode Control of a 2-DOF Direct-Drive Robot Arm. *IEEE Transactions on Systems, Man, and Cybernetics. Part B, Cybernetics, 38*(6), 1561–1570. doi:10.1109/TSMCB.2008.928227 PMID:19022726

Efe, M. Ö. (2011). Fractional order systems in industrial automation—a survey. *IEEE Transactions on Industrial Informatics, 7*(4), 582–591. doi:10.1109/TII.2011.2166775

Efe, M. Ö., & Kasnakoğlu, C. (2008). A fractional adaptation law for sliding mode control. *International Journal of Adaptive Control and Signal Processing, 22*(10), 968–986. doi:10.1002/acs.1062

Ellner, S., Gallant, A. R., McCaffrey, D., & Nychka, D. (1991). Convergence rates and data requirements for Jacobian-based estimates of Lyapunov exponents from data. *Physics Letters. [Part A], 153*(6), 357–363. doi:10.1016/0375-9601(91)90958-B

Engheta, N. (1997). On the Role of Fractional Calculus in Electromagnetic Theory. *IEEE Transact. on Antennas Propagation, 39*(4), 35-46.

Faieghi, M. R., Naderi, M., & Jalali, A. A. (2011). Design of fractional-order PID for ship roll motion control using chaos embedded PSO algorithm. In *Control, Instrumentation and Automation (ICCIA), 2011 2nd International Conference on Control, Instrumentation and Automation* (pp. 606–610). IEEE. Retrieved from http://ieeexplore.ieee.org/abstract/document/6356727/

Farges, C., Moze, M., & Sabatier, J. (2010). Pseudo-state feedback stabilization of commensurate fractional order systems. *Automatica, 46*(10), 1730–1734. doi:10.1016/j.automatica.2010.06.038

Fridman, E., & Dambrine, M. (2009). Control under quantization, saturation and delay: An LMI approach. *Automatica*, *45*(10), 2258–2264. doi:10.1016/j.automatica.2009.05.020

Fu, Z.-J., Xie, W.-F., & Na, J. (2016). Robust adaptive nonlinear observer design via multi-time scales neural network. *Neurocomputing*, *190*, 217–225. doi:10.1016/j.neucom.2016.01.015

Gallegos, J. A., Duarte-Mermoud, M. A., Aguila-Camacho, N., & Castro-Linares, R. (2015). On fractional extensions of Barbalat Lemma. *Systems & Control Letters*, *84*, 7–12. doi:10.1016/j.sysconle.2015.07.004

Gammoudi, I. E., & Feki, M. (2013). Synchronization of integer order and fractional order Chua's systems using robust observer. *Communications in Nonlinear Science and Numerical Simulation*, *18*(3), 625–638. doi:10.1016/j.cnsns.2012.08.005

Gao, T. G., Chen, G. R., Chen, Z. Q., & Cang, S. (2007). The generation and circuit implementation of a new hyper-chaos based upon Lorenz system. *Physics Letters. [Part A]*, *361*(1), 78–86. doi:10.1016/j.physleta.2006.09.042

Gao, X., & Yu, J. (2005). Chaos in the fractional order periodically forced complex Duffing's oscillators. *Chaos, Solitons, and Fractals*, *24*(4), 1097–1104. doi:10.1016/j.chaos.2004.09.090

Gao, X., & Yu, J. (2005). Synchronization of two coupled fractional-order chaotic oscillators. *Chaos, Solitons, and Fractals*, *26*(1), 141–145. doi:10.1016/j.chaos.2004.12.030

Gao, Y.-F., Sun, X.-M., Wen, C., & Wang, W. (2017). Observer-Based Adaptive NN Control for a Class of Uncertain Nonlinear Systems With Nonsymmetric Input Saturation. *IEEE Transactions on Neural Networks and Learning Systems*, *28*(7), 1520–1530. doi:10.1109/TNNLS.2016.2529843 PMID:28113478

Gao, Y., & Liu, Y. J. (2016). Adaptive fuzzy optimal control using direct heuristic dynamic programming for chaotic discrete-time system. *Journal of Vibration and Control*, *22*(2), 595–603. doi:10.1177/1077546314534286

Gao, Y., Zhang, X., Lu, G., & Zheng, Y. (2011). Impulsive synchronization of discrete-time chaotic systems under communication constraints. *Communications in Nonlinear Science and Numerical Simulation*, *16*(3), 1580–1588. doi:10.1016/j.cnsns.2010.07.002

Geng, L., Yu, Y., & Zhang, S. (2016). Function projective synchronization between integer-order and stochastic fractional-order nonlinear systems. *ISA Transactions*, *64*, 34–46. doi:10.1016/j.isatra.2016.04.018 PMID:27156677

Ge, Z. M., & Chen, Y. S. (2004). Synchronization of unidirectional coupled chaotic systems via partial stability. *Chaos, Solitons, and Fractals*, *21*(1), 101–111. doi:10.1016/j.chaos.2003.10.004

Ge, Z.-M., & Li, S.-Y. (2011). Chaos generalized synchronization of new Mathieu–Vander Pol systems with new Duffing–Van der Pol systems as functional system by GYC partial region stability theory. *Applied Mathematical Modelling*, *35*(11), 5245–5264. doi:10.1016/j.apm.2011.03.022

Ghaderi, R., Hosseinnia, S. H., & Momani, S. (2012). *Control and Synchronization of Chaotic Fractional-Order Coullet System via Active Controller*. arXiv preprint arXiv:1206.2415

Ginarsa, I. M., Soeprijanto, A., & Purnomo, M. H. (2013). Controlling chaos and voltage collapse using an ANFIS-based composite controller-static var compensator in power systems. *International Journal of Electrical Power & Energy Systems*, *46*, 79–88. doi:10.1016/j.ijepes.2012.10.005

Giresse, T. A., & Crépin, K. T. (2017). Chaos generalized synchronization of coupled Mathieu-Van der Pol and coupled Duffing-Van der Pol systems using fractional order-derivative. *Chaos, Solitons, and Fractals*, *98*, 88–100. doi:10.1016/j.chaos.2017.03.012

Gould, H. W. (1981). A history of the Fibonacci Q-matrix and a higher-dimensional problem. *Fibonacci Quart*, *19*(3), 250–257.

Grigorenko, I., & Grigorenko, E. (2003). Chaotic Dynamics of the Fractional Lorenz System. *Physical Review Letters*, *91*(3), 034101. doi:10.1103/PhysRevLett.91.034101 PMID:12906418

Grunwald, A. (1867). Ueber be grenz te Derivationen und deren Anwe dung. *Z. Math. Phys.*, *12*, 441–480.

Guermah, S., Bettayeb, M., & Djennoune, S. (2009). A New Approach for Stability Analysis of Linear Discrete-Time Fractional-Order Systems. In New Trends in Nanotechnology and Fractional Calculus Applications (pp 151-162). Springer Netherlands.

Guermah, S., Bettayeb, M., & Djennoune, S. (2008). Controllability and the observability of linear discrete-time fractional-order systems. *International Journal of Applied Mathematics and Computer Science*, *18*(2), 213–222. doi:10.2478/v10006-008-0019-6

Guo, Y., & Ma, B. (2016). Stabilization of a class of uncertainnonlinear system via fractional sliding mode controller. In *Proceedings of 2016 Chinese Intelligent Systems Conference, Lecture Notes in Electrical Engineering*. Springer. 10.1007/978-981-10-2338-5_34

Guo, T., & Chen, W. (2016). Adaptive Fuzzy Decentralized Fault-Tolerant Control for Uncertain Nonlinear Large-Scale Systems with Unknown Time-Delay. *IET Control Theory & Applications*, *10*(18), 2437–2446. doi:10.1049/iet-cta.2016.0471

Gura, N., Patel, A., Wander, A., Eberle, H., & Shantz, S. C. 2004, August. Comparing elliptic curve cryptography and RSA on 8-bit CPUs. CHES, 4, 119-132.

Habib, M., Mehmood, T., Ullah, F., & Ibrahim, M. 2009, November. Performance of wimax security algorithm (the comparative study of rsa encryption algorithm with ecc encryption algorithm). In *Computer Technology and Development, 2009. ICCTD'09. International Conference on* (vol. 2, pp. 108-112). IEEE.

Haddad, W. M., & Chellaboina, V. S. (2007). *Nonlinear dynamical systems and control: A Lyapunov-based approach*. Princeton University Press.

Hale, J. K. (1997). Diffusive coupling, dissipation, and synchronization. *Journal of Dynamics and Differential Equations*, *9*(1), 1–52. doi:10.1007/BF02219051

Hamamci, S.-E. (2012). Stabilization of fractional-order chaotic system via a single state adaptive-feedback controller. *Nonlinear Dynamics*, *68*(1), 45–51.

Hamel, S., & Boulkroune, A. (2016). A generalized function projective synchronization scheme for uncertain chaotic systems subject to input nonlinearities. *International Journal of General Systems*, *45*(6), 689–710. doi:10.1080/03081079.2015.1118094

Hamiche, H., Ghanes, M., Barbot, J. P., Kemih, K., & Djennoune, S. (2013b). Hybrid dynamical systems for private digital communications. *International Journal of Modeling, Identification and Control*, *20*(2), 99–113. doi:10.1504/IJMIC.2013.056182

Hamiche, H., Guermah, S., Djennoune, S., Kemih, K., Ghanes, M., & Barbot, J.-P. (2013). Chaotic synchronisation and secure communication via sliding-mode and impulsive observers.*International Journal of Modelling. Identification and Control.*, *20*(4), 305–318. doi:10.1504/IJMIC.2013.057564

Hamiche, H., Guermah, S., Saddaoui, R., Hannoune, K., Laghrouche, M., & Djennoune, S. (2015a). Analysis and implementation of a novel robust transmission scheme for private digital communications using Arduino Uno board. *Nonlinear Dynamics*, *81*(4), 1921–1932. doi:10.100711071-015-2116-z

Hamiche, H., Kassim, S., Djennoune, S., Guermah, S., Lahdir, M., & Bettayeb, M. (2015b). Secure data transmission schemebased on fractional-order discrete chaotic system. *International Conference on Control, Engineering and Information Technology (CEIT'2015)*. 10.1109/CEIT.2015.7233065

Hamri, N. (2011). Chaotic Dynamics of the Fractional Order Nonlinear Bloch System. *Electronic Journal of Theoretical Physics*, *8*(25), 233–244.

Han, S., Ha, H., & Lee, J. (2016). Barrier Lyapunov function-based model-free constraint position control for mechanical systems. *Journal of Mechanical Science and Technology*, *30*(7), 3331–3338. doi:10.100712206-016-0642-3

Harsoyo, A. (2007). Weyl's Fractional Operator Expression of Skin Effect of a Good Conductor. In *Proceedings of the International Conference on Electrical Engineering and Informatics*. InstitutTeknologi Bandung, Indonesia.

Hartley, T. T., Lorenzo, C. F., & Qammer, H. K. (1995). Chaos in fractional order Chua's System. *IEEE Transactions on Circuits and Systems. I, Fundamental Theory and Applications*, *42*(8), 485–490. doi:10.1109/81.404062

Hasler, M., Maistrenko, Y., & Popovych, O. (1998). Simple example of partial synchronization of chaotic systems. *Physical Review. E*, *58*(5), 6843–6846. doi:10.1103/PhysRevE.58.6843

Hassard, B. K. (1982). *Theory and Applications of Hopf Bifurcation*. Cambridge, UK: Cambridge University Press.

Heaviside, O. (1971). *Electromagnetic Theory*. New York: Chelsea Pub. Co.

He, S. B., Sun, K. H., & Wang, H. H. (2015). Complexity analysis and DSP implementation of the fractional-order Lorenz hyperchaotic system. *Entropy (Basel, Switzerland)*, *17*(12), 8299–8311. doi:10.3390/e17127882

He, S. B., Sun, K. H., & Wang, H. H. (2016). Solution and dynamics analysis of a fractional-order hyperchaotic system. *Mathematical Methods in the Applied Sciences*, *39*(11), 2965–2973. doi:10.1002/mma.3743

He, S. B., Sun, K. H., & Wang, H. H. (2016). Synchronisation of fractional-order time delayed chaotic systems with ring connection. *The European Physical Journal. Special Topics*, *225*(1), 97–106. doi:10.1140/epjst/e2016-02610-3

He, S. B., Sun, K. H., & Zhu, C. X. (2013). Complexity analyses of multi-wing chaotic systems. *Chinese Physics B*, *22*(5), 050506. doi:10.1088/1674-1056/22/5/050506

He, W., David, A. O., Yin, Z., & Sun, C. (2016). Neural Network Control of a Robotic Manipulator With Input Deadzone and Output Constraint. *IEEE Transactions on Systems, Man, and Cybernetics. Systems*, *46*(6), 759–770. doi:10.1109/TSMC.2015.2466194

He, W., Yin, Z., & Sun, C. (2017). Adaptive Neural Network Control of a Marine Vessel With Constraints Using the Asymmetric Barrier Lyapunov Function. *IEEE Transactions on Cybernetics*, *47*(7), 1641–1651. doi:10.1109/TCYB.2016.2554621

Hilfer, R. (2000). *Applications of Fractional Calculus in Physics*. Singapore: World Scientific Publishing. doi:10.1142/3779

Hilfer, R. (2001). *Applications of fractional calculus in physics*. World Scientific.

Hirsch, M. M. (1974). *Differential Equations: Dynamical Systems and Linear Algebra*. New York: Academic Press.

Hoggat Koshy, T. (2011). *Fibonacci and Lucas numbers with applications*. John Wiley & Sons.

Ho, H. F., Wong, Y. K., & Rad, A. B. (2009). Adaptive fuzzy sliding mode control with chattering elimination for nonlinear SISO systems. *Simulation Modelling Practice and Theory*, *17*(7), 1199–1210. doi:10.1016/j.simpat.2009.04.004

Holzfuss, J., & Lauterborn, W. (1989). Lyapunov Exponents from a Time Series of Acoustic Chaos. *Physical Review A.*, *39*(4), 2146–2152. doi:10.1103/PhysRevA.39.2146 PMID:9901470

HosseinNia, S. H. (2010). Control of chaos via fractional order state feedback controller. In New trends in nanotechnology and fractional calculus applications. Berlin: Springer-Verlag.

Hosseinnia, S. H., Ghaderi, R., Ranjbar, A., Abdous, F., & Momani, S. (2010). *Control of Chaos via Fractional-Order State Feedback Controller: New Trends in Nanotechnology and Fractional Calculus Applications*. Springer Verlag-Berlin. doi:10.1007/978-90-481-3293-5_46

Hosseinnia, S., Ghaderi, R., Mahmoudian, M., & Momani, S. (2010). Sliding mode synchronization of an uncertain fractional order chaotic system. *Computers & Mathematics with Applications (Oxford, England)*, *59*(5), 1637–1643. doi:10.1016/j.camwa.2009.08.021

Huang, L., Wang, L., & Shi, D. (2016). Discrete fractional order chaotic systems synchronization based on the variable structure control with a new discrete reaching-law. *IEEE/CAA Journal of Automatica Sinica*. doi:10.1109/JAS.2016.7510148

Huang, X., Wang, Z., Li, Y., & Lu, J. (2014). Design of fuzzy state feedback controller for robust stabilization of uncertain fractional-order chaotic systems. *Journal of the Franklin Institute*, *351*(12), 5480–5493. doi:10.1016/j.jfranklin.2014.09.023

Huang, Y. J., Kuo, T. C., & Chang, S. H. (2008). Adaptive Sliding-Mode Control for NonlinearSystems with Uncertain Parameters. *IEEE Transactions on Systems, Man, and Cybernetics. Part B, Cybernetics*, *38*(2), 534–539. doi:10.1109/TSMCB.2007.910740 PMID:18348934

Hwang, E., Hyun, C., Kim, E., & Park, M. (2009). Fuzzy model based adaptive synchronization of uncertain chaotic systems: Robust tracking control approach. *Physics Letters. [Part A]*, *373*(22), 1935–1939. doi:10.1016/j.physleta.2009.03.057

Ibeas, A., & DelaSen, M. (2007). Robust Sliding Control of Robotic Manipulators Based on a Heuristic Modification of the Sliding Gain. *Journal of Intelligent & Robotic Systems*, *48*(4), 485–511. doi:10.100710846-006-9124-7

Ichise, M., Nagayanagi, Y., & Kojima, T. (1971). An analog simulation of non-integer order transfer functions for analysis of electrode process. *Journal of Electroanalytical Chemistry and Interfacial Electrochemistry*, *33*(2), 253–265. doi:10.1016/S0022-0728(71)80115-8

Illing, L., Gauthier, D. J., & Roy, R. (2007). Controlling optical chaos, spatio-temporal dynamics, and patterns. *Advances in Atomic, Molecular, and Optical Physics*, *54*, 615–697. doi:10.1016/S1049-250X(06)54010-8

Ioannou, P. A., & Sun, J. (1996). *Robust adaptive control*. Englewood Cliffs, NJ: Prentice Hall.

Iqbal, M., Rehan, M., Hong, K. S., Khaliq, A., & Saeed-ur-Rehman. (2015). Sector-condition based results for adaptive control and synchronization of chaotic systems under input saturation. *Chaos, Solitons, and Fractals*, *77*, 158–169. doi:10.1016/j.chaos.2015.05.021

Isermann, R., & Münchhof, M. (2011). *Identification of dynamic systems: An introduction with applications*. Springer-Verlag Berlin Heidelberg. doi:10.1007/978-3-540-78879-9

Ishteva, M., Boyadjiev, L., & Scherer, R. (2005). On the Caputo operator of fractional calculus and C-Laguerre functions. *Mathematical Sciences Research Journal*, *9*(6), 161.

Jafari, H., & Daftardar-Gejji, V. (2006). Positive solutions of nonlinear fractional boundary value problems using Adomian decomposition method. *Applied Mathematics and Computation*, *180*(2), 700–706. doi:10.1016/j.amc.2006.01.007

Jafrasteh, B., & Fathianpour, N. (2017). A hybrid simultaneous perturbation artificial bee colony and back-propagation algorithm for training a local linear radial basis neural network on ore grade estimation. *Neurocomputing*, *235*, 217–227. doi:10.1016/j.neucom.2017.01.016

Jenson, V. G., & Jeffreys, G. V. (1977). *Mathematical Methods in Chemical Engineering*. London: Academic Press.

Jesus, I. S., Machado, J. A. T., & Cunha, J. B. (2006).Application of genetic algorithms to the implementation of fractional electromagnetic potentials. *Proceedings of The Fifth International Conference on Engineering Computational Technology (ECT'06)*. 10.4203/ccp.84.58

Jiang, J. A., Yang, J. Z., Lin, Y. H., Liu, C. W., & Ma, J. C. (2000). An adaptive PMU based fault detection/location technique for transmission lines. I. Theory and algorithms. *IEEE Transactions on Power Delivery*, *15*(2), 486–493. doi:10.1109/61.852973

Jiang, W., & Ma, T. (2013). Synchronization of a class of fractional-order chaotic systems via adaptive sliding mode control. In *Proceedings of the Int. IEEE Conf. Vehicular Electronics and Safety (ICVES)* (pp. 229-233). Dongguan, China: IEEE. 10.1109/ICVES.2013.6619637

Jing, C. G., He, P., Fan, T., Li, Y., Chen, C., & Song, X. (2015). Single state feedback stabilization of unified chaotic systems and circuit implementation. *Open Physics*, *13*, 111–122.

Kadir, A., Wang, X. Y., & Zhao, Y.-Z. (2011). Robust adaptive fuzzy neural tracking control for a class of unknown chaotic systems. *Pramana – Journal of Physics*, *76*(6), 887–900.

Karnik, N. N., & Mendel, J. M. (1998). Type-2 fuzzy logic systems: type-reduction. *Proceedings of the IEEE International Conference on Systems, Man, and Cybernetics*, 2046-2051.

Karnik, N. N., Mendel, J. M., & Liang, Q. (1999). Type-2 fuzzy logic systems. *IEEE Transactions on Fuzzy Systems*, *7*(6), 643–658. doi:10.1109/91.811231

Karthikeyan, R., & Sundarapandian, V. (2014). Hybrid Chaos Synchronization of Four–Scroll Systems via Active Control. *Journal of Electrical Engineering*, *65*(2), 97–103. doi:10.2478/jee-2014-0014

Kassim, S., Hamiche, H., Djennoune, S., & Bettayeb, M. (2017). A novel secure image transmission scheme based on synchronization of fractional-order discrete-time hyperchaotic systems. *Nonlinear Dynamics*, *88*(4), 2473–2489. doi:10.100711071-017-3390-8

Kassim, S., Hamiche, H., Djennoune, S., Megherbi, O., & Bettayeb, M. (2016). A novel robust image transmission scheme based on fractional-order discrete chaotic systems. *International Workshop on Cryptography and its Applications (IWCA)*.

Kaveh, A. (2014). *Advances in Metaheuristic Algorithms for Optimal Design of Structures*. Springer.

Khettab, K., Bensafia, Y., & Ladaci, S. (2017). Robust Adaptive Fuzzy Control for a Class of Uncertain Nonlinear Fractional Systems. In Lecture Notes in Electrical Engineering: Vol. 411. Recent Advances in Electrical Engineering and Control Applications. Springer International Publishing.

Khettab, K., Bensafia, Y., & Ladaci, S. (2017). Robust Adaptive Fuzzy Control for a Classof Uncertain Nonlinear Fractional Systems. In Recent Advances in Electrical Engineering and Control Applications. Springer.

Khettab, K., Ladaci, S., & Bensafia, Y. (2017). Fuzzy adaptive control of fractional order chaotic systems with unknown control gain sign using a fractional order Nussbaum gain. *IEEE/CAA Journal of Automatica Sinica, 4*(4). DOI: 10.1109/JAS.2016.7510169

Khettab, K., Ladaci, S., & Bensafia, Y.(2016) Fuzzy adaptive control of a fractional order chaotic system with unknown control gain sign using a fractional order nussbaum gain. *IEEE/CAA Journal of Automatica Sinica, 1*-8.

Khettab, Ladaci, & Bensafia. (2017). Fuzzy adaptive control of fractional order chaotic systems with unknown control gain sign using a fractional order Nussbaum gain. IEEE/CAA Journal of Automatica Sinica, 4(3), 1-8.

Khettab, K., Bensafia, Y., & Ladaci, S. (2014). Robust Adaptive Fuzzy control for a Class of Uncertain nonlinear Fractional Systems. *Proceedings of the Second International Conference on Electrical Engineering and Control Applications ICEECA'2014.*

Khettab, K., Bensafia, Y., & Ladaci, S. (2015). Fuzzy adaptive control enhancement for non-affine systems with unknown control gain sign. *Proc. 16th Int. IEEE Conf. on Sciences and Techniques of Automatic control and computer engineering, STA'2015*, 616-621. 10.1109/STA.2015.7505141

Khettab, K., Bensafia, Y., & Ladaci, S. (2017). Robust Adaptive Interval Type-2 Fuzzy Synchronization for a Class of Fractional Order Chaotic Systems. In A. T. Azar & ... (Eds.), *Fractional Order Control and Synchronization of Chaotic Systems, Series: Studies in Computational Intelligence 688* (pp. 203–224). Springer-Verlag Germany. doi:10.1007/978-3-319-50249-6_7

Khettab, K., Bensafia, Y., & Ladaci, S. (2017d). Chattering Elimination in Fuzzy Sliding Mode Control of Fractional Chaotic Systems Using a Fractional Adaptive Proportional Integral Controller. *International Journal of Intelligent Engineering and Systems*, *10*(5), 255–265. doi:10.22266/ijies2017.1031.28

Kiani, B. A., Fallahi, K., Pariz, N., & Leung, H. (2009). A chaotic secure communication scheme using fractional chaotic systemsbased on an extended fractional Kalman filter. *Communications in Nonlinear Science and Numerical Simulation*, *14*(3), 863–879. doi:10.1016/j.cnsns.2007.11.011

Kilbas, A. A., Srivastava, H. M., & Trujillo, J. J. (2006). *Theory and application of fractional differential equations*. Amsterdam: Editor Elsevier.

Kilbas, A. A., Srivastava, H. M., & Trujillo, J. J. (2006). *Theory and applications of fractional differential equations* (1st ed.). Amsterdam: Elsevier.

Kocarev, L., Amato, P., Ruggiero, D., & Pedaci, I. 2004. Discrete Lyapunov exponent for Rijndael block cipher. *Proc. 2004 International Symposium on Nonlinear Theory and its Applications (NOLTA 2004)*, 609-612.

Kocarev, L., & Parlitz, U. (1996). Generalized synchronization, predictability, and equivalence of unidirectionally coupled dynamical systems. *Physical Review Letters*, *76*(11), 1816–1819. doi:10.1103/PhysRevLett.76.1816 PMID:10060528

Kolumban, G., & Kennedy, M. P. (2000). Communications using chaos/spl Gt/MINUS. III. Performance bounds for correlation receivers. *IEEE Transactions on Circuits and Systems. I, Fundamental Theory and Applications*, *47*(12), 1673–1683. doi:10.1109/81.899919

Korsch, H. J., Jodl, H. J., & Hartmann, T. (2008). Chaos A Program Collection for the PC (3rd ed.). Academic Press.

Kulish, V., & Jose, L. (2002). Lage application of fractional calculus to fluid mechanics. *Journal of Fluids Engineering*, *124*(3), 803–806. doi:10.1115/1.1478062

Kuntanapreeda, S. (2015). Tensor product model transformation based control and synchronization of a class of fractional-order chaotic systems. *Asian Journal of Control*, *17*(2), 371–38. doi:10.1002/asjc.839

Kwan, C., & Lewis, F. L. (2000). Robust backstepping control nonlinear systems using neural networks. *IEEE Transactions on Systems, Man, and Cybernetics. Part A, Systems and Humans*, *30*(6), 753–766. doi:10.1109/3468.895898

Ladaci, S., & Bensafia, Y. (2015). Fractional order Self-Tuning Control. In *Proceedings of the IEEE 13th International Conference on Industrial Informatics (INDIN'15)* (pp. 544-549). Cambridge, UK: IEEE. 10.1109/INDIN.2015.7281792

Ladaci, S., & Bensafia, Y. (2016). Indirect fractional order pole assignment based adaptive control. *Engineering Science and Technology, an International Journal*, *19*(1), 518–530.

Ladaci, S., & Bensafia, Y. (2016). Indirect fractional order pole assignment based adaptive control. *Engineering Science and Technology, an International Journal, 19*, 518-530.

Ladaci, S., & Charef, A. (2012). Fractional order adaptive control systems: A survey. In Classification and Application of Fractals. Nova Science Publishers, Inc.

Ladaci, S., &Bensafia, Y. (2016). Indirect fractional order pole assignment based adaptive control. *Engineering Science and Technology, an International Journal, 19*(1), 518–530.

Ladaci, S., Assabaa, M., & Charef, A. (2009).Fractional Order Integro-differential Adaptive Control. *10th Int. Conf. on Sciences and Techniques of Automatic Control and Computer Engineering, STA'2009*, 181–188.

Ladaci, S., & Charef, A. (2002). Commande adaptative à modèle de référence d'ordre fractionnaire d'un bras de robot. (in French) Communication Sciences & Technologie. *ENSET Oran, Algeria., 1*, 50–52.

Ladaci, S., & Charef, A. (2006). An Adaptive Fractional PIλDμ Controller. *Proceedings of the Sixth Int. Symposium on Tools and Methods of Competitive Engineering, TMCE 2006*, 1533-1540.

Ladaci, S., & Charef, A. (2006). On Fractional Adaptive Control. *Nonlinear Dynamics, 43*(4), 365–378. doi:10.100711071-006-0159-x

Ladaci, S., Charef, A., & Loiseau, J. J. (2009). Robust fractional adaptive control based on the strictly positive realness condition. *International Journal of Applied Mathematics and Computer Science, 19*(1), 69–76. doi:10.2478/v10006-009-0006-6

Ladaci, S., & Khettab, K. (2012). Fractional Order Multiple Model Adaptive Control. *International Journal of Automation & Systems Engineering, 6*(2), 110–122.

Ladaci, S., Loiseau, J. J., & Charef, A. (2008). Fractional Order Adaptive High-Gain Controllers for a Class of Linear Systems. *Communications in Nonlinear Science and Numerical Simulation, 13*(4), 707–714. doi:10.1016/j.cnsns.2006.06.009

Ladaci, S., Loiseau, J. J., & Charef, A. (2010). Adaptive Internal Model Control with Fractional Order Parameter. *International Journal of Adaptive Control and Signal Processing, 24*(11), 944–960. doi:10.1002/acs.1175

Ladaci, S., & Moulay, E. (2008). Lp-stability analysis of a class of nonlinear fractional differential equations. *Journal of Automation and Systems Engineering, 2*(1), 40–46.

Lai, G., Liu, Z., Zhang, Y., Chen, C. L. P., Xie, S., & Liu, Y.-J. (2017). Fuzzy Adaptive Inverse Compensation Method to Tracking Control of Uncertain Nonlinear Systems With Generalized Actuator Dead Zone. *IEEE Transactions on Fuzzy Systems, 25*(1), 191–204. doi:10.1109/TFUZZ.2016.2554152

Lamb, D., Chamon, L. F. O., & Nascimento, V. H. (2016). Efficient filtering structure for Spline interpolation and decimation. *Electronics Letters, 52*(1), 39–41. doi:10.1049/el.2015.1957

Lan, Y.-H., Huang, H.-X., & Zhou, Y. (2012). Observer-based robust control of a ($1 \leq a < 2$) fractional-order uncertain systems: A linear matrix inequality approach. *IET Control Theory & Applications, 6*(2), 229–234. doi:10.1049/iet-cta.2010.0484

Lan, Y.-H., & Zhou, Y. (2013). Non-fragile observer-based robust control for a class of fractional-order nonlinear systems. *Systems & Control Letters, 62*(12), 1143–1150. doi:10.1016/j.sysconle.2013.09.007

Larrondo, H. A., González, C. M., Martin, M. T., Plastino, A., & Rosso, O. A. (2005). Intensive statistical complexity measure of pseudorandom number generators. *Physica A, 356*(1), 133–138. doi:10.1016/j.physa.2005.05.025

Lashab, M., Ladaci, S., Abdelliche, F., Zebiri, C., & Benabdelaziz, F. (2010). Fractional spline wavelet for numerical analysis in electromagnetic. In *Proceedings of the International Multi-Conference on Systems Signals and Devices (SSD)*. Amman, Jordan: Academic Press. 10.1109/SSD.2010.5585573

Lazarević, M.-P., & Spasić, A.-M. (2009). Finite-time stability analysis of fractional order time-delay systems: Gronwall's approach. *Mathematical and Computer Modelling*, *94*(3-4), 475–481. doi:10.1016/j.mcm.2008.09.011

Lian, S., Sun, J., & Wang, Z. (2005). A block cipher based on a suitable use of the chaotic standard map. *Chaos, Solitons, and Fractals*, *26*(1), 117–129. doi:10.1016/j.chaos.2004.11.096

Li, C. L., Han, Q. T., & Xiong, J. B. (2016). Linear control for mixed synchronization of a fractional-order chaotic system. *Optik-International Journal for Light and Electron Optics*, *127*(15), 6129–6133. doi:10.1016/j.ijleo.2016.04.105

Li, C. L., Xiong, J. B., & Li, W. (2014). A new hyperchaotic system and its generalized synchronization. *Optik-International Journal for Light and Electron Optics*, *125*(1), 575–579. doi:10.1016/j.ijleo.2013.07.013

Li, C., & Chen, G. (2004). Chaos and hyperchaos in the fractional-order Rössler equations. *Physica A*, *341*(1–4), 55–61. doi:10.1016/j.physa.2004.04.113

Li, C., & Chen, G. (2004b). Chaos in the fractional order Chen system and its control. *Chaos, Solitons, and Fractals*, *22*(3), 549–554. doi:10.1016/j.chaos.2004.02.035

Li, C., & Deng, W. H. (2006). Chaos synchronization of fractional order differential systems. *International Journal of Modern Physics B*, *20*(07), 791–803. doi:10.1142/S0217979206033620

Li, C., Gong, Z., Qian, D., & Chen, Y. Q. (2010). On the bound of the Lyapunov exponents for the fractional differential systems. *Chaos (Woodbury, N.Y.)*, *20*(1), 013127. doi:10.1063/1.3314277 PMID:20370282

Li, C., & Peng, G. (2004). Chaos in Chen's system with a fractional order. *Chaos, Solitons, and Fractals*, *22*(2), 443–450. doi:10.1016/j.chaos.2004.02.013

Li, C., Su, K., Zhang, J., & Wei, D. (2013). Robust control for fractional-order four-wing hyperchaotic system using LMI. *Optik-International Journal for Light and Electron Optics*, *124*(22), 5807–5810. doi:10.1016/j.ijleo.2013.04.054

Li, C., & Tong, Y. (2013). Adaptive control and synchronization of a fractional-order chaotic system. *Pramana Journal of Physics*, *80*(4), 583–592. doi:10.100712043-012-0500-5

Li, C., & Wang, J. (2014). Robust adaptive observer for fractional order nonlinear systems: an LMI approach. In *Control and Decision Conference (2014 CCDC), The 26th Chinese* (pp. 392-397). IEEE. 10.1109/CCDC.2014.6852179

Li, D.-J., Li, J., & Li, S. (2016). Adaptive control of nonlinear systems with full state constraints using Integral Barrier Lyapunov Functionals. *Neurocomputing*, *186*, 90–96. doi:10.1016/j.neucom.2015.12.075

Li, G. H. (2006). Projective synchronization of chaotic system using backstepping control. *Chaos, Solitons, and Fractals*, *29*(2), 490–598. doi:10.1016/j.chaos.2005.08.029

Li, H., Bai, L., Wang, L., Zhou, Q., & Wang, H. (2017). Adaptive Neural Control of Uncertain Nonstrict-Feedback Stochastic Nonlinear Systems with Output Constraint and Unknown Dead Zone. *IEEE Transactions on Systems, Man, and Cybernetics. Systems*, *47*(8), 2048–2059. doi:10.1109/TSMC.2016.2605706

Li, H., Wang, J., Lam, H. K., Zhou, Q., & Du, H. (2016a). Adaptive sliding mode control for interval type-2 fuzzy systems. *IEEE Transactions on Systems, Man, and Cybernetics. Systems*, *46*(12), 1654–1663. doi:10.1109/TSMC.2016.2531676

Li, L., & Sun, Y. (2015). Adaptive Fuzzy Control for Nonlinear Fractional-Order Uncertain Systems with Unknown Uncertainties and External Disturbance. *Entropy (Basel, Switzerland)*, *17*(12), 5580–5592. doi:10.3390/e17085580

Li-Ming, W., Yong-Guang, T., Yong-Quan, C., & Feng, W. (2014). Generalized projective synchronization of the fractional-order chaotic system using adaptive fuzzy sliding mode control. *Chinese Physics B, 23*(10), 100501. doi:10.1088/1674-1056/23/10/100501

Lim, Y.-H., Oh, K.-K., & Ahn, H.-S. (2013). Stability and Stabilization of Fractional-Order Linear Systems Subject to Input Saturation. *IEEE Transactions on Automatic Control, 58*(4), 1062–1067. doi:10.1109/TAC.2012.2218064

Lin, T. C., Kuo, C. H., & Balas, V. E. (2011). Uncertain Fractional Order Chaotic Systems Tracking Design via Adaptive Hybrid Fuzzy Sliding Mode Control. I*nt. J. of Computers, Communications & Control, 6*(3), 418-427.

Lin, T. C., Kuo, M. J., & Hsu, C. H. (2010). Robust Adaptive Tracking Control of Multivariable Nonlinear Systems Based on Interval Type-2 Fuzzy approach. *International Journal of Innovative Computing, Information, & Control, 6*(1), 941–961.

Lin, T. C., & Lee, T. Y. (2011). Chaos synchronization of uncertain fractional-order chaotic systems with time delay based on adaptive fuzzy sliding mode control. *IEEE Transactions on Fuzzy Systems, 19*(4), 623–635. doi:10.1109/TFUZZ.2011.2127482

Lin, T. C., Lee, T. Y., & Balas, V. E. (2011). Adaptive fuzzy sliding mode control for synchronization of uncertain fractional order chaotic systems. *Chaos, Solitons, and Fractals, 44*(10), 791–801. doi:10.1016/j.chaos.2011.04.005

Lin, T. C., Lee, T.-Y., & Balas, V. E. (2011). Synchronization of Uncertain Fractional Order Chaotic Systems via Adaptive Interval Type-2 Fuzzy Sliding Mode Control. *Proceedings of the IEEE International Conference on Fuzzy Systems.* 10.1109/FUZZY.2011.6007354

Lin, T. C., Liu, H. L., & Kuo, M. J. (2009). Direct adaptive interval type-2 fuzzy control of multivariable nonlinear systems. *Engineering Applications of Artificial Intelligence, 22*(3), 420–430. doi:10.1016/j.engappai.2008.10.024

Lin, T.-C., Chen, M.-C., Roopaei, M., & Sahraei, B. R. (2010). Adaptive type-2 fuzzy sliding mode control for chaos synchronization of uncertain chaotic systems. *Proceedings of the IEEE International Conference on Fuzzy Systems (FUZZ).* 10.1109/FUZZY.2010.5584444

Lin, T.-C., & Kuo, C. H. (2011). synchronization of uncertain fractional order chaotic systems: Adaptive fuzzy approach. *ISA Transactions, 50*(4), 548–556. doi:10.1016/j.isatra.2011.06.001 PMID:21741648

Li, R., & Chen, W. (2014). Lyapunov-based fractional-order controller design to synchronize a class of fractional-order chaotic systems. *Nonlinear Dynamics, 76*(1), 785–795. doi:10.100711071-013-1169-0

Li, T., Wang, Y., & Yang, Y. (2014). Designing synchronization schemes for fractional-order chaotic system via a single state fractional-order controller. *International Journal for Light and Electron Optics, 125*(22), 6700–6705. doi:10.1016/j.ijleo.2014.07.087

Liu, B., & Marquez, H. J. (2008). Uniform stability of discrete delay systems and synchronization of discrete delay dynamical networks via Razumikhin Thechnique. *IEEE Transactions on Circuits and Systems. I, Regular Papers, 55*(9), 2795–2805. doi:10.1109/TCSI.2008.923163

Liu, H., Li, S. G., Sun, Y. G., & Wang, H. X. (2015a). Adaptive fuzzy synchronization for uncertain fractional-order chaotic systems with unknown non-symmetrical control gain. *Acta Physica Sinica, 64*(7), 070503.

Liu, H., Li, S. G., Wang, H. X., & Li, G. J. (2017a). Adaptive fuzzy synchronization for a class of fractional-order neural networks. *Chinese Physics B, 26*(3), 030504. doi:10.1088/1674-1056/26/3/030504

Liu, H., Li, S., Cao, J., Li, G., Alsaedi, A., & Alsaadi, F. E. (2017b). Adaptive fuzzy prescribed performance controller design for a class of uncertain fractional-order nonlinear systems with external disturbances. *Neurocomputing*, *219*, 422–430. doi:10.1016/j.neucom.2016.09.050

Liu, H., Li, S.-G., Sun, Y.-G., & Wang, H.-X. (2015b). Prescribed performance synchronization for fractional-order chaotic systems. *Chinese Physics B*, *24*(9), 090505. doi:10.1088/1674-1056/24/9/090505

Liu, H., Li, S., Wang, H., Huo, Y., & Luo, J. (2015c). Adaptive synchronization for a class of uncertain fractional-order neural networks. *Entropy (Basel, Switzerland)*, *17*(10), 7185–7200. doi:10.3390/e17107185

Liu, H., Pan, Y., Li, S., & Chen, Y. (2017c). Adaptive fuzzy backstepping control of fractional-order nonlinear systems. *IEEE Transactions on Systems, Man, and Cybernetics. Systems*, *47*(8), 2209–2217. doi:10.1109/TSMC.2016.2640950

Liu, K., & Jiang, W. (2013a). Uniform stability of fractional neutral systems: A Lyapunov-Krasovskii functional approach. *Advances in Difference Equations*, *2013*(1), 379. doi:10.1186/1687-1847-2013-379

Liu, S., Jiang, W., Li, X., & Zhou, X. F. (2016b). Lyapunov stability analysis of fractional nonlinear systems. *Applied Mathematics Letters*, *51*, 13–19. doi:10.1016/j.aml.2015.06.018

Liu, X. (2016). Optimization design on fractional order PID controllerbased on adaptive particle swarm optimization algorithm. *Nonlinear Dynamics*, *84*(1), 379–386. doi:10.100711071-015-2553-8

Liu, Y. J., Gao, Y., Tong, S., & Li, Y. (2016a). Fuzzy Approximation-Based Adaptive Backstepping Optimal Control for a Class of Nonlinear Discrete-Time Systems With Dead-Zone. *IEEE Transactions on Fuzzy Systems*, *24*(1), 16–28. doi:10.1109/TFUZZ.2015.2418000

Liu, Y. J., & Tong, S. (2013b). Adaptive Fuzzy Control for a Class of Nonlinear Discrete-Time Systems with Backlash. *IEEE Transactions on Fuzzy Systems*, *22*(5), 1359–1365. doi:10.1109/TFUZZ.2013.2286837

Liu, Y. J., & Tong, S. (2014). Adaptive Fuzzy Identification and Control for a Class of Nonlinear Pure-Feedback MIMO Systems with Unknown Dead Zones. *IEEE Transactions on Fuzzy Systems*, *23*(5), 1387–1398. doi:10.1109/TFUZZ.2014.2360954

Liu, Y. J., & Tong, S. (2015b). Adaptive fuzzy control for a class of unknown nonlinear dynamical systems. *Fuzzy Sets and Systems*, *263*, 49–70. doi:10.1016/j.fss.2014.08.008

Liu, Y. J., & Tong, S. (2016). Barrier Lyapunov Functions-based adaptive control for a class of nonlinear pure-feedback systems with full state constraints. *Automatica*, *64*, 70–75. doi:10.1016/j.automatica.2015.10.034

Liu, Y. J., & Tong, S. (2017). Barrier Lyapunov functions for Nussbaum gain adaptive control of full state constrained nonlinear systems. *Automatica*, *76*, 143–152. doi:10.1016/j.automatica.2016.10.011

Liu, Y. J., & Zheng, Y. Q. (2009). Adaptive robust fuzzy control for a class of uncertain chaotic systems. *Nonlinear Dynamics*, *57*(3), 431–439. doi:10.100711071-008-9453-0

Liu, Y.-H., Huang, L., Xiao, D., & Guo, Y. (2015a). Global adaptive control for uncertain nonaffine nonlinear hysteretic systems. *ISA Transactions*, *58*, 255–261. doi:10.1016/j.isatra.2015.06.010 PMID:26169122

Liu, Y.-J., Tong, S., Chen, C. L. P., & Li, D.-J. (2017). Adaptive NN Control Using Integral Barrier Lyapunov Functionals for Uncertain Nonlinear Block-Triangular Constraint Systems. *IEEE Transactions on Cybernetics*, *47*(11), 3747–3757. doi:10.1109/TCYB.2016.2581173 PMID:27662691

Li, X.-J., & Yang, G.-H. (2016). FLS-Based Adaptive Synchronization Control of Complex Dynamical Networks With Nonlinear Couplings and State-Dependent Uncertainties. *IEEE Transactions on Cybernetics*, *46*(1), 171–180. doi:10.1109/TCYB.2015.2399334 PMID:25720020

Li, Y., Chen, Y. Q., & Podlubny, I. (2009). Mittag–Leffler stability of fractional order nonlinear dynamic systems. *Automatica*, *45*(8), 1965–1969. doi:10.1016/j.automatica.2009.04.003

Li, Y., Chen, Y., & Podlubny, I. (2010). Stability of fractional-order nonlinear dynamic systems: Lyapunov direct method and generalized Mittag–Leffler stability. *Computers & Mathematics with Applications (Oxford, England)*, *59*(5), 1810–1821. doi:10.1016/j.camwa.2009.08.019

Li, Y., & Li, J. (2014). Stability analysis of fractional order systems based on T-S fuzzy model with the fractional order α: $0 < α < 1$. *Nonlinear Dynamics*, *78*(4), 2909–2919. doi:10.100711071-014-1635-3

Li, Y., & Tong, S. (2016b). Adaptive fuzzy output-feedback stabilization control for a class of switched nonstrict-feedback nonlinear systems. *IEEE Transactions on Cybernetics*, *47*(4), 1007–1016. doi:10.1109/TCYB.2016.2536628 PMID:26992190

Li, Y., Tong, S., & Li, T. (2013). Direct adaptive fuzzy backstepping control of uncertain nonlinear systems in the presence of input saturation. *Neural Computing & Applications*, *23*(5), 1207–1216. doi:10.100700521-012-0993-3

Li, Y., Tong, S., & Li, T. (2015a). Observer-Based Adaptive Fuzzy Tracking Control of MIMO Stochastic Nonlinear Systems with Unknown Control Directions and Unknown Dead Zones. *IEEE Transactions on Fuzzy Systems*, *23*(4), 1228–1241. doi:10.1109/TFUZZ.2014.2348017

Li, Y., Tong, S., & Li, T. (2015b). Hybrid Fuzzy Adaptive Output Feedback Control Design for MIMO Time-Varying Delays Uncertain Nonlinear Systems. *IEEE Transactions on Fuzzy Systems*. doi:10.1109/TFUZZ.2015.2486811

Li, Y., Tong, S., & Li, T. (2015c). Composite Adaptive Fuzzy Output Feedback Control Design for Uncertain Nonlinear Strict-Feedback Systems with Input Saturation. *IEEE Transactions on Cybernetics*, *45*(10), 2299–2308. doi:10.1109/TCYB.2014.2370645 PMID:25438335

Li, Z., Santi, F., Pastina, D., & Lombardo, P. (2017). Passive Radar Array With Low-Power Satellite Illuminators Based on Fractional Fourier Transform. *IEEE Sensors Journal*, *17*(24), 8378–8394. doi:10.1109/JSEN.2017.2765079

Li, Z., & Xu, D. (2004). A secure communication scheme using projective chaos synchronization. *Chaos, Solitons, and Fractals*, *22*(2), 477–481. doi:10.1016/j.chaos.2004.02.019

Lorenz, E. (1963). Deterministic Nonperiodic Flow. *Journal of the Atmospheric Sciences*, *20*(2), 130–141. doi:10.1175/1520-0469(1963)020<0130:DNF2.0.CO;2

Lu, J. C., Chen, G., Yu, X., & Leung, H. (2004). Design and Analysis of Multi-Scroll Chaotic Attractors from Saturated Function Series. *IEEE Transactions on Circuits and Systems*, *12*(51), 2476–2490. doi:10.1109/TCSI.2004.838151

Lu, J. G. (2005). Chaotic dynamics and synchronization of fractional-order Arneodo's systems. *Chaos, Solitons, and Fractals*, *26*(4), 1125–1133. doi:10.1016/j.chaos.2005.02.023

Lu, J. G. (2006). Chaotic dynamics of the fractional-order Lü system and its synchronization. *Physics Letters. [Part A]*, *354*(4), 305–311. doi:10.1016/j.physleta.2006.01.068

Lu, J. G., & Chen, G. (2006). A note on the fractional-order Chen system. *Chaos, Solitons, and Fractals*, *27*(3), 685–688. doi:10.1016/j.chaos.2005.04.037

Lu, J., Wu, X., Han, X., & Lü, J. (2004). Adaptive feedback synchronization of a unified chaotic system. *Physics Letters. [Part A]*, *329*(4), 327–333. doi:10.1016/j.physleta.2004.07.024

Luo, J., & Liu, H. (2014). Adaptive Fractional Fuzzy Sliding Mode Control for Multivariable Nonlinear Systems. *Discrete Dynamics in Nature and Society*.

Machado, J. T., Kiryakova, V., & Mainardi, F. (2011). Recent history of fractional calculus. *Communications in Nonlinear Science and Numerical Simulation*, *16*(3), 1140–1153. doi:10.1016/j.cnsns.2010.05.027

Mandelbrot, B., & Van Ness, J. W. (1968). Fractional Brownian motions, fractional noises and applications. *SIAM Review*, *10*(4), 422–437. doi:10.1137/1010093

Ma, S., Xu, Y., & Yue, W. (2012). Numerical solutions of a variable-order fractional financial system. *Journal of Applied Mathematics*.

Matignon, D. (1996). Stability result on fractional differential equations with applications to control processing. In IMACS-SMC proceedings (pp. 963-968). Lille.

Matignon, D. (1996, July). Stability results for fractional differential equations with applications to control processing. In Proceeding of Computational engineering in systems applications (vol. 2, pp. 963-968). Lille, France: IMACS, IEEE-SMC.

Matignon, D. (1996). Stability results for fractional differential equations with applications to control processing. *Proceedings of IMACS, IEEE-SMC, Computational Engineering in Systems and Application Multi-conference*, *2*, 963–968.

Matouk, A. E. (2009). Stability Conditions, Hyperchaos and Control in a novel Fractional Order Hyperchaotic System. *Physics Letters. [Part A]*, *373*(25), 2166–2173. doi:10.1016/j.physleta.2009.04.032

Matouk, A. E. (2011). Chaos, Feedback Control and Synchronization of a Fractional-Order Modified autonomous Van Der Pol-Duffing Circuit. *Communications in Nonlinear Science and Numerical Simulation*, *16*(2), 975–986. doi:10.1016/j.cnsns.2010.04.027

Matouk, A. E., & Elsadany, A. A. (2017). Dynamical analysis, stabilization and discretization of a chaotic fractional-order GLV model. *Nonlinear Dynamics*, *85*(3), 1597–1612. doi:10.100711071-016-2781-6

Maus, A., & Sprott, J. C. (2013). Evaluating Lyapunov exponent spectra with neural networks. *Chaos, Solitons, and Fractals*, *51*(51), 13–21. doi:10.1016/j.chaos.2013.03.001

Maybhate, A., & Amritkar, R. E. (1999). Use of synchronization and adaptive control in parameter estimation from a time series. *Physical Review. E*, *59*(1), 284–293. doi:10.1103/PhysRevE.59.284

McGarry, K., Sarfraz, M., & MacIntyre, J. (2007). Integrating gene expression data from microarrays using the self-organising map and the gene ontology. *Pattern Recognition in Bioinformatics*, 206-217.

Megherbi, O., Kassim, S., Hamiche, H., Djennoune, S., Bettayeb, M., & Barbot, J-P. (2017). Robust image transmission scheme based on coupled fractional-order chaotic maps. *SIAM Conference on Control and its Application*. 10.1137/1.9781611975024.8

Megherbi, O., Guermah, S., Hamiche, H., Djennoune, S., & Ghanes, M. (2013). A novel transmission scheme based on impulsivesynchronization of two Colpittschaotic systems. *3rd International Conference on Systems and Control, ICSC'13*. 10.1109/ICoSC.2013.6750845

Megherbi, O., Hamiche, H., Djennoune, S., & Bettayeb, M. (2017). A new contribution for the impulsive synchronization of fractional-order discrete-time chaotic systems. *Nonlinear Dynamics*, *90*(3), 1519–1533. doi:10.100711071-017-3743-3

Mendel, J. M., & John, R. I. B. (2002). Type-2 fuzzy sets made simple. *IEEE Transactions on Fuzzy Systems*, *10*(2), 117–127. doi:10.1109/91.995115

Miao, B., & Li, T. (2015). A novel neural network-based adaptive control for a class of uncertain nonlinear systems in strict-feedback form. *Nonlinear Dynamics*, *79*(2), 1005–1013. doi:10.100711071-014-1717-2

Miller, K., & Ross, B. (1993). *An introduction to the fractional calculus and fractional differential equations*. New York: Wiley.

Miller, K., & Ross, B. (1993). *An Introduction to the Fractional Calculus and Fractional Differential Equations*. New York: Wiley.

Mishina, A. P. (1965). *Higher Algebra*. Moscow: Nauka.

Mitschke, F., & Flüggen, N. (1984). Chaotic behavior of a hybrid optical bistable system without a time delay. *Applied Physics. B, Lasers and Optics*, *35*(2), 59–64. doi:10.1007/BF00697423

Mizumoto, I., Fujii, S., & Ikejiri, M. (2015). Control of a magnetic levitation system via output feedback based two DOF control with an adaptive predictive feedforward input. In *Control Applications (CCA), 2015 IEEE Conference on* (pp. 71-76). IEEE. 10.1109/CCA.2015.7320612

Momani, S., & Odibat, Z. (2008). A Novel Method for Nonlinear Fractional Partial Differential Equations: Combination of DTM and Generalized Taylor's Formula. *Journal of Computational and Applied Mathematics*, *1-2*(220), 85–95. doi:10.1016/j.cam.2007.07.033

Morgül, Ö., & Solak, E. (1996). Observer based synchronization of chaotic systems. *Physical Review. E*, *54*(5), 4803–4811. doi:10.1103/PhysRevE.54.4803 PMID:9965660

Morgul, Ö., & Solak, E. (1997). On the synchronization of chaotic systems by using state observers. *International Journal of Bifurcation and Chaos in Applied Sciences and Engineering*, *7*(6), 1307–1322. doi:10.1142/S0218127497001047

Moze, M. &. (2005). Lmi Tools for Stabilty Analysis of Fractional Systems. *Proc. of ASME International Design Engineering Technical Conferences, Computers and and Information in Information in Engineering Conference*.

Muthukumar, P., Balasubramaniam, P., & Ratnavelu, K. (2015). Sliding mode control design for synchronization of fractionalorder chaotic systems and its application to a new cryptosystem. *International Journal of Dynamics and Control*, *5*(1), 115–123. doi:10.100740435-015-0169-y

N'Doye, I., & Laleg-Kirati, T. M. (2015). Fractional-order adaptive fault estimation for a class of nonlinear fractional-order systems. In American Control Conference (ACC), 2015 (pp. 3804-3809). IEEE. doi:10.1109/ACC.2015.7171923

N'doye, I., Laleg-Kirati, T.-M., Darouach, M., & Voos, H. (2017). $\mathcal{H}\infty$ Adaptive observer for nonlinear fractional-order systems. *International Journal of Adaptive Control and Signal Processing*, *31*(3), 314–331. doi:10.1002/acs.2699

Na, J., Ren, X., Shang, C., & Guo, Y. (2012). Adaptive neural network predictive control for nonlinear pure feedback systems with input delay. *Journal of Process Control*, *22*(1), 194–206. doi:10.1016/j.jprocont.2011.09.003

Neçaibia, A., & Ladaci, S. (2014). Self-tuning fractional order PIλDμ controller based on extremum seeking approach. International Journal of Automation and Control. *Inderscience*, *8*(2), 99–121.

Neçaibia, A., Ladaci, S., Charef, A., & Loiseau, J. J. (2014). Fractional Order Extremum Seeking Control. *Proceedings of the 22nd Mediterranean Conference on Control and Automation*, 459-462.

Neçaibia, A., Ladaci, S., Charef, A., & Loiseau, J. J. (2015). Fractional order extremum seeking approach for maximum power point tracking of photovoltaic panels. *Frontiers in Energy*, *9*(1), 43–53. doi:10.100711708-014-0343-5

Nijmeijer, H., & Van der Schaft, A. J. (1990). *Nonlinear dynamical control systems*. New York: Springer-Verglag. doi:10.1007/978-1-4757-2101-0

Nikdel, N., Badamchizadeh, M., Azimirad, V., & Nazari, M. A. (2016). Fractional-order adaptive backstepping control of robotic manipulators in the presence of model uncertainties and external disturbances. *IEEE Transactions on Industrial Electronics*, *63*(10), 6249–6256. doi:10.1109/TIE.2016.2577624

Odibat, Z. (2010). Analytic Study on linear Systems of Fractional Differential Equations. *Computers & Mathematics with Applications (Oxford, England)*, *59*(3), 1171–1183. doi:10.1016/j.camwa.2009.06.035

Odibat, Z. M. (2010). Adaptive feedback control and synchronization of non-identical chaotic fractional order systems. *Nonlinear Dynamics*, *60*(4), 479–487. doi:10.100711071-009-9609-6

Odibat, Z., & Momani, S. (2006). Application of Variational Iteration Method to Nonlinear Differential Equations of Fractional Order. *International Journal of Nonlinear Sciences and Numerical Simulation*, *7*(1), 27–34. doi:10.1515/IJNSNS.2006.7.1.27

Odibat, Z., & Momani, S. (2008). Modified Homotopy Perturbation Method: Application to Quadratic Riccati Differential Equation of Fractional Order. *Chaos, Solitons, and Fractals*, *36*(1), 167–174. doi:10.1016/j.chaos.2006.06.041

Oldham, K. B., & Spanier, J. (2006). The Fractional Calculus: Theory and Applications of Differentiation and Integration to Arbitrary Order (mathematics in science and engineering, Vol. 111). Richard Bellman.

Oldham, K. B. (1974). *The Fractional Calculus: Theory and applications of Differentiation and Integration to Arbitrary Order*. Academic Press.

Oldham, K. B., & Spanier, J. (1974). *The fractional Calculus, Theory and applications of Differentiation and integration to arbitrary order*. London: Academic Press Inc.

Oldham, K. B., & Spanier, J. (1974). *The fractional calculus*. New York: Academic Press.

Oliveira, T. R., Peixoto, A. J., & Hsu, L. (2010). Sliding Mode Control of Uncertain Multivariable Nonlinear Systems With Unknown Control Direction via Switching and Monitoring Function. *IEEE Transactions on Automatic Control*, *55*(4), 1028–1034. doi:10.1109/TAC.2010.2041986

Onufriyenko, V. M., & Lewykin, V. M. (2002) Integro-Differential Potentials for the Analysis of a Fractal cover Properties. *Proceedings of the IX Conference on Mathematical Methods for electromagnetic Theory (MMET'02)*. 10.1109/MMET.2002.1106932

Oppo, G. L., Brambilla, M., & Lugiato, L. A. (1994). Formation and evolution of roll patterns in optical parametric oscillators. *Physical Review A.*, *49*(3), 2028–2032. doi:10.1103/PhysRevA.49.2028 PMID:9910454

Othman, A. A., Noorani, M. S. M., & Al-Sawalha, M. M. (2016). Adaptive dual synchronization of chaotic and hyperchaotic systems with fully uncertain parameters. *Optik-International Journal for Light and Electron Optics*, *127*(19), 7852–7864. doi:10.1016/j.ijleo.2016.05.139

Oustaloup, A. S. (2008). An Overview of the Crone Approach in System Analysis, Modelling and Identification, Observation and Control. 17th World Comgress IFAC, 14254-14265.

Oustaloup, A. (1991). *Commande Robuste d'ordre non Entier. In The CRONE control (La commande CRONE)*. Paris: Hermès.

Oustaloup, A. (1991). *La Dérivation non entière*. Paris: Hermès.

Oustaloup, A. (1991). *The CRONE control (La commande CRONE)*. Paris: Hermès.

Oustaloup, A. (1995). *La dérivation non entière: théorie, synthèse et applications*. Hermès-Paris.

Oustaloup, A. (1999). *La Commande CRONE: Commande Robuste d'Ordre Non Entier*. Paris: Editions Hermès.

Panagou, D., & Stipanovi, D. M. (2016). Distributed coordination control for multi-robot networks using Lyapunov-like barrier functions. *IEEE Transactions on Automatic Control*, *61*(3), 617–632. doi:10.1109/TAC.2015.2444131

Pan, I., & Das, S. (2012). Chaotic multi-objective optimization based design of fractional order PIλDμ controller in AVR system. *International Journal of Electrical Power & Energy Systems*, *43*(1), 393–407. doi:10.1016/j.ijepes.2012.06.034

Pan, L., Zhou, W., Fang, J., & Li, D. (2010). Synchronization and anti-synchronization of new uncertain fractional-order modified unified chaotic systems via novel active pinning control. *Communications in Nonlinear Science and Numerical Simulation*, *15*(12), 3754–3762. doi:10.1016/j.cnsns.2010.01.025

Pan, Y., & Yu, H. (2015). Dynamic surface control via singular perturbation analysis. *Automatica*, *57*, 29–33. doi:10.1016/j.automatica.2015.03.033

Pan, Y., & Yu, H. (2016). Composite learning from adaptive dynamic surface control. *IEEE Transactions on Automatic Control*, *61*(9), 2603–2609. doi:10.1109/TAC.2015.2495232

Pecora, L. M., & Carroll, T. L. (1990). Synchronization in chaotic systems. *Physical Review Letters*, *64*(8), 821–824. doi:10.1103/PhysRevLett.64.821 PMID:10042089

Peng, G. (2007). Synchronization of fractional order chaotic systems. *Physics Letters. [Part A]*, *363*(5-6), 426–432. doi:10.1016/j.physleta.2006.11.053

Perez, R. E., & Behdinan, K. (2007). Particle swarm approach for structural design optimization. *Computers & Structures*, *85*(1), 1579–1588. doi:10.1016/j.compstruc.2006.10.013

Perruquetti, W., & Barbot, J.-P. (2006). *Chaos in Automatic Control*. CRC Press.

Petráš, I. (2011). *Fractional-order nonlinear systems: Modeling, analysis and simulation*. Higher Education Press.

Pétras, I. (2011). *Fractional-Order Nonlinear Systems: Modeling, Analysis and Simulation, Series: Nonlinear Physical Science*. Springer-Verlag. doi:10.1007/978-3-642-18101-6

Petras, I. (2011). *Fractional-Order Nonlinear Systems: Modeling, Analysis and Simulation*. Berlin: Springer-Verlag; doi:10.1007/978-3-642-18101-6.

Pettiaux, N. P., Ruo-Ding, L., & Mandel, P. (1989). Instabilities of the degenerate optical parametric oscillator. *Optics Communications*, *72*(3-4), 256–260. doi:10.1016/0030-4018(89)90407-0

Pham, V. T., Kingni, S. T., Volos, C., Jafari, S., & Kapitaniak, T. (2017). A simple three-dimensional fractional-order chaotic system without equilibrium: Dynamics, circuitry implementation, chaos control and synchronization. *International Journal of Electronics and Communications*, *78*(1), 220–227. doi:10.1016/j.aeue.2017.04.012

Pham, V. T., Vaidyanathan, S., Volos, C., Jafari, S., & Kingni, S. T. (2016). A no-equilibrium hyperchaotic system with a cubic nonlinear term. *Optik-International Journal for Light and Electron Optics*, *127*(6), 3259–3265. doi:10.1016/j.ijleo.2015.12.048

Phillip, P. A., Chiu, F. L., & Nick, S. J. (2009). Rapidly detecting disorder in rhythmic biological signals: A spectral entropy measure to identify cardiac arrhythmias. *Physical Review. E*, *79*(1), 011915. doi:10.1103/PhysRevE.79.011915 PMID:19257077

Pikovsky, A. S., Rosenblum, M. G., Osipov, G. V., & Kurths, J. (1997). Phase synchronization of chaotic oscillators by external driving. *Physica D. Nonlinear Phenomena*, *104*(3-4), 219–238. doi:10.1016/S0167-2789(96)00301-6

Pisano, A., Rapaić, M. R., Jeličić, Z. D., & Usai, E. (2010). Sliding mode control approaches to the robust regulation of linear multivariable fractional-order dynamics. *International Journal of Robust and Nonlinear Control*, *20*(18), 2045–2056. doi:10.1002/rnc.1565

Plestan, F., Shtessel, Y., Bregeault, V., & Poznyak, A. (2010). New methodologies for adaptive sliding mode control. *International Journal of Control*, *83*(9), 1907–1919. doi:10.1080/00207179.2010.501385

Podlubny, I. (1998). *Fractional differential equations: An introduction to fractional derivatives, fractional differential equations, some methods of their solution and some of their applications*. San Diego, CA: Academic Press.

Podlubny, I. (1999). *Fractional Differential Equations*. New York: Academic Press.

Podlubny, I. (1999). *Fractional differential equations*. San Diego, CA: Academic Press.

Podlubny, I. (1999). *Fractional differential Equations*. San Diego, CA: Academic Press.

Podlubny, I. (1999). Fractional order systems and PIλDμ controllers. *Trans. Automatic Control*, *44*(1), 208–214. doi:10.1109/9.739144

Poursamad, A., & Davaie-Markazi, A. H. (2009). Robust adaptive fuzzy control of unknown chaotic systems. *Applied Soft Computing*, *9*(3), 970–976. doi:10.1016/j.asoc.2008.11.014

Precup, R. E., & Tomescu, M. L. (2015). Stable fuzzy logic control of a general class of chaotic systems. *Neural Computing & Applications*, *26*(3), 541–550. doi:10.100700521-014-1644-7

Precup, R. E., Tomescu, M. L., & Dragos, C. A. (2014). Stabilization of Rössler chaotic dynamical system using fuzzy logic control algorithm. *International Journal of General Systems*, *43*(5), 413–433. doi:10.1080/03081079.2014.893299

Pyragas, K. (1992). Continuous control of chaos by self-controlling feedback. *Physics Letters. [Part A]*, *170*(6), 421–428. doi:10.1016/0375-9601(92)90745-8

Qilian, L., & Mendel, J. M. (2000). Interval type-2 fuzzy logic systems: Theory and design. *IEEE Transactions on Fuzzy Systems*, *8*(5), 535–550. doi:10.1109/91.873577

Rabah, K., Ladaci, S. & Lashab, M. (2016). Stabilization of a Genesio-Tesi Chaotic System Using a Fractional Order PIλDμ Regulator. *International Journal of Sciences and Techniques of Automatic Control & Computer Engineering*, *10*(1), 2085–2090.

Rabah, K., Ladaci, S. & Lashab, M. (2017) Bifurcation-based Fractional Order PIλDμ Controller Design Approach for Nonlinear Chaotic Systems. *Frontiers of Information Technology & Electronic Engineering*. DOI: 10.1613/FITEE.1601543

Rabah, K., Ladaci, S., &Lashab, M. (2017). Bifurcation-based Fractional Order PIλDμ Controller Design Approach for Nonlinear Chaotic. *Frontiers of Information Technology & Electronic Engineering*.

Rabah, K., Ladaci, S., Lashab, M. (2016). Stabilization of a Genesio-Tesi Chaotic System Using a Fractional Order PIλDμ Regulator. *International Journal of Sciences and Techniques of Automatic Control & Computer Engineering*, *10*(1), 2085–2090.

Rabah, K., Ladaci, S., & Lashab, M. (2015). Stabilization of Fractional Chen Chaotic System by Linear Feedback Control. In *Proceedings of the 3rd Int. IEEE Conf. on Control, Engineering & Information Technology (CEIT2015)*. Tlemcen, Algeria: IEEE. 10.1109/CEIT.2015.7232990

Rabah, K., Ladaci, S., & Lashab, M. (2016). Stabilization of a Genesio-Tesi Chaotic System Using a Fractional Order PIλDµ. *International Journal of Sciences and Techniques of Automatic Control & Computer Engineering, IJ-STA, 10*(1), 2085–2090.

Rabah, K., Ladaci, S., & Lashab, M. (2017b). (to appear). Bifurcation-based Fractional Order PI^λD^µ Controller Design Approach for Nonlinear Chaotic Systems. *Frontiers of Information Technology & Electronic Engineering*.

Rabah, K., Ladaci, S., & Lashab, M. (2017b). A novel fractional sliding mode control configuration for synchronizing disturbed fractional-order chaotic systems. *Pramana, 89*(46).

Rădac, M. B., Precup, R. E., Petriu, E. M., & Preitl, S. (2014). Iterative Data-Driven Tuning of Controllers for Nonlinear Systems With Constraints. *IEEE Transactions on Industrial Electronics, 61*(11), 6360–6368. doi:10.1109/TIE.2014.2300068

Ren, C., Tong, S., & Li, Y. (2012). Fuzzy adaptive high-gain-based observer backstepping control for SISO nonlinear systems with dynamical uncertainties. *Nonlinear Dynamics, 67*(1), 941–955. doi:10.100711071-011-0036-0

Richman, J. S., & Moorman, J. R. (2000). Physiological time-series analysis using approximate entropy and sample entropy. *American Journal of Physiology. Heart and Circulatory Physiology, 278*(6), 2039–2049. doi:10.1152/ajpheart.2000.278.6.H2039 PMID:10843903

Rigatos, G., Zhu, G., Yousef, H., & Boulkroune, A. (2016). Flatness-based adaptive fuzzy control of electrostatically actuated MEMS using output feedback. *Fuzzy Sets and Systems, 290*, 138–157. doi:10.1016/j.fss.2015.08.027

Rivest, R. L., Shamir, A., & Adleman, L. (1978). A Method for Obtaining Digital Signatures and Public-Key Cryptosystems. *Communications of the ACM, 21*(2), 120–126. doi:10.1145/359340.359342

Rodríguez, A., De León, J., & Fridman, L. (2008). Quasi-continuous high-order sliding-mode controllers for reduced-order chaos synchronization. *International Journal of Non-linear Mechanics, 43*(9), 948–961. doi:10.1016/j.ijnonlinmec.2008.07.007

Roohi, M., Aghababa, M. P., & Haghighi, A. R. (2015). Switching adaptive controllers to control fractional-order complex systems with unknown structure and input nonlinearities. *Complexity, 21*(2), 211–223. doi:10.1002/cplx.21598

Roopaei, M., & Jahromi, M. Z. (2008). Synchronization of two different chaotic systems using novel adaptive fuzzy sliding mode control. *Chaos (Woodbury, N.Y.), 18*(3), 033133. doi:10.1063/1.2980046 PMID:19045471

Roseinstein, M. T., Collins, J. J., & De Luca, C. J. (1993). A Practical Method for Calculating Largest Lyapunov Exponents from Small Data Sets. *Physica D. Nonlinear Phenomena, 65*(1-2), 117–134. doi:10.1016/0167-2789(93)90009-P

Rosenblum, M. G., Pikovsky, A. S., & Kurths, J. (1996). Phase synchronization of chaotic oscillators. *Physical Review Letters, 76*(11), 1804–1807. doi:10.1103/PhysRevLett.76.1804 PMID:10060525

Rössler, O. E. (1976). An equation for continuous Chaos. *Physics Letters, 5*(5), 397–397. doi:10.1016/0375-9601(76)90101-8

Rostami, M., & Haeri, M. (2015). Undamped oscillations in fractional-order Duffing oscillator. *Signal Processing, 107*, 361–367. doi:10.1016/j.sigpro.2014.03.042

Rubezic, V., & Ostojic, R. (2000). *Breaking chaotic switching using generalized synchronization*. Academic Press.

Sabatier, J., Agrawal, O. P., & Tenreiro Machado, J. A. (Eds.). (2007). *Advances in fractional calculus: theoretical developments and applications in physics and engineering*. Dordrecht: Springer. doi:10.1007/978-1-4020-6042-7

Sadeghian, H., Salarieh, H., Alasty, A., & Meghdari, A. (2011). On the control of chaos via fractional delayed feedback method. *Computers & Mathematics with Applications (Oxford, England), 62*(3), 1482–1491. doi:10.1016/j.camwa.2011.05.002

Sastry, S., & Bodson, M. (1989). *Adaptive Control: Stability, Convergence and Robustness*. New York: Prentice-Hall.

Scherer, R., Kalla, S. L., Tang, Y., & Huang, J. (2011). The Grünwald-Letnikov method for fractional differential equations. *Computers & Mathematics with Applications (Oxford, England)*, *62*(3), 902–917. doi:10.1016/j.camwa.2011.03.054

Sejdic, E., Djurovic, I., & Stankovic, L. (2011). Fractional Fourier transform as a signal processing tool: An overview of recent developments. *Signal Processing*, *91*(6), 1351–1369. doi:10.1016/j.sigpro.2010.10.008

Shahiri, M., Gharderi, R., Ranjbar, A. N., Hosseinnia, S. H., & Momani, S. (2010). Chaotic Fractional-Order Coullet System: Synchronization and Control Approach. *Communications in Nonlinear Science and Numerical Simulation*, *15*(3), 665–674. doi:10.1016/j.cnsns.2009.05.054

Shahnazi, R. (2016). Observer-based adaptive interval type-2 fuzzy control of uncertain MIMO nonlinear systems with unknown asymmetric saturation actuators. *Neurocomputing*, *171*, 1053–1065. doi:10.1016/j.neucom.2015.07.098

Shahverdiev, E. M., Hashimova, L. H., Bayramov, P. A., & Nuriev, R. A. (2014). Chaos synchronization between Josephson junctions coupled with time delays. *Journal of Superconductivity and Novel Magnetism*, *27*(10), 2225–2229. doi:10.100710948-014-2599-8

Shannon, C. E. (1949). Communication theory of secrecy systems. *The Bell System Technical Journal*, *28*(4), 656–715. doi:10.1002/j.1538-7305.1949.tb00928.x

Sharkowskii, A. (1964). Cycles Coexistence of Continuous Tranformation of Line in Itself. *Ukrainian Mathematical Journal*, *1*(26), 61–71.

Shaw, R. (1981). Strange Attractors, Chaotic Behavior and Information Flow. *Zeitschrift fur Naturforschung. Section A. Physical Sciences*, *36*(1), 80–112. doi:10.1515/zna-1981-0115

Shen, E. H., Cai, Z. J., & Gu, F. J. (2005). Mathematical foundation of a new complexity measure. *Applied Mathematics and Mechanics*, *26*(9), 1188–1196. doi:10.1007/BF02507729

Sheng, D., Wei, Y., Cheng, S., & Shuai, J. (2017). Adaptive backstepping control for fractional order systems with input saturation. *Journal of the Franklin Institute*, *354*(5), 2245–2268. doi:10.1016/j.jfranklin.2016.12.030 PMID:28683926

Shen, J., & Lam, J. (2014). Non-existence of finite-time stable equilibria in fractional-order nonlinear systems. *Automatica*, *50*(2), 547–551. doi:10.1016/j.automatica.2013.11.018

Sheu, L. J., Chen, H.-K., Chen, J.-H., Tam, L.-M., Chen, W.-C., Lin, K.-T., & Kang, Y. (2008). Chaos in the Newton-Leipnik System with Fractional Order. *Chaos, Solitons, and Fractals*, *36*(1), 98–103. doi:10.1016/j.chaos.2006.06.013

Shi, W. (2015a). Observer-based fuzzy adaptive control for multi-input multi-output nonlinear systems with a nonsymmetric control gain matrix and unknown control direction. *Fuzzy Sets and Systems*, *236*, 1–26. doi:10.1016/j.fss.2014.05.015

Shi, W. (2015b). Observer-based direct adaptive fuzzy control for single-input single-output non-linear systems with unknown gain sign. *IET Control Theory & Applications*, *9*(17), 2506–2513. doi:10.1049/iet-cta.2015.0076

Shukla, M. K., & Sharma, B. B. (2017). Stabilization of a class of uncertain fractional order chaotic systems via adaptive backstepping control. In *Proceedings of the IEEE 2017 Indian Control Conference (ICC)*. IIT Guwahati. 10.1109/INDIANCC.2017.7846518

Shukla, M. K., & Sharma, B. B. (2017a). Backstepping based stabilization and synchronization of a class of fractional order chaotic systems. *Chaos, Solitons, and Fractals*.

Shukla, M. K., & Sharma, B. B. (2017b). Stabilization of a class of fractional order chaotic systems via backstepping approach. *Chaos, Solitons, and Fractals*, *98*, 56–62. doi:10.1016/j.chaos.2017.03.011

Shukla, M. K., & Sharma, B. B. (2018). Control and Synchronization Of A Class Of Uncertain Fractional Order Chaotic Systems Via Adaptive Backstepping Control. *Asian Journal of Control.*

Shyu, K. K., Liu, W. J., & Hsu, K. C. (2005). Design of large-scale time-delayed systems with dead-zone input via variable structure control. *Automatica, 41*(7), 1239–1246. doi:10.1016/j.automatica.2005.03.004

Si-Ammour, A., Djennoune, S., & Bettayeb, M. (2009). A sliding mode control for linear fractional systems with input and state delays. *Communications in Nonlinear Science and Numerical Simulation, 14*(5), 2310–2318. doi:10.1016/j.cnsns.2008.05.011

Si, G., Sun, Z., Zhang, Y., & Chen, W. (2012). Projective synchronization of different fractional-order chaotic systems with non-identical orders. *Nonlinear Analysis Real World Applications, 13*(4), 1761–1771. doi:10.1016/j.nonrwa.2011.12.006

Silva, C. P. (1993). Shilnikov's Theorem - a Tutorial. *IEEE Transactions on Circuits and Systems, I*(40), 675–682. doi:10.1109/81.246142

Sira-Ramirez, H., & Rouchon, P. (2001). Exact delayed reconstruction in nonlinear discrete-time system. *European Union Nonlinear Control Network Workshop.*

Slotine, J. J. E. (1991). *Applied Nonlinear Control.* Prentice Hall.

Soukkou, A., Boukabou, A., & Leulmi, S. (2016). Prediction-based feedback control and synchronization algorithm of fractional-order chaotic systems. *Nonlinear Dynamics, 85*(4), 2183–2206. doi:10.100711071-016-2823-0

Soukkou, A., & Leulmi, S. (2017). Elaboration of a generalized approach to control and to synchronize the fractional-order chaotic systems. *International Journal of General Systems, 46*(8), 853–878. doi:10.1080/03081079.2017.1324854

Staliunas, K., & Sanchez-Morcillo, V. J. (1998). Spatial-localized structures in degenerate optical parametric oscillators. *Physical Review A., 57*(2), 1454–1457. doi:10.1103/PhysRevA.57.1454

Stamova, I., & Stamov, G. (2013). Lipschitz stability criteria for functional differential systems of fractional order. *Journal of Mathematical Physics, 54*(4), 043502. doi:10.1063/1.4798234

Stamova, I., & Stamov, G. (2014). Stability analysis of impulsive functional systems of fractional order. *Communications in Nonlinear Science and Numerical Simulation, 19*(3), 702–709. doi:10.1016/j.cnsns.2013.07.005

Standard, A. E. (2001). *Federal information processing standard (fips) publication 197.* Washington, DC: National Bureau of Standards, US Department of Commerce.

Standard, D. E. (1977). *Federal information processing standards publication 46.* National Bureau of Standards, US Department of Commerce.

Sui, S., Li, Y., & Tong, S. (2016). Observer-based adaptive fuzzy control for switched stochastic nonlinear systems with partial tracking errors constrained. *IEEE Transactions on Systems, Man, and Cybernetics. Systems, 46*(12), 1605–1617. doi:10.1109/TSMC.2016.2523904

Sui, S., Tong, S., & Li, Y. (2015). Observer-based fuzzy adaptive prescribed performance tracking control for nonlinear stochastic systems with input saturation. *Neurocomputing, 158*, 100–108. doi:10.1016/j.neucom.2015.01.063

Sun, H. H., Abdelwahab, A. A., & Onaral, B. (1984). Linear approximation of transfer function with a pole of fractional power. *IEEE Transactions on Automatic Control, 29*(5), 441–444. doi:10.1109/TAC.1984.1103551

Sun, J., & Zhang, Y. (2004). Impulsive control and synchronization of Chua's oscillators. *Mathematics and Computers in Simulation, 66*(6), 499–508. doi:10.1016/j.matcom.2004.03.004

Sun, K. H., He, S. B., & Zhu, C. X. (2013). Analysis of chaotic complexity characteristics based on C_0 Algorithm. *Tien Tzu Hsueh Pao*, *41*(9), 1765–1771.

Sun, K. H., Wang, X., & Sprott, J. C. (2010). Bifurcations and chaos in fractional-order simplified Lorenz system. *International Journal of Bifurcation and Chaos in Applied Sciences and Engineering*, *20*(4), 1209–1219. doi:10.1142/S0218127410026411

Sun, K., & Sprott, J. C. (2009). Bifrucations of Fractional-Order Diffusionless Lorenz System. *Electronic Journal of Theoretical Physics*, *6*(22), 123–134.

Tabatabaei, S. M., & Arefi, M. M. (2016). Adaptive neural control for a class of uncertain non-affine nonlinear switched system. *Nonlinear Dynamics*, *83*(3), 1773–1781. doi:10.100711071-015-2446-x

Takagi, T., & Sugeno, M. (1985). Fuzzy Identification of Systems and Its Applications to Modeling and Control. *IEEE Transactions on Systems, Man, and Cybernetics*, *15*(1), 116–132. doi:10.1109/TSMC.1985.6313399

Tang, S., Chen, H. F., Hwang, S. K., & Liu, J. M. (2002). Message encoding and decoding through chaos modulation in chaotic optical communications. *IEEE Transactions on Circuits and Systems. I, Fundamental Theory and Applications*, *49*(2), 163–169. doi:10.1109/81.983864

Tang, Y., Cui, M., Hua, C., Li, L., & Yang, Y. (2012). Optimum design of fractional order PIλDμ controller for AVR system using chaotic ant swarm. *Expert Systems with Applications*, *39*(8), 6887–6896. doi:10.1016/j.eswa.2012.01.007

Tarasov, V. E. (2016). On chain rule for fractional derivatives. *Communications in Nonlinear Science and Numerical Simulation*, *30*(1–3), 1–4. doi:10.1016/j.cnsns.2015.06.007

Tavazoei, M. S. (2008b). Limitations of Frequency Domain Approximation for Detecting Chaos in Fractional Order Systems. *Nonlinear Analysis - Theory Methods and Applications*, (69), 1299-1320.

Tavazoei, M. S. (2012). Comments on "Chaos Synchronization of Uncertain Fractional-Order Chaotic Systems With Time Delay Based on Adaptive Fuzzy Sliding Mode Control". *IEEE Transactions on Fuzzy Systems*, *20*(5), 993–995. doi:10.1109/TFUZZ.2012.2188637

Tavazoei, M. S., & Haeri, M. (2007). Unreliability of frequency-domain approximation in recognizing chaos in fractional-order systems. *Signal Processing IET*, *1*(4), 171–181. doi:10.1049/iet-spr:20070053

Tavazoei, M. S., & Haeri, M. (2008). Stabilization of unstable fixed points of chaotic fractional order systems by a state fractional PI controller. *European Journal of Control*, *3*(3), 247–257. doi:10.3166/ejc.14.247-257

Tavazoei, M. S., & Haeri, M. (2008). Synchronization of chaotic fractional-order systems via active sliding mode controller. *Physica A*, *387*(1), 57–70. doi:10.1016/j.physa.2007.08.039

Tavazoei, M. S., & Haeri, M. (2008a). Chaotic Attractors in incommensurate Fractional Order Systems. *Physica D. Nonlinear Phenomena*, *237*(20), 2628–2637. doi:10.1016/j.physd.2008.03.037

Tavazoei, M. S., Haeri, M., Bolouki, S., & Siami, M. (2009). Using fractional-order integrator to control chaos in single-input chaotic systems. *Nonlinear Dynamics*, *55*(1), 179–190. doi:10.100711071-008-9353-3

Terry, J. R., & Thornburg, K. S., Jr. (2009). Experimental synchronization of chaotic lasers. *Physical Review Let*, *72*.

Tian, X., Fei, S., & Chai, L. (2014). Adaptive Control of a Class of Fractional-order Nonlinear Complex Systems with Dead-zone Nonlinear Inputs. *Proceedings of the 33rd Chinese Control Conference*. 10.1109/ChiCC.2014.6896919

Tong, S. C., Li, Y. M., Feng, G., & Li, T. S. (2011). Observer-based adaptive fuzzy backstepping dynamic surface control for a class of MIMO nonlinear systems. *IEEE Transactions on Systems, Man, and Cybernetics. Part B, Cybernetics*, *41*(4), 1124–1135. doi:10.1109/TSMCB.2011.2108283 PMID:21317084

Tong, S., & Li, Y. (2013). Adaptive fuzzy output feedback control of MIMO nonlinear systems with unknown dead-zone inputs. *IEEE Transactions on Fuzzy Systems*, *21*(1), 134–146. doi:10.1109/TFUZZ.2012.2204065

Tong, S., Li, Y., & Shi, P. (2012). Observer-based adaptive fuzzy backstepping output feedback control of uncertain MIMO pure-feedback nonlinear systems. *IEEE Transactions on Fuzzy Systems*, *20*(4), 771–785. doi:10.1109/TFUZZ.2012.2183604

Tong, S., Sui, S., & Li, Y. (2015). Fuzzy adaptive output feedback control of MIMO nonlinear systems with partial tracking errors constrained. *IEEE Transactions on Fuzzy Systems*, *23*(4), 729–742. doi:10.1109/TFUZZ.2014.2327987

Travazoei, M. S. (2010). A Note on Fractional-Order Derivatives of Periodic Functions. *Automatica*, *46*(5), 945–948. doi:10.1016/j.automatica.2010.02.023

Travazoei, M. S., Haeri, M., & Nazari, N. (2008). Analysis of Undamped Oscillations Generated by Marginally Stable Fractional Order Systems. *Signal Processing*, *88*(12), 2971–2978. doi:10.1016/j.sigpro.2008.07.002

Travazoei, M., & Haeri, M. (2009). A Proof for Non Existence of Periodic Solutions in Time invariant Fractional Order Systems. *Automatica*, *45*(8), 1886–1890. doi:10.1016/j.automatica.2009.04.001

Ushio, T. (1995). Chaotic synchronization and controlling chaos based on contraction mappings. *Physics Letters. [Part A]*, *198*(1), 14–22. doi:10.1016/0375-9601(94)01015-M

Ushio, T., & Yamamoto, S. (1999). Prediction-based control of chaos. *Physics Letters. [Part A]*, *264*(1), 30–35. doi:10.1016/S0375-9601(99)00782-3

Utkin, V. I. (1992). *Sliding modes in control optimization*. Berlin: Springer-Verlag. doi:10.1007/978-3-642-84379-2

Vaidyanathan, S. (2015). Global chaos synchronization of the Lotka-Volterra biological systems with four competitive species via active control. *International Journal of Pharm Tech Research*, *8*(6), 206–217.

Vargas-De-León, C. (2015). Volterra-type Lyapunov functions for fractional-order epidemic systems. *Communications in Nonlinear Science and Numerical Simulation*, *24*(1-3), 75–85. doi:10.1016/j.cnsns.2014.12.013

Vinagre, B. M., Petras, I., Podlubny, I., & Chen, Y.-Q. (2002). Using Fractional Order Adjustment Rules and Fractional Order Reference Models in Model-Reference Adaptive Control. *Nonlinear Dynamics*, *29*(1/4), 269–279. doi:10.1023/A:1016504620249

Vishal, K., Agrawal, S. K., & Das, S. (2016). Hyperchaos control and adaptive synchronization with uncertain parameter for fractional-order Mathieu–van der Pol systems. *Pramana-. Journal of Physics*, *86*(1), 59–75.

Wang, C.H., & Chen, C.Y. (2015). Intelligent chaos synchronization of fractional order systems via mean-based slide mode controller. *International Journal of Fuzzy Systems*, *17*(2), 144-157.

Wang, C. N., Li, S. R., Ma, J., & Jin, W. Y. (2010). Synchronization transition in degenerate optical parametric oscillators induced by nonlinear coupling. *Applied Mathematics and Computation*, *216*(2), 647–654. doi:10.1016/j.amc.2010.01.101

Wang, C.-H., Liu, H.-L., & Lin, T.-C. (2002). Direct Adaptive Fuzzy-Neural Control with State Observer and Supervisory Controller for Unknown Nonlinear Dynamical Systems. *IEEE Transactions on Fuzzy Systems*, *10*(1), 39–49. doi:10.1109/91.983277

Wang, F., Yang, Y., Xu, X., & Li, L. (2017). Global asymptotic stability of impulsive fractional-order BAM neural networks with time delay. *Neural Computing & Applications*, *28*(2), 345–352. doi:10.100700521-015-2063-0

Wang, H., Liu, X., & Liu, K. (2015a). Adaptive neural data-based compensation control of non-linear systems with dynamic uncertainties and input saturation. *IET Control Theory & Applications*, *9*(7), 1058–1065. doi:10.1049/iet-cta.2014.0709

Wang, J. W., & Zhang, Y. B. (2009). Synchronization in coupled non identical incommensurate fractional-order systems. *Physics Letters. [Part A]*, *374*(2), 202–207. doi:10.1016/j.physleta.2009.10.051

Wang, J., Chen, L., & Deng, B. (2009). Synchronization of Ghostburster neuron in external electrical stimulation via H∞ variable universe fuzzy adaptive control. *Chaos, Solitons, and Fractals*, *39*(5), 2076–2085. doi:10.1016/j.chaos.2007.06.070

Wang, J., Zhang, Z., & Li, H. (2008). Synchronization of FitzHugh–Nagumo systems in EES via H∞ variable universe adaptive fuzzy control. *Chaos, Solitons, and Fractals*, *36*(5), 1332–1339. doi:10.1016/j.chaos.2006.08.012

Wang, L. X. (1993). Stable Adaptive Fuzzy Control of Nonlinear Systems. *IEEE Transactions on Fuzzy Systems*, *1*(1), 146–155. doi:10.1109/91.227383

Wang, L. X. (1994). *Adaptive fuzzy systems and control: design and stability analysis*. Englewood Cliffs, NJ: Prentice-Hall.

Wang, L. X. (1994). *Adaptive fuzzy systems and control: Design and stability analysis*. Englewood Cliffs, NJ: Prentice-Hall.

Wang, L. X. (1994). *Adaptive Fuzzy Systems and Control: Design and Stability Analysis*. Englewood Cliffs, NJ: Prentice-Hall.

Wang, L. X., & Mendel, J. M. (1992). Fuzzy basis function, universal approximation, and orthogonal least square learning. *IEEE Transactions on Neural Networks*, *3*(5), 807–814. doi:10.1109/72.159070 PMID:18276480

Wang, Q., Zhou, B., & Duan, G.-R. (2015b). Robust gain scheduled control of spacecraft rendezvous system subject to input saturation. *Aerospace Science and Technology*, *42*, 442–450. doi:10.1016/j.ast.2015.02.002

Wang, S., & Yu, Y. G. (2012). Application of multistage homotopy-perturbation method for the solutions of the chaotic fractional order systems. *International Journal of Nonlinear Science*, *13*(1), 3–14.

Wang, S., Yu, Y. G., Wang, H., & Rahmani, A. (2014). Function projective lag synchronization of fractional-order chaotic systems. *Chinese Physics B*, *23*(4), 040502. doi:10.1088/1674-1056/23/4/040502

Wang, X. Y., & Wang, M. (2007). Dynamic Analysis of the Fractional- Order Liu System and its Synchronization. *Chaos (Woodbury, N.Y.)*, *17*(3), 033106. doi:10.1063/1.2755420 PMID:17902988

Wang, X., & Chen, G. (2012). A Chaotic System with Only one Stable Equilibrium. *Communications in Nonlinear Science and Numerical Simulation*, *17*(3), 1264–1272. doi:10.1016/j.cnsns.2011.07.017

Wang, X., He, Y., & Wang, M. (2009). Chaos control of a fractional order modified coupled dynamos system. *Nonlinear Analysis: Theory. Methods & Applications*, *71*(12), 6126–6134.

Wang, X., Zhang, X., & Ma, C. (2012). Modified projective synchronization of fractional order chaotic systems via active sliding mode control. *Nonlinear Dynamics*, *69*(1-2), 511–517. doi:10.100711071-011-0282-1

Wang, Y., & Li, C. (2007). Does the Fractional Brusselator with Efficient Dimension Less than 1 have a Limit Cycle. *Physics Letters. [Part A]*, *363*(5-6), 414–419. doi:10.1016/j.physleta.2006.11.038

Wang, Z., Huang, X., Li, Y. X., & Song, X.-N. (2013). A new image encryption algorithm based on the fractional-order hyperchaotic Lorenz system. *Chinese Physics B*, *22*(1), 010504. doi:10.1088/1674-1056/22/1/010504

Wei, Y., Chen, Y., Liang, S., & Wang, Y. (2015). A novel algorithm on adaptive backstepping control of fractional order systems. *Neurocomputing*, *165*, 395–402. doi:10.1016/j.neucom.2015.03.029

Wei, Y., Sun, Z., Hu, Y., & Wang, Y. (2015). On fractional order composite model reference adaptive control. *International Journal of Systems Science*. doi:10.1080/00207721.2014.998749

Wei, Y., Tse, P. W., Yao, Z., & Wang, Y. (2016). Adaptive backstepping output feedback control for a class of nonlinear fractional order systems. *Nonlinear Dynamics*, *86*(2), 1047–1056. doi:10.100711071-016-2945-4

Wen, C., Zhou, J., Liu, Z., & Su, H. (2011). Robust Adaptive Control of Uncertain Nonlinear Systems in the Presence of Input Saturation and External Disturbance. *IEEE Transactions on Automatic Control*, *56*(7), 1672–1678. doi:10.1109/TAC.2011.2122730

Wen, G., Zhao, Y., Duan, Z., Yu, W., & Chen, G. (2016). Containment of higher-order multi-leader multi-agent systems: A dynamic output approach. *IEEE Transactions on Automatic Control*, *61*(4), 1135–1140. doi:10.1109/TAC.2015.2465071

Wiggins, S. (2003). *Introduction to Applied Nonlinear Dynamical Systems and Chaos*. New York: Springer-Verlag.

Wolf, A., Swift, J. B., Swinney, H. L., & Vastano, J. A. (1985). Determining Lyapunov exponents from a time series. *Physica D. Nonlinear Phenomena*, *16*(3), 285–317. doi:10.1016/0167-2789(85)90011-9

Wu, G. C., & Baleanu, D. (2014). Chaos synchronization of the discrete fractional logistic map. *Signal Processing*, *102*, 96–99. doi:10.1016/j.sigpro.2014.02.022

Wu, G. C., & Lee, E. W. M. (2010). Fractional variational iteration method and its application. *Physics Letters. [Part A]*, *374*(25), 2506–2509. doi:10.1016/j.physleta.2010.04.034

Wu, X. J., Lu, H. T., & Shen, S. L. (2009). Synchronization of a new fractional-order hyperchaotic system. *Physics Letters. [Part A]*, *373*(27–28), 2329–2337. doi:10.1016/j.physleta.2009.04.063

Wu, X., Wang, H., & Lu, H. (2012). Modified generalized projective synchronization of a new fractional-order hyperchaotic system and its application to secure communication. *Nonlinear Analysis Real World Applications*, *13*(3), 1441–1450. doi:10.1016/j.nonrwa.2011.11.008

Xin, B., Liu, L., Hou, G., & Ma, Y. (2017). Chaos synchronization of nonlinear fractional discrete dynamical systems via linear control. *Entropy (Basel, Switzerland)*, *19*(7), 351. doi:10.3390/e19070351

Xu, B., Yang, C., & Pan, Y. (2015). Global Neural Dynamic Surface Tracking Control of Strict-Feedback Systems With Application to Hypersonic Flight Vehicle. *IEEE Transactions on Neural Networks and Learning Systems*, *26*(10), 2563–2575. doi:10.1109/TNNLS.2015.2456972 PMID:26259222

Xu, Y., Li, Y., Liu, D., Jia, W., & Huang, H. (2013). Responses of Duffing oscillator with fractional damping and random phase. *Nonlinear Dynamics*, *74*(3), 745–753. doi:10.100711071-013-1002-9

Xu, Y., & Wang, H. (2013). Synchronization of Fractional-Order Chaotic Systems with Gaussian Fluctuation by Sliding Mode Control. *Abstract and Applied Analysis*, *948782*, 1–7.

Xu, Y., Wang, H., Liu, D., & Huang, H. (2015). Sliding mode control of a class of fractional chaotic systems in the presence of parameter perturbations. *Journal of Vibration and Control*, *21*(3), 435–448. doi:10.1177/1077546313486283

Xu, Y., Wang, H., Li, Y., & Pei, B. (2014). Image encryption based on synchronization of fractional chaotic systems. *Communications in Nonlinear Science and Numerical Simulation*, *19*(10), 3735–3744. doi:10.1016/j.cnsns.2014.02.029

Yacoub, R. R., Bambang, R. T., Harsoyo, A., & Sarwono, J. (2014). *DSP* Implementation of Combined FIR-Functional Link Neural Network for Active Noise Control. *International Journal of Artificial Intelligence*, *12*(1), 36–47.

Yang, X-S., & Bekdaş, G. (2015). *Metaheuristics and Optimization in Civil Engineering*. Springer.

Yang, N., & Liu, C. (2013). A novel fractional-order hyperchaotic system stabilization via fractional sliding-mode control. *Nonlinear Dynamics*, *74*(3), 721–732. doi:10.100711071-013-1000-y

Yang, Q., Wei, Z., & Chen, G. (2010). An unusual 3d Autonomous Quadratic Chaotic System with two Stable Node-Foci. *International Journal of Bifurification and Chaos*, *20*(4), 1061–1083. doi:10.1142/S0218127410026320

Yang, T., & Chua, L. O. (1997). Impulsive stabilization for control and synchronization of chaotic systems: Theory and application to secure communication'. *IEEE Transactions on Circuits and Systems. I, Fundamental Theory and Applications*, *44*(10), 976–978. doi:10.1109/81.633887

Yang, Y., & Chen, G. (2015). Finite-time stability of fractional order impulsive switched systems. *International Journal of Robust and Nonlinear Control*, *25*(13), 2207–2222. doi:10.1002/rnc.3202

Yan, J., & Li, C. (2005). Generalized projective synchronization of a unified chaotic system. *Chaos, Solitons, and Fractals*, *26*(4), 1119–1124. doi:10.1016/j.chaos.2005.02.034

Yan, P., Liu, D., Wang, D., & Ma, H. (2016). Data-driven controller design for general MIMO nonlinear systems via virtual reference feedback tuning and neural networks. *Neurocomputing*, *171*, 815–825. doi:10.1016/j.neucom.2015.07.017

Yazdani, M., & Salarieh, H. (2011). On the Existence of Periodic Solutions in Time Invariant Fractional Order Systems. *Automatica*, *47*(8), 1834–1837. doi:10.1016/j.automatica.2011.04.013

Yin, C., Zhong, S., & Chen, W. (2012). Design of sliding mode controller for a class of fractional-order chaotic systems. *Communications in Nonlinear Science and Numerical Simulation*, *17*(1), 356–366. doi:10.1016/j.cnsns.2011.04.024

Yin-He, W., Yong-Qing, F., Qing-Yun, W., & Yun, Z. (2012). Adaptive feedback stabilization with quantized state measurements for a class of chaotic systems. *Communications in Theoretical Physics*, *57*(5), 808–816. doi:10.1088/0253-6102/57/5/11

Yin, S., Gao, H., Qiu, J., & Kaynak, O. (2017). Descriptor reduced-order sliding mode observers design for switched systems with sensor and actuator faults. *Automatica*, *76*, 282–292. doi:10.1016/j.automatica.2016.10.025

Yuan, J., Shi, B., & Yu, Z. (2014). Adaptive Sliding Control for a Class of Fractional Commensurate Order Chaotic Systems. *Mathematical Problems in Engineering*.

Yue, H., & Li, J. (2012). Output-feedback adaptive fuzzy control for a class of non-linear time-varying delay systems with unknown control directions. *IET Control Theory & Applications*, *6*(9), 1266–1280. doi:10.1049/iet-cta.2011.0226

Yu, W., Li, Y., Wen, G., Yu, X., & Cao, J. (2017). Observer design for tracking consensus in second-order multi-agent systems: Fractional order less than two. *IEEE Transactions on Automatic Control*, *62*(2), 894–900. doi:10.1109/TAC.2016.2560145

Yu, Y., Li, H., Wang, S., & Yu, J. (2009). Dynamic analysis of a fractional-order Lorenz chaotic system. *Chaos, Solitons, and Fractals*, *42*(2), 1181–1189. doi:10.1016/j.chaos.2009.03.016

Yu, Z., & Du, H. (2011). Adaptive neural control for uncertain stochastic nonlinear strict-feedback systems with time-varying delays: A Razumikhin functional method. *Neurocomputing*, *74*(12-14), 2072–2082. doi:10.1016/j.neucom.2010.12.030

Yu, Z., Li, S., & Yu, Z. (2016). Adaptive neural control for a class of Pure-Feedback Nonlinear Time-Delay Systems with Asymmetric Saturation Actuators. *Neurocomputing*, *173*(3), 1461–1470. doi:10.1016/j.neucom.2015.09.020

Zadeh, L. A. (1975). The concept of a linguistic variable and its application to approximate reasoning. *Information Sciences*, *8*(3), 199–249. doi:10.1016/0020-0255(75)90036-5

Zeghlache, S., Ghellab, M. Z., & Bouguerra, A. (2017). Adaptive Type-2 Fuzzy Sliding Mode Control Using Supervisory Type-2 Fuzzy Control for 6 DOF Octorotor Aircraft. *International Journal of Intelligent Engineering and Systems*, *10*(3), 47–57. doi:10.22266/ijies2017.0630.06

Zeng, X., Pielke, R. A., & Eykholt, R. (1992). Extracting Lyapunov Exponents from Short Time Series of Low Precision. *Modern Physics Letters B, 6*(2), 55–75. doi:10.1142/S0217984992000090

Zhang, F., & Li, C. (2011). Stability analysis of fractional differential systems with order lying in (1, 2). *Advances in Difference Equations, 1*, 213–485.

Zhang, R., Tian, G., Yang, S., & Cao, H. (2015). Stability analysis of a class of fractional order nonlinear systems with order lying in (0, 2). *ISA Transactions, 56*, 102–110. doi:10.1016/j.isatra.2014.12.006 PMID:25617942

Zhang, R., & Yang, S. (2011). Adaptive synchronization of fractional-order chaotic systems via a single driving variable. *Nonlinear Dynamics, 66*(4), 831–837. doi:10.100711071-011-9944-2

Zhang, S., Yu, Y., Wen, G., & Rahmani, A. (2016). Lag-generalized synchronization of time-delay chaotic systems with stochastic perturbation. *Modern Physics Letters B, 30*(1), 1550263. doi:10.1142/S0217984915502632

Zhang, W., Li, J., & Ding, C. (2016a). Anti-synchronization control for delayed memristor-based distributed parameter NNs with mixed boundary conditions. *Advances in Difference Equations, 1*(1), 320. doi:10.118613662-016-1017-x

Zhang, Z., Duan, G., & Hou, M. (2017). Robust adaptive dynamic surface control of uncertain non-linear systems with output constraints. *IET Control Theory & Applications, 11*(1), 110–121. doi:10.1049/iet-cta.2016.0456

Zhang, Z., Feng, X., & Yao, Z. (2016b). Chaos control of a Bose–Einstein condensate in a moving optical lattice. *Modern Physics Letters B, 30*(19), 165–238. doi:10.1142/S0217984916502389

Zhang, Z., Xu, S., & Zhang, B. (2015). Exact tracking control of nonlinear systems with time delays and dead-zone input. *Automatica, 52*, 272–276. doi:10.1016/j.automatica.2014.11.013

Zheng, Y. (2015). Fuzzy prediction-based feedback control of fractional-order chaotic systems. *International Journal for Light and Electron Optics, 126*(24), 5645–5649. doi:10.1016/j.ijleo.2015.08.164

Zheng, Y. A., Nyan, Y. B., & Liu, Z. R. (2003). Impulsive synchronization of discrete chaotic systems. *Chinese Physics Letters, 20*(2).

Zheng, Y. I., Nian, Y. B., & Liu, Z. R. (2002). Impulsive control for the stabilization of discrete chaotic system. *Chinese Physics B, 19*(9), 251–1253.

Zhen, W., Xia, H., Ning, L., & Xiao-Na, S. (2012). Image encryption based on a delayed fractional-order chaotic logisticsystem. *Chinese Physics B, 21*(5).

Zhen, W., Xia, H., Yu-Xia, L., & Xiao-Na, S. (2013). A new image encryption algorithm based on the fractional-order hyperchaoticLorenz system. *Chinese Physics B, 22*(1).

Zhou, P., & Ding, R. (2012). Control and synchronization of the fractional-order Lorenz chaotic system via fractional-order derivative. *Mathematical Problems in Engineering*. doi:.10.1155/2012/214169

Zhou, P., & Ding, R. (2012). Modified function projective synchronization between different dimension fractional-order chaotic systems. Abstract and Applied Analysis, ID 862989.

Zhou, P., & Bai, R. (2015). The adaptive synchronization of fractional-order chaotic system with fractional-order 1<q <2 via linear parameter update law. *Nonlinear Dynamics, 80*(1-2), 753–765. doi:10.100711071-015-1903-x

Zhou, Q., Wang, L., Wu, C., Li, H., & Du, H. (2017). Adaptive Fuzzy Control for Nonstrict-Feedback Systems With Input Saturation and Output Constraint. *IEEE Transactions on Systems, Man, and Cybernetics. Systems, 47*(1), 1–12. doi:10.1109/TSMC.2016.2557222

Zhu, H., Zhou, S., & Zhang, J. (2009). Chaos and synchronization of the fractional order Chua's system. *Chaos, Solitons, and Fractals*, *39*(4), 1595–1603. doi:10.1016/j.chaos.2007.06.082

Zouari, F., Boulkroune, A., & Ibeas, A. (2017). Neural adaptive quantized output-feedback control-based synchronization of uncertain time-delay incommensurate fractional-order chaotic systems with input nonlinearities. *Neurocomputing*, *237*, 200–225. doi:10.1016/j.neucom.2016.11.036

Zouari, F., Boulkroune, A., Ibeas, A., & Arefi, M. M. (2016). Observer-based adaptive neural network control for a class of MIMO uncertain nonlinear time-delay non-integer-order systems with asymmetric actuator saturation. *Neural Computing & Applications*, 1–18.

Zouari, F., Boulkroune, A., Ibeas, A., & Arefi, M. M. (2017a). Observer-based adaptive neural network control for a class of MIMO uncertain nonlinear time-delay non-integer-order systems with asymmetric actuator saturation. *Neural Computing & Applications*, *28*(S1), 993–1010. doi:10.100700521-016-2369-6

About the Contributors

Abdesselem Boulkroune received his Engineering degree from Setif University in 1995, his Master grade from the military polytechnic school (EMP) of Algiers in 2002, his Ph.D. degree in Automatic from the national polytechnic school (ENP) of Algiers in 2009, in Algeria. In 2003, he joined the automatic control department at Jijel University, in Algeria, where he is currently a full professor. His research interests are in nonlinear control, chaos synchronization, fractional-order systems, induction motor drives, fuzzy control and adaptive control.

Samir Ladaci received the State Engineer degree in Automatics from the Polytechnic School of Algiers in 1995 and the Magister degree in Industrial Automation from Annaba University, Algeria in 1999. He received his Ph.D. and HDR degree (Habilitation à diriger les Recherches) from the department of Electronics, Mentouri University of Constantine, Algeria in 2007 and 2009 respectively. From 2001 to 2013, he was an assistant professor and then associate professor (Maitre de conférence 'A') in the Department of Electrical Engineering at Skikda University, Algeria. On December 1rst, 2013, he joined the National Polytechnic School of Constantine, Algeria where he is a Full Professor since January 2015. His current research interests include Fractional order Systems and Control, Adaptive Control, Robust Control.

* * *

Yassine Bensafia was born in Béjaia, Algeria, in 1978. He received the Engineering and Magister degrees in Electrical Engineering from the Béjaia University, in 2003 and 2006, respectively. Recently, he obtained his Science Doctorate in Automatic Control from the Department of Electrical Engineering, University of the 20th August 1955 of Skikda, Algeria. Since 2015, he joined the University of Bouira as an assistant professor. His research interests include fractional systems control, Adaptive control, Robust control.

Maamar Bettayeb received the B.S., M.S., and Ph.D. degrees in Electrical Engineering from University of Southern California, Los Angeles, in 1976, 1978 and 1981, respectively. He worked as a Research Scientist at the Bellaire Research Center at Shell Oil Development Company, Houston, Texas, USA, in the development of seismic signal processing de-convolution algorithms for the purpose of Gas and Oil exploration during 1981/1982. From 1982 to 1988, He directed the Instrumentation and Control Laboratory of High Commission for Research in Algeria, where He led various research and development projects in the field of modeling, simulation, and control design of large scale energy systems, specifically, model reduction, identification and control of computer-controlled systems with applications to nuclear, solar and electric power systems.

Amina Boubellouta received bachelor and master degrees from automatic control department, University of Jijel, Algeria, in 2013 and 2015, respectively. She is currently a PhD student at the same University. Her research interests include nonlinear control, fuzzy control, chaos synchronization, systems and applications.

Abdelkrim Boukabou received the Dr. Eng. degree and his habilitation in electronics from the University of Constantine Algeria in 2006 and 2008, respectively. Currently, he is a full professor at the University of Jijel. His research interests include nonlinear control theory, robotics and automation, power-line communications, and smart grids.

Bachir Bourouba graduated from Ferhat Abbes University of Setif (UFAS), Algeria, in 2000. He received the Magister degree in Automatics from UFAS in 2005, Algeria. He obtained his PhD from Mentouri University of Constantine, Algeria, in 2018, He is an Assistant Professor at the Ferhat Abbes University of Setif (UFAS). His research interests include optimisation, fractional-order systems and control, adaptive and robust control, nonlinear systems.

Amel Bouzeriba was born in Taher-Jijel, Algeria, in 1983. She received the Engineer degree in Electronics in 2006 and the Magister degree in Automatic control and Signal Processing in 2011, from the Jijel University, Jijel, Algeria. Currently, she is an Associate Professor at the Jijel University. Her research interests are in nonlinear control, adaptive Control, fuzzy control and synchronization of fractional-order chaotic systems.

Said Djennoune received his PhD in Electrical Engineering from University of Tizi-Ouzou, Algeria in 1999. His research interest is in model order reduction, singular perturbation, nonlinear control, fractional order systems, robust control, hybrid systems, sliding-mode control, hybrid systems, synchronisation and observation of chaotic systems, which are applied to cryptography.

Hamid Hamiche received his PhD degree in Automatic Control from the Mouloud MAMMERI University of Tizi-Ouzou of Algeria and National School of Electronics and Applications of Cergy-Pontoise (France) in 2011. His research activities deal with sliding-mode control, hybrid systems, synchronization and observation of chaotic systems, which are applied to cryptography, digital data transmission and watermarking.

Nasr-eddine Hamri is currently a full professor in the mathematics department at the University of Mila, Algeria which he joined in 2009, where he is also Vice-President and the Director of Mathematics and their interactions Laboratory of Mila (Melilab), and the head of the Dynamical Systems, Complexity and Chaos team, after a long career at University of Constantine, Algeria. He earned a Ph.D from the University of Nice - Sophia- Antipolis, France in 1994. His PhD thesis was entitled "Continuité de la demi-application de Poincaré dans le circuit de Chua". He has received the State doctorate (Doctorate d'état) in mathematics from the University of Constantine, Algeria. His research interest is in qualitative study of ODE, Nonlinear Dynamical systems, Chaos, Complex systems, Control and Synchronization of chaotic Fractional systems and properties of nonlinear circuits.

Shaobo He obtained his Phd degree in Central South University and now is enrolled in Hunan University of Arts and Science as a lecture. His research interests are fractional-order nonlinear dynamics, complexity analysis and applications.

Sarah Kassim received his Master research in Electrical Engineering in 2013 from the Mouloud MAMMERI University of Tizi-Ouzou. Currently she is a PhD student in Electrical Engineering from the Mouloud MAMMERI University. His research activities deal with synchronization and observation of chaotic systems, which are applied to cryptography, digital data transmission and watermarking.

Khatir Khettab graduated from Ferhat Abbes University of Sétif (UFAS), Algeria, in 2001. He received the M.Sc. degree from UFAS, Algeria in 2005, and obtained his Ph.D. degree in Advanced Automatic from Skikda University, Algeria in 2016. He works currently as an assistant professor at the Mohamed Boudiaf University of M'sila, Algeria. His research interests include robotics and automation, especially the Robust fractional systems control, chaos synchronization and fractional adaptive intelligent control.

Crépin Kofane Timoleon is professor of physics at the University of Yaoundé I, Cameroon. He completed his PhD at the University of Bourgogne, France. In October 1988, he returned to Cameroon and began to teach physics at the University of Yaoundé and has since then created a successful nonlinear dynamics and chaos group. His research touches on subjects ranging from nonlinear excitations and coherent structures such as soliton theory to dynamical systems and chaos. He has also been studying the "Bose-Einstein condensate". The ICTP has provided the opportunity for all of his 33 PhD students and colleagues to visit the centre to carry out research for up to three months duration. Kofané is a member of the Cameroon Academy of Sciences, African Academy of Sciences and the international board of editors, African Physical Review.

Mohamed Lashab received the DES degree in physics and electronics from Constantine University, Constantine, Algeria, in 1985, and the M Phil.in Electronics instrumentation, from Trent polytechnic Nottingham, UK in 1988. He obtained the Phd degree in Electronic Communication in 2012 from Skikda university, Algeria. He joined Skikda university from 1994 to 2016, he is actually at Larbi Ben M'hidi university, Oum El-Bouaghi, Algeria. He is interested in numerical techniques in electromagnetics, fractional processes, wireless and optical communications, microwave components.

Ouerdia Megherbi received his Master research in Electrical Engineering in 2013 from the Mouloud MAMMERI University of Tizi-Ouzou. Currently she is a PhD student in Electrical Engineering from the Mouloud MAMMERI University. His research activities deal with impulsive synchronization and observation of chaotic systems, which are applied to cryptography and digital data transmission.

Karima Rabah received the State Engineer degree in Electronic option: system's control in 2003 and the Magister degree in 2006 from, Mentouri University of Constantine. She is currently, in finalization of Ph.D at the University of Skikda on Contribution to the modeling and control of Fractional order chaotic systems in Skikda University. Her current research interests include Fractional order Chaotic Systems and Control, Adaptive Control, Robust Control.

Ammar Soukkou received his habilitation in electronics from the University of Jijel Algeria in 2017. Currently, he is an Associate Professor at the University of Jijel. His research interests include nonlinear control theory, hybrid systems and fractional order systems.

Kehui Sun is a Professor in School of Physics and Electronics, Central South University. His current research interests are nonlinear dynamics, circuits design of chaotic systems and applications of chaotic systems.

Alain Giresse Tene is a PhD student at the University of Dschang, Department of Physics. He is holder of two Masters Degrees: the first in Mathematical Science with strong component in programming and the second in Physics particularly in information processing tasks. He started his university studies in 2010 at the University of Dschang Cameroon in the department of Physics and got his Bachelor Degree in physics three years later (2013) afterward he started the first year master in 2014 where he completed with success after a year. During his second year master, he got a scholarship to study at AIMS (African Institute for Mathematical Science) which is a Pan-African center of excellence that recruits and trains young and talented students from all countries in Africa with a strong background in Applied Mathematics, Physics, Pure Mathematics, and Computer Sciences in 2015. After completing the program in one year, he returned back to his home University to complete his Master degree in Physics in November 2016. Since then, he is currently working as a PhD student.

Huihai Wang obtained his PhD degree in Central South University and now is enrolled in Central South University. His research interests are circuit design of fractional-order nonlinear system and ts applications.

Farouk Zouari was born in Tunis, Tunisia, on August 27, 1980. He received his Engineer degree in Electrical Engineering, his magister degree in Automatic and Signal Processing, and his PhD degree in Electrical Engineering from the "National Engineering School of Tunis, University of Tunis El Manar, Tunisia, in 2004, 2005 and 2014, respectively. He is currently a researcher at Laboratoire de Recherche en Automatique (LARA), École Nationale d'Ingénieurs de Tunis, Université de Tunis El Manar. His current research interests include singular systems, neural control theory, nonlinear control, and intelligent adaptive control.

Index

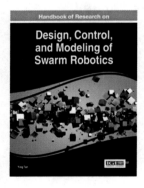

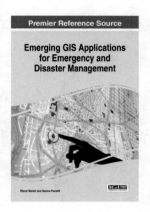 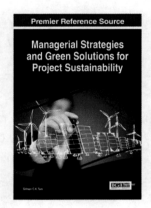  

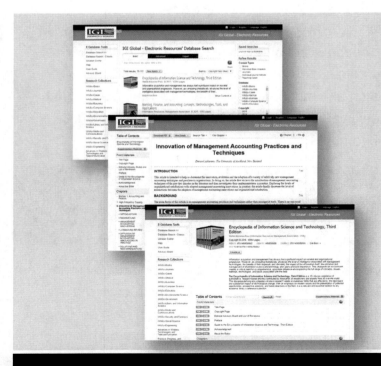

Printed in the United States
By Bookmasters